Global Writing for Public Relations

Global Writing for Public Relations: Connecting in English with Stakeholders and Publics Worldwide provides multiple resources to help students and public relations practitioners learn best practices for writing in English to communicate and connect with a global marketplace. Author Arhlene Flowers has created a new approach on writing for public relations by combining intercultural communication, international public relations, and effective public relations writing techniques.

Global Writing for Public Relations offers the following features:

- Insight into the evolution of English-language communication in business and public relations, as well as theoretical and political debates on global English and globalization.
- An understanding of both a global thematic and customized local approach in creating public relations campaigns and written materials.
- Strategic questions to help writers develop critical thinking skills and understand how to create meaningful communications materials for specific audiences.
- Storytelling skills that help writers craft compelling content.
- Real-world global examples from diverse industries that illustrate creative solutions.
- Step-by-step guidance on writing public relations materials with easy-to-follow templates to reach traditional and online media, consumers, and businesses.
- Self-evaluation and creative thinking exercises to improve cultural literacy, grammar, punctuation, and editing skills for enhanced clarity.
- Supplemental online resources for educators and students.

English is the go-to business language across the world, and this book combines the author's experience training students and seasoned professionals in crafting public relations materials that resonate with global English-language audiences. It will help public relations students and practitioners become proficient and sophisticated writers with the ability to connect with diverse audiences worldwide.

Arhlene A. Flowers is associate professor of Integrated Marketing Communications at Ithaca College.

Global Writing for Public Relations

Connecting in English with Stakeholders and Publics Worldwide

Arhlene A. Flowers

Routledge
Taylor & Francis Group

NEW YORK AND LONDON

Please visit the companion website at www.routledge.com/cw/

First published 2016
by Routledge
711 Third Avenue, New York, NY 10017

and by Routledge
2 Park Square, Milton Park, Abingdon, Oxon, OX14 4RN

Routledge is an imprint of the Taylor & Francis Group, an informa business

Library of Congress Cataloging in Publication Data
Flowers, Arhlene A.
    Global writing for public relations: connecting in English with
    stakeholders and publics worldwide / Arhlene A. Flowers.
    pages cm
    Includes bibliographical references and index.
    1. Public relations. 2. Public relations—Authorship. 3. Mass media—
    Authorship. 4. Press releases. 5. English language—Globalization.
    6. Intercultural communication. I. Title.
    HM1221.F65 2015
    659.2—dc23
    2015016744

ISBN: 978-0-415-74883-4 (hbk)
ISBN: 978-0-415-74884-1 (pbk)
ISBN: 978-1-315-77425-1 (ebk)

Typeset in Abode Caslon and Times New Roman
by Florence Production Ltd, Stoodleigh, Devon, UK

MIX
Paper from
responsible sources
FSC® C014174

Printed and bound in the United States of America by Sheridan Books, Inc. (a Sheridan Group Company).

Brief Contents

List of Exercises   xiii
List of Exhibits   xiv
List of Figures   xvi
Preface   xxi
About the Author   xxiv

Part One GOING GLOBAL IN
PUBLIC RELATIONS   1

1 Exploring the Evolution of
  English as "Globish"   3

2 Understanding Global Perspectives
  in Public Relations   27

3 Changing Global Media Landscape
  and Ethical and Legal Issues   52

Part Two DEVELOPING
INTERCULTURAL
COMMUNICATION SKILLS
AND SENSITIVITIES   81

4 Appreciating Cultural Similarities
  and Accepting Differences   83

5 Decoding Nonverbal
  Communication and Imagery
  Worldwide   105

6 Mastering the Fine Art of
  Storytelling in International
  Public Relations   129

Part Three HONING ENGLISH
WRITING SKILLS FOR
GLOBAL AUDIENCES   161

7 Applying Consistency of Style   163

8 Acing Grammar and Punctuation   178

9 Sharpening Editing Skills for
  Global Audiences   208

Part Four GENERATING AND
MANAGING NEWS WORLDWIDE   233

10 Crafting Global News Releases for
   Mainstream and Social Media   235

11 Composing Global Media Kits
   and Online Newsrooms   263

12 Using Other Media Relations
   Techniques for Local or
   Global Campaigns   294

Part Five CONNECTING ONLINE
AND USING EXTERNAL
COMMUNICATION TOOLS
GLOBALLY   331

13 Writing for the Internet and
   Social Media Worldwide   333

14 Shaping Speeches and Scripts   357

15 Controlling Content with Brand
   Journalism and Corporate-Produced
   Materials   379

Part Six WRITING INTERNATIONAL
PLANS, REPORTS, AND BUSINESS
CORRESPONDENCE   405

16 Creating and Presenting Public
Relations Plans for Local or
Global Markets   407

17 Preparing Global Business
Correspondence and Internal
Reports   429

Appendix A
Examples of English-Language
Public Relations Industry Trade
Outlets   461

Appendix B
Public Relations Industry Groups
Worldwide   464

Appendix C
Examples of English-Language
Television Broadcasters Worldwide   470

Appendix D
Answers to Selected Exercises   474

Index   479

Contents

List of Exercises   *xiii*
List of Exhibits   *xiv*
List of Figures   *xvi*
Preface   *xxi*
About the Author   *xxiv*

Part One GOING GLOBAL IN
PUBLIC RELATIONS   1

1   Exploring the Evolution of
       English as "Globish"   3
       1.1   Introduction to the World
             of English   3
       1.2   English Evolves from More
             Than 350 Languages   5
             1.2.1   English from the Roman
                     Empire to Today   5
       1.3   English: Today's Lingua Franca
             of Global Business and
             Diplomacy   12
       1.4   English Language Education
             and World Englishes   15
             1.4.1   Variations of English   18
             1.4.2   Foreign-Language
                     Education in English-
                     Language Countries   20
       1.5   The Future of English and
             Reality for Contemporary
             Public Relations   21
             1.5.1   Efforts to Create a New
                     Universal Language and
                     to Simplify English   21
             1.5.2   English as the Global
                     Language of Public
                     Relations   22
       1.6   Learning Objectives and
             Key Terms   23
       References   24

2   Understanding Global Perspectives
       in Public Relations   27
       2.1   Introduction to Globalism and
             Global Public Relations   27
       2.2   Rise of Multinationals and
             International Nongovernmental
             Organizations   30
             2.2.1   Corporations Comprise
                     Almost Half of the
                     World's Largest
                     Economies   30
             2.2.2   INGOs and Public
                     Affairs   31
       2.3   Globalization of the Public
             Relations Industry   31
             2.3.1   International Public
                     Relations Services   32
             2.3.2   Global Collaboration:
                     Public Relations Trade
                     Groups   35
       2.4   Glocalization and Public
             Relations   38
             2.4.1   Think Locally, Act
                     Globally   38
             2.4.2   Think Globally, Act
                     Locally   39
             2.4.3   Global and Glocal
                     Public Relations   41
       2.5   Global Careers in Public
             Relations   42
             2.5.1   Short-Term Living
                     Abroad Experiences   43
             2.5.2   International Skill-
                     Building Opportunities
                     without Leaving Home   44
             2.5.3   Full-Time International
                     Positions   45
             2.5.4   Multiculturals and Global
                     Cosmopolitans   47

2.6   Learning Objectives and Key
       Terms   48
References   49

3   Changing Global Media Landscape
    and Ethical and Legal Issues   52
    3.1   Introduction to Evolving Global
           Communications   52
    3.2   Global Connectivity, Social
           Media, and Portable Technology 53
           3.2.1   Opportunities and
                    Challenges in Public
                    Relations   56
    3.3   Global Print and Broadcast Media 58
           3.3.1   Changes in Traditional
                    Media Worldwide   60
    3.4   Global Ethical and Legal
           Considerations in Public
           Relations Writing   62
           3.4.1   Ethics in Public Relations 64
           3.4.2   Legal Considerations in
                    Public Relations   64
    3.5   Global Media Ethics and Issues 73
    3.6   Learning Objectives and Key
           Terms   76
    References   77

Part Two DEVELOPING
INTERCULTURAL
COMMUNICATION SKILLS
AND SENSITIVITIES   81

4   Appreciating Cultural Similarities
    and Accepting Differences   83
    4.1   Introduction to Culture   83
    4.2   Culture and Communication   85
    4.3   Intercultural Dimensions Relevant
           to Public Relations Strategists and
           Writers   88
           4.3.1   Time Orientation   88
           4.3.2   Level of Diplomacy and
                    Expressiveness   95
           4.3.3   Sense of Power and Self 96
           4.3.4   Adherence to Rules and
                    Traditions   99

4.4   Learning Objectives and Key
       Terms   102
References   103

5   Decoding Nonverbal
    Communication and
    Imagery Worldwide   105
    5.1   Introduction to Visual Imagery
           in Public Relations   105
    5.2   Cultural Interpretations of Body
           Language   107
           5.2.1   Dimensions of Visual
                    Interactions of People 111
    5.3   Cultural Interpretations of
           Colors   114
           5.3.1   Colorful Blunders   116
    5.4   Cultural Perspectives on
           Numbers   118
    5.5   Symbols Across Cultures   121
           5.5.1   Religious, National, and
                    Political Symbols   121
           5.5.2   Popular Cultural Icons 123
           5.5.3   Imagery of Animals and
                    Flowers   124
    5.6   Learning Objectives and Key
           Terms   126
    References   126

6   Mastering the Fine Art of
    Storytelling in International
    Public Relations   129
    6.1   Introduction to Worldwide
           Storytelling Past and Present 129
    6.2   Storytelling in the Global
           Digital Era   133
           6.2.1   Make It Real: Tell
                    Stories about People or
                    Animals   133
           6.2.2   Show Us the
                    Possibilities   141
           6.2.3   Engage Our Senses   143
           6.2.4   Seek Our Participation 148
           6.2.5   Make It Timely   153
    6.3   Learning Objectives and Key
           Terms   158
    References   158

Part Three HONING ENGLISH
WRITING SKILLS FOR
GLOBAL AUDIENCES   161

7 Applying Consistency of Style 163
   7.1   Introduction to Style Usage for
         Public Relations Writers   163
   7.2   The Evolution of English-
         Language Standards   164
         7.2.1   "Words of the Year":
                 Three Global
                 Perspectives   171
   7.3   "Style Wars": English-Language
         Stylebooks   172
   7.4   Customized Style Guides for
         Unified Voices   175
   7.5   Learning Objectives and
         Key Terms   176
   References   176

8 Acing Grammar and Punctuation 178
   8.1   Introduction to the Importance
         of Grammar   178
   8.2   The Art of Sentence Structure 180
         8.2.1   Sentences, Clauses, and
                 Phrases—and Common
                 Errors   182
   8.3   Direction of the Nine Parts of
         Speech   186
         8.3.1   Nouns: Protagonists of
                 Your Sentences   186
         8.3.2   Pronouns: Understudies
                 for Nouns   188
         8.3.3   Verbs: Action, Timing,
                 and Mood of Your
                 Story   190
         8.3.4   Adjectives: Props,
                 Makeup, and Costumes 192
         8.3.5   Adverbs: Stunt Actors
                 and Special Effects   193
         8.3.6   Prepositions: Scene
                 Transitions and
                 Relationships Among
                 Characters   193
         8.3.7   Conjunctions: Editing
                 Tools   193
         8.3.8   Interjections: Dramatic
                 Sound Effects, Emotions,
                 and Surprise   194
         8.3.9   Articles: Definite and
                 Indefinite   194
         8.3.10 Grammar Rules Evolve
                 and Some Become
                 Archaic   194
   8.4   Punctuation as a "Tour Guide" for
         Readers: American- and British-
         English Versions   194
   8.5   Learning Objectives and Key
         Terms   205
   References   205

9 Sharpening Editing Skills for Global
   Audiences   208
   9.1   Introduction to Editing   208
   9.2   Tone and Relevance   209
         9.2.1   Edit Nonstandard Words 210
         9.2.2   Be Mindful of Clichés,
                 Idioms, and Slang   210
         9.2.3   Be Sensitive to
                 Generational Gaps—
                 and Greater
                 Transcultural Gaps 213
   9.3   Clarity, Simplicity, and Precision 214
         9.3.1   Delete Superfluous
                 Words   214
         9.3.2   Avoid Hype and
                 Superlatives   214
         9.3.3   Replace Vague Words
                 with Specific Terms 215
         9.3.4   Edit Phrasal Verbs for
                 ESL/EFL Speakers   215
         9.3.5   Edit Negative Language 215
         9.3.6   Use Foreign Words
                 Selectively   216
         9.3.7   Use the Right Words for
                 Religions and Nations 216
         9.3.8   Apply Correct Terms for
                 Gender, Race, Age, and
                 Sexual Orientation 217
         9.3.9   Use Numbers and
                 Abbreviations Clearly 219
   9.4   Commonly Misused Words and
         Confusing Expressions   219

9.4.1 Mangling and Tangling
Words with "Baited"
Breath   221
9.5   Cultural Blunders and Translation
Issues   223
9.6   Proofreading Techniques   225
9.6.1 Real-World Snafus   225
9.6.2 Proofreading Solutions 227
9.7   Learning Objectives and Key
Terms   229
References   230

Part Four GENERATING AND
MANAGING NEWS WORLDWIDE   233

10 Crafting Global News Releases for
Mainstream and Social Media   235
10.1 Introduction to News Releases
and Industry Issues   235
10.2 News Release Strategies   237
10.3 Writing Techniques   239
10.3.1 News Release Topics 239
10.3.2 Content and
Considerations   241
10.3.3 Organization and
Formatting   244
10.3.4 Social Media News
Releases   251
10.4 Imagery and Captions   253
10.5 Delivery of News Releases   258
10.6 Learning Objectives and Key
Terms   259
References   260

11 Composing Global Media Kits
and Online Newsrooms   263
11.1 Introduction to Newsroom
Writing in Public Relations 263
11.2 Types of Media Kits   264
11.2.1 Printed and Digital
Formats   264
11.2.2 Online Media Kits and
Newsrooms   274
11.3 Core Written Media Kit
Components   276

11.3.1 Fact Sheets   277
11.3.2 Executive Profiles   281
11.3.3 Backgrounders   285
11.4 Audiovisual Libraries for
Global and Glocal Media Kits 287
11.5 Learning Objectives and Key
Terms   292
References   292

12 Using Other Media Relations
Techniques for Local or
Global Campaigns   294
12.1 Introduction to Other Methods of
Communicating with Reporters 294
12.2 Global and Glocal Media
Relations   296
12.3 Story Ideas and Pitches   298
12.4 Face-to-Face Media Events   302
12.4.1 Media Alerts   303
12.4.2 Formal Invitations   307
12.4.3 Media Tours and
Editorial Briefings 309
12.4.4 Statements   312
12.4.5 Press Familiarization
Trips   318
12.5 Techniques for Voicing Opinions
in Media Outlets   323
12.5.1 Letters to the Editor 323
12.5.2 Op-Eds   324
12.5.3 Bylined Articles   327
12.6 Learning Objectives and Key
Terms   328
References   328

Part Five CONNECTING ONLINE
AND USING EXTERNAL
COMMUNICATION TOOLS
GLOBALLY   331

13 Writing for the Internet and
Social Media Worldwide   333
13.1 Introduction to Web Writing for
Public Relations   333
13.1.1 Strategic
Considerations   334

13.2 Blogs and the Blogosphere   338
  13.2.1 Best Practices in
      Blogging   340
13.3 Microblogs and the Twitterverse 343
  13.3.1 Taste and Judgment   345
13.4 Social Networking and Photo
  and Video Sharing Sites   346
13.5 Wikipedia   350
13.6 Learning Objectives and Key
  Terms   353
References   354

14 Shaping Speeches and Scripts   357
14.1 Introduction to Writing for
  the Ear   357
14.2 Speeches for Glocal and
  Global Audiences   359
  14.2.1 The Preparation Process 359
  14.2.2 Structural and
      Presentation
      Considerations   362
  14.2.3 Benefits of Learning
      from the Masters   363
14.3 The Art of Making Short
  Introductions   367
14.4 Video Applications in Public
  Relations   369
  14.4.1 B-Roll Footage and
      Video News Releases   370
  14.4.2 Writing Audiovisual
      Scripts   371
  14.3.3 Public Service
      Announcements   374
14.5 Learning Objectives and Key
  Terms   376
References   377

15 Controlling Content with Brand
Journalism and Corporate-Produced
Materials   379
15.1 Introduction to Brand
  Journalism   379
15.2 Organizational Magazines
  and Newsletters   380
15.3 Branded Online Newsroom
  Content   385

15.4 White Papers   387
15.5 Brochures and Posters   391
15.6 Advertorials and Native
  Advertising   400
15.7 Learning Objectives and Key
  Terms   401
References   402

Part Six WRITING INTERNATIONAL
PLANS, REPORTS, AND BUSINESS
CORRESPONDENCE   405

16 Creating and Presenting
Public Relations Plans for
Local or Global Markets   407
16.1 Introduction to Public
  Relations Proposals   407
16.2 The New Business Planning
  Process   408
16.3 Writing Public Relations
  Proposals for Local or
  Global Campaigns   410
  16.3.1 Step-by-Step Guidelines
      on Proposal Writing   410
16.4 Presenting Public Relations
  Plans   422
  16.4.1 How to Avoid "Death
      by PowerPoint"
      Presentations   423
16.5 Learning Objectives and Key
  Terms   428
References   428

17 Preparing Global Business
Correspondence and Internal
Reports   429
17.1 Introduction to Business
  Communication in Public
  Relations   429
17.2 Business Correspondence   431
  17.2.1 Preparing Formal
      Business Letters   431
  17.2.2 Crafting Business
      Memos   437
  17.2.3 Writing Business
      Emails   439

17.3 New Business Letters and
      Responses to Complaints   441
      17.3.1 Preparing Sales Letters
              in Public Relations   441
      17.3.2 Responding to
              Complaints in Writing   443
17.4 Written Materials for Meetings 445
      17.4.1 Preparing Meeting
              Agendas   446
      17.4.2 Recording Meeting
              Minutes   450
17.5 Public Relations Reporting   454
      17.5.1 Preparing Activity
              Reports   454
      17.5.2 Documenting Media
              Monitoring Updates   457
17.6 Learning Objectives and Key
      Terms   458
References   459

Appendix A
Examples of English-Language
Public Relations Industry Trade
Outlets   461

Appendix B
Public Relations Industry Groups
Worldwide   464

Appendix C
Examples of English-Language
Television Broadcasters Worldwide   470

Appendix D
Answers to Selected Exercises   474

Index   479

Exercises

1.1	Self-Evaluation: Origins of English Words	11
1.2	Insights: Your Experiences with Languages	22
2.1	Insights: Public Relations Agency Global Scope and Capabilities	34
2.2	Insights: Your Nearest Public Relations Trade Group	36
3.1	Insights: Traditional Media Outlets	60
3.2	Self-Evaluation: Ethical and Legal Issues in Public Relations	63
4.1	Self-Evaluation: Circles Test on Perception of Time: Past, Present, and Future	90
4.2	Self-Evaluation: Writing with Diplomacy and Tact	97
5.1	Self-Evaluation: Cross-Cultural Interpretations of Hand Gestures	108
6.1	Creative Thinking: Sensory Story Ideas for a Travel Destination	146
6.2	Creative Thinking: Telling Timely Stories about Life Passages	154
7.1	Self-Evaluation: American (Webster's) and British (Oxford) English Spelling	167
8.1	Self-Evaluation: Pronouns	190
8.2	Self-Evaluation: Punctuation	196
9.1	Self-Evaluation: Geographic Knowledge of Religions of the World	217
9.2	Self-Evaluation: Cross-Cultural Meanings of English Words	221
10.1	Insights: Analysis of News Releases	252
10.2	Insights: Media Placements Generated from a News Release	258
11.1	Creative Thinking: Tactical Media Kit Ideas	273
11.2	Insights: Investigating Online Newsrooms	276
11.3	Creative Thinking: Fact Sheet Topics	281
11.4	Creative Thinking: Topics for Backgrounders	287
12.1	Insights: Press Conferences	318
12.2	Insights: Op-eds	326
13.1	Insights: Blogs	343
13.2	Insights: Organizational Social Networking Sites	351
14.1	Insights: Public Service Announcements	375
15.1	Insights: Evaluation of White Papers	391
15.2	Insights: Assessment of Advertorials or Native Advertising	401
16.1	Creative Thinking: Preparing Colorful Table of Content Headings	412
17.1	Insights: Your Experiences with Meetings	430

Exhibits

1.1	English-Language Career Requirements at Multinational Organizations	16
1.2	World's Most Widely Spoken Languages	17
2.1	"Big Five" Communication Conglomerates	33
2.2	Reports and Rankings on Public Relations Agencies Worldwide	35
2.3	International Public Relations Industry Associations	37
3.1	Timeline of Major Technological Innovations Post-Google	56
3.2	Global Alliance for Public Relations and Communication Management Code of Ethics	65
3.3	International Public Relations Association Code of Conduct	66
3.4	International Journalism Organizations	74
3.5	International Public Relations Association Charter on Media Transparency	76
4.1	Intercultural Scholars: Hall, Hofstede, Trompenaars, and Hampden-Turner	89
4.2	12-Hour and 24-Hour Clocks	93
4.3	Seasons in the Northern and Southern Hemispheres	94
4.4	Cultural Dimensions and Communication Considerations	100
5.1	Examples of Cultural Interpretations of Colors	117
5.2	Examples of Positive and Negative Meanings of Numbers	120
6.1	Freytag's Dramatic Storytelling Sequences	133
6.2	Aesop's Brand Storytelling Survey Criteria	143
6.3	Seven Types of Imagery	145
7.1	Differences between American (Webster's) and British (Oxford) English Spelling	165
7.2	English-Language Dictionaries Worldwide	170
7.3	English-Language Style Guides Worldwide	174
8.1	Sentence Types	183
8.2	Clauses, Modifiers, and Phrases	184
8.3	Personal Pronouns	188
8.4	Verb Moods	191
8.5	American and British English Punctuation	204
9.1	Examples of Religious Terms	216
9.2	Same Words with Different Meanings in American and British English	222
9.3	Cultural Blunders in Translation	223
10.1	Traditional News Release Template	244
10.2	Other News Release Formatting Tips	251
11.1	Fact Sheet Template (two-column format)	278
11.2	Sample of a Biography Questionnaire	282
11.3	Executive Profile Example	284
12.1	Email Pitch Template	300

12.2	Media Alert Template	304
12.3	Media Tour Appointment Template	312
12.4	Statement Template	316
12.5	Example of a Statement	317
12.6	Press Trip Itinerary Example	321
13.1	Writing Tips on Blogs, Microblogs, and Social Media	336
13.2	Tips on Visual Sharing Social Media Sites	347
14.1	Video News Release Template	372
15.1	Resources Containing White Papers on Public Relations	390
15.2	Resources on Graphic Design Associations and Awards Worldwide	399
16.1	Scope of Public Relations Tactics	418
16.2	Barcelona Declaration of Measurement Principles	419
16.3	Considerations for Public Relations Proposal Presentations	425
17.1	Traditional Business Letter Format in Block Style	432
17.2	Resources for Formal Titles of Address	437
17.3	Response to a Complaint Template (by email)	444
17.4	Example of Meeting Agenda with Specific Times	447
17.5	Example of Meeting Agenda without Specific Timeframes	448
17.6	Meeting Minutes Template with More Details	451
17.7	Example of At-a-Glance Meeting Minutes	452

Figures

1.1   Map of the contemporary English-speaking world   4
1.2   Grainger, "The First Descent of Julius Caesar on the Coast of Britain,"
      1808, engraving   6
1.3   Sole surviving manuscript of *Beowulf* (11th century). British Library
      shelfmark: c13187–11; Cotton Vitelius A. XV f.105   7
1.4   August Benziger, "King Alfred Visiting a Monastery School," 1894,
      engraving   7
1.5   Detail of the Bayeux Tapestry depicting the Norman Invasion of England in
      the 11th century   8
1.6   William Shakespeare, English poet and playwright. Engraving from
      The Leisure Hour Magazine, April 1864   9
1.7   Imperial Federation, map of the world showing the extent of the British
      Empire in 1886   10
1.8   Pilots in the cockpit need to communicate clearly with air traffic controllers
      anywhere   14
1.9   Image of the Speak Good English Movement campaign in Singapore   18
1.10 Diagram based on the model of three concentric language circles developed
      by sociolinguist Braj Kachru (1985)   19
1.11 Diagram based on the ranges of language proficiencies from high to low in
      English Next, published by the British Council in 2006   20
2.1   Definitions of public relations   28
2.2   The Melbourne Mandate Diagram   38
2.3   Example of French-made product at Disneyland Paris; Ladurée branded
      macaroons   40
2.4   Volunteers also can gain international experience   44
2.5   Image of multicultural staff members   47
3.1   Cartoon depicts the changes in communication tools   54
3.2   Cartoon conveys the power of Google   55
3.3   Cartoon depicts transparency issues on the Web   58
3.4   The *Idol* television franchise has spread around the globe. Image shows
      performers in the 2013 American Idols Live! Tour in Sacramento, Calif.   61
3.5   Copyright symbol   68
3.6   Trademark symbol   70
3.7   Stock exchange market trading concepts   72
4.1   Cartoon by Global Integration depicts some of the questions that can arise
      during international travels   84
4.2   Iceberg metaphor illustrates dimensions of culture   86
4.3   Cartoon illustrates the various meanings of deadlines   91

4.4   Cartoon shows how creative types can express themselves differently   95
5.1   Kevin Carter received the Pulitzer prize in journalism (feature photography)
       in 1994 for this image of the famine in the Sudan   106
5.2   Cartoon shows how nonverbal communication may be simpler for some   107
5.3   Examples of hand gestures—but "keep your hands to yourself" is sage advice
       since not all gestures have universal meanings   108
5.4   President George W. Bush gestured the "hook 'em horns," the salute of the
       University of Texas Longhorns, as he watched the Inaugural Parade with
       his family and friends from the reviewing stand in front of the White House,
       January 20, 2005   110
5.5   Stamp printed in Barbuda, circa 1974, was dedicated to the centenary
       of the birth of Sir Winston S. Churchill and depicted his "V for victory"
       hand gesture   111
5.6   Cultural cartoon on attitudes about bikinis and burkas   112
5.7   The exchange of business cards has different traditions   114
5.8   Bridal white is popular in many Western cultures   115
5.9   White also can be the color of mourning. People shown attending a funeral
       in Suratthani, Thailand   116
5.10   Some cultures consider Friday 13th to be an unlucky day   119
5.11   August 8, 2008 was considered an auspicious date to open the Summer
       Olympics in Beijing. Image shows spectators cheering for the Chinese
       team prior to a Group C match between China and Belgium at the
       Olympic Games soccer tournament   119
5.12   Lady Gaga uses religious imagery in her fashion and performances; shown
       here performing on stage for an NBC *Today Show* concert at Rockefeller
       Plaza, New York City, in 2010   122
5.13   Dogs may be considered beloved pets in many cultures, but not in all. PR
       practitioners should be careful in selecting appropriate imagery of animals   124
5.14   The type of flower and their colors can have different meanings, so writers
       should check the symbolism of flowers for specific markets   125
6.1   Javanese performance presents the story of Ramayana and Mahabharata in
       wayang kulit (shadow puppetry) at the Sonobudoyo Museum in Yogyakarta,
       Indonesia   130
6.2   World premiere of Walt Disney Animation Studios' *Frozen* in Los Angeles   131
6.3   Actress Audrey Tautou at the Los Angeles premiere of *Coco Before Chanel*   134
6.4   Employees of all levels, whether in front or behind-the-scenes of a company,
       can tell compelling stories   136
6.5   Isaiah Mustafa (left) and Fabio at a public appearance to promote the Epic
       Old Spice Challenge in Los Angeles   139
6.6   Logo of the Internet Cat Video Festival held at the Walker Art Center in
       Minneapolis, Minnesota   140
6.7   Grumpy Cat at the 2014 MTV Movie Awards at the Nokia Theatre LA Live   140
6.8   Sebastian Vettel racing in his Red Bull Racing car during 2012 Formula 1
       Singtel Singapore Grand Prix   142
6.9   Rescued baby bats at the Australian Bat Clinic & Wildlife Trauma Centre   144
6.10   Taughannock Falls, a waterfall near Ithaca, N.Y.   147

6.11   PepsiMax presents the "unbelievable" bus shelter in London with the help
       of augmented reality   149
6.12   "Nutella® 50 years full of stories" campaign   150
6.13   2014 Share a Coke promotion   150
6.14   Examples of three job descriptions from Australia's Best Jobs in the World
       Campaign   152
6.15   World Vegan Day stamp   154
6.16   Visitors can explore 44 holes at Hobbiton Movie Set Tours, which were
       reconstructed in 2011 for *The Hobbit* trilogy   155
6.17   After three straight days of competition at the 2013 Rubik's Cube World
       Championship in Las Vegas, Feliks Zemdegs of Australia bested his
       fellow competitors with the fastest average time for solving the classic
       3x3 Rubik's Cube of 8.18 seconds, completing his fastest single solve
       in 7.36 seconds   156
6.18   IBM employees, retirees, clients, and business partners worldwide donated
       their time and expertise during the company's 100th anniversary   157
6.19   IBM Centennial Day of Service in Rio de Janeiro, Brazil   157
7.1   Cartoon illustrates how Dr. Johnson had a challenging mission   166
7.2   "Noah Webster, The Schoolmaster of the Republic," print by Root & Tinker   168
7.3   Photo of Sir James Murray, first editor of the Oxford English Dictionary,
       in his office   169
7.4   Selfie (noun, informal) was named Oxford Dictionaries' international Word
       of the Year 2013   172
8.1   Cartoon depicts the "grammar police"   179
8.2   Jackson Pollock, "Number 14: Gray," 1948, enamel over gesso on paper   181
8.3   Jackson Pollock, "Stacking Hay" (formerly "Harvest"), ca. 1935–36,
       lithograph (double-sided)   181
8.4   "A Cautionary Tale" cartoon illustrates the power of a comma   195
9.1   Cartoonist Ron Therien illustrates how football means different things   212
9.2   The gaffe by Tony Hayward, the former BP CEO, about the Gulf of Mexico
       oil spill was widely commented on in all forms of media and lampooned by
       cartoonists   225
9.3   Cartoonist shares a new perspective on editing and proofreading marks   228
10.1   A Fedex Panda Express just seconds after landing at Edinburgh Turnhouse
       Airport carries two Giant Pandas Tian Tian and Yang Guang to Edinburgh
       Zoo in Edinburgh, Scotland, on December 4, 2011   254
10.2   Four globular clusters in Fornax   255
10.3   Artist's reconstruction of the huge groundhog-like animal that once lived
       on Madagascar   256
10.4   The new North Wing exterior rendering, Corning Museum of Glass,
       Corning, N.Y.   257
10.5   Interior rendering of the North Wing Contemporary Gallery, Corning
       Museum of Glass, Corning, N.Y.   257
11.1   Musikmesse USB in the shape of a guitar   265
11.2   Aquatica, SeaWorld's Waterpark in San Antonio, provided journalists with
       photos, videos, and news releases on a USB shaped like a stingray   266

11.3	Self-contained Heavy Rain media kit mailer constructed of hard cardboard unfolds into a jewel-case box containing the SONY PlayStation 3 game	266
11.4	Kraken Black Spiced Rum media kit box with seven forms of "proof"	267
11.5	Kraken Black Spiced Rum media kit box with "scientific journal"	268
11.6	Lindt media kit packaged with chocolate samples	269
11.7	Daisy Marc Jacobs Pop Art edition media kit	270
11.8	FIAT 500 media kit. FIAT is a registered trademark of Fiat Group Marketing & Corporate Communication S.p.A., used under license by Chrysler Group LLC	270
11.9	Universal Orlando's Halloween Horror Nights media kit packaged in a locked trunk containing a faux head	271
11.10	Nike "Write the Future" World Cup media kit	272
11.11	Nike "Write the Future" media kit also included a display stand for hand-carved crayons with the likeness of six World Cup soccer players	272
11.12	Close-up images of crayons carved by Diem Chau in the Nike "Write the Future" World Cup media kit	273
11.13	Example of a portrait image for a profile, eportfolio, or other biographical use	283
11.14	The Jelly Belly Jelly Bean infographic	288
11.15	Spilling the Beans infographic	289
11.16	Visiting Jelly Belly infographic	290
11.17	Love It or Leave It? infographic	291
12.1	Hourglass metaphor shows a technique in news reporting	295
12.2	The kabob metaphor illustrates another way to organize a story	296
12.3	Popular Dutch DJ Armin Van Buuren (center) and English musician Christian Burns (to his left) speak at a press conference in Moscow	302
12.4	Front cover of invitation for the National Maritime Historical Society's annual awards dinner	309
12.5	Inside spread of invitation for the National Maritime Historical Society's annual awards dinner	310
13.1	Cartoon illustrates the challenges in creating hashtags	335
13.2	American Red Cross blog screenshot	342
13.3	Edison's Desk blog screenshot	342
13.4	Cartoonist depicts how clichéd content on Instagram can be	348
13.5	Honda celebrates Halloween on Vine with VACula; screenshot No. 1	349
13.6	Honda celebrates Halloween on Vine with VACula; screenshot No. 2	349
13.7	The American Red Cross also celebrates Halloween on Vine	350
13.8	Wikipedia website	351
14.1	Receiving enthusiastic applause after you speak can be rewarding	360
14.2	Knowing the setup of where you will be speaking is essential	361
14.3	Spot where "I Have a Dream" speech was delivered by American civil rights activist Martin Luther King, Jr. on August 28, 1963, from the steps of the Lincoln Memorial in Washington, D.C.	364
14.4	Author J. K. Rowling at the press conference for An Evening with Harry, Carrie and Garp author book readings to benefit Doctors Without Borders, Radio City Music Hall, New York, in 2006	365

14.5   Close-up of an Apple iMac computer displaying the www.apple.com front
        page tribute to former chief executive Steve Jobs, who died on October 5,
        2011   366
14.6   Connecting with your audience is essential   368
14.7   "Dumb Ways to Die" screenshot of public service announcement created
        by Metro Trains Melbourne, Australia, to promote rail safety   376
15.1   Front page of *The Furrow* from 1897   381
15.2   Cover page of *The Furrow*, September/October 2014 issue   382
15.3   Cover of *Stronger*, an Interpublic publication on corporate citizenship,
        from 2014   383
15.4   Screenshot of *BlueNotes*, an online publication on ANZ's newsroom   384
15.5   Screenshot of *The Network,* Cisco's Technology News Site   386
15.6   Volkswagen "Green Guts" brochure; front and back covers   392
15.7   Volkswagen "Green Guts" brochure shown opened front and back panels   392
15.8   Volkswagen "Green Guts" brochure on display at consumer show exhibitions
        in Toronto and Vancouver   393
15.9   Close-up image of Volkswagen "Green Guts" brochure on display at consumer
        show exhibitions in Toronto and Vancouver   394
15.10 Example of an Earth Hour poster   395
15.11 Half-fold brochure   397
15.12 Six-panel gate fold brochure   397
15.13 Tri-fold brochure   397
15.14 Z-fold brochure   397
15.15 Multi-panel accordion-fold brochure   398
16.1   Cover of public relations proposal for Emmy's Organics   411
16.2   Creative example of a bio in the form of a motorcoach ticket   421
17.1   Dilbert cartoon captures how meeting time can be misused   430
17.2   Learning how to write clear agendas and minutes can make meetings more
        productive for all participants   445

Preface

Welcome to Global Writing for Public Relations

I have created a new approach to a book on writing for public relations that combines intercultural communication, international public relations, and effective public relations writing techniques for today's global arena. *Global Writing for Public Relations: Connecting in English with Stakeholders and Publics Worldwide* is designed to help public relations students and practitioners become proficient and sophisticated writers to connect with diverse audiences. Public relations practitioners will need to navigate within an increasingly global world in English, the lingua franca of business, spoken by one-third of the world's population—and within the transnational, borderless quality of the Internet, where approximately 80% of electronically stored information is in English.

Worldwide technological innovations, as well as social, economic, and political changes, have broadened the importance of public relations. For organizations to thrive in a competitive marketplace, they need to diversify in international markets. New opportunities abound in China, Russia, India, Brazil, South Korea, and elsewhere—and many people in business and diplomacy, regardless of location, are conversant in English. English also has become the dominant language in education.

Global Writing for Public Relations provides multiple resources to help students and public relations practitioners learn best practices to communicate with global audiences in English. This book focuses on writing public relations materials in English that can be understood and appreciated by journalists, businesses, and consumers in approximately 75 countries with English as an official or special-status language, as well as by other English-speaking audiences worldwide. The book will help writers develop competencies to reach diverse international markets and multicultural users of multiple media platforms for information and news who prefer simpler, less commercial language in an increasingly savvy, yet distracted and cluttered environment.

This new book offers the following features:

- Insight into the evolution of English-language communication in business and public relations, as well as theoretical and political debates on global English and globalization.
- An overview of the growth of international public relations operations and industry efforts for universal standards.
- An understanding of both a global thematic and customized local approach in creating public relations campaigns and written materials.
- Ongoing and evolving innovations in social media and mobile communications worldwide—and their impact on public relations writing.
- The importance of navigating intercultural business communications and developing writing skills to resonate with international audiences.

- An appreciation of the differences between Oxford and Webster's English, as well as other English-language dictionaries and stylebooks around the globe.
- Strategic questions to help writers develop critical thinking skills and understand how to create meaningful communications materials for specific audiences.
- Storytelling skills that help writers craft compelling content to inspire others to read, share, and engage with.
- Real-world examples from different countries and diverse industries that illustrate creative solutions.
- Academic insights that apply to real-world situations in the public relations field.
- Step-by-step guidance on writing public relations materials with easy-to-follow templates to reach traditional and online media, consumers, and businesses.
- Self-evaluation and creative thinking exercises to improve cultural literacy, grammar, punctuation, and editing skills for enhanced clarity.
- Supplemental online resources for educators and students.

The book combines my experience training students and seasoned professionals and my background in crafting public relations materials that resonate with global English-language audiences. Although I am focusing on English-language writing skills in this book, I also address the growing demand for bilingual and multilingual skills. Today's public relations practitioners face an exciting time to be in the field, with an increasingly diverse global marketplace and ongoing technological tools to maintain a dialogue and share words and images.

I hope this new resource proves to be helpful and insightful. I would welcome your comments by email at PRresearch@ithaca.edu.

What You Will Learn

Global Writing for Public Relations is divided into six parts:

- ***Part One: Going Global in Public Relations*** traces the evolution of English and its current status as the lingua franca of business; looks at the world's language landscape and variations of English; examines the impact of globalism on the public relations industry and international career opportunities; and addresses the changes in social media and traditional media, as well as ethical and legal issues affecting public relations writers worldwide.
- ***Part Two: Developing Intercultural Communication Skills and Sensitivities*** examines intercultural theories to help public relations practitioners navigate within a global marketplace; addresses nonverbal interpretations relevant to public relations writers when selecting visual imagery; and describes storytelling approaches that are relevant to contemporary public relations writers communicating with diverse audiences locally or worldwide on multiple platforms.
- ***Part Three: Honing English Writing Skills for Global Audiences*** reviews writing basics and covers variations in English standards and English-language stylebooks worldwide; presents techniques for improving grammar and punctuation; outlines editing skills for greater cultural clarity and preferred terms for gender, race, age, and sexual orientation; and reviews translation issues and proofreading techniques for public relations materials.

- *Part Four: Generating and Managing News Worldwide* focuses on writing tools for communicating with journalists; explains how to write news releases for traditional and digital media; illustrates different types of media kits and online newsrooms for global audiences; and focuses also on writing tools for media events, press visits, and opinion pieces that are used by public relations practitioners to generate coverage in global and "glocal" media outlets.
- *Part Five: Connecting Online and Using External Communication Tools Globally* examines writing techniques for blogs, microblogs, and social networking sites; covers writing for the ear and eye to craft speeches and video scripts; and outlines controlled content options for writers, including corporate-produced magazines and newsletters, branded online newsrooms, brochures and posters, and advertorials and native advertising.
- *Part Six: Writing International Plans, Reports, and Business Correspondence* explains how to prepare, compose, and present public relations plans on a local, regional, or global scale to clients or in-house decision makers; and outlines how to prepare various types of business correspondence, meeting agendas and minutes, and activity and monitoring reports, as well as addresses cultural considerations and levels of formality.

Acknowledgments

I particularly want to offer my gratitude to Linda Bathgate, communication and media studies publisher at Routledge/Taylor & Francis Group, as well as to Ross Wagenhofer, editorial assistant; Bonita Glanville-Morris, production editor; the publishing house's other staff members; and the external reviewers for their feedback. I want to thank four graduate assistants at Ithaca College's Roy H. Park School of Communications: Benjamin Daumas (Class of 2014) and Suzanne Chouman (2014) for their help during the final stages; and Sarah Rosemarino (2011) and Jacqueline Adelewitz (2012) for their assistance during the preliminary research process, as well as professors Cory L. Young and Harold Kalman for arranging the assistantships. I greatly appreciate the companies, nonprofits, and individuals for their support in providing visual imagery and exhibits for free or at a discount. I also am thankful to my husband, Steven Lovass-Nagy, for providing feedback throughout the entire manuscript process, as well as to my family and friends who were patient and understanding while I opted out of social activities and spent many hours during weeknights, weekends, and holidays working on the manuscript. In addition, I am very grateful to my colleagues, particularly during my earlier years in the business, for their guidance and advice in helping me learn how to communicate more effectively with the media and diverse stakeholders around the world. To conclude, I am indebted to many of my students at Ithaca College for their ongoing encouragement.

About the Author

Global Writing for Public Relations draws on Arhlene Flowers's experience as both an academic and a practitioner in international public relations. Having conducted business for more than two decades while representing organizations on all continents except for Antarctica, Arhlene is proficient in communicating in English to diverse international and multicultural audiences. She has represented a wide range of nonprofits, government organizations, and public and private companies.

Prior to joining Ithaca College's Roy H. Park School of Communications, Arhlene held senior management positions at leading global companies on both sides of the business: global agencies headquartered in New York City, such as Ruder Finn and Hill and Knowlton, serving a variety of clients; and in-house corporate marketing departments. On the client side, she served as corporate public relations director worldwide at Four Seasons Hotels and Resorts, based in its corporate headquarters in Toronto, during a time of global expansion when it was a publicly held company. She has developed and managed public relations campaigns to launch new products and services, revitalize existing brands, reach new markets, overcome crises and challenges, and enhance awareness among shareholders. In the crisis communications arena, she dealt with crime, hijackings, accidents, hurricanes, floods, earthquakes, boycotts, labor disputes, and food poisonings.

This global experience has helped her acquire an appreciation and understanding of English as a common language for global audiences. She is well versed in the nuances of cultural differences and sensitivities. She also managed internal public relations staff and public relations agencies in multiple countries, in which she learned how to apply a "glocal" approach, blending the global mission of the organizations with the specific needs of the local markets and media. Her professional background spans all elements of public relations writing for internal and external audiences, reaching the media, businesses, consumers, and shareholders in North America and international markets.

In 2006, she segued to academia and transferred her skills to training a new generation of communicators. She started as an assistant professor in Ithaca College and was granted tenure and promoted to associate professor in 2012. She has been teaching courses in public relations, including Writing for Public Relations, in the Department of Strategic Communication and its two undergraduate degree programs: Integrated Marketing Communications, which offers students interrelated disciplines of public relations, advertising, and marketing; and Communication Management and Design in its Corporate Communication concentration. She also has taught public relations in the department's graduate program in Communication.

Her research in integrated marketing and public relations has been published in a variety of peer-reviewed academic publications. She also has presented papers at regional, national, and international conferences in the U.S., Europe, and Asia.

Born in Hawaii and raised in New York, she holds a Bachelor of Arts from New York University and a Master of Professional Studies from the New School for Social Research in New York City. She is a member of the Public Relations Society of America and also serves as the faculty advisor to Ithaca College's Chapter of the Public Relations Student Society of America.

Part One

GOING GLOBAL IN PUBLIC RELATIONS

Part One contains three chapters that review the evolution of English and its role as the lingua franca of business; the impact of globalism on public relations; and the changes in social and traditional media, as well as ethical and legal issues affecting public relations writers worldwide.

Chapter 1 Exploring the Evolution of English as "Globish"

- Traces the evolution of English and looks at the language landscape of the world—and explains why public relations practitioners need to be fluent in today's lingua franca.
- Provides examples of multinational corporations and diplomatic and trade groups that have adopted English as their official language or one of their official languages.
- Looks at world languages, differences in English-language education, and the growing demand in developing skills to communicate in written and spoken English, as well as in other languages.
- Covers ways to prepare for a career in international public relations, as well as considerations for working abroad.

Chapter 2 Understanding Global Perspectives in Public Relations

- Examines the evolution of international public relations, definitions of public relations, and the proliferation of industry trade groups on an international, regional, and local level.
- Reviews efforts by global trade groups to develop universal standards in public relations.
- Looks at the growth of international communication conglomerates, as well as the growing importance of verbal and written English proficiency for careers in business and public relations.
- Explains a "glocal" approach, communicating core messages and localizing content to the needs of the local market.

Chapter 3 Changing Global Media Landscape and Ethical and Legal Issues

- Investigates evolving social networking platforms around the globe and the growth of portable and participatory technology.
- Examines the evolution of the 24/7 news reporting cycle at international media outlets and changes facing traditional media as they embrace social media.
- Reviews major ethical and legal issues so that public relations practitioners understand them and know when to seek legal counsel to follow a country's regulations.

1 Exploring the Evolution of English as "Globish"

This is the interactive, ever-changing world of global English. At the beginning of the twenty-first century, rarely has a language and its culture enjoyed such an opportunity to represent the world. In crude numbers alone, English is used, in some form, by approximately 2 billion people on earth, one-third of the planet, and only outnumbered by the speakers of Chinese, approximately 350 million of whom also speak some kind of English.

—Robert McCrum, author of *Globish: How English Became the World's Language*

1.1 Introduction to the World of English

The morphing of "global" and "English" into "globish" reflects the ubiquity of English in the new millennium. English has become the world's **lingua franca**—the most commonly used language by people who speak other languages to communicate collectively—in international business and in the public relations field. Popular movies and music, academic conferences and scientific research, international diplomacy and economics, international sports competitions, multinational[1] corporations, and global advocacy groups all have one thing in common: English. English is now the required language of business for several multinational corporations, as well as for international maritime and air traffic control. English also dominates the Internet, as the language of approximately 80% of electronically stored information worldwide (Mydans, 2007). More than half of the world is predicted to gain some level of proficiency in English by 2050 ("Triumph of English," 2001).

Public relations agencies and in-house corporate communication departments also have been impacted by worldwide technological innovations, as well as by social, economic, and political changes. For organizations to thrive in a competitive marketplace, they must diversify in international markets. New opportunities abound in economies around the globe—and a rising number of consumers, business executives, and journalists are reading English, particularly on the Web, and conversing in English as the common language for business.

New talent and seasoned public relations practitioners can now easily connect with a global audience in English with the borderless quality of the Internet. They also need to communicate with users of multiple media platforms for information and news who prefer simpler, more direct and less commercial language in an increasingly distracted and cluttered environment. According to Nielsen Company (2010), blogs and social networking sites are visited by three-quarters of global consumers who access the Internet.

The proliferation of English also means that people, regardless of their location, from many walks of life—academics, diplomats, intellectuals, journalists, business executives, government officials, nonprofit directors, and public relations professionals—need to have proficiency in the language to communicate in the global arena.

Naomi Buck (2006), a Toronto-born journalist who has lived in a number of countries, reflected on the ubiquity of English in public debate—and the disadvantages of not having a voice in English to reach a broader audience. Buck also provided a colorful description of the language's evolution:

> Maybe some comfort can be taken in the fact that English has been sashaying, reconnoitring and kowtowing its way around the world for a long time. It knows how to beg, borrow and steal but also how to integrate, share and age—with grace and not. (para. 16)

Linguist David Crystal summed up the situation: "Global English can lead to Global Understanding" (2001a, p. 27). Approximately 335 million people speak English as a first language in 101 countries (Lewis, Simons, & Fennig, 2015). English is spoken in more countries than any other language—people from American Samoa to Zimbabwe speak English as a national or official language (see Figure 1.1). In addition, English serves as the de facto national working language in Bahrain, Bhutan, the Maldives, and the United Arab Emirates, as well as in other countries by substantial immigrant groups.

Although the total number of countries in the world is debated due to disputed territories, a widely used number is 193, based on the member nations of the United Nations, which includes its most recent member country, South Sudan, in 2011 (United Nations, 2015a), or 195, including the UN's two non-member observer states (the Holy See, which is the jurisdiction

Figure 1.1—MAP OF THE CONTEMPORARY ENGLISH-SPEAKING WORLD.
Source: © Svein-Tore Griff With.

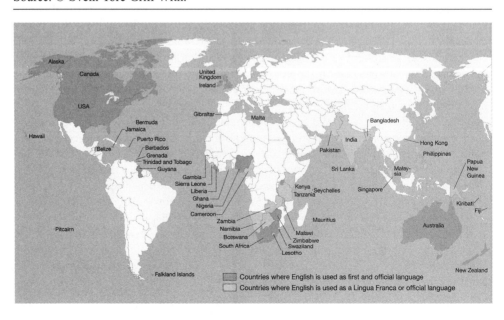

in Rome of the Catholic Church, and the State of Palestine). Currently, the International Olympic Committee is represented by 205 National Olympic Committees, including 192 United Nations members (with the exception of South Sudan) and one of its observers, Palestine. The 12 other non-United Nations members or observers include Cook Islands, Kosovo, Hong Kong (as an administrative region of China), Taiwan, as well as four U.S. territories, three British territories, and one Netherlands territory. The National Olympic Committees maintain responsibility for supervising the bidding process of host cities, as well as developing, selecting, and sending teams in their nations to compete in the international Olympic Games (Olympic.org, 2015).

1.2 English Evolves from More Than 350 Languages

The history of English is a fascinating narrative on how a language spoken by tribes in northwest England about 2,000 years ago spread around the globe. Authors McCrum, Cran, and MacNeil of *The Story of English* (1986) explain why:

> The story of all languages is full of surprises. The year the Anglo-Saxons first crossed the sea to the former Roman province of Britannia, in AD 450, the odds against English becoming a world language were about a million to one. (p. 48)

Understanding the evolution of English can help us better appreciate how the language thrives today. Let us start by looking at your knowledge of the language by trying to answer the following questions:

- Can you identify the Latin roots of English-language words, such as the Latin equivalents of *both*, *stars* and *outer space*, *all*, and *city*? See the Pre-English period in the next section.
- Can you name a few Anglo-Saxon words that are still used in English? See Early Old English.
- Can you identify a few English words with Viking roots? See Later Old English.
- How many thousands of French words influenced English? See Middle English.
- Which British monarch was the first to set up trading posts around the world? See Early Modern English.
- When was the first English-language printed book published? See Early Modern English.
- Can you estimate how many words Shakespeare added to the English vocabulary? See Early Modern English.
- When did Noah Webster publish the first American-English dictionary? See Modern English.
- What developments have influenced the spread of English since the mid-20th century? See Late Modern English.

1.2.1 English from the Roman Empire to Today

According to linguist David Graddol (1997), English has evolved over the following seven time periods:

1. **Pre-English period** (before A.D. 450)

   Latin became the lingua franca in administration and education when Julius Caesar and the Roman Empire invaded Britain in 55 B.C. (see Figure 1.2). The Celtic-speaking population in Britain then spoke two main branches similar to today's Gaelic and Welsh. The names of places such as Chester and Manchester derive from *castra*, the Latin word for *camp* (McCrum et al., 1986). English words with Latin origins remain today. *Ambi* (both), *astro* (stars and outer space), *omni* (all), and *urb* (city) are just a few examples.

2. **Early Old English** (c. 450 to c. 850)

   Germanic tribes from Continental Europe—Angles, Saxons, and Jutes—invaded Britain in A.D. 449, influencing the development of Early Old English. Basic Anglo-Saxon words have evolved and are still used today: *is*, *here*, *the*, *there*, and *you*, as well as words reflecting farming, celebrations, and emotions—*earth*, *field*, *sheep*, *glee*, *laughter*, and *mirth* (McCrum et al., 1986). This period also sparked the "Anglo-Saxon love of ambiguity, innuendo and word-play" (McCrum et al., 1986, p. 62), with a rich oral tradition of storytelling and new English literature. Today's readers would be bewildered trying to read the original Anglo-Saxon epic poem of *Beowulf* (see Figure 1.3), yet the legend continues to live on in contemporary film and games.

3. **Later Old English** (c. 850 to 1100)

   The Viking invasion of Scandinavian peoples brought over other linguistic influences to the development of English. King Alfred, known as Alfred the Great, was instrumental in having Latin texts translated into English and setting up English-language education (see Figure 1.4). Up to 900 words of Viking origin remain in English today.

Figure 1.2—"THE FIRST DESCENT OF JULIUS CAESAR ON THE COAST OF BRITAIN" ENGRAVING BY GRAINGER. Source: Image courtesy of antiqueprints.com.

The first descent of Julius Cæsar on the Coast of Britain.

Figure 1.3—SOLE SURVIVING MANUSCRIPT OF *BEOWULF* (11TH CENTURY).
British Library shelfmark: c13187–11; Cotton Vitelius A. XV f. 105. Source: © The British
Library Board.

**Figure 1.4—"KING ALFRED VISITING A MONASTERY SCHOOL" ENGRAVING
BY AUGUST BENZIGER.** Source: Project Gutenberg.

Many of these words refer to the human body, food, living things, and family members, as well as commonly used pronouns and verbs—*ankle, freckle, cake, egg, steak, reindeer, kid, husband, sister, both, their, get, take,* and *want* (Baugh & Cable, 2002; Butterfield, 2008).

4. **Middle English** (c. 1100 to 1450)

   The Norman Conquest changed the official language from English to French, creating a trilingual culture with Latin still in use for religion and scholarship. (See Figure 1.5 with a section of the Bayeux Tapestry depicting the Norman Conquest with Latin inscriptions.) Approximately 10,000 French words were assimilated into English, of which 75% still remain (McCrum, 2010). English strengthened nonetheless in literature and common usage; the Hundred Years War with France instilled loyalty to the English language, and the Peasants' Revolt and the Black Death led to a rise of leadership of the common English-speaking workers (McCrum et al., 1986). The literature of Geoffrey Chaucer can be understood to some degree by today's readers, particularly *The Canterbury Tales*, which was published in 1425.

5. **Early Modern English** (c. 1450 to 1750)

   This period comprises the Renaissance and the reign of Elizabeth I, rich with economic growth and cultural and scientific achievements. Between 5 and 7 million people spoke English during the reign of Queen Elizabeth I from 1558 to 1603 (Crystal, 1985). British ships sailed to the Americas and set up the first colony in Jamestown, Virginia, and to the Caribbean and India, establishing the first trading posts, thereby spreading the use of English while adopting words from other languages. The first printed English-language book was published in 1473—18 years after Johannes Gutenberg, the inventor of the printing press with metal movable type, printed *The Gutenberg Bible* in Latin. The first English-language bibles also appeared

Figure 1.5—DETAIL OF THE BAYEUX TAPESTRY DEPICTING THE NORMAN INVASION OF ENGLAND IN THE 11TH CENTURY. Source: © jorisvo/Shutterstock.com.

Figure 1.6—WILLIAM SHAKESPEARE, ENGLISH POET AND PLAYWRIGHT.
Engraving from *The Leisure Hour Magazine*, April 1864. Source: © Stocksnapper/Shutterstock.
com.

during this time period; the *King James Bible*, which was authorized by the English
Church, remains in use today. Scientific, religious, and literary works were published
in English by the likes of Thomas More, Francis Bacon, John Milton, William
Shakespeare (see Figure 1.6), and Isaac Newton. The Renaissance added between
10,000 and 12,000 new words to English from Latin, Greek, French, Spanish, and
Dutch, among other languages. Shakespeare's work reflected his vast vocabulary of
approximately 30,000 words (McCrum et al., 1986) and his creativity in coining
1,700 new words (Crystal, 2008).

6. **Modern English** (c. 1750 to 1950)
Mass migrations of colonists, traders, settlers, and missionaries continued to spread
English throughout North America, the Caribbean, Africa, the Middle East, Asia,
Australia, New Zealand, and the Pacific islands, as well as to the tip of South America
(see Figure 1.7 of a map of the British Empire in 1886). Serious efforts to standardize
the language began in the late 18th century with dictionaries and grammar books in
Britain, while the American War of Independence inspired Noah Webster to formulate
a distinctive American-English vocabulary. English also became the official language
or widely used as the second language in commerce, as global trade grew and more
products were produced during the Industrial Revolution. Technological innovations,
from the telegraph and radio to cinema and television, also spread English.

7. **Late Modern English** (c. 1950 to present)
At the beginning of Queen Elizabeth II's reign in 1952, an estimated 250 million
people worldwide spoke English as a first language (Crystal, 1985). Although British
English still remains used in former British colonies, many countries have adapted

Figure 1.7—IMPERIAL FEDERATION, MAP OF THE WORLD SHOWING THE EXTENT OF THE BRITISH EMPIRE IN 1886. Source: Map reproduction courtesy of the Norman B. Leventhal Map Center at the Boston Public Library.

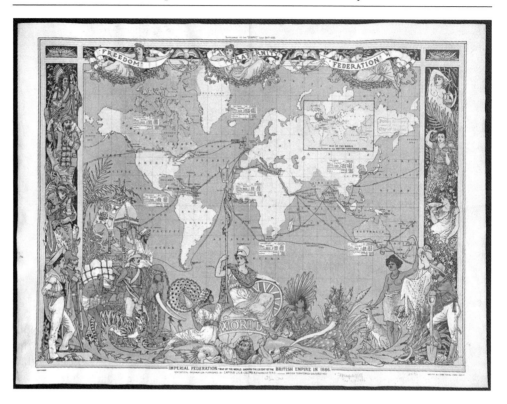

their own form of English usage, resulting in specialized dictionaries and English-language tools that recognize their unique heritage and evolution. Technological innovations—satellites, 24/7 cable news, the Internet, social media, and mobile technology—and the worldwide dissemination of movies and music have enhanced the familiarity of American English globally. English-language training also has proliferated worldwide due to the language's prominence in the media and business.

This linguistic evolution over two millennia has made contemporary English rich, with its roots in Dutch and German and absorption of words borrowed or adapted from Norman French, Old Norse Latin, Greek, and over 350 languages (Crystal, 2001b; Butterfield, 2008). Try Exercise 1.1 and see if you can identify the linguistic origins of words used in the English language today.

English continues to develop with new words and changing definitions from global usage, pop culture, and contemporary slang. A writer for *The Economist* said, "When it comes to new words, English puts up few barriers to entry" ("The Triumph of English," 2001, para. 3). According to the Global Language Monitor (2014), the English language acquires a new word every 98 minutes (approximately 14.7 words per day) and includes 1,025,109.8 words

Exercise 1.1

Self-Evaluation: Origins of English Words

The English language has absorbed over 350 languages. Try to match the language origins of these words used in contemporary English. Each English word below has one primary origin.

English Words

1. Agile
2. Algebra
3. Amok
4. Bigot
5. Boss
6. Berserk
7. Boomerang
8. Catamaran
9. Catastrophe
10. Coach
11. Face-off
12. Fest
13. Galore
14. Ghetto
15. Gung-ho
16. Hurricane
17. Juggernaut
18. Kayak
19. Ketchup
20. Khaki
21. Klutz
22. Lanai
23. Ombudsman
24. Robot
25. Safari
26. Sauna
27. Terrapin
28. Trek
29. Troika
30. Tycoon
31. Yogurt

Origins

a. Afrikaans
b. Algonquin
c. Arabic
d. Australian Aboriginal
e. Canadian English
f. Cantonese
g. Czech
h. Dutch
i. Finnish
j. French
k. Gaelic
l. German
m. Greek
n. Hawaiian
o. Hindi
p. Hungarian
q. Inuit
r. Italian
s. Japanese
t. Latin
u. Malay
v. Mandarin
w. Old Norse
x. Russian
y. Spanish
z. Swahili
aa. Swedish
bb. Turkish
cc. Tamil
dd. Urdu
ee. Yiddish

Please refer to Appendix D for answers.

(as of January 1, 2014), while having passed the one millionth word threshold with "Web 2.0" in 2009. The Oxford English Dictionary now contains more than 600,000 words. The Oxford Corpus, an electronic collection of oral and written English text, contains more than two billion words from around the globe. The Corpus follows codes and analyzes 21st-century English in all forms from print media and literature to Internet exchanges. Jeremy Butterfield, author of the *Damp Squid: The English Language Laid Bare* and editor of dictionaries, described the scope of words in the Corpus: "if you laid all the words in the Corpus end to end the line would stretch from the northern tip of Scotland to the Southern tip of New Zealand" (2008, p. 4).

1.3 English: Today's Lingua Franca of Global Business and Diplomacy

Since the 20th century, a number of new multinational organizations in international trade, transportation, and diplomacy were formed, bringing together diverse people around the globe to share their opinions, discuss serious topics, and work out collective solutions. These organizations also had to decide what language or languages to communicate in. Ku and Zussman (2010), academics and economists based in the U.S. and Israel respectively, examined English as the lingua franca in business in more than 100 countries over 30 years, concluding that English-language proficiency aids in promoting foreign trade by "overcoming historically determined language barriers" (p. 259) with trade partners.

English was chosen as the official or one of the official languages of the following global organizations:

- The **International Monetary Fund** (founded in 1945), based in Washington, D.C., works with 188 countries and describes what it does as follows: "promotes international financial stability and monetary cooperation. It also seeks to facilitate international trade, promote high employment and sustainable economic growth, and reduce poverty around the world" (International Monetary Fund, 2015, para. 1). The IMF also provides its staff with language instruction and requires written and spoken proficiency in English. Its Language Services group offers interpretation and translation services in Arabic, Chinese, English, French, German, Portuguese, Russian, and Spanish (International Monetary Fund, n.d.).
- The 193 member nations of the **United Nations** (set up in 1945) address significant peacekeeping and humanitarian issues facing the globe. Based in New York City, the United Nations also is linked to 30 specialized organizations, including the International Monetary Fund, the World Bank, and World Health Organization. The United Nations has six official languages (Arabic, Chinese, English, French, Russian, and Spanish), which are equally celebrated through United Nations Language Days. For example, English Language Day is held on the birthday of William Shakespeare. With more than 44,000 staff stationed in the New York headquarters and UN offices in Geneva, Vienna, Nairobi, and other locations, the United Nations Secretariat uses English and French as its working languages, while delegates may choose other official languages (United Nations, 2015b).
- Based in Washington, D.C., the **World Bank** (established in 1944) aims to share prosperity and to decrease poverty by providing loans and financial services to

developing countries and by negotiating trade agreements and trade disputes between nations. While English is the working language among its staff of approximately 10,000 based in more than 120 offices worldwide, the World Bank also translates reports into other languages, and data are available in 34 languages on Google (Barton, 2010).

- The **North Atlantic Treaty Organization** (formed in 1949) focuses on freedom and security of its 28 member nations. Based in Brussels, NATO uses English and French as its official languages (North Atlantic Treaty Organization, 2015).
- The multilateral **Organization of the Petroleum Exporting Countries** (established in 1960) oversees the petroleum policies of 12 oil-exporting nations. Based in Vienna, OPEC employs staff from approximately 38 countries and maintains English as its working language (Organization of the Petroleum Exporting Countries, 2015).
- The **Organisation for Economic Co-operation and Development** (established in 1961) works with 34 member countries to promote policies to improve the economic and social well-being of people around the world. Based in Paris, the OECD's official languages are English and French (Organisation for Economic Co-operation and Development, 2014).
- The **World Trade Organization** (set up in 1995) serves as a global forum for rules of trade between countries by negotiating trade agreements and trade disputes between nations. Based in Geneva, the WTO maintains English, French, and Spanish as its official languages, and requires staff to be fluent in at least two of these languages (World Trade Organization, 2015).

The demand for a universal language takes on a life-and-death dimension in international aviation. The worst civil aviation crash in history happened in 1977 in Tenerife in the Canary Islands when a KLM Boeing 747 pilot and an air traffic controller misunderstood one another. The pilot radioed the control tower that the plane was at takeoff or taking off (the transmission tapes were unclear), and the air traffic controller thought the pilot meant that the plane was at the takeoff position. The pilot taxied down the foggy runway directly into the path of a Pan Am Boeing 747 (McCreary, Pollard, Stevenson, & Wilson, 1998). This "ambiguous phraseology" led to the loss of 583 people. In 1990, a misunderstood dialogue between Spanish-speaking pilots of an Avianca flight from Bogota and an English-speaking air traffic controller at John F. Kennedy International Airport led to the plane running out of fuel before attempting to land in New York City, crashing and killing 73 of the 158 people aboard. The International Civil Aviation Organization now requires proficiency in English, beyond the standard ICAO Radiotelephony Phraseology, for air traffic controllers and flight crew members (see Figure 1.8) involved with international flights. The director of ICAO's Air Navigation Bureau explained its language testing initiatives: "In response to fatal accidents in which the lack of proficiency in English was identified as a contributing factor, ICAO adopted standards to strengthen language proficiency for pilots and air traffic controllers involved in international operations" (International Civil Aviation Organization, 2011, para. 3).

Malcolm Gladwell, author of *Outliers: The Story of Success*, examined the intercultural communication complexities beyond language to ethnocentricity and power distance in the cockpit and the air traffic control tower as the cause for a few plane accidents. Gladwell (2008) interviewed the retired Delta Air Lines vice president who was brought back to run Korean Air's flight operations and re-train pilots after a few plane crashes. The trainer explained that

Figure 1.8—PILOTS IN THE COCKPIT NEED TO COMMUNICATE CLEARLY WITH AIR TRAFFIC CONTROLLERS ANYWHERE. Source: © Tatiana Popova/Shutterstock.com.

the pilots "needed an opportunity to step outside those roles when they sat in the cockpit, and language was the key to that transformation" (p. 219), and that English allowed the pilots to "participate in a culture and language with a very different legacy" (p. 219). In 1999, Korean Air faced a poor safety record, financial losses, and a tarnished reputation; it was suspended from the SkyTeam airline alliance and banned as a carrier for employees by the United States Department of Defense. Since that time, Korean Air has strengthened its reputation, financial solvency, and safety record, resulting in many industry awards, including a Phoenix Award by *Air Transport World* for overcoming challenges in global aviation.

For many companies, lack of communication would not be as fatal, but misunderstandings could result in lost revenues, increased layoffs, poor employee morale, image problems, and botched projects. Staff members at headquarters and offices of multinational corporations worldwide have to be able to communicate collectively to exchange information, brainstorm ideas, conduct research, make decisions, manage teams, and create marketing and public relations plans on a global, regional, and local level. Four *Businessweek* editors in Paris, Rome, and Stuttgart co-authored an article titled "The Great English Divide" that explained the economic value and necessity of conducting global business in English, calling the language "an industrial tool now as basic as the screwdriver" (Baker, Resch, Carlisle, & Schmidt, 2001, para. 5).

Airbus, Daimler AG, Nokia, Lenovo, and Rakuten are a few examples of multinational corporations that have adopted English as their official language of business regardless of the location. This process requires strategic planning, a language policy, and resources for English-language training. Chris Allen Thomas, a specialist in educational linguistics, examined language policies in multinational organizations and their challenges for both employees and management in adopting English as a global language; a policy that does not fully recognize the value of linguistic diversity. Thomas (2007) advocates for "the need to develop creative and enlightened language planning to improve both the quality and value of intercultural communication" (p. 101). Multinational corporations may have language policies on different levels; the official language (or languages) of the country of the company's headquarters usually determines the company's language. If English is not an official language of the country of the headquarters, the company may have two official corporate languages used in the headquarters and among staff at all offices. In addition, staff within the local office or subsidiary also may communicate in the official language (or languages) of the country where it is based.

When you look at the career sections for major multinationals, international non-governmental organizations, and global advertising and public relations agencies, you will find a common theme: requirement for proficiency in English, and in some cases, bilingual or multilingual competencies. See Exhibit 1.1 for a few examples of English-language requirements for internships, graduate training programs, and other job openings. Korn/Ferry International, an international executive search firm, found that English was identified as the most frequent language in demand by 88% of the recruiters surveyed in Asia, Europe, and Latin America. In addition, recruiters ranked bilingualism as "critical" in business, with some regional differences: 95% in Latin America, 88% in Asia, 85% in Europe, and 34% in North America (Purdum, 2005).

1.4 English Language Education and World Englishes

According to Ethnologue (Lewis et al., 2015), people around the world speak 7,102 living languages out of a population of approximately 7.1 billion. Can you name the top 10 languages spoken today? Exhibit 1.2 lists the world's most widely spoken languages, of which English ranks third, yet it has been dominant in foreign-language education (Graddol, 2006). As the lingua franca of international business, English has become "the key to prosperity" (Skapinker, 2007, p. 5), making it a highly desirable and pragmatic language to learn.

Terms in English-language education use many acronyms, illustrating widely diverse and debated teaching methods (Graddol, 2006). Two English-language teaching models began in the 19th century. **English as a Second Language** (ESL) refers to the English primarily taught in countries that were former British colonies in Africa, Asia, and the Caribbean that continue to use English. **English as a Foreign Language** (EFL) has been dominant in the 20th century, which focuses on emulating native English speakers while learning about their culture. Newer models of English-language education have emerged that reflect today's realities. **English for Young Learners** (EYL) reflects the growing demand for bilingual education for children to develop proficiency. **English as a Lingua Franca** (ELF) also can refer to English spoken between speakers whose first language is not English. Other terms on the global application of English include **English as a Global Language** (EGL) or **English as an International**

Exhibit 1.1—ENGLISH-LANGUAGE CAREER REQUIREMENTS AT MULTINATIONAL ORGANIZATIONS

Company	Headquarters	Requirements (from corporate websites)
Airbus (aircraft manufacturer)	Toulouse, France	"We look for high-achieving dynamic graduates who are fluent in written and spoken English." (Direct Entry Graduate Programme requirement)
BRAC (formerly the Bangladesh Rural Advancement Committee)	Dhaka, Bangladesh	"BRAC receives foreign interns who have no knowledge of Bangla every year. BRAC also offers translator services if requested by an intern, especially when engaged in field work. Interns have to pay for these translators' services, as well as for their food and accommodation. Most BRAC staff stationed in the head office can communicate fluently in English." (Internships)
Burson-Marsteller (public relations agency)	New York, New York, U.S.	"For local applicants, excellent verbal and written communication skills in both Chinese and English are a must. For expatriate applicants, excellent verbal and written communication skills in English are a basic requirement and Chinese language skills are preferred but not required." (about careers in China)
Teva Pharmaceuticals Industries	Petah Tikva, Israel	"Fluent in English; Second language fluently, further European languages recommended." (requirement for Future Teva Leadership European Programme)
Microsoft (software corporation)	Redmond, Washington, U.S.	"Do I need to speak English fluently to work at Microsoft? English is the language we use to conduct business around the world, though you may also need to be fluent in the local language[s] of the country[s] in which you work." (Careers)
Nestlé (food and beverage company)	Vevey, Switzerland	"Adapting quickly to different cultures isn't always easy. All of which makes it important to combine a flexible approach with fluent English and two other languages." (International Development Programme)
Rakuten (electronic commerce and Internet company)	Tokyo, Japan	"What is the ideal skill set that you look for? We welcome applicants with Daily Conversation Level English [TOEIC 600 or above]. Even if you don't meet the above requirements, your application is welcome. We welcome people who have a desire to learn." (Careers)
Renault (vehicle manufacturer)	Boulogne, France	"International profiles carry great value at Renault. All executives joining the Group need a minimum score of 750 points in the TOEIC test of English for international communication." (Careers)
Samsung (electronics company)	Seoul, South Korea	"In this role it is important that you have excellent communication-and project management skills . . . You will need good Danish and English skills." (Samsung Accelerate Program, Graduate Program-Marketing, in Denmark)

Exhibit 1.2—WORLD'S MOST WIDELY SPOKEN LANGUAGES. Source: Lewis, M. P., Simons, G. F., & Fennig, C. D. (2015). *Ethnologue: Languages of the World* (18th ed.). Dallas, TX: SIL International. Retrieved from http://www.ethnologue.com/statistics/size.

Language	Approximate number of speakers in millions (with at least 50 million first-language speakers)
1. Chinese	1,197
2. Spanish	399
3. English	335
4. Hindi	260
5. Arabic	242
6. Portuguese	203
7. Bengali	189
8. Russian	166
9. Japanese	128
10. Lahnda*	88.7

* Lahnda is a macrolanguage spoken in Pakistan, which includes Khetrani, Northern Hindko, Pahari-Potwari, Saraiki, Southern Hindko, and Western Punjabi.

Language (EIL). Since the 1990s, new terms on English spoken in international business settings have become widespread: **English as a Business Language** (EBL), **English for International Business** (EIB), or **Business English as a Lingua Franca** (BELF), which means the use of English as the lingua franca in business communication for both people who speak **English as a Mother Tongue** (EMT) and ELF speakers, who may be ESL or EFL. For example, business transactions between executives in China and Brazil or in Abu Dhabi and India would probably be in English.

Some governments have mandated English as an official language or as a requirement in education. After Singapore became independent in 1965, the government kept English as one of its official languages, which is widely used in business, administration, and education; its other three official languages are Chinese, Malay, and Tamil, which reflect the country's ethnic diversity. Singapore is home to Chinese (74.2% of the population), Malays (13.3%), Indians (9.2%), and Eurasians and other Asians (3.3%), as well as expatriates from around the globe, who all need to communicate in a common language, yet maintain their own linguistic heritage (Singapore Tourism Promotion Board, 2013). In 2000, Singapore began its "Speak Good English Movement" (see Figure 1.9) to promote usage of standardized English, thereby attempting to lessen Colloquial Singapore English, also known as Singlish.

English-language education in China began in 1862 and has accelerated rapidly since the 1960s as the first foreign language required in middle school education and the preferred language in courses and majors at universities, making English more dominant than Russian

Figure 1.9—IMAGE OF THE SPEAK GOOD ENGLISH MOVEMENT CAMPAIGN IN SINGAPORE. Source: Provided with the courtesy of the Speak Good English Movement website.

was earlier in the mid-20th century (Chang, 2006). Bahrain, for example, uses English widely in business, and it is a compulsory second language in education. Chile has established an "English Opens Doors" elementary and high school educational program, with the long-term intention to make 15 million Chileans bilingual in English and Spanish within a generation (Rohter, 2004).

Edgar Schneider (2010), a linguist and academic in Germany, explained how English played a neutral role in politics in multilingual cultures. For example, in Nigeria, "it was nobody's ethnic tongue, so all ethnic groups were treated equally" (p. 215) and its role as "a language of liberalization" (p. 214), such as when English became the language of the African National Congress in South Africa. Ethnologue (Lewis et al., 2015) lists 526 living languages for Nigeria and 44 living languages for South Africa. Speaking of linguistic complexity, Papua New Guinea boasts more living languages than any other country: 839 (Lewis et al., 2015). However, New Guinea's principle languages are English and Tok Pisin.

1.4.1 Variations of English

Scholars also have been examining new variations of Englishes—Singlish, Japlish, Hinglish, Chinglish, Taglish or Filipino English, and Spanglish, among others—and debating what versions constitute standard usage of English today. *World Englishes*, an academic journal published by the International Association for World Englishes, covers global issues and cross-cultural perspectives on language, literature, and pedagogy.

How are English speakers defined? Braj Kachru, a sociolinguist and professor emeritus of the University of Illinois at Urbana-Champaign, coined the term **"World Englishes"** and developed a model of three concentric language circles (Kachru, 1985; Graddol, 2006) that defined English by location as follows (see Figure 1.10):

- The **inner circle** includes countries in which English is the first language of the majority of the population, such as the U.S., U.K., Australia, New Zealand, and other English-speaking countries, with approximately 320 to 380 million speakers.
- The **outer circle** encompassed approximately 150 to 300 million English speakers in India, Kenya, Singapore, and in other former colonies under British or American

Figure 1.10—DIAGRAM BASED ON THE MODEL OF THREE CONCENTRIC LANGUAGE CIRCLES DEVELOPED BY SOCIOLINGUIST BRAJ KACHRU (1985).

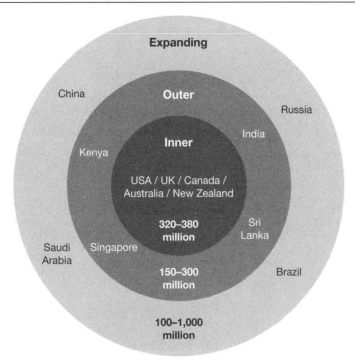

rule, in which English has been a popular second language or additional language, whether English is an official language or has been used historically.

- The **expanding circle** reaches 100 million to 1,000 million English speakers, where English is a foreign language, such as Japan, China, Brazil, and Russia, following British or American English standards, whether taught in school or applied in international business.

Why do you think this model would be debated today and how would you update it? Although the model was well respected, it also was criticized for disregarding globalization, the changing nature of English-language education, and language proficiencies beyond geographic borders (Graddol, 2006). Paul Bruthiaux (2003), an English professor in the U.S., argued that the model enforces rigid standards by disregarding dialects within the inner circle, such as African-American English in the U.S., and instead focuses on the language spoken by the minority, such as White South African English, in a diverse multilingual country. Bruthiaux also raises other location, historical, and political limitations in all circles. Kachru proposed a newer model with an expanded inner circle of 500 million highly proficient speakers that includes bands of varying levels of proficiency from high to low (see Figure 1.11), in which he explained how "the 'inner circle' is now better conceived of as the group of highly proficient speakers of English—those who have 'functional nativeness' regardless of how they learned or use the language" (Graddol, 2006, p. 110).

**Figure 1.11—DIAGRAM BASED ON THE RANGES OF LANGUAGE PROFICIEN-
CIES FROM HIGH TO LOW IN *ENGLISH NEXT* BY DAVID GRADDOL, WHICH
WAS PUBLISHED BY THE BRITISH COUNCIL IN 2006.**

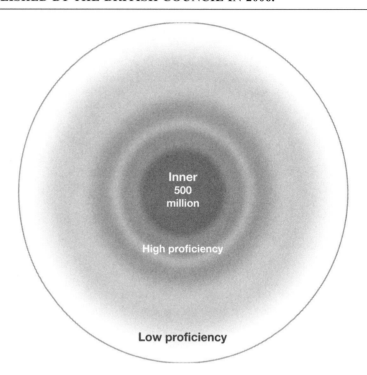

1.4.2 Foreign-Language Education in English-Language Countries

You can travel 3,000 miles (4,828 kilometers) across mainland U.S. and hear English mostly everywhere in schools, offices, and the media. Americans envy continental Europeans, in particular, for their multilingual skills. Think about how many different languages are spoken in continental Europe when you travel 2,060 miles (3,315.25 kilometers) from Lisbon, Portugal, to Tallinn, Estonia. Although the U.S. is a multicultural society with 21% of its population age 5 and older speaking a language other than English at home (Ryan, 2013), America still lags behind in competency in foreign-language skills. Francisco Marmolejo (2010), an international educational administrator and a supporter of foreign-language skills in the U.S., explained the number-one excuse: "The rationale used by many who justify this widespread second-language deficiency is that English is today's lingua franca" (para. 3). The United States Department of Education (2012) established its first articulated international strategy for 2012–2016 to prepare today's young Americans to become globally competent citizens by developing skills in languages, cultural awareness, and critical and creative thinking, among others. The goals are to help the new generation face complex global challenges, enter a workforce with increasing economic and employment competitiveness, and function effectively within America's diverse multicultural society.

The U.K. government also wants to reverse the decline in foreign language skills. Michael Shackleton, the former head of the European Parliament Information Office in London, stated on the BBC that poor foreign language skills have resulted in the underrepresentation of the British workforce in the European Parliament and Commission (Hargreaves, 2011). The director of strategy for the British Council stated in a report proposing foreign language initiatives: "But in the UK we must accept that speaking English alone is not enough in a world where multilingualism is becoming the norm" (Tinsley & Board, 2014, p. 2). Australia set up a National Asian Languages and Studies in Schools Program to encourage children to learn the languages of its neighboring countries, particularly Mandarin (Macgibbon, 2011).

1.5 The Future of English and Reality for Contemporary Public Relations

Will English remain the global language? Graddol (2006) speculates about the future of the dominance of the English language, with population shifts and the growth of other languages further shrinking the number of English-language speakers. Remember that Latin was once the lingua franca when globalism was on a much smaller scale. More recently, French was the lingua franca of international diplomacy, primarily from the 18th century to World War I, and remains an official language in international trade and diplomacy by European and African multilateral organizations. After English, French is the second most widely studied foreign language worldwide, with nearly 120 million students and 500,000 teachers outside of France (French Ministry of Foreign Affairs and International Development, 2014).

Another important consideration for the future of languages is the Internet, which has not just spread English around the world, it also has become a "new global impetus" (Burns, 2003, p. 24) for speakers of all languages.

1.5.1 Efforts to Create a New Universal Language and to Simplify English

"Inteligentaj personoj lernas la internacian lingvon." That is Esperanto for "Intelligent people learn the international language." **Esperanto** was a linguistic effort in 1887 to create an unbiased, simple second language for universal use. Dr. Ludwig L. Zamenhof, an ophthalmologist born in Bialystok, Russian Empire (now Poland), was fluent in Russian, German, Yiddish, Polish, and other European languages. He founded Esperanto (which means "hope") as a solution to the complexities of communication with a politically neutral language. Based on European languages, Esperanto is spoken by approximately 2 million people worldwide (Lewis et al., 2015); its monolingual dictionary contains more than 16,000 words. Although Esperanto has its own publications and an online presence, it has not become an official language of any country.

Jean-Paul Nerrière, a retired IBM consultant whose native language is French, developed another language approach for international communication. As an international vice president of marketing at IBM, Nerrière worked in Asia and traveled extensively, observing English-language transactions of native and non-native English-speaking people conducting business. As a non-native English speaker with an accent, he discovered "that international clients understood him better than they did his Texan boss" (Skapinker, 2012, para. 4). In 2004, he began publishing a series of books on simplified English, called "**Globish**," with a total vocabulary of 1,500 English words, stripped down to essentials without idiomatic expressions and popular cultural references. In an interview in the *New York Times* (Blume, 2005), Nerrière describes Globish: "It is not a language, it is a tool . . . A language is the vehicle of a culture. Globish doesn't want to be that at all. It is a means of communication" (para. 3). The Globish-English dictionary excludes the term "public relations," but describes "public" as "of the community or the people" and "relation" as "connections between people." Nerrière's website, www.globish.com, provides more on his language philosophy and the global English term he had trademarked.

1.5.2 English as the Global Language of Public Relations

The reality is that English has become the global language of business. Public relations practitioners benefit by knowing how to write clearly in English to reach diverse international publics and to communicate with colleagues, clients, journalists, consumers, and other stakeholders in multiple countries. They also need to secure approvals from decision-makers, whether they are clients or in-house executives, for expenditures to support their multinational or national campaigns. Developing cultural sensitivities to navigate within the global arena is extremely important, as is connecting within multicultural communities within your own country.

Try Exercise 1.2 and reflect on your experiences with English and other languages, as well as your perspective on what the future of English will be in business, specifically in the

---

Exercise 1.2

Insights: Your Experiences with Languages

1. What are the languages in your country? If English is an official or widely spoken language in your country, do you know the history of the English language in your country?

2. What languages do you speak fluently or have some proficiency in?

3. What type of English is considered the standard where you live, such as American, British, or another version? Look at Kachru's concentric language circles of English. What circle does the English in your country fall into?

4. Have you ever had any challenges communicating with someone who speaks another version of English? Do you recall the words or expressions that you found confusing?

5. Have you ever struggled to understand a different version of English in a song, a novel, a television program, or a movie? Do you recall why?

6. What language or languages have you used in education or in business for part- or full-time jobs or internships?

7. Do you plan on studying another language for business?

8. What do you think the future of English will be in business, particularly in the public relations industry, over the next 10 years?

public relations field. Being able to communicate in other languages, beyond English, is not only an advantage, but a requirement when undertaking campaigns in specific countries that must be manned with local staff who are proficient in business English and fluent in the local languages. Although fluency in other languages is a benefit for the staff members in the headquarters or primary office responsible for supervising multinational campaigns, they should gain some proficiency in writing and speaking other languages to read communiques, engage in some dialogue, and travel within that country. Even knowing some basic words in another language can show effort and respect with international business colleagues. The widely disseminated quote about the power of language in negotiation from the late Nelson Mandela means a great deal in all walks of life: "If you talk to a man in a language he understands, that goes to his head. If you talk to him in his language, that goes to his heart" ("Mandela in his own words," 2008).

1.6 Learning Objectives and Key Terms

After reading Chapter 1, you should be able to:

- Understand the importance of communicating clearly in English worldwide since the language has become the lingua franca of trade, business, and diplomacy, as well as in public relations.
- Trace the evolution of the English language over seven time periods from the pre-English period during the Roman Empire to Late Modern English.
- Identify a number of multinational organizations that have named English as their official or one of their official languages.
- Explain why the International Civil Aviation Organization requires proficiency in English for communication between airline pilots and air traffic controllers.
- Describe why English has become important for multinational corporations.
- Provide an overview of different approaches in English-language education.
- Summarize the concept of World Englishes and Kachru's three concentric language circles.
- Discuss challenges facing English-speaking countries that want to enhance their foreign-language education.
- Identify efforts to create a universal language and a simplistic version of global English.

This chapter covers the following key terms:

Lingua franca (p. 3)	Pre-English Period (p. 6)
Early Old English (p. 6)	Later Old English (p. 6)
Middle English (p. 8)	Early Modern English (p. 8)
Modern English (p. 9)	Late Modern English (p. 9)
ESL (p. 15)	EFL (p. 15)
EYL (p. 15)	ELF (p. 15)
EGL (p. 15)	EIL (p. 15)
EBL (p. 17)	BELF (p. 17)
EMT (p. 17)	World Englishes/Kachru (p. 18)
Esperanto (p. 21)	Globish-English (p. 22)

Note

1   Although different definitions exist on what constitutes a multinational or transnational corporation, I am using the general term multinational, which seems to be the most widely used term, based on my research.

References

Baker, S., Resch, I., Carlisle, K., & Schmidt, K. A. (2001, August 12). The great English divide. *Businessweek*. Retrieved from http://www.businessweek.com.

Barton, L. (2010, October 7). World Bank data now available in 34 languages on Google. *Inside the web: The intersection of the web and the World Bank* [Web log]. Retrieved from http://blogs.worldbank.org/insidetheweb/world-bank-data-now-available-in-34-languages-on-google.

Baugh, A. C., & Cable, T. (2002). *A history of the English language* (5th ed.). London: Routledge.

Blume, M. (2005, April 22). If you can't master English, try Globish. *New York Times*. Retrieved from http://www.nytimes.com.

Bruthiaux, P. (2003). Squaring the circles: Issues in modeling English worldwide. *International Journal of Applied Linguistics, 13*(2), 159–178. doi: 10.1111/1473–4192.00042.

Buck, N. (2006, May 15). The medium is English. *signandsight.com*. Retrieved from http://www.signandsight.com/features/752.html.

Burns, A. (2003). Opportunities or threats? The case of English as a global language. *Publishing Research Quarterly, 18*(4), 18–25. doi: 10.1007/s12109–003–0011–9.

Butterfield, J. (2008). *Damp squid: The English language laid bare*. Oxford: Oxford University Press.

Chang, J. (2006). Glocalization and English in Chinese higher education. *World Englishes, 25*(3/4), 513–525. doi: 10.1111/j.1467–971X.2006.00484.x.

Crystal, D. (1985). How many millions? The statistics of English today. *English Today, 1*, 7–9. Retrieved from http://www.davidcrystal.com/David_Crystal/articles.htm.

Crystal, D. (2001a). Global understanding for global English. *Moscow State University Bulletin, 19*(4), 13–28. Retrieved from http://www.davidcrystal.com/David_Crystal/articles.htm.

Crystal, D. (2001b). English as a classical language. *Omnibus, 42*, 21–22. Retrieved from http://www.davidcrystal.com/David_Crystal/articles.htm.

Crystal, D. (2008). *Think on my words: Exploring Shakespeare's language*. Cambridge: Cambridge University Press.

French Ministry of Foreign Affairs and International Development. (2014). *Francophony: Spreading the French language is a priority for French diplomacy*. Retrieved from http://www.diplomatie.gouv.fr/en/french-foreign-policy-1/promoting-francophony/.

Gladwell, M. (2008). *Outliers: The story of success*. New York, NY: Little, Brown and Company.

Global Language Monitor. (2014). *Number of words in the English language: 1,025,109.8*. Retrieved from http://www.languagemonitor.com/one-millionth-word/.

Graddol, D. (1997). *The future of English? A guide to forecasting the popularity of the English language in the 21st century*. British Council. Retrieved from http://www.britishcouncil.org/learning-elt-future.pdf.

Graddol, D. (2006). *English next: Why global English may mean the end of "English as a foreign language."* British Council. Retrieved from http://www.britishcouncil.org/learning-research-english-next.pdf.

Hargreaves, G. (2011, May 9). Poor language skills "leave Britons out of EU jobs." *BBC News*. Retrieved from http://www.bbc.co.uk/news/education-13314147.

International Civil Aviation Organization. (2011, October 13). *ICAO promotes aviation safety by endorsing English language testing.* Retrieved from http://www.icao.int/Newsroom/News%20Doc/PIO.21.11.EN.pdf.

International Monetary Fund. (n.d.). *Language services.* Retrieved from http://www.imf.org/external/np/adm/rec/job/langsvc.htm.

International Monetary Fund. (2015, March 27). *Factsheet: The IMF at a glance.* Retrieved from http://www.imf.org/external/np/exr/facts/glance.htm.

Kachru, B. B. (1985). Standards, codification and sociolinguistic realism: The English language in the outer circle. In R. Quirk and H. G. Widdowson (Eds.), *English in the world: Teaching and learning the language and literatures* (pp. 11–30). Cambridge: Cambridge University Press.

Ku, H., & Zussman, A. (2010). Lingua franca: The role of English in international trade. *Journal of Economic Behavior & Organization, 75*, 250–260. doi: 10.1016/j.jebo.2010.03.013

Lewis, M. P., Simons, G. F., & Fennig, C. D. (Eds.). (2015). *Ethnologue: Languages of the world* (18th ed.). Dallas, TX: SIL International. Retrieved from http://www.ethnologue.com.

Macgibbon, A. (2011, February 7). A nation lost in translation. *Sydney Morning Herald*. Retrieved from http://www.smh.com.au.

Mandela in his own words. (2008, June 26). *CNN.com*. Retrieved from http://edition.cnn.com/2008/WORLD/africa/06/24/mandela.quotes/.

Marmolejo, F. (2010, November 9). Deficiency in foreign language competency: What is wrong with the U.S. educational system? *The Chronicle of Higher Education*. Retrieved from http://chronicle.com/blogs/worldwise/deficiency-in-foreign-language-competency-what-is-wrong-with-the-u-s-educational-system/27558.

McCreary, J., Pollard, M., Stevenson, K., & Wilson, M. B. (1998). Human factors: Tenerife revisited. *Journal of Air Transportation World Wide, 3*(1), 23–32.

McCrum, R. (2010). *Globish: How English became the world's language.* New York, NY: W. W. Norton & Company.

McCrum, R., Cran, W., & MacNeil, R. (1986). *The story of English.* New York, NY: Elisabeth Sifton Books, Viking.

Mydans, S. (2007, May 14). Across cultures, English is the word. *New York Times*. Retrieved from http://www.nytimes.com.

Nielsen Company. (2010, June 15). *Social networks/blogs now account for one in every four and a half minutes online.* Retrieved from http://blog.nielsen.com/nielsenwire/global/social-media-accounts-for-22-percent-of-time-online/

North Atlantic Treaty Organization. (2015). *Frequently asked questions: What are the official languages of NATO?* Retrieved from http://www.nato.int/cps/en/natolive/faq.htm.

Olympic.org. (2015). *205 National Olympic Committees (NOC).* Retrieved from http://www.olympic.org/national-olympic-committees.

Organisation for Economic Co-operation and Development. (2014). *About the OECD.* Retrieved from http://www.oecd.org/about/.

Organization of the Petroleum Exporting Countries. (2015). *Working for OPEC.* Retrieved from http://www.opec.org/opec_web/en/32.htm.

Purdum, T. (2005, March 9). Survey: Bilingual executives in demand. *IndustryWeek.* Retrieved from http://www.industryweek.com.

Rohter, L. (2004, December 29). Learn English, says Chile, thinking upwardly global. *New York Times.* Retrieved from http://www.nytimes.com.

Ryan, C. (2013). Language use in the United States: 2011. *U.S. Census Bureau.* Retrieved from http://www.census.gov/prod/2013pubs/acs-22.pdf.

Schneider, E. W. (2010). *English around the world: An introduction.* Cambridge: Cambridge University Press.

Singapore Tourism Promotion Board. (2013). *About Singapore: Culture, language and people.* Retrieved from http://www.yoursingapore.com/content/traveller/en/browse/aboutsingapore/people-lang-culture.html.

Skapinker, M. (2007, November 8). Whose language? *Financial Times.* Retrieved from http://www.ft.com.

Skapinker, M. (2012, February 29). Executives speak a language of their own: The secret to aiming higher than Globish. *Financial Times.* Retrieved from http://www.ft.com.

Thomas, C. A. (2007). Language policy in multilingual organizations. *Working Papers in Educational Linguistics, 22*(1), 81–104.

Tinsley, T., & Board, K. (2014, November). Languages for the future: Which languages the UK needs most and why. *British Council.* Retrieved from http://www.britishcouncil.org/sites/britishcouncil.uk2/files/languages-for-the-future.pdf.

Triumph of English: A world empire by other means. (2001, December 20). *The Economist.* Retrieved from http://www.economist.com

United Nations. (2015a). *Growth in United Nations membership, 1945-present.* Retrieved from http://www.un.org/en/members/growth.shtml.

United Nations. (2015b). *UN official languages.* Retrieved from http://www.un.org/en/aboutun/languages.shtml.

United States Department of Education. (2012, November). *Succeeding globally through international education and engagement: U.S. Department of Education international strategy 2012–2016.* Retrieved from http://www2.ed.gov/about/inits/ed/internationaled/international-strategy-2012–16.pdf.

World Trade Organization. (2015). *General information on recruitment in the World Trade Organization.* Retrieved from http://www.wto.org/english/thewto_e/vacan_e/recruit_e.htm.

2 Understanding Global Perspectives in Public Relations

If the World were 100 People: . . .
There would be:
60 Asians
15 Africans
14 people from the Americas
11 Europeans.

—100 People: A World Portrait

2.1 Introduction to Globalism and Global Public Relations

This excerpt from *100 People: A World Portrait* (2012) describing a potential gathering of 100 people could be a reality if you were a public relations executive representing a multinational organization. You most likely would attend planning sessions and collaborate with such diverse staff from countries spanning the globe. Developing global competencies has become essential in public relations since the field offers career opportunities with multinational corporations, private companies seeking international markets, public diplomacy beyond the country's borders, and international nongovernmental organizations. Public relations agencies, whether independent or part of a conglomerate, also have expanded worldwide with wholly owned offices or developed affiliate relationships with local agencies. E-commerce enables products to be sold anywhere. The borderless world of the Internet means that content can be read or viewed by anyone anywhere.

To better understand how public relations and globalization intersect, let us look at the definitions of public relations and globalization, both of which have widely debated meanings. How do you define public relations (see Figure 2.1)? If you were to ask 10 public relations practitioners to define public relations, you may receive 10 different answers—and find few commonalities. The industry at large has been grappling with a consolidated definition of the field. The world's largest public relations trade group, the **Public Relations Society of America** (PRSA), called out to its members and other international industry trade associations in 2011 to help update its 13-word definition of public relations from 1982: "Public relations helps an organization and its publics adapt mutually to each other" (Public Relations Society of America, 2014a, para. 2). After the PRSA received almost 1,500 public votes on its short list

Figure 2.1—DEFINITIONS OF PUBLIC RELATIONS. Source: © Rafal Olechowski/
Shutterstock.com.

of three definitions culled from 927 suggestions, the trade group announced its latest 17-word
version in 2012: "Public relations is a strategic communication process that builds mutually
beneficial relationships between organizations and their publics" (Public Relations Society of
America, 2014b, para. 3).

The term **international public relations** (also called **global public relations**) can be
defined as "the planned and organized efforts of a company, institution, or government to
establish and build relationships with the publics of other nations" (Wilcox, Cameron, Reber,
& Shin, 2013, p. 288). Some scholars distinguish the practice of public relations based on
how the organizations operate worldwide (Sylvie, Wicks, Hollifield, Lacy, & Sohn, 2008):

- **International** (representation for organizations that produce products or services for
  local markets, which are adapted to the needs of other countries);
- **Multinational** (public relations for organizations headquartered in one country with
  autonomous operations in other international markets);
- **Global** (products distributed around the world); and
- **Transnational** (when foreign subsidies adapt plans from the headquarters to promote
  within the local market and also develop their own products for the local market).

Nilanjana Bardhan (2011), a professor at Southern Illinois University Carbondale and a
former practitioner in India and the U.S., proposes **transcultural public relations** as a
departure from the term multinational that focuses on the limitations of "the 'countries as
culture' logic" (p. 79). She argues that a transcultural approach extends beyond the confines
of national cultures, which are not fixed and exclude other cultural characteristics that people

may identify with, such as "ethnicity, religion, race, gender, region, diasporic status, sexual orientation, and so on" (p. 79).

Jacquie L'Etang, director of a graduate program in public relations at the University of Stirling in Scotland, adds an **intercultural** perspective to the public relations field:

> PR practitioners have an intercultural role, both between organizational cultures and within increasingly multicultural contexts. PR arises at points of societal change and resistance. PR is the discursive and relational function present in public communication processes, visible and invisible. (2009, p. 609)

The term **globalization** also has many definitions from different perspectives—positive, neutral, or negative—based on economics, sociology, religion, culture, politics, and communications. Manfred Steger (2009), a professor of global studies at the Royal Melbourne Institute of Technology, shares a Buddhist parable to illustrate the debate among scholars on defining globalization. In essence, four blind scholars try to determine what an elephant looks like, each scholar stubbornly sticking to a different interpretation of an elephant and all bickering among themselves.

Two perspectives on globalism focus on interdependence and shifting relationships. British sociologist Anthony Giddens (2006) explains that "we all increasingly live in one world, so that individuals, groups and nations become ever more *interdependent*" (p. 50), and he attributes the creation of globalization to "the coming together of political, social, cultural and economic factors" (p. 50), including the rise of information and communication technology. Arjun Appadurai (1990), an Indian-born social-cultural anthropologist and a professor at New York University, developed the following five dimensions of global cultural flows, which also have relevance to the field of public relations:

- **Ethnoscapes** refer to the shifting populations in the world of expatriates, whether voluntary or not, as well as to tourists. According to the *International Migration Report* (United Nations, Department of Economic and Social Affairs, Population Division, 2013), international migrants worldwide reached 232 million, which showed an increase of 77 million people, representing a 50% rise between 1990 and 2013. Europe is home to the largest population of immigrants, followed by Asia and North America. Public relations practitioners should investigate diversity further when identifying audiences due to increasingly multicultural populations.
- **Technoscapes** describe the "global configuration, also ever fluid, of technology, and of the fact that technology, both high and low, both mechanical and informational, now moves at high speeds across various kinds of previously impervious boundaries" (Appadurai, 1990, p. 297). Technoscapes have a huge impact on the public relations business. The Holmes Report/International Communications Consultancy Organisation (2013) report on global public relations surveyed 500 heads of public relations agencies and identified mastering digital and other new technologies as a significant issue in 2013. The public relations leaders regarded the evolving technology "as a challenge rather than an opportunity" (p. 34), addressing concerns of adapting with enough speed and coping with competitors.
- **Finanscapes** of megamonies are being traded and exchanged with "vast absolute implications for small differences in percentage points and time units" (Appadurai, 1990, p. 298), which can result in a global recession. The collapse of Lehman

Brothers, the global financial services firm, became the largest bankruptcy in U.S. history in 2008 and marked the beginning of economic chaos worldwide. Five years later, the World PR Report by the Holmes Report/ICCO (2013) found that 37.6% of agency principals still listed overall economic conditions as a major challenge.

- **Mediascapes** convey a world of instantly available multimedia news, information, and entertainment, providing "narrative-based accounts of strips of reality" (Appadurai, 1990, p. 299) by people, companies, and governments. These 24/7 evolving communication platforms provide public relations writers with numerous opportunities to share stories, maintain a dialogue, and monitor the pulse of public sentiment.

- **Ideoscapes** reflect debates on freedom, rights, and political ideologies, as well as counter-ideologies on democracy and enlightenment beyond Europe and America. Public relations professionals should remain updated on current events and changing points of view to better understand their publics and issues affecting the organizations they represent.

2.2 Rise of Multinationals and International Nongovernmental Organizations

Economic globalization has led to a proliferation of multinationals and nongovernmental agencies (NGOs), resulting in an increased demand for public relations worldwide. In addition, governments around the globe seek talented communicators to manage a dialogue within and outside their own borders.

2.2.1 Corporations Comprise Almost Half of the World's Largest Economies

The "direct ancestors of today's multinational corporations" (Gabel & Bruner, 2003, p. 22) were established in the 17th century—the English East India Co. (1600), the Dutch East India Co. (1602), and the Hudson Bay Co. (1670). An estimated 77,000 multinational corporations now span the globe with more than 770,000 foreign affiliates (United Nations Conference on Trade and Development, 2007). According to Forbes Global 2000, the countries with the largest number of multinationals include the U.S. with 543 companies, followed by Japan with 251, and China with 136 (DeCarlo, 2013).

Statistics from Global Trends (Keys & Malnight, 2012) illustrate the powerful economic presence of multinational corporations:

- In 2010, 58% of the world's 150 largest economic entities were corporations.
- Walmart ranked as the 25th largest economy in the world in 2010; to put that into perspective, Walmart's economy was ahead of the Gross Domestic Product of 171 countries, such as Norway and Iran. Walmart employs 2.1 million people, which is the equivalent of 43% of Norway's population.
- The revenues of AXA Group, a global insurance company headquartered in France, exceeded the economy of Romania.
- ING, the financial services company based in Amsterdam, generated revenues greater than the economy of New Zealand.

The public relations practice takes on an important role in these organizations worldwide as the "ambassador" and "conscience" in diverse industries and markets. The largest industry sectors of multinationals are diverse—automotive, energy, chemicals, pharmaceuticals, construction and construction materials, forestry, electronics, computer software and the Internet, telecommunications, commercial banks, transportation, postal services, legal services, food services, advertising, media and entertainment, management consulting, accounting, and retail (Gabel & Bruner, 2003).

2.2.2 INGOs and Public Affairs

The United Nations originated the term **nongovernmental organization** (NGO) to apply to a legal entity formed by private persons or organizations without involvement from any government, whether they pertain to local, national, or international levels (Union of International Associations, 2014). According to the United Nations, the other term for an NGO is a **civil society organization** (CSO). Other related terms are **international nongovernmental organizations** (INGO), such as Oxfam and Save the Children, and **intergovernmental organizations** (IGO), referring to organizations of sovereign states or other intergovernmental organizations, such as the United Nations or the World Bank (United Nations Global Compact, n.d.).

Concurrent with the prominence of multinationals, INGOs also have risen and play a "watchdog role" in keeping track of the activities of corporations on employment practices, environmental factors, and other important issues. For example, Greenpeace persuaded Nestlé, one of the world's largest multinationals, to change its practices in harvesting palm oil in Indonesia through an international public relations campaign that raised global awareness of the destruction of rainforests, which have become the endangered habitat for orangutans and indigenous peoples. INGOs also play a powerful role in delivering aid to developing countries and relief during political strife or after natural disasters. Some INGOs draw from considerable financial resources. The combined revenues of eight leading INGOs—World Vision International, Oxfam International, Save the Children International, Plan International, Médecins Sans Frontières, CARE International, CARITAS International, and ActionAid International—exceeded USD11.7 billion in 2011, a 40% increase since 2005 (Morton, 2013).

Governments also need support for public diplomacy and international relations, as they liaise with other countries and promote tourism, trade, and other resources. Public relations agencies (also called **public affairs** in the government sector) and lobbyists aim to influence legislation affecting the businesses of their clients. Two major hubs for lobbying are located in Washington, D.C., and in Brussels, the headquarters of the European Union. The Center for Public Integrity, a U.S.-based nonprofit, stated that 1,150 companies, with headquarters in approximately 100 nations, have hired lobbyists in the U.S. over a six-year period (Wilcox et al., 2013).

2.3 Globalization of the Public Relations Industry

To thrive in a global marketplace today, public relations agencies have expanded globally to provide their clients with worldwide services. In addition, in-house public relations departments have needed to hire talent in local markets, whether they hire full-time staff or public relations agencies for support in specific countries. Burson-Marsteller, Ogilvy Public Relations, FleishmanHillard, Golin, Porter Novelli, Ketchum, Hill+Knowlton Strategies, and Cohn & Wolfe all have one thing in common: these public relations agencies are part of publicly held multinational communication conglomerates, with a collection of agencies offering advertising, branding, and other creative services. Public relations agencies belonging to conglomerates handle an estimated 60% of the global public relations business (Wilcox et al., 2013). Exhibit 2.1 provides background on the "big five" communication conglomerates: Dentsu, headquartered in Tokyo; WPP Group in London; Publicis Groupe based in Paris; and Interpublic Group and Omnicom, both in New York. Two of the companies almost joined forces to form what would have been the world's largest communications conglomerate. Omnicom and Publicis announced a merger in July 2013 that would have brought together more than 130,000 employees with plans to relocate to the Netherlands, a neutral location with tax benefits, but the merger was terminated in May 2014.

Wholly owned or affiliate agencies around the world offer clients extensive integrated communication services almost anywhere, thereby providing global capabilities and streamlined management. Consolidated services can be a benefit to clients who receive one invoice, deal with a primary global contact, and conduct meetings or conference calls simultaneously with team members from each office. Not only agencies that are part of multinational conglomerates offer this capability, smaller independent agencies also have been partnering with like-minded agencies in other parts of the world on an ad hoc basis or as part of independent agency networks, such as the Public Relations Global Network. Large independent agencies, such as Edelman, Waggener Edstrom Worldwide, and APCO Worldwide, also operate wholly owned offices around the globe.

2.3.1 International Public Relations Services

Public relations agencies with international proficiency should be able to offer the following services:

- **Spoken and written proficiency in English** that is clear and understandable by the agency's employees, clients, publics, and stakeholders worldwide, as well as international offices manned with staff fluent in English and languages widely used in their countries.
- **Intercultural skills internally and externally** to navigate the complexities of verbal and nonverbal communications among global staff, clients, and media.
- **Client counseling** as a valued, trusted resource and partner who can provide insight on the global political and economic situation, media consumption, and ethical and legal differences.
- **Strategic planning and management of staff** in their headquarters and diverse international talent in offices around the globe.
- **Research analysis**, whether primary or secondary, providing clients with a level of insight that can identify opportunities, trends, and potential issues in different markets.
- **Up-to-date Web and mobile capabilities** from the design and writing of websites to the creation of social media content and promotions.
- **Comprehensive global monitoring** of traditional media and social media.
- **Crisis communication and issues management** that can impact clients globally and within local markets.
- **Management of complex budgets** and fluctuating currencies.
- **Evaluation and measurement** that capture the results of local and international campaigns in ways meaningful to their clients.

Exhibit 2.1—"BIG FIVE" COMMUNICATION CONGLOMERATES.

Company/Ticker Symbol	Headquarters	Brief Description
(Global reach, number of employees, and examples of PR agencies; facts from corporate websites)		
Dentsu Inc. Tokyo: 4324; ISIN: JP3551520004	Tokyo	Approximately 37,000 employees Offices in 124 countries and territories Advertising and public relations, among others Acquired Aegis Group in 2013 and established a new global operating unit, Dentsu Aegis Network, in London. PR agencies: Dentsu Public Relations, Mitchell Communications
Interpublic Group NYSE: IPG	New York City	Approximately 48,000 employees More than 100 offices worldwide Advertising, public relations, digital marketing, media buying, and other areas of communications PR agencies: Golin, Weber Shandwick
Omnicom Group Inc. NYSE: OMC	New York City	More than 5,000 clients (no numbers on employees) Offices in more than 100 countries Advertising, strategic media planning and buying, digital and interactive marketing, direct and promotional marketing, public relations, and other specialty communications services PR agencies: FleishmanHillard, Ketchum, Porter Novelli, Cone, Brodeur Partners, Clark & Weinstock, and Kreab Gavin Anderson
Publicis Groupe Euronext Paris: FR0000130577	Paris	Approximately 75,000 employees Offices in 108 countries Digital and consulting services, corporate communications, public affairs, media strategy, planning and buying, healthcare communications, brand asset production PR agencies: MSLGROUP, Public Healthcare Communications Group
WPP Group LSE: WPP; NASDAQ: WPPGQ	London	Approximately 175,000 employees 3,000 offices located in 110 countries Advertising, public relations and public affairs, branding and identity, digital and relationship marketing, among other creative services PR agencies: Burson-Marsteller, Cohn & Wolfe, Hill+Knowlton Strategies, Ogilvy Public Relations

Many public relations agencies effectively use their websites to provide extensive content on their capabilities and credentials. See Exercise 2.1 for an in-depth look at a public relations agency of interest to you and examine your chosen firm's resources based on its website content.

Public relations practitioners must keep abreast of current events and industry trends that affect their clients' businesses, as well as new developments and successful campaigns in the public relations industry at large. Industry publications around the globe publish current news, examples of best practices, case studies, skill-building tips, job opportunities, and analyses and reports on trends. Many publications also invite award submissions for peer-reviewed work on public relations campaigns and specific tactics, including media kits and other written documents. See Appendix A for a listing of industry publications, in which some of the content is offered free online for non-subscribers. Databases, such as LexisNexis, also enable you to search and download complete articles from many trade publications.

Industry rankings quickly become dated with mergers, acquisitions, closures, and startups affecting the public relations agency world. Exhibit 2.2 lists a number of annual public relations industry rankings on a global and regional basis and their websites, so you can access the most current available information.

Exercise 2.1

Insights: Public Relations Agency Global Scope and Capabilities

Select a public relations agency that interests you. Look at the agency's website and try to answer the following questions:

1. Which public relations agency did you select?
2. Where is the company's headquarters?
3. Is it an independent agency or part of a communication conglomerate?
4. Which countries (or regions) does the agency have offices in or affiliate relationships with other agencies?
5. How does the agency discuss its global resources?
6. What services does the agency claim to offer?
7. Does the agency indicate specializations in specific areas, such as industries?
8. Does the agency provide a list of current or former clients?
9. Does the website include case studies of client work?
10. What other type of content does the company share to promote its capabilities, such as newsrooms, white papers, reports, blogs, or other social media?
11. Was the career section easy to find with job openings? Did it include information on training?
12. Did you think the website could be enhanced with other content? If so, please provide a few examples.

Exhibit 2.2—REPORTS AND RANKINGS ON PUBLIC RELATIONS AGENCIES WORLDWIDE.

Source	Reports or Rankings	Website
AdAge's Agency Report	Provides data on revenue on a worldwide, U.S., and non-U.S. basis of the giant multinational conglomerates, many of which own PR agencies.	http://adage.com
The Holmes Report's World PR Report	Covers the top 250 agencies worldwide by fee income, tracking both independent and multinational PR agencies. Publishes a series of regional "agency report cards," with analyses and trends. In 2013, the International Communication Consultancy Organisation collaborated with The Holmes Report to create a rebranded World PR Report, including the annual Global Rankings by The Holmes Report with data from ICCO national associations worldwide.	www.holmesreport.com
O'Dwyer's Directory of PR Firms	Publishes an annual review of both independent and conglomerate PR agencies, with a focus on U.S.-based PR firms. It also includes a cross-client index, so you can find out which companies are represented at what agencies.	www.odwyerpr.com
PR Report	Monthly newsletter covering the PR industry in Australia. Covers an annual ranking of PR agencies in Australia.	www.theprreport.com
PRWeek's Top 150 Consultancies	Ranks PR agencies operating in London and throughout the U.K., as well as the top 25 or 50 agencies by industry specialization.	www.prweek.com/uk
PRWeek Agency Business Report	Publishes an annual report, with profiles and rankings of PR agencies in the U.S.	www.prweek.com/us

2.3.2 Global Collaboration: Public Relations Trade Groups

Krishnamurthy Sriramesh (2009), a communications professor and scholar in global public relations, raises an important point that globalism is not new and has taken place over different time periods. In the last century for example, globalism led to cooperative efforts among nations, such as the rebuilding of Europe after World War II, the creation of the United Nations in 1945, and the Bandung conference held in Indonesia in 1955, which brought together 29 African and Asian nations to discuss initiatives on peace, economic development, and post-colonial solidarity. Collaboration on a global scale also led to the formation of **public relations trade groups**, which initially began on a regional basis in the U.S. in the mid-20th century and have since expanded around the globe. Trade groups may have different names, such as associations, clubs, councils, forums, institutes, or societies. These organizations provide professional networking opportunities, codes of conduct, and other resources to keep members abreast of evolving trends and technological innovations. They also host regular meetings and annual conferences, while some groups offer accreditation credentials and workshops—and writing is a popular topic. In addition, a few industry groups specialize in an industry sector (National Investor Relations Institute) or by ethnicity (National Black Public Relations Society). Look at the public relations trade association closest to you and examine the scope of services available to its members (the association may have student memberships), ethical guidelines, calendar of events, and other industry resources (see Exercise 2.2).

Economic expansion after World War II in the late 1940s sparked the development of public relations trade groups in North America, Europe, and Australia. Established in 1947 in New York City, the **Public Relations Society of America** merged with the East Coast-based National Association of Accredited Publicity Directors, which was established in 1936, and the West Coast-based American Council on Public Relations, which was founded in 1939 by Rex Harlow, a Stanford University professor, who became the first full-time public relations educator (Heath & Coombs, 2006). Today, more than 22,000 professionals belong to PRSA and more than 11,000 students and faculty advisers belong to its student division. The **Chartered Institute of Public Relations** in London and the **Canadian Public Relations Society** were established in 1948; the **Public Relations Institute of Australia** began the following year.

Since the 1950s, a number of international, regional, country-specific, and industry-specific public relations trade groups were formed. In 1955, the first multinational public relations industry group was established as the **International Public Relations Association** in London,

Exercise 2.2

Insights: Your Nearest Public Relations Trade Group

Go online and look at the public relations trade association that is closest to you. (See the Appendix for a list of national, regional, and international groups worldwide.) Please answer the following questions about your selected trade association:

1. Which group did you choose?
2. What geographic areas are the members from?
3. Does your chosen group have a student membership division? If so, what does the student division offer its members?
4. Does the group have a code of conduct/ethics policy posted on its website?
5. Does it host an annual conference, regional ones, or other local events or workshops?
6. Does the group offer awards for work undertaken by its members?
7. Does the group conduct any research? If so, what kind?
8. Does the group publish any magazines or newsletters, whether print or digital?
9. Does the website list job openings or other career resources?
10. What other benefits does the group offer its members?

which today has members from more than 80 countries. The Inter-American Federation of Public Relations, representing the U.S. and countries in the Caribbean and Central South America, was formed in 1960; it was renamed the **Inter-American Confederation of Public Relations** in 1985. San Francisco-based **International Association of Business Communicators** debuted in 1970, and its current members span public relations, corporate communications, editorial services, and other communication fields in over 70 countries. In Nairobi, Kenya, the Federation of African Public Relations Associations was formed in 1975, which was later renamed as the **African Public Relations Association**. The London-based **International Communications Consultancy Organisation** brought together public relations agency professionals worldwide in 1989; today's membership includes over 2,000 public relations agencies in 31 countries. The **Global Alliance for Public Relations and Communication Management** was officially launched in Lugano, Switzerland, in 2002, focusing on global ethics and competencies, and now has more than 160,000 practitioners and academics as members. Exhibit 2.3 contains a list of examples of multinational public relations trade groups. See Appendix B for a comprehensive list of public relations groups by region and country.

Developing consistent worldwide standards has been the focus of many international trade groups. For example, members of the Global Alliance for Public Relations and Communication Management developed the **Melbourne Mandate** (named after the city in which the 2012 forum was held) as new principles for practitioners. The Melbourne Mandate proposes that public relations practitioners "define and maintain an organisation's character and values; to build a culture of listening and engagement; and to instill responsible behaviours by individuals and organisations" (2012, p. 1). The diagram in Figure 2.2 shows how its core DNA interconnects three strands of main principles: values, leadership, and culture.

Exhibit 2.3—INTERNATIONAL PUBLIC RELATIONS INDUSTRY ASSOCIATIONS.
This list includes examples of large international public relations trade groups. (For an extensive list of industry trade groups worldwide, please see Appendix B.)

PR Industry Group	Website	Member Countries (approximate)
Global Alliance for Public Relations and Communication Management (based in Switzerland)	http://www.globalalliancepr.org	30
International Association of Business Communicators (based in the U.S.)	http://www.iabc.com	70+
International Communications Consultancy Organisation (based in England)	http://www.iccopr.com	31
International Public Relations Association (based in England)	http://www.ipra.org	80

Figure 2.2—THE MELBOURNE MANDATE DIAGRAM. Source: Property of the Global Alliance for Public Relations and Communication Management.

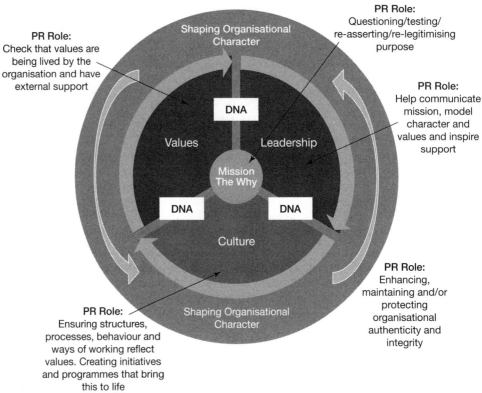

2.4 Glocalization and Public Relations

Roland Robertson, a British sociologist and academic, defined **glocalization**, the portmanteau of "globalization" and "local," from an economic perspective as "'micro-marketing': the tailoring and advertising of goods and services on a global or near-global basis to increasingly differentiated local and particular markets" (1994, p. 36). Robertson explained how the term glocalization has agricultural roots from the Japanese word "dochakuka" ("living on one's own land"), meaning to adapt farming techniques to local conditions. The concept later was adopted by Japanese businesses in making Japanese products appealing beyond local markets. From a public relations perspective, glocalization means adapting global brand messages and strategies to appeal to the values, tastes, and needs of the local markets. The term can be interpreted as "think locally, act globally" or "think globally, act locally."

2.4.1 Think Locally, Act Globally

The phrase, "think local, act global," is generally attributed to Japanese Internet pioneer Izumi Aizu, who coined the expression in 1985 while protecting a forest outside of Tokyo from being bulldozed by the Japanese government to build U.S. military housing. Aizu secured support online from both American and Japanese legislators (Wakefield, 2009). Thomas Friedman, author of *The World is Flat* (2007), referred to the "glocalization of the local" (p. 479), an expression coined by Indrajit Banerjee, an Indian-born scholar and expert in media and communications. Banerjee described glocalization as "globalization in reverse" (p. 480), giving an example of how local Asian media are reaching millions of Asian expatriates worldwide, who are seeking news from their home countries in their native languages. Friedman provided other examples and concluded that "globalization will finally become, well, *global*—both culturally and commercially—a process no longer driven from America and Europe but from all four corners of the flat world" (p. 488).

Shifting economies are a reality. The shifting economic global landscape is estimated to show increasing gains in emerging markets. According to research by McKinsey & Company (Dobbs, Remes, Smit, Manyika, Woetzel, & Agyenim-Boateng, 2013), Fortune Global 500 companies could rise to 45% of the total share in emerging economies by 2025, with an estimated 40% of the 5,000 new large companies based in the China region. In 1990, only 5% of the Fortune Global 500 companies were based in emerging regions, and by 2010, 17% of those companies were located in these regions. The researchers provided a rationale for the shift:

> That's because while three-quarters of the world's 8,000 companies with annual revenue of $1 billion or more are today based in developed economies, we forecast that an additional 7,000 could reach that size in little more than a decade—and 70 percent of them will most likely come from emerging markets. To put this dramatic shift in the balance of global corporate power in perspective, remember that many of the world's largest companies have maintained their current status for generations: more than 40 percent of the 150 Western European companies in last year's Fortune Global 500 had been founded before 1900. (para. 2)

Euromonitor International predicts that China, India, Russia, Brazil, and Mexico will comprise five of the world's top 10 economies by 2020, accounting for a combined USD47 trillion in GDP in purchasing power parity terms (Boumphrey & Bevis, 2013), which means in simple terms that goods should cost the same in Country A and Country B when the exchange rates are equivalent (Moffatt, 2014).

In addition, technology has enabled local organizations based anywhere to communicate effectively with audiences in any country. Chairman Patrick Liotard-Vogt of ASMALLWORLD, a private, international lifestyle club with invitation-only membership capped at 250,000, explained the value of the Internet in an article in *Marketing Week*: "In the old days a brand had to work hard and spend a lot of money to be global. Now a small brand can be global very cheaply and easily" (Cooper, 2010, para. 29).

2.4.2 Think Globally, Act Locally

The origin of this widely used motto, "think globally, act locally," is attributed to environmentalists, who enhanced awareness of local issues on a global scale to promote their overall causes, not business leaders as one might suspect (Wakefield, 2009). Although the person who actually coined the phrase is debated, the originator may be René Dubos (1901–1982), a molecular biologist and Nobel Laureate, who also chaired an advisory group of scientists for the United Nations Conference on the Human Environment in 1972, positing that raising concerns about global environment and education would bring awareness and support to local and regional environmental issues (Gough, 2013).

This term has been adapted and applied by many multinational brands that have revised their global products to cater to local tastes. The World of Coca-Cola interactive museum in Atlanta, Georgia, features a Coca-Cola Freestyle touch-screen soda fountain, where visitors can sample more than 100 different flavored beverages sold around the globe. Look at McDonald's menus and you'll find significant variations from its American offerings in other markets, such as the McCurry and the Big Spicy Paneer Wrap in India, McRice Burger in parts of Southeast Asia, and McMollete in Mexico.

When the Walt Disney Company opened Euro Disney in Paris in 1992, the company followed its American model, thereby becoming a case study in how *not* to export American standards to another country. Jonathan Matusitz (2010), a professor of human communication at the University of Central Florida, examined how Disney undertook four glocalized changes to transform its failed theme park into its more viable Disneyland Paris:

- reducing the price, which was initially higher than its U.S. parks, to a more affordable level and reducing rates at the Disney-managed area hotels;
- turning shows and settings into French style with less glitzy and tacky décor, adding European-themed attractions, toning down logos on products and providing different items for sale (see Figure 2.3 for an example of a French-made product), and changing

Figure 2.3—EXAMPLE OF FRENCH-MADE PRODUCT AT DISNEYLAND PARIS; LADURÉE BRANDED MACAROONS. Source: © Ladurée.

colors in graphics and architecture (less purple and pink, which are considered colors with negative associations in parts of Europe);

- adjusting the food menus and eating habits by serving alcohol, offering more French and international menu options, accommodating the preferred meal times, and providing table-service restaurants; and
- hiring local management staff and changing Disney's stringent labor standards on appearance and behavior by allowing more choice in physical appearance, including altering the "smile factory" tradition from America.

FreshIntelligence, a market research company in Toronto, analyzed global brands, such as Coca-Cola, Colgate, Nescafé, Nike, and Nokia, by conducting a cross-cultural study of brand messaging and perceptions, consumer values, and sales performance in Australia, Brazil, Canada, China, Russia, and the U.S. The company developed a "glocalization score" based on 22 values. For example, FreshIntelligence found that feeling safe and protected ranked among the top five values of all six countries, while being beautiful and physically attractive was highly valued by Brazilians, Russians, and Chinese (Churkina, 2013). Its research findings determined that brands scoring higher on glocalization adapted to local values, which resonated more with the local consumers, resulting in higher usage of the products and higher sales. For example, Coca-Cola communicates messages about innovation in developing countries, while conveying family values and security in North America (Shaw, 2011).

2.4.3 Global and Glocal Public Relations

Creating public relations plans and strategies is not as simple as changing products and services. How should public relations strategies be implemented in diverse global markets? The public relations planning worldwide traditionally originates from the organization's headquarters and the corporate public relations agency, along with feedback and, ideally, a dialogue with public relations staff from both within the organization and its global regional and local offices *and* externally with its corporate public relations agency and other contracted public relations firms worldwide. The headquarters may mandate that the overall theme maintains some level of consistency to adapt to different geographic markets. The glocal approach communicates relevant core messages and localizes content to the needs of the local market.

James Grunig (2009), professor emeritus at the University of Maryland, theorized that global public relations operates in the middle between standard and individual practices by following "a set of generic principles that *could* be applied universally but that at a local level these principles *should* be applied differently in different locations" (pp. 1–2). **Generic principles** refer to ones that are universally understood in public relations and can be practiced in most places. A few examples of generic principles include empowerment of public relations managers, strategic management, integrated communications, two-way and symmetrical communication, and ethical and social responsibility initiatives.

Frank Ovaitt, Jr. (1988), who has served as the president and CEO of the Institute for Public Relations, interviewed more than 40 public relations practitioners with extensive international experience and determined that the following four strategies were successful in implementing and managing local public relations campaigns:

1. to enable local public relations talent to choose or customize standardized elements of public relations program elements;

2. to identify governmental barriers to trade and developing relations with local influentials in non-commercial settings;
3. to align global campaigns with the client's business strategies; and
4. to understand the value in unified planning and processes of global campaigns, "whether or not the company pursues a high degree of program standardization" (p. 8).

Local public relations talent can provide global organizations with valuable insight for country-specific campaigns. They offer an in-depth understanding of cultural differences, local communication and media relations practices, and translation services. A local public relations expert can serve as a "**strategic decoder**: one who decodes discourses and then appropriates selected parts to in turn encode public relations materials" (Curtin & Gaither, 2007, p. 93) for the local market. This requires that global management supervisors, whether agency or in-house, allow the local talent a level of flexibility and autonomy to interpret global messages to connect with local markets. At the same time, the global account manager must establish clear reporting guidelines and approval processes.

The following services are required for local offices, with writing playing a significant role:

- Adapting the global public relations plan by evaluating local publics and making necessary adjustments that would be effective in the local market.
- Analyzing and adapting the global messages to appeal to local market needs and specific audiences.
- Communicating on a regular basis with the primary public relations agency or company headquarters, as well as preparing required reports on activities and results.
- Extending the existing global corporate social responsibility program to the local market or identifying other local causes.
- Understanding how print and broadcast media really operate in that country and identifying which outlets are considered credible (requiring a level of insight that may not be easily obtained from secondary sources).
- Utilizing social media that the local audiences follow and understanding any censorship or issues with freedom of speech.
- Revising written materials to comply with the most widely used English in the country or region, and editing content for cultural nuances and sensitivities.
- Selecting appropriate visual imagery for local media and consumers.
- Translating and interpreting services by staff fluent in the local language or languages and English are crucial. Have you ever used Google's translator? The results are instant, yet the translated words may be transformed into gibberish, lacking clarity and sense. Although bilingual dictionaries are useful tools, the reality is that language contains many nuances that only someone who speaks both languages fluently will understand.

2.5 Global Careers in Public Relations

The public relations profession offers diverse career opportunities in the international arena, whether you want to stay in your own country or work abroad. You can find in-house public relations and communications positions at multinational companies, NGOs, and trade associations. Governments also hire communication professionals to promote countries for tourism, trade, economic development, or even on-location filming, among other areas. The diplomatic corps needs multilingual, culturally sophisticated staff for positions at embassies around the globe. On the public relations agency side, multinational and independent agencies have offices around the globe, representing diverse industries. You also can have a promising career in global public relations, *without* leaving your home, particularly if you are living in a major city or area with a large commercial base or with global nonprofits.

The Report of the Commission on Public Relations Education (VanSlyke Turk, 2006) states that the public relations field is "becoming a global profession in an increasingly-connected world where mutual understanding and harmony are more important than ever" (p. 35). Stacie Nevadomski Berdan, an American public relations professional who had worked in Hong Kong and author of a book on international careers, shares valid advice:

> Working in another country can expand your horizons professionally and personally in ways you might never have considered. Overseas assignments can enhance your reputation and set you apart from your peers. Doors will open for you, because companies need more people who can apply international experience to local business challenges. Knowledge and understanding of foreign cultures, regulations, economies, consumers and work habits are now crucial for corporate survival—and they can be your ticket to the fast track. (2011, para. 4)

If you are a student aiming to enter the public relations profession, a junior-level public relations practitioner desiring to work in the international arena, or a college-educated professional seeking a career transition, you can best prepare for a career in international public relations by exploring the following opportunities, whether you travel abroad or stay in your home country.

2.5.1 Short-Term Living Abroad Experiences

- Many higher-educational institutions offer **study abroad courses, exchange programs, or scholarships** to study in other countries.
- In addition, many countries also offer unaccredited **language programs** or immersive language programs in which students live with a local family and take language classes.
- **Teaching English as a second language** is an opportunity for college graduates who can join programs sponsored by governments or nonprofits. A few programs in Asia are well established. The Japan Exchange and Teaching Programme (JET) sets up temporary jobs for teaching English, as well as other opportunities, as an international exchange between Japan and other nations. JET welcomed approximately 4,372 participants from 40 countries in 2013. The English Program in Korea (EPIK) also offers teaching positions for college graduates, as well as educational scholarships for college students to teach English in rural communities.
- Opportunities for **volunteer work abroad** abound (see Figure 2.4). The San Francisco-based Foundation for Sustainable Development offers four collaborative and sustainable programs to support underserved communities in Africa, Asia, and Latin America. Cross-Cultural Solutions has offices in the U.S. (its headquarters), the U.K., Canada, and Australia, and arranges volunteer abroad trips throughout nine countries. These are only two examples of organizations that coordinate volunteer excursions from start to finish.

Figure 2.4—VOLUNTEERS ALSO CAN GAIN INTERNATIONAL EXPERIENCE.
Source: © Mangostock/Shutterstock.com.

- **Short-term internships or training positions**, particularly related to public relations or communications, are offered through higher-education institutions or through companies directly.
- **Traveling and exploring places** on your own or with a friend or friends also can provide insight. The preferred method is to become immersed with **local experiences** by staying with local residents, if possible, or at farm stays or small locally owned places, while seeking more authentic experiences beyond the touristy hotels, eateries, and attractions.

2.5.2 International Skill-Building Opportunities without Leaving Home

- Courses in **international public relations, communications, marketing, or business** are offered at many universities at an undergraduate or graduate level. Online courses also can be an option.
- Studying **languages** is beneficial, particularly gaining proficiency to conduct business. The demand for people to speak Mandarin, Spanish, Russian, and Arabic will most likely increase.

- **Internships or executive training positions** (for college graduates) are available at public relations agencies handling international clients or local clients reaching international markets, as well as with in-house communication departments at companies or NGOs with international causes, volunteers, and stakeholders. Many universities also can arrange internships in exchange for credit. Volunteering locally at nonprofits with global reach is another way to gain experience without traveling.
- Students can become active with **international-related clubs** on campus where they can attend events to meet international students.
- **Other face-to-face local opportunities** include cross-cultural chambers of commerce or other cultural organizations.

2.5.3 Full-Time International Positions

International full-time job opportunities may be limited by language skills, level of professional experience and education, and work visas and immigration restrictions. Companies may not want to pay the extra legal fees and relocation expenses, particularly for a junior-level position. Obtaining work visas can be more difficult if you don't have extensive work experience. For example in the U.S., the U.S. Citizen and Immigration Services offers an O-1 visa for an initial stay of up to three years. The stipulation, however, is the classification of "alien of extraordinary ability or achievement," which is also called a "genius visa."

Being an expatriate can be rewarding, but the experience may present challenges too—and can be much more daunting for long-term jobs. Visiting a country as a tourist or studying abroad for a semester *and* working and living in a country full-time are very different experiences. Expatriates may be quite surprised, positively or negatively, about the differences in taxation, employment benefits, quality of life, and cost of living between their home country and their new country. Having financial obligations in your home country also can result in problems if the currency exchange rate becomes unfavorable in your new country. The relocation experience would be simpler for someone who is single. Relocating with a domestic partner/spouse or children requires taking their needs into consideration. The best solution is to be prepared.

If you have a job offer in another country, you should explore the following logistics:

- **Salary**—What is the take-home pay? You should know how much your income will be taxed and what other mandatory deductions will be taken out of your paycheck. If you are relocating to a country with higher taxes, you may be able to negotiate a tax equalization. Also, check on the tax policies of your home country as an expatriate.
- **Cost of Living**—How far will your income will go? Look at how much it costs to rent or buy a place to live, as well as other expenses (utilities and routine maintenance fees), transportation, car insurance, taxes on goods and services, food shopping, and other essentials. If you own an apartment or house in your home country, you will need to factor in those expenses as well. If you rent out your property, you will need to hire someone to help or you will become a long-distance landlord or landlady, which may be difficult to manage.
- **Benefits**—What benefits are offered and what do you need to pay for? Are there any other special allowances? In the U.S., medical insurance plans can be quite costly, particularly if you are covering benefits for a spouse and children. Other considerations include supplemental insurances (dental, vision, disability, or life), retirement

packages (some plans may require a minimum contribution), education (tuition reimbursement and language courses) and other benefits, such as stock options for a publicly held company. Will the organization pay for your relocation expenses and short-term housing and storage, if needed?

- **Time Expectations and Time Off**—What are the office hours? What are the weekends? What are the expectations for availability in the evenings and weekends? Some cultures work six-day weeks, which can be a major adjustment for people who are used to five-day work weeks. How much time off will you have, factoring in days when offices are closed for national and religious holidays, as well as paid vacation time? Europeans are accustomed to more generous paid time off than employees in other countries. Will you be able to take off religious holidays, if they are not part of the culture you are moving to?

- **Quality of Living**—What is the social life like? What will you do during your spare time? Does the location offer culture, entertainment, recreation, and other comparable experiences that you have been enjoying in your home country? You may want to talk to other expatriates in that country to find out their experiences.

- **Family**—If you are relocating with a domestic partner/spouse or children, you will have to look at how the relocation would affect their education, careers, and overall quality of life. Would your partner/spouse, for example, be able to work legally in the country? What are the language barriers? What is the educational system for your children—and how much does it cost? Are there any support systems, such as clubs, for expatriates? What community, religious, and recreational or leisure activities will your family be able to enjoy? If your family members are unhappy with the move, you could experience enormous stress, particularly on a short-term basis. If these issues are not resolved, expatriates may find themselves returning home with their families earlier than expected. What about your family members and friends back home—will they plan on visiting you and where will they stay, or do you plan on traveling back home during vacations? You may find yourself spending all or most of your vacation time visiting family and friends back home.

- **Other Considerations**—If you have student loans or other consumer debt in your home country, you will need to include those expenses into your budget. Be prepared for currency exchange fluctuations that may affect your discretionary income positively or negatively.

The initial euphoria of relocating to another country can wane when the exotic becomes familiar and the day-to-day realities come into play. Also, expatriates may underestimate the impact of home sickness from being away from their friends and family, as well as the familiarity of their home country. Nonetheless, many expatriates can thrive in a new environment that becomes their long-term or permanent home.

Recent multicultural research indicates positive effects of living abroad and adapting to new environments. Scholars at Northwestern University and INSEAD (Maddux, Adam, & Galinsky, 2010) conducted experiments with MBA and undergraduate students in the U.S. and France to investigate how multicultural learning facilitates creativity. Their findings indicated intellectual and creative benefits:

> Learning within and about a foreign culture—in particular, learning that certain behaviors one has long grown accustomed to as natural and inevitable can suddenly have very different functions in a

different cultural environment—may help individuals perceive and understand why cultural differences occur. These experiences then seem to enhance cognitive complexity and flexibility, heightening the ability to approach problems from new and multiple perspectives and ultimately enhancing the creative process. (p. 738)

2.5.4 Multiculturals and Global Cosmopolitans

A new term for highly desirable international executives has emerged: **multiculturals**, who transcend specific geographic boundaries and ethnic backgrounds. The public relations field also attracts multiculturals, who can flourish in the profession that requires cultural sophistication and communication skills and offers diverse international career opportunities (see Figure 2.5). Becoming a multicultural has enormous career benefits. Multiculturals are a highly desirable group for international management positions. They share the ability to navigate the verbal and nonverbal intercultural communication in businesses with people from anywhere. They tend to be exceptionally astute listeners and acute observers. Based on their extensive experiences traveling and working outside of their own country and culture, they are usually devoid of prejudice and ethnocentric beliefs. Some may have grown up with families from different cultures and gained bilingual and intercultural sensitivity skills as a child. Creativity is another skill multiculturals offer: "foreign culture experiences may not only enhance creativity but also, perhaps literally, as well as figuratively, broaden the mind" (Maddux et al., 2010, p. 739). Others may have studied, lived, or worked abroad for extended amounts of time. You may fit the description of a multicultural or have met people who do.

Figure 2.5—IMAGE OF MULTICULTURAL STAFF MEMBERS. Source: © Monkey Business Images/Shutterstock.com.

Linda Brimm (2010), a psychology professor and author of *Global Cosmopolitans: The Creative Edge of Difference*, uses the term **global cosmopolitans** to describe this "talented population of highly educated, multilingual people that have lived, worked and studied for extensive periods in different cultures" (p. 4). Brimm identifies five characteristics shared by this group:

1. Global Cosmopolitans see change as normal.
2. As outsiders to fixed cultural rules, they rely on creative thinking.
3. They reinvent themselves and experiment with new identities.
4. They are expert at the subtle and emotional aspects of transition.
5. They easily learn and use new ways of thinking. (p. 29)

Hae-Jung Hong, an academic at the Rouen Business School in France, and Yves Doz, an emeritus professor at INSEAD, examined the management approach used by L'Oréal, the global cosmetics company based in France, with a portfolio of brands from France and other cultures, including Maybelline, The Body Shop, Giorgio Armani, and Shu Uemura, in more than 130 countries. Their research (2013) found that the company hired multicultural professionals in new-product development since more than 50% of the company's sales originate from new markets beyond Europe and North America. L'Oréal also set up teams headed by multicultural managers from the company's international subsidiaries, drawing upon professionals with experience in sales and marketing, new recruits from other global companies, and graduates of leading international business schools.

These concepts are based on earlier sociological research (Useem, Useem, & Donoghue, 1963) on children raised by expatriates, in which the children navigate between two cultures of their family's home country and the country they grew up in, giving them insight into a blended **third culture**.

2.6 Learning Objectives and Key Terms

After reviewing Chapter 2, you should be able to:

- Identify different terms about international public relations.
- Define globalization from Appadurai's dimensions of global "scapes" as relevant to public relations.
- Describe the rise of multinational corporations and international nongovernmental organizations.
- Understand how globalism has impacted public relations agencies and in-house public relations departments.
- Outline how public relations trade associations have expanded on a local, regional, and global basis.
- Define the concept of glocalization and the distinctions between thinking globally, acting locally, and thinking locally, acting globally.
- Summarize the variety of international educational experiences and public relations career opportunities, whether you stay within your own country or go abroad.
- Define multiculturals and global cosmopolitans and explain why they offer desirable skills in the global workforce.

This chapter covers the following key terms:

International public relations (p. 28)   Multinational public relations (p. 28)
Global public relations (p. 28)   Transnational public relations (p. 28)
Transcultural public relations (p. 28)   Intercultural role (p. 29)
Ethnoscapes (p. 29)   Technoscapes (p. 29)
Finanscapes (p. 29)   Mediascapes (p. 30)
Ideoscapes (p. 30)   Nongovernmental organizations (p. 31)
Civil society organizations (p. 31)   Intergovernmental organizations (p. 31)
Public relations trade groups (p. 35)   Glocalization (p. 38)
Generic principles (p. 41)   Multiculturals (p. 47)
Global cosmopolitans (p. 48)   Third culture (p. 48)

References

100 People: A World Portrait. (2012). Statistics. Retrieved from http://www.100people.org/statistics_100stats.php?section=statistics.

Appadurai, A. (1990). Disjuncture and difference in the global cultural economy. *Theory, Culture & Society, 7*, 295–310. doi: 10.1177/026327690007002017.

Bardhan, N. (2011). Culture, communication, and third culture building in public relations within global flux. In N. Bardhan and C. K. Weaver (Eds.), *Public relations in global cultural contexts: Multi-paradigmatic perspectives* (pp. 77–107). New York, NY: Routledge.

Berdan, S. N. (2011, November 9). Interested in a global career? Consider PR. *The Huffington Post*. Retrieved from http://www.huffingtonpost.com/stacie-nevadomski-berdan/interested-in-a-global-ca_b_1080421.html.

Boumphrey, S., & Bevis, E. (2013). Reaching the emerging middle classes beyond BRIC. *Euromonitor International*. Retrieved from http://go.euromonitor.com/rs/euromonitorinternational/images/Reaching%20the%20Emerging%20Middle%20Classes%20Beyond%20BRIC.pdf?mkt_tok=3RkMMJWWfF9wsRoivqzBZKXonjHpfsX+7uwpWKa+lMI/0ER3fOvrPUfGjI.

Brimm, L. (2010). *Global cosmopolitans: The creative edge of difference*. Basingstoke, Hampshire: Palgrave Macmillan.

Churkina, O. (2013). *Glocalization: A measure of global brands' adaptation to local cultures*. Research presented at the Insight Innovation eXchange North America 2013, Philadelphia, PA. Retrieved from http://www.slideshare.net/InsightInnovation/glocalization-a-measure-of-global-brands-adaptation-to-local-cultures-by-olga-churkina-of-fresh-intelligence-presented-at-the-insight-innovation-exchange-north-america-2013.

Cooper, L. (2010, June 29). Five strategies for a successful global brand. *Marketing Week*. Retrieved from http://www.marketingweek.co.uk.

Curtin, P. A., & Gaither, T. K. (2007). *International public relations: Negotiating culture, identity, and power*. Thousand Oaks, CA: Sage Publications.

DeCarlo, S. (2013, April 17). The world's biggest companies. *Forbes.com*. Retrieved from http://www.forbes.com.

Dobbs, R., Remes, J., Smit, S., Manyika, J., Woetzel, J., & Agyenim-Boateng, Y. (2013, October). Urban world: The shifting global business landscape. *McKinsey & Company*. Retrieved from http://www.mckinsey.com/insights/urbanization/urban_world_the_shifting_global_business_landscape.

Friedman, T. L. (2007). *The world is flat: A brief history of the twenty-first century* (3rd ed.). New York, NY: Picador.

Gabel, M., & Bruner, H. (2003). *Global Inc.: An atlas of the multinational corporation.* New York, NY: The New Press.

Giddens, A. (2006). *Sociology* (5th ed.). Cambridge: Polity Press.

Global Alliance for Public Relations and Communication Management. (2012, November). *The Melbourne Mandate: A call to action for new areas of value in public relations and communication management.* Retrieved from http://melbournemandate.globalalliancepr. org/wp-content/uploads/2012/11/Melbourne-Mandate-Text-Draft-for-WPRF-final.pdf.

Gough, N. (2013). Thinking globally in environmental education: A critical history. In Robert Stevenson, Michael Brody, Justin Dillon, & Arjen Wals (Eds.), *International handbook of research on environmental education* (pp. 33–44). Washington, DC: American Educational Research Association/Routledge.

Grunig, J. E. (2009). Paradigms of global public relations in an age of digitalisation. *PRism, 6*(2). Retrieved from http://www.prismjournal.org/fileadmin/Praxis/Files/globalPR/ GRUNIG.pdf.

Heath, R. L., & Coombs, W. T. (2006). *Today's public relations: An introduction.* Thousand Oaks, CA: Sage.

Holmes Report/International Communications Consultancy Organisation. (2013). *World PR report.* Retrieved from http://worldreport.holmesreport.com/sites/all/themes/global250/ WorldReport-2013.pdf.

Hong, H., & Doz, Y. (2013, June). L'Oréal masters multiculturalism: The cosmetics giant manages to be very global—yet very French. *Harvard Business Review,* 114–118.

Keys, T. S., & Malnight, T. W. (2012). Corporate clout distributed: The influence of the world's largest 100 economic entities. *Global Trends.* Retrieved from http://www.globaltrends.com/ reports/?doc_id=500537&task=view_details.

L'Etang, J. (2009). Public relations and diplomacy in a globalized world: An issue of public communication. *American Behavioral Scientist, 53*(4), 607–626. doi: 10.1177/0002764 209347633.

Maddux, W. W., Adam, H., & Galinsky, A. D. (2010). When in Rome . . . Learn why the Romans do what they do: How multicultural learning experiences facilitate creativity. *Personality and Social Psychology Bulletin, 36*(6), 731–741. doi: 10.1177/01461672 10367786.

Matusitz, J. (2010). Disneyland Paris: A case analysis demonstrating how glocalization works. *Journal of Strategic Marketing, 18*(3), 223–237. doi: 10.1080/09652540903537014.

Moffatt, M. (2014). A beginner's guide to purchasing power parity theory (PPP Theory). *Economics.about.com.* Retrieved from http://economics.about.com/cs/money/a/purchasing power.htm.

Morton, B. (2013, September). Case study 7: An overview of international NGOs in development cooperation. In *Working with civil society in foreign aid: Possibilities for south-south cooperation?* (pp. 325–352). Beijing, China: United Nations Development Programme. Retrieved from http://www.undp.org/content/dam/undp/documents/partners/ civil_society/publications/2013_UNDP-CH-Working-With-Civil-Society-in-Foreign-Aid_EN.pdf.

Ovaitt, F., Jr. (1988). PR without boundaries: Is globalization an option? *Public Relations Quarterly, 33*(1), 5–9.

Public Relations Society of America. (2014a). *PRSA's old definition of public relations.* Retrieved from http://www.prsa.org/AboutPRSA/PublicRelationsDefined/Old%20Definition#.UqiFwNJDuZc.

Public Relations Society of America. (2014b). *What is public relations? PRSA's widely accepted definition.* Retrieved from http://www.prsa.org/AboutPRSA/PublicRelationsDefined/#.U9Zl-fldWSo.

Robertson, R. (1994). Globalisation or glocalisation? *The Journal of International Communication, 1*(1), 33–52. doi: 10.1080/13216597.1994.9751780.

Shaw, H. (2011, May 20). "Glocalization" rules the world: Brand marketing adapts to global customers. *Financial Post.* Retrieved from http://business.financialpost.com/2011/05/20/glocalization-rules-the-world/.

Sriramesh, K. (2009). Globalisation and public relations: The past, present, and the future. *PRism, 6*(2). Retrieved from http://www.prismjournal.org/fileadmin/Praxis/Files/globalPR/SRIRAMESH.pdf.

Steger, M. (2009). *Globalization: A very short introduction* (2nd ed.). Oxford: Oxford University Press.

Sylvie, G., Wicks, L. J., Hollifield, C.A., Lacy, S., & Sohn, A. B. (2008). *Media management: A casebook approach.* New York, NY: Lawrence Erlbaum.

Union of International Associations. (2014). *What is a non-governmental organization (NGO)?* Retrieved from http://www.uia.org/faq/yb2.

United Nations Conference on Trade and Development. (2007). *The universe of the largest transnational corporations.* Retrieved from http://unctad.org/en/Docs/iteiia20072_en.pdf.

United Nations, Department of Economic and Social Affairs, Population Division. (2013). *International migration report 2013.* Retrieved from http://www.un.org/en/development/desa/population/publications/pdf/migration/migrationreport2013/Full_Document_final.pdf#zoom=100.

United Nations Global Compact. (n.d.). *Civil society organizations.* Retrieved from http://www.unglobalcompact.org/participantsandstakeholders/civil_society.html.

Useem, J., Useem, R. H., & Donoghue, J. (1963). Men in the middle of the third culture: The roles of American and non-Western people in cross-cultural administration. *Human Organization, 22*(3), 169–179.

VanSlyke Turk, J. (Ed.). (2006, November). Public relations education for the 21st century: The professional bond—public relations education and the practice. *The Report of the Commission on Public Relations Education.* Retrieved from http://www.commpred.org/_uploads/report2-full.pdf.

Wakefield, R. I. (2009). Public relations contingencies in a globalized world where even "glocalization" is not sufficient. *Public Relations Journal, 3*(4). Retrieved from http://www.prsa.org/Intelligence/PRJournal/Vol3/No4/#.U96MV_ldWSo.

Wilcox, D. L., Cameron, G. T., Reber, B. H., & Shin, J. (2013). *Think public relations* (2nd ed.). Upper Saddle River, NJ: Pearson.

3 Changing Global Media Landscape and Ethical and Legal Issues

In the globalized world that is ours, maybe we are moving towards a global village, but that global village brings in a lot of different people, a lot of different ideas, lots of different backgrounds, lots of different aspirations. I think respect and understanding will help that village function better than it does today.

—Lakhdar Brahimi, Algerian diplomat

3.1 Introduction to Evolving Global Communications

The widely used term "global village" was coined by the late Canadian academic and scholar Marshall McLuhan in *The Gutenberg Galaxy* in 1962. His book examined human consciousness since the mid-15th century, when the Gutenberg Press's movable type became the industry standard for mass-produced printing over 400 years,[1] making books more easily accessible to the public, not just the wealthy. Many scribes who created books by hand may have groused about Gutenberg's invention—in fact, "monks were put out of work in perhaps the first technological layoffs" (Waite, 2001, p. 7). The invention of the mass-produced book increased literacy, inspired thought, and even sparked revolutions. Book reading also became a pleasurable activity, resulting in the novel, which McLuhan (1962) called: "one of the most radical of new literary conventions of the market society of the eighteenth century" (p. 273).

As communication tools change, people generally fall into two extreme categories: early adopters who are the first to experience the latest technology and resisters who may fear the newest tool and avoid trying it. Going back further in time to Classical Greece, Plato complained that writing utensils would weaken the mind and ruin one's ability to memorize. "What hath God wrought?" was the first telegraph message sent by Samuel Morse, who invented the Morse code system of dots and dashes that enabled operators to telegraph messages back in the mid-19th century. Businesses were the most receptive markets to sell telephones to back in the late 1800s, yet some people feared telephones as an invasion of privacy and a cause for hearing disorders. The trifecta of inappropriate content, particularly for children: "advertising, sex, and violence—are concerns that have been raised with each wave of new technology" (Wartella & Jennings, 2000, p. 38). Radio dissenters believed the new medium would undermine reading and religious practices, while exposing children to advertising, crime, and violence. The volume of detractors amplified with television—and even heightened with the Internet as an interactive virtual playground, full of harmless fun along with sexually explicit content and dangerous predators.

Every new medium also offers positive attributes. Radio, film, television, and the Internet have transformed the way people consume news and find, read, and share information. Ongoing technological innovations enable people to communicate instantly and cheaply with anyone around the globe from their smartphones, tablets, laptops, or desktop computers.

Today's public relations practitioners function in a "global village," a faster interconnected world than McLuhan had predicted. At the beginning of the chapter, I quoted from Lakhdar Brahimi, an Algerian United Nations diplomat, who emphasized that the global village requires respect and understanding of its significant differences during a "Conversations with History" interview conducted by the Institute of International Studies, University of California, Berkeley, (Kreisler, 2005). Patricia Wallace, author of *The Psychology of the Internet* (1999), believes that the Internet functions not quite like a global village: "With respect to human interaction, it is more like a huge collection of distinct neighborhoods where people with common interests can share information, work together, tell stories, joke around, debate politics, help each out, or play games" (p. 9).

Thomas Friedman envisioned a flat, leveled world with more equal opportunities due to globalization as outlined in his international bestselling book, *The World is Flat: A Brief History of the Twenty-first Century*. Researchers at George Mason University and the University of Maryland conceptualized the world map with spikes in major financial and commercial hubs. In terms of innovations, nearly two-thirds of world patents originated from the U.S. and Japan, while 85% of the inventors were from Japan, the U.S., South Korea, Germany, and Russia (Florida, 2005).

Whether you prefer the flat or spiky world metaphor, public relations writers can thrive with the borderless and instant accessibility of information on the Internet. The field has progressed far beyond the role of serving as a "press agent," generating publicity in traditional media outlets, to one that requires strategic engagement on multiple platforms for all types of dialogues with businesses, consumers, journalists, and other stakeholders anywhere. The Internet has enabled public relations practitioners to bypass the "gatekeepers" of media outlets—newspaper and magazine editors or radio and television producers and bookers— and to tell their stories directly and engage in conversations with their audiences online.

3.2 Global Connectivity, Social Media, and Portable Technology

"Old media are not being displaced. Rather, their functions and status are shifted by the introduction of new technologies," said Henry Jenkins, an American author and academic, in his book *Convergence Culture: Where Old and New Media Collide* (2006, p. 14). Jenkins refers to how past and present media have converged and how delivery technologies evolve. Think of what you might consider "dinosaurs" of delivery technologies in your time—the different technological tools you have used over the years to listen to music, watch TV, read a news story, access the Web, write a letter, take a photograph, or make a phone call.

The cartoon in Figure 3.1 illustrates the desk of a communicator from the past and present. How we communicate continues to evolve. What would this illustration look like 5, 10, or 20 years from now? What is considered the state-of-the-art delivery tool today quickly becomes antiquated.

Figure 3.1—CARTOON DEPICTS THE CHANGES IN COMMUNICATION TOOLS.
Source: © John Atkinson, Wrong Hands.

The public relations field has claimed "ownership" of social media, and practitioners must be conversant in navigating in and writing for the digital world. Do you remember the world before Google or the most popular search engine in your country? The word Google is a noun and now a verb—the *Oxford English Dictionary* and *Merriam-Webster's Collegiate Dictionary* and their online editions officially made google a verb, with a lowercase "g," in 2006 (Lombardi, 2006).

Roz Chast's cartoon from the *New Yorker* (see Figure 3.2) uses humor to illustrate the ubiquity of Google. Have you ever tried to google someone or something and found nothing? This would be quite a rare occurrence and make you wonder how a person or topic has no footprint on Google or on another popular search engine—unless that person opted to delete content, which is an option that Google now offers in some countries.

The impact of the Internet is substantial—and recent surveys indicate that its reach will continue to be pervasive worldwide. According to the Boston Consulting Group, almost half the world will be on the Internet, and if the Internet were a country, its national economy would be the world's fifth largest, behind the U.S., China, Japan, and India, by 2016 (Dean et al., 2012). More than 40% of the world's population has Internet access with more than 3 billion users by the end of 2014, showing a growth of 7.9% over the previous year (Internet Live Stats, 2014). More than 80% of the population is online in North America, Australia,

Figure 3.2—CARTOON CONVEYS THE POWER OF GOOGLE. Source: © Roz Chast, The New Yorker Collection/The Cartoon Bank.

New Zealand, Japan, Singapore, South Korea, most of Europe, and some of the Gulf Arab states and Caribbean islands. China ranks the highest in terms of total number of Internet users by country, with more than 641 million people online; however, the country's percentage of total population with Internet access is 46.03% (Internet Live Stats, 2014). eMarketer (2014) predicts that nearly 70% of the global population will have cellphones by 2017, of which 50% will be smartphones.

The Pew Research Center's Internet & America Life Project (Purcell, Rainie, Mitchell, Rosenstiel, & Olmstead, 2010) examined multiple platforms that Americans use to receive, forward, and customize news. Its survey determined that news has become portable (33% access news on their cellphones), personalized (28% customize their home page), and participatory (37% create, comment, or share news). Although the survey focused on the U.S., the three Ps—portable, personalized, and participatory—transcend borders. Do you use your cellphone to access news? Think about how many different sites or multiple media platforms you access to follow news. How much content do you customize on your phone or computer? Do you contribute to news content, comment on, or share postings on social media?

3.2.1 Opportunities and Challenges in Public Relations

Public relations practitioners have more opportunities to communicate in portable, personalized, and participatory platforms to exchange ideas, spread news, solicit feedback, and share documents and visual imagery. Doreen Starke-Meyerring (2005), a professor at McGill University in Montreal, said that for communicators "this shift toward communicating in open, participatory, and networked genres means that they need to understand how to connect and communicate across diverse cultural contexts to build, navigate and manage these communication and information networks" (p. 476). The choice of communication tools continues to expand, requiring that public relations professionals stay current and understand the potential for new technologies. See Exhibit 3.1 for a list of some of the major technological innovations when portable tools became readily available and examples of popular English-language social networking sites since the debut of Google in 2008.

The Plank Center for Leadership in Public Relations (Berger, 2012) conducted a cross-cultural study of 4,484 global public relations leaders in 23 countries. Two-thirds of the respondents identified four digital issues as the most important:

1. managing the volume and velocity of information (23%);
2. keeping abreast of new developments and the increase of social media (15.3%);
3. improving measurement of digital platforms (12.2%); and
4. coping with fast-moving crises (11.9%).

Exhibit 3.1—TIMELINE OF MAJOR TECHNOLOGICAL INNOVATIONS POST-GOOGLE. This list includes examples of technological innovations and social networking platforms, many of which are popular in English, since Google was launched in 1998.

RSS	1999	Twitter	2006
iPod	2001	iPhone	2007
Wikipedia	2001	Tumblr	2007
LinkedIn	2002	Foursquare	2009
Second Life	2003	iTablet	2010
MySpace	2003	Quora	2010
Skype	2003	Pinterest	2010
Facebook	2004	Instagram	2010
Digg	2004	Google+	2011
Wikinews	2004	Snapchat	2011
Flickr	2004	Vine	2013
Reddit	2005	Apple Watch	2014
YouTube	2005		

How are social media impacting the public relations field and the way people communicate?

- **Speed**—We have more speed and ways to communicate, yet less control. Public relations writers still need time, even though the turnaround time to research and draft content for approval and then make any necessary edits has accelerated. We cannot control the public commentary, but we can manage how we monitor and respond to feedback. The two-way dialogue requires responsiveness and transparency.
- **Convergence**—Jenkins (2006) describes convergence as "a cultural shift as consumers are encouraged to seek out new information and make connections among dispersed media content" (p. 3). He explains how traditional media have to re-examine older assumptions about programming and marketing, particularly since consumers have gone from "passive" to "active," from "predictable" and "loyal" to "migratory," from "isolated" to "socially connected," and from "silent" and "invisible" to "noisy" and "public" (pp. 18–19). Public relations professionals also need to pay attention to these behavioral shifts.
- **Consumer Empowerment**—Just as communicators have more ways and ease to share content, consumers are empowered as well. Consumers can actively express their opinions in multiple online forums. Anyone with a cellphone can capture events through photographs and video clips. People who are first on the scene of a crisis incident can become **citizen journalists**, providing imagery that can be shared instantly on social media networks and widely disseminated by mainstream media.
- **Citizen Activism**—Online platforms can mobilize people to protest and voice their dissatisfactions, particularly before a government interferes and shuts down access. A social networking site brought attention to the slain Khaled Mohamed Said, a 28-year-old Egyptian who became the "face" symbolizing torture and oppression during the Mubarak regime. The Facebook page, Kullena Khaled Said ("We Are All Khaled Said"), became the virtual organizational hub for the Egyptian protests in 2011. Wael Ghonim, the creator of the Facebook page, tells the full story in his memoir, *Revolution 2.0: The Power of the People is Greater than the People in Power*, which illustrates the power of social media.
- **Conversational and Visual Content**—Communication demands more of a conversation online—and a conversation that must be compelling with not just words but with images and video clips. Writing styles and tone must reflect less of an institutional voice. The Internet also allows one to provide global and local content in multiple languages.
- **Evolutionary**—Keeping track of enhancements of existing social media sites and new technological innovations can be time-intensive yet necessary. The fact that a new tool exists does not mean that it should be adopted by an organization. The new technology should be investigated first and then determined if it can be applied and measured strategically as part of the public relations planning.
- **Transparency**—The *New Yorker* cartoon in Figure 3.3 illustrates the issue of anonymity on the Internet since anyone can craft an online persona. Transparency is essential; laws also are catching up to prevent fakery online.

Although the Internet offers many positive features, the digital world also presents an environment for cyberbullying, cyberstalking, cybercrimes (invasion of privacy, identity theft,

Figure 3.3—CARTOON DEPICTS TRANSPARENCY ISSUES ON THE WEB. Source: © Robert Leighton, The New Yorker Collection/The Cartoon Bank.

"Instead of creating life, I've decided just to establish an online persona."

and scams), and other challenges. Evgeny Morozov, author of *The Net Delusion: The Dark Side of Internet Freedom*, rails against cyberutopian views and shares the downside of the Internet in a dictatorship:

> Failing to anticipate how authoritarian governments would respond to the Internet, cyber-utopians did not predict how useful it would prove for propaganda purposes, how masterfully dictators would learn to use it for surveillance, and how sophisticated modern systems of Internet censorship would become. (2011, p. xiv)

3.3 Global Print and Broadcast Media

"I'm thinking about joining the dark side," said a reporter to a public relations practitioner. I was the public relations practitioner listening to this comment from a journalist, who was acting like a wanderlust Jedi, on the editorial staff of a leading U.S. lifestyle magazine. This *Star Wars* metaphor shocked me. It was the first time I had heard the public relations business being referred to as the "dark side." I never thought of myself or my colleagues as Siths on the side of evil, with the likes of Darth Vader. I have regarded myself as a trusted, reliable resource with ethical principles—and, with a few rare exceptions, have worked with and met other highly ethical public relations practitioners.

When you hear the word press, what comes to mind? *Merriam-Webster* defines *press* from a journalistic perspective four ways:

a) the gathering and publishing or broadcasting of news: journalism;
b) newspapers, periodicals, and often radio and television news broadcasting;
c) news reporters, publishers, and broadcasters;
d) comment or notice in newspapers and periodicals <is getting a good press>. ("Press," 2014a)

The online *Oxford Dictionaries* differs in describing **press** as "newspapers or journalists viewed collectively" and "coverage in newspapers and magazines" ("Press," 2014b). The important distinction is that outside of the U.S., the term press generally refers to print media, not broadcast media. *Oxford Dictionaries* defines **media** in both its American and British/global English versions as: "the main means of mass communication (television, radio, and newspapers) regarded collectively" ("Media," 2014). For international dialogue, public relations practitioners should use the term *media* when they are referring to both print and electronic media.

Media relations is the term widely used for public relations interactions with journalists at traditional media outlets (also called mainstream or legacy media). One of the goals of public relations practitioners is to provide meaningful story ideas and assistance to journalists. This relationship can be very rewarding, particularly when you can see your efforts come to life in the form of an actual story published in a blog, magazine, or newspaper or aired on a TV or radio program. An effective approach for practitioners is to identify the most relevant media outlets and then the specific journalists, whether they are editors, columnists, freelancers, producers, or bookers. Public relations professionals must understand the media's reporting styles, topics of interest, and deadlines. Identifying the most influential media that your target audiences follow is more effective than reaching mass media. Media relations should not be a numbers game, focusing on total circulation, audience, and viewership; instead it should be strategic and relevant.

Public relations practitioners should gain the respect of journalists by becoming a valued resource about the industries they represent and by providing worthwhile story ideas and imagery, as well as access to spokespeople. Maintaining relationships with the most important journalists in your industry is essential—and reaching journalists is getting harder overall since they are bombarded with email, voicemail, and social media messages. Journalists employed by outlets that have downsized may have less time to attend media events or meet face to face with public relations practitioners.

Generating positive exposure about the clients or organizations you represent can result in stories that are read, seen, heard, downloaded, or shared by your targeted publics. What do you believe more: an advertisement or editorial? This third-party editorial endorsement is considered more believable and credible than paid-for content that is completely controlled by the organization. Complete Exercise 3.1 by evaluating a news media outlet, whether in print or broadcast or digital formats, that you follow and respect.

Exercise 3.1

Insights: Traditional Media Outlets

Identify a recent news story you recall from a traditional media outlet—one that you read in a magazine or newspaper, watched on TV news, or listened to on the radio—that inspired you to think about something differently or to do something, such as to see a movie, go to a concert, visit a specific place, volunteer for a nonprofit, vote for a candidate, or buy a product. You also can look at the online content or social media created by the mainstream media outlet.

Please answer the following questions:

1. What is the name of the newspaper, magazine, or TV or radio program?
2. What did this media outlet inspire you to do or think about?
3. How often do you follow this media outlet?
4. Does this outlet also connect with its audiences on social media?
5. What format or combinations of formats do you use to follow this media outlet? Print, TV, radio, online, or app?
6. Who is this media outlet aiming to reach?
7. What are the appeals of this media outlet? Do you like the reporter(s), the style of the content, the specific topics covered, or what other elements?
8. What makes you trust the opinions of this media outlet? Do you know other people who follow this media outlet?

3.3.1 Changes in Traditional Media Worldwide

Just as the public relations field has dealt with changes in media consumption and social media, traditional media have been facing challenges with more consumers obtaining news online. Newspapers, magazines, and television and radio outlets have been adopting social media. Print and broadcast journalists now write blogs, tweet, post content on social media, or stream live videos on YouTube. Traditional media outlets also engage their viewers, readers, and listeners on social media, while soliciting their participation and feedback.

Let us look at a few trends that have been impacting traditional media:

- **Traditional Journalists Going Digital**—Oriella PR Network conducted its Global Digital Journalism Study (2013) of over 500 journalists in 14 countries, discovering that more than one-third believe "digital first" (p. 2) in breaking news online and one-fourth create multiple versions of the same story online. The survey also found that nearly 50% produce video in-house and 34% use externally produced video. Mobile is growing as a platform to generate revenue. The Oriella survey also revealed that journalists are relying on blogs and microblogs for sources and verification, with more than 50% using Twitter, from trusted sources.
- **Print Circulation up 2% Yet More Digital Enhancements**—The World Association of Newspapers and News Publishers (WAN-IFRA) releases an annual World Press Trends survey. Its 2014 survey revealed that print circulation rose by 2% in 2013,

but it has declined by a negative 2% over the past five years. The total number of worldwide readership still remains significant: 2.5 billion people read newspapers and 800 million read newspapers on digital platforms. Findings also show that newspapers are trying to find sustainable solutions for digital news by measuring and enhancing their social media engagement while improving the online experience.

- **More 24/7 TV News Programs in English and Other Languages**—Since the advent of 24/7 television news programming on CNN in 1980, all-day television news programming has spanned the globe. English-language content airs around the globe on CNN, BBC, and others, while foreign-language media outlets have started to produce English-language content, such as Al Jazeera (Graddol, 2006). Concurrently, English-language television channels have expanded programming in other languages. (See Appendix C for a list of global English-language broadcast media.)

- **More Entertainment TV News Programming and Reality Shows**—An international study investigated global trends since the 1980s and found that the news media in many countries have become more entertainment- and market-oriented due to an increase in privately owned TV channels, deregulation of commercial broadcasters, and shrinking audiences (Curran, Iyengar, Lund, & Salovaara-Moring, 2009). Reality entertainment TV formats also have proliferated worldwide. The *Idol* franchise began in the U.K. in 2001 and has since expanded to local versions in the U.S. (see Figure 3.4) and to over 50 different countries (Oren & Shahaf, 2012).

Figure 3.4—THE *IDOL* TELEVISION FRANCHISE HAS SPREAD AROUND THE GLOBE. Image shows performers in the 2013 American Idols Live! Tour in Sacramento, California. Source: © Randy Miramontez/Shutterstock.com.

Truly understanding global media requires knowing the biases of specific media, whether they are government controlled or pulpits for political viewpoints. Is journalism in the country regarded as a "watchdog," reporting and investigating stories objectively on any subject, or a "lapdog," disseminating propaganda and avoiding controversy? Which media outlets do the public respect and regard as accurate? What topics would be censored? Not all traditional media follow a model of democracy, such as in North America, Europe, Australia, and New Zealand. Some media in parts of Asia, including Mainland China, Vietnam, and Cambodia, believe their "most important role is to communicate the policies and views of the government" (Devereux & Peirson-Smith, 2009, p. 38). Even media outlets in democratic societies may have a conservative, moderate, or liberal bias, showing support for a political party or candidate. In the U.S., for example, Fox News is reputed to have a conservative, pro-Republican slant, whereas MSNBC reflects a more liberal, pro-Democratic voice.

Public relations practitioners handling international media relations must understand how the media operate differently from country to country. Ming-Yi Wu (2011), a communications scholar, compared media relations practices in Japan, South Korea, Taiwan, and the U.S. Relationships and face-to-face social activities have a higher value in Asia than in the U.S. For example, the Japanese media function within a press club culture (*kisha kurabu*) structured by industry for news gathering and reporting. *Cheong* (long-term relationships) flourishes in Korea and *guanxi* (close interpersonal relationships) thrives in China and Taiwan, requiring that public relations executives establish strong relationships built on trust with journalists.

3.4 Global Ethical and Legal Considerations in Public Relations Writing

Public relations practitioners will encounter different ethical and legal situations throughout their careers, with the complexity increasing in the global arena. They need to understand legal issues regarding contracts for employment, clients, and freelance talent; intellectual property to protect their company's or client's creative output and how to legally use the work of others; defamation and privacy of people; and commercial and government regulations that impact how organizations can promote their products and services in specific countries.

Your company most likely will have you sign a contract; public relations agencies are very concerned about non-compete agreements to protect their client base. Whether you work for a public relations agency or in-house, you most likely will hire freelance writers, designers, illustrators, photographers, and videographers, as well as other creative talent—and you need to make sure that your contractual agreements work for both parties. You may want to use existing audiovisual or written material from other sources, which would entail understanding who owns the copyright.

Although public relations practitioners are not expected to be lawyers, they do need to understand legal issues that could impact the work they perform or the freelance talent they may use for creative services. Serious breaches could result in lawsuits, ruined reputations, or even time in prison for such major offenses as insider trading. Corporations, nonprofits, and public relations agencies usually have in-house legal counsel or a retainer with a law firm. When in doubt with any potential legal issue, check with your supervisor. Try answering the "what if" questions to determine what ethical or legal issue you would need to consider in Exercise 3.2.

Exercise 3.2

Self-Evaluation: Ethical and Legal Issues in Public Relations

What would you do if you were an account executive at a public relations agency and the following situations occurred (If you don't know the exact answers, what would you need to find out?):

1. Your tourist board client wants you to invite journalists to join a press trip. The client will pay for the airfare, hotels, meals, and tours. Is this trip ethical?

2. Your agency receives a Request for Proposal (a formal invitation to submit credentials and a plan) to bid on a huge account. However, it is a conflict of interest with an existing account. Do you still pursue the new business opportunity?

3. Your real estate client has altered a digital image dramatically. The image shows an exterior of a new condominium development *without* its unsightly electrical power lines. Should you post the retouched image on the online newsroom?

4. You have been asked by a colleague to add activities that you have not undertaken to an activity report on work completed for the client. How do you handle that?

5. You are preparing a new business proposal to a prospective client. Can you include information about a competitive client that you no longer represent? The information was considered confidential by your former client.

6. You are planning on setting up your own public relations agency and want to bring along a few accounts from your current company. What do you need to consider?

7. Your client would like you to buy expensive gifts, over USD500 each, for journalists who have written or produced stories about the company. Do you recommend this?

8. Your client asks you to describe a new product as a "game changer in the industry" in a release. You have no factual evidence to substantiate this claim. What can you do to avoid a legal issue?

9. You have written a news release on financial earnings for a publicly held company that has not yet been issued. Can you share this information with a relative or friend before the facts are made public? Is this legal? Why or why not?

10. You are working with a website designer on behalf of your client. Your client wants to add artwork she found from an outside source on the company's home page. What do you need to do to use the visuals?

11. Your client wants to use an image of a deceased celebrity in the publicity material. Can you do so without permission? Why or why not?

12. Your restaurant client is unhappy with some of the online reviews and wants you to arrange for writers to assume fake identities as loyal customers extolling the client's services with glowing online reviews. Do you recommend this?

13. Your client wants to post stories that appeared in media outlets on the company's website. What do you need to do before posting the content?

14. Your entertainment client wants you to use only part of a quote from a movie review. The film critic wrote, "What an amazing waste of talent and time." Your client wants you to quote only one word "amazing." Should you do so? Why or why not?

Please see Appendix D for answers.

3.4.1 Ethics in Public Relations

How do you define ethics in public relations? Unlike laws that are developed and enforced by governments, ethics are less black and white, falling into grayer shades. **Business ethics** provide guidelines on moral and professional standards based on relationships and interactions with both internal and external audiences. Internal audiences in public relations could span clients, employers, colleagues, freelance talent, and other providers of services. External audiences could include journalists, bloggers, analysts, investors, customers, other external stakeholders, the society at large, and peers in public relations and other industries.

Dean Kruckeberg (2000), professor emeritus at the University of North Carolina at Charlotte, recommends another dimension of **"strategic ethics,"** rather than tactical ethics that assesses the organization in respect to the physical and social environment, human rights, or cultural differences. Kruckeberg stated "that public relations practitioners look more broadly, more *strategically*, at their role as interpreters and ethicists and social-policy makers in guiding organizational behavior and take strategic responsibility in influencing and reconciling public perceptions of their organizations within a global context" (p. 38).

Public relations trade associations and many public relations agencies have established industry codes and ethics in the profession. A study analyzed the similarities among ethical codes of 17 public relations associations worldwide, finding that the most popular key words included "values, honesty, transparency, loyalty and conduct" (Skinner, Mersham, & Valin, 2003, p. 17).

Exhibit 3.2 on the Global Alliance for Public Relations and Communication Management Code of Ethics and Exhibit 3.3 on the International Public Relations Association Code of Conduct show how two multinational public relations trade groups spell out professional standards for their members. These guidelines illustrate best practices in relationships with clients, the public, stakeholders, the media, and other internal and external audiences.

Ethics—as well as laws in some cases—affect managing campaigns and writing for public relations in such areas as follows:

- Quality of information in all forms of written and visual communication should be accurate, honest, and devoid of deception, such as false or unsubstantiated claims.
- Content should be fair and and transparent in all forms of communications.
- Confidentiality to the client or employer must be followed. Even if an A-list journalist pressures a public relations executive for information that could make or break a story being covered, the executive would be unable to disclose information that would be considered confidential. The solution would be to double-check with the client and receive approval in writing—or to forgo the opportunity.

3.4.2 Legal Considerations in Public Relations

Charles J. Glasser, Jr., global media counsel for Bloomberg News, edited the *International Libel & Privacy Handbook* (2013) and illustrated the complexity of international law:

> Spend five minutes at the United Nations or any international congress—where arguing about the shape of a meeting table can go on for a day—and it will come as no surprise that media law around the world is a crazy patchwork quilt of laws, with each square reflecting a nation's cultural biases, political history, and economic structure. (p. ix)

Exhibit 3.2—GLOBAL ALLIANCE FOR PUBLIC RELATIONS AND COMMUNICATION MANAGEMENT CODE OF ETHICS. Source: Reprinted with permission. © Global Alliance for Public Relations and Communication Management.

---

1. CODE OF PROFESSIONAL STANDARDS

We are committed to ethical practices, preservation of public trust, and the pursuit of communication excellence with powerful standards of performance, professionalism, and ethical conduct.

Advocacy

We will serve our client and employer interests by acting as responsible advocates and by providing a voice in the market place of ideas, facts, and viewpoints to aid informed public debate.

Honesty

We will adhere to the highest standards of accuracy and truth in advancing the interests of clients and employers.

Integrity

We will conduct our business with integrity and observe the principles and spirit of the Code in such a way that our own personal reputation and that of our employer and the public relations profession in general is protected.

Expertise

We will encourage members to acquire and responsibly use specialized knowledge and experience to build understanding and client/employer credibility. Furthermore we will actively promote and advance the profession through continued professional development, research, and education.

Loyalty

We will insist that members are faithful to those they represent, while honoring their obligations to serve the interests of society and support the right of free expression.

Public relations writers should gain an understanding of four legal areas: 1) intellectual property, 2) defamation and invasion of privacy, 3) commercial and government regulations, and 4) contractual and employment laws.

Intellectual Property

Intellectual property refers to legal protection of completed creative work and inventions, such as patents, copyrights, trademarks, industrial designs, and geographical indications. Intellectual property rights protect creators from having their work used by others, without their approval, and enable them to negotiate payment for use of their work. The United Nations created a self-funding agency with 188 member states, the World Intellectual Property Organization, which helps people obtain international protection for their intellectual property through services, collaborative network, technical platforms, and free databases. Its "mission is to lead the development of a balanced and effective international intellectual property (IP)

Exhibit 3.3—INTERNATIONAL PUBLIC RELATIONS ASSOCIATION CODE OF CONDUCT.
Source: Reprinted with permission by the International Public Relations Association. © International Public Relations Association.

The "IPRA Code of Conduct"

Adopted in 2011 the IPRA Code of Conduct is an affirmation of professional and ethical conduct by members of the International Public Relations Association and recommended to public relations practitioners worldwide.

The Code consolidates the 1961 Code of Venice, the 1965 Code of Athens and the 2007 Code of Brussels.

RECALLING the Charter of the United Nations which determines "to reaffirm faith in fundamental human rights, and in the dignity and worth of the human person";

RECALLING the 1948 "Universal Declaration of Human Rights" and especially recalling Article 19;

RECALLING that public relations, by fostering the free flow of information, contributes to the interests of all stakeholders;

RECALLING that the conduct of public relations and public affairs provides essential democratic representation to public authorities;

RECALLING that public relations practitioners through their wide-reaching communication skills possess a means of influence that should be restrained by the observance of a code of professional and ethical conduct;

RECALLING that channels of communication such as the Internet and other digital media, are channels where erroneous or misleading information may be widely disseminated and remain unchallenged, and therefore demand special attention from public relations practitioners to maintain trust and credibility;

RECALLING that the Internet and other digital media demand special care with respect to the personal privacy of individuals, clients, employers and colleagues.

In the conduct of public relations practitioners shall:

1. Observance

Observe the principles of the UN Charter and the Universal Declaration of Human Rights;

2. Integrity

Act with honesty and integrity at all times so as to secure and retain the confidence of those
with whom the practitioner comes into contact;

3. Dialogue

Seek to establish the moral, cultural and intellectual conditions for dialogue, and recognise
the rights of all parties involved to state their case and express their views;

4. Transparency

Be open and transparent in declaring their name, organisation and the interest they
represent;

5. Conflict

Avoid any professional conflicts of interest and to disclose such conflicts to affected parties
when they occur;

6. Confidentiality

Honour confidential information provided to them;

---

continued

7. Accuracy

Take all reasonable steps to ensure the truth and accuracy of all information provided;

8. Falsehood

Make every effort to not intentionally disseminate false or misleading information, exercise proper care to avoid doing so unintentionally and correct any such act promptly;

9. Deception

Not obtain information by deceptive or dishonest means;

10. Disclosure

Not create or use any organisation to serve an announced cause but which actually serves an undisclosed interest;

11. Profit

Not sell for profit to third parties copies of documents obtained from public authorities;

12. Remuneration

Whilst providing professional services, not accept any form of payment in connection with those services from anyone other than the principal;

13. Inducement

Neither directly nor indirectly offer nor give any financial or other inducement to public representatives or the media, or other stakeholders;

14. Influence

Neither propose nor undertake any action which would constitute an improper influence on public representatives, the media, or other stakeholders;

15. Competitors

Not intentionally injure the professional reputation of another practitioner;

16. Poaching

Not seek to secure another practitioner's client by deceptive means;

17. Employment

When employing personnel from public authorities or competitors take care to follow the rules and confidentiality requirements of those organisations;

18. Colleagues

Observe this Code with respect to fellow IPRA members and public relations practitioners worldwide.

IPRA members shall, in upholding this Code, agree to abide by and help enforce the disciplinary procedures of the International Public Relations Association in regard to any breach of this Code.

Adopted by the IPRA Board 5 November 2010

system that enables innovation and creativity for the benefit of all" (World Intellectual Property Organization, 2014a, para. 2). This organization also administers a few treaties, including the Berne Convention for the Protection of Literary and Artistic Works (the oldest copyright treaty, established in 1886) that has been ratified by more than 160 countries to establish minimum standards of copyright protection of copyright holders. According to the Berne Convention principles (World Intellectual Property Organization, 2014b), "automatic protection" applies from when a qualifying work is in a tangible form. Questions can arise from country to country on copyright registration requirements, definition of a qualifying work, duration of the copyright, and transfer of moral rights (identification of author, integrity, and divulgation of work), and economic rights (ability to reproduce, distribute copies, and communicate and transform work).

The digital age, with the ability to instantly post and share content, has also created new legal complexities. The World Economic Forum describes the importance of intellectual property: "Intellectual property (IP) is about promoting progress and innovation. The global IP system should be seen as a tool to regulate and facilitate trade, information and knowledge in innovative and creative goods and services" (2013, p. 4).

Public relations professionals would primarily be involved with copyright, trademarks, and geographic indications:

Copyright protects creators with regard to the use of their tangible work in a fixed form—whether it is a drawing, painting, play, novel, choreography, musical composition, film, documentary, software program, or another form of creative expression in multiple disciplines (see Figure 3.5 of the copyright symbol). An idea, however, is not copyrightable. The challenge is that copyright follows the laws of individual countries, meaning that "international copyright" law does not truly exist.

Public domain categorizes works that are not protected by copyright, which means that the copyright has expired or the works were never copyrightable. **Fair dealing** and **fair use** allow usage of copyrighted material to such non-commercial educational ventures as academic research and teaching, and to news reporting, satire, criticism, and reviews. However, restrictions do apply and the concept of fair dealing varies from country to country.

If you are designing a website or a brochure or selecting content for social media for a corporation and want to add illustrations and photographs, you would need to request

Figure 3.5—COPYRIGHT SYMBOL. Source: ©Yuriy Vlasenko/Shutterstock.com.

permission from the copyright holders, which could be a third party, such as a publisher. If you are writing an audiovisual presentation, you also would need to check on music, video, and other imagery. You would need to let the copyright holders know details about how you intend to use the creative work, such as the formats, number of copies to be produced, and in which geographic areas. In many cases, you would need to pay a fee for using their creative work. All agreements must be in writing.

Public relations practitioners must receive permission to post or reprint stories from other copyrighted sources. For example, a public relations firm in Las Vegas was sued by a copyright enforcement company for alleged copyright infringement for posting a story published in the city's daily newspaper about the agency's celebrity client, without permission, on the agency's website (Green, 2010).

Trademarks and **service marks** are considered valuable brand assets for organizations. Trademarks can be a logo, brand name, slogan, package design, or another indicator that clearly identifies products that can be distinguished from competitors. Nike's corporate logo forms a "swoosh," design trademark that clearly identifies the shoe and clothing manufacturer, and the symbol is incorporated into all of the brand's tangible and digital imagery. Slogans (also called taglines), whether one word or a few words, instantly convey the brand's image. Look at the following car company slogans: Acura, the road will never be the same; BMW, the ultimate driving machine; Ford, go further; Mazda, zoom zoom; Porsche, there is no substitute; and Volvo, for life. A service mark (or servicemark) applies to services literally, instead of products. For example, the name of a restaurant chain, such as McDonald's, is a registered service mark for its restaurant services; the names of its food products would be trademarks.

The World Intellectual Property Organization (WIPO) also administers the Madrid System of International Registration of Marks (which originated in 1891) and the Protocol Relating to the Madrid Agreement (adopted in 1989), which allow international registration of trademarks. The WIPO's website (www.wipo.int) provides extensive information and lists its member countries; 95 members were posted as of April 15, 2015. As with copyright law, trademark registrations and rights vary from country to country. Most trademarks are labeled. For example, the ® symbol and Reg. abbreviation indicate registration in one or more countries; "TM" (trademark; see Figure 3.6) and "SM" (service mark) usually mean an intent to claim trademarks, while some countries use other symbols and designations, such as "Marca Registrada" or "MR" in Spanish-language countries (International Trademark Association, 2012). The International Trademark Association's website (www.inta.org) contains extensive background information on trademarks. Many companies also set up policies on how public relations materials should identify trademarks. See the section on style guides in Chapter 7.

Geographic indications apply to names of places that identify unique products from a specific location. This copyright law would be important if you were handling public relations for certain food and beverage products. The term Champagne only refers to wine produced from grapes grown in the Champagne region of France. Other examples include Cognac, Tequila, Darjeeling tea, Parma ham, Roquefort and Parmigiano-Reggiano cheese, and Colombian and Jamaican Blue Mountain coffee. WIPO's website offers detailed facts on geographic indications.

Defamation and Invasion of Privacy

Defamation is defined as a false statement—whether it is slander, a spoken falsehood, or libel, a printed untruth in words or an image—that damages the reputation of a person or an

Figure 3.6—TRADEMARK SYMBOL. Source: © Nasirkhan/Shutterstock.com.

organization. A universal defamation law does not exist, meaning that proving defamation varies from country to country.

The **right of publicity** (also called personality rights and appropriation) protects people, including employees, from having their names or likeness used by others, without permission or payment, for commercial purposes. For example, marketers must receive permission from people, whether they are celebrities, employees, or average citizens, to use their name, image, or voice—or recognizable sound-alikes and lookalikes—to promote products or services. The laws vary from country to country and from state to state in the U.S. Michael G. Parkinson and L. Marie Parkinson, authors of *Public Relations Law* (2008), recommend that "anyone producing advertisements or commercial communication would be well advised to secure a specific written release, prepared by competent legal counsel, from everyone whose name or image is used" (p. 39). Misappropriation of personality also applies to the deceased. You could not go ahead and use an image of Princess Diana or Michael Jackson without approval from their estates.

Commercial and Government Regulations

To protect consumers and fair trade, many governments have **commercial regulations** that need to be adhered to. In addition, pharmaceutical, health care, insurance, banking, and other industries are heavily regulated. Public relations practitioners in these fields should gain familiarity with regulations that would impact how they can promote products and services in multimedia, including social media, in specific countries.

Information released to the public in any form should be accurate, truthful, and fair, avoiding misleading information about the product or service. For example, a news release should avoid hype and unsubstantiated claims. The only place acceptable for puffery is in the form of a quotation containing an opinion from a company executive or identified spokesperson. Rules also can apply to visual imagery, such as retouching of photographs that are deceptive in altering reality, and terms for contests and competitions.

The Internet is another area rife with changing regulations, particularly with **astroturfing**, when public relations staff or paid spokespeople post positive or negative commentary online, such as on review sites or blogs, without identifying themselves or masking their identity as a disinterested party. The Taiwanese Federal Trade Commission fined Samsung Electronics in Taiwan approximately USD340,000 for violating its Fair Trade Act for paying writers and employees to post unfavorable comments about a competitor online (Chen, 2013).

Is the sandwich really a foot long or was an inch of bread missing? Lawsuits were filed in two U.S. states against Subway, the sandwich franchise, for its deceptive 11-inch sandwich. The uproar actually started in Australia via Facebook and spread throughout other social media and traditional media (Allen, 2013).

Formed in 1992, the International Consumer Protection and Enforcement Network (ICPEN) is composed of consumer protection authorities from more than 50 countries, thereby helping consumers settle file claims cross-border and find out more about scams.

Handling public relations for publicly held companies requires strict adherence to **security and exchange regulations**. Michael G. Parkinson and L. Marie Parkinson explain: "Reporting about stocks, advertising the sale of bonds, and communicating about all kinds of securities are important tasks for communications practitioners because communication has an extraordinary impact on the value of the securities themselves" (2008, p. 111). Writers need to fully understand what a *material* announcement means: information that would affect the decision-making process of buying or selling shares needs to be disclosed at specified times so that no single person has an advantage (see Figure 3.7). Rules and regulations also apply to companies filing an initial public offering during the pre-filing, waiting, and post-effective quiet periods, thereby preventing companies and their investment bankers from inflating the stock. Public relations practitioners also need to provide accurate information—and avoid hype and misleading information—in news releases and other forms of communication. Many news releases for publicly held companies include forward-looking statements on future performance. Releases on financial performance and major news that could impact the company's revenues are traditionally vetted by senior investor relations staff, the chief financial officer, and legal counsel. The U.S. Securities and Exchange Commission describes insider trading as:

> Illegal insider trading refers generally to buying or selling a security, in breach of a fiduciary duty or other relationship of trust and confidence, while in possession of material, nonpublic information about the security. Insider trading violations may also include "tipping" such information, securities trading by the person "tipped," and securities trading by those who misappropriate such information. (2013, para. 2)

This means that any individual with insider knowledge would be unable to benefit directly from insider knowledge and would be forbidden to share information with colleagues, friends, family members, or any person.

Contractual and Employment Laws

Public relations professionals traditionally deal with the following contracts, which would need to conform to local laws and regulations:

- **Employment agreements** must clearly indicate the date of hire, title, compensation, benefits, and overall terms of employment. Public relations agencies also may have

Figure 3.7—STOCK EXCHANGE MARKET TRADING CONCEPTS. Source: ©
Rawpixel/Shutterstock.com.

a separate noncompetition contract (also called covenant not to compete) that outlines
a time period after employees leave the agency, in which they are unable to approach
the agency's clients for employment or as clients at another agency. This agreement
helps the agency protect its client base for a specific timeframe, which is usually a
minimum of one year. Public relations professionals also should understand
employment contracts in terms of copyright laws. In the U.S., for example, the work
produced by employees, whether they are employed directly by an organization or a
public relations agency, falls under "work for hire," which means that the copyright
belongs to the employer or client, not to the employee.

- **Independent service contracts** are required when you hire freelance talent for such
  services as graphic design, writing, videography, or photography. These contracts
  must clearly state the payment and terms of use of the work, particularly if it is for
  a specific region or global distribution, and applicable copyright laws.
- **Public relations agency client contracts** outline the agreement between the two
  parties, covering the fees for staff (usually on a monthly retainer basis, along with
  hourly rates for services beyond the specified retainer), out-of-pocket transactions
  (for expenses on behalf of the client), length of contract, renewal and termination

terms, indemnification (for both sides), and confidentiality, as well as other relevant content on the working relationship. Many contracts also have a noncompetition agreement that covers which companies the client considers a conflict of interest, thereby restricting the public relations agency from representing these organizations while under contract with the current client. Work produced by an agency on behalf of a client traditionally remains the property of the client, meaning the client owns the copyright.

3.5 Global Media Ethics and Issues

As with global intellectual property, global media ethics are not universal. Although public relations practitioners may find more similarities than differences when dealing with global media, they should be aware of ethical and legal issues, as well as government regulations that may restrict content. Media codes for a specific newspaper, magazine, or television or radio station are traditionally posted online. National official codes for government-controlled media in some countries in the Middle East, Africa, and Asia may censor content and public debates on religion, royalty, and politicians (Hafez, 2002). As with the public relations industry, journalists also have collaborated to form local, regional, and international trade groups to address such issues as ethics, industry trends, and censorship. Exhibit 3.4 includes examples of international journalism trade groups.

In addition, watchdog groups also look at journalists and other professions to protect the freedom of expression. The **Index on Censorship** began sharing the voices of dissidents behind the former Iron Curtain in the 1970s and evolved to defending the Universal Declaration of Human Rights, which the UN General Assembly adopted in 1948, specifically Article 19: "Everyone has the right to freedom of opinion and expression; this right includes freedom to hold opinions without interference and to seek, receive and impart information and ideas through any media and regardless of frontiers" (United Nations, 2014). Based in London, the Index on Censorship (2014) monitors threats to global free expression that apply to journalists, bloggers, artists, and other citizens worldwide: digital (such as surveillance and censorship), authoritarian (suppression of media content, voices of people and public protests), policies and society (restrictions and regulations blocking free speech), access (barriers and impediments), and religion and culture (discrimination, blasphemy, and self-censorship). Its website (www.indexoncensorship.org) provides news and reports on trends and issues of interest to international public relations practitioners.

The International Public Relations Association (IPRA) launched a campaign for media transparency in 2001 by creating a **Charter on Media Transparency** (see Exhibit 3.5) to establish international ethical standards. As of 2015, the charter has been adopted by approximately 50 national and international public relations trade groups and 250,000 practitioners in more than 100 countries, as well as by media organizations with an estimated half-million media executives and journalists in at least 115 countries (International Public Relations Association, 2015). The charter focuses on five areas: editorial, identification, solicitation, sampling, and policy statement. I have added commentary in each section relevant to public relations.

- **Editorial** departments traditionally operate independently of advertising, which is considered the preferred professional practice. However, some media outlets may

Exhibit 3.4—INTERNATIONAL JOURNALISM ORGANIZATIONS. This chart includes examples of international organizations for journalists and news organizations.

Associations/Website	Headquarters	Countries/Members	Descriptions (from the organizations' websites)
International Center for Journalists (www.icfj.org)	U.S.	More than 80,000 professional and citizen journalists and media managers from 180 countries over the past 30 years	"The International Center for Journalists advances quality journalism worldwide. Our hands-on programs combine the best professional practices with new technologies. We believe that responsible journalism empowers citizens and holds governments accountable."
International Federation of Journalists (www.ifj.org)	Belgium	Around 600,000 members in more than 100 countries	"The IFJ promotes international action to defend press freedom and social justice through strong, free and independent trade unions of journalists."
International Press Institute (www.freemedia.at)	Austria	Global network of editors, media executives and journalists; members in more than 120 countries	". . .dedicated to the furtherance and safeguarding of press freedom, the protection of freedom of opinion and expression, the promotion of the free flow of news and information, and the improvement of the practices of journalism."
Reporters without Borders (http://en.rsf.org)	France	Activities carried out on five continents through its network of over 150 correspondents	"Reporters Without Borders is one of the world's leading independent organisations dedicated to promoting and defending freedom of information. . .Reporters Without Borders strives daily to maintain a free press in every corner of the globe."
World Press Freedom Committee (www.wpfc.org)	U.S.	44 affiliates of national and international news media organizations on six continents	"The World Press Freedom Committee has provided leadership for more than 30 years in the fight against licensing of journalists, mandatory codes of conduct, mandatory tasks for journalists and other news controls."

give their high-spending advertisers greater consideration for editorial content, and advertisers may receive a courtesy call before a negative story appears. Public relations practitioners may encounter a media outlet, usually a smaller, independent one with limited resources, that will request an advertisement in exchange for editorial coverage.

- **Identification** in the case of transparency is the responsibility of the media outlet. For example, editors who have accepted a hosted press trip or a product sample may identify the sponsor in the story, thereby being transparent with their readers, listeners, or viewers. Public relations practitioners creating video news releases should clearly identify the source of the footage. Advertorials—defined as paid advertisements that look like editorial—are handled by the media outlet's advertising departments in which the advertiser has control over the content and visuals in exchange for a fee. Unless the advertising staff or agency manages advertorials, public relations professionals would be involved in placing and writing advertorials. Paid placements, such as advertorials, are covered further in Chapter 15.

- **Solicitation** for payment by either a journalist or a public relations professional should not be in exchange for editorial content. In some cases, travel may be covered to attend a press conference, an event, or a press trip. In Ghana, for example, public relations practitioners may pay transportation expenses for journalists, who are underpaid and would be unable to attend without help (Curtin & Gaither, 2007). The reality is that some lifestyle television programs on such topics as home décor, gardening, travel, and food may request payment for production and travel costs. Whether overseen by public relations or advertising executives, product placements in cinema and non-news television programs require payment based on the extent of coverage—if the star mentions the product, the amount of airtime, and other factors. The "granddaddy" of product placement is Reese's Pieces in Steven Spielberg's *E.T. The Extra-Terrestrial*, in which the peanut butter candy plays a role in the script.

- As a common practice, public relations professionals also may provide **sampling of products** to help journalists better understand products or services. Check the media outlet's code of ethics, if it is publicly available; some outlets would be unable to receive any product samples or accept any subsidies. Sharing samples with journalists is no guarantee for editorial exposure, even if an outlet may be able to accept samples. Food and wine samples are not expected to be returned. Public relations staff should receive approval in advance before providing journalists with more expensive and non-perishable items. Guidelines on returning products should be clear. It is not an uncommon practice for public relations practitioners to arrange face-to-face product or service demonstrations on an individual or small group basis with journalists. Chapter 12 also covers how to write materials for hosting press visits on a partially subsided or complimentary basis for journalists to gain firsthand experiences.

- **Policy statements and ethical guidelines** are available on many websites of media outlets that outline terms of interest to public relations practitioners, such as the outlet's ability to accept product samples, tickets, meals, and travel arrangements. The "gray" area can be on what terms apply to freelancers of media outlets. For example, freelance travel writers may be able to accept subsidized trips to cover the costs of airfare and hotels, particularly if the media outlets will not cover travel expenses.

Exhibit 3.5—INTERNATIONAL PUBLIC RELATIONS ASSOCIATION CHARTER ON MEDIA TRANSPARENCY. Source: Reprinted with permission by the International Public Relations Association. © International Public Relations Association.

IPRA members observe three codes—the IPRA code of professional conduct, the international code of ethics, and the charter on environmental communications. IPRA members expect editorial providers to observe the following:

Editorial. Editorial appears as a result of the editorial judgement of the journalists involved, and not as a result of any payment in cash or in kind, or barter by a third party.

Identification. Editorial which appears as a result of a payment in cash or in kind, or barter by a third party will be clearly identified as advertising or a paid promotion.

Solicitation. There should be no suggestion by any journalist or members of staff of an editorial provider, that editorial can be obtained in any way other than through editorial merit.

Sampling. Third parties may provide samples or loans of products or services to journalists where it is necessary for such journalists to test, use, taste or sample the product or service in order to articulate an objective opinion about the product or service. The length of time required for sampling should be agreed in advance and all loaned products or services should be returned after sampling.

Policy statement. Editorial providers should prepare a policy statement regarding the receipt of gifts or discounted products and services from third parties by their journalists and other staff. Journalists and other staff should be required to read and sign acceptance of the policy. The policy should be available for public inspection.

3.6 Learning Objectives and Key Terms

By studying Chapter 3, you should be able to:

- Examine the evolving technological changes and the opportunities and challenges they present to the public relations field worldwide.
- Describe how portable, participatory, and personalized technology has impacted the way people consume news.
- Pinpoint opportunities and challenges facing public relations practitioners today.
- Define media relations in public relations.
- Name a few trends affecting traditional media worldwide.
- Identify ethical issues impacting the public relations business and standards initiated by global public relations trade groups.
- Understand what legal considerations would apply to the public relations industry and specifically to public relations writing.
- Discuss issues facing the global media in terms of ethics and relationships with public relations practitioners.

This chapter covers the following key terms:

Convergence (p. 57)	Consumer empowerment (p. 57)
Citizen activism (p. 57)	Press (p. 59)
Media (p. 59)	Media relations (p. 59)
Business ethics (p. 64)	Strategic ethics (p. 64)
Intellectual property (p. 65)	Copyright (p. 68)
Public domain (p. 68)	Fair use/fair dealing (p. 68)
Trademarks (p. 69)	Service marks (p. 69)
Geographic indications (p. 69)	Defamation (p. 69)
Right of publicity (p. 70)	Commercial regulations (p. 70)
Astroturfing (p. 71)	Security and exchange regulations (p. 71)
Employment agreements (p. 71)	Independent service contracts (p. 72)
Client contracts (p. 72)	Charter on Media Transparency (p. 73)

Note

1　Although movable type was invented earlier in China in the 11th century and later in other parts of Asia, the Gutenberg Press is considered the first applied for mass printing production.

References

Allen, K. (2013, January 25). Lawsuits aggravate Subway's "footlong" PR crisis. *Ragan's PR Daily*. Retrieved from http://www.prdaily.com.

Berger, B. (2012, October). Key themes and findings: The cross-cultural study of leadership in public relations and communication management. *The Plank Center for Leadership in Public Relations*. Retrieved from http://plankcenter.ua.edu/wp-content/uploads/2012/10/Summary-of-Themes-and-Findings-Leader-Survey.pdf.

Chen, B. X. (2013, October 24). Samsung Electronics fined for fake online comments. *New York Times*. Retrieved from http://bits.blogs.nytimes.com/2013/10/24/samsung-electronics-fined-for-fake-online-comments/?_php=true&_type=blogs&_r=0.

Curran, J., Iyengar, S., Lund, A. B., & Salovaara-Moring, I. (2009). Media system, public knowledge and democracy: A comparative study. *European Journal of Communication, 24*(1), 5–26. doi: 10.1177/0267323108098943.

Curtin, P. A., & Gaither, T. K. (2007). *International public relations: Negotiating culture, identity, and power*. Thousand Oaks, CA: Sage Publications.

Dean, D., DiGrande, S., Field, D., Lundmark, A., O'Day, J., Pineda, J., & Zwillenberg, P. (2012, March 19). The Internet economy in the G-20: The $4.2 trillion growth opportunity. *BCG Perspectives*. Retrieved from https://www.bcgperspectives.com/content/articles/media_entertainment_strategic_planning_4_2_trillion_opportunity_internet_economy_g20/.

Devereux, M. M., & Peirson-Smith, A. (2009). *Public relations in Asia Pacific: Communicating effectively across cultures*. Singapore: John Wiley & Sons.

eMarketer. (2014, January 16). *Smartphone users worldwide will total 1.75 billion in 2014*. Retrieved from http://www.emarketer.com/Article/Smartphone-Users-Worldwide-Will-Total-175-Billion-2014/1010536.

Florida, R. (2005, October). The world in numbers: The world is spiky. *The Atlantic Monthly*. Retrieved from http://www.theatlantic.com.

Glasser, C., Jr. (Ed.). (2013). *International libel & privacy handbook: A global reference for journalists, publishers, webmasters, and lawyers* (3rd ed.). New York, NY: Bloomberg Press.

Graddol, D. (2006). English next: Why global English may mean the end of "English as a foreign language." *British Council*. Retrieved from http://www.britishcouncil.org/learning-research-english-next.pdf.

Green, S. (2010, September 1). PR firm Kirvin Doak sued by Righthaven over Celine Dion story it promoted. *Vegas Inc*. Retrieved from http://www.vegasinc.com.

Hafez, K. (2002). Journalism ethics revisited: A comparison of ethics codes in Europe, North Africa, the Middle East, and Muslim Asia. *Political Communication, 19*(2), 225–250. doi: 10.1080/10584600252907461.

Index on Censorship. (2014). *About index*. Retrieved from http://www.indexoncensorship.org/about-index-on-censorship/.

International Public Relations Association. (2015). *Campaign for media transparency*. Retrieved from http://www.ipra.org/secciones.php?sec=2&subsec=5.

International Trademark Association. (2012). *Trademark basics: A guide for business*. Retrieved from http://www.inta.org/Media/Documents/2012_TMBasicsBusiness.pdf.

Internet Live Stats. (2014). *Internet users*. Retrieved from http://www.internetlivestats.com/internet-users/.

Jenkins, H. (2006). *Convergence culture: Where old and new media collide*. New York, NY: New York University Press.

Kreisler, H. (2005, April 5). Lakhdar Brahimi interview: Conversations with history. *Institute of International Studies, University of California, Berkeley*. Retrieved from http://globetrotter.berkeley.edu/people5/Brahimi/brahimi-con6.html.

Kruckeberg, D. (2000, Fall). The public relations practitioner's role in practicing strategic ethics. *Public Relations Quarterly*, *45*(3), 35–39.

Lombardi, C. (2006, July 6). Google joins Xerox as a verb. *CNET.com*. Retrieved from http://news.cnet.com.

McLuhan, M. (1962). *The Gutenberg galaxy: The making of typographic man*. Toronto: University of Toronto Press.

Media. (2014). In *Oxford Dictionaries online*. Retrieved from http://www.oxforddictionaries.com/definition/english/media.

Morozov, E. (2011). *The net delusion: The dark side of internet freedom*. New York, NY: PublicAffairs.

Oren, T. & Shahaf, S. (2012). Introduction: television formats—a global framework for TV studies. In T. Oren & S. Shahaf (Eds.), *Global television formats: Understanding television across borders* (pp. 1–20). New York, NY: Routledge.

Oriella PR Network Global Digital Journalism Study. (2013). *The new normal for news: Have global media changed forever?* Retrieved from http://www.oriellaprnetwork.com/sites/default/files/research/Brands2Life_ODJS_v4.pdf.

Parkinson, M. G., & Parkinson, L. M. (2008). *Public relations law: A supplemental text*. New York, NY: Routledge.

Press. (2014a). In *Merriam-Webster's online dictionary*. Retrieved from http://www.merriam-webster.com/dictionary/press.

Press. (2014b). In *Oxford Dictionaries online*. Retrieved from http://www.oxforddictionaries. com/definition/english/press.

Purcell, K., Rainie, L., Mitchell, A., Rosenstiel, T., & Olmstead, K. (2010, March 1). Understanding the participatory news consumer. *Pew Research Center*. Retrieved from http://www.pewinternet.org/2010/03/01/understanding-the-participatory-news-consumer/.

Skinner, C., Mersham, G., & Valin, J. (2003). Global protocol on ethics in public relations. *Journal of Communication Management, 8*(1), 13–28. doi: 10.1108/13632540410807510.

Starke-Meyerring, D. (2005). Meeting the challenges of globalization: A framework for global literacies in professional communication programs. *Journal of Business and Technical Communication, 19*(4), 468–499. doi: 10.1177/1050651905278033.

United Nations. (2014). *The universal declaration of human rights*. Retrieved from http:// www.un.org/en/documents/udhr/index.shtml.

U.S. Securities and Exchange Commission. (2013). *Insider trading*. Retrieved from http:// www.sec.gov/answers/insider.htm.

Waite, J. (2001). *The unsung heroes, a history of print* [Teaching notes]. Retrieved from http://www.digitalmedia.tech.uh.edu/learn/course-materials/3350/materials/religion_and_ print.html.

Wallace, P. (1999). *The psychology of the internet*. Cambridge: Cambridge University Press.

Wartella, E. A., & Jennings, N. (2000). Children and computers: New technology—old concerns. *Children and Computer Technology*, *10*(2), 31–43. Retrieved from http://future ofchildren.org/publications/journals/article/index.xml?journalid=45&articleid=201.

World Association of Newspapers and News Publishers. (2014). *World press trends: Print and digital together increasing newspaper audiences*. Retrieved from http://www. wan-ifra.org/press-releases/2014/06/09/world-press-trends-print-and-digital-together- increasing-newspaper-audienc.

World Economic Forum. (2013, October). *Intellectual property rights in the global creative economy*. Retrieved from http://www3.weforum.org/docs/GAC/2013/WEF_GAC_Intel lectualPropertyRights_GlobalCreativeEconomy_Report_2013.pdf.

World Intellectual Property Organization. (2014a). *Inside WIPO: What is WIPO?* Retrieved from http://www.wipo.int/about-wipo/en/.

World Intellectual Property Organization. (2014b). *Summary of the Berne Convention for the Protection of Literary and Artistic Works (1886)*. Retrieved from http://www.wipo.int/ treaties/en/ip/berne/summary_berne.html.

Wu, M. (2011). Comparing media relations in Japan, South Korea, Taiwan, and the United States: A metaresearch analysis. *China Media Research, 7*(1), 5–15.

Part Two

DEVELOPING INTERCULTURAL COMMUNICATION SKILLS AND SENSITIVITIES

Part Two contains three chapters focusing on intercultural communication, nonverbal interpretations, and storytelling approaches that are relevant to contemporary public relations writers communicating with diverse audiences locally or worldwide.

Chapter 4 Appreciating Cultural Similarities and Accepting Differences

- Focuses on the importance of understanding how to navigate in a global marketplace in business, and provides an overview of definitions of culture, as well as potential barriers to successful intercultural communication.
- Covers academic theories from Hall, Hofstede, Trompenaars, and Hampden-Turner that provide useful insight for real-world applications for public relations strategists and writers.
- Examines delivery of writing style based on cultural preferences, such as formal/informal, direct/indirect, and reserved/expressive.

Chapter 5 Decoding Nonverbal Communication and Imagery Worldwide

- Reviews different cultural interpretations of body language and gestures, as well as spatial relationships among people.
- Examines positive and negative meanings of colors, and interpretations of symbolism related to religion, national emblems, local heroes and foes, and flowers and animals.

- Covers real-world examples of cross-cultural mishaps, illustrating how public relations writers need to carefully select visual imagery for use in any type of print or digital platform.

Chapter 6 Mastering the Fine Art of Storytelling in International Public Relations

- Traces the appeals of storytelling from the past to the present and discusses how public relations practitioners serve as contemporary storytellers, who have an increasing number of new platforms for expression.
- Covers different approaches in storytelling to connect with diverse audiences on a global or glocal basis.
- Explains how to tell stories about real people or animals; how to show people new possibilities and how to make the unfamiliar familiar; how to develop stories that inspire and excite the senses; how to seek people's participation; and how to tell stories in sync with the seasons, holidays, life passages, or other occasions.

4 Appreciating Cultural Similarities and Accepting Differences

The new global market opportunities and the need to communicate differently should be seen as a challenge rather than an obstacle. In the emerging global economic and market convergence, the corporate communicator has no option but to confront the new realities of doing business optimistically. It will demand hard work, the eagerness to know others, and the ability to see others the way they see themselves and not the way others want them to be.

—Augustine Ihator, communications professor

4.1 Introduction to Culture

This quote by Augustine Ihator (1999, p. 26), a professor of communications at Jacksonville State University in Alabama, illustrates the necessity of becoming a global communicator in today's world. A well-used passport from studying abroad or traveling for pleasure may give people greater insight about cultural differences. However, conducting business abroad requires an even greater level of sophistication of cultural values, ideologies, and idiosyncrasies. Understanding the importance of navigating in a global marketplace in business is essential for international public relations professionals. Respecting intercultural differences is vital to effective public relations writing, whether you are writing for local, regional, or international audiences. Intercultural business communication requires gaining knowledge—and, preferably, firsthand experience in that community, country, or countries—of the multicultural differences, such as levels of formality, body language, perception of time, appropriate discussion topics, acceptance of gifts, relationship dynamics, and language style orally and in writing. Look at the cartoon (Figure 4.1) depicting people meeting at the international arrivals terminal at an airport as an example of a potentially confusing transcultural scenario.

No one-size-fits-all solution exists. Communication is with individuals, who are influenced by their background, their experience with other cultures, the style of the organization they work for, and other factors. Your client, for example, could have been born in Germany to Chinese parents, college educated in France and the U.S., and worked in five different countries—easily fitting the description of a multicultural or global cosmopolitan. Conversely, your clients could have never traveled beyond their country's borders and live within a closely knit homogenous community in an urban or suburban area.

One may have a **self-reference criterion**, an unconscious reference with "the tendency to view other cultures through the lens of one's own culture" (Cavusgil, Knight, & Riesenberger,

Figure 4.1—CARTOON BY GLOBAL INTEGRATION DEPICTS SOME OF THE QUESTIONS THAT CAN ARISE DURING INTERNATIONAL TRAVELS. Source: Reprinted with permission by www.global-integration.com.

2008, p. 149). Be wary of stereotypes that can form biases and prejudices—they can result in ethnocentric behavior, in which people may regard their own culture as superior. Negative perceptions are counterproductive to communicating and maintaining meaningful relationships. **Deductive stereotypes** occur when a broad cultural generalization is applied to all people within a culture; **inductive stereotypes** develop when we make assumptions about a culture based on only one experience or a few observations.

Are all stereotypes bad? Nancy Adler and Allison Gundersen, authors of *International Dimensions of Organizational Behavior*, argue that **effective stereotyping** can be helpful in certain situations to provide a context on "descriptive rather than evaluative" (2008, p. 77) attributes of shared characteristics of groups. For example, you can read travel guides about a specific country and acquire an overview of a country's cultural traditions. This knowledge can serve as a foundation that can be modified based on firsthand experiences. Milton Bennett (1998), an American scholar on intercultural communication, explains that cultural generalizations also help researchers develop theories and establish shared patterns in intercultural communication.

Academic theories also look at ethnocentricity relevant to public relations. Patricia A. Curtin and T. Kenn Gaither (2007), who are both academics in the U.S., described three different orientations:

- The **ethnocentric theory** in international public relations maintains the belief that "public relations is no different in other countries than in its country of origin" (p. 113).
- The **polycentric model** (also called culturally relative perspective) is the complete opposite, believing that public relations practices should be different in every country (p. 114).
- The more realistic **hybrid approach** blends the two contrasting theories, "suggesting there are some generic public relations principles appropriate to all cultures and societies" (p. 114; Verčič, Grunig, & Grunig, 1996). Based on my experiences as a former public relations practitioner, I have found that the hybrid approach is the most commonly applied approach in managing and implementing global public relations campaigns.

4.2 Culture and Communication

Defining culture is fraught with complexities. The term "culture" has more than 110 accepted definitions and another 400 terms related to culture in anthropology (Sriramesh, 2009). The late American anthropologist Clifford Geertz (1973) defined culture in relation to social structure of interactive behavior: "Culture is the fabric of meaning in terms of which human beings interpret their experience and guide their action; social structure is the form that action takes, the actually existing network of social relations" (p. 145).

Culture can be looked at broadly from two views: objective and subjective. Milton Bennett (1998), an intercultural communication specialist, described **objective culture** as culture with a "capital C," such as the arts, music, and literature of a country, which reflect "behavior that has become routinized into a particular form" (p. 2). Harry Triandis (2002), a Greek-born emeritus professor of psychology at the University of Illinois at Urbana-Champaign, calls this **material culture**, describing how we dress, what we eat, what type of housing we live in, the tools and machines we use, and other explicit and tangible aspects.

Bennett raises a valid point: "Understanding objective culture may create knowledge, but it doesn't necessarily generate competence" (1998, p. 2). Although insight on objective culture can provide useful background information about a country and its people, the real value of intercultural competence requires gaining knowledge of culture with a "small c," the **subjective culture** of the psychological side and levels of abstraction. Bennett defines subjective culture as "learned and shared patterns of beliefs, behaviors, and values of groups of interacting people" (1998, p. 2). He recommends understanding your own culture and others by examining assumptions and values about ethnicity, religion, gender, lifestyle, individualism, socioeconomic class, and professional status.

Triandis (2002) suggests understanding patterns of shared culture and how they relate to a language (such as distinctive regional dialects), historical time periods (generational differences), and geographic regions (having a shared language, for example, does not necessarily mean shared cultures). Countries may share commonalities and be home to diverse subcultures of people based on many factors—gender, age, religion, education, income, professions, and ethnic background, among others. The terminology **subculture** in no way means inferiority; instead, it signifies "a level of analysis below that of broad cultures" (Guirdham, 2005, p. 66).

Anthropologists have used a visual metaphor to better understand the levels of culture: an iceberg (see Figure 4.2). The top part visible above the surface signifies high culture, the objective, easily observable culture of the fine arts, theater, and literature. Right below the top layer, but still visible above the water, the middle part is the apparent cultural makeup, such as the folk culture, etiquette, humor, diet, dress, and rites of passage. In the layer below the surface lies the deep culture, which contains the more complex cultural elements, such as value judgments, family and work relationships, gender roles, interpretations of beauty, nonverbal communication, and other less visible characteristics (Cavusgil et al., 2008). Public relations practitioners need to see both the visible and less visible parts of the iceberg.

No culture should be considered right or wrong or superior or inferior to another culture, meaning that different cultures have different values and standards. Cultural values are acquired from society and learned from others, and they are "not about individual behavior" (Cavusgil et al., 2008, p. 129), but about societies with shared cultures, in which some individuals may exhibit nonconformist behavior that would not define the cultural values of a specific group of people or residents of an entire country.

Figure 4.2—ICEBERG METAPHOR ILLUSTRATES DIMENSIONS OF CULTURE.
Source: © PointaDesign/Shutterstock.com.

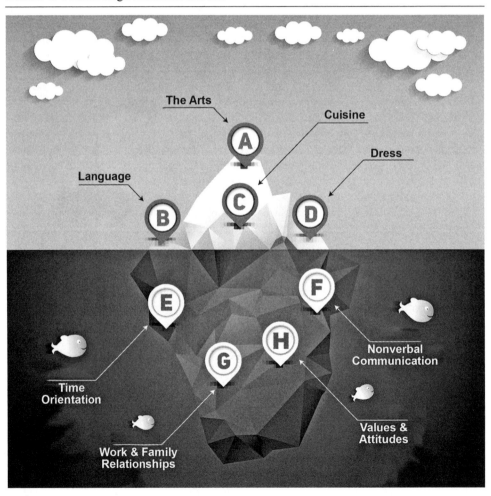

If you have worked as an intern or held full- or part-time jobs, you may have observed how the company itself has a culture of its own. In the workforce, employees are influenced and socialized by three distinctive cultures (Terpstra & David, 1991; Cavusgil et al., 2008):

- The **national culture** of the country would be prevalent where the headquarters or the individual offices are located.
- The **professional culture** is based on the values of the industry or industries which one works in, such as the field of public relations and the different types of industry sectors represented by the organization or the public relations agency.
- The **corporate culture** (also referred to as organizational or business culture) refers to the management style, office operations, ethics and values, as well as behavioral patterns of the specific company, government office, or nongovernmental organization.

Do you think a major multinational corporation would give a few employees the opportunity for an immersive cultural experience by living for a year in another country of their choice, *without* having to work, while getting paid their full-time salary? This experience could be a reality for selected employees at Samsung Electronics. The South Korean company launched its regional specialist program in 1990. In a *Businessweek* article, the president of Samsung's Human Resources Center explained the rationale of the program that has sent more than 5,000 employees to more than 80 countries between 1990 and 2013: "They are given three missions: Learn the local language, learn the local culture, and become an expert in their specialty" (Grobart, 2013, para. 3).

Weber Shandwick, a global public relations agency, created a 10x10 interoffice exchange program that gives 10 employees every year the opportunity to spend a week with their colleagues in another office in a different country. The agency's CEO Andy Polansky explained his company's global mindset in an interview with *The Public Relations Strategist* (Jacobs, 2014):

> The maturation of the PR business on a global basis will continue. Those that have the global mindset will be rewarded. Multinational companies looking for growth aren't looking to the United States, but many PR companies are still focusing on the United States. What we do for our senior leadership is the Weber Shandwick 10x10 program, where we send 10 midlevel managers and high-potential employees around the world, for their personal development and to bring more of a global viewpoint back to their offices. (para. 22)

Most people, however, will not have the opportunity to enjoy such an all-expenses-paid immersive experience. Instead, they will need to take advantage of every opportunity to learn as much as possible about different cultures when they are traveling on business or meeting face-to-face with international clients or business associates in their home country. Being sensitive to other cultures requires accepting and appreciating both the differences and similarities—and making the effort to communicate in ways that will resonate with individuals.

Curtin and Gaither (2007) refer to public relations practitioners as "cultural intermediaries," who they define as "mediators between producers and consumers who actively create meanings by establishing an identification between products or issues and publics" (p. 210). Developing intercultural skills will make you a more effective, responsible, and successful public relations practitioner. Learning to write clearly and succinctly, with multicultural sensitivities, is a must to connect with global and glocal audiences in English.

4.3 Intercultural Dimensions Relevant to Public Relations Strategists and Writers

This section examines perspectives on intercultural communication, which I have based on theories developed by scholars Edward T. Hall, Geert Hofstede, Fons Trompenaars, and Charles Hampden-Turner, who have made significant contributions in their respective fields of anthropology, psychology, and cross-cultural communication. Exhibit 4.1 provides brief biographical information on the four scholars. Their theories can provide insight on cultural dimensions relevant to business communication, as well as to public relations. However, their theories serve as a platform, not as a definitive answer to communicating with all types of people within a specific culture. Although Hofstede's cultural dimensions research is one of the most widely cited sources on intercultural business, some scholars have found limitations. Iris Varner, professor emeritus from Illinois State University, explained during a panel discussion on global business communication: "Yet Hofstede makes no distinction between a largely shared culture in a nationality (say, Japan or Poland) and a nationality whose people are culturally distinct and even adversarial (say, Belgium, Canada or South Africa)" (Victor, 2012, p. 14).

Each of the following four segments begins with an overview of the theories and then provides practical applications on how these insights can improve communication skills in negotiating with diverse staff and clients and writing clearly and appropriately with different audiences:

- Time orientation covers a continuum of perspectives from time urgency to time flexibility.
- Level of diplomacy and expression examines a variety of communication styles, such as formality and restraint to frankness and expressiveness.
- Sense of power, self, and control includes a range of perspectives from egalitarian and individualistic values to hierarchical and collective dimensions.
- Adherence to rules and traditions encompasses a continuum from flexible to rigid structures, with varying levels of acceptance of uncertainty.

4.3.1 Time Orientation

Understanding how people perceive time is important for conducting business and communicating in writing or in person. Time sensitivity can be particularly pertinent in public relations. The field requires deadlines with pre-planned activities fitted into timetables: issuing news in multiple formats, responding to media inquiries based on a reporter's deadline, planning events and speaking engagements, posting updates and responding to social media, and implementing other components of plans. Scholars have examined intercultural differences on time from a number of perspectives, some of which overlap.

Long-Term or Short-Term Orientation

Hofstede (2011) developed **long-term versus short-term orientation dimensions** when he examined 10 differences in how societies view past, present, and future events and traditions. Long-term orientation societies value thrift, perseverance, and adaptability based on circumstances, while delaying gratification for the future. Short-term orientation societies focus on the present, thereby seeking more immediate gratification while valuing personal stability,

Exhibit 4.1—INTERCULTURAL SCHOLARS: HALL, HOFSTEDE, TROMPENAARS, AND HAMPDEN-TURNER

We should never denigrate any other culture but rather help people to understand the relationship between their own culture and the dominant culture. When you understand another culture or language, it does not mean that you have to lose your own culture.

—Edward T. Hall (Sorrells, 1998, para. 70)

U.S. anthropologist Edward T. Hall (1914–2009) is dubbed the "father of intercultural communication" for his contributions to the field of nonverbal intercultural communication. Throughout his varied career, Hall conducted fieldwork living on U.S. reservations and studying the Navajos and Hopis. He also served in the U.S. Army during World War II in Europe and in the Philippines, trained U.S. State Department personnel for overseas assignments, and taught anthropology at a few universities. These experiences led to practical and academic studies in which Hall developed concepts on polychronic and monochronic time, proxemics (spatial relationships), and high- and low-context cultures.

Culture is the collective programming of the mind that distinguishes the members of one group or category of people from others.

—Geert Hofstede (2011, p. 3)

Dutch social psychologist Geert Hofstede (1928–) is considered "the man who put corporate culture on the map" (Hindle, 2008, p. 251) for his research on intercultural communication. Hofstede's career has spanned both corporate management and academia. As the founder and manager of the Personnel Research Department for IBM in Europe from 1965 to 1971, he conducted one of the most extensive surveys on cultural values in the workplace by analyzing a database of IBM employees in more than 70 countries. This undertaking eventually led to a five-year research project from 1973 to 1978 and later to the first edition of *Culture's Consequences* in 1980. Hofstede initially identified four dimensions of national cultures (power distance, uncertainty avoidance, individualism versus collectivism, and masculinity versus femininity), adding a fifth dimension, long-term versus short-term orientation, in 1991, and a sixth dimension, indulgence versus restraint, in 2010.

A fish discovers its need for water only when it is no longer in it. Our own culture is like water to a fish. It sustains us. We live and breathe through it. What one culture may regard as essential—a certain level of material wealth, for example—may not be so vital to other cultures.

—Fons Trompenaars with Charles Hampden-Turner (1998, p. 20)

Alfons "Fons" Trompenaars (1952–), a Dutch organizational theorist, brings a corporate perspective to intercultural communication, having served in management positions for Shell Oil Company in nine countries and as a consultant for Fortune 500 countries. He is also the author of books on culture and management. *The Harvard Business Review* has identified Trompenaars as one of the 50 most influential management gurus. In collaboration with Charles Hampden-Turner (1934–), a British management consultant and research associate, Trompenaars developed seven cultural dichotomies: universalism (consistent rules for all) versus particularism (flexibility based on situation); individualism (self oriented) versus communitarianism (community oriented); affective (expressive) versus neutral (restrained);

specific (direct, transparent) versus diffuse (indirect, evasive); achievement (respect expertise and competence) versus ascription (respect status and influence); sequential (one activity at a time, measureable time) versus synchronic (multiple activities, diffuse time); and internal (inner directed, control) versus external control (harmony, flexible).

Sources

Hindle, T. (2008). *The Economist guide to management ideas and gurus.* London: Profile Books/The Economist Newspaper.

Hofstede, G. (2011). Dimensionalizing cultures: The Hofstede model in context. *Online Readings in Psychology and Culture, 2*(1). doi: 10.9707/2307-0919.1014.

Sorrells, K. (1998). Gifts of wisdom: An interview with Dr. Edward T. Hall. *The Edge: The E-Journal of Intercultural Relations, 1*(3). Retrieved from http://people.umass.edu/~leda/comm494r/The%20Edge%20Interview%20Hall.htm.

Trompenaars, F., & Hampden-Turner, C. (1998). *Riding the waves of culture: Understanding diversity in global business* (2nd ed.). New York, NY: McGraw-Hill.

---

spending, and consumption. Countries in East Asia and Eastern and Central Europe ranked high in long-term orientation; medium in South Asia and South- and North-European countries; and short-term orientation in the U.S. and Australia, along with Latin American, African, and Muslim countries.

Past-present-future orientation (Trompenaars & Hampden-Turner, 2012) can be illustrated by following the "circles test" developed by psychologist Thomas Cottle (1967). Please take a moment and complete Exercise 4.1 to determine your perspective on time.

After you have completed the exercise, you can compare your observations to Cottle's intercultural research in which he asked participants from different countries to reflect on their relationships with the past, present, and future. He then asked them to visualize these timeframes in circles and draw three circles in any configuration that best reflected their feelings, which resulted in the following four broad configurations by countries:

- Although the sizes of the circles varied indicating a different emphasis on time periods, the circles did not overlap, thereby indicating a distinct separation between the past, present, and future (China, Hong Kong, Mexico, Russia, and Venezuela).
- Time integration showed all three time periods fully overlapping (Japan and Malaysia).

Exercise 4.1

Self-Evaluation: Circles Test on Perception of Time: Past, Present, and Future

Take out a blank sheet of paper and think about your perception of time by drawing three circles that represent the past, the present, and the future. Arrange the circles in any way—your circles can be different sizes, and they may be separate, touch one another, or overlap. Label each circle to indicate your three perspectives on time.

Please see Appendix D for comments.

- Partial overlapping of circles, with the circle sizes varying considerably, demonstrated a link between different times, with some cultures showing more balance between time periods and others more focused on the future (Belgium, Canada, France, Germany, Korea, Sweden, the U.K., and the U.S.).
- All same-sized circles touched without overlapping showing a sequential flow of time that gave each time period nearly equal value (India and Nigeria).

Time Urgency or Flexibility

Monochronic versus polychronic (Hall, 1976) and **sequential versus synchronic cultures** (Trompenaars & Hampden-Turner, 2012) explain the cultural differences in perceiving and valuing time. Monochronic time adherents value deadlines and punctuality, and they tend to accomplish tasks sequentially in a logical order, following strict schedules and to-do lists. The U.S. and many Western cultures fall into this category. Although the term multitasking is widely used in the U.S. workforce, particularly in public relations as an ability to work on different projects or clients simultaneously, polychronic cultures do not regard multitasking "as a way to be more productive" (Kent & Taylor, 2011, p. 65). Polychronic cultures (also referred to as synchronic) value relationships more than schedules and do not adhere to strict timetables and may not start or end meetings as scheduled. Synchronically oriented people are comfortable handing multiple tasks simultaneously and shifting priorities, primarily based on the relationships with the people involved.

Expressing clarity on deadlines can create less stress for all parties. When you ask someone to respond "as soon as possible" or "at your convenience," how does the receiver interpret that request? This can be interpreted many ways. Will the receiver react immediately, the same day, the next day, next week, next month, whenever, or never? (See Figure 4.3 of Drew Dernavich's cartoon from the *New Yorker* on "The Graveyard of Past Deadlines.")

Figure 4.3—CARTOON ILLUSTRATES THE VARIOUS MEANINGS OF DEADLINES.
Source: © Drew Dernavich, The New Yorker Collection/The Cartoon Bank.

Be specific about when something is due and explain why. If you know that the receiver regards time with greater flexibility, you will have to give ample advance notice along with a specific deadline, and you will need to be prepared to follow up to obtain feedback or approvals. The other option is to call the person directly and discuss the time urgency, particularly in a time-sensitive or crisis situation.

Are schedules strictly adhered to or regarded with flexibility? Does your client or supervisor follow every word in your public relations plan or is your plan collecting dust in a filing cabinet or filed electronically and forgotten? Both extremes present challenges. Monochronic time followers need to be reassured that all activities are conducted in a timely manner based on original plans. They would require detailed explanations if the sequential order or pre-planned activity is changed. They may spend so much time deliberating about a decision that last-minute opportunities may be never be approved in time. Whereas polychronic time adherents may not pay attention to consecutive order and may alter plans considerably, so that the original plan becomes almost unrecognizable.

What would motivate the reader to care and respond to your message? People with a short-term orientation would be more motivated to react by receiving immediate gratification and being receptive to new ideas as long as the benefits are clearly articulated, whereas people with long-term orientation would be more interested in what could happen years from now. Writers preparing public relations plans, in particular, need to be able to communicate the potential short- or long-term benefits to get the plans approved.

When negotiating a new business contract, is it more important to work out the deal directly or solidify a relationship first? Polychronic cultures value building long-term relationships. For example a public relations agency wanting to win a new business contract would need to invest time in traveling and meeting face-to-face with the prospective client and the decision-makers for selecting agency talent. Interactions also would require scheduling purely social events *without* business discussions to nurture and develop a relationship. Whereas a monochronic culture regards time as equaling money, thereby solidifying the deal quickly without investing much time in socializing.

Clarifying Tangible Aspects of Time

Writers communicating with international audiences also need to be clear about the following usage of time to avoid any confusion:

- **Dates**
  What does 1/8/18 mean? Dates are written two ways: month day, year (January 8, 2018) or day month year (8 January 2018). Avoid using numbers when writing dates, such as 1/8/18 or 8/1/18. Depending on the reader, the date could be interpreted as January 8 or August 1.
- **Clock Time**
  Time is read two ways. The **12-hour clock**, which is used in the U.S., Canada, and a few other countries, divides time into two cycles: a.m. (ante meridiem, Latin for before midday) from midnight, 12 a.m., to 11:59 a.m.; and p.m. (post meridiem, Latin for after midday) from noon, 12 p.m., to 11:59 p.m. English speakers following the 12-hour clock say 11 in the morning, instead of 11 a.m., or 11 at night, instead of 11 p.m.; however, in written materials, the a.m. and p.m. are used. The most widely used time worldwide is the **24-hour clock** (except for the U.S. and Canada, where

Exhibit 4.2—12-HOUR AND 24-HOUR CLOCKS.

12-Hour Clock	24-Hour Clock	12-Hour Clock	24-Hour Clock
12 a.m. (Midnight)	00:00 (Midnight start of day); 24:00 (Midnight end of day)	12 p.m. (Noon)	12:00 (Noon)
1 a.m.	01:00	1 p.m.	13:00
2 a.m.	02:00	2 p.m.	14:00
3 a.m.	03:00	3 p.m.	15:00
4 a.m.	04:00	4 p.m.	16:00
5 a.m.	05:00	5 p.m.	17:00
6 a.m.	06:00	6 p.m.	18:00
7 a.m.	07:00	7 p.m.	19:00
8 a.m.	08:00	8 p.m.	20:00
9 a.m.	09:00	9 p.m.	21:00
10 a.m.	10:00	10 p.m.	22:00
11 a.m.	11:00	11 p.m.	23:00

it is also called military time), which runs from midnight beginning of day (00:00) to midnight end of day (24:00), with noon reading 12:00. The 24-hour clock uses zeros before the one-digit number, such as 01:00 (1 a.m. in the 12-hour clock). Exhibit 4.2 outlines time in both the 12- and 24-hour clocks. Writers should use the terms midnight and noon for either time usage to avoid confusion. Stylebooks also contain specific rules in writing and expressing time.

- **Time Zones**

Greenwich Mean Time (GMT) originated in Greenwich, England, to monitor navigation of the world's waterways and was first adopted for land use by the British railroads before becoming the universal standard in 1884 (Time and Date, 2015). You may have heard time being referred to as a specific number of hours ahead or behind GMT. The new time zone standard since 1972 is referred to as Coordinated Universal Time (UTC, not CUT), which is based on the same zero degree longitude as GMT in a world divided into 24 time zones using a 24-hour clock, but with a more accurate atomic clock with leap seconds (Rosenberg, 2014). In other words, midnight in Greenwich is UTC±00:00. Time zones are expressed as the number of hours east (+) or west (−) of GMT or UTC, with the Republic of Kiribati, an island nation in the central Pacific Ocean, being the first place to greet the new day (UTC+14:00), to the westernmost time zone, with the nearly uninhabited U.S. territories of Howland and Baker islands in the southwestern Pacific Ocean being the last to see the new day (UTC-12:00).

Exhibit 4.3—SEASONS IN THE NORTHERN AND SOUTHERN HEMISPHERES.

Season	Northern Hemisphere	Southern Hemisphere
Fall (Autumn)	September to November	March to May
Winter	December to February	June to August
Spring	March to May	September to November
Summer	June to August	December to February

- **Daylight Saving Times**
  Be mindful that not all countries use UTC when referring to multiple time zones within their own countries—and some countries follow daylight saving time. This can create confusion, particularly when setting up conference calls between time zones in the same country or different countries. The U.S., for example, follows nine time zones (such as Eastern Standard Time or EST) and daylight saving times (Eastern Daylight Time or EDT) from 2 a.m. on the second Sunday in March, with clocks set ahead an hour, to 2 a.m. on the first Sunday in November, with clocks set back an hour. However, most of Arizona, Hawaii, and U.S. territories do not follow daylight saving time. Australia has three time zones: Australian Eastern Standard Time (AEST), Australian Central Standard Time (ACST), and Australian Western Standard Time (AWST). Australia also observes daylight saving time, except in Queensland, the Northern Territory, or Western Australia. And in the Southern Hemisphere, daylight saving time is the reverse, with clocks set one hour forward at 2 a.m. on the first Sunday in October and set back one hour on the first Sunday in April.
- **Seasons**
  When is winter in Australia and Canada or summer in Japan or South Africa? The seasons are the complete opposites in the Northern and Southern hemispheres as illustrated in Exhibit 4.3.
- **Business Hours and Days of Operations**
  Not all businesses operate officially from 9 a.m. to 5 p.m. and maintain five-day weeks. Office hours and work days vary considerably. Some countries follow religious observances: Sunday (Christian influenced), Saturday (Jewish), and Friday (Islamic). Offices in parts of Asia, for example, may have six-day workweeks, with half-day office hours on Saturdays.
- **Holidays (Religious, National, and Public) and Major Public Events**
  It is important to become familiar with the major religious, national, and public holidays in which offices may be closed. This knowledge would determine the timing of basic business transactions and the best days to host events or announce news.
- **Peak Vacation Seasons**
  Know when your clients, business associates, and target audiences usually take off time for vacations (which are also called "holidays" in British English). Vacation times would affect timing of campaigns, business correspondence, and meetings, as well as requiring approvals in advance or establishing guidelines for another person temporarily in charge to make decisions. Some cultures take time-off seriously, meaning separating personal and business life, so that business voicemail and email remain unchecked during personal time.

4.3.2 Level of Diplomacy and Expressiveness

Understanding acceptable dimensions of expression and emotion can help communicators determine the appropriate level of formalities, depth of information, and tone of expressions. (See Figure 4.4 of a cartoon by Tom Fishburne, where he uses humor to illustrate the challenges in providing meaningful feedback while reviewing creative work.)

Direct or Indirect

High- and low-context cultures (Hall, 1976) illustrate the differences between how people interpret the meaning of words based on the situation. High-context cultures use indirect, formal language, in which the actual meaning is derived from social relationships and nonverbal cues, whereas low-context cultures focus on facts and logic, applying meaning to the explicit, direct language. Many Western low-context cultures derive meaning from the actual words and prefer candid, expedient language. In high-context cultures, the meaning is implied by the status of the speaker and his or her relationship with the receivers.

As another version of high- or low-context cultures, the theory of **specific versus diffuse cultures** refers to communication extremes that require reconciliation particularly in business

Figure 4.4—CARTOON SHOWS HOW CREATIVE TYPES CAN EXPRESS THEMSELVES DIFFERENTLY. Source: © Tom Fishburne.

(Trompenaars & Hampden-Turner, 2012). Specific-oriented (low context) people use direct, transparent language consistently; diffuse-oriented (high context) people apply more indirect, ambiguous language that varies based on the people and context.

Saving face is an extremely important concept to understand. I believe that no person in any culture wants to be criticized, humiliated, or embarrassed publicly. Western people are accustomed to a direct style that could be interpreted as rude, disrespectful, or confrontational in other cultures. People in many Asian cultures prefer to avoid using the word *no*. Instead, they will make indirect comments and use body language to convey their real intent that people outside these cultures may not comprehend. Learning to decipher nuances of *yes*, *maybe*, and *no* takes keen observation and time. Public relations communicators not only need to be sensitive to saying *no*, but they also must avoid correcting someone's mistake publicly and instead talk to that person privately or ignore the error.

A popular television show illustrates the concept of saving face. China's *Super Girl* talent contest is the country's equivalent to the American television singing competition, *American Idol*. Unlike the U.S. program where judges publicly criticize and eliminate the candidates without apologies, the judges in *Super Girl* spend more time on the losers by showing support and consoling them ("Cult of 'face,'" n.d.).

Warm or Reserved

Affective versus neutral cultures (Trompenaars & Hampden-Turner, 2012) illustrate the level of emotion in how people communicate. People in affective cultures express warmth, enthusiasm, and emotions without constraint. Trompenaars cautions that although people in neutral cultures tend to avoid displaying emotion, they "are not necessarily cold or unfeeling, nor are they emotionally constipated or repressed" (p. 87). These communicative extremes can create challenges in the global workforce: affectively oriented people may find neutrally oriented people detached, cold, and unlikeable, and the latter may find the other group chaotic, irrational, and unprofessional. Writers need to find the right blend of reserve and warmth. Copy with just the facts could be interpreted as uncaring in affective cultures or appropriate in neutral cultures.

4.3.3 Sense of Power and Self

The following theories look at the interplay of power, status, and sense of self as an individual or as part of a group:

Low or High Power Distance

The **power distance dimension** (Hofstede, 2011) examines how societies view equality and inequality. Low-power distance cultures exhibit a more egalitarian approach with less stringent hierarchies, whereas high-power distance cultures accept hierarchy and inequality. Asian, African, Latin, and Eastern European countries received higher Power Distance Index scores than Germanic- and English-speaking countries.

Are you on a first or last name basis? It is important not to make assumptions and to err on the side of formality. Make sure to use correct titles when speaking and writing. In North America, Australia, New Zealand, and parts of Europe, a first-name relationship may be established immediately that transcends job titles and years of experience. Even so, the public relations agency staff should follow the lead of the client. Formalities also apply to writing

---

Exercise 4.2

Self-Evaluation: Writing with Diplomacy and Tact

Assume you are a public relations executive at a public relations agency and you are communicating with your client. Rewrite the sentences below to convey more diplomacy.

1. I'm not available since that meeting doesn't work out for my schedule.
2. I don't have the time to talk now.
3. This idea doesn't make sense at all.
4. There's no way to do the work you want within that budget.
5. That deadline is unrealistic.
6. Your social media presence is awful.
7. The journalist needs an answer now.
8. I don't know the answer.

Please see Appendix D for suggested answers.

---

both basic and complex correspondence. A new account executive at an American public relations agency addressed an email to a new Asian client as *Hi, Ravi*. The email was forwarded to the agency's principal with a complaint. All future correspondence was *Dear Mr. Khan*.

High-power distance people expect diplomatic and formal language in business. How would you re-word the sentences in Exercise 4.2 to reflect diplomacy and tact, as well as to switch the focus to the needs of the receiver of the message, not of the sender?

People who have a high regard for power distance also can be sensitive about the way staff members interact with others internally and with public relations agency staff. The most senior person of a company may expect to receive all correspondence, whether by mail or email, from the most senior counterpart in the agency. In other words, a peer-to-peer dialogue would have to be maintained between staff on both sides of equal rank. This dynamic can result in ghostwritten documents prepared by the person supervising the account on behalf of the agency's CEO, partner, or other senior executive. Preparing an account team chart that outlines every person's key responsibilities can be helpful to demonstrate the role each person will play.

Junior-level staff and young agency executives, even in more senior positions, can face challenges in gaining the respect of high-power distance clients, who may prefer to work directly with older executives. The most senior-ranking person would need to introduce the staff members and showcase their talents to build up the client's confidence level.

The power distance also can be an issue with relationships between public relations staff, whether in-house or agency side, and journalists. A Latin American client was miffed that an agency account executive treated American journalists like peers during a press trip. She felt that the agency representative was having too much fun with the reporters and that the journalists should be lectured to and told what to think. The American executive felt he was behaving appropriately with the U.S. writers and had to write a follow-up letter thanking the client for her feedback while explaining diplomatically how the U.S. media prefer to be treated. The press trip resulted in positive feature stories, so the client stopped complaining about dynamics during future press visits.

I or We

The **individualism versus collectivism dimension** (Hofstede, 2011) contrasts individualistic societies ("I conscious"), in which people focus on looking after themselves and their immediate family while working in a competitive environment, and collectivist cultures ("we conscious") that extend ties and loyalties to extended families or cohesive groups, seeking harmony and loyalty. Western and developed countries scored high in Hofstede's individualism dimension, whereas Eastern countries received low scores, and Japan ranked in the middle. **Individualism and communitarianism dichotomies** (Trompenaars & Hampden-Turner, 2012) illustrate extreme differences, particularly in international management, which can result in dilemmas in how people negotiate with one another and motivate diverse teams. Pronouns should be carefully selected. Individualistic societies can be self-oriented or community-oriented, yet they use the first person "I" frequently and value autonomy, whereas communitarians prefer to use "we" and work collectively.

Mary M. Devereux and Anne Peirson-Smith, a public relations executive and academic respectively based in Asia, developed a new model of hierarchy of needs based on Abraham Maslow's original concept, in which Maslow created a pyramid model starting with the most basic survival needs at the lowest level to the ultimate level of self-actualization. In their **Asia Pacific Communication Universe model**, the self is at the center in an Asian collectivist society:

> This means that the collectivist social self in the Asian context frequently dominates the individualistic private self and is the prime motivator for decision making. In this context, the public relations professional should articulate more collectivist wants and affiliations in public relations messages in order to connect with stakeholders in a more relevant and engaging manner. (2009, p. 19)

Collective societies respond better to messages and incentives that benefit the group or emphasize the shared responsibilities of the community. Collective praise is preferred in a culture that values modesty, harmony, and responsibility to the team. Extolling individual accomplishments would be considered appropriate in individualistic cultures that acknowledge personal gain and solo achievements.

Bragging is generally not a beneficial trait anywhere. Be careful about being too boastful of one's abilities since it could result in poor relationships and lost business opportunities. Here is a cautionary tale of a behind-the-scenes encounter between executives of an American public relations agency, which was one of two finalist agencies for a new business opportunity, and the chauffeur of a multinational European company. The first agency team was picked up by the chauffeur, who also happened to be the CEO's chauffeur—a detail the agency executives did not know. While being driven from the airport to the company's headquarters, the public relations agency team boasted about how the account would be so easy to win and talked about ways to try to get more money beyond the monthly retainer. During the presentation, the first team seemed qualified, yet somewhat arrogant and boastful. These traits were noticed by most of the decision-makers, including those who felt that the agency's written proposal was the best one received. The other competing public relations agency, which had similar capabilities and resources offered by the first agency, conveyed a more caring and humble demeanor. This agency team also behaved more professionally in transit with the chauffeur. After the presentations, the decision-making committee was uncertain about the final selection. However, the chauffeur later shared the in-transit conversations with the CEO and the head of public relations. Who got the account? The moral of the story is to be careful about what you say, wherever you are. The first agency team members assumed the chauffeur was "invisible" while conducting a private discussion, which resulted in losing the new business opportunity.

Achievements or Ascriptions

Achievement versus ascription orientations (Trompenaars & Hampden-Turner, 2012) illustrate the differences between achievement-focused people who value competence and expertise and ascription-focused individuals who respect status and hierarchy. Achievement-oriented cultures admire what someone has recently accomplished; ascription-oriented cultures look at a person's family background and personal connections. Trompenaars uses a clear example on views on education: *what* did you study (achievement-focus) versus *where* did you study (ascription-focus).

Writers communicating with ascription-focus people need to convey status and established relationships with well-known people or businesses. For new business materials, public relations agencies would need to promote their name-brand clients. Whereas achievement-focused prospective clients would care more about recent case studies that show strategy, creativity, and results.

Internal or External

Internal versus external control dichotomies (Trompenaars & Hampden-Turner, 2012) indicate the extremes between internal- and external-oriented cultures in how motivations and values are derived within an environment, whether it is nature or a government or a business. Internal-oriented people focus from within, on the individual, one's own group or organization, expressing control of the environment and discomfort over changes. External-oriented cultures view the environment as more powerful than individuals, exhibiting comfort with natural changes, as well as flexibility and harmony. Trompenaars gave an example of different motivations and relationships with the environment. The chairman of Sony was inspired to invent the Walkman (Sony's portable audio cassette player launched in 1979 that later became an MP3 player) as a way for an individual to listen to music without disturbing other people, thereby remaining in harmony with the environment.

4.3.4 Adherence to Rules and Traditions

Intercultural theories also examined different cultures' tolerance of uncertainty, needs for gratification or restraint, and adherence to rules and regulations.

Avoidance or Acceptance of Uncertainty

Uncertainty avoidance (Hofstede, 2011) examines the comfort level of a society's acceptance of ambiguity and structure. Strong uncertainty cultures impose strict rules and codes of conduct, with limited acceptance of deviances from the determined norm. Weak uncertainty avoidance societies display tolerance of diverse opinions and beliefs, imposing fewer rules and standards. Eastern and Central Europe, Latin America, and Japan, as well as German-speaking countries, received high scores in the Uncertainty Avoidance Index. Scandinavia, English-speaking countries, and China-culture countries scored lower.

Exhibit 4.4—CULTURAL DIMENSIONS AND COMMUNICATION CONSIDERATIONS.

Cultural Dimensions	Communication Considerations	Cultural Dimensions (Opposite Spectrum)	Communication Considerations
Short-term Orientation	Focus on new ideas and innovations Messages: Immediacy, flexibility, creativity, near future, quick results	Long-term Orientation	Focus on tradition and authority Messages: Thrift, perseverance, commitment, far future, long-term investment
Monochronic	Deal focused, schedules and agendas essential Messages: Efficiency, punctuality, accomplishments	Polychronic	Relationship-focused, fluid schedules and agendas Messages: Flexibility, spontaneity
Sequential	To-do lists, clear timetables, focus on accomplishing one task at a time Messages: Guidelines, logic, efficiency, time is money	Synchronic	Multiple tasks not in order, fluid plans and deadlines, relationships more important than time Messages: Flexibility, time is intangible
Low-context culture	Emphasis on words and messages, explicit, details Messages: Constructive criticism, direct, literal, factual, transparency	High-context culture	Nonverbal cues and status of deliverer, interpretive Messages: Noncritical, indirect, implicit, respectful, diplomatic
Specific culture	Separation of business and private lives Messages: Structure, direct	Diffuse culture	Integration of business and personal lives Messages: Fluid, indirect
Affective	Emotional connections, relationships Messages: Expressiveness, warmth, enthusiasm, passion	Neutral	Rational and logical explanations Messages: Restraint, control, realism
Low-power distance	Consensus, teamwork, equal opportunities Messages: Egalitarian, independence, expressiveness, shared debates, resourceful, autonomy	High-power distance	Respectful of rankings, deference to seniority, status, and age Messages: Hierarchical, interdependence, loyalty, obedience, authority

Exhibit 4.4—Continued

Cultural Dimensions	Communication Considerations	Cultural Dimensions (Opposite Spectrum)	Communication Considerations
Individualism	Individual rewards, freedom of expression, quick decisions Messages: Self-satisfaction, self-pride, personal achievement, privacy, individual praise	Collectivism	Shared responsibilities, close ties, group harmony, slow decisions Messages: Community, humility, cooperation, solidarity, cohesiveness, group praise
Achievement orientation	Importance of personal accomplishments and merit Messages: Skills, capabilities, results, action, recent successes, resourcefulness	Ascription orientation	Importance of title, social standing, and personal connections Messages: Prestige, recognition, status symbols, family, connections, hierarchy, privilege
Internal control	Inner directed, control of one's destiny and nature, less faith in luck Messages: Opportunistic, dominance, personal efforts, competitiveness	External control	Outer directed, cannot control nature or destiny Messages: Harmony, peace, patience, acceptance
Low uncertainty avoidance	Fluid plans, receptive to innovation and new opportunities Messages: Adaptable, flexibility, nonconformity, do-it-yourself, exploration, adventure, risk-taking	High uncertainty avoidance	Structured plans, emphasis of previous successes, clear explanations for any changes Messages: Low-risk, assurance, safety, conformity, traditions, security, expertise, familiarity
Indulgence	Freedom and happiness, receptive to feedback and interactivity Messages: Gratification, hedonism, pleasure, optimism, personal control	Restraint	Formality and structure, community focus Messages: Discipline, order, procedures, predictable
Universalism	Rules more important than relationships Messages: Professional, business oriented, impersonal, contractual obligations	Particularism	Relationships more important than rules Messages: Personal, friendships, flexibility, mutual trust

Copy appealing to high uncertainty avoidance cultures would need to convey lower risks and greater predictability. New business would need to showcase similar campaigns that were successful and achieved results. Consumer communications also should focus on success stories and offer product samples or other low commitment opportunities, as well as messages on security, safety, and assurance.

Indulgence or Restraint

The **indulgence versus restraint dimension** (Hofstede, Hofstede, & Minkov, 2010; Hofstede, 2011) is based on research analyzing the level of happiness in a society. Indulgence means seeking happiness by gratifying personal desires, whereas restraint stands for adhering to societal norms and forgoing personal gratifications. According to Hofstede, indulgence prevails in Western Europe and North and South America, as well as in parts of Sub-Saharan Africa; restraint in Eastern Europe and Asia, as well as in Muslim countries; and Mediterranean Europe falls in the middle.

Rules or Flexibility

Universalism and particularism dichotomies developed by Trompenaars and Hampden-Turner (2012) recommend reconciliation between universalism, with strict adherence to equitable yet consistent rules and procedures, and particularism, which encourages flexibility based on the particular situation. Extreme universalism can result in bureaucratic procedures and inflexible contracts. For example, the marketing and public relations departments in a corporate headquarters following universalism may demand that its in-house staff and public relations agencies worldwide follow their rules, without allowing adaptability to connect with the local markets. The other spectrum is flexibility, where rules, procedures, and contracts are fluid based on the situation and the relationship with the people involved. The extreme particularistic approach could result in chaos and inequitable treatment.

Exhibit 4.4 provides a chart of the different intercultural dimensions covered in this chapter, including their distinctive characteristics and potential messages for public relations writers to consider.

4.4 Learning Objectives and Key Terms

After reading Chapter 4, you should be able to:

- Identify potential barriers to effective intercultural communication.
- Discuss three different interpretations of ethnocentricity and how these approaches would impact public relations operations.
- Explain different meanings of culture.
- Understand intercultural dimensions developed by Hall, Hofstede, Trompenaars, and Hampden-Turner that have relevance to public relations strategists and writers.
- Apply cultural theories—time orientation, level of diplomacy and expressiveness, sense of power and self, and adherence to rules and tradition—to communication strategies and written materials in public relations.

This chapter covers the follows key terms:

Self-reference criterion (p. 83)

Deductive stereotypes (p. 84)

Inductive stereotypes (p. 84)

Effective stereotyping (p. 84)

Ethnocentric theories (p. 85)

Objective culture (p. 85)

Subjective culture (p. 85)

Subculture (p. 85)

National culture (p. 87)

Professional culture (p. 87)

Corporate culture (p. 87)

Long- and short-term orientation (p. 88)

Past-present-future orientation (p. 90)

Monochronic vs. polychronic cultures
(p. 91)

Sequential vs. synchronic cultures
(p. 91)

High- and low-context cultures (p. 95)

Specific vs. diffuse cultures (p. 95)

Affective vs. neutral cultures (p. 96)

Power distance dimension (p. 96)

Individualism vs. collectivism dimension
(p. 98)

Individualism and communitarianism
dichotomies (p. 98)

Achievement vs. ascription orientations (p. 99)

Internal vs. external control (p. 99)

Uncertainty avoidance dimension (p. 99)

Indulgence vs. restraint dimension
(p. 102)

Universalism vs. particularism dichotomies
(p. 102)

References

Adler, N. J., & Gundersen, A. (2008). *International dimensions of organizational behavior* (5th ed.). Mason, OH: Thomson Higher Education.

Bennett, M. J. (1998). Intercultural communication: A current perspective. In Milton J. Bennett (Ed.), *Basic concepts of intercultural communication: Selected readings* (pp. 1–34). Yarmouth, ME: Intercultural Press.

Cavusgil, S. T., Knight, G., & Riesenberger, J. R. (2008). *International business: Strategy, management, and the new realities*. Upper Saddle River, NJ: Pearson Education.

Cottle, T. J. (1967). The circles test: An investigation of perceptions of temporal relatedness and dominance. *Journal of Projective Techniques & Personality Assessment, 31*(5), 58–71. doi:10.1080/0091651X.1967.10120417.

Cult of "face" (n.d.). *China Mike* [Blog]. Retrieved from http://www.china-mike.com/chinese-culture/understanding-chinese-mind/cult-of-face/.

Curtin, P. A., & Gaither, T. K. (2007). *International public relations: Negotiating culture, identity, and power*. Thousand Oaks, CA: Sage Publications.

Devereux, M. M., & Peirson-Smith, A. (2009). *Public relations in Asia Pacific: Communicating effectively across cultures*. Singapore: John Wiley & Sons.

Geertz, C. (1973). *The interpretations of cultures*. New York, NY: Basic Books.

Grobart, S. (2013, April 4). Samsung's year abroad. *Businessweek.com*. Retrieved from http://www.businessweek.com/articles/2013–04–04/samsungs-year-abroad.

Guirdham, M. (2005). *Communicating across cultures at work* (2nd ed.). West Lafayette, IN: Ichor Books.

Hall, E. T. (1976). *Beyond culture*. New York, NY: Anchor Books.

Hofstede, G. (2011). Dimensionalizing cultures: The Hofstede model in context. *Online Readings in Psychology and Culture, 2*(1). doi: 10.9707/2307–0919.1014.

Hofstede, G., Hofstede, G. J., & Minkov, M. (2010). *Cultures and organizations: Software of the mind* (Rev. 3rd ed.). New York, NY: McGraw-Hill.

Ihator, A. (1999, December). When in Rome. . . *Communication World, 17*(1), 24–26.

Jacobs, K. (2014, April 8). 7 skills PR leaders need to succeed in the coming years: Do you have what it takes? *The Public Relations Strategist.* Retrieved from http://www.prsa.org/Intelligence/TheStrategist/Articles/view/10605/1092/7_Skills_PR_Leaders_Need_to_Succeed_in_the_Coming#.VEwTDfnF-S.

Kent, M., & Taylor, M. (2011). How intercultural communication theory informs public relations practices in global settings. In N. Bardhan and C. K. Weaver (Eds.), *Public relations in global cultural contexts: Multi-paradigmatic perspectives* (pp. 50–76). New York, NY: Routledge.

Rosenberg, M. (2014). GMT vs. UTC: An overview of Greenwich Mean Time and Coordinated Universal Time. *Geography.About.com.* Retrieved from http://geography.about.com/od/timeandtimezones/a/gmtutc.htm.

Sriramesh, K. (2009). Globalisation and public relations: An overview looking into the future. *PRism, 6*(2). Retrieved from http://praxis.massey.ac.nz/prism_on-line_journ.html.

Terpstra, V., & David, K. H. (1991). *The cultural environment of international business.* Cincinnati, OH: South-Western Publishing Co.

Time and Date. (2015). UTC—the world's time standard. Retrieved from http://www.timeanddate.com/time/aboututc.html.

Triandis, H. C. (2002). Subjective culture. In W. J. Lonner, D. L. Dinnel, S. A. Hayes, & D. N. Sattler (Eds.), *Online readings in psychology and culture* (Unit 15, Chapter 1). Bellingham, WA: Center for Cross-Cultural Research, Western Washington University.

Trompenaars, A., & Hampden-Turner, C. (2012). *Riding the waves of culture: Understanding diversity in global business* (3rd ed.). New York, NY: McGraw-Hill.

Verčič, D., Grunig, L. A., & Grunig, J. E. (1996). Global and specific principles of public relations: Evidence from Slovenia. In H. M. Culbertson & N. Chen (Eds.), *International public relations: A comparative analysis* (pp. 31–65). Mahwah, NJ: Lawrence Erlbaum.

Victor, D. A. (2012). Global advances in business communication from multiple perspectives: A panel discussion from experts in the field. *Global Advances in Business Communication, 1*(1), Art. 2.

5 Decoding Nonverbal Communication and Imagery Worldwide

> Of all of our inventions for mass communication, pictures still speak the most universally understood language.
>
> —Walt Disney, founder of the Walt Disney Company

5.1 Introduction to Visual Imagery in Public Relations

Although Walt Disney, the founder of the company that still thrives under his name, was referring to cinema in his quote above, he did make an important point about the universal power of imagery that can transcend any language. Visual imagery is powerful, whether used to illustrate joy, love, achievement, or sorrow. Public relations practitioners must be adept in selecting images to bring their stories to life. You may be responsible for buying existing imagery or hiring new talent, whether they are photographers, videographers, illustrators, cartoonists, or Web designers.

Have you even seen the Pulitzer Prize-winning photographs in photojournalism? I viewed "Capture the Moment: The Pulitzer Prize Photographs," in Philadelphia, which was a traveling exhibit throughout the U.S. and abroad of more than 150 Pulitzer Prize photographs from the award's inception in 1942 to 2013. The photojournalists captured scenes from wars, natural disasters, heroic feats, and significant events, evoking such emotions as pain, rage, relief, happiness, or exhilaration. Many of the images previously appeared on the front pages of newspapers and magazines. Each image in the exhibit was accompanied by a brief description about the circumstances and the photographer's involvement.

I found Kevin Carter's image of an emaciated Sudanese child collapsed in front of a stalking vulture to be the most haunting and heartbreaking photograph (see Figure 5.1). The caption explained how photojournalists covering the famine in the Sudan in 1993 were not permitted to touch the victims for fear of spreading diseases. Although the photographer said he chased away the vulture, he did not know if the child survived. I later read that the photograph ran in the *New York Times* and in major newspapers around the globe, prompting outcries from editors and readers wanting to know the toddler's fate. An article in *Time* covered reactions to Carter's iconic photograph of the African famine, as well as background on his life as a photojournalist and his suicide at age 33 in 1994:

Others questioned his ethics: "The man adjusting his lens to take just the right frame of her suffering," said the St. Petersburg (Florida) Times, "might just as well be a predator, another vulture on the scene." Even some of Carter's friends wondered aloud why he had not helped the girl. (MacLeod, 2001, para. 19)

Although not all imagery used in public relations may be as dramatic, it could be if you were representing an INGO or NGO illustrating social causes. The goal of this chapter is to explain nonverbal communication, which can take on another level of complexity in international communications. Public relations writers need to understand cross-cultural interpretations of visual imagery that they select for social media, brochures, posters, infographics, websites, online newsrooms, or any other promotional purposes. This knowledge would help practitioners make better decisions when choosing imagery for products, services, or causes. According to some scholars, nonverbal behavior accounts for 60 to 65% of interpersonal communication (Burgoon, Guerrero, & Floyd, 2009). Gestures and body language appropriate in one culture could be considered offensive or perplexing in another. The same applies to images that show people interacting and how they dress. Colors and numbers also have different positive or negative associations. Popular icons and symbols may not transcend borders, whether the imagery represents heroes, religious or political figures, or animals and flowers. (See Figure 5.2 of a cartoon that shows how one animal in particular conveys strong nonverbal cues.)

Figure 5.1—KEVIN CARTER RECEIVED THE PULITZER PRIZE IN JOURNALISM (FEATURE PHOTOGRAPHY) IN 1994 FOR THIS IMAGE OF THE FAMINE IN THE SUDAN. Source: © Kevin Carter/Sygma/Corbis.

Figure 5.2—CARTOON SHOWS HOW NONVERBAL COMMUNICATION MAY BE SIMPLER FOR SOME. Source: Courtesy of Terry P. Smith.

5.2 Cultural Interpretations of Body Language

American anthropologist Ray Birdwhistell coined the term **kinesics**, based on the Greek word "kinesis" (motion), for the study of body language—facial expressions, posture, and gestures—in nonverbal communications. Within the study of nonverbal communications, other terms apply to studying specific body language. **Oculesics** refers to the study of eye behavior, in which direct or indirect eye contact can be interpreted differently, as well as the length of time someone gazes at another person. **Haptics** is the term for examining the behavior of touch, particularly the different cultural customs of rituals, when people greet one another, bid farewell, or show public displays of affection.

Gestures that have positive connotations in one culture could be considered obscene in others. Can you recall an incident when you were baffled or even offended by hand gestures or body language made by people from another culture? Take the quiz in Exercise 5.1 and see if you can identify what these hand gestures signify in different countries—and try to do the exercise before you continue to read the chapter. (See Figure 5.3 of a montage of different types of hand gestures.)

"Keep your fingers to yourself" is sage advice. Let us look at examples of popular hand gestures, with extremely different meanings from country to country:

- **The "OK" Sign**

  The gesture with the thumb and index finger forming the letter O is not universal. In the U.S. for example, it means "OK" or "yes," yet it means "zero" in France and "money" in Japan (Cotton, 2013). In parts of Latin America and the Middle East, as well as in other countries, the "OK" sign is a highly obscene gesture. In fact, a company unaware of the negative interpretation of "OK" in Latin America printed

Exercise 5.1

Self-Evaluation: Cross-Cultural Interpretations of Hand Gestures

Try to identify what these hand gestures signify in specific countries. (You can use the words "obscene" or "offensive" to describe lewd gestures.)

1. What does the "corna" ("horn sign" formed by holding up the pinkie and index finger from one's fist) mean in Brazil?
2. What does the "corna" gesture mean in the U.S., particularly in the state of Texas?
3. What does the "thumbs up" gesture mean in Portugal?
4. What does the "thumbs up" gesture signify in the U.S.?
5. What does the "chin flick" mean when people brush their finger tips in a forward motion under their chin in France?
6. What does the thumb and index finger forming the letter "O" gesture mean in Japan?
7. What does the "V" sign mean with the palm facing outward in the U.K.?
8. What does the "V" sign signify with the palm facing inward mean in Australia?
9. What does it mean when the elbow is tapped with one's palm in Mexico and most of South America?
10. What does the same elbow-tapping gesture mean in Austria and Germany?

Please see Appendix D for answers.

Figure 5.3—EXAMPLES OF HAND GESTURES—BUT "KEEP YOUR HANDS TO YOURSELF" IS SAGE ADVICE SINCE NOT ALL GESTURES HAVE UNIVERSAL MEANINGS. Source: © Tribalium/Shutterstock.com.

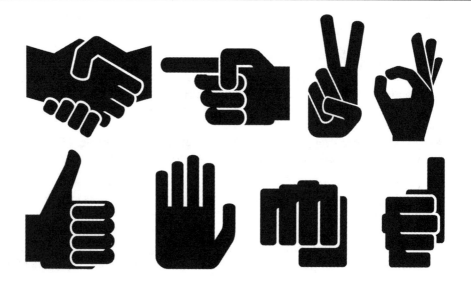

a catalogue with the "OK" motif on each page. The mistake was not only embarrassing but costly with reprinting fees (Hummel, 2010).

- **"Thumbs-Up" or "Thumbs-Down"**
  The "thumbs-up" gesture has positive connotations ("great job" or "recommend this") in the U.S. and some other countries. The "thumbs-down" motion means the exact opposite ("awful" or "don't recommend"). The gesture of a "thumbs-up" thrust upward, however, is an insult in Australia, Greece, and Russia, as well as in parts of Latin America, Western Africa, and the Middle East (Cotton, 2013; Lefevre, 2011).

- **Sign of Bull Horns or Devil Horns ("Corna")**
  This gesture is formed by raising one's fist and extending the index finger and little finger. Does the "sign of the horns" gesture mean you are a fan of a heavy metal band or a sports team or does it signify marital woes? You may use this gesture at a rock concert in the U.K., but it means "your wife is unfaithful" in the Baltics, Brazil, Colombia, Italy, Portugal, and Spain (Lefevre, 2011). Some African countries consider this gesture a curse. In the U.S., the "hook 'em horns" is a salute to the Longhorns at the University of Texas at Austin, a football team named after Longhorn cattle. Former President and longtime Texan resident George W. Bush used this salute to greet the University of Texas marching band during the parade for his second inauguration (see Figure 5.4). However, the salute was lost in translation when photographs were disseminated around the world in traditional and social media, generating some negative exposure and commentary.

- **"V" Sign**
  When Winston Churchill celebrated the end of World War II, he used the "V" sign to signify "victory" (see Figure 5.5). In the U.S., protestors against the Vietnam War and the hippies in the 1960s formed the "V" sign to signify "peace." However, be careful of the direction of the "V" sign formation in some countries. When the sign is formed with the index and middle finger facing the signer's palm inward, along with a few upward thrusts, it has a completely different meaning—an obscene one in the U.K., Ireland, Australia, New Zealand, and other English-speaking countries (Link, 2010).

- **Other Gestures**
  Here are examples of other hand gestures that are considered rude in some cultures:

  - The "finger" with the middle finger pointing with the palm facing the gesturer is the most lewd gesture in the U.S. However, in some countries, the middle finger is used to point—and the index finger is considered rude.
  - The "beckoning gesture" is formed by curling up one's index finger with the palm facing the gesturer. The gesture means "come here" in the U.S., but not in many parts of North Africa and Asia where it should only be used to beckon dogs, not people (Cotton, 2013).
  - The open hand or "moutza" gesture means "stop" or "enough" to many Westerners, but it may be considered an insult in Greece, Pakistan, and many countries in Africa and Asia (Cotton, 2013).
  - Touching one's elbow can have different meanings. The "tacaño" gesture means "stingy" when the elbow is tapped with one's palm in Mexico and most of South America, whereas the same gesture in Austria and Germany stands for "idiot" (Lefevre, 2011).

Figure 5.4—PRESIDENT GEORGE W. BUSH GESTURED THE "HOOK 'EM HORNS," SALUTE OF THE UNIVERSITY OF TEXAS LONGHORNS, AS HE WATCHED THE INAUGURAL PARADE WITH HIS FAMILY AND FRIENDS FROM THE REVIEWING STAND IN FRONT OF THE WHITE HOUSE, JAN. 20, 2005. Source: Photo by Paul Morse. Courtesy of the George W. Bush Presidential Library and Museum.

Body language and visual dynamics of people in photographs and video also should be considered for cultural misinterpretations. Let us investigate a few other potential problem areas:

- *Bottom of Feet or Soles of Shoes*
  Is it appropriate for people to stretch out their legs and show the soles of their shoes? This pose may signify relaxation in the U.S., but the same body language can be perceived as disrespectful in parts of the Middle East and Africa. A U.S. phone company aiming to sell its services in Saudi Arabia produced an advertisement of an executive chatting on the phone with his feet propped up on the desk. Saudis would consider it inappropriate to show the sole of one's shoes (Hummel, 2010). The feet are viewed as dirty, the lowest part of the body on the ground. Muslims remove their shoes to pray, and shoes are disallowed in mosques. Hitting someone with a shoe is an insult. Do you recall the images of Iraqis throwing shoes at the toppled statue of Saddam Hussein in 2003? An Iraqi journalist threw a shoe at U.S. President George W. Bush during a press conference in Baghdad in 2008. CBS correspondent Richard Roth (2008) explained the significance of the gesture in a

Figure 5.5—STAMP PRINTED IN BARBUDA, CIRCA 1974, WAS DEDICATED TO THE CENTENARY OF THE BIRTH OF SIR WINSTON S. CHURCHILL AND DEPICTED HIS "V FOR VICTORY" HAND GESTURE. Source: © Neftali/ Shutterstock.com.

television news report: "The symbolism wouldn't have been lost on Iraqis, for whom shoes can be used to show extreme contempt." Showing the sole of one's foot when crossing one's legs also can be interpreted as rudeness in Japan and other countries in the Middle East. Removing shoes is a common custom when entering someone's home in parts of Asia and the South Pacific.

- *Left Hands*
  Be careful to avoid showing people in photographs using their left hands, particularly for eating and passing food. In parts of Africa, India, and the Middle East, the right hand is considered the appropriate "clean" hand.

- *Heads*
  Patting a child or an adult on the head is considered an affectionate gesture in some Western countries. However, this gesture would be deemed highly inappropriate in Thailand and Indonesia, where one's head is valued as sacred (Morrison & Conaway, 2006).

5.2.1 Dimensions of Visual Interactions of People

Other visual dynamics to consider are interactions between men and women, particularly physical displays of affection, in imagery. How people dress should be analyzed for appropriateness. I recall representing a resort in Bali that created a promotional brochure, with a photograph of a woman taking a shower—a rather blurry image but you could tell she was nude—in the outdoor garden of a villa. The feedback varied considerably: the European sales force thought the image was staid and the Americans thought it was racy—and customs officials in a Middle Eastern country felt the brochures should be censored and confiscated all the boxes. Look at what imagery is considered culturally appropriate for how women or men are dressed—and in various stages of undress—such as women clad in bikini swimsuits or bra and underwear, or bare-chested men in underwear. See Malcolm Evans' cartoon (Figure 5.6) on the different interpretations of acceptable women's attire between the bikini and the burka.

Visual representations of how people interact with brands also have different meanings. Western consumers value uniqueness of the product and how the individual enjoys it; Eastern cultures respond to similarity and group togetherness (Kastanakis & Voyer, 2014).

There is no shortage of "cautionary tales" about companies that did not consult local talent for assistance with promotional materials. Procter & Gamble's television commercial in Japan showed a women bathing while her husband enters the bathroom. Although this scene would not seem out of place in many Western countries, the Japanese found it inappropriate since it depicted an invasion of privacy (Fromowitz, 2013).

IKEA, the global furniture company based in Sweden, faced a cross-cultural dilemma when the company edited its catalogue for the Saudi Arabian market by removing all imagery of women to comply with a culture where women rarely appear in advertisements and promotional materials. This approach followed the religious and cultural norms of a society

Figure 5.6—CULTURAL CARTOON ON ATTITUDES ABOUT BIKINIS AND BURKAS. Source: © Malcolm Evans.

where women in public are completely covered, except for their eyes, and exposed body parts are routinely censored in international magazines (Ritter, 2012). Known for being a progressive company, IKEA faced a backlash in its home country for erasing women from the catalogue. IKEA released a statement as reported in the *Guardian* (Quinn, 2012): "We should have reacted and realised that excluding women from the Saudi Arabian version of the catalogue is in conflict with the Ikea Group values" (para. 5).

Olay launched its new line of beauty skin cream in Saudi Arabia and the United Arab Emirates by celebrating the beauty of eyes with its "Olay Eyes of Arabia" beauty pageant, thereby following conservative social norms. More than 82,000 women participated in the pageant as a judge or contestant in the digital campaign that was promoted through Web banner advertisements, blogs, and social media, resulting in a spike of 806% of website traffic and selling 57% more Olay eye products than the previous year (Dubai Lynx, 2011).

Public relations practitioners also should be sensitive to selecting visual imagery that shows ethnic diversity of people and a variety of age groups and genders. Material used for local markets can be customized further to reflect the specific races, religions, social customs, dress, and body language appropriate for that culture.

Physical Space

Anthropologist Edward T. Hall invented the theory of **proxemics** in *The Hidden Dimension* (1966). He analyzed cultural dimensions of space: the intimate space with close friends and loved ones; the social and consultative space of routine social interactions with colleagues, acquaintances, or strangers; and the public space of impersonal and anonymous interactions. Hall argued that understanding the human sense of space in an intercultural context can enhance communications:

> It is essential that we learn to read the silent communications as easily as the printed and spoken ones. Only by doing so can we also reach other people, both inside and outside our national boundaries, as we are increasingly required to do. (p. 6)

Think about how important the concept of space is to interactions with people. How much space do you believe is appropriate when sitting next to a stranger on a bench? How close do you stand next to your boss at work? Have you ever been surprised by the sense of space from someone from other country, who may have been too close or too far out of your comfort zone? How did you perceive that person? Your perspective may not be the same as people from other countries. The sense of space between North Americans and Europeans may be quite similar, whereas Middle Easterners maintain a tighter sense of space, and the Japanese prefer to keep a greater distance. The location even within a culture may change dynamics. The exception for physical closeness in Japan takes place in Tokyo's subway system, where its professional, impeccably groomed white-gloved "pushers" cram commuters safely into packed subway cars.

What is the appropriate protocol in touching someone, particularly a business colleague or even a loved one in public? Some cultures exchange enthusiastic hugs and kisses and others don't touch. It's important to understand the personal space requirements of a different culture, so that you're not perceived as being rude or aloof (by standing too far away) or pushy and aggressive (by standing too close). Be mindful of spatial considerations when selecting visual imagery of people interacting as couples, families, strangers, or business colleagues.

Figure 5.7—THE EXCHANGE OF BUSINESS CARDS HAS DIFFERENT TRADITIONS.
Source: © Reo/Shutterstock.com.

Body language applies to basic business transactions from greeting people, saying farewells, and handing out business cards. An Asian client expressed to me his concern about how business cards are exchanged: "Americans hand out business cards like a deck of playing cards." It's true that some Americans flick their business cards across a conference table to other people. In Asia, business cards are treated with great respect. Cards are presented carefully with the presenter holding the two outer edges in both hands with the business card (see Figure 5.7), preferably with the translated side facing the reader. Cards remain kept out during a meeting, preferably in the order in which people are seated. This arrangement also can help people keep track of names when meeting for the first time.

5.3 Cultural Interpretations of Colors

The late Roger Axtell, who was an author of books on cultural blunders and international business travel, summed up the different perceptions of colors with strong imagery: "symbolism among colors can vary as much as sushi differs from succotash" (2007, p. 64). Public relations writers also need to understand different interpretations of color in the visual imagery they select for print, video, or digital formats. Colors play an important role in rites of passages—births, weddings, and funerals. What is the color most widely associated with weddings in your culture? What about funerals? White may be the color for bridal dresses in many Western countries (see Figure 5.8), yet it is the color worn by mourners in many countries in Asia, Africa, and the Middle East (see Figure 5.9). Writers also should be mindful of colors of money (not all money is green as in the U.S.), religious colors (green is the color of Islam and should not be used in promotional material), flag colors of a specific country, and other symbolic uses of color.

Colors of the stock market are *almost* universal. However, the color green signifies an up market and red a down market in all countries, including Hong Kong, except for Mainland China (Jiang, Lu, Yao, Yue, & Au, 2013). Refer to Exhibit 5.1 with examples of symbolic colors in different countries and regions.

Colors can be discriminatory, even unintentionally. What is the color "nude" or "flesh"? Crayola, the company best known for its crayons, has grappled with this question. In 1962 during the civil rights movement in the U.S., Crayola changed its crayon color called Flesh, which was in its original box of 64 crayons, to Peach (Crayola.com, 2014a). Crayola launched its Multicultural Crayons in 1992 with Apricot, Burnt Sienna, Mahogany, Peach, Sepia,

Figure 5.8—BRIDAL WHITE IS POPULAR IN MANY WESTERN CULTURES.
Source: © Alena Ozerova/Shutterstock.com.

Figure 5.9—WHITE ALSO CAN BE THE COLOR OF MOURNING. People shown attending a funeral in Suratthani, Thailand. Source: © Settawat Udom/Shutterstock.com.

Tan, and Black and White for blending colors. The company's website explains why: "Multiculturalism is an important issue in early childhood education today because it is important for each child to build a positive sense of self, and to respect the cultural diversity in others" (Crayola.com, 2014b, para. 2). The crayon manufacturer also faced another issue in 1999 about its Indian Red, another shade in the original box, when teachers complained that the reddish-brown color referred to the skin color of American Indians. Although Crayola claimed the color was based on a red shade in India, the company requested feedback from consumers to change the name and selected the new name, Chestnut, after sifting through 250,000 suggestions ("Chestnut replaces a color Crayola called Indian Red," 1999).

5.3.1 Colorful Blunders

Marketers have experienced color-related cultural blunders that exhibited a lack of awareness of the local customs and political sensitivities. Let us look at a few examples:

- Back in the 1950s, Pepsi found itself losing market share to Coca-Cola in parts of Southeast Asia when Pepsi changed its vending machines from a dark blue to light blue, a color signifying death and mourning (Wooten, 2011a).
- UPS repainted its brown trunks in Spain since they looked like hearses (Cateora & Graham, 2005).

Exhibit 5.1—EXAMPLES OF CULTURAL INTERPRETATIONS OF COLORS. Source: De Bortoli, M., & Maroto, J. (2001). Colors across culture: Translating colors in interactive marketing communications. In R. Russow & D. Barbereau (Eds.), *Elicit 2001: Proceedings of the European Languages and the Implementation of Communication and Information Technologies (Elicit) conference* (pp. 3–4). UK: Paisley University Language Press.

Attribute	Color (examples of regions/countries; religious and cultural differences may vary within many countries)	Visual examples (as relevant)
Buddhism	Orange (parts of Asia) Red (Thailand)	Robes of Buddhist monks
Communism	Red (Russia, Commonwealth of Independent States)	Red Square
Environment Nature	Brown (Australia, Brazil, New Zealand) Gold (Turkey) Green (North America, Caribbean, Latin America, Mexico, Europe, India) Red (Turkey) Purple (Turkey) Yellow (Caribbean, China, Japan, parts of Asia, India) White (Northern Europe, Australia, New Zealand)	Ecological symbols, rainforests, earth, outdoors, stones, mountains, plants, snow, red fruits, oceans, deserts
Female Femininity	Pink (North America)	Clothing of baby girls (North America)
Funerals Mourning	Black (North America, Europe, Central and South America, parts of Asia, Iran) Blue (Latin America, Mexico, Italy, South Korea) Orange (India) Red (parts of Africa) Purple (Brazil) White (Japan, China, other parts of Asia and Middle East)	Funeral clothing, cleric robes, Hindu monks' robes
Hinduism	Blue Orange	Krishna (sacred color of blue) Hindu monks' robes
Islam	Green	Cloak of the prophet
Judaism	Blue	Star of David in the flag of Israel
Male Masculinity	Blue (North America) Silver (Japan)	Clothing of baby boys (North America)
Nobility	Gold (parts of Europe, Russia) Purple (North America, Western Europe, Japan) Yellow (Malaysia)	
Wealth	Blue (Turkey) Gold (North America, Caribbean, Latin America, Mexico, South America, Egypt, China, other parts of Asia)	Gold, jewelry
Weddings	Red (India, Indonesia, China) White (North America, Europe, Central and South America, Israel)	Bridal clothing

- A Japanese-American executive prevented a cultural mishap when he discovered that his American company was about to send Christmas cards to its Japanese clients with all red ink. The color red is traditionally used for funeral notices in Japan (Martin & Chaney, 2006).
- Orange may have bright and sunny meanings in some cultures, but not for the entire population in Northern Ireland. Orange is a brand name of France Telecom, and its slogan was "The Future's Bright—the Future's Orange." This slogan would have an unintended meaning for Catholics in religiously divided Northern Ireland, where the color orange is associated with the Orange Order, an Irish Protestant society (Wooten, 2011a).
- A U.S. company placed yellow stickers on products that passed inspection—and discovered that the color yellow stood for defects in China (Martin & Chaney, 2006).

Colors reflecting moods, emotions, and opinions are highly idiomatic. Expressions such as "feeling blue" or "green with envy" do not always translate with the same meaning in other languages. Keep this in mind if you are writing global materials or having material translated.

5.4 Cultural Perspectives on Numbers

Do you believe that certain numbers are lucky or unlucky? Have you ever noticed missing floors in buildings? Many buildings in the West lack a 13th floor or the 13th floor is used for storage or maintenance. In fact, renters or buyers of condos in Manhattan and Brooklyn would have a challenging time finding a designated 13th story—with less than 5% of mid- or high-rise residential inventory containing the unlucky numbered floor (Tanaka, 2013). These superstitious roots go back to Christianity when the 13th guest at the Last Supper with Jesus was a traitor. The fourth floor—or even numbers with a four in them—may be skipped in some buildings in Hong Kong, and hotels and hospitals in Japan may not number floors or rooms containing the numbers four or nine (Smartling.com, n.d.). Four in Cantonese, Mandarin, Korean, and Japanese sounds like the word for "death," and nine in Japanese sounds like "suffering." Fours should be avoided overall in Asia, even when packaging products. For example, a manufacturer of golf balls experienced challenges selling the products in packs of four in Japan (Hummel, 2010). The number 17 is avoided for floors and room numbers in Italy, as well as for row numbers in many Alitalia planes, since an anagram of the Roman numeral translates into "I have lived," meaning "I'm dead" (Harris, 2007). Combinations of days and numbers also have superstitious connotations for generating bad luck: Friday the 13th throughout the West (see Figure 5.10); Friday the 17th in Italy; and Tuesday the 13th in Greece, Mexico, and other Spanish-speaking countries.

Numbers also reflect positive associations. Eights are widely coveted in parts of Asia. The Beijing 2008 Olympic Games opened on August 8, 2008, considered an auspicious date (see Figure 5.11). Bidding on a license plate for the number 8888 is an expensive proposition in a number of countries in Asia. Retailers in Asia like to use eights in price tags (Ang, 1997). In the West, the number seven is considered lucky by many cultures. Journalist and author Alex Bellos (2014) conducted online research that revealed number seven as the world's favorite number. Seven historically has been popular in fact and fiction—seven seas, seven continents, seven wonders, seven dwarves, seven gods, and seven sins, among others.

How do numbers affect public relations writers? This could impact selections of visual imagery with numbers of people or items, dates selected for events, prices of goods and

Figure 5.10—SOME CULTURES CONSIDER FRIDAY 13TH TO BE AN UNLUCKY DAY. Source: © Everett Collection/Shutterstock.com.

Figure 5.11—AUGUST 8, 2008 WAS CONSIDERED AN AUSPICIOUS DATE TO OPEN THE SUMMER OLYMPICS IN BEIJING. Image shows spectators cheering for the Chinese team prior to a Group C match between China and Belgium at the Olympic Games soccer tournament. Source: © fstockfoto/Shutterstock.com.

services, numbers of product samples sent to reporters, and usage of numbers in written content. Numbers should be carefully considered for product numbers and telephone numbers, such as avoiding the use of fours in Asia. Even though not all people may follow the popular positive or negative interpretations of numbers in their culture, communicators may want to consider the potentially undesirable meanings. Exhibit 5.2 provides a few cultural examples of interpretations of numbers. Local public relations talent also could shed insight on which numbers—and combination of numbers—to avoid in written and visual materials. Odd and even numbers also have different meanings: the Japanese, for example, prefer odd numbers while many Western cultures like symmetrical even numbers.

Exhibit 5.2—EXAMPLES OF POSITIVE AND NEGATIVE MEANINGS OF NUMBERS. Sources: Ang, S. H. (1997). Chinese consumers' perception of alpha-numeric brand names. *Journal of Consumer Marketing, 14*(3), 220–233; Axtell, R. E. (2007). *Essential do's and taboos: The complete guide to international business and leisure travel.* Hoboken, NJ: John Wiley & Sons; Skurie, J. (2013, September 14). Superstitious numbers around the world: Numbers carry different meanings depending on what country you are in. *National Geographic News.* Retrieved from http://news.nationalgeographic.com/news.

Number	Positive Interpretations	Negative Interpretations
1	Unity, beginning (China) Favorable number (Japan)	
2	Duality (China)	
3	Growth, lucky number (China) Favorable number (Japan, Sweden)	Bad luck (Vietnam, three people in a photograph)
4		Unlucky and unpopular number, sounds like "death" (China, Japan, most of Asia)
5	Balanced, central position (China) Favorable number (Japan)	
6	Auspicious, sounds like "wealth" (China)	
7	Lucky (some countries in Europe and North America)	Unlucky numbers ending in 7 (some African countries)
8	Lucky, favorable, prosperity (China, Japan, other Asian countries)	
9	Longevity, auspicious (China)	Suffering (Japan)
10	Completeness, auspicious with 6 or 8 (China)	
13	Lucky (some parts of Italy)	Unlucky (many Western countries); Friday the 13th, considered an unlucky day in most of the West; Tuesday the 13th in Latin America
17		Unlucky (parts of Italy)
39		Unlucky (Afghanistan)
250		"Imbecile" (Mandarin)
666	Lucky, "Things going smoothly" (parts of Asia)	Number of the devil (Christianity)
7456		Anger, "make me mean" (Mandarin)

5.5 Symbols Across Cultures

Public relations writers also need to be sensitive to symbols representing religions, nations, and political parties. Celebrities and icons in popular culture may not have the same universal appeals. Visual imagery of animals and flowers also convey different meanings.

5.5.1 Religious, National, and Political Symbols

Unless you represent a religious organization or a controversial artist, you should avoid using religions icons and figures in any visual imagery. One of the most dramatic examples of a controversy over the use of religious imagery took place in 2005 when a Danish cartoonist inflamed Muslims and sparked demonstrations and boycotts of Danish products around the globe for his depictions of the Prophet Muhammad in *Morgenavisen Jyllands-Posten*, a Danish daily newspaper. Denmark's Prime Minister Anders Rasmussen called the situation "Denmark's worst international crisis since World War II" (Curry, 2008, para. 10). A short-lived example was when Prince Harry acquired a new nickname, "Harry the Nazi," for attending a costume party wearing a desert uniform and a swastika armband in 2005. British and international media coverage was far from positive—and Prince Harry did apologize for his lack of taste. Although the costume would be inappropriate on any occasion, the timing was even more sensitive since the party took place a few weeks before the 60th anniversary of the liberation of Auschwitz, the Nazi concentration camp in Poland.

In literature, film, television, fine arts, or music, blasphemy can be condemned, debated, or celebrated as an art form. Popular music performers can star as "kings and queens of controversy," particularly with provocative religious lyrics and iconography in their videos or live performances for deliberate shock value. Raised in a Catholic household, the singer Madonna has reveled in overt religious icons and lyrics in her music and performances. Her album titled "Immaculate Collection" sold millions around the globe. Another singer with a Catholic upbringing, Lady Gaga (see Figure 5.12), more recently simulated sex, swallowed a rosary, donned a nun's habit in red latex and a white robe with red crosses with matching underwear, featuring a less-than-subtle inverted red cross phallic symbol, in an 8-minute video called "Alejandro."

Indian British author Salman Rushdie's *The Satanic Verses* received not only positive literary reviews, but also provoked outrage within the Muslim world, resulting in book-burning demonstrations and such serious death threats that the British government provided the author with police protection.

Gaining insight on religious differences is essential when promoting controversial products or services, particularly "cigarettes, alcohol, contraceptives, underwear, and political advertising" (Fam, Waller, & Erdogan, 2004, p. 542). If you were representing a food company or restaurant, you would have to be aware of different food consumption patterns and cultural taboos. For example, you would avoid recipes or menu items with beef for Hindus or pork for devout Jews or Muslims.

Not all cultures celebrate the same holidays, and secular holiday icons should be examined for relevance. Modern Christmas images, for example, may not travel in cultures with few Christian residents. Make sure that it is appropriate to showcase visuals of Santa Claus, reindeer, elves, wreaths, trees with lights and ornaments, or wrapped presents with bows for Christmas, as well as Easter imagery of bunnies, decorated eggshells, or baskets with candy. American communities have been restricting holiday displays or adding icons from other faiths to reflect the country's multicultural diversity. Americans now refer to Christmas cards as "holiday cards."

Figure 5.12—LADY GAGA USES RELIGIOUS IMAGERY IN HER FASHION AND PERFORMANCES; SHOWN HERE PERFORMING ON STAGE FOR AN NBC *TODAY SHOW* **CONCERT AT ROCKEFELLER PLAZA, NEW YORK CITY, IN 2010.** Source: © Everett Collection/Shutterstock.com.

Have you noticed how flags are used during protests, whether they are proudly displayed or burned, ripped, or defaced? Desecrating a national flag can be a criminal offense in some countries. Understanding the protocol of flags is important. Some cultures allow flags to be placed almost anywhere and, in other countries, flags must be treated with respect along with restrictions in usage. PUMA, a German-based international apparel company, created limited-edition athletic shoes with the colors of the United Arab Emirates flag to celebrate the country's 40th National Day. The shoes were pulled off the shelves and widely criticized. Why? The flag is not only considered sacred, but wearing the flag on one's shoes would be considered highly disrespectful. As reported in *Business Insider* (Zeveloff, 2011), PUMA issued the following statement:

PUMA took the feedback from our consumers very seriously and has indefinitely actioned the removal of the shoe from all stores. PUMA apologises for any trouble caused on this matter. The shoe was never intended to upset or offend our customers here in the Middle East, but to give the people of the UAE a piece of locally created design as a symbol of recognition of this great occasion. (para. 6)

Another leading athletic shoe company also experienced cultural problems. In 1997, Nike launched four basketball shoe lines with a flaming air logo with the Arabic word for "air." Muslims felt that the logo looked too similar to the word for "Allah" in Arabic script, thereby threatening a worldwide boycott of Nike products. Nike recalled the product, issued apologies, and donated money to an elementary school playground (Starnes, 1997).

McDonald's attempted to celebrate Mexico's Flag Day (Día de la Bandera) in its restaurants in Mexico City by printing the Mexican flag on its napkins and tray placements. Customers were less than happy to drip "ketchup on a symbol of national pride" (Wooten, 2011b, para. 7), so government agents confiscated the commemorative paper goods.

5.5.2 Popular Cultural Icons

Who are the popular icons in the culture you are trying to communicate with? Would Hollywood or Bollywood be of appeal? Who are the local heroes and villains, whether they are real people or characters from legend and lore? These questions are not that simple. The answers require significant insight into the local culture and knowledge of current events. Popularity can be precarious. Well-respected public figures can lose their reputation over a scandal or from the public's changing fads and tastes, while other celebrities can be revered in one culture and reviled in another.

International public relations campaigns require investigating the image of a personality before that person is used in a promotional campaign in any form. Personalities could be actors and actresses from movies, theater, or television; popular writers, artists, dancers, or musicians; sports figures from the Olympics or other spectator sports; or other figures in positions of authority or people of accomplishments.

Let us look at a few examples of cross-cultural dilemmas:

- In China, Nike ran a television commercial with LeBron James, an American basketball player, battling a dragon and Chinese elders wearing traditional garb. What were the problems? Dragons are not just mythological figures in China, they are considered auspicious and the most revered sign in the Chinese zodiac. Chinese treat elders with respect. What was the reaction in China? The "Chamber of Fear" ad was banned. As reported in the *China Daily* ("China bans Nike TV ad as national insult," 2004), the State Administration for Radio, Film and Television issued a statement that the Nike advertisement "violates regulations that mandate that all advertisements in China should uphold national dignity and interest and respect the motherland's culture" (para. 4).
- A respected personality in one culture may not be admired in other cultures. Fiat discovered this when the Italian automaker launched its TV advertising campaign in China, starring the popular American actor Richard Gere driving its Lancia Delta model in Tibet. Gere's support of the Dalai Lama and Tibet is not shared in China (Castonguay, 2008).
- A celebrity who may have a positive or neutral image can turn into a negative one, particularly when the star criticizes the values or actions of a country. Christian Dior,

the French fashion house, dropped actress Sharon Stone from its advertising campaign in China after Stone shared her opinions about China's relationship with Tibet during an interview at the Cannes Film Festival. As quoted in the *New York Times* (Jolly, 2008), Stone said:

> I'm not happy about the way the Chinese are treating the Tibetans because I don't think anyone should be unkind to anyone else. And then the earthquake and all this stuff happened, and then I thought, is that karma? When you're not nice that the bad things happen to you? (para. 5)

Dior later released a statement from the actress in which she apologized for her "inappropriate words and acts during the interview" (Jolly, 2008, para. 4) and offered to help with the post-earthquake relief effort.

5.5.3 Imagery of Animals and Flowers

The symbolism of animals and flowers is not universal. Public relations practitioners should investigate the significance of mammals, reptiles, birds, insects, aquatic animals, and flowers in specific cultures before they invest the money in using the imagery in promotional materials. Owls may stand for wisdom in many Western countries, yet they mean "wise guy" in Taiwan or can be considered bad luck to Eastern Indians and some Native American tribes (Lu, 1998).

Figure 5.13—DOGS MAY BE CONSIDERED BELOVED PETS IN MANY CULTURES, BUT NOT IN ALL. PR practitioners should be careful in selecting appropriate imagery of animals. Source: © bikeriderlondon/Shutterstock.com.

Figure 5.14—THE TYPE OF FLOWERS AND THEIR COLORS CAN HAVE DIFFERENT MEANINGS, SO WRITERS SHOULD CHECK THE SYMBOLISM OF FLOWERS FOR SPECIFIC MARKETS. Source: © Steve Herrmann/Shutterstock.com.

Bald eagles are the national birds in the U.S., but eagles symbolize bad luck in China and Saudi Arabia (Martin & Chaney, 2006). Guinea pigs may be pets in North America, Europe, Australia, and New Zealand, yet they are popular on the menu in many countries in South America.

Dogs may be adored as "man's best friend" in the West and in other countries (see Figure 5.13), but they are seen as dirty or low animals by some people in parts of the Middle East, China, and other Asian countries (Zhu, 2010). A cologne manufacturer trying to sell its product in Muslim countries failed when its promotional materials depicted a pastoral scene with a man and his dog. The company should have realized that dogs are considered unclean by many residents in the Middle East and that connecting canine imagery with a skin product would not resonate with consumers there (Hummel, 2010).

Flowers convey different meanings and symbolize diverse events, based on their color and type (see Figure 5.14). If you are showing images of weddings, you should know which flowers and colors of flowers are actually used for those celebrations. The same applies to other celebrations and occasions. Be particularly careful to avoid flowers that signify death and are widely seen at funerals or cemeteries in certain countries: white gladiolus in China; white carnations in France and Germany; chrysanthemums in many European countries; white flowers in Islamic countries and some countries in Asia; purple flowers in Brazil; and purple and yellow flowers in Mexico and other South American countries. Some types of flowers also symbolize good or bad luck, and whether a small bouquet of flowers is arranged in odd or even numbers (Martin & Chaney, 2006).

5.6 Learning Objectives and Key Terms

By studying Chapter 5, you should be able to:

- Develop cultural awareness of the use of visual imagery in public relations materials.
- Identify various hand gestures and other body language that may be misinterpreted in different cultures, as well as in public relations campaigns.
- Define the concept of proxemics and its importance in visual imagery.
- Understand the importance of selecting colors carefully in digital and print materials in different markets.
- Consider numbers that may have negative or positive associations in different cultures.
- Develop sensitivities to using religions, national, and political symbols, as well as cultural icons and images of flowers and animals.

This chapter covers the following key terms:

Kinesics (p. 107)	Oculesics (p. 107)
Haptics (p. 107)	Proxemics (p. 113)

References

Ang, S. H. (1997). Chinese consumers' perceptions of alpha-numeric brand names. *Journal of Consumer Marketing, 14*(3), 220–233. doi: 10.1108/07363769710166800.

Axtell, R. E. (2007). *Essential do's and taboos: The complete guide to international business and leisure travel*. Hoboken, NJ: John Wiley & Sons.

Bellos, A. (2014, April 8). "Seven" triumphs in poll to discover world's favourite number: The results of an online survey reveal a world in love with numbers that stand out and feel exceptional. *Guardian*. Retrieved from http://www.theguardian.com/science/alexs-adventures-in-numberland/2014/apr/08/seven-worlds-favourite-number-online-survey.

Burgoon, J. K., Guerrero, L. K., & Floyd, K. (2009). *Nonverbal communication*. Boston, MA: Allyn & Bacon.

Castonguay, G. (2008, June 20). Fiat apologizes to China for TV ad for new car. *Reuters*. Retrieved from http://www.reuters.com/article/2008/06/21/industry-fiat-china-dc-idUSL20 30648920080621.

Cateora, P. R., & Graham, J. L. (2005). *International marketing* (12th ed.). Boston, MA: McGraw-Hill Irwin.

Chestnut replaces a color Crayola called Indian Red. (1999, July 27). *Chicago Tribune*. Retrieved from http://articles.chicagotribune.com/1999–07–27/news/9907280062_1_ crayola-red-color.

China bans Nike TV ad as national insult. (2004, December 7). *China Daily*. Retrieved from http://www.chinadaily.com.cn/english/doc/2004–12/07/content_397920.htm.

Cotton, G. (2013, June 13). Gestures to avoid in cross-cultural business: In other words, "keep your fingers to yourself!" *Huffington Post*. Retrieved from http://www.huffingtonpost.com/gayle-cotton/cross-cultural-gestures_b_3437653.html.

Crayola.com. (2014a). *Frequently asked questions. Why does the color "flesh" not appear in the 1958 limited edition box of 64?* Retrieved from http://www.crayola.com/faq/another-topic/why-does-the-color-quotfleshquot-not-appear-in-the-1958-limited-edition-box-of-64/.

Crayola.com. (2014b). *Frequently asked questions. When did you introduce Crayola Multi-cultural products?* Retrieved from http://www.crayola.com/faq/another-topic/when-did-you-introduce-crayola-multicultural-products/.

Curry, A. (2008, January 30). Is cartoon controversy history? Danish library wants to preserve inflammatory drawings. *Spiegel International Online*. Retrieved from http://www.spiegel.de/international/europe/is-cartoon-controversy-history-danish-library-wants-to-preserve-inflammatory-drawings-a-532057.html.

Dubai Lynx. (2011). *2011 winners & shortlists: Eyes of Arabia, Procter & Gamble*. Retrieved from http://www.dubailynx.com/winners/2011/promo/entry.cfm?entryid=2017&award=99&order=0&direction=1.

Fam, K. S., Waller, D. S., & Erdogan, B. Z. (2004). The influence of religion on attitudes towards the advertising of controversial products. *European Journal of Marketing, 38*(5/6), 537–555. doi: 10.1108/03090560410529204.

Fromowitz, M. (2013, October 7). Cultural blunders: Brands gone wrong. *Campaign Asia-Pacific*. Retrieved from http://www.campaignasia.com/BlogEntry/359532,Cultural+blunders+Brands+gone+wrong.aspx.

Hall, E. T. (1966). *The hidden dimension*. Garden City, NY: Doubleday.

Harris, N. (2007, November 15). Bad omen for Italy as their unlucky number comes up. *Independent*. Retrieved from http://www.independent.co.uk/sport/football/european/bad-omen-for-italy-as-their-unlucky-number-comes-up-400380.html.

Hummel, D. (2010, January 3). Ten cross-cultural blunders to remember. *UniversalConsensus.com* [Blog]. Retrieved from http://denisehummel.wordpress.com/2010/01/03/ten-cross-cultural-blunders-to-remembe/.

Jiang, F., Lu, S., Yao, X., Yue, X., & Au, W. T. (2013). Up or down? How culture and color affect judgments. *Journal of Behavioral Decision Making, 27*(3), 226–234. doi: 10.1002/bdm.1800.

Jolly, D. (2008, May 29). Dior drops Sharon Stone from its China ads for Tibet remark. *New York Times*. Retrieved from http://www.nytimes.com/2008/05/29/business/worldbusiness/29iht-29lux.13308544.html?_r=0.

Kastanakis, M. N., & Voyer, B. G. (2014). The effect of culture on perception and cognition: A conceptual framework. *Journal of Business Research, 67*(4), 425–433. doi: 10.1016/j.jbusres.2013.03.028.

Lefevre, R. (2011). *Rude hand gestures of the world: A guide to offending without words*. San Francisco, CA: Chronicle Books.

Link, M. (2010, July 26). Dangerous body language abroad. *AOL Travel*. Retrieved from http://news.travel.aol.com/2010/07/26/dangerous-body-language-abroad/.

Lu, M. (1998). Meeting the challenge of designing multimedia for an international audience. *Information Technology in Education and Training*, *35*(4), 272–274. doi: 10.1080/09523 98980350409.

MacLeod, S. (2001, June 24). The life and death of Kevin Carter. *Time.com*. Retrieved from http://content.time.com/time/magazine/article/0,9171,165071,00.html.

Martin, J. S., & Chaney, L. H. (2006). *Global business etiquette: A guide to international communication and customs*. Westport, CT: Praeger.

Morrison, T., & Conaway, W. A. (2006). *Kiss, bow, or shake hands* (2nd ed.). Avon, MA: Adams Media.

Quinn, B. (2012, October 1). Ikea apologises over removal of women from Saudi Arabia catalogue. *Guardian*. Retrieved from http://www.theguardian.com/world/2012/oct/02/ikea-apologises-removing-women-saudi-arabia-catalogue.

Ritter, K. (2012, October 1). Ikea deleted women from Saudi version of catalog. *Associated Press*. Retrieved from http://bigstory.ap.org/article/ikea-deleted-women-saudi-version-catalogue.

Roth, R. (2008, December 16). Bush shrugs off shoe attack. *CBSNews.com*. Retrieved from http://www.cbsnews.com/videos/bush-shrugs-off-shoe-attack/.

Smartling.com. (n.d.). *I've got your number: Negative meanings & numerical superstitions around the globe* [Infographic]. Retrieved from http://www.smartling.com/static/pdf/Smartling_Infographic_IveGotYourNumber.pdf

Starnes, R. (1997, June 25). Boycott threat forces Nike into recall. *The Ottawa Citizen*, p. A8.

Tanaka, S. (2013, September 5). A 13th-floor condo? No such luck. *Wall Street Journal*. Retrieved from http://online.wsj.com/news/articles/SB1000142412788732332490457904498343509225.

Wooten, A. (2011a, January 21). International business: Color meanings can be lost and found in translation. *Deseret News*. Retrieved from http://www.deseretnews.com/article/705364808/Color-meanings-can-be-lost-and-found-in-translation.html?pg=all.

Wooten, A. (2011b, August 5). International business: Marketers beware of using international flags in campaigns. *Deseret News*. Retrieved from http://www.deseretnews.com/article/705388697/Marketers-beware-of-using-international-flags-in-campaigns.html?pg=all.

Zeveloff, J. (2011, November 28). The United Arab Emirates is up in arms over this pair of Puma sneakers. *Business Insider*. Retrieved from http://www.businessinsider.com/puma-sneakers-flag-colors-uae-2011-11.

Zhu, P. (2010). Cross-cultural blunders in professional communication from a semantic perspective. *Journal of Technical Writing and Communication, 40*(2), 179–196. doi: 10.2190/TW.40.2.e.

6 Mastering the Fine Art of Storytelling in International Public Relations

There's an ancient grammar to story that opens our mental locks, and gives us the joy of story. A tablet computer is a bit like the clay tablet from 3000 BC or the printing press from 1450—a technology that is radically changing how we consume stories, without changing the fundamental elements of the stories themselves.

—Jonathan Gottschall, literary scholar

6.1 Introduction to Worldwide Storytelling Past and Present

The art of storytelling can be traced back to prehistoric times when cave paintings depicted hunting scenes; perhaps the hunter was promoting his prowess as a hunter for hire or just sharing his adventures. Storytelling is a universal craft. Tomb paintings in ancient Egypt illustrated the pharaoh's life and journey into the underworld. In China, the Song dynasty (960 to 1279) became the time when professional storytellers served as the "'university' of ordinary people" (Børdahl, n.d., para. 3) by sharing myths and legends with the public, whether in private homes or in the community's marketplace. Storytellers still thrive from the griots in West Africa who sing, dance, and recite stories to the Indonesian shadow puppeteers (as seen in Figure 6.1) who entertain residents and tourists alike. As noted in the quote at the opening of the chapter by Jonathan Gottschall (2013, para. 10), an American literary scholar, the craft of storytelling remains, but the methods in which we tell and share stories change. Tales and traditions still live on and many have come back to life in new forms of theater, cinema, television, games, and social media:

- The 650-plus tales of morality recorded in *Aesop's Fables* are attributed—and disputed by others—to a real person, Aesop, a slave and storyteller from ancient Greece. You may recall the fable of the boastful hare that believes he has no worries winning a race against his contender, the slow and steady tortoise.
- For 1,001 nights, Scheherazade, a legendary sultana, discovered that storytelling was the only way to spare her life as the newlywed of an embittered Persian sultan. Angered by his unfaithful first wife, the sultan had her executed and then developed a habit of marrying a virgin at night and ending her life the next day. Scheherazade regaled her husband with cliffhanger stories about 9th-century life in Baghdad and other

Figure 6.1—JAVANESE PERFORMANCE PRESENTS THE STORY OF RAMAYANA AND MAHABHARATA IN WAYANG KULIT (SHADOW PUPPETRY) AT THE SONOBUDOYO MUSEUM, IN YOGYAKARTA, INDONESIA. Source: © Aleksandar Todorovic/Shutterstock.com.

parts of the Middle East, ensuring that he would put off the execution to hear more the next day. Her *Arabian Nights* stories brought to life magic lamps, flying carpets, and such colorful figures as Aladdin, Ali Baba, and Sinbad the Sailor.

- In Britain and Ireland, bards were professional storytellers or poets-for-hire, many of whom regaled the aristocracy with tales of their patron's feats past and present and their illustrious family members. Shakespeare became known as the "Bard of Avon."

- Written story tales became popular in the 17th century when Charles Perrault in France wrote *The Tales of Mother Goose*, bringing to life "Puss in Boots," "Sleeping Beauty," "Little Red Riding Hood," and "Cinderella," among others. In Germany in the early 19th century, Jacob and Wilhelm Grimm, known as the Brothers Grimm, collected and adapted story tales from Perrault and many others. "Rapunzel," "Hansel and Gretel," and "The Frog Prince" are just a few examples. While in Denmark during the same century, Hans Christian Andersen immortalized such stories as "The Little Mermaid," "The Ugly Duckling," and "The Snow Queen" (which was adapted by Disney for its 3D animated film, *Frozen*, in 2013; see Figure 6.2).

Public relations practitioners serve as contemporary storytellers, sharing the narratives of companies, governments, nonprofits, and personalities through multimedia. Professionals in the field have been called flacks and spin doctors. The word "**flack**" originally had no pejorative connotations. *Variety*, the U.S. entertainment industry publication, coined the term to refer to a person practicing public relations in the 1930s, in homage to Gene Flack, who was a well-respected movie publicist (Edson, 2006; Pedersen, 1999). Have you ever heard the expression: "that's just PR"? This expression stands for making exaggerations, distorting or hiding the truth, or putting lipstick on a pig.

Being an effective **storyteller in public relations** requires creativity, research, and ethical behavior; high-quality stories must be truthful and devoid of meaningless hype. The word **story** in this context refers to a nonfictional account of events, information about a particular topic, or news of interest to the media. Public relations professionals still share story ideas with traditional media to spread in print and electronic media. However, they no longer have to rely exclusively on their story ideas being vetted by editors of newspapers or magazines

Figure 6.2—WORLD PREMIERE OF WALT DISNEY ANIMATION STUDIOS' *FROZEN* IN LOS ANGELES. Source: © Joe Seer/Shutterstock.com.

or producers of radio and television programs. Public relations practitioners can craft stories of their own on the Web, which is like a virtual street corner for the storyteller, trying to engage busy and distracted passers-by to stop and listen. Practitioners now have more opportunity to share stories on social media, portable media players, or smartphones. Storytelling today has become "*the* universal human currency, now giving unprecedented circulation and impact through the social web" (Mighall, 2013, para. 6).

Stories are an integral part of our daily life—they are what we share with our friends, families, colleagues, or classmates. The content may cover what is happening in our personal lives; current events about our company, university, community, country, or other parts of the globe; entertainment fantasies and recaps of what we read in literature or see on film, TV, or the Web; or visions and dreams about the future. Videos, images, and words can go viral on the Web, considered the "virtual water coolers" of personal and business lore, where people spread gossip and share news.

Storytelling is a particularly popular topic in marketing, advertising, and public relations. It is important to understand the differences between the verbs "convince" and "persuade." I could most likely convince you that smoking is dangerous to your health by sharing research and statistics on smoking-related deaths and illnesses. Persuading you to stop smoking is much more difficult, requiring you to act and make a change, one that may take great effort. What could be the trigger to persuade you to give up smoking? Perhaps I could share a story about someone who once lived a healthy, vibrant life and who is now suffering with an advanced form of cancer. I could videotape this person telling his or her story or share before-and-after images—or I can introduce you to the once-healthy-smoker at the hospice. This personal approach could provide greater emotional appeal and power to be unforgettable. The not-yet-ill smoker now may be more receptive to information on cessation treatment programs from health organizations.

Screenwriting coach Robert McKee (Fryer, 2003) argues that beyond the use of conventional rhetoric—an intellectual approach traditionally using statistics, facts, and authoritative sources—that the more compelling way to persuade people "is by uniting an idea with an emotion" (para. 6) through storytelling. He advises writers to give up the lifeless lists and, instead, tell creative and imaginative stories that arouse emotions.

Screenwriter Jeffrey Hirschberg gives this advice as one of his "laws of great storytelling": "assume everyone has ADD" (2009, p. 224). Attention-deficit disorder seems to be endemic, so this principle particularly applies to public relations writers, competing to attract preoccupied audiences who are being courted by so many other brands, products, services, and causes. Think about what stories from social or traditional media, books, plays, or films that struck you as memorable; look at what qualities those stories conveyed to make you pay attention.

Dr. Paul Zak, a neuroeconomics scientist at Claremont Graduate University, has been studying the neurobiology of narrative by monitoring the neural activity of hundreds of people who viewed a simple narrative in public service announcements that followed the **dramatic arc** created by the 19th-century novelist and critic Gustav Freytag—exposition, rising action, climax, falling action, and dénouement (see Exhibit 6.1). Dr. Zak discovered that these dramatic stories evoked empathetic emotional responses associated with brain responses, namely **oxytocin**, which he dubbed the "moral molecule," resulting in action by the participants who actually donated money and gifts to the charity after watching its public service announcements (Zak, 2013).

Exhibit 6.1—FREYTAG'S DRAMATIC STORYTELLING SEQUENCES.

Sequences	Characteristics
Exposition	Inciting moment: Introduction of the story that explains the major characters, the setting, and the overall situation, as well as narrative tension
Complication	Rising action: Events and challenges the protagonist(s) encountered that lead up to the next sequence
Climax	Turning point: Considered the peak of the story
Reversal	Falling action: Events happening after the climax
Dénouement	Moment of release/conclusion: Wrap up of the story and resolutions

6.2 Storytelling in the Global Digital Era

Storytelling is a particularly important feature in public relations writing. This section examines five different approaches to storytelling in public relations:

- **Make It Real**—tell stories about real people, whether dead or living, to provide a personal connection with causes, products, and services.
- **Show Us the Possibilities**—craft stories that illustrate how to improve our lives and make the unfamiliar more familiar.
- **Engage Our Senses**—develop stories that inspire and excite the senses, thereby encouraging the reader or viewer to become immersed with the experience.
- **Seek Our Participation**—create stories that engage us to act or react with a brand, company, nonprofit, or personality.
- **Make the Story Timely**—weave stories that are in sync with the seasons, holidays, life passages, or opportunistic occasions.

6.2.1 Make It Real: Tell Stories about People or Animals

The protagonists of your stories could be people deceased or living—or even animals. Have you ever read fundraising appeals from nonprofits? Appeals from animal shelters usually tell the story of an abused or neglected animal that was rescued, restored to good health, and adopted by a loving family. An illness that people may have no familiarity with becomes real with a story of a person suffering with that illness, thereby helping one form a personal, relatable connection beyond statistics. The joys or tragedies we read about or follow on the Internet become more powerful when we see a face of someone affected by the situation.

Finding real protagonists for stories may require a combination of identifying the obvious and sleuthing for the less obvious. You also need to think about your audiences and ask yourself who they would relate to. You may need to identify people from different walks of life and countries—local heroes, celebrities, public opinion leaders, company executives and staff, customers, volunteers, donors, and other people who can spread voices globally or be customized locally.

A CEO's or celebrity's involvement with a social cause or charity can seem contrived if that person exudes no real passion or genuine interest. One would not question the involvement of a CEO who lost a child to a disease when that executive becomes involved with raising funds to combat that disease. The situation becomes more poignant than just supporting any cause.

Many organizations tell stories about their founders or top-level people. Not all organizations are headed by the most dynamic people, although they may be quite accomplished in managing the business or nonprofit. Of course, there are many dynamic founders past and present. Can you think of charismatic and interesting entrepreneurs? Richard Branson, Steve Jobs, Henry Ford, and Coco Chanel are just a few examples. Let's look at Chanel (1883–1971), whose legacy as a fashion icon and her company thrive today. Her widely disseminated quote still has meaning: "Fashion fades, only style remains the same." Chanel's life story has drama:

Figure 6.3—ACTRESS AUDREY TAUTOU AT THE LOS ANGELES PREMIERE OF *COCO BEFORE CHANEL.* Source: © s_bukley/Shutterstock.com.

starting as an orphan with no advantages to succeeding as an innovator of 20th-century fashion, whose fashion, fragrance, makeup, and accessories remain popular today. If you have ever seen photographs of Chanel or the 2009 biopic film (see Figure 6.3), you most likely will be able to recall vividly her distinctive appearance and personality.

Success stories of founders are more interesting when they include conflict and challenges that were overcome. Frankly, perfection can be painfully dull—and some organizations may not be willing to paint anything but a perfect picture. Conveying a more realistic approach does not mean outlining flaws. The story can show the process of innovation and trial-and-error research until a better solution is uncovered, the virtue of optimism when naysayers expressed doubts, and the ups and downs of the journey.

What type of stories could you develop about the founder or leader of a company or a nonprofit? The best way to start is by conducting secondary research. Look at all aspects of his or her life. Find out what stories have been told in traditional media and on the Web. See if the person has presented speeches or written articles, books, blogs, or white papers. Look at the person's curriculum vitae. Be completely prepared with insightful questions before you invest the time in interviewing the person. Understand which audiences you want to reach and in what types of forums, whether in traditional media and social media or in bylined articles or speaking engagements. Story ideas could cover the following areas:

- Inspiration for starting the company or nonprofit—what sparked the idea, what was the process for bringing the idea to life, and what lessons were learned? If the person is not the original founder, you can find out more about the legacy of the founder, the shared vision, and the organization's evolution since it was established.
- Management philosophy—what is the person's leadership style and his or her opinions on recruiting and retaining talent in the headquarters and at offices worldwide?
- Philanthropy—what is the rationale for supporting different causes, the person's direct involvement, and future goals?
- Accomplishments—which ones are deemed the proudest and which ones have yet to be achieved?
- Personal dimensions—what aspects of the person's personal life does he or she want to share? Stories can range considerably on one's hobbies, athletic or recreational pursuits, cultural interests, religious involvement, community service, or family life.

Writers also can look beyond the executive offices when identifying storytellers within a company. Although the public relations executives for a luxury hotel company generated positive stories about its founder, they found fresh opportunities when thinking beyond the corporate offices. For example, they looked at the people who look after the guests for new stories (see Figure 6.4):

- The head housekeeper provided spring cleaning tips on how to maintain streak-free windows, expunge dust bunnies from under furniture, and freshen up your home's closets, pantries, and public spaces.
- The shoeshine expert responsible for polishing over 100 shoes nightly explained how to care for your shoes and keep a perfect shine.
- The valet who really understands how to fold different fabrics shared suitcase packing advice on how to minimize wrinkled clothes.
- The floral designer with experience in staging celebrity-studded events showed how to buy cut flowers and make impressive floral centerpieces for in-home entertaining.

- The concierge staff explained how to use their services before, during, and after your trips, including whimsical stories about how they found obscure gifts, arranged surprise marriage proposals, and organized last-minute parties for their guests.
- The chef at a resort provided recipes for picnicking in hot weather locales, while demonstrating how to pack picnic baskets for elegant al fresco dining.
- The doorman at a prominent urban hotel shared stories about his multi-decade career of welcoming famous and not-so-famous people.

Let us look at a few examples of high-quality storytelling from employees, volunteers, and even an advertising character.

Figure 6.4—EMPLOYEES OF ALL LEVELS, WHETHER IN FRONT OR BEHIND-THE-SCENES OF A COMPANY, CAN TELL COMPELLING STORIES. Source: © stockyimages/Shutterstock.com.

The multinational information technology company **Hewlett-Packard** launched its annual Global Wellness Challenge in 2011, which engaged the participation of its workforce in nearly 90 countries on a voluntary 12-week health and fitness initiative. This internal communications campaign included telling "Winning with Wellness Heroes" stories of employees of all levels, not just the CEO and senior management. The promotional material also showed real people who were actual employees, not just fit and lean models (Public Relations Society of America, 2012a).

charity: water, a nonprofit dedicated to helping developing nations have access to clean, safe water, explains its accomplishments by sharing stories about the people of all ages who directly benefit by these sustainable, community-built projects. Its website has a "stories" tab organized by countries, with each story supported by photographs. Here is an excerpt from "Will the Beautiful Women of the World Please Stand Up" (Straw, n.d.), a story about a woman in Uganda and her enthusiasm about the community's new freshwater well, as told by a charity: water project water manager:

> "I am happy now," Helen beamed. "I have time to eat, my children can go to school. And I can even work in my garden, take a shower and then come back for more water if I want! I am bathing so well."
>
> A few of the men chuckled to hear a woman talk about bathing. But all I noticed was Helen's glowing face, the fresh flowers in her hair, and the lovely green dress she wore for special occasions. Touching her forearm, I replied, "Well, you look great."
>
> "Yes," she paused. Placing both hands on my shoulders and smiling, she said, "Now, I am beautiful." (paras. 10–12)

Willis Group, a global risk advisor, insurance and reinsurance broker based in London, undertook its Willis Resilience Expedition to the South Pole to showcase the company's analytical, technological, and scientific capabilities and credentials. The expedition illustrated human endurance and was led by Parker Liautaud, a 19-year-old explorer and Yale University student with experience leading three expeditions to the North Pole. Liautaud accomplished the fastest-ever walk from the edge of Antarctica to the South Pole and became the youngest person to reach both poles on foot (Willis Group, 2013). His 400-mile trek was captured on video and available for viewing on the company's website, as well as on dedicated social media channels and a series of television shows. Willis Group's Chief Communications Officer Josh King explained the resilience theme:

> More people summit Mount Everest every year than have ever touched the South Pole in human history, and yet conditions there can advance our ability to build greater resilience for a risky world. We are proud to enable Parker to conduct his important research and share his unfolding journey, day-by-day, with those on every continent whose lives, businesses and organizations are affected by these issues and who are fascinated by the extraordinary human endeavor Parker is undertaking. (Willis Group, 2013, para. 9)

Old Spice, a line of male grooming products established in 1938, needed to revitalize its products to appeal to a younger audience in the U.S. Part of its rebranding campaign starred Isaiah Mustafa (see Figure 6.5), an American actor and former National Football League athlete, in a series of television advertisements. "The Man Your Man Could Smell Like" was the first ad that showed Mustafa with a towel wrapped around his waist in a steamy bathroom, telling ladies how their man could not only smell like a man, but their man also could treat the ladies like a man. The imagery quickly segued from a bathroom to a boat, with Mustafa holding an opened oyster with two tickets "to the thing you love" that morphed to diamonds and then to the product, and concluded with Mustafa sitting on a horse at a beach.

Old Spice's public relations campaign complemented the advertisements by encouraging consumers to post questions on Twitter and Facebook for the "Old Spice Guy" to personally answer. Over a three-day period, Mustafa starred in nearly 200 personalized YouTube video responses to consumers, as well as to such celebrities as Ashton Kutcher and Alyssa Milano. The setting was the opening scene of the commercial: a tiled bathroom with Mustafa, wearing a towel around his waist, standing in front of the shower, along with a few props. Mustafa also appeared on major television programs and was interviewed by leading U.S. media outlets, serving as a charming Old Spice spokesperson who told stories about the making of the commercials and conveyed messages about the brand. In an interview in *Newsweek* (Ellison, 2010), Mustafa said:

> The character says a lot of things that men would want to say, but also wouldn't want to say. And he says a lot of things that women would want to hear, or what we think women want to hear. But he's very tongue-in-cheek. He knows he's full of, you know, whatever. But he also knows he can get away with it. He's one of those guys in the mold of an Indiana Jones or James Bond, which you don't see much anymore. (para. 3)

A tribute to a successful campaign is parody. A spoof aired on *Sesame Street*, a popular children's television program in the U.S.; a trailer parody ran in movie theaters promoting *Puss in Boots*, a computer-animated film produced by DreamWorks in 2011; and everyday people created YouTube posts. Did this rejuvenate Old Spice? The campaign definitely did enhance the brand, resulting in a 107% spike in sales and more than 279 million viewers watched Mustafa's YouTube responses, "just shy of the viewership of two and a half Super Bowls" (Summers, 2012, para. 14). For non-football fans, the Super Bowl is the annual championship of the National Football League in the U.S. Considered the most viewed television program, the Super Bowl also has become a sports extravaganza for advertising, not just for showcasing the most expensive advertisements, but for being an annual forum for reviews, commentary, and rankings on the advertisements themselves.

Animals also can be powerful protagonists in stories, but be careful that certain animals may not have universal appeal. Chapter 5 covers cross-cultural issues about animals. **FedEx** continues to illustrate its shipping capabilities more dramatically with stories about transporting exotic animals—pandas, elephants, eagles, penguins, and beluga whales—safely to zoos and nature reserves around the world.

"Move over, Cannes, Minneapolis might just be home to the greatest film festival ever" was the description in the Huffington Post about a new type of film festival: one that is not about bipeds, instead it took advantage of an Internet trend ("Internet cat video film festival," 2012, para. 1). CBS News (Blackstone, 2013) reported that 15% of all Internet videos center on cats. A few of the Internet cat sensations on YouTube have drawn millions of viewers, including Maru, a Scottish Fold cat from Japan, with a yen for jumping into boxes; Grumpy, a sour-faced Snowshoe Siamese from Arizona; and Henri the existential cat, a long-haired Tuxedo from Seattle, famous in French-language videos (subtitled in English). The **Walker Art Center** in Minneapolis took advantage of this craze and launched its first Internet Cat

Figure 6.5—ISAIAH MUSTAFA (LEFT) AND FABIO AT A PUBLIC APPEARANCE TO PROMOTE THE EPIC OLD SPICE CHALLENGE IN LOS ANGELES. Source: © Helga Esteb/Shutterstock.com.

Video Festival in 2012 (see logo in Figure 6.6), receiving more than 10,000 submissions from around the world. In a news release, the Walker Art Center (2014) provided more background:

> In August 2012, the Walker Art Center planned a small experiment as part of its outdoor summer programming on Open Field, the greenspace adjacent to the building. What if there was an evening program dedicated to the internet phenomenon of cat videos? Would anyone come to watch videos what they could easily view with a few clicks at home or work? How would this solo hobby translate to a public setting? Word of the program quickly spread internationally via social media and the press including coverage as varied as the *New York Times*, the BBC, Japanese television, Australian talk shows, Brazilian newspapers, CNN, NPR, the *Wall Street Journal, Cat Fancy, Slate, Time, CHEEZburger*, and many more. The result was 10,000 people gathered on Open Field enjoying the first Internet Cat Video Festival—together. (para. 9)

The first Golden Kitty award went to "Henri 2: Paw de Deux" and "The Original Grumpy Cat" won the following year. Both of these cats have become celebrities (see Figure 6.7 of Grumpy Cat at the MTV Movie Awards).

Figure 6.6—LOGO OF THE INTERNET CAT VIDEO FESTIVAL HELD AT THE WALKER ART CENTER IN MINNEAPOLIS, MINNESOTA. Source: Courtesy of the Walker Art Center.

Figure 6.7—GRUMPY CAT AT THE 2014 MTV MOVIE AWARDS AT THE NOKIA THEATRE LA LIVE. Source: © Jaguar PS/Shutterstock.com

When I was representing an international airline, our account team uncovered a small news item in a French newspaper about a wayward American cat from the Midwest that became an unexpected stowaway in a cargo container of paper shipped to a company in France. Starving and thirsty, Emily the cat endured three weeks in a container until a surprised worker discovered the tabby wearing a collar with an identification tag containing the telephone number of the cat's veterinarian. While my agency staff and I were working out logistics with our airline client about bringing the cat back home, **Continental Airlines** had already made arrangements to provide free business class airfare to the tabby, along with an airline escort, and reunite the cat with her family in Wisconsin. The airline held press conferences at airports in France and the U.S., distributed a news release, and pitched stories to media on both sides of the Atlantic, resulting in positive and entertaining human interest stories.

6.2.2 Show Us the Possibilities

Explaining benefits, instead of listing features of a product or service, makes a huge difference in bringing stories to life. Show people—whether they are customers, investors, volunteers, or donors—the possibilities in what the product, service, or cause can do for them. Messages can illustrate how to make your life better in many dimensions—how to make you smarter and more attractive; how to save you money; how to renovate your house or apartment; how to have a wonderful trip or a great meal; how to find a better job; how to help others in need; or how to benefit from whatever is of appeal.

Shoes worn by a celebrity you admire can look more desirable all of a sudden. Fashion magazines showcase pricey haute couture fashion or less costly brands for the same look. Fashion, cosmetics, home décor, and other products can come alive with before-and-after stories and images. Service-related stories also can showcase before-and-after transformations from the poorly behaved dog to the well-trained pet thanks to the pet trainer, the undisciplined spender to master saver with the help of the financial consultant, or the out-of-shape couch potato to svelte marathon runner with the support of a private trainer at the fitness center.

Stories also can convey qualities about the brand. The **Red Bull** Stratos project created by Red Bull, the Austrian-based energy drink, dramatically illustrated "energy" with a record-breaking feat. In 2012, Austrian Felix Baumgartner jumped from the highest manned balloon ascent of 128,177.5 feet (39,068.5 meters) in just 4 minutes and 20 seconds, becoming the first person to break the speed of sound in freefall, without the protection of propulsion or a vehicle, while breaking eight world records for maximum vertical speed, exit (jump) altitude, and vertical distance of freefall, along with others (Sampiero, 2013). The event also broke records as the most-watched live webcast through 280 digital partners, which drew 52 million Web views, when people watched Baumgartner leap from the capsule in space and land on his feet back on Earth (Zmuda, 2013). In addition, the Red Bull Stratos event aired on nearly 80 TV stations in 50 countries, resulting in an increase of worldwide sales of its energy drink by 13% over the previous year (Zmuda, 2013). Red Bull Media House received an Emmy award for "Outstanding New Approaches—Sports Event Coverage."

In addition, Red Bull has been involved with numerous airplane, motorcar, motorcyle, and yacht races worldwide, which emphasize the brand's endurance and strength themes (see Figure 6.8).

Stories can spark debates and share emotional connections with brands. Jonah Sachs (2013), CEO of a branding agency and author, explained how "stories act like cultural DNA—tiny packets of information that build tribes and societies. The stories we love most tell us

Figure 6.8—SEBASTIAN VETTEL RACING IN HIS RED BULL RACING CAR DURING 2012 FORMULA 1 SINGTEL SINGAPORE GRAND PRIX IN SINGAPORE.
Source: © Jordan Tan/Shutterstock.com.

what people like us value, what they don't, and what they want for the future" (para. 4). Sachs described four steps in myth making for a brand, using the **Dove** Campaign for Real Beauty as an example.

> Explanation: Society makes women believe they're less beautiful than they are.
> Meaning: "You are more beautiful than you think"
> Story: Dove shows, not tells, these points through people its audience can relate to.
> Ritual: Sharing the message becomes an act of defiance. (paras. 8–11)

By creating a dialogue about perceptions of beauty and idealized images in the media and advertising, the Dove Campaign for Real Beauty differentiated Dove's hair and skin care products from the competition. The campaign triggered a vibrant discussion that resulted in stories in traditional media and commentary on social media. The campaign theme stemmed from research conducted in 10 countries about women's attitudes about their appearance. The findings revealed that only 2% of women describe themselves as "beautiful" and just 13% expressed satisfaction with their body weight and shape, while 75% strongly agreed that women could be more accurately portrayed in advertisements and in the media (Public Relations Society of America, 2006).

Any product no matter how utilitarian can become more dynamic with storytelling. **Fairy Liquid** dish-washing products, a Procter & Gamble line that originated in the U.K., tell stories "around virtues, such as mildness and domestic harmony" (Bacon, 2013, para. 20). Fairy's website and social media cover family recipes, family rituals, such as bedtime stories, and household cleaning solutions and tips. This storytelling strategy resulted in Fairy being ranked

Exhibit 6.2—AESOP'S BRAND STORYTELLING SURVEY CRITERIA. Source: Aesop. (2014). *The brand storytelling survey results 2014*. Retrieved from http://aesopagency.com/wp-content/uploads/2014/07/Aesop-Storytelling-survey-2014.pdf.

Aesop, a brand communications agency based in London, launched an annual survey on the U.K.'s leading storytelling brands, asking consumers to identify brands based on the following nine storytelling elements:

1. Which of these brands do you consider to have a unique character/personality?
2. Which of these brands have a clear opinion?
3. Which of these brands has vision or purpose?
4. Which of these brands are you intrigued to know what they'll do next?
5. Which of these brands tell a credible story?
6. Which of these brands create their own world?
7. Which of these brands produce content you want to share or talk about?
8. Which of these brands are entertaining?
9 Which of these brands are memorable?

as one of the top 10 storytelling brands in the U.K. within the cosmetics, toiletries, and household category in a poll conducted by Aesop, a London-based brand and communications agency. See Exhibit 6.2 for a list of the nine criteria examined in the brand storytelling survey. These elements also could be useful in crafting stories for a public relations campaign.

Make the unfamiliar familiar also can mean make the scary less so. What do you think of bats, the only mammals that truly fly? The **Australian Bat Clinic & Wildlife Trauma Centre** in South East Queensland has told stories effectively about rescuing orphaned baby bats from a flood and a heat wave, and how their volunteers serve as surrogate mothers to baby bats. The supporting visual images and video clips truly enhance the stories. Have you even seen baby bats wrapped up in pastel colored blankets (see Figure 6.9) or videos of volunteers petting and feeding them? "Prepare to have your opinion about bats changed forever" ("Lil' Drac," 2011) was the first line of a Huffington Post story about a video of an orphaned fruit bat. Positive commentary spread in mainstream media, blogs, and social media about the bats, with many people expressing surprise about the bats' visual charm while spreading educational messages about the importance of bats in our ecosystem. The Australian Bat Clinic's mission seems to be fulfilled:

> To provide the best practices medical care to all species of sick, injured, and orphaned Bats. To create an environment that educates and inspires the general public to accept Bats and other native fauna as part of our lives. (Australian Bat Clinic, 2014, para. 1)

6.2.3 Engage Our Senses

Stories have the power to provoke imagery that evokes the senses, helping the reader actually see, hear, smell, touch, or taste something. See Exhibit 6.3 for an overview of the seven types of imagery that relate to the senses. Can you think of stories that were so vivid they transported you to a place you could walk through and enjoy the scenery, listen to the people and sounds, smell the indoor and outdoor spaces, feel the rain or snow, or savor a dessert and sip a drink?

Figure 6.9—RESCUED BABY BATS AT THE AUSTRALIAN BAT CLINIC & WILDLIFE TRAUMA CENTRE. Source: Photo by Luke Marsden/Newspix.

Stories can affect the way we feel about something and someone. Are the stories full of twists and surprises, leaving cliffhangers that spark desire for us to find out more? Or are the stories so evocative that you can visualize a new environment, whether you are thinking about buying paint or new furniture to spruce up your apartment or booking a trip to a place you have been yearning to visit?

Let us look at travel for a moment. Travel is not a product you can pick up and examine and buy and bring home. Travel truly requires activating the senses as a guide in selecting the place to go for a vacation or celebrate a special occasion, such as a honeymoon, an anniversary, or a family reunion. Logistical considerations include how much time you can spare and when you can travel, how much money you have to spend, and the needs of others you may be traveling with. After you have the logistics in place, you then have the difficult choice: where to go?

Exhibit 6.3—SEVEN TYPES OF IMAGERY.

Evocative language can help the reader experience different sensations through the following types of imagery:

Type of Imagery	Description
Visual	Representation of the sense of sight—images, shapes, colors, tones, brightness, and descriptions that help people see the setting
Auditory	Representation of the sense of hearing—sounds and pitches from whispers to howls and from rustling to screeching
Olfactory	Representation of the sense of smell—odors from such pleasant aromas as perfume scents or cakes in the oven to such unpleasant smells as mildew and rotten garbage
Gustatory	Representation of the sense of taste—from bland and mild to hot and spicy, and from sweet to bitter
Tactile	Representation of the sense of touch—from feeling softness, such as silk, to hardness, such as metal, or from cold to hot
Organic	Representation of personal experiences and internal sensations, such as what someone feels, whether hunger, fear, or exhaustion
Kinesthetic	Representation of a physical action, such as movement, or a natural bodily function, such as a pulse or a breath

Try Exercise 6.1 in which you are the public relations executive for a tourist board in your city, town, or country—or select a location you have firsthand experience in. The next step is to identify potential travelers that your tourist board aims to attract. Think about different story ideas that would evoke the senses. Consider content you could share in different media—such as story ideas to pitch to journalists and bloggers, as well as stories you could post on the tourist board's website and social media. Determine at least one story angle per topic and think of topics that have strong sensual appeal.

I have outlined examples of story ideas based on Ithaca, New York, a college town in upstate New York's Finger Lakes region, where I currently live. My target audience is the urban drive market, focusing on young college-educated professionals residing in the cities of Rochester, New York, and Philadelphia, who are seeking affordable getaways.

Food and Beverages:
- Ithaca has more restaurants per capita than New York City. This upstate New York college town is home to people from across the U.S. and around the globe who come here to teach, study, and live. You can share nachos, sushi, tacos, antipasti, dim sum, Buffalo wings, hummus platters, or local cheese plates—at affordable prices too.
- Your urban greengrocers sell products that were grown at the farms in and nearby Ithaca. You can pluck the freshest bounty during the growing season at U-pick farms and orchards for fruits and vegetables. Chefs at many of the local restaurants also feature fresh produce on their menus.

Exercise 6.1

Creative Thinking: Sensory Story Ideas for a Travel Destination

You are a public relations executive and your client, a tourist board (in your city or pick another place that you know well), needs your help in developing story angles that would appeal to potential travelers. You'll need to identify the most desirable travelers—where they are from (within driving distance or from another country) and what type (budget or luxury travelers, honeymooners, or families; or what other special interests do they share). Brainstorm story ideas evoking different senses that you could share with journalists or bloggers, as well as post on the tourist board's website and social media. What stories could you develop about the following themes relevant to the location you have selected?

1. Food and beverages in your selected area—such as restaurants, markets, farms, wineries, or distilleries.
2. Performing or visual arts—dance, music, theater, museums, galleries, or art studios.
3. Festivals—annual events, fairs, or special events that celebrate the area's history, agriculture, sports and recreation, arts and culture, or seasonal attributes.
4. Sightseeing—the great outdoors, historic architecture, the urban life, or other attractions.
5. Fun trivia—unusual attributes; whether facts, history, or folklore about famous people, innovations, or events.

- Take the Cayuga Lake Wine Trail—the first and oldest one in America—and enjoy tastings from more than 15 wineries, many with views of Cayuga Lake. Some call the Finger Lakes wine region the "Napa Valley of the East," with its wineries receiving over 5,300 national and international wine-related medals. Don't worry about drinking and driving; trolley vans and private limousines can whisk people from vineyard to vineyard.

Performing or Visual Arts:
- Free is the operative word here—you can listen to live music almost every night at bars and restaurants, and enjoy outdoors concerts in parks and plazas during the summer and at the colleges throughout the semester. The Greater Ithaca Art Trail allows you to visit about 50 different artists in their studios where you can see them at work, look at their latest creations, and talk to them about their inspirations and creative energy.

Festivals:
- Have you seen a Volvo ballet? Yes, one in which the cars actually wear tutus. You can see the Volvo dancers parade by during the annual four-day Ithaca Festival held in early summer, which also celebrates the community's artists, poets, dancers, and musicians in a place called "10 square miles surrounded by reality" for its liberal, sustainable vibe.

Sightseeing:
- "Ithaca is gorges" is the tourist board's slogan—and for good reason. You can see more than 100 gorgeous gorges within 10 miles of downtown. Nearby 215-foot-high Taughannock Falls (see Figure 6.10) is taller than Niagara Falls. You can even swim in some of the gorges and hike on zero-grade paths or choose steeper trails.

Fun Trivia:
- Ithaca is the official birthplace of the ice cream sundae. The inventors—a team effort by a local fountain owner and a reverend—discovered how sensational ice cream can be when topped off with syrup, whipped cream, and a cherry back on a Sunday in 1892. The city is also home to Purity, a local ice cream company and parlor, serving sundaes with brownies and other delectable flavors.

Figure 6.10—TAUGHANNOCK FALLS, A WATERFALL NEAR ITHACA, N.Y.
Source: © Nicholas Piccillo/Shutterstock.com.

Another strategy to inspire the senses positively is to create events, which can serve as a creative platform to tell your story through words and visual imagery. Here are two examples from a fashion company and a beverage manufacturer:

Burberry, the British luxury fashion house, created theatrical events to tell its brand story with consumers in Shanghai, emphasizing its British heritage with multimedia sets of backdrops of scenes from London, as well as from Shanghai, with music, models, and fashion. Burberry's CEO explained in an interview in *The Business of Fashion*:

> Tonight language doesn't matter—no matter where you are from, when you do something properly, people respond to that. It always surprises me how many people discover Burberry through our music projects for example. It's important to keep innovating with your product and keep telling different stories with it. History and heritage is important to have as a foundation, but you have to build on top of that to keep it moving forward. Technology helps us do that. (Harilela, 2014, para. 4)

With the help of computer-generated simulations, marketers of **Pepsi Max** transformed the wait for commuters at a London bus shelter into a surprising and thrilling experience. The bus riders were treated to a fantastic world when they looked at the poster promoting the Pepsi Max "unbelievable" campaign, where a hidden camera brought the theme to life with images of crashing meteors, flying spaceships, a lion at large, a tentacled monster emerging from the manhole, and a giant robot with laser-beam eyes (see Figure 6.11). The creative talent behind the brand also created a "PepsiMax Presents Unbelievable Bus Shelter" YouTube clip that showed how the bus stop was set up by technicians and the subsequent reactions of commuters and passers-by enjoying the "end of the world" adventure. The video clip has attracted more than 7 million views (as of June 2015). The general manager at a company specializing in augmented reality discussed the Pepsi Max campaign in an article in *Mobile Marketing*:

> "This is a great example of how technologies like augmented reality offer a highly memorable and captivating experience," said Annie Weinberger, general manager of Aurasma at HP Autonomy, San Francisco. "No one who was at the bus stop that day will forget that any time soon."
>
> "Augmented reality—whether mobile or stationary like this example—helps brands cut through the noise to deliver a memorable experience," she said. (Tode, 2014, paras. 14–15)

6.2.4 Seek Our Participation

David Meerman Scott (2013), an author of books on marketing and public relations, shared an important point: "People want participation, not propaganda" (p. 36). Events and social media offer public relations practitioners the chance to engage the consumer or advocate by encouraging them to become active participants with the brand, sharing their experiences, voicing their opinions, voting and ranking content, doing something to help a cause, or testing their creativity by submitting videos, drawings, or writing samples.

You can engage consumers by personalizing the product itself. **Nutella**®, the hazelnut spread, celebrated its 50th anniversary by allowing its customers to customize their own labels on limited-edition jars of Nutella® in exchange for sharing their experiences with Nutella® hazelnut spread (see Figure 6.12). Fans in the U.K. and Ireland were invited to submit their stories in text, photo, or video to www.nutellastories.com. In addition, in Belgium, the Nutella® marketing team created a Facebook tab for fans to create their own jar labels. A Ferrero spokesperson explained the impetus of the "thank you" campaign (MacLeod, 2014):

Figure 6.11—PEPSIMAX PRESENTS THE "UNBELIEVABLE" BUS SHELTER IN LONDON WITH THE HELP OF AUGMENTED REALITY. Source: Courtesy of OMD Agency.

Nutella always elicits a strong response and its fans have a fantastic emotional connection to the product. When it came to celebrating the 50th anniversary, it seemed obvious to us that we should place the fans at the centre of our anniversary activities to thank them for their continued support of the brand. (para. 5)

Coca-Cola also got personal with customers through its "Share a Coke" campaign that was launched in Australia in 2011 and later exported to countries in Europe, Asia, South America, the Middle East, and the U.S. The campaign encouraged consumers to personalize Coca-Cola bottle labels physically and virtually with people's names (see Figure 6.13). Coca-Cola's managing director in the South Pacific said:

We are using the power of the first name in a playful and social way to remind people of those in their lives they may have lost touch with, or have yet to connect with.

This is the first time in its 125-year history that Coca-Cola has made such a major change to it [*sic*] packaging and the limited edition bottles are expected to fly off shelves as people search for their friend's [*sic*] names. (Coca-Cola Journey, 2013, paras. 3 and 4)

The "Share a Coke" Australia campaign won a series of competitive awards and resulted in a 7% increase in consumption by young adults, as well as more than 18.3 million media impressions and an increase of 870% traffic on Facebook and a spike of page likes by 39% (Grimes, 2013).

To dramatize living without shoes, **TOMS Shoes** began its "One Day Without Shoes" as an annual event in 2007 to encourage people to go barefoot for a brief moment, an hour, or a full day to serve as a platform to spark dialogue globally about poverty and to spread

Figure 6.12—"NUTELLA® 50 YEARS FULL OF STORIES" CAMPAIGN. Source: © Ferrero S.p.A.

Figure 6.13—2014 SHARE A COKE PROMOTION. Source: © bagwold/Shutterstock. com.

awareness about how a pair of shoes can give children access to schools and to better health. The event complements the company founder's "One for One" mission, in which every pair of shoes purchased results in a pair of shoes donated to a child in need. The "One for One" shoe giving model later expanded to each eyewear purchase, in which the company donates money to helping an individual restore his or her eyesight through surgery or prescription glasses, and coffee purchases, in which each bag sold provides a person in need with one week of clean water.

What's the most desirable thing anyone would want during a global economic recession? A great job was the answer from **Tourism Queensland**, Australia, when it launched its "Best Job in the World" campaign in 2009. The campaign's only advertisements for its "Island Caretaker" were classifieds in the employment section of major newspapers around the globe, a very affordable option. Quinn, a New York-based public relations agency, managed the U.S. part of the campaign, and placed the following 72-word ad in the *Wall Street Journal* (Seitel & Doorley, 2012):

THE BEST JOB IN THE WORLD

Island Caretaker

Islands of the Great Barrier Reef, Australia

Full-time, live-in position with flexible hours. AUD $150,000 for a six-month contract. Accommodation provided—luxury home on Hamilton Island, overlooking Australia's Great Barrier Reef. Responsibilities: Explore the islands and report back; clean the pool; feed the fish; collect the mail. Apply to Tourism Queensland at islandreefjob.com. Anyone can apply. (Refer to the terms and conditions at islandreefjob.com.)

(p. 31)

Job applicants were required to create a one-minute video on why they were the right candidate and post it on the tourist office's website. Tourism Queensland received nearly 35,000 video job applications from 197 countries (which is four more than the total number of member countries of the United Nations), while attracting over 8 million unique visits on its website with an average time spent of 8.25 minutes (Interactive Advertising Bureau, n.d.). The campaign featured three stages, with each phase attracting stories in traditional media, website engagement, and a social media dialogue worldwide: the global search for the candidate, the finalists in Australia, and the winner's experiences in Queensland that were documented in his weekly blog.

The next version of the campaign took place in 2013 and extended to "Best Jobs in the World," with six different positions, promoting the variety of potential working holiday experiences available to visitors throughout Australia: park ranger in Queensland, outback adventurer in the Northern Territory, taste master in Western Australia, lifestyle photographer in Victoria, chief funster in New South Wales, and wildlife caretaker in South Australia (see Figure 6.14). **Tourism Australia** received more than 330,000 applications from 196 countries (Tourism Australia, 2013). Ben Southall, the winner of the initial "Best Job in the World" competition, starred in a promotional video on the new "job offices" and also gave advice to applicants on the Queensland blog. Here is the opening of Southall's blog post that demonstrates his breezy conversational and entertaining writing style:

Most of you probably remember when Tourism Queensland launched the Best Job in the World campaign advertising the position of "Island Caretaker" here in Queensland. Well, I was the lucky sod who won!

At the time, I questioned if it was worth going to the effort of creating a video but look where it got me—a fun job in a new country and I found my sweetheart here too!

So if you're still twiddling your thumbs about whether to enter or not—stop procrastinating—you have to be in it to win it.

(Southall, 2013, paras. 1–3)

Dela, a Dutch funeral-insurance company, created a campaign that addressed a very sensitive topic of conversation for many people: death. "Why wait until it's too late? Say something wonderful today" was the campaign theme that encouraged people to share their feelings to loved ones before it is too late on its website. Selected stories also were adapted for the company's advertising. One of the judges of the Cannes Lions International Festival

Figure 6.14—EXAMPLES OF THREE JOB DESCRIPTIONS FROM AUSTRALIA'S BEST JOBS IN THE WORLD CAMPAIGN. Source: Courtesy of Tourism Australia.

of Creativity explained in an *AdvertisingAge* article why Dela won the media Grand Prix: "It checked all the boxes—it's very human, very measurable. And every piece builds toward the next . . . It brilliantly touched everyone's heart, and the results were fantastic" (Wentz, 2013, para. 4).

6.2.5 Make It Timely

Early in my career, my supervisor was an avid gardener and explained public relations planning in terms of the value of "planting perennials" that can be counted on to "bloom" and thrive during specific times every year with advance planning. Every season has perennials: the weather creates different demands for consumers to buy and do different things; and the holidays prompt people to buy gifts, decorate their homes, prepare different recipes, or entertain friends and family. Think of all the story opportunities you have to tell for each season—and how extensive they would be on a global scale due to different climates, religious celebrations, and secular holidays.

Many causes have declared months or days of celebration with consumer awareness campaigns and fundraising events within a country or multiple countries. October is **Breast Cancer Awareness Month** in the U.S. and in other parts of the globe, thereby educating people about detection and prevention while raising funds for a disease that knows no boundaries. According to the International Agency for Research on Cancer (2014), the year 2012 resulted in 14.1 million new cancer cases (excluding non-melanoma skin cancer), 8.2 million cancer deaths, and 32.6 million people living with cancer (within 5 years of diagnosis). Although the numbers alone illustrate the impact of the disease, many nonprofits tell stories of firsthand accounts by real people who have survived cancer to provide a more personal connection.

The food industry and other informal groups, primarily in the U.S., also have created their own thematic food-related days, weeks, or months. In the U.S., you could celebrate approximately 175 foods a year, with **Apple Week** being one of the early examples in 1904, which became Apple Month in the 1970s, and expanded to a three-month celebration in the 1990s (Severson, 2007). You can celebrate New Year's Day in the U.S. with **National Bloody Mary Day** and end the year with **National Vinegar Day** or **National Champagne Day**, according to Foodimentary.com. A few examples of global food holidays include the Vegan Society's **World Vegan Day** on November 1 (see Figure 6.15) and the North American Vegetarian Society's **World Vegetarian Day**, officially on October 1, which was endorsed by the International Vegetarian Union.

A popular resource on events is *Chase's Calendar of Events*, which was started by two American brothers, a journalist and a social scientist, back in 1957, with a 32-page edition. Today, the book is nearly 800 pages, with both print and digital editions, and contains background on many types of days, with some international content: astronomical phenomena (such as moon phases); religious observances (Christian, Jewish, Muslim, and Bahá'í faiths, as well as others); U.S. and international observances and civic holidays; special days, weeks, and months (such as Black History Month); U.S. presidential proclamations; events and festivals (U.S. and international); anniversaries (historic, biographic, and milestones); and birthdays today (living celebrities). People can submit an entry suggestion before mid-April for the next annual edition.

Other timely storytelling angles include milestones and anniversaries, as well as opportunistic ones that tie in a product, service, or cause to a current event or a popular art form, such as a movie. Passages of life from birth to death also offer provide fodder for stories, which would be of particular interest to insurance companies and financial institutions appealing to singles, newlyweds, parents, and retirees. Try Exercise 6.2 on creating story ideas for different life passages for a financial services company.

Timely campaigns can be opportunistic. *The Lord of the Rings* film trilogy followed by *The Hobbit* trilogy not only revitalized interest in J. R. R. Tolkien's books, but also sparked Tolkien tourism in New Zealand. The website of **Tourism New Zealand** promotes 10-day *Lord of the Rings* self-guided adventures and describes how tourists can visit Middle-earth

Figure 6.15—WORLD VEGAN DAY GRUNGE RUBBER STAMP. Source: © ducu59us/ Shutterstock.com.

Exercise 6.2

Creative Thinking: Telling Timely Stories about Life Passages

Your client is a local financial services and insurance company that wants you to develop timely story ideas to illustrate its range of services for people in different stages of their lives. Think about which time periods—such as specific seasons, national or religious holidays, or other occasions in your community—and thematic stories that would make the following current or prospective customers more aware of your client's service:

1. young single professionals joining the workforce;
2. newlyweds merging finances and saving for the immediate future;
3. first-time home buyers;
4. new parents planning for their children's education;
5. second home buyers or home owners undergoing renovations or taking out home equity loans; and
6. retirees looking at retirement saving options, as well as wills and estate planning.

and see over 150 locations. See Figure 6.16 of the Hobbiton Movie Set from *The Lord of the Rings* and *The Hobbit* film trilogies.

Another movie helped revitalize a 1980s craze. **Rubik's Cube**, the three-dimensional puzzle, played a supporting role in *The Pursuit of Happyness* in 2006; the most memorable scene was when the protagonist (played by actor Will Smith) solved the puzzle during a short cab ride scene, thereby impressing an important business contact who found the puzzle "impossible" and landing a job interview. Tyson Mao, a 22-year-old speed-cuber who also trained the actor to master the puzzle, was the spokesperson for a multimedia public relations campaign to rejuvenate the product. Rubik's Cube champions also continue to play a role in promoting the puzzle (see Figure 6.17). Rubik's Cube holds the distinction of ranking among the top 10 best-selling products, along with the iPhone and Sony's PlayStation, as well as the most successful single toy product with more than 350 million cubes sold worldwide (Calio, Frohlich, & Hess, 2014). This puzzle also has a fascinating story. Rubik's Cube was named after its inventor, Erno Rubik, a Hungarian architecture professor, who created the puzzle as a teaching tool on spatial relationships in 1974 and became the wealthiest individual in then Communist Hungary.

Anniversary milestones are not always newsworthy, particularly if the promotional material is self-congratulatory. **IBM**, however, celebrated its centennial in 2011 (see Figures 6.18 and 6.19) by staging the world's largest corporate volunteerism program and engaging more than

Figure 6.16—VISITORS CAN EXPLORE 44 HOLES AT HOBBITON MOVIE SET TOURS, WHICH WERE RECONSTRUCTED IN 2011 FOR *THE HOBBIT* TRILOGY.
Source: © Ian Brodie c/o Tourism New Zealand.

Figure 6.17—AFTER THREE STRAIGHT DAYS OF COMPETITION AT THE 2013 RUBIK'S CUBE WORLD CHAMPIONSHIP IN LAS VEGAS, FELIKS ZEMDEGS OF AUSTRALIA BESTED HIS FELLOW COMPETITORS WITH THE FASTEST AVERAGE TIME FOR SOLVING THE CLASSIC 3×3 RUBIK'S CUBE OF 8.18 SECONDS, COMPLETING HIS FASTEST SINGLE SOLVE IN 7.36 SECONDS. Source: Rubik's Cube® used by permission of Rubik's Brand Ltd.

300,000 employees, retirees, and their families and friends to pledge more than 3.2 million hours to undertake more than 5,000 service projects in 120 countries (IBM100, 2011). The Public Relations Society of America (2012b) Silver Anvil award case study stated the importance of IBM's glocal approach: "Corporate volunteerism needs to be relevant to local markets, given the effects of globalization" (para. 5). This campaign resulted in giving service to local communities on six continents with an estimated volunteerism value at USD100 million, while garnering extensive media exposure and social media interaction about the volunteers' stories. IBM's centennial events also extended the company's messages on "innovation" and "making the world better" with "Icons of Progress" online stories, business school lectures, a research colloquia, and a traveling exhibition in 12 countries.

Figure 6.18—IBM EMPLOYEES, RETIREES, CLIENTS, AND BUSINESS PARTNERS WORLDWIDE DONATED THEIR TIME AND EXPERTISE DURING THE COMPANY'S 100TH ANNIVERSARY. Source: © IBM.

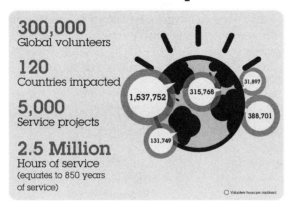

Figure 6.19—IBM CENTENNIAL DAY OF SERVICE IN RIO DE JANEIRO, BRAZIL. Source: © IBM.

6.3 Learning Objectives and Key Terms

By studying Chapter 6, you should be able to:

- Understand the universal appeal of storytelling from prehistoric times to the present.
- Explain why storytelling is a significant skill for public relations writers to acquire.
- Develop story themes in public relations campaigns and materials that would resonate with different audiences in multimedia platforms—showing human interest appeals, bringing benefits to life, creating sensory experiences, motivating people to participate, and making the stories timely.
- Provide examples of real-world campaigns that successfully connected with their audiences.

This chapter covers the following key words and terms:

Storytelling in PR (p. 131)	Flack (p. 131)
Freytag's dramatic arc (p. 132)	Visual imagery (p. 145)
Auditory imagery (p. 145)	Olfactory imagery (p. 145)
Gustatory imagery (p. 145)	Tactile imagery (p. 145)
Organic imagery (p. 145)	Kinesthetic imagery (p. 145)

References

Australian Bat Clinic. (2014). *Mission of ABC* [Web copy]. Retrieved from http://australian batclinic.com.au/?page_id=111.

Bacon, J. (2013, July 18). Brand storytelling: Narrative theory. *MarketingWeek*. Retrieved from http://www.marketingweek.co.uk/trends/brand-storytelling-narrative-theory/40072 79.article.

Blackstone, J. (2013, September 2). Cat videos take over Internet, marketing world. *CBS News*. Retrieved from http://www.cbsnews.com/videos/cat-videos-take-over-internet-marketing-world/.

Børdahl, V. (n.d.). Chinese storytelling: A short introduction. *Shuoshu.org*. Retrieved from http://www.shuoshu.org/chinese_storytelling/intro.shtml.

Calio, V., Frohlich, T. C., & Hess, A. E. M. (2014, May 18). 10 best-selling products of all time. *USA Today*. Retrieved from http://www.usatoday.com/story/money/business/2014/05/18/24-7-wall-st-the-best-selling-products-of-all-time/9223465/.

Coca-Cola Journey. (2013, November 11). *Local idea goes global: Share a Coke*. Retrieved from http://www.coca-colajourney.com.au/stories/local-idea-goes-global-share-a-coke.

Edson, A. S. (2006, Summer). Flak vs. flack: That is the question. *Cheklist*. Retrieved from http://www.edsonpr.com/NEWS/Cheklist_summer06.pdf.

Ellison, J. (2010, December 16). Isaiah Mustafa and the secret to his Old Spice success. *Newsweek*. Retrieved from http://www.newsweek.com/isaiah-mustafa-and-secret-his-old-spice-success-69101.

Fryer, B. (2003, June). Storytelling that moves people: A conversation with screenwriting coach Robert McKee. *Harvard Business Review*. Retrieved from http://hbr.org/2003/06/storytelling-that-moves-people/ar.

Gottschall, J. (2013, October 27). Story 2.0: The surprising thing about the next wave of narrative. *Fast Company Co.Create*. Retrieved from http://www.fastcocreate.com/3020047/story-20-the-surprising-thing-about-the-next-wave-of-narrative.

Grimes, T. (2013, July 24). What the Share a Coke campaign can teach other brands. *Guardian*. Retrieved from http://www.theguardian.com/media-network/media-network-blog/2013/jul/24/share-coke-teach-brands.

Harilela, D. (2014, April 26). Storytelling key to Burberry's China strategy, says Christopher Bailey. *The Business of Fashion*. Retrieved from http://www.businessoffashion.com/2014/04/storytelling-key-burberrys-china-strategy.html.

Hirschberg, J. (2009). *Reflections of the shadow: Creating memorable heroes and villains for film and TV*. Studio City, CA: Michael Wiese Productions.

IBM100. (2011). *A worldwide celebration of service: Explore the global impact*. Retrieved from http://www-03.ibm.com/ibm/history/ibm100/us/en/service/.

Interactive Advertising Bureau. (n.d.). *Campaign name: The best job in the world* [Case study]. Retrieved from http://www.iab.net/media/file/Sample_Case_Study.pdf.

International Agency for Research on Cancer. (2014). *All cancers (excluding non-melanoma skin cancer): Estimated incidence, mortality and prevalence worldwide in 2012* [Fact sheet]. Retrieved from http://globocan.iarc.fr/Pages/fact_sheets_cancer.aspx.

Internet cat video film festival to be held in Minneapolis. (2012, July 11). *Huffington Post*. Retrieved from http://www.huffingtonpost.com/2012/07/11/internet-cat-video-film-festival-minneapolis-_n_1665369.html.

Lil' Drac: Orphaned short-tailed fruit bat rescued by bat world sanctuary. (2011, December 10). *Huffington Post*. Retrieved from http://www.huffingtonpost.com/2011/12/10/lil-drac-orphaned-bat_n_1141191.html.

MacLeod, I. (2014, February 13). Nutella spreads thank you message to fans to celebrate 50 years in first global campaign. *The Drum*. Retrieved from http://www.thedrum.com/news/2014/02/13/nutella-spreads-thank-you-message-fans-celebrate-50-years-first-global-campaign.

Mighall, R. (2013, November 12). The demise of the brand: Why technology will usher in a new era of storytelling. *Marketing*. Retrieved from http://www.marketingmagazine.co.uk/article/1220497/demise-brand-why-technology-will-usher-new-era-storytelling.

Pedersen, W. (1999, September 26). A flack or a flak [Letter to the editor]. *New York Times*. Retrieved from http://www.nytimes.com/1999/09/26/style/l-a-flack-or-a-flak-666823.html.

Public Relations Society of America. (2006). *Dove Campaign for Real Beauty. 2006 Silver Anvil winner—marketing consumer products—packaged goods* [Case study].

Public Relations Society of America. (2012a, January 1). *HP global wellness challenge. 2012 Silver Anvil award of excellence winner—internal communications—business* [Case study].

Public Relations Society of America. (2012b, January 1). *IBM at 100: Modernizing the way the world sees big blue. 2012 Silver Anvil award winner—integrated communications—business to business* [Case study].

Sachs, J. (2013, August 15). Three steps to better storytelling for brands. *Guardian*. Retrieved from http://www.theguardian.com/sustainable-business/three-steps-better-story-telling-brands.

Sampiero, J. (2013, February 22). Red Bull Stratos world records confirmed. *RedBull.com*. Retrieved from http://www.redbull.com/en/adventure/stories/1331582371669/red-bull-stratos-world-records-confirmed.

Scott, D. M. (2013). *The new rules of marketing & PR: How to use social media, online video, mobile applications, blogs, news releases, and viral marketing to reach buyers directly* (4th ed.). Hoboken, NJ: John Wiley & Sons.

Seitel, F. P., & Doorley, J. (2012). *Rethinking reputation: How PR trumps marketing and advertising in the new media world*. New York, NY: Palgrave Macmillan.

Severson, K. (2007, May 30). Having a snack? Make it a holiday. *New York Times*. Retrieved from http://www.nytimes.com/2007/05/30/dining/30holi.html?pagewanted=all.

Southall, B. (2013, March 21). How to get the best job in the world. *Queensland Blog*. Retrieved from http://blog.queensland.com/2013/03/21/how-to-get-best-job-in-the-world/.

Straw, B. (n.d.). Will the beautiful women of the world please stand up. *Charity: water*. Retrieved from http://www.charitywater.org/projects/stories/i-feel-beautiful-for-the-first-time/.

Summers, N. (2012, March 19). New wave of advertisers consider consumers the new medium. *Newsweek*. Retrieved from http://www.newsweek.com/new-wave-advertisers-consider-consumers-new-medium-63721.

Tode, C. (2014, April 1). How Pepsi is elevating message delivery via augmented reality. *Mobile Marketer*. Retrieved from http://www.mobilemarketer.com/cms/news/software-technology/17493.html.

Tourism Australia. (2013). *About the campaign—Best jobs in the world*. Retrieved from http://www.tourism.australia.com/campaigns/Global-Youth-about-the-campaign.aspx.

Walker Art Center. (2014, June 25). *Walker Art Center's Internet Cat Video Festival Golden Kitty award public voting now open* [News release]. Retrieved from http://www.walkerart.org/press/browse/press-releases/2014/walker-art-centers-internet-cat-video-festiva.

Wentz, L. (2013, June 18). Dutch funeral-insurance company Dela snares top Media Lion at Cannes: Win brings Ogilvy's Grand Prix total to three. *AdvertisingAge*. Retrieved from http://adage.com/article/special-report-cannes-2013/netherlands-dela-wins-top-media-prize-cannes/242186/.

Willis Group. (2013, December 2). *The Willis Resilience expedition arrives in Antarctica* [News release]. Retrieved from http://www.prnewswire.com/news-releases/the-willis-resilience-expedition-arrives-in-antarctica-234081381.html.

Zak, P. J. (2013, December 17). How stories change the brain. *Greater Good*. Retrieved from http://greatergood.berkeley.edu/article/item/how_stories_change_brain.

Zmuda, N. (2013, September 2). Red Bull's Stratos "space jump" wowed the world—while selling a lot of product. *AdvertisingAge*. Retrieved from http://adage.com/article/special-report-marketer-alist-2013/red-bull-stratos-space-jump-helped-sell-a-lot-product/243751/.

Part Three

HONING ENGLISH WRITING SKILLS FOR GLOBAL AUDIENCES

Part Three includes three chapters that cover different writing styles, grammar and punctuation, and editing and proofreading strategies relevant to public relations writers.

Chapter 7 Applying Consistency of Style

- Discusses the different writing styles in English, with a focus on the two major standards in English: American English (Webster's) and British (Oxford) English.
- Outlines the evolution of English-language dictionaries in specific countries or regions.
- Covers the most widely used stylebooks in different parts of the English-speaking world.
- Shows how a style sheet can capture the most commonly used words and formatting consistency tailored to the requirements of an organization in different markets.

Chapter 8 Acing Grammar and Punctuation

- Reviews grammar basics and encourages readers to evaluate their own knowledge and identify areas for improvement.
- Demonstrates how proper use of punctuation makes copy easier to follow and understand.
- Looks at the major differences between American and British punctuation, as well as different English-language stylebooks.

Chapter 9 Sharpening Editing Skills for Global Audiences

- Addresses the power of words and how to write clearly to reach diverse audiences and to develop cultural sensitivities for terms used in race, gender, religion, and sexual orientation.

- Reviews how to avoid slang, idiomatic expressions, and local cultural references that may not be widely understood.
- Provides editing tips that demonstrate how to simplify copy and select the less complex word, use specific versus general words, and apply positive language to strengthen sentences.
- Shows how to avoid hype, puffery, jargon, and clichés.
- Covers commonly confused words—and words that have different meanings in different versions of English.
- Shares proofreading blunders and covers techniques on how to fact-check and proof copy.

7 Applying Consistency of Style

It is our job to communicate clearly and effectively, to be understood without difficulty, and to offer viewers and listeners an intelligent use of language which they can enjoy. Good writing is not a luxury; it is an obligation.

—John Allen, author of the *BBC News Styleguide*

7.1 Introduction to Style Usage for Public Relations Writers

The quotation above from John Allen, the author of the *BBC News Styleguide* (2003), is an excerpt from the answer to the question, "Why does the BBC need a styleguide?" (p. 7). As the world's largest public service broadcaster, the British Broadcasting Corporation airs throughout the U.K. and around the world in English, and the BBC World Service Group offers news in 27 languages to more than 250 million people every week. The style manual helps BBC journalists communicate in a unified, consistent voice, whether by TV, radio, or online. (A newer style guide is available on the BBC News website; Allen's version can still be downloaded.)

Practically every media company has its own style manual or follows someone else's. In addition, many organizations—whether they are nonprofits, government offices, publicly or privately held companies, or their creative agencies—have established guidelines on writing, such as which dictionaries and style manuals to follow in all types of business communication, spanning advertising, public relations, sales promotions, and Web and social media content.

Language is fluid and ever-changing; and the English language is particularly complex in its diverse spellings, definitions, and pronunciations. Today's public relations writers need to follow specific dictionaries and style manuals for consistency in how they write in English, as well as how to communicate in different forms of English.

Theater or *theatre*, *color* or *colour*, *program* or *programme*? The two broad usages are **American English** (also called **Webster's** or **U.S. English**), widely spoken in the United States and its five territories, where approximately two-thirds of English speakers live, as well as in some other countries; and **British English** (also called **U.K.**, **Oxford**, **Commonwealth**, or the **Queen's English**) that is used in the United Kingdom and many of its current and former Commonwealth countries. However, this broad category is not so simple. Canadian

English blends British and American spellings and pronunciations, along with its own distinctions. Although based on British English, the versions of English used in Australia, New Zealand, South Africa, Nigeria, and Jamaica have evolved with unique variations in each country. People learning English as a second or foreign language may learn British, American, or another variation of English. Geographic proximity can be a factor. Europeans tend to learn British English, whereas South Americans most likely are educated in American English. Organizations usually follow the English used in the country of their headquarters, if English is one of the official or de facto official languages. Otherwise, the English most widely taught in educational institutions may apply. Companies also may use other English versions in material produced for specific geographic areas.

See Exhibit 7.1 for an overview of some of the major differences between American and British spellings. Writers should check dictionaries to make sure they are using the correct spelling. *Glamour*, for example, is more commonly spelled with the "ou" in both American and British English language dictionaries.

7.2 The Evolution of English-Language Standards

How do words officially become words and how should they be spelled and defined? A look at the historical evolution of setting standards in English usage helps to explain the complexity. If you have ever tried to read original versions of correspondence before the 18th century, you will find huge variations in how words are spelled.

The earliest English-language dictionaries were Latin-English to help educate schoolboys (very few girls received formal education back then) preparing for the ministry in the 15th century, followed by other bilingual dictionaries. Starting in the 1500s, a few English schoolmasters began creating new teaching tools to help students learn how to spell, parse, pronounce, and understand definitions. The most comprehensive monolingual dictionary of that time was Robert Cawdrey's dictionary in 1604 that listed the spellings and brief descriptions of 2,543 words. Cawdrey explained what his dictionary offered (the spelling and punctuation follow the original text):

> A Table Alphabeticall, conteyning and teaching the true writing, and understanding of hard usuall English, wordes, gathered from the Hebrew, Greeke, Latine, or French. &c. With the interpretation thereof by plaine English words, gathered for the benefit & helpe of Ladies, Gentlewomen, or any other unskilfull persons. (as cited in Starnes & Noyes, 1991, p. 13)

It is quite obvious that spelling standards and definitions have changed dramatically. "Hard words" refer to English words borrowed from foreign or ancient languages; a distinction we would not make today.

Three significant lexicologists created standardizations in English: Samuel Johnson's *Dictionary of the English Language* in 1755; Noah Webster with his *American Dictionary of the English Language* in 1828; and Sir James A. H. Murray, primary editor of what is now known as the *Oxford English Dictionary* that was completed in 1928.

Dr. Samuel Johnson, an Oxford-educated writer born in Lichfield, England, in 1709, aimed to create a new authoritative yet practical dictionary to bring order to the language. See the cartoon in Figure 7.1 that uses humor to illustrate the anarchy in English spelling at that time—and proves why Dr. Johnson had a serious mission.

Exhibit 7.1—DIFFERENCES BETWEEN AMERICAN (WEBSTER'S) AND BRITISH (OXFORD) ENGLISH SPELLING. This chart shows examples of some of the major differences between American and British English.

Spellings	American	British
-ce OR -se	Defense (noun); defensive (adverb) License (noun and verb)	Defence (noun); defensive (adverb) Licence (noun); licence or license (verb)
e OR ae or oe	Archeology or Archaeology Esophagus	Archaeology Oesophagus
e OR dropped e	Aging Judgment Sizable	Ageing Judgement Sizeable
-ize and -ization OR -ise and -isation	Globalization Realize	Globalisation or globalization Realise or realize
l OR double l	Enroll; enrollment Jewelry	Enrol; enrolment Jewellery
-og OR -ogue	Analog Dialog or dialogue	Analogue Dialogue
-or OR -our	Color, colorful Neighbor, neighborhood Vigor, vigorous	Colour, colourful Neighbour, neighbourhood Vigour, vigorous
-ter OR -tre	Center; centering Theater	Centre; centring Theatre
-yze or -yse	Analyze Catalyze	Analyse Catalyse
Miscellaneous	Aluminum Check (money) Curb (pavement) Gray Program Specialty Story (building level)	Aluminium Cheque (money) Kerb (pavement) Grey Programme Speciality Storey (building level)

Figure 7.1—CARTOON ILLUSTRATES HOW DR. JOHNSON HAD A CHALLENGING MISSION. Source: © Fran, CartoonStock.

BUT DR JOHNSON, OF WAT YUSE WIL THIS DICSHUNARY OF YOURS BE?

Dr. Johnson explained the challenges his faced during his time in the following excerpt in his dictionary's preface:

> When I took the first survey of my undertaking, I found our speech copious without order, and energetick without rules: wherever I turned my view, there was perplexity to be disentangled, and confusion to be regulated; choice was to be made out of boundless variety, without any established principle of selection; adulterations were to be detected, without a settled test of purity; and modes of expression, to be rejected or received, without the suffrages of any writers of classical reputation or acknowledged authority. (as cited in Besalke, 2013, para. 4)

Dr. Johnson analyzed the nuances of words and interpretations from writers and intellectuals: William Shakespeare, creator of new words in the 16th century, with his vast vocabulary, along with Jonathan Swift, Francis Bacon, John Milton, and others. Dr. Johnson and six assistants spent nine years writing the dictionary, compiling over 40,000 words, along with illustrations and 114,000 quotations, in 80 large notebooks—without the benefit of a library to cull resources from (McCrum, Cran, & McNeil, 1986). Johnson's dictionary was a success, particularly appealing to the growing middle classes of the 18th century. This dictionary was not only readable; it also conveyed a distinctive voice and occasional humor. For example, Johnson defined a *lexicographer* as "A writer of dictionaries; a harmless drudge, that busies himself in tracing the original, and detailing the signification of words" ("Lexicographer," 1755).

Noah Webster's adaptation of English reflected the spirit of independence of the newly formed United States and a departure from British-English traditions in spelling and pronunciation. Born in 1758 in Hartford, Connecticut, Webster experienced the American Revolution and was influenced by Benjamin Franklin's "Scheme for a New Alphabet and a

Reformed Mode of Spelling" proposal in 1768 that called for a distinctive American English voice (McCrum et al., 1986). Educated at Yale and originally set for a career in law, Webster became an educator and found many classrooms full of new immigrants learning from British-English language books on writing and spelling that did not reflect the language of the new country. He started writing bestselling books on spelling and a smaller dictionary before embarking on his *American Dictionary of the English Language*, a 22-year-long undertaking (see Figure 7.2 illustrating Webster's publications). Webster studied the roots of 26 languages from Anglo-Saxon to Sanskrit, along with the Bible and classical literature, to present an American substitution for Johnson's dictionary (Merriam-Webster, 2013a). The dictionary was published in 1828 and contained more than 70,000 entries. Webster's writing style is more straightforward than Johnson's. Webster defined a lexicographer as: "The author of a lexicon or dictionary" ("Lexicographer," 1828). However, Webster became "the father of American English" by introducing spelling reform from the British tradition, most of which remains today—*humor* for *humour*, *jail* for *gaol*, and *traveled* for *travelled*, among others—and popularizing new American words, such as *skunk* and *chowder*. Try Exercise 7.1 and see if you master both American and British spelling.

The term "Webster" has become synonymous with an American-English dictionary. Publishers George and Charles Merriam set up their company in 1831 and bought the rights to Webster's dictionary in 1843. Merriam-Webster continues to publish dictionaries, while other publishers also use the Webster name in their titles since the copyright has elapsed.

Exercise 7.1

Self-Evaluation: American (Webster's) and British (Oxford) English Spelling

Try to convert the words below (1 to 10) in American English to British English and vice versa (11 to 20).

Convert the words below from American English to British English	Change the words in British English to American English
1. Practice (noun and verb)	11. Pyjamas
2. Organization	12. Tyre
3. Counseling	13. Haulier
4. Cozy	14. Paralyse
5. Honor	15. Marvellous
6. Mustache	16. Paediatrics
7. Acknowledgment	17. Savour
8. Skeptic	18. Skilful
9. Airplane	19. Plough
10. Artifact	20. Fibre

See Appendix D for answers.

Figure 7.2—"NOAH WEBSTER, THE SCHOOLMASTER OF THE REPUBLIC,"
PRINT BY ROOT & TINKER. Source: Courtesy of the Library of Congress, Division of
Prints and Photographs Online.

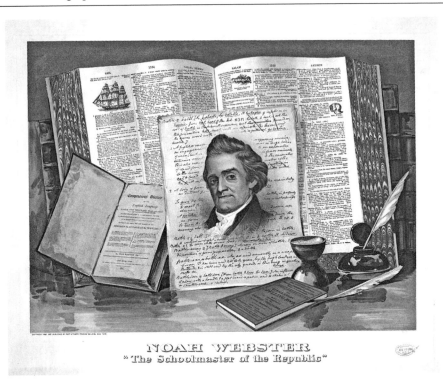

NOAH WEBSTER
"The Schoolmaster of the Republic"

Sir James A. H. Murray (1837–1915; see Figure 7.3), a Scottish lexicographer, teacher,
and scholar, devoted the last four decades of his life researching and editing a new type of
dictionary by providing a historical evolution of English words from the obsolete to the present.
Although Sir Murray originally estimated that the project would take 10 years, he and his
team took five years to complete the A to Ant section (Burchfield, 2004). The entire 10 volumes,
with more than 400,000 words, were completed in 1928, 13 years after Murray's death, and
called *A New English Dictionary on Historical Principles*, published by the Oxford University
Press. The ***Oxford English Dictionary***, also abbreviated as the OED, now uses the slogan,
"The definitive record of the English language," and describes its scope as "More than 600,000
words . . . over 3 million quotations . . . over 1000 years of English" (OED, 2013).

Oxford University Press now publishes dictionaries in American, Australian, Canadian,
and South African English. Other publishers around the globe have created country-specific
English dictionaries. The University of the West Indies published the first English-language
dictionary in the Caribbean, the *Dictionary of Jamaican English*, in 1967. *The Macquarie
Dictionary* debuted in 1981 and set the standard for Australian English. Oxford University
Press, Merriam-Webster, and other publishers also offer editions on modern slang, English
as a second language, and business English covering both American and British terms. Exhibit
7.2 highlights examples of English-language dictionaries around the world.

Figure 7.3—PHOTO OF JAMES MURRAY, FIRST EDITOR OF THE OXFORD ENGLISH DICTIONARY, IN HIS OFFICE. Source: Reprinted by permission of the Secretary to the Delegates of Oxford University Press.

Computer software programs also provide English-language choices. You can select from 16 versions of English on Microsoft Office Word 2010—Australia, Belize, Canada, Caribbean, India, Ireland, Jamaica, Malaysia, New Zealand, Philippines, Singapore, South Africa, Trinidad and Tobago, U.K., U.S., and Zimbabwe.

Contemporary dictionaries continue to capture words becoming widely used in popular culture. Have you ever heard the animated character Homer Simpson's say *d'oh* or have you used the expression? This exclamation from *The Simpsons*, the American animated television series from 1989 to 2013, now continues in reruns around the globe, but its characters have coined words now found in dictionaries. Here are definitions from two dictionaries:

Exhibit 7.2—ENGLISH-LANGUAGE DICTIONARIES WORLDWIDE. This list includes examples of English-language dictionaries around the world.

Dictionary/Publisher/Website	Year First Published
Merriam-Webster Dictionary, Merriam-Webster, U.S.; www.merriam-webster.com	1847
Oxford English Dictionary, Oxford University Press, U.K.; www.oed.com (also free content on www.oxforddictionaries.com)	1884–1928
American College Dictionary, Random House, U.S.; www.randomhouse.com	1947
Dictionary of Jamaican English, University of the West Indies Press, Jamaica; www.uwipress.com	1967
Collins English Dictionary, HarperCollins, U.K.; www.harpercollins.co.uk	1979
Macquarie Dictionary, Macquarie Dictionary Publishers, Australia; www.macquariedictionary.com.au	1981
Canadian Oxford Dictionary, Oxford University Press, U.K./Canada; www.oupcanada.com	1998
Dictionary of Caribbean English Usage, University of the West Indies Press, Jamaica; www.uwipress.com	1996
Australian Concise Oxford Dictionary, Oxford University Press Australia & New Zealand; www.oup.com.au	1999
Longman Business English Dictionary, Pearson Longman, U.S.; www.longmanhomeusa.com/	2000
South African Concise Oxford Dictionary, Oxford University Press Southern Africa; South Africa; www.oxford.co.za	2002
A Dictionary of Nigerian English Usage, Enicrownfit Publishers, Nigeria; www.africanbookscollective.com/publishers/enicrownfit-publishers	2002
New Zealand Oxford Dictionary, Oxford University Press Australia & New Zealand; www.oup.com.au	2005
Oxford Business English Dictionary for Learners of English, Oxford University Press, U.K.; www.oed.com	2005
A Dictionary of South African Indian English, UCT Press, South Africa; www.uctpress.co.za	2010
Collins Canadian English Dictionary, Harper Collins Publishers Canada; www.harpercollins.ca	2011
A Dictionary of Hong Kong English: Words from the Fragrant Harbor, Hong Kong University Press; www.hkupress.org	2011
Cambridge Business English Dictionary, Cambridge University Press, U.K.; www.cambridge.org	2011
Collins COBUILD International Business English Language Dictionary HarperCollins Publishers, U.K.; www.harpercollins.co.uk	2011

- "Doh (also d'oh) exclamation, informal— Used to comment on a foolish or stupid action, especially one's own: 'I keep crashing cars. Doh! What a dummy!'" ("Doh," 2014) in the *Oxford Dictionaries*.
- "*D'oh* interjection—used to express sudden recognition of a foolish blunder or an ironic turn of events" ("D'oh," 2014) in *Merriam-Webster*.

Computer terms also are keeping lexicologists busy as technology evolves. Lexicographers may take time to approve new words and meanings. For example, the term *tweet* (meaning to write on Twitter) debuted in 2006 and entered the *Oxford English Dictionary* in 2013 (Simpson, 2013). Conversely, words also are dropped in updated editions of some dictionaries. Can you think of any words that should be axed for being obsolete or irrelevant? *Cramoisie* (crimson cloth), *octandrious* (having eight stamens), and *prolan* (either of two pituitary hormones that are no longer in scientific use) were deleted from *Merriam-Webster's Collegiate Dictionary*; *Panama Red* (1970s slang for a type of marijuana) and *cassette memory* (obsolete technology) were removed from *The American Heritage Dictionary* (Doll, 2013).

The fact that a word exists in the dictionary does not mean it should be applied to more formal writing, such as in public relations materials. Dictionaries contain slang and nonstandard English, such as *ain't*. The online *Oxford Dictionaries* ("Ain't," 2015) explains:

> The use of ain't was widespread in the 18th century and is still perfectly normal in many dialects and informal contexts in both North America and Britain. Today, however, it does not form part of standard English and should not be used in formal contexts.

7.2.1 "Words of the Year": Three Global Perspectives

Language evolves and many of the world's leading dictionaries promote their new words, generating exposure in traditional media, the blogosphere, and other social media.

The online *Oxford Dictionaries* publishes updates on new word additions four times per year and also promotes its enhanced vocabulary and "Word of the Year." In 2013, editors of the *Oxford Dictionaries* named *selfie* (see Figure 7.4)—defined as "a photograph that one has taken of oneself, typically one taken with a smartphone or webcam and uploaded to a social media website"—as the "Word of the Year," with its frequency of use surging 17,000% within a 12-month time period (Oxford Dictionaries, 2013). Editors in both the U.K. and U.S. compile the shortlist and vote on the finalists. *Selfie* transcended both sides of the Atlantic in 2013. *Oxford Dictionaries* also created an infographic on its 2013 choice, illustrating its earliest known usage, different words for *selfies* around the world, popular spin-offs, shortlist contenders for "Word of the Year," and previous selections. For those who want immediate gratification, you can sign up to receive *Oxford Dictionaries'* "Word of the Day" by email or follow it on Twitter.

In the U.S., *Merriam-Webster*'s 2013 "Word of the Year" was surprisingly *science*, which became a widely searched word with a 176% increase on its online dictionary. The editor-at-large at *Merriam-Webster* explained the selection:

> A wide variety of discussions centered on science this year, from climate change to educational policy. We saw heated debates about "phony" science, or whether science held all the answers. It's a topic that has great significance for us. And it fascinates us–enough so that it saw a 176% increase in lookups this year over last, and stayed a top lookup throughout the year. (Merriam-Webster, 2013b, para. 2)

Figure 7.4—SELFIE (NOUN, INFORMAL) WAS NAMED OXFORD DICTIONARIES' INTERNATIONAL WORD OF THE YEAR 2013. Source: © Peter Bernik/Shutterstock.com.

Merriam-Webster's online edition also posts a "Word of the Day" or you can subscribe to receive daily posts by email or listen to its daily podcast.

The 2013 "Word of the Year" committee of the *Macquarie Dictionary*, based in Australia, selected *infovore*, defined as "a person who craves information, especially one who takes advantage of their ready access to it on digital devices" (Macquarie Dictionary, 2014). The committee's rationale was based on how the proliferation of smartphones provides instant accessibility to find out anything at any time, becoming a potential addiction for the digiterati. The online dictionary also posts "Aussie Word of the Week" and "Word of the Day," which also can be followed on social media or received by email subscriptions.

Public relations writers should follow specific dictionaries—and then the next step is to choose specific style manuals for greater consistency.

7.3 "Style Wars": English-Language Stylebooks

"4 Copy Editors Killed in Ongoing AP Style, Chicago Manual Gang Violence" (2013) was the title of an article in *The Onion*, a weekly online satirical publication in the U.S., that reported a mock news story on the "ongoing violence between two rival gangs divided by their loyalties" (para. 1) to the two most popular stylebooks in the U.S., vying to gain control over American English, while other stylebook adherents became victims in the gang wars. Should the graffiti read *anti-social* or *antisocial*? Loyalists to specific stylebooks can be quite persnickety about word usage—and you will meet many of them in the classroom and in the workforce. This article refers to the following four **stylebooks**:

- *The Associated Press Stylebook and Briefing on Media Law* is considered the most popular resource for U.S. journalists and public relations practitioners. The first edition debuted in 1953, and it is now updated annually, with new listings on technology and social media, industry-specific terms from fashion to sports, medical definitions, new words or phrases, and grammatical changes. The Associated Press is a not-for-profit cooperative owned by more than 1,400 U.S. newspapers, with staff operating in more than 280 locations worldwide.
- Whereas *The Chicago Manual of Style* goes back to 1891 when the University of Chicago Press opened and created its own style sheet to help academics with consistency in preparing manuscripts. This style manual continues to be used in the publishing industry, spanning magazines, academic literature, and mainstream fiction and nonfiction. Some companies also follow this style guide for printed documents and website content.
- Published by the Modern Language Association, the *MLA Handbook* was released in 1883 and today is primarily used in academia in approximately 100 countries.
- And then *The Onion* story acknowledges the Oxford serial comma, based on the *New Oxford Style Manual* from Oxford University Press. This edition combines *New Hart's Rules*, which debuted in 1893, and the *New Oxford Dictionary for Writers and Editors*, originally from 1905. This comma is widely debated, particularly by *Associated Press Stylebook* users. The serial comma is placed before the last coordinating conjunction (*and*, *or*, *nor*) in a list of three or more items. A widely disseminated cartoon on the Web dramatizes the use of the comma: "With the Oxford comma, we invited the strippers, JFK, and Stalin" is the caption above an illustration of the two former leaders along with two strippers wearing G-strings and high heels. The caption of the second panel reads, "Without the Oxford comma, we invited the strippers, JFK and Stalin," and the illustration depicts just JFK and Stalin dressed as strippers.

Writing and editing would be simpler if there were just a few options. The reality is that numerous style manuals exist in publishing, journalism, business, and academia, including editions for specific countries. Journalists and public relations practitioners worldwide also may follow a stylebook published by a leading media outlet, such as the British Broadcasting Corporation (BBC), Australian Broadcasting Corporation, *Times* (London), *Wall Street Journal*, *New York Times*, or Associated Press, among others. Academics also may write for publications or conferences requiring the *Publication Manual of the American Psychological Association* (also called the APA), the Harvard System of Referencing, or other industry-specific manuals in law, music, science, and medicine, as well as the *MLA Handbook* or *The Chicago Manual of Style*. Public relations writers would need to follow one of the academic guides to write citations and references in white papers and other reports.

Deborah Cameron (1996), a professor of English and linguistics at Oxford, studied the institutional style guides of British newspapers and their conformity to create an "institutional voice" that follows "'the four Cs': correctness, consistency, clarity and concision" (p. 319). Stylebooks of all kinds help writers make decisions and answer many questions that may arise when writing material:

- Which spelling is correct when the dictionary has more than one choice?
- What are the best ways to describe someone's race, health, religion, gender, lifestyle, or nationality?
- How are titles of novels, movies, TV programs, or musical compositions written?
- How should technological terms be written?
- What words should be capitalized or not?
- How should the word or words be abbreviated—or is it appropriate to do so?
- Should the words be combined as one word, written as two words, or be hyphenated?
- When do you use the figure or spell out the number?
- What words should be avoided? The *BBC Styleguide*, for example, cautions about Americanisms when communicating with a British audience: "Many American words and expressions have impact and vigour, but use them with discrimination or your audience may become a tad irritated" (Allen, 2003, p. 21).
- What words should be edited or deleted for brevity?

The goal is not to memorize the stylebook content, but to develop familiarity with the style guide's philosophy and know which terms to look up. Avoid making assumptions on word usage by double-checking listings in the specific stylebook. Some stylebooks also have free downloads or paid subscriptions for online databases or phone apps. See Exhibit 7.3 for examples of English-language style guides used around the globe.

Exhibit 7.3—ENGLISH-LANGUAGE STYLE GUIDES WORLDWIDE. This list includes examples of English-language style manuals in the U.S., the U.K., and other countries.

Stylebook (Country of Origin)	Website
Associated Press Stylebook and Briefing on Media Law (U.S.)	www.apstylebook.com
Australian Broadcasting Corporation Style Guide (Australia)	style.radionational.net.au
BBC News Styleguide (U.K.)	www.bbc.co.uk/academy/journalism/news-style-guide
Butcher's Copy-editing: The Cambridge Handbook for Editors, Copy-editors and Proofreaders (U.K.)	www.cambridge.org
Canadian Press Stylebook (Canada)	www.thecanadianpress.com
Canadian Style: A Guide to Writing and Editing (Canada)	www.dundurn.com
Chicago Manual of Style (U.S.)	www.chicagomanualofstyle.org
Economist Style Guide (U.K.)	www.theeconomist.com/styleguide
Guardian Style Guide (U.K.)	www.theguardian.com/guardian-observer-style-guide-a
New Oxford Style Manual (U.K.)	ukcatalogue.oup.com
Style Manual for Authors, Editors and Printers (Australia)	au.wiley.com/WileyCDA/

Public relations professionals should adhere to specific stylebooks for consistency in how they write, thereby ensuring that the work they produce for their organizations or clients maintains a unified appearance. Most public relations agencies and in-house public relations departments have guidelines on the choice of stylebooks and dictionaries; international organizations also may have selected stylebooks for writing material for journalists and publics in specific countries or regions.

7.4 Customized Style Guides for Unified Voices

Style guides do not have all words, particularly ones that may be frequently used by the organization you are representing. Dictionaries may not have all the answers too. How do I describe the product features? Which version of English should I use in specific markets? Learning how to create a **customized style guide** (also called a **house guide** or a **style sheet**) for an organization can answer these questions, capture the most commonly used words, and provide guidelines on formatting consistency tailored to the requirements of an organization. Customized style guides also apply to the visual identity of the company or nonprofit in all printed materials and digital content. The goal is to ensure that the organization provides a uniform appearance in communicating to internal and external audiences in all areas, such as sales, marketing, advertising, customer service, investor relations, human resources, and public relations.

Brand identity guidelines include how the logo can be used and placed in all visual print and electronic formats, including trademarks, templates, font selections, color variations, and paper stock. Although this content is traditionally developed by marketing, advertising, and Web designers, the public relations staff members also should contribute to establishing standards for written documents and the visual identity, particularly on the appearance of the online newsroom and other print or digital materials for the media and the public.

Creating a corporate style guide becomes increasingly important for global companies that institute English as an official business language. This reference should contain commonly used terms in the industry, which can be particularly helpful to multilingual staff members who may have varying levels of proficiency in English.

Customized style guides should be comprehensive and updated regularly. They can easily be posted on the organization's Intranet. The following components should be considered for style sheets:

- **Preferred stylebooks and dictionaries** for all materials or for specific markets. For example, a company may decide to use the English spoken in the country of its headquarters in all materials, or opt to create specific English-language versions for other markets.
- **Messaging and tone guidelines** provide consistency when describing and positioning the brand and its products and services on a global basis, as well as in specific regions or countries. This section also could cover the core brand messages and regional and local nuances.
- **Composition guidelines and templates** explain how writers can present and convey information in multiple forms—business correspondence by mail and email, website content, social media, blogs, microblogs, reports, brochures, news releases, visual presentations, and other internal and external communiqués.

- **Visual brand consistency** provides layout guidelines and standards in selecting fonts and colors for logos in multiple digital and print formats, as well as for underlined, boldface, and italicized copy. This part can include selection of photographs and videos, particularly to showcase imagery of multicultural audiences.
- **Punctuation and writing style preferences** offer guidelines on consistency when writing frequently used abbreviations, acronyms, trademarks, numbers, and word use related to the organization. Recommended grammar usage can cover preferred tenses and voice, such as active over passive, as well as punctuation guidelines.
- **International and multicultural guidelines** can cover how to best express terms, such as nationalities, time, currencies, and dimensions, as well as other guidelines on writing content in English that will be translated into other languages. Bias-free copy and cultural sensitivities should be addressed. This part also can include which English version should be used for specific geographic markets.
- A **glossary** in alphabetical order of commonly used words can be a helpful reference. It also could include different English-language versions.

"Small disciplines repeated with consistency every day lead to great achievements gained slowly over time" (Maxwell, 2012, p. 73). Consistency is one of John C. Maxwell's laws in *The 15 Invaluable Laws of Growth: Live Them and Reach Your Potential*. Public relations writers also can benefit in developing consistency in their writing styles and following different styles seamlessly with the help of dictionaries, style manuals, and in-house style guides, particularly when communicating with diverse geographic audiences. The goal of style manuals is to provide consistency of an "institutional voice," yet not one that stifles all creativity.

7.5 Learning Objectives and Key Terms

After reading Chapter 7, you should be able to:

- Outline the evolution of English-language standards and demand for dictionaries that reflect different versions of English around the world.
- Identify some of the major differences between Webster's and Oxford English spellings.
- Understand the challenges facing lexicologists as they acquire new terms in technology and popular usages, as well as delete obsolete words.
- Explain the usefulness of style guides in writing and editing public relations materials.
- Identify elements that should be considered for inclusion in customized style guides for organizations.

This chapter covers the following key terms:

Webster's English (p. 163)   American English (p. 163)
British English (p. 163)   Oxford English Dictionary (p. 168)
Stylebooks (p. 173)   Customized style guides (p. 175)

References

4 copy editors killed in ongoing AP style, Chicago Manual gang violence. (2013, January 7). *The Onion*. Retrieved from http://www.theonion.com/articles/4-copy-editors-killed-in-ongoing-ap-style-chicago,30806/.

Ain't. (2015). In *Oxford Dictionaries online*. Retrieved from http://www.oxforddictionaries. com/us/definition/american_english/ain't.

Allen, J. (2003). *BBC News Styleguide*. BBC News Training & Development.

Besalke, B. (Ed.). (2013). *A dictionary of the English language: A digital edition of the 1755 classic by Samuel Johnson*. Retrieved from http://johnsonsdictionaryonline.com.

Burchfield, R. W. (2004). Murray, Sir James Augustus Henry, lexicographer (1837–1915). *Oxford Dictionary of National Biography*. Retrieved from http://www.oxforddnb.com/public/dnb/35163.html.

Cameron, D. (1996). Style policy and style politics: A neglected aspect of the language of the news. *Media, Culture & Society, 18*(2), 315–333. doi: 10.1177/016344396018002008.

Doh. (2014). In *Oxford Dictionaries online*. Retrieved from http://www.oxforddictionaries.com/us/definition/american_english/doh.

D'oh. (2014). In *Merriam-Webster's online dictionary*. Retrieved from http://www.merriam-webster.com/dictionary/d'oh.

Doll, J. (2013, September). How to edit a dictionary: What to keep and what to cut? You can start by checking the Internet. *The Atlantic*, 24.

Lexicographer. (1755). In *A dictionary of the English language: A digital edition of the 1755 classic by Samuel Johnson*. Retrieved from http://johnsonsdictionaryonline.com/?p=4848.

Lexicographer. (1828). In *Webster dictionary 1828 online edition*. Retrieved from http://webstersdictionary1828.com.

Macquarie Dictionary. (2014, February 4). *Winning word of the year 2013*. Retrieved from https://www.macquariedictionary.com.au/news/view/article/83/.

Maxwell, J. C. (2012). *The 15 invaluable laws of growth: Live them and reach your potential*. New York, NY: Center Street.

McCrum, R., Cran, W., & MacNeil, R. (1986). *The story of English*. New York, NY: Elisabeth Sifton Books, Viking.

Merriam-Webster. (2013a). *About us: Noah Webster and America's first dictionary*. Retrieved from http://www.merriam-webster.com/info/noah.htm.

Merriam-Webster. (2013b, December 3). *2013 word of the year* [News release]. Retrieved from http://www.merriam-webster.com/info/2013-word-of-the-year.htm.

OED. (2013). *About*. Retrieved from http://public.oed.com/about/.

Oxford Dictionaries. (2013, November 19). *Oxford Dictionaries Word of the Year 2013: SELFIE is named Oxford Dictionaries Word of the Year 2013*. Retrieved from http://blog.oxforddictionaries.com/press-releases/oxford-dictionaries-word-of-the-year-2013/.

Simpson, J. (2013). A heads up for the June 2013 OED release. *Oxford English Dictionary*. Retrieved from http://public.oed.com/the-oed-today/recent-updates-to-the-oed/previous-updates/june-2013-update/a-heads-up-for-the-june-2013-oed-release/.

Starnes, D. T., & Noyes, G. E. (1991). *The English dictionary from Cawdrey to Johnson, 1604–1755*. Amsterdam, The Netherlands: John Benjamins Publishing.

8 Acing Grammar and Punctuation

> The bridge between the words *glamour* and *grammar* is magic. According to the OED, *glamour* evolved from *grammar* through an ancient association between learning and enchantment. There was a time when grammar described not just language knowledge but all forms of learning, which in a less scientific age included things like magic, alchemy, astrology, even witchcraft.
>
> —Roy Peter Clark, author and scholar

8.1 Introduction to the Importance of Grammar

Roy Peter Clark, author of *The Glamour of Grammar*, discovered the relationship of these words while browsing the *Oxford English Dictionary* for verification. Clark traced the roots connecting *grammar* and *glamour* from gothic stories with the word *glamor* (noun/verb without a *u*) as a witch's magic potion and a vampire's spell to a *glamorous* celebrity strutting down the red carpet at an awards ceremony, which is an occasion when "we sometimes hear the words *magical, alluring*, and *enchanting*" (2010, p. 3). Trying to make the topic of grammar entertaining is no easy feat. With texting and tweeting becoming so ubiquitous, parsing and punctuation may seem passé. Grammar has the power to be glamorous; correct usage can make words enjoyable and entertaining that resonate with readers. Sloppy grammar, however, is far from glamorous. It can be distracting and confusing to readers—and to the "grammar police" as illustrated in the *New Yorker* cartoon in Figure 8.1.

Think about this quote: "Nobody ever made a grammatical error in a non-literate society" (McLuhan, 1962, p. 238). Literacy rates globally continue to increase: 87% of female youth and 92% of male youth have basic literacy skills, while 60% of the countries with data reported youth literacy rates of 95% or higher in 2012 (UNESCO Institute for Statistics, 2014). We are living in an increasingly literate world, so applying proper grammar makes it easier to communicate in English—and to write material that can be easily translated into other languages.

The formal rules of grammar may not apply to our daily lives. Our dialogue with our friends, particularly when we are texting, may be full of slang and abbreviations. Movies, music, television, literature, social media, and other popular cultural forms tend to use expressive, informal language. Lyrics to music can ignore the rules; many songs are full of misused pronouns, double negatives, and other grammatical errors. If you try to correct the titles or lyrics from pop music past and present, they may lose their zing and rhyme. The

Figure 8.1—CARTOON DEPICTS THE "GRAMMAR POLICE." Source: © Michael Maslin, The New Yorker Collection/The Cartoon Bank.

"Sorry, but I'm going to have to issue you a summons for reckless grammar and driving without an apostrophe."

Rolling Stones' "(I Can't Get No) Satisfaction" would not work as effectively as "(I Can't Get Any) Satisfaction" or "I'm Unable to Be Satisfied" for a title of a rock song. "Hello It's Me" was a hit solo by Todd Rundgren in 1973, and still remains a rock classic while becoming a downloadable ringtone for mobile phones. "Hello It's I" would sound too stilted. Lady Gaga and Tony Bennett collaborated to sing "It Don't Mean a Thing (If It Ain't Got That Swing)," while mangling grammar. But would "It Doesn't Mean a Thing (If It Hasn't Got That Swing)" sound right? Rapper Timbaland's "The Way I Are" song also may not resonate with correct grammar.

However, when writing in academia and for business and public relations, the rules of grammar do apply. Just search any major bookstore in person or online, and you will find no shortage of grammar and writing books. Although many of the book titles are straightforward, some books have more whimsical titles to appeal to broader audiences beyond grammar enthusiasts—and public relations writers also may find them helpful:

- *Woe Is I: The Grammarphobe's Guide to Better English in Plain English*
- *Lapsing into a Comma: A Curmudgeon's Guide to the Many Things That Can Go Wrong in Print—and How to Avoid Them*
- *The Bugaboo Review: A Lighthearted Guide to Exterminating Confusion About Words, Spelling, and Grammar*
- *Grammar Snobs Are Great Big Meanies: A Guide to Language for Fun and Spite*

- *The Elephants of Style: A Trunkload of Tips on the Big Issues and Gray Areas of Contemporary American English*
- *Eats, Shoots & Leaves: The Zero Tolerance Approach to Punctuation.*

The last book on the list by British writer Lynne Truss became a bestseller in the U.S. and the U.K., and was subsequently translated into other languages, becoming "the go-to grammar book for those studying English as a second language" (Solomon, 2005, para. 3). The clever title about the panda description mishap and the cover illustration of a panda deleting the unwanted comma may have helped sell the book. Eats, shoots and leaves (all verbs) or eats shoots and leaves (verb followed by two nouns) mean two completely different things. As a *New York Times* reviewer pointed out: "Or maybe Ms. Truss has indeed touched a nerve of latent pedantry in a world in which, as she writes, increasing numbers of people 'don't know their apostrophe from their elbow'" (Lyall, 2004, para. 8). Nonetheless, this book on punctuation is entertaining reading.

Public relations writing is nonfiction—with a few exceptions, such as when a company is promoting a fictional advertising character. Not all grammar rules are alike between American and British English, as well other forms of English. The goal of this chapter is to help you evaluate your own knowledge and to identify areas for improvement. I have not yet encountered any person, no matter how erudite, who masters every rule of grammar or punctuation without needing to refer to a dictionary or stylebook from time to time. Writing is a never-ending learning process for everyone.

8.2 The Art of Sentence Structure

I have heard a common lament from faculty and experienced public relations practitioners in the U.S. and abroad that students, interns, and junior staff seem to lack basic skills in grammar. It's not uncommon for public relations agencies to give grammar quizzes and other writing exercises to determine if an entry-level job candidate can handle the basics. Some agencies also give quizzes on the most popular stylebook used in the country, such as the *Associated Press Stylebook* in the U.S.

In my writing classes, I like to start off the session on grammar by showing works of well-known abstract painters and ask the students if they think these artists had traditional art training. Let us look at Jackson Pollock (1912–1956), the late American abstract expressionist painter with the nickname, "Jack the Dripper," whose work produced during his most prolific years ("Drip Period") in the mid-20th century can be seen at leading museums in the U.S. and around the world (see Figure 8.2). Do you think Pollock received formal art training or he just started off with drip paintings?

During Pollock's early years, he studied at the Art Students League of New York in New York City, painting the human figure, still lifes, and landscapes before he began exploring other art styles and techniques (see Figure 8.3). Pollock discovered the freedom of liquid paint from the Mexican muralist David Alfaro Siqueiros, which sparked the development of his own painting style for which he became famous. The moral of my art example is that one must grasp and apply the basics before moving forward to greater levels of creativity.

And in writing, the basics include **grammar**. What is grammar? Linguist David Crystal has a valid explanation:

Figure 8.2—"NUMBER 14: GRAY" BY JACKSON POLLOCK. Enamel over gesso on paper. Sources: Yale University Art Gallery Katharine Ordway Collection. © 2014 The Pollock-Krasner Foundation/Artists Rights Society (ARS), New York.

Figure 8.3—"STACKING HAY" (FORMERLY "HARVEST") BY JACKSON POLLOCK. Lithograph (double-sided). Sources: Yale University Art Gallery Everett V. Meeks, B.A. 1901, Fund. © 2014 The Pollock-Krasner Foundation/Artists Rights Society (ARS), New York.

Grammar is one of the most exciting, creative, relevant subjects I know. It is sometimes described as the skeleton of a language, but it is much more than bones. It is the language's heartbeat, its nervous system, its intelligence. For without grammar, there can be no meaningful or effective communication. (Crystal, 2004, para. 2)

Just as a painter needs to understand composition and form and a sculptor creates an armature as a foundation, writers need to know how to craft sentences that express their thoughts to others. Grammar has rules, some of which vary based on the type of English. John Algeo (2006), professor emeritus in English at the University of Georgia, Athens, wrote a 364-page book on the similarities and differences between American and British grammar. He explains how the language evolves on both sides of the Atlantic Ocean:

Although many, few of the grammatical differences between British and American are great enough to produce confusion, and most are not stable because the two varieties are constantly influencing each other, with borrowing both ways across the Atlantic and nowadays via the Internet. When a use is said to be British, that statement does not necessarily mean that it is the only or even the main British use or that the use does not occur in American also, but only that the use is attested in British sources and is more typical of British than of American English. (p. 2)

Grammarians also may debate about standards and contemporary usage. Grammar can be **organic**, incorporating the common language we acquire to express ideas, or **prescriptive**, following grammatical rules taught at school (Connatser, 2004). You should have an understanding of both the prescriptive rules and the organic language style used in the cultures you are trying to connect with.

Understanding the specific names of grammatical terms can make it easier to understand the language structure and to describe to others how to improve their writing and make edits and corrections. Some of you may have studied grammar formally, so this content may be familiar. If so, I do hope the content serves as a refresher, and you discover some new tips.

8.2.1 Sentences, Clauses, and Phrases—and Common Errors

Sentences simply express a complete thought with words, at minimum a subject (unless it is implied, such as *Eat!*) and a verb, and they begin with a capitalized word and end with a period (called a full stop in Oxford English), question mark, or an exclamation mark. Refer to Exhibit 8.1 for descriptions of different types of sentences and their structures—simple, complex compound, and compound-complex—and Exhibit 8.2 for definitions of clauses, phrases, and modifiers, which will help make sense of sentence formations, if you are not familiar with the terms. This section examines some of the most common sentence structure errors.

- **Incomplete sentences** occur when writing a sentence with a missing verb or when mistaking a dependent clause as a sentence. In informal usage or dialogue, we may express our thoughts without forming full sentences and the readers or listeners may still understand the context. *Of course!* However, public relations writing should avoid incomplete sentences.

  Example: *Because the flight was delayed.* What's wrong with this sentence? This is a dependent clause trying to masquerade as a simple sentence. How can I improve

Exhibit 8.1—SENTENCE TYPES.

Types of Sentences	Descriptions	Examples
Simple	Contain one independent clause, including a noun and a verb.	The flight arrived two hours late.
Complex	Contain an independent clause and at least one dependent clause. Subordinating conjunctions link dependent clauses to independent clauses in complex sentences.	After we present our public relations recommendations to the prospective client (*dependent clause*), we will conduct a 20-minute question-and-answer session (*independent clause*).
Compound	Contain a minimum of two independent clauses, which are usually linked by a conjunction (such as *and* or *but*).	Natalia completed her undergraduate studies in communications, *and* she hopes to begin a career in public relations at a bilingual agency in Miami.
Compound-complex	Contain a minimum of two independent clauses and at least one dependent clause.	We wanted to relocate our office outside the downtown area (*independent*), but our employees (*start of second independent clause*), who enjoy the city center and take public transportation (*dependent clause*), complained that the location was inconvenient (*end of second independent clause*).
Declarative	State facts or opinions.	I hope you understand the value of proper grammar.
Exclamatory	Express levels of emotion, such as surprise, anger, or stress, ending with exclamation marks.	Don't rely on the computer spell-check program!
Imperative	Give instructions or make a command or a polite request.	Please complete the self-evaluation exercises on grammar.
Interrogative	Ask questions or make requests, ending with question marks.	What is the Oxford serial comma debate about?

this? Taking out the preposition is one solution. *The flight was delayed.* If I continue the sentence, I also would be able to provide more context. *Because the flight was delayed, I missed the meeting with our new client.*

- **Comma splices** happen when a comma is added between two independent clauses. They can be corrected a variety of ways: by forming two sentences; placing a semicolon between the two sentences; adding a coordinating conjunction (such as *for, and, nor, but, or, yet, so*) or a subordinating conjunction (such as *after, because, while*) and a comma; or rewriting the sentence in other ways.

Exhibit 8.2—CLAUSES, MODIFIERS, AND PHRASES.

Terms	Definitions
Dependent clauses (also called clauses)	Cannot stand on their own as complete sentences, subordinate even though they contain a subject and verb.
	Support adjectives, adverbs, and nouns by providing more information.
	Depend on an independent clause linked with a subordinating conjunction (*as*, *if*, *since*) or a relative pronoun (*that*, *which*, *who*) to form a complete sentence.
	Fall into two categories: **restrictive relative clauses** (also called defining relative or essential clauses) and **non-restrictive relative clauses** (also called non-defining relative or nonessential clauses).
Independent clauses (also called main clauses)	Contain a subject and verb and can stand on their own as a complete thought or as a simple sentence.
Modifiers	Refer to a word, phrase, or clause that further defines the meaning of another word, phrase, or clause.
Phrases	Can be words used together to create an idiomatic expression, such as "nuts and bolts."
	Provide more description and context within clauses in sentences.
	Support other words—**noun phrases** center around nouns; **verbal phrases** cluster around verbs; **adjectival phrases** support adjectives; **adverbial phrases** add words before or after adverbs; and **prepositional phrases** add more information starting with a preposition.

Example: *I want to understand grammar, it will improve my writing.* How can I correct this sentence? I can turn the clauses into two separate sentences, which may be a bit choppy. *I want to understand grammar. It will improve my writing.* I can insert a semi-colon between the two sentences. *I want to understand grammar; it will improve my writing.* Or I could add a subordinating conjunction and a comma. *I want to understand grammar, because it will improve my writing.* The sentence also could be edited in other ways. *If I master grammar, I will be able to improve my writing.*

- **Run-on sentences** (also called fused sentences) occur when two independent clauses lack punctuation between them.

Example: *My professor is intelligent I've learned a lot from her.* This sentence can be corrected by forming two sentences. *My professor is intelligent. I've learned a lot from her*. A better solution would be to add a semi-colon since they are short, interrelated sentences. *My professor is intelligent; I've learned a lot from her*.

• **That or Which Hunting**—To understand the challenges in selecting *that* or *which*, we will need to understand the differences between restrictive and nonrestrictive relative clauses:

– **Restrictive relative clauses** (also known as defining relative or essential clauses) provide essential information about the noun preceding the clause. In other words, the reader would be confused if that information is not included. These sentences require the relative pronoun *that* in American English, whereas in British English *that* or *which* can be used when referring to things, not to people ("Relative clauses," 2014). Commas are unnecessary.

Example: *The stream that flows past my house is flooded*. The clause explains which stream is flooded.

– **Nonrestrictive relative clauses** (also called non-defining relative or nonessential clauses) add information that is not essential to the meaning of the sentence. These clauses could be left out, and the reader would still understand the meaning of the sentence. *Which* is the most commonly used pronoun in nonessential sentences. Commas are necessary.

Example: *The stream, which usually floods in the spring, flows past my house*. You would still understand which stream the writer is referring to without the clause, making this information nonessential to the meaning of the sentence.

• **Appositives** are nouns or noun phrases that can be placed before or after the word or phrases they are describing. The tricky part is whether appositives provide essential or nonessential meaning to the sentence. Nonessential appositives require commas; essential ones do not.

Example: Does Lena have more than one sister based on the following sentence?

Lena's sister Felicia lives in Barcelona. Yes, Lena has more than one sister. The sentence *without* commas indicates more than one sister. Adding Felicia's name provides essential meaning to understanding the sentence.

• **Misplaced modifiers** usually result in nonsensical sentences, but they can be overlooked when one is writing quickly. Misplaced modifiers cause confusion when they are separated from the word or words they describe. Dangling modifiers are misplaced phrases or clauses, usually at the beginning of the sentence, that do not match the word or words they are referring to.

Example: *The patient waited in the clinic's lobby reading old magazines*. Who was reading the old magazines? Not the clinic's lobby. This sentence needs to be edited to make it clear that the last three words modify the actions of the patient.

Example: *When dipped in cocktail sauce, I really enjoy the shrimp*. Are you being dipped in the cocktail sauce? This sentence needs to be rewritten to indicate that the shrimp was being dipped in the sauce.

Example: *While waiting at the airport, John's flight arrived two hours late.* Who was waiting for John at the airport? This sentence needs to be rewritten for clarity on who was waiting for the flight to arrive.

- **Faulty parallelism** happens when a series of words, phrases, or clauses do not balance logistically in the same grammatical form. Corrections can be made simply by matching words, phrases, or clauses within the same grammatical construction.

Example: *She likes to windsurf, swim, and sailing.* Be consistent with the infinitives. She likes to windsurf, swim, and sail.

8.3 Direction of the Nine Parts of Speech

Think of yourself in the dual role of producer and director of a movie, who is overseeing the final script and managing the entire filming process. Select words carefully so that your audience clearly understands your characters, the action, the settings, the costumes, and the entire experience. You will apply the **nine parts of speech**—nouns, pronouns, verbs, adjectives, adverbs, prepositions, conjunctions, interjections, and articles—to create "award-winning" grammar that would resonate with your audiences in English anywhere.

8.3.1 Nouns: Protagonists of Your Sentences

Think of nouns as the leading and supporting characters, and you are trying to select the best cast to tell your story. Select nouns carefully—and know how to treat them with the respect they deserve. "The difference between the *almost right* word and the *right* word is really a large matter—'tis the difference between the lightning-bug and the lightning," wrote American humorist and writer Mark Twain more than a century ago (Bainton, 1891, pp. 87–88). This advice still has merit today: know when to use crackling lightning or the gentle flicker of a lightning bug.

Avoid vague terms such as *thing, facility, venue, gadget, stuff,* or *creature.* Are you referring to an *emerald* or a *rhinestone,* a *palace* or a *shack,* an *amphitheater* or a *gym,* a *laptop* or *smartphone, treasures* or *junk,* an *orangutan* or a *tarantula,* or an *ogre* or a *princess*? I have seen too many news releases and brochures full of lifeless nouns. **Concrete nouns** describe the person, place, animal, or other physical thing. If you use a specific term that may not be familiar to your audiences, you should consider adding more description or a brief definition in parentheses to describe the unfamiliar with the familiar. For example, a *yurt* is not a common dwelling worldwide, so a writer should explain what it is: *yurt* (a circular domed tent). **Abstract nouns** express feelings, ideas, and other intangibles. Choose the noun that clearly describes, but be careful of meanings that may not have the same definitions in all cultures like *beauty, liberty, love, freedom,* or *happiness.*

Watch out for **nominalizations**. These words are verbs, adjectives, and even other nouns transformed into new nouns, such as *finalization, conceptualization, experimentation,* and *connectivity.* Helen Sword, an academic and writer based in New Zealand, calls nominalizations "zombie nouns" appropriately, "because they cannibalize active verbs, suck the lifeblood from adjectives and substitute abstract entities for human beings" (2012, para. 2). Many articles in academic journals are plagued with nominalizations. Too much business correspondence and public relations materials are littered with nominalizations. Although nominalizations can be useful to some extent, public relations writers should use them with caution.

Make sure **double-duty** noun-verbs are clear, particularly for international audiences. English contains nouns that also can function as verbs. Here is an A–Z list of examples of double-duty words: *Answer, benefit, cause, drink, estimate, function, guarantee, help, influence, judge, kiss, level, mind, notice, object, place, quote, reason, ship, type, use, voice, wave, x-ray, yield,* and *zone.* This attribute can be entertaining for crossword puzzle fans, but confusing for non-native speakers and even native speakers. Chapter 9 on editing covers this topic in greater depth.

Nouns also can morph into "zombie verbs," otherwise known as **verbification of a noun.** Some nouns take time to evolve into acceptable verbs, such as *microwave* and *google.* But leave *inbox, architect,* and *author* to remain as nouns.

Use the right noun-verb agreement. **Collective nouns** refer to more than one person, place or thing, such as an *army, audience, class, committee, conglomerate, couple, family, government, group, jury, media, people, public,* or *team.* The tricky part is whether these nouns are singular or plural, which may depend on context in some cases. Follow a specific stylebook or dictionary if in doubt. In American English, many collective nouns are treated as singular. The online style guide created by *The Economist Style Guide* (2014a) explains the flexibility of collective nouns: "There is no firm rule about the number of a verb governed by a singular collective noun. It is best to go by the sense—that is, whether the collective noun stands for a single entity" (para. 1). However, *The Economist Style Guide* outlines a few exceptions that are always singular: the name of a company, a political party, or country, regardless if the word looks like a plural noun (such as General Motors and the Philippines); *-ics* words without a definite article (*the*), such as statistics and politics; and words that may seem plural like propaganda, billiards, and darts. Plural examples include the names of sports team, whether they look singular or plural.

Be careful to be consistent with the proper pronoun use, particularly with company names and pronouns: Sony announces *its* (not *their*) expansion plans. When you feel that the collective noun doesn't read right, such as *committee, jury,* or *faculty,* consider adding *members of,* which will automatically make the collective noun plural. For example: *Members of the committee are busy analyzing the reports.*

Know which nouns can be counted. **Count nouns** can form plurals (*pens, offices, calories,* and *restaurants*), whereas non-count nouns cannot form plurals (*time, homework,* and *weather*). These distinctions are important to understand with the following adjectives:

Countable and uncountable: *any, enough, no, some*
Countable: *few, fewer, many, several*
Uncountable: *less, little, much.*

Another cause for confusion arises between *a number of,* which is plural, and *the number of,* which is singular: *a number of students are . . .; the number of students is*

Singular and plural **Latin nouns** also can create confusion, and, in some cases, the rules have changed in modern English. Although *data* is considered the correct plural form of datum, the word is used as both a singular and plural noun today. How often do you hear the singular form *datum*? The word *media* is also widely debated, particularly when it is used as a collective noun, referring to print and electronic media outlets or social media. Some dictionaries would argue that media can be singular in this context. Speakers of contemporary English also prefer *agenda* (which is plural for *agendum* in Latin) as a singular noun and *agendas* for plural usage. Many Latin words, however, have not been disputed, such as *crisis* (singular) and *crises* (plural). Double-check your chosen style guide and dictionary for guidance.

8.3.2 Pronouns: Understudies for Nouns

Pronouns can replace nouns and save space, but writers should be careful that the reader understands who or what you are referring to. Unlike some other languages that have "status markers" of different second-person singular pronouns that distinguish relationships of familiarity and formal respect, English has one form of *you*. Most pronouns are gender-neutral; except gender-specific pronouns when referring to people of a specific sex in the third person (*he* or *she*). People may use *she* when referring to a ship or *he* or *she* for pets. See Exhibit 8.3 for a chart on pronouns. Try Exercise 8.1 to check your familiarity with pronouns.

Some writers may find some pronouns deceptively pesky. Personal pronouns substitute for nouns four ways:

- The **subjective case** (also called nominative) is used when one is doing the action, when the pronoun is the subject of the sentence, or when the pronoun follows linking verbs. Linking verbs do not express action; instead they link the subject of the verb with additional facts. Popular linking verbs include *be*, *become*, and *seem*, as well as verbs related to the *senses*.

  Example: *She* is writing the speech.

- The **objective case** (also called dative) applies when the pronoun is the object of the verb or preposition. Objective pronouns cannot be the subject of the sentence.

  Example: The journalist interviewed *him*.

- The **possessive case** (also called genitive) provides an indication of ownership or relationship.

  Example: The blue car is *mine*.

- The **reflexive case** (also called intensive) is used when the receiver of an action is the same as the doer. It can be used for emphasis.

  Example: I see *myself* in the mirror.

  Example: The president *himself* visited the victim in the hospital.

Exhibit 8.3—PERSONAL PRONOUNS.

Person	Subjective (nominative)	Objective (dative)	Possessive (genitive)	Reflexive (intensive)
First Person	I (singular) We (plural)	Me (singular) Us (plural)	My, mine (singular) Our, ours (plural)	Myself (singular) Ourselves (plural)
Second Person	You (singular and plural)	You (singular and plural)	Your (singular) Yours (plural)	Yourself (singular) Yourselves (plural)
Third Person	He, she, it (singular) They (plural)	Him, her, it (singular) Them (plural)	His, hers, its (singular) Their, theirs (plural)	Himself, herself, itself (singular) Themselves (plural)

Beyond personal pronouns, other types of pronouns also substitute for nouns the following ways:

- **Reciprocal pronouns** express shared actions or feelings or serve as possessives.

  Example: *Each other* traditionally refers to two people; *one another* to more than two people.

- **Indefinite pronouns** refer to unspecific persons or things.

  Singular: *Another, anybody, anyone, anything, each, either, everybody, everyone, everything, neither, nobody, no one, nothing, one, somebody, something*

  Plural: *Both, few, many, others, several*

  Singular or Plural: *All, any, more, most, none, some, such*

- **Demonstrative pronouns** (also called noun markers) point directly to nouns.

  Example: *That* man is an exceptional speaker. (singular)

  Example: Have you read *this*? (singular)

  Example: *These* are excellent books. (plural)

  Example: *Those* were the days. (plural)

  John R. Kohl (2008), a technical writer and author of a book on writing global English for translatable documents, recommends avoiding demonstrative pronouns when writing for international audiences, particularly for translated documents. *This*, *that*, and *these* pronouns should only be used as adjectives.

  Example: *These* are easy to understand. Explain what *these* are referring to. The preferred usage would be: *These guidelines* are easy to follow.

- **Interrogative pronouns** ask questions.

  Example: *Who* is at the door? (subjective case; *he* or *she* is at the door)

  Example: To *whom* should the letter be addressed? (objective case; the letter should be addressed to *him* or *her*)

  Example: *What* is the situation?

  Example: *Which* key opens the door?

  Example: *Whose* car is this?

- **Relative pronouns** introduce dependent clauses, which include a verb and noun but are not complete sentences, and refer to nouns, whether a person or a thing, previously mentioned in the sentence. This group includes *who, whom, whoever, whomever, whose, that,* and *which*. The most widely misused ones are *who* or *whom* (see interrogative pronouns) and *that* and *which* (see "that and which hunting" for essential and nonessential clauses).

  Be sure that pronouns are clear by avoiding **premature pronouns**.

Example: If *it* wins the award, the *public relations agency* will invite the entire staff to attend the awards ceremony. Using the noun first instead of the pronoun would make the sentence easier to understand. If the *public relations agency* wins the award, *it* will invite the entire staff to attend the awards ceremony.

Pronouns can be murky when the reader may not know what noun the pronoun is referring to.

Example: John told Albert that *he* will open an office in Miami next year. Who's *he*? It could be John or Albert. Reword for clarity. If it is John, the sentence should read: John told Albert that *he, John,* will open an office in Miami next year.

Try Exercise 8.1 to check your familiarity with pronouns.

8.3.3 Verbs: Action, Timing, and Mood of Your Story

Verbs explain the actions and moods of the actor, cinematographer, stage animal, or movie studio. How do you want to direct the characters' movements? Should they tiptoe, skip, sashay, strut, stagger, run, crawl, jog, trip, or walk? How do you want to direct their moods?

Exercise 8.1

Self-Evaluation: Pronouns

Choose the grammatically correct words in the following sentences.

1. My client and (me / I) went to the public relations workshop.
2. Will Juan or (him / he) be promoted to senior vice president?
3. Ali writes better than (me / I).
4. Between you and (I / me), I would prefer to be the keynote speaker.
5. John invited Anna and (I / me) to a beach party.
6. The award was presented to my colleague and (me / I).
7. My parents do not approve of (me / my) smoking.
8. The company has (it's / its) own cafeteria for employees.
9. Each of these reports (examine / examines) the challenges.
10. Everyone in her agency (is / are) required to maintain weekly timesheets online.
11. Everybody who can meet these requirements (is / are) welcome to apply.
12. Five passengers were in the damaged helicopter, but none (was / were) hurt.
13. Neither his personal trainer nor his physical therapist (were / was) available without an appointment.
14. Either debit cards or credit credits (is / are) accepted at this restaurant.
15. The public relations executive (whom / who) rented the office left the door unlocked.
16. The public relations executive to (who / whom) the office was rented left the door unlocked.

Please refer to Appendix D for answers.

In public relations writing, the third person (*it*, meaning the name of the organization, or *he* or *she* when referring to a person) is most frequently used when communicating to journalists. The exception is the use of quotations from a company spokesperson, which would be in the first-person singular (*I*) or plural (*we*). For communications in social media and to the consumer in multiple media, the first person singular or plural (*I* or *we*) and second person (*you*) are more widely used to convey a more conversational tone. Unlike other languages, English does not have status markers like Thai, Japanese, and some other Asian and European languages that have two verb formations in second person, the formal and familiar (Bennett, 1998).

Public relations writing traditionally requires the present tense to talk about what is happening now or about to happen. Except for some irregular verbs, tenses in English are not that complex. Double-check verbs when you are unsure of the correct tenses. I find that *lie* (to rest or recline) and *lay* (to place something or put something on something) are the most commonly misused verbs. Exhibit 8.4 provides an overview of **verb moods**, including the indicative, interrogative, imperative, conditional, and subjunctive.

Can or *may*? Most writers have no problems with *can* to indicate the ability to do something. Using *can* or *may* for asking or granting permission is debatable. This distinction has blurred in widespread usage, but many grammarians recommend *may* as the more polite verb in formal usage.

Exhibit 8.4—VERB MOODS.

Moods	Definitions	Examples
Conditional	Expresses a condition, such as what might happen if certain things occur ("if clauses").	If I win that new account, I will be able to hire more staff.
Indicative	States a fact.	The college offers both undergraduate and graduate programs in communications.
Imperative	Makes a command, warning, or request.	Don't be late! Please make sure to arrive a few minutes early.
Interrogative	Asks a question.	When will the presentation be held?
Subjunctive	Expresses wishes, hopes, demands, expectations, doubts, or hypothetical situations. All verbs use the infinitive without "to," such as *write* or *read*. The only exception is the verb *be*, in which *was* becomes *were* (even for first and third person singular).	She wishes she *were* independently wealthy. If I *were* you, I would book the flight way in advance. The agency principal recommended that John and Susan *be* promoted to vice president. The executive board decided that the museum *extend* its hours on Thursdays.

Should or *would*? Use *should* to express obligations, predictions, and expectations; and select *would* to express wishes, intents, or habitual action.

Most grammar guides recommend using the **active voice** instead of the **passive voice**. Exceptions may occur when the person or people doing the action do not want to be identified or when the focus is on the receiver of the action. Politicians like to use the following expression when things go wrong: "Mistakes were made." In this case, the passive voice is deliberate when no blame is attributed to a specific person or persons. The other situation is when you want to emphasize the person or object receiving the action. The *fugitive* was nabbed by the police. The fugitive is of greater interest than the police in this context.

8.3.4 Adjectives: Props, Makeup, and Costumes

Edit adjectives ruthlessly and be selective. You don't want to have props and costumes that distract or confuse the audience. Your characters should be dressed appropriately, and the scenery should help your audience better understand the story. Adjectives describe nouns or pronouns, helping to provide more description and well as answering the necessary 5Ws—who, what, where, when, and why—and sometimes how.

Mark Twain shared the following advice in a letter to a student back in 1880 (Mark Twain Project, 2007), which still has relevance today:

> I notice that you use plain, simple language, short words, & brief sentences. That is the way to write English—it is the modern way, & the best way. Stick to it; don't let fluff & flowers & verbosity creep in. When you catch an adjective, kill it. No, I don't mean that, utterly, but kill the most of them—then the rest will be valuable. They weaken when they are close together, they give strength when they are wide apart. An adjective-habit, or a wordy, diffuse, or flowery habit, once fastened upon a person, is as hard to get rid of as any other vice. (para. 9)

Follow Twain's advice and have no mercy editing adjectives. The worst offenders are non-defining adjectives—*unique*, *state-of-the-art*, *unparalleled*, *world-class*, and *revolutionary*. These adjectives should be used selectively or deleted. What do these adjectives really describe to the reader? I have heard many journalists complain about public relations practitioners using meaningless hype in press materials. Try to explain why something is special, instead of applying these overused adjectives. Be careful to make sure that *unique* means one of a kind; writing more unique or less unique is poor grammar.

One- or two-syllable adjectives traditionally form **comparisons** with -er endings, such as *thinner* and *heavier*, whereas adjectives with more than two syllables begin with more (*more outrageous*). **Superlatives** are the most overused adjectives: This new product is the *most innovative* of all. Consider rewriting sentences when you write one-or-two syllable adjectives ending in -est (*the poshest*) or adjectives with three or more syllables with the most (*the most extraordinary*)—unless the superlatives are truly accurate. If so, superlatives work more effectively in a quotation by a company spokesperson. Be careful of using correct **irregular comparative adjectives**: *good*, *better*, *best*; *bad*, *worse*, *worst*; and *little*, *less*, *least*. Although the hierarchy of adjectives has been debated by some grammarians, the British Council (n.d.) recommends the following order: General opinion (*good*, *nice*); specific opinion (*delicious*, *intelligent*); size (*tall*, *short*); shape (*rectangular*, *circular*); age (*historic*, *contemporary*); color (*silver*, *chartreuse*); nationality (*Japanese*, *Norwegian*); and material (*wool*, *stone*) and then the noun. Although better writers would avoid using so many adjectives in one sentence, the recommended logical word order can be helpful as a guideline.

8.3.5 Adverbs: Stunt Actors and Special Effects

Adverbs help verbs express information about how (*gently*), where (*indoors*), when (*early*), and to what degree (*frequently*). Adverbs modify action verbs (adjectives often follow linking verbs), adjectives, and other adverbs. The publicist *diplomatically* expressed her opinions. The new business presentation went *badly*. The client responded *very quickly* to my email. Arthur Plotnik (2007), an author of books on editing and publishing, recommends applying "joltingly fresh adverbs" (p. 37) by transforming adjectives with -ly endings creatively to adverbs in unusual ways, such as "ridiculously early" or "witheringly cute" (p. 38). Think of adverbs as great stunts beyond hackneyed car chase scenes.

Understand the differences between irregular adjectives (*bad*) and adverbs (*badly*). Chris feels *bad* (use the adjective form in this context, not *badly*, an adverb), which can mean sorry or unhealthy. If you write Chris feels *badly*, you are referring to how his skin feels, perhaps it is dry when you touch it, or that Chris has problems with his ability to feel.

8.3.6 Prepositions: Scene Transitions and Relationships Among Characters

You are editing your movie and you need to put together scenes in a logical, relevant order to tell your story. Prepositions provide connections to time, place, conditions, and cause and effect. These words connect nouns or pronouns to other words; examples include *about, above, across, among, at, before, behind, below, beneath, between, by, down, during, except, for, from, in, like, of, off, on, over, since, though, to, toward, under, up, with,* and *without*.

Prepositions have two roles as adjectival phrases, defining the noun, or adverbial phrases, supporting the verb, which are groups of words starting with prepositions and concluding with nouns or pronouns. Mignon Fogarty, author of the *Grammar Girl* series, explains that "prepositions are notoriously hard to pin down" (2013, p. 2), with numerous definitions, differences from country to country, and regional differences within countries. Fogarty recommends Google Books Ngram Viewer as a "secret weapon" (2013, p. 3) that allows you to search words or phrases and compare the frequencies of usage from a corpus of millions of books published from 1500 to 2008 in English, as well as in Chinese (simplified), French, German, Hebrew, Italian, Russian, and Spanish. For example, if you type in *different from, different than,* and *different to*, you will see a graph that indicates how *different from* is the most widely used phrase from 1800 to 2000. You can change the settings for specific year spans and languages—English (published in all countries), American English, British English, English Fiction, English One Million (books from 1500 to 2008, in which all early books are tracked and a random sample of later years), and other languages.

8.3.7 Conjunctions: Editing Tools

Conjunctions join words, phrases, or clauses together in a sentence, while some conjunctions also serve as prepositions. Conjunctions are particularly helpful in explaining time (*after, before, since, until*) and conditions (*even if, if, so that, unless*). They are classified in three ways:

- **Coordinating conjunctions** include *for, and, nor, but, or, yet, so*. Think FANBOYS. These simple words help connect independent clauses, and each conjunction can serve many purposes.

- **Correlative conjunctions** work in tandem to join elements together—*both, and*; *not only, but also*; *either, or*; *neither, nor*; and *whether, or*.
- **Subordinating conjunctions** establish the connection between a dependent clause and the remainder of the sentence.
  Example: *Because* Russell enjoyed writing and planning, he decided to pursue a career in public relations.

8.3.8 Interjections: Dramatic Sound Effects, Emotions, and Surprise

Avoid using interjections in more formal writing. *Pow! Wham! Wow! Oh!* They are usually punctuated with an exclamation mark; some are followed by commas. Generally, you do not find interjections in academic writing or rarely in public relations writing, except in social media, less formal communiqués, and fundraising appeal letters.

8.3.9 Articles: Definite and Indefinite

Articles always precede nouns, and sometimes are placed before the modifiers of the noun. *A* is applied before a consonant, *an* before a vowel or vowel-sounding noun, and *the* before a consonant or vowel. *A* and *an* are indefinite articles that do not refer to a specific person, place, or thing (person, residence, or apple); *the* is a definite article referring to a specific noun or a superlative (the most wonderful). Roy Peter Clark (2010) shares an effective way to understand articles by switching *a* and *the* in well-known titles of titles of books, songs, and movies: *Harry Potter and a Philosopher's Stone, A Hobbit, A Godfather,* and *To Kill the Mockingbird*. Be careful of nouns starting with an "h" that sound like a vowel, such as *hour*, which would use the article *an*. Other confusing words are acronyms when read aloud sound as if they begin with vowels. Is the student studying for *an* MBA? Double-check your stylebook for rules.

8.3.10 Grammar Rules Evolve and Some Become Archaic

Patricia O'Conner's *Woe is I: The Grammarphobe's Guide to Better English in Plain English* (2003) contains a chapter appropriately titled "The Living Dead" on archaic rules. Let us look at a few examples that deserve tombstones:

- Never split infinities. One of the most widely quoted examples is from the opening narrative by Captain Kirk in *Star Trek*: "Space, the final frontier. These are the voyages of the starship Enterprise. Its 5-year mission: to explore strange new worlds, to seek out new life and new civilizations, to *boldly* go where no man has gone before."
- Never end a sentence with a preposition. That's a rule most people won't put up *with*.
- Never begin a sentence with *and* or *but*. *And* why not? *But* don't overdo this exception.

8.4 Punctuation as a "Tour Guide" for Readers: American- and British-English Versions

"Just a side comment here," "stop and pay attention," "these are words from someone else," and "here's the conversion to that number" are a few of the many "directions" writers use to guide the readers. Think of **punctuation** as the tour guide for readers, helping to steer them

Figure 8.4—"A CAUTIONARY TALE" CARTOON ILLUSTRATES THE POWER OF A COMMA. Source: © Lauren Farnsworth.

in the right direction, highlight points of interest, and pace the timing right. Improper punctuation—whether misused or neglected—confuses readers, resulting in eye fatigue and potential misunderstandings. Look at the difference a comma can make in describing the steak in the cartoon shown in Figure 8.4.

Public relations writers should understand how and when to use the following forms of punctuation: ampersands, apostrophes, capitalizations, colons, commas, dashes, ellipses, exclamation points, hyphens, parentheses, periods, quotation marks, and semi-colons. Try Exercise 8.2 for a self-evaluation exercise on punctuation.

Ampersand (&)

An ampersand is not always a substitute for the conjunction *and.* In formal writing, only use the ampersand when it is the formal part of a company name, such as Ogilvy & Mather, or a brand name or a title of a creative work.

Apostrophes (' or ')

A retired journalist in the U.K. set up the Apostrophe Protection Society to protect this "threatened species" (Richards, n.d.). The most mangled and No. 1 offender of apostrophes is *it's.* These three letters—*i-t-s*—create havoc. *It's* is always the contraction for *it is* or *it has*—and cannot serve as a possessive pronoun, which is *its. Its'* with the apostrophe does not exist. Watch out for unnecessary apostrophes, also called **apostroflies**: "like an insect— an apostrofly—over the dining table, alighting where it will" (Mayes, 2002, para. 3). Apostroflies tend to land on store signs, posters on campus, email messages, and all forms of social media. Watch out for misused apostrophes as plurals of nouns (*oysters'* on sale) and the wrong contraction (*you're* for *your* or *they're* for *their*).

Apostrophes serve many useful purposes, such as the following applications:

• *Possessives* (clarity on who owns what or is doing something)

  Example: *Anne's* house

Exercise 8.2

Self-Evaluation: Punctuation

Try to correct the punctuation in the following sentences.

1. Let's eat grandpa. (What can you do to avoid having grandpa for dinner?)
2. It was a moose with huge antlers. We have all seen it using binoculars in the woods at the nature reserve.
3. The chef finds inspiration in cooking her family and her dogs. (How can we stop the chef from turning her family and pets into a meal? This sentence is based on a fake magazine cover for pet lovers that went viral online of Rachel Ray, an American celebrity chef.)
4. A woman without her man is nothing. (How would you punctuate this sentence from a feminist point of view?)
5. A woman without her man is nothing. (How would you punctuate this sentence from a male chauvinist point of view?)
6. Colin said, I'm trying to understand the differences in punctuation between American and British English. (How would you add quotations marks from an American perspective?)
7. Colin said, I'm trying to understand the differences in punctuation between American and British English (How would you punctuate this sentence from a British perspective?)
8. She will resign as soon as she can. (How can I prevent her from leaving her job?)
9. The agency executive said the client was challenging. (How can I edit this sentence to make it clear that the client was challenging in American English?)

Please see Appendix D for answers.

Example: *Dick and Jane's* apartment (they both own the apartment)

Example: The pharmaceutical company is considering public relations proposals from two public relations agencies: *Agency X's and Agency Y's* (two different agencies)

Example: *Journalists'* code of ethics

Example: *Caracas'* international airport (double-check your stylebook on names ending in s; some stylebooks would prefer Caracas's)

Example: *girls'* names (plural nouns ending in s)

• *Omitted Letters or Numbers*

Example: *I'm* (contractions)

Example: the *'60s* (meaning the 1960s)

• *Single Letters*

Example: We dotted the *i's* and crossed the *t's*.

Capitalizations

Although capitalizations may seem simple, not all stylebooks share the same rules on their usage. Formal names are consistently capitalized: names of people (*John Doe*); names of states, provinces, and countries (*Idaho, Ontario, Canada*); addresses (*Main Street, Madison Avenue*); bodies of water (*Lake Tanganyika, Pacific Ocean, Black Sea, Thames River*); names of religions, religious scriptures, religious figures, and holidays (*Christianity, Bible, Jesus, Christmas*); time periods and events (*Monday through Sunday, January through December, Iron Age, St. Patrick's Day*); political movements and parties (*Communism, Democratic Party*); names of companies and brands, unless noted by the trademark name (*Microsoft, Toyota, iPod*); and titles of creative works from music, cinema, television, and literature (*The Magic Flute, Avatar, Doctor Who, Harry Potter and the Philosopher's Stone*).

Here are other popular usages for capitalizations. Please check your selected stylebook. These examples follow the rules of the *Associated Press Stylebook*.

- ***Formal Titles***

  Example: *Prime Minister* Tony Abbott (Titles are capitalized before names.)

  Example: Tony Abbott is the 28th *prime minister* of Australia.

- ***Plurals of Common Nouns***

  Common nouns—mountains, seas, oceans, streets, avenues, and parties—remain lowercase when used as plurals with formal names.

  Example: *the Baltic, Black and Caspian seas.*

  Example: *Conservative, Labour and Liberal Democrat parties.*

  Example: *between Park and Madison avenues.*

- ***Geographic Directions***

  Double-check rules in your style guide on geographic areas, which are traditionally capitalized, but not compass directions.

  Example: They traveled *west* to reach the *Midwest*.

- ***Derivatives of Proper Nouns***

  Derivatives of proper nouns may not be capitalized when their original meaning has changed to a new meaning. A few examples include *scotch* and soda, *venetian* blinds and *pasteurize* (Cappon, 2003).

Colons (:)

Public relations writers should consider using the colon for the following purposes:

- ***Division in Sentences to Indicate Lists***

  Example: *The writer referred to three sources: a dictionary, a thesaurus, and a stylebook.* Some stylebooks, such as the *Associated Press Stylebook*, would object to the second comma, which is called a **serial comma**.

- ***Emphasis to Alert the Reader to Pay Attention***

    Example: *The company had one goal: profitability.*

- ***Time and Ratios***

    Example: *9:30 p.m.*

    Example: *3:1.*

- ***Question-and-answer Interviews***

    Example: *Q: What is your next project?*

- ***Before Quotations Over One Sentence***

    Example: *W. Somerset Maugham said: "There are three rules for writing a novel. Unfortunately, no one knows what they are."* Some stylebooks may debate this usage, so double-check your chosen one.

- ***Titles with Subheads***

    Example: *When Bad Grammar Happens to Good People: How to Avoid Common Errors in English.*

Commas (,)

Lynne Truss summed up the significance of a comma: "More than any other mark, the comma requires the writer to use intelligent discretion and to be simply alert to potential ambiguity" (2003, p. 96). Truss illustrated her point with the following examples of sentences that have misplaced or missing punctuation:

1. Leonora walked on her head, a little higher than usual.
2. The driver managed to escape from the vehicle before it sank and swam to the river-bank.
3. Don't guess, use a timer or watch.
4. The convict said the judge is mad. (p. 97)

Let us take a moment and try to fix these four sentences for clarity and sense.

1. Is Leonora walking on her head? No, you need to place the comma after *on* and prevent Leonora from having a headache. *Leonora walked on, her head a little higher than usual.*
2. Who is swimming to the river-bank? Have you ever seen a car swim? Although I believe Truss was addressing a missing comma after the word *sank* to indicate that the driver was the swimmer, I would recommend a better solution by adding a comma and a pronoun: *The driver managed to escape from the vehicle before it sank, and she swam to the river-bank.*
3. For greater clarity, replace the comma with a semi-colon to advise the reader to avoid guessing by using a timer or watch. *Don't guess; use a timer or watch.*
4. Who is mad? The convict or the judge? Without punctuation, the convict may believe that the judge is mad. If the judge is making the comment about the convict, quotation marks should be inserted between *the convict* and *is mad*; commas need to be added before *said* and before *is*. *"The convict," said the judge, "is mad."*

Commas serve many purposes to help readers understand relationships between words and clauses. Public relations writers should be familiar with the following usages:

- *Separation of Equal Adjectives, Substituting for the Word "and"*

  Example: *the careful, efficient timekeeper.*

- *Introduction to Direct Speech*

  Some stylebooks recommend a colon if the quote is over one sentence.

  Example: *He said, "I can do it."*

- *Separation of Full Dates and Numbers Over 999*

  Example: *January 1, 2015* (This is an example of American English usage.)

  Example: *1,101* (Please note that some countries may use periods or no punctuation.)

- *Separation of Names of Cities and Countries or Cities and States*

  Example: *The flight departs Amman, Jordan, at noon.*

- *Separation of Elements in a Series*

  Stylebooks vary on the usage of the serial comma, the final comma before "and."

  Example: *The inn serves breakfast, brunch, and dinner.* Oxford English and other style manuals apply the serial comma, whereas the *Associated Press Stylebook* recommends deleting the last comma.

- *Separation of Adverbial Clauses, Compound Sentences, and One or More Dependent Clauses Introduced by a Preposition*

  Example: *After suffering from jet lag, she slept for nine hours.*

  Example: *Hassan wants to attend graduate school, but he decided to work for a few years after finishing his bachelor's degree.*

  Example: *The hotel concierge, after calling the city's most popular restaurants, reserved a table for six at a highly recommended French bistro.*

- *Separation of Nonessential Clauses* (also called nonrestrictive relative clauses)

  Example: *Donna, who has two children, is the new account executive.* The fact that she has children is not essential to the meaning of the sentence.

Dashes (—)

Dashes have two forms: **en dash** (the size of an n) and **em dash** (the size of an m). Microsoft Word has an automatic feature that inserts en dashes (–) when you type a word, add a space, type a hyphen, add a space, and type the next word (word – word); and the program forms em dashes (—) when you type a word without a space, followed by two hyphens, and the next word without a space (word—word). Dashes are helpful punctuation marks for the following usages:

- *Additional Information, Emphasis, or Attribution*

  This quotation shows two usages; 1) emphasis and 2) attribution of the source at the end of a quotation.

  Example: *"There's a fine line between funny and annoying—and it's exactly the width of a quotation mark."—Martha Brockenbrough*

  When used in pairs, dashes can indicate additional but nonessential information, usually a series of extra facts within a phrase or an abrupt train of thought.

  Example: *Agatha squeezed everything she could into one carry-on pack—one suit, an evening dress, work-out clothes, three pairs of shoes, a cosmetics bag, and a nightgown—and smiled when she finally was able to close the zipper.*

- *Substitute for the Word "To"*

  Example: *Pages 20–50.*

  Example: *1900–1975.*

Exclamation Marks (!): Also Called Exclamation Points

F. Scott Fitzgerald said: "Cut out all these exclamation marks. An exclamation mark is like laughing at your own joke" (as cited in Graham & Frank, 1958, pp. 197–198). Exclamation marks follow warnings (Watch out!), commands (Sit down!), and emphasis (No!). The Internet has spawned the multiple-exclamation-mark frenzy: *Oh, really!!!!!* Public relations writers should ignore these marks—or use exclamation marks selectively to express caution or extreme emotions.

Be careful to apply exclamation marks to formal names, unless your stylebook states otherwise. Can you recall any company names with exclamation marks? *Yahoo!* and *Yum!* are two examples. Company names with exclamation marks cannot receive registered trademarks in the European Union. *JOOP!*, a German clothing and perfume company, tried to keep the exclamation mark and lost its case ("Exclamation marks not trademarks!" 2009). Can you name a town that has two exclamation marks in its name, the only one in the world to have such distinctive punctuation? Here's a clue: it is located in Quebec. The town is *Saint-Louis-du-Ha! Ha!* You may be thinking about which places have names with one exclamation mark: *Westward Ho!* in England and *Hamilton!* in Ohio. *Westward Ho!* was named after a book by Charles Kingsley in the mid-19th century. Hamilton became *Hamilton!* in 1986, gaining worldwide publicity for its point, but the punctuation has not been widely accepted throughout the community, such as on street signs and signage on police cars (Kemme, 2001).

Hyphens (-)

Stylebooks and dictionaries are scaling back on hyphens, with many words merging. The *Oxford English Dictionary* dropped 16,000 hyphens in its sixth edition in 2007, generating global media coverage. *Newsweek* magazine called it "punctuational genocide" (Braiker, 2007, para. 3). An op-ed in the *New York Times* ran an illustration of a tombstone with this engraving: "Here lies the nearly-departed, seldom-understood, soon-to-be-forgotten HYPHEN" (McGrath, 2007). *The Economist*'s online style guide (2014b) ends with a quote from the

Oxford University Press Style Manual: "If you take hyphens seriously, you will surely go mad." Let's try to keep our sanity and have a look at how hyphens can help guide readers. Hyphens still serve a purpose—and keep stylebooks in print since many guides will disagree. June Casagrande (2006), a columnist and author on grammar, calls hyphens "Life-sucking, mom-and-apple-pie-hating, mime-loving, nerd-fight-inciting daggers of the damned" (p. 61). Casagrande tells a story about two copy editors arguing about hyphens, illustrating the madness of hyphens:

"You had no right to put a hyphen in the story I edited about the orange juice salesman."

"You should have hyphenated it. In that context, 'orange' and 'juice' are forming a compound modifier and therefore require a hyphen. 'Orange-juice salesman.'"

"But reasonable use dictates that 'orange' and 'juice' form a familiar compound, one a reader can recognize without the hyphen."

"But without the hyphen, it's not clear whether you're talking about a man who sells orange juice or an orange man who sells some other kind of juice."

"Oh yeah? Well . . . your mama dangles her participles!" (2006, pp. 61–62)

- *Phrasal Adjectives (with two or more words before a noun; also called compound modifiers)*

    Example: Hyphens can help clarify the relationship of words. Is it a *man eating fish* or a *man-eating fish*? The hyphen would make a big difference to readers, as well as to piranhas and the man. Is it a *small business woman* or a *small-business woman*?

    Example: *a follow-up call* (as an adjective, but not as a verb, such as to *follow up* with a phone call)

- *Prefixes and Suffixes*

    Many prefixes and suffixes do not require hyphens. The exceptions are the prefixes *all, ex* and *self* and prefixes before capitalized words, letters or numbers (*all-encompassing, ex-spouse, self-explanatory, pro-Republican, U-shaped, mid-1900s*). *Elect, odd*, and *free* are three suffixes that require hyphens (*president-elect, fifty-odd, smoke-free*). Some prefixes forming double vowel words use hyphens, as well as suffixes forming triple consonants. Be careful of words that have different meanings whether they are hyphenated or not, such as *re-cover* or *recover*, *re-sign* or *resign*, or *coop* or *co-op*. According to the *Associated Press Stylebook* and others, adverbs ending in *-ly* do not require hyphens. However, a stylebook may exist that differs since I see this rule ignored in some print and online content.

    Example: *Small-business entrepreneur* (clarity of modifiers)

    Example: *Re-sign* (certain prefixes)

    Example: *Shell-like* (certain suffixes)

    Example: *Chinese-Australian* (paired nationalities)

    Example: The *co-op* board would not allow chicken coops on the balconies.

    Example: The event was *beautifully done*. (But you can use hyphens with adjectives ending in *-ly*, such as a *family-owned* business.)

- *Numbers and Ages*

  Compound numbers require hyphens (*twenty-three*), as well as numbers as adjectives before nouns (*15-acre estate*). Ages as adjectives before the noun require hyphens.

  Example: *50-kilometer drive* (but the drive was *50 kilometers*)

  Example: *23-year-old woman* (but she is *23 years old*)

- *Missing Words*

  Suspended hyphens indicate missing words that do not need to be repeated when the final adjective in the series is hyphenated.

  Example: It will be a *one- to two-hour* wait.

Parentheses ( ): Also Called Brackets or Round Brackets

Here are a few examples when parentheses can be helpful in providing the reader with additional information.

- *Conversions of Length, Pressure, Temperature, Volume, and Weight*

  When communicating with an international audience, writers should convert U.S. customary units and metric systems of measurements.

  Example: *10 ounces (283.5 grams)*

  Example: *100 kilometers (62.1 miles)*

  Example: *20° Celsius (68° Fahrenheit)*

- *Definitions and Other Supporting Information*

  Writers may want to provide a definition to a less commonly used word or translate a foreign word. Parentheses can be helping in providing dates, such as lifespans.

  Example: *Schadenfreude (joy derived from the troubles of others)*

  Example: *Pablo Picasso (1881–1973)*

Periods (.): Also Called Full Stops

Periods seem quite simple to conclude sentences and to indicate websites and emails. They can be more confusing with abbreviations, initials, and decimals since style manuals may differ in usage. Some stylebooks require one or two spaces between sentences.

- *Conclusion of Sentences, Websites, and Emails*

  Example: This is the end. (conclusion of sentence)

  Example: *www.google.com* (websites and emails; usually referred to as "dot")

  Example: *Dr., Mrs., St.* (American English) Note: *Dr, Mrs, St* (British English, titles and words are not punctuated, if they include the first and last letters of the abbreviated word)

Example: *etc.* (Latin words)

Example: *Mon.* (days of the week)

Example: *Jan. 1* (Some stylebooks only allow abbreviations of multisyllabic months when the day is included. March, May, June, and July are not abbreviated.)

Example: *USA* (British English) and *U.S.A.* or *USA* (American English, depending on the style guide).

Question Marks (?)

The question mark originates from the Latin word *quaestio*. Some grammarians believe that the mark was the evolution of the abbreviation of the first and last letter, *q* and *o*, which eventually became *?*, the symbol we use today. Question marks can be used to express uncertainty. However, I would recommend that public relations writers use the question mark for one primary purpose:

- ***Interrogative Sentences***

- Example: *When is the report due?*

Quotation Marks ("Quote and Unquote")

Cited material and dialogue requires quotation marks. Differences apply between American and British usage.

- ***Direct Quotations***

  Quotations are required before and after people's words whether spoken or written. American English uses double quotations and keeps commas and periods within the quotation. British English uses single quotations and places commas and periods after the quotation.

  Example: *"I'll be back," said the Terminator.*

  Example: *'I'll be back', said the Terminator.*

- ***Quotes within Quotes***

  In American English, quotations within quotes use single quotation marks; British English uses double quotation marks.

- ***Composition Titles***

  Double-check your stylebook for usage of quotations or italics (or no punctuation) for titles of books, plays, music, movies, artwork, TV shows, and other creative works.

Semi-Colons (;)

Semi-colons may have an identity crisis. One of my students even called them "evil."

Let us look at perspectives from two writers. Kurt Vonnegut is not a fan of semi-colons: "Here is a lesson in creative writing. First rule: Do not use semicolons. They are transvestite hermaphrodites representing absolutely nothing. All they do is show you've been to college"

Exhibit 8.5—AMERICAN AND BRITISH ENGLISH PUNCTUATION. This chart includes commonly used punctuation marks and some of their major applications, as well as differences between American English and British English.

Symbol	Punctuation Terms	Examples of Common Usages
&	Ampersand	Substitution for "and" in the formal name of an organization or brand name.
' or '	Apostrophe	Possessives; omitted letters and numbers; plurals of single letters and others. *Style guide rules vary, particularly for plural possessives.*
[ ]	Brackets (AE) Square brackets (BE)	Explanations within quoted language; use of [sic] to indicate misspellings in original copy within quotation marks. *Associated Press avoids brackets since these punctuation marks cannot be transmitted over newswires.*
:	Colons	Divisions in sentences to indicate lists; emphasis; time; ratios; question-and-answer interviews; before quotations over one sentence and some direct speech; titles with subheads; legal citations. *Other usages apply; refer to chosen style book.*
,	Comma	Separation of elements in a series (stylebooks vary on usage of serial comma); introduction of direct speech; separation of full dates in AE; separation of numbers 1,000 and up in AE; separation of cities and countries, cities, states, or provinces; separation of nonessential clauses. *Many other comma usages apply; refer to style manual.*
– (en) —em)	Dashes en dash (width of an "n") em dash (width of an "m")	Abrupt change in thought or interruption; emphasis; censorship of obscene words; long appositive phrases; substitution for "to" with ranges of page numbers, times, and dates. *Check your stylebook for usage. Associated Press, for example, does not use an en dash (short dash) or em dash (long dash).*
. . .	Ellipses	Omitted words in a quotation; pause in speech.
!	Exclamation point (AE)	Exclamation mark (BE or AE); dramatic effect; astonishment; warnings and commands. *Note: Use selectively in public relations writing.*
-	Hyphen	Compound modifiers; certain prefixes and suffixes; paired nationalities; ages as adjectives; some numbers as adjectives; suspended words. *Other usages apply; stylebook rules vary; differences between AE and BE usage.*
( )	Parentheses (AE) Brackets or round brackets (BE)	Additional information; metric and American measurement conversions.
.	Period (AE) Full stop (BE)	Conclusion of sentence; websites and emails (usually referred to as "dot"); courtesy titles in AE (titles and words are not punctuated in BE, if abbreviations include both first and last letters of words); some Latin abbreviations; days of the week; abbreviations of some countries; decimals. *Refer to style manual; differences between BE and AE.*
?	Question mark	End of question; uncertainty.
" " (double) (AE) ' ' (single)	Quotation marks (AE) Inverted commas, speech marks, or quotation marks (BE)	Before and after people's words spoken or written (AE uses double quotations and keeps commas and periods within the quotation; BE uses single quotations and places commas and periods after the quotation); quotations within quotes using quotation marks (AE uses single quotation marks; and BE uses double quotation marks); composition titles when not italicized; irony. *Other rules apply; refer to style manual; differences between BE and AE.*
;	Semicolon	Clarity in a sentence with multiple commas; separation of two independent clauses (stronger than a comma, but less separate than a period). *Other rules apply; refer to style manual.*

(2007, p. 23). Whereas Pico Iyer has a more favorable impression: "the semicolon brings clauses and thoughts together with all the silent discretion of a hostess arranging guests around her dinner table" (2001, para. 8). Here are two ways semi-colons can be useful:

- ***Clarity in a Sentence with Multiple Commas***

  Example: *The airline flies to Kyoto, Japan; Jakarta, Indonesia; and Mumbai, India.*

- ***Connection Between Two Independent Clauses*** (stronger than a comma, but less separate than a period)

  Example: *I love to write; words are my passion.*

The chart in Exhibit 8.5 includes a brief overview of the different forms of punctuation and highlights some of the major differences in nomenclature and usage between American and British English.

8.5 Learning Objectives and Key Terms

After reading Chapter 8, you should be able to:

- Explain the importance of applying proper grammar to public relations materials.
- Identify grammatical terms in sentences, clauses, phrases, and modifiers.
- Correct common sentence structure errors.
- Name the nine parts of grammar and describe the role each part plays.
- Identify grammatical areas that you may need to improve upon.
- Apply proper punctuation to public relations materials by understanding fundamental usages.
- Differentiate basic applications of American and British punctuation.

This chapter covers the following key terms:

Grammar (p. 180)	Organic grammar (p. 182)
Prescriptive grammar (p. 182)	Sentence types (p. 183)
Comma splices (p. 183)	Phrases (p. 184)
Clauses (p. 184)	Run-on sentences (p. 184)
Modifiers (p. 184)	Misplaced modifiers (p. 185)
Parallelism (p. 186)	Nine parts of speech (p. 186)
Nominalizations (p. 186)	Collective nouns (p. 187)
Count nouns (p. 187)	Active and passive voice (p. 192)
Punctuation (p. 194)	

References

Algeo, J. (2006). *British or American English? A handbook of word and grammar patterns*. Cambridge: Cambridge University Press.

Bainton, G. (Ed.) (1891). *The art of authorship: Literary reminiscences, methods of work, and advice to young beginners, personally contributed by leading authors of the day*. New York, NY: D. Appleton and Company.

Bennett, M. J. (1998). Intercultural communication: A current perspective. In M. J. Bennett (Ed.), *Basic concepts of intercultural communication: Selected readings* (pp. 1–34). Yarmouth, ME: Intercultural Press.

Braiker, B. (2007, September 25). Books: A dictionary drops 16,000 hyphens. *Newsweek*. Retrieved from http://www.newsweek.com/books-dictionary-drops-16000-hyphens-100795.

British Council (n.d.). Order of adjectives. Retrieved from http://learnenglish.britishcouncil.org/en/english-grammar/adjectives/order-adjectives.

Cappon, R. J. (2003). *The Associated Press guide to punctuation*. Cambridge, MA: Perseus Publishing.

Casagrande, J. (2006). *Grammar snobs are great big meanies: A guide to language for fun and spite*. New York, NY: Penguin Books.

Clark, R. P. (2010). *The glamour of grammar: A guide to the magic and mystery of practical English*. New York, NY: Little, Brown and Company.

Connatser, B. R. (2004). Reconsidering some prescriptive rules of grammar and composition. *Technical Communication, 51*(2), 264–275.

Crystal, D. (2004, April 30). In word and deed. *TES Newspaper*. Retrieved from http://www.tes.co.uk/article.aspx?storycode=393984.

Economist. (2014a). Singular or plural: Collective nouns. *The Economist style guide*. Retrieved from http://www.economist.com/style-guide/singular-or-plural.

Economist. (2014b). Hyphens. *The Economist style guide*. Retrieved from http://www.economist.com/style-guide/hyphens.

Exclamation marks not trademarks! (2009, September 30). *BBC News*. Retrieved from http://news.bbc.co.uk/2/hi/business/8282967.stm.

Fogarty, M. (2013, August 29). Prepositions: The fascinating history of English prepositions and a secret weapon to find the right one. *QuickandDirtyTips.com*. Retrieved from http://www.quickanddirtytips.com/education/grammar/prepositions.

Graham, S., & Frank, G. (1958). *Beloved infidel: The education of a woman*. New York, NY: Holt.

Iyer, P. (2001, June 24). In praise of the humble comma. *Time*. Retrieved from http://content.time.com/time/magazine/article/0,9171,149453,00.html.

Kemme, S. (2001, September 21). City's gimmick made a point: But 15 years later, Hamilton's punctuation mark has faded. *The Cincinnati Enquirer*. Retrieved from http://enquirer.com/editions/2001/09/21/loc_citys_gimmick_made.html.

Kohl, J. R. (2008). *The global English style guide: Writing clear, translatable documentation for a global market*. Cary, NC: SAS Institute.

Lyall, S. (2004, January 5). Writes, punctuation book and finds it's a best seller. *New York Times*. Retrieved from http://www.nytimes.com/2004/01/05/books/05GRAM.html.

Mark Twain Project. (2007). *SLC to David Watt Bowser, 20 March 1880*. Retrieved from http://www.marktwainproject.org/xtf/view?docId=letters/UCCL01772.xml;style=letter;brand=mtp.

Mayes, I. (2002, September 30). It's in its rightful place: The readers' editor on . . . the plague of the apostrofly. *Guardian*. Retrieved from http://www.theguardian.com/comment/story/0,,801364,00.html.

McGrath, C. (2007 October 7). Death-knell. Or death knell [Op-ed]. *New York Times*. Retrieved from http://www.nytimes.com/2007/10/07/weekinreview/07mcgrath.html?_r=0.

McLuhan, M. (1962). *The Gutenberg galaxy: The making of typographic man*. Toronto: University of Toronto Press.

O'Conner, P. T. (2003). *Woe is I: The grammarphobe's guide to better English in plain English*. New York, NY: Riverhead Books.

Plotnik, A. (2007). *Spunk & bite: A writer's guide to bold, contemporary style*. New York, NY: Random House.

Relative clauses. (2014). *Oxford Dictionaries online*. Retrieved from http://www.oxforddiction aries.com/us/words/relative-clauses.

Richards, J. (n.d). The Apostrophe Protection Society. Retrieved from http://www.apostrophe. org.uk/page3.html.

Solomon, D. (2005, November 20). Lynne Truss has another gripe with you. *New York Times*. Retrieved from http://www.nytimes.com/2005/11/20/magazine/20truss.html?pagewanted= print.

Sword, H. (2012, July 23). Zombie nouns [Blog]. *New York Times*. Retrieved from http://opinion ator.blogs.nytimes.com/2012/07/23/zombie-nouns/?_php=true&_type=blogs&_r=0.

Truss, L. (2003). *Eats, shoots & leaves: The zero tolerance approach to punctuation*. New York, NY: Gotham Books.

UNESCO Institute for Statistics. (2014, July 17). *International literacy data 2014*. Retrieved from http://www.uis.unesco.org/literacy/Pages/data-release-map-2013.aspx.

Vonnegut, K. (2007). *A man without a country* [Paperback edition]. New York, NY: Random House.

9 Sharpening Editing Skills for Global Audiences

But the last several decades have brought New Journalism and its rude vitality; in-your-face media; manic Internet blab; the voices of ethnic, pop, youth, and other subcultures; globalization; class meltdown; and mass attention deficit. In this sometimes disparaging, sometimes liberating environment, expressiveness calls for a break-a-leg performance. It demands rock-solid command of the language, yes, but also aggressiveness, surprise, exuberance, responsiveness, intensity, *rebelliousness*—most of which White seemed to disdain, except in his own prose.

—Arthur Plotnik, editor and author

9.1 Introduction to Editing

This above quote is in reaction to the Strunk and White classic book on writing, *The Elements of Style*, which debuted in 1919, and continues to be published today. This small paperback still contains useful, basic information on writing. My favorite is rule 17 to omit needless words, part of which reads: "A sentence should contain no unnecessary words, a paragraph no unnecessary sentences, for the same reason that a drawing should have no unnecessary lines and a machine no unnecessary parts" (Strunk & White, 2000, p. 23). Arthur Plotnik, an author and publishing executive, updated new standards in his *Spunk & Bite: A Writer's Guide to Bold, Contemporary Style* (2007), in which he debates that some of Strunk and White's rules are outdated and out of sync with today's readers, a group he describes as: "half focused, half distracted; half in the armchair savoring the well-chosen word, half seeking thrills in the electronic wilds" (p. 2). Plotnik also refers to how E. B. White digressed from his own Strunk and White's rules in his children's classics, *Charlotte's Web* and *Stuart Little*.

Learning how to edit is extremely important for public relations writers, who will need to customize content for diverse audiences, whether the copy is English for any global audience or catered to a specific audience or geographic region. Editing requires an understanding of the following techniques that are covered in this chapter:

- Using the most relevant tone from formal to informal, based on the intended audience.
- Avoiding nonstandard English, even when writing informally.
- Simplifying copy appropriately by deleting superfluous words.
- Selecting precise terms for greater clarity.
- Purging hype, jargon, clichés, slang, and idiomatic expressions that may not be widely understood.

- Developing cultural sensitivities about humor and references to race, gender, nationalities, religion, and sexual orientation.
- Checking polysemic words for accuracy and choosing other words to avoid confusing the reader.
- Proofreading strategies to write clear and logical content and to ferret out typographical and grammatical errors.

9.2 Tone and Relevance

Applying the right **tone** can make the difference in having your copy read, saved, and shared *or* unread and discarded. Peter Newmark (1988), who was an English professor at the University of Surrey specializing in translation, demonstrated the range of writing styles from officialese to taboo:

Officialese: The consumption of any nutriments whatsoever is categorically prohibited in this establishment.
Official: The consumption of nutriments is prohibited.
Formal: You are requested not to consume food in this establishment.
Neutral: Eating is not allowed here.
Informal: Please don't eat here.
Colloquial: You can't feed your face here.
Slang: Lay off the nosh!
Taboo: Lay off the fucking nosh! (p. 14)

These examples may be a bit extreme, but they do illustrate the huge variety of tone. Selecting the right tone depends on the personality of the organization or the brand, the audiences you are trying to reach, and the medium you are using. Although the officialese and official styles would seem too stilted or bureaucratic in many written materials, these styles would apply to forward-looking statements in financial news releases for publicly held companies and disclaimers about pharmaceutical brands and other products. Formal writing would pertain to white papers or reports. Public relations writers would write in the neutral tone for corporate media kit materials. Social media communication and audiovisual material would fall mostly into the informal style. Colloquial language could be used selectively, mostly in social media and public service announcements, if you know your audience would relate to it and that you are fluent in that voice. Applying less formal language does not mean ignoring the rules of grammar and sprinkling copy with vulgarities; it means using a conversational voice with familiar words that are relevant. Slang and taboo styles would most likely confuse international audiences or be considered rude by most readers.

Popular language has become pervasive—and the instant voice of social media discourse spreads fresh expressions that should be devoid of corporate gobbledygook. Bland copy regurgitated from reports will most likely be ignored. In Chapter 7, we looked at how dictionaries are acquiring new words, mostly originating from pop culture and technological innovations, every year. Edmund Weiner, principal philologist of the *Oxford English Dictionary*, was quoted in the *New York Times*: "'One hundred years ago it wasn't respectable to put a lot of colloquial language and slang words into print . . . It's only been in the last century that the gap between written and spoken language has narrowed" (Lyall, 2000, p. E1). This quote also appeared in Leslie Savan's book, *Slam Dunks and No-Brainers*, in which the author explained how politicians and businesses started adopting pop expressions from the 1960s counterculture and anti-establishment rock music to sell causes and products, a practice that continues today to reflect contemporary mainstream street language. Savan (2005) stated, "When corporations pitch rebellious, anticorporate attitude and when the public accepts it, without a blink, as cool, then the pressure is on language to likewise hold corporate and anticorporate values simultaneously" (p. 41).

Public relations writers mostly write immediate or short-term communiqués in print or digital formats, while competing to be read, seen, or heard within a distracted environment abuzz with promotional messages. Even if you want to write in a conversational style, you should be aware of the following guidelines to ensure that readers understand you.

9.2.1 Edit Nonstandard Words

Public relations writers should avoid usage of nonstandard words and grammar in all written forms, including blogs and social media commentary. Nonstandard English should be limited to lyrics and dialogue in novels, movie, or TV shows—or for informal conversation among friends. Here are a few examples:

Nonstandard Usage	*Proper Usage*
irregardless	regardless
could of	could have
gonna	going to (or will)
wanna	want to
would of	would have
have went	would have gone
kinda	kind of
ain't	isn't
don't have nothing	don't have anything

9.2.2 Be Mindful of Clichés, Idioms, and Slang

Most writing books suggest selecting simpler words for all audiences. This approach would be particularly relevant for the general global reader and recommended for social media and writing for the ear. However, if you are addressing an academic audience or a well-educated professional group, you may want to use more complex, multisyllabic words that are widely used by people in those fields. Writers must edit carefully to avoid idiomatic expressions that would be confusing for the reader, listener, or viewer. Be careful of expressions that may not transcend a particular region or country, such as clichés, euphemisms, idioms, humor, slang, colloquialisms, regionalisms, jargon, tech lingo, and neologisms.

Clichés are overused phrases that many consider trite. Patricia O'Conner, author of *Woe is I*, states that not all clichés need "to be summarily executed" (2004, p. 168) and shares a reality: "There's no way to eliminate all clichés. It would take a roomful of Shakespeares to replace them with fresh figures of speech, and before long those would become clichés, too. Vivid language is recycled precisely because it's vivid" (p. 168).

O'Conner compares clichés to familiar condiments you may use with foods. I think of clichés as old clothes, the ones you have loved wearing for comfort. You may have a hard time giving up your favorites until the stains, rips, or moth holes start to become too obvious.

Clichés bring attention to those "clothes beyond repair." The worst clichés are those that don't have a "passport," so they should remain within their own geographic borders. How many clichés can you find in this paragraph?

> At the crack of dawn, the student was scared out of her wits when she sat in front of the blank computer screen glaring as white as snow. Five minutes lasted an eternity as she searched her brain for the right words. She knew that the cat got her tongue. Time was running out. She looked at the printout of the homework assignment over and over again. She drew a blank and nothing came to mind. She was banging her head against the brick wall. Her professor had had it up to here with her excuses. Her dog really did eat her homework and made a pig's breakfast out of it. She really was a sick puppy when the flu epidemic descended upon the college like the plague. She decided to give it the old college try and grabbed the bull by the horns. Before she knew it, she completed the assignment in the nick of time.

The Oxford Dictionaries (2014) defines a **euphemism** as: "A mild or indirect word or expression substituted for one considered to be too harsh or blunt when referring to something unpleasant or embarrassing." Although some public relations practitioners seem to wear "glittering tiaras" of euphemisms, writers should be cautious when trying to hide the obvious. *Realigning human resources* or *rightsizing* are euphemisms for *layoffs*; *downsizing* also has become a popular euphemism and more commonly used term for *layoffs*. Other euphemisms have become commonplace: *collateral damage* for *civilian casualties* during warfare; and *passed away* for *died*.

Idioms have a few meanings according to *Merriam-Webster*:

- an expression that cannot be understood from the meanings of its separate words but that has a separate meaning of its own;
- a form of a language that is spoken in a particular area and that uses some of its own words, grammar, and pronunciations;
- and a style or form of expression that is characteristic of a particular person, type of art, etc. ("Idiom," 2014, paras. 1–3)

Idioms present serious challenges for international writers. **Sports references**, for example, are highly idiomatic and should be avoided, unless you know your audience follows that sport and understands these expressions. In the U.S., football is a completely different sport from the football played outside of America, which would be called soccer in the U.S. (see Figure 9.1 for a humorous interpretation). Confusions abound when Americans use sports terms when writing and speaking with international audiences. Here are a few examples from American football: *drop the ball* (make a mistake), *game plan* (strategy), and *take the ball and run with it* (finish or develop something further). Baseball terms are commonly used in business, primarily in the U.S.: *step up to the plate* (to take responsibility and do something), *a home run* (a success), *cover all bases* (be defensive and prepared), *in the ballpark* (estimate), *throw a curveball* (a surprise, usually a negative one), and *pinch hit* (substitute for someone, usually last minute).

Be careful of **humor** that may bewilder audiences or could be considered offensive in other cultures. Is this an example of humor or anti-American sentiment? Subway fast food franchises in Germany set up a promotion with *Super Size Me*, an Academy Award-nominated documentary on the consequences of a 30-day diet exclusively on food from McDonald's, which is also Subway's major competitor. Subway's promotional tray liners were decorated

Figure 9.1—CARTOONIST RON THERIEN ILLUSTRATES HOW FOOTBALL MEANS DIFFERENT THINGS. Source: © Ron Therien, CartoonStock.

with an illustration of an obese Statue of Liberty holding fries instead of a torch and a burger in her other hand with the heading "Warum sind die Amis so fett?" ("Why are Americans so fat?). The term "Amis" is the slang equivalent of "Yanks," which Subway's founder and president claimed was not meant to be "pejorative, but rather a shortened German word for 'American'" ("Group calls Subway ad 'unpatriotic,'" 2004, para. 10). A U.S.-based advocacy group called the promotion anti-American. Subway's corporate headquarters in the U.S. demanded a discontinuation of the promotion and issued an apology on behalf of the German franchisees (Jones, 2008).

The Oxford Dictionaries (2014) describes **slang** as: "A type of language consisting of words and phrases that are regarded as very informal, are more common in speech than writing, and are typically restricted to a particular context or group of people." Apply slang judiciously since this informal language is used inclusively within social or professional circles, with some groups residing within narrow geographic areas. Slang comes from a large family of related terms—*argot, cant, colloquialism, jargon, lingo, neologism, patois,* and *shoptalk.* Let us look at relevant synonyms of interest to public relations writers.

- **Colloquialisms** and **regionalisms** are informal expressions used within a community. The challenge is that they may not be understood beyond the borders of the geographic area. For example, an American public relations account executive dumfounded a group of European female executives, when she asked: "What do you guys think about this idea?" "You guys" in slang is considered the plural "you." My colleague from the Midwest uses the word "pop" for "soda," which confuses people outside that region. The *Dictionary of American Regional English* (dare.wisc.edu) documents dialects in the U.S.

- Purge your copy of **jargon**—words or terms used by people within a specific profession—unless you are writing directly to that professional group. Otherwise, the reader may be completely confused. You may have heard of the term *legalese*, meaning legal terms than people outside of the legal profession may not understand. However, be careful of hackneyed jargon that is overused by professionals in any field. My former colleague at a public relations agency was a fan of "BS bingo," particularly the *marketingese* version that follows the bingo rules of five columns and five rows, with numbers in each grid (in this case, a word or words are used), except for a free space in the middle. You would be surprised how easily one can fill in the squares with chips (or coins) when certain words or phrases are used during a conference call on marketing and public relations—such as *engagement, game plan, impact, paradigm, proactive, synergy, leverage, low-hanging fruit*, and *think outside the box*.

- Keep **tech lingo** out of business correspondence. Tweets, texts, and email messages can be full of extra letters for emphasis (*Whaaaat?*), initialisms (*LOL* for "laughing out loud," which some political leaders have mistakenly used as "lots of love"), and **emoticons**, such as :-) for smiling.

- **Neologisms** are newly coined words or expressions that may not be popular in mainstream usage. Grammar.monster.com provides an explanation of different types of neologisms: "A completely new word (e.g., oversharers); A new combination of existing words (e.g., digital detox); and A new meaning for an existing word (e.g., sick)" (Shrives, n.d., para. 3). Can you think of any other neologisms past and present? I also address neologisms in the upcoming section on generational gaps.

- Be mindful of **semantics** in terms of words that can have several interpretations and provoke either positive or negative reactions from people in different cultures. What does the word or phrase mean in the cultures you are trying to reach? For example, *Diet Coke* was renamed *Coke Light*, since the word *diet* had negative, embarrassing connotations in Japan (Cateora & Graham, 2004).

9.2.3 Be Sensitive to Generational Gaps—and Greater Transcultural Gaps

As words age, they can take on new meanings or become passé. Generations who grew up with "geezer terms" (Plotnik, 2007, p. 232) may want to update their vocabulary. My personal favorite—and one that my students say they cringe when they hear their parents say the words—is *hook up*, which now means to engage in casual sexual activity in slang, and formerly meant to meet or associate with someone, who could be a friend, a date, or a business associate. Popular music introduces new terms, such as *phat* (meaning tempting, gratifying, or excellent) in rap, that may confuse older people. Common words can change meanings completely, depending on the context and inflection. The word *sick* in American slang can mean "great; amazing; 'cool'; 'awesome'" ("Sick," 2014). *Bad, crazy, insane*, and *wicked* also have positive connotations in slang that may confuse generations and international audiences.

Technology introduces new terms that can date someone. A U.S. Republican senator was 82 years old when he was widely mocked by traditional and social media for referring to the Internet as "a series of tubes" in a public speech (Williams, 2006). The term *information superhighway* now seems very 1990s.

References to movies and television programs also change in popularity and familiarity by generation—and may not transcend transculturally except within a specific region or among movie buffs of a certain genre.

9.3 Clarity, Simplicity, and Precision

Simple editing techniques can make your writing clearer, simpler, and more precise. This section looks at superfluous words, hype and superlatives, vague terms, negative language, and foreign words, as well as preferred terms for religions, nations, and people.

9.3.1 Delete Superfluous Words

Go on a hunt for superfluous words that can be deleted without changing the sentence.

Wordy	*Shortened*
Look into	Find, search
It was the public relations agency that	The public relations agency
There are many solutions	Many solutions
The field of public relations	Public relations
Make editorial changes	Edit
The people who live in the city of New York	New York City residents (or New Yorkers)
The charts illustrated in the	The charts in the
Some of the businesses	Some businesses
It is usually the case	Usually
Proposals that are submitted after	Proposals submitted after
Off of	Off
Company X is proud to announce the opening of its . . .	Company X opens its . . .

9.3.2 Avoid Hype and Superlatives

Edit copy carefully to delete hype and unnecessary descriptions that do not add to the meaning. Be careful of *very* and superlatives. Try to describe why something is important, instead of using puffery or self-serving copy that sounds like a poorly written advertisement. Develop a "BS detector" for copy and releases littered with hype and promotional copy (Fernando, 2011, p. 10).

Words to Edit	*Improved*
Very unique	Unique (nothing can be more or less unique; this word means one of kind; make sure a product or service has earned this distinction).

The most extraordinary	Reword; why is it so extraordinary?
Revolutionary	Reword; why is it revolutionary?
State-of-the-art	Reword; explain why.
The only	Make sure this claim is true or edit.
The first	Is it really the first? Check for accuracy.

9.3.3 Replace Vague Words with Specific Terms

Careful writers should select the clearest word to describe a thing, place, event, or person, particularly when the word is first introduced (unless there is reason for the vague term). Concrete nouns also were covered in Chapter 8 on grammar.

Vague Terms	*Questions to Ask*
Venue	What is it?
Place to stay	What type of place?
Person	What type of person?
Thing	What thing?
Color	Which color?
Emotion	What emotion?

9.3.4 Edit Phrasal Verbs for ESL/EFL Speakers

Find substitutes for phrasal verbs that can be confusing to people whose first language is not English.

Phrasal Verbs	*Clearer Meanings*
Check up on	Investigate
Come down with	Fall ill
Come up with	Raise money, fund
Get away with	Escape blame
Hang out	Stay, linger, relax
Look in on	Visit
Put some thought to	Consider
Pull through	Survive
Put up with	Tolerate
Talk back to	Answer rudely

9.3.5 Edit Negative Language

An excellent example of why to avoid writing the word *not* is from Richard Nixon, the 37th president of the U.S. When Nixon was trying to defend himself during the 1973 Watergate scandal, he said, "I am not a crook." He should have said, "I am honest." *Time* magazine listed Nixon's quote as one of the "Top 10 Unfortunate Political One-Liners" (2008).

Negative Language	*Less Negative or Neutral Language*
He was not able to participate.	He was unable to participate.
I am not available.	I am available at (a specific time).

I cannot do this now.	I can take care of this later (or indicate when).
She didn't arrive on time.	She arrived late.

9.3.6 Use Foreign Words Selectively

Many grammar books mandate that writers should not use foreign words. Linguist Edgar Schneider (2010) explains how English "is being localized, fusing with indigenous language input to yield new dialects suitable for the expression of local people's hearts and minds" (p. 229). Use the non-English word, if it best describes what you are trying to express. Plotnik (2007) explains how the Japanese word *umami* contains "all the qualities of a foreign term word worth borrowing" (p. 93). Not one English word can replace the meaning of *umami*, meaning a savory taste, a fifth taste sensation beyond sweet, sour, bitter, and salty.

9.3.7 Use the Right Words for Religions and Nations

Double-check that you are using the right terms in describing religions, such as the correct noun for the name of the religion, the noun for adherents, and adjectives referring to the religion. Writers also should avoid using religious words that have other secular meanings, such as the word *mecca* as a popular place or *nirvana* as an ideal place. Many stylebooks address preferred religious terms. The Association of Religion Data Archives (ARDA) also maintains a dictionary on its website (http://www.thearda.com). Refer to Exhibit 9.1 for examples of religious terminology.

Public relations writers should be aware of what religions are practiced in a particular region for planning PR campaigns and writing materials appropriately. Try Exercise 9.1 to test your awareness about religions around the world.

Exhibit 9.1—EXAMPLES OF RELIGIOUS TERMS.

Religion (noun)	Adherents of the religion (noun, plural examples)	Adjective
Bahá'í	Bahá'ís	Bahá'í
Buddhism	Buddhists	Buddhist
Christianity	Christians	Christian
Confucianism	Confucianists	Confucianist
Hinduism	Hindus	Hindu
Islam	Muslims	Islamic or Muslim
Jainism	Jainists or Jains	Jainist or Jain
Judaism	Jews	Jewish
Shintoism or Shinto	Shintoists	Shintoist or Shintoistic
Sikhism	Sikhs	Sikh
Taoism	Taoists	Taoist

Exercise 9.1

Self-Evaluation: Geographic Knowledge of Religions of the World

Try to answer the following questions about religious geography.

1. Which country has the world's largest Islamic population?
2. Which country has the second largest Islamic population?
3. Which regions in the world have the largest Catholic population?
4. Which city has the world's largest Jewish population?
5. Which city has the second largest Jewish population?
6. Which country has the highest proportion of Buddhists?
7. Which two countries have the highest proportion of Hindus?
8. Which country has the largest population of Bahá'í followers?
9. Which county has the largest number of Shintoist followers?
10. Which country has the largest population of Confucianists?

Please see Appendix D for answers.

Be mindful of changes of the names of countries and cities. Many names of Indian cities were renamed in the 1990s; Bombay is officially *Mumbai* and Madras became *Chennai*, among others. *Guangzhou*, China, is no longer called Canton. The *Czech Republic* and *Slovakia* are the correct names of the former Czechoslovakia. If you google Myanmar or Burma, you will uncover debates over the country's name. However, the *Associated Press Stylebook* recommends *Myanmar*. The terms *domestic*, *national*, or *countrywide* must be explicit to the reader or should be rewritten to indicate the specific geographic area.

9.3.8 Apply Correct Terms for Gender, Race, Age, and Sexual Orientation

Stylebooks may differ about terms that are considered politically correct when referring to gender, age, race, and the LGBT community.

The most common solutions for writing gender-neutral terms are taking out the "man" or "men" out of words referring to professionals or selecting more contemporary terms describing occupations. Here are a few examples:

Gender-Specific	*Preferred Gender-Neutral Usage*
Businessman	Business executive
Chairman	Chair
Congressman	Congressional representative
Fireman	Firefighter
Mailman	Postal worker or letter carrier
Policeman	Police
Salesman	Sales representative or salesperson

Stewardess	Flight attendant
Workmen	Workers

An effective way to avoid the clunky *he* or *she* is by using the plural *they*. Avoid terms such as *lady doctor* or *male nurse* when doctor or nurse alone would be sufficient. Other gender-neutral preferred terms apply to *parents*, instead of *mothers* or *fathers*, as well as to *spouses*, instead of *wives* and *husbands*. The U.S.-based National Council of Teachers of English posts a useful reference called Guidelines for Gender-Fair Use of Language on its website (http://www.ncte.org).

GLAAD, the U.S.-based lesbian, gay, bisexual, and transgender (LGBT) media advocacy group, publishes a downloadable *Media Reference Guide*, with a comprehensive section on glossary of terms and language, on its website (http://www.glaad.org). GLAAD defines *gay* and *LGBT/GLBT* as follows:

Gay: The adjective used to describe people whose enduring physical, romantic and/or emotional attractions are to people of the same sex (e.g., *gay man*, *gay people*). Sometimes *lesbian* (n. or adj.) is the preferred term for women. Avoid identifying gay people as "homosexuals," an outdated term considered derogatory and offensive to many lesbian and gay people. (GLAAD, 2014, p. 6)

LGBT/GLBT: Acronym for "lesbian, gay, bisexual and transgender." LGBT and/or GLBT are often used because they are more inclusive of the diversity of the community. Care should be taken to ensure that audiences are not confused by their use . . . (GLAAD, 2014, p. 7)

Writers also should be sensitive to addressing age. The International Longevity Center-USA and Aging Services of California issued a *Styleguide for Journalism, Entertainment and Advertising* with the subhead *Media Takes: On Aging* (Dahmen & Cozma, 2009). Its glossary includes a list of preferred terms, and recommends *older* as the preferred adjective, such as *older people* or *older individuals*, instead of such terms as *seniors*, *senior citizens*, or the *elderly*, which can be perceived as discriminatory or offensive.

The National Association of Black Journalists (http://www.nabj.org) publishes an online style guide with an explanation of how to use the terms *African*, *African American*, and *black*:

Hyphenate when using African American as an adjective. Not all black people are African Americans (if they were born outside of the United States). Let a subject's preference determine which term to use. In a story in which race is relevant and there is no stated preference for an individual or individuals, use black because it is an accurate description of race. Be as specific as possible in honoring preferences, as in Haitian American, Jamaican American or (for a non-U.S. citizen living in the United States) Jamaican living in America. Do not use race in a police description unless the report is highly detailed and gives more than just the person's skin color. In news copy, aim to use black as an adjective, not a noun. Also, when describing a group, use black people instead of just blacks. In headlines, blacks, however, is acceptable. (n.d., para. 4)

Many style guides also address how to refer to people of other ethnic backgrounds properly. For example in the *Associated Press Stylebook* (Christian, Froke, Jacobsen, & Minthorn, 2014), *Asian* is the preferred term over *Oriental*. In the U.S., *Native American* or *American Indian* or the specific name of the tribe is the preferred usage over *Indian*, which would be the correct term when referring to people from the country of India. The only other proper usage for *Indians* would be when referring to one of the indigenous groups collectively called *Alaska Natives*.

9.3.9 Use Numbers and Abbreviations Clearly

Make it clear what currency you are referring to. Dollars, dinars, pesos, and rupees are used by different countries. The International Organization for Standardization (www.iso.org) posts a list online of standard currency codes referred to as ISO 4217 for both alphabetic and numeric codes (for languages that do not use Latin scripts and computerized systems). The three-letter code helps avoid confusion when you are communicating with multinational audiences. Here are examples of dollars: AUD for Australian Dollar, CAD for Canadian Dollar, JMD for Jamaican Dollar, NZD for New Zealand Dollar, and USD for United States Dollar.

You also can provide conversion rates in documents by using parentheses: USD100 (EUR74.8). Writers should add the source and date of currency exchange when providing cost estimates and budgets in proposals. Fluctuations can happen frequently and unexpectedly.

Measurements and dimensions fall predominately into three categories: 1) the metric system, which is formally called the International System of Units; 2) U.S. standard units, which is also referred to as the U.S. customary system; and 3) the imperial system, which is also called the British imperial system, that has been replaced by the metric system in many countries. Although many British Commonwealth countries have switched to the metric system, metrication in the U.K. began in 1965 and still seems to be a debated issue. Apparently, the U.S., Liberia, and Myanmar remain the only three countries reluctant to adopt metrication in daily life (Villarreal, 2013). Some industries at large have adopted the metric system. Americans may be more familiar with the metric system than they think. Wine and distilled spirits have been sold in metric units since the early 1980s in the U.S.; while other industries, such as health care, automotive, and some consumer products, have converted to the metric system (National Institute of Standards and Technology, 2014).

Americans should avoid the single prime symbol for feet (3′) and the double prime symbol for inches (3″). Writers should convert different systems using parentheses, particularly the metric system to U.S. standard units and vice versa.

The most basic and most widely confusing numbers are dates in international usage. Always spell out months since different cultures do not follow the same order for day, month, and year. Clarity on terms about time is addressed in depth in Chapter 4.

Unless you are certain that your audience is familiar with acronyms and abbreviations, you may want to avoid using them. When I googled CIA, the first reference was the Culinary Institute of America, followed by the Central Intelligence Agency, and the Cleveland Institute of Art. Unless you have a tight word count on a microblog post or are writing an academic paper, you may want to avoid using many of the Latin abbreviations in public relations writing, such as *etc.*, *et al.*, and *e.g.*

9.4 Commonly Misused Words and Confusing Expressions

English is littered with many polysemic words that play multiple roles and sound or appear very similar, yet they may have different meanings, creating confusion for even seasoned writers. *Affect* or *effect*, *premiere* or *premier*, and *a while* or *awhile* are among the many commonly confused words in English. Your computerized spell check program will not catch these errors.

- **Homonyms** are words that share the same spellings and pronunciations, *but* they have different meanings (This definition follows *Merriam-Webster*; some dictionaries define homonyms as words sharing the same spellings or pronunciations.)

  I can't *bear* seeing a brown *bear* in my backyard.

  The country *fair* was *fair*.

  The hospital *patient* was quite *patient* while waiting for the doctor.

  I'm sorry I told a *lie*, and now I need to *lie* down for a while.

- **Homophones** are subsets of homonyms that have the same pronunciations, *but* they have different spellings and meanings.

  I *knew* the *new* account executive at another agency.

  I will be *right* there to *write* up the story about the religious *rite*.

  My *son* enjoys being out in the *sun*.

  They're meeting us *there*, not at *their* office.

- **Homographs** share the same spellings, *but* they have different meanings and sometimes different pronunciations. **Heteronyms** are words with the same spellings, *but* they have different pronunciations and meanings.

  I'll *graduate* in the spring and then I'll finally be a *graduate*.

  The conductor wearing the *bow* tie took a *bow*.

  The advocates *lead* the initiative to ban *lead* paint in toys.

- **Capitonyms** are words with the same spelling, *but* the words mean different things when capitalized.

  Our set of *china* was made in *China*.

  The *march* is slated for early *March*.

- **Contronyms** (also spelled contranyms) are the same words used to define contrary meanings. The verb *sanction*, for example, can mean to approve or to penalize.

  I'll use the paper clips to *clip* together the clippings that I just *clipped* out of the magazines. (The verb *clip* can mean to attach or to cut, among other definitions.)

- **Cultural usage** also adds another layer of complexity. Another linguistic definition of heteronyms applies to different words used to refer to the same thing, which could be a noun or verb, in different geographic areas, whether they are spoken in the same country or in different countries. Have you encountered confusing words within your own country or while traveling on the road? Speakers of Webster's and Oxford English use different word choices for identical terms. Try taking your car to a mechanic, if you are an American in the U.K. or vice versa, for an instant lesson in different word usage. *Hood, bonnet, boot,* and *trunk* are just a few examples of basic words that have different meanings in American and British English. Try Exercise 9.2 and see if you can match which words mean the same things in American and British English.

  Conversely, some of the same words may have very different meanings in American and British English. See Exhibit 9.2 for a few examples that could create confusion.

Exercise 9.2

Self-Evaluation: Cross-Cultural Meanings of English Words

Match the different American and British words that have the **same meaning**.

American English Words	British English Words
1. Apartment	a. Aubergine
2. Baby carriage	b. Autumn
3. Closet	c. Biscuit
4. Cookie	d. Bonnet
5. Diaper	e. Boot
6. Drug store/pharmacist	f. Chemist
7. Dumpster	g. Dummy
8. Eggplant	h. Flat
9. Elevator	i. Full stop
10. Eraser	j. Holiday
11. Exhausted	k. Jumper
12. Fall	l. Knackered
13. Flashlight	m. Lift
14. Garbage	n. Lorry
15. Gas	o. Nappy
16. Hood	p. Petrol
17. Line	q. Pinch
18. Pacifier	r. Pram
19. Period	s. Queue
20. Sneakers	t. Rubber
21. Steal	u. Rubbish
22. Subway	v. Skip
23. Sweater	w. Torch
24. Truck	x. Trainers
25. Trunk	y. Underground
26. Vacation	z. Wardrobe

Please see Appendix D for answers.

9.4.1 Mangling and Tangling Words with "Baited" Breath

The Rivals, a play by Richard Brinsley Sheridan (1907), may be best known for one of its characters, Mrs. Malaprop, the aunt meddling with her niece's love affairs—and mangling the English language. **Malapropisms** are humorous misuses of words, whether accidental or intentional. "He is the very pine-apple of politeness!" (p. 59) was how Mrs. Malaprop described a suitor, substituting *pineapple* for *pinnacle*. She also confused *illiterate* for *obliterate*, *dissolve* for *resolve*, *preposition* for *proposition, illegible* for *eligible, exploded* for *exposed*,

Exhibit 9.2—SAME WORDS WITH DIFFERENT MEANINGS IN AMERICAN AND BRITISH ENGLISH. Some words have very different meanings between Webster's and Oxford English. Here are a few examples that can potentially cause confusion. (Please note that some of these words also have other definitions.)

Word	American English	British English
First floor	Ground floor of building	Floor above ground floor
Football	American football	Soccer
Homely	Ugly, unattractive	Comfortable, homey
Momentarily	At any moment; very soon	For a very short time
Moot	Pointless discussion	Open to discussion
Randy	A first name of a man	Sexually excited (informal)
Quite	Very	Somewhat, fairly
Table (verb)	Postpone consideration	Present formally

among others. These comedic misuses prompted audiences to laugh. The "sister" term is **dogberryism**, also based on a character in a play: Officer Dogberry in William Shakespeare's *Much Ado About Nothing*, who struggled with the differences between *comprehended* and *apprehended* and *auspicious* and *suspicious*.

Mondegreens also can easily bring entertainment to grammar. Can you think of a song in which you thought the lyrics were different? Writer Sylvia Wright coined this phrase in 1954 after mishearing "And laid him on the green" for "And Lady Mondegreen" from a 17th-century Scottish ballad (Fogarty, 2007).

Have you ever laid an eggcorn? In 2003, linguist professors introduced **eggcorns**, the mutation of *egg corns* for *acorns*, to the lexicon of confused English terms, defining misheard or misinterpreted words or phrases. Linguist professor Mark Liberman (2003) explains the distinctions of eggcorns on his Language Log blog:

> It's not a malapropism, because "egg corn" and "acorn" are really homonyms (at least in casual pronunciation), while pairs like "allegory" for "alligator," "oracular" for "vernacular" and "fortuitous" for "fortunate" are merely similar in sound (and may also share some aspects of spelling and morphemic content).
>
> It's not a mondegreen because the mis-construal is not part of a song or poem or similar performance. (paras. 5–6)

Liberman's blog and other bloggers have been building the list of eggcorns: with *baited* (bated) breath, *new leash* (lease) on life, and *mating* (maiden) name, among many other creative word replacements.

9.5 Cultural Blunders and Translation Issues

Cultural blunders can happen to anyone and to any organization. The best solutions to prevent blunders are to be well prepared and seek the counsel of global and local experts who can help provide guidance with all forms of communications. Mishaps should be corrected as quickly as possible. Refer to Exhibit 9.3 for examples of real-world translation blunders. Many of these mistakes could have been prevented if seasoned translators—and ones who really master the local language and popular slang, as well as cultural trends—were hired.

Exhibit 9.3—CULTURAL BLUNDERS IN TRANSLATION.

Company or Product	Cultural Mishaps
American Motors Corporation, Matador (car)	"Matador" traditionally stands for courage and strength, but it means "killer" in Puerto Rico.
Clairol Mist Stick (curling iron)	"Mist" is the slang word for "manure" in German.
Colgate Cue (toothpaste)	"Cue" is the name of a pornographic magazine in France.
Coors (beer)	Slogan "turn it loose" was translated into "suffer from diarrhea" in Spanish.
Electrolux (vacuum cleaners)	"Nothing sucks like an Electrolux" became the slogan in English.
Fresca (soft drink)	Drink name is the same as the Mexican slang word for "lesbian."
IKEA (furniture and home décor)	Bed product named after a town in Norway, "Redalen," which sounds similar to an obscene term for sex in Thailand.
KFC (fast food restaurant chain)	"Finger lickin' good" was translated as "eat your fingers off" in China.
Mazda Laputa (minivan)	"La puta" means "prostitute" in Spanish
Parker Pens (ballpoint pens)	"It won't leak in your pocket and embarrass you" became "It won't leak in your pocket and make you pregnant" in Mexico.
Pepsi (soft drink)	Original slogan, "Pepsi brings you back to life," was translated as "Pepsi brings your ancestors back from the grave" in China.
Puffs (tissues)	"Puff" is a colloquial expression for "whorehouse" in German.
Salem (cigarettes)	"Salem—feeling free" slogan became "When smoking Salem, you will be so refreshed that your mind seems to be free and empty" in Japan.
Schweppes Tonic Water	Translated as "Schweppes Toilet Water" in Italy.
U.S. Dairy Association	"Got milk?" slogan was translated to "Are you lactating?" for Mexican campaign.

Linguistic nuances can be quite problematic. "We care about the small people," said the British Petroleum Chairman Carl-Henric Svanberg, who is Swedish, during a meeting at the White House with President Obama in 2010 to express sympathy to the American people about the Gulf Coast oil spill. This quote was widely disseminated as the headline in traditional media outlets in the U.S. and abroad, as well as on social media. Although Svanberg speaks English proficiently, he was unaware of the negative and condescending meaning of "small people" as inconsequential and unimportant. He later issued an apology as reported on CNN ("BP chief to testify to uncertainty of efforts to stop oil leak," 2010):

> I spoke clumsily this afternoon, and for that, I am very sorry . . . What I was trying to say—that BP understands how deeply this affects the lives of people who live along the Gulf and depend on it for their livelihood—will best be conveyed not by any words but by the work we do to put things right for the families and businesses who've been hurt. Like President Obama, I believe we made some good progress toward that goal today. (para. 24)

Svanberg was trying to restore British Petroleum's reputation two months after a gaffe by another BP executive—and one whose native language is English—became known for crafting the "crisis-P.R. sound bite from hell: 'I'd like my life back'" (Reed, 2012, para. 4). This comment from former BP CEO Tony Hayward was in reaction to the worst oil spill in U.S. history when a BP well erupted below the Deepwater Horizon oil rig in the Gulf of Mexico in April 2010. To be fair, Hayward did make other more sensitive comments, but his apology ended with these five words, becoming the most widely quoted sentence about the oil spill in both traditional and social media. Hayward also issued another apology the next day on Facebook about his statement, as reported in *Business Insider* (Lubin, 2010):

> I made a hurtful and thoughtless comment on Sunday when I said that "I wanted my life back." When I read that recently, I was appalled. I apologize, especially to the families of the 11 men who lost their lives in this tragic accident. Those words don't represent how I feel about this tragedy, and certainly don't represent the hearts of the people of BP—many of whom live and work in the Gulf—who are doing everything they can to make things right. My first priority is doing all we can to restore the lives of the people of the Gulf region and their families—to restore their lives, not mine. (para. 2)

Nonetheless, his insensitive quote lives on as a "poster child" for an ineffectual response to a crisis. Cartoonists skewered BP, capturing public sentiment during the crisis, and later when Hayward stepped down as CEO, got his life back, and received a USD18 million payout. See cartoonist Dave Granlund's depiction of Hayward in Figure 9.2.

Four academics from universities in the U.S., New Zealand, and Hong Kong researched 100 multinational companies entering China and discovered translation complexities in converting the company and brand name into Chinese characters with their varying meanings. They concluded that companies have four choices: no adaptation in sound or meaning, sound adaptation, meaning adaptation, and dual adaptation (Fetscherin, Alon, Littrell, & Chan, 2012). Their survey revealed that 22% of multinationals entering the Chinese market applied dual adaptations and rebranded their name for both phonetic and semantic associations. Dual adaptations of the translated name in Chinese characters can have a positive and relevant connotation of the brand. For example, Nike was translated as "endurance conquers."

A widely disseminated mistranslation on the Web is Coca-Cola's logo in Chinese characters into "bite the wax tadpole" when the products were introduced in China. Apparently, the true

Figure 9.2—THE GAFFE BY TONY HAYWARD, THE FORMER BP CEO, ABOUT THE GULF OF MEXICO OIL SPILL WAS WIDELY COMMENTED ON IN ALL FORMS OF MEDIA AND LAMPOONED BY CARTOONISTS. Source: © 2010 Dave Granlund—All Rights Reserved.

story is that Chinese shopkeepers were responsible for the unusual interpretation when they crafted their own signs for the soft drinks. Coca-Cola translated its name into Chinese characters that sound close to the brand name with a more positive connotation, "permit the mouth to be happy" (Hollis, 2012).

9.6 Proofreading Techniques

Proofreading is a "fine art," and one that should not be overlooked. Typo tales abound—and you may have a few to share. Understanding the limitations of computerized proofreading programs is essential. Look at how many newspapers, e-zines, and blogs run corrections every day, primarily due to misspellings and fact-checking errors.

9.6.1 Real-World Snafus

Here are a few real-world scenarios that illustrate what problems typos can cause:

- **Missing Letters and Unintended Meanings**
  One of the classic mistakes in public relations typos is the missing letter *l* out of *public*. A major public relations agency almost submitted a *pubic* relations proposal to a prospective client. An astute team member discovered the mistake a few hours before the required copies were due and had the covers quickly re-printed. A university with a School of Public Affairs, however, printed its commencement program without the *l* in public. A public relations manager for a new hotel overlooking the Brooklyn

Bridge almost posted a fact sheet online about the hotel's stunning view of the Brooklyn *Bride*.

- **Missing Words and Misinterpretations**

  Leaving out a word can change the entire meaning of a sentence. Back in 1631, royal printers of the King James Bible mistakenly created a "Wicked Bible" by omitting one word—*not*— in the Seventh Commandment: "Thou shalt commit adultery." The printers lost their license, paid a stiff fine, destroyed their stock, and attempted to recall all sold copies. The exact number of surviving bibles is unknown; an antiquarian recently sold an original for USD89,500 (Gekoski, 2010).

- **Reversal of Letters and Meanings**

  A public relations agency submitted a proposal to a global company based in Europe, with a focus on reaching the *Untied* States. The prospective client, who was originally from New York, smiled and said, "The country may seem that way to some." Voters in a state in America were asked to cast their ballots for president/vice president of the *Untied* States.

- **Similar Spellings or Pronunciations Yet Different Meanings**

  A manager of a print shop, who thought he was being helpful, changed *naval* to *navel* on the greetings inside holiday cards for a historical maritime association. Someone did catch the typo before the holiday cards were mailed out, and the printer reprinted the cards without charging. A billboard for a children's educational program read: "So fun, they won't even know *their* learning." Grammar-savvy parents would be less than inspired to enroll their children, even if the program is so entertaining that their kids wouldn't know *they are* learning lessons.

- **Additional Letters and New Definitions**

  A university's communications department almost posted Web copy about its new bachelor of fine *farts* program. The computerized spellcheck program did not flag the unwanted *f*.

- **Wrong Numbers and Serious Problems**

  A company lost millions on the stock exchange when it missed some digits on its listed share price. And an airline left two digits off the fare of its trans-Atlantic flights and had to absorb the lost income when a few thousand passengers bought the discounted tickets online. Printing the wrong telephone numbers also can create havoc, with frustrated callers and perplexed people answering the wrong-number calls. The same applies to misspelled websites and social media.

- **Faulty Punctuation**

  What would have been the first interplanetary space probe mission, set for Venus, by America's National Aeronautics and Space Administration (NASA) in 1962 was a failure when it veered off course and self-destructed less than 5 minutes after take-off. One of the factors was a missing hyphen in the computer code (National Aeronautics and Space Administration, 2014), resulting in the most expensive punctuation mistake made in history.

  Punctuation could save a life. This story, fact or fiction, also illustrates how crucial a comma can be. Tsar Alexander III apparently issued a death warrant: "Pardon impossible, to be sent to Siberia." His wife transposed the comma: "Pardon, impossible to be sent to Siberia," thereby freeing the criminal.

- **Incongruous Computer Spellcheck Solutions**
  Have you ever smiled when your computerized spellcheck program provided you with a "correction" that is far from accurate? A student once handed in a mock new business letter assignment with an embarrassing autocorrection for the misspelling of *position*: "We are confident that our public relations recommendations will *poison* your company . . ." According to Ben Zimmer (2007), a lexicographer and editor at the Oxford University Press, writers and translators working for the European Union gave this malady a name, the *Cupertino effect*, since *Cupertino* (the name of a city in California) was the suggested correction to the word *cooperation* by a computer spell-check program with a dictionary that did not contain *co-operation* with a hyphen. Although computer dictionaries have improved, the Cupertino effect still creates havoc. Zimmer shared a few other examples of computerized "corrections": a lawyer's brief with the Latin phrase *sua sponte* (meaning "of one's accord") turned to *sea sponge*; a newswire article transformed Pakistan's *Muttahida Quami Movement* to the *Muttonhead Quail Movement*; and a magazine misprinted the surnames of *Beavais* to *Beavers* and of *Gareis* to *Agrees*.
- **When Typos Need to Remain**
  Editors of a history book containing letters from the 16th century decided to correct the spellings when transcribing the documents and explained the editing in the preface. Before dictionaries were commonplace, letters and documents included inconsistent spelling formations. (See Chapter 7 for more on the standardization of English.) The publisher, however, asked the editors to put the original spellings back. Using original copy also applies to citing directly from written sources, past or present; the typos stay in. The abbreviation *sic* from the Latin words *sic erat scriptum* ("thus was it written") can be useful to let the reader know that the mistakes are from the original material.

9.6.2 Proofreading Solutions

What can you do to prevent pesky typos and present clearly written copy that your readers will understand? You can proofread carefully after you have edited the copy—and here are a few techniques:

- Double-check all facts first. The most severe typographic errors include incorrect numbers for prices, dates, addresses, and telephone numbers; misspelled names of people, companies, and products; and inaccurate online sources, such as websites and social media.
- Read for clarity overall since you may have overlooked content during the editing process. Does the content make sense? Is the information explained clearly and logically? Are the right messages being conveyed for your audiences? Is the content appropriate—cultural nuances, sensitivities, and expressions—for the specific audience or geographic area?
- Go ahead and use the computerized spell check in your preferred version of English—but be mindful of the limitations and be careful of autocorrect functions that may result in additional errors. If you are a master of British English and are editing material for a U.S. audience, you may want to consult someone proficient in U.S. English—and vice versa.

Figure 9.3—CARTOONIST SHARES A NEW PERSPECTIVE ON EDITING AND PROOFREADING MARKS. Source: Graphic courtesy of Eve Corbel and *Geist* magazine (geist.com).

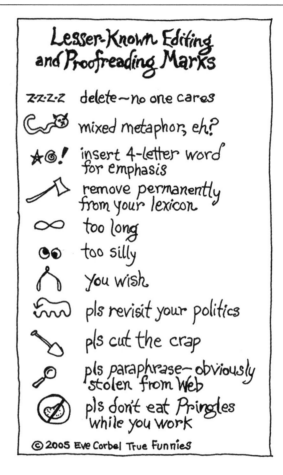

- Read again for grammar, punctuation, and typographical errors, as well as for consistency in style. Make sure you are consistent with the version of English you want to use? Follow your selected stylebook and dictionary.
- Finally, check for formatting consistency—fonts and sizes; headers and footers; bullets, indentations, and margins; italicized, boldfaced, or underscored copy; and capitalizations of headings and subheads.
- And as a final step, print out two copies and read your copy aloud to another person, preferably someone who was not involved in preparing the material, who can listen to you and follow the print-out as well. Lawrence Block (1988), an American fiction writer who also taught writing at the university level, explained another benefit of reading your work aloud: "he is apt to be struck by those unfortunate turns of phrase, those awkward verbal constructions that seemed perfectly acceptable when they were just sitting there on the page" (p. 11).

- If you are unable to seek the assistance of another person, you may want to read your copy backwards, so that you will focus on reading every single word. This technique, however, works more effectively for shorter documents.
- Collective editing also presents challenges when a few people are involved in editing and proofreading the same documents. In this case, it is important that all editors use the same online system to track changes or the same set of proofreading marks when working on hardcopies. If you are reviewing printed materials, you may want to share a copy of proofreaders' marks (which can found in a stylebook or dictionary) to all of the editors to follow for consistency. The reality is that not everyone may be familiar with the standard proofreading symbols, resulting in people creating their own marks that may not be understood by all parties involved with the editing process. (See Figure 9.3 of cartoonist Eve Corbel's interpretation of creative editing and proofreading marks.)

And, if typos do happen, you can re-issue material. Web copy and social media are the easiest content to change, and corrections should be made immediately. The challenge may be that the content was widely shared before the correction or deletion was made. Printed materials, however, may not be so easy to reprint. Apologize, if needed, and do so graciously. Bill Walsh, author of *Lapsing into a Comma*, wrote in his preface: "To write about usage is to tempt the gods and the gremlins, and so I fully expect this book to contain errors. If you find one, please be gentle" (2000, p. x). Your bosses or clients, however, may be less forgiving about serious errors.

9.7 Learning Objectives and Key Terms

After reading Chapter 9, you should be able to:

- Apply the right tone to documents that would be relevant to the audiences you are intending to reach.
- Edit nonstandard words and copy with slang and idiomatic expressions that may be confusing to your readers.
- Develop a level of sensitivity to generational and transcultural gaps.
- Hone skills in simplifying copy and selecting more precise terms.
- Understand the importance of double-checking the most appropriate terms for religions, nations, gender, race, age, and sexual orientation.
- Express numbers and abbreviations clearly when writing to global audiences.
- Identify commonly confused words—homonyms, homophones, homographs, heteronyms, capitonyms, and contronyms—that you will need to double-check for accuracy.
- Write more carefully when applying words that have different meanings in different versions of English, such as American and British English.
- Explain the importance of sophisticated translation when adapting content into other languages.
- Acquire techniques to improve proofreading skills.

The chapter contains the following key terms:

Tone (p. 209)   Cliché (p. 210)
Euphemism (p. 211)   Idiom (p. 211)

Slang (p. 212)	Colloquialism (p. 212)
Jargon (p. 213)	Tech lingo (p. 213)
Neologism (p. 213)	Semantics (p. 213)
Homonym (p. 220)	Homophone (p. 220)
Homograph (p. 220)	Heteronym (p. 220)
Capitonym (p. 220)	Contronym (p. 220)
Malapropism (p. 221)	Dogberryism (p. 222)
Mondegreen (p. 222)	Eggcorn (p. 222)

References

Block, L. (1988). *Spider, spin me a web: Lawrence Block on writing fiction*. Cincinnati, OH: Writer's Digest Books.

BP chief to testify to uncertainty of efforts to stop oil leak. (2010, June 16). *CNN*. Retrieved from http://www.cnn.com/2010/US/06/16/gulf.oil.disaster/.

Cateora, P. R., & Graham, J. L. (2004). *International marketing* (12th ed.). Boston, MA: McGraw-Hill.

Christian, D., Froke, P., Jacobsen, S., & Minthorn, D. (Eds.) (2014). *Associated Press Stylebook and Briefing on Media Law* (15th ed.). New York, NY: Associated Press.

Dahmen, N. S., & Cozma, R. (2009). Styleguide for journalism, entertainment and advertising: Media takes: On aging. *International Longevity Center—USA and Aging Services of California*. Retrieved from http://www.ilc-alliance.org/images/uploads/publication-pdfs/Media_Takes_On_Aging.pdf.

Euphemism. (2014). In *Oxford Dictionaries online*. Retrieved from http://www.oxford dictionaries.com/definition/english/euphemism.

Fernando, A. (2011, May–June). Doing PR in the era of social media: Whatever became of the social media release? *Communication World, 28*(3).

Fetscherin, M., Alon, I., Littrell, R., & Chan, A. (2012, September). In China? Pick your brand name carefully. *Harvard Business Review*. Retrieved from http://hbr.org/2012/09/in-china-pick-your-brand-name-carefully/ar/1.

Fogarty, M. (2007, June 15). Spoonerisms, mondegreens, eggcorns, and malapropisms. *QuickandDirtyTips.com*. Retrieved from http://www.quickanddirtytips.com/education/grammar/spoonerisms-mondegreens-eggcorns-and-malapropisms?page=all.

Gekoski, R. (2010, November 25). The wicked Bible: The perfect gift for collectors, but not for William and Kate. *Guardian*. Retrieved from http://www.theguardian.com/books/books blog/2010/nov/25/wicked-bible-gift-william-kate.

GLAAD. (2014). *GLAAD media reference guide* (9th ed.). Retrieved from http://www.glaad.org/reference.

Group calls Subway ad "unpatriotic." (2004, July 30). *CNNMoney*. Retrieved from http://money.cnn.com/2004/07/30/news/international/subway_protest/.

Hollis, N. (2012, September 20). What's in a __? How to name a company in a global economy. *The Atlantic*. Retrieved from http://www.theatlantic.com/business/archive/2012/09/whats-in-a-how-to-name-a-company-in-a-global-economy/262377/.

Idiom. (2014). In *Merriam-Webster's online dictionary*. Retrieved from http://www.merriam-webster.com/dictionary/idiom.

Jones, S. (2008, July 7). Subway ends "fat Statue of Liberty" campaign. *CNSnews.com*. Retrieved from http://cnsnews.com/news/article/subway-ends-fat-statue-liberty-campaign.

Liberman, M. (2003, September 23). Egg corns: Folk etymology, malapropism, mondegreen, ??? *Language Log* [Blog]. Retrieved from http://itre.cis.upenn.edu/~myl/languagelog/archives/000018.html.

Lubin, G. (2010, June 2). BP CEO Tony Hayward apologizes for his idiotic statement: "I'd like my life back." *Business Insider*. Retrieved from http://www.businessinsider.com/bp-ceo-tony-hayward-apologizes-for-saying-id-like-my-life-back-2010–6.

Lyall, S. (2000, April 10). Staid know-it-all goes hip and online; O.E.D. enters the dot-com world. *New York Times*, p. E1.

National Aeronautics and Space Administration. (2014, August 26). *Mariner 1. National Space Science Data Center*. Retrieved from http://nssdc.gsfc.nasa.gov/nmc/spacecraftDisplay.do?id=MARIN1.

National Association of Black Journalists. (n.d.). *NABJ style guide*. Retrieved from http://www.nabj.org/?styleguide.

National Institute of Standards and Technology. (2014). *SI base units*. Retrieved from http://www.nist.gov/pml/wmd/metric/si-units.cfm.

Newmark, P. (1988). *A textbook of translation*. Hertfordshire, England: Prentice Hall.

O'Conner, P. (2004). *Woe is I: The grammarphobe's guide to better English in plain English* (2nd ed.). New York, NY: Penguin Group.

Plotnik, A. (2007). *Spunk & bite: A writer's guide to bold, contemporary style*. New York, NY: Random House.

Reed, S. (2012, September 2). Tony Hayward gets his life back. *New York Times*. Retrieved from http://www.nytimes.com/2012/09/02/business/tony-hayward-former-bp-chief-returns-to-oil.html?pagewanted=all&_r=0.

Savan, L. (2005). *Slam dunks and no-brainers: Language in your life, the media, business, politics, and, like, whatever*. New York, NY: Alfred A. Knopf.

Schneider, E. W. (2010). *English around the world: An introduction*. Cambridge: Cambridge University Press.

Sheridan, R. B. (1907). *The rivals*. New York, NY: T. Y. Crowell & Co.

Shrives, C. (n.d.). What is a neologism? (with examples). *GrammarMonster.com*. Retrieved from http://www.grammar-monster.com/glossary/neologism.htm.

Sick. (2014). In *The Online Slang Dictionary*. Retrieved from http://onlineslangdictionary.com/meaning-definition-of/sick.

Slang. (2014). In *Oxford Dictionaries online*. Retrieved from http://www.oxforddictionaries.com/us/definition/american_english/slang.

Strunk, W., Jr., & White, E. B. (2000). *The elements of style* (4th ed.). Needham Heights, MA: Allyn & Bacon.

Top 10 unfortunate political one-liners. (2008, November 16). *Time*. Retrieved from http://content.time.com/time/specials/packages/article/0,28804,1859513_1859526_1859514,00.html.

Villarreal, R. (2013, March 2). America, Liberia, Myanmar: The anti-metric system holdouts. *International Business Times*. Retrieved from http://www.ibtimes.com/america-liberia-myanmar-anti-metric-system-holdouts-1109357.

Walsh, B. (2000). *Lapsing into a comma: A curmudgeon's guide to the many things that can go wrong in print—and how to avoid them*. Lincolnwood, IL: Contemporary Books.

Williams, G. (2006, October 17). Is your tech speak out of date? *Entrepreneur.* Retrieved from http://www.entrepreneur.com/article/169114.

Zimmer, B. (2007, November 1). When spellcheckers attack: Perils of the Cupertino effect. *Oxford University Press* [Blog]. Retrieved from http://blog.oup.com/2007/11/spellchecker/.

Part Four

GENERATING AND MANAGING NEWS WORLDWIDE

Part Four includes three chapters on writing news releases, media kits, and online newsrooms, and writing techniques utilized by public relations practitioners worldwide to generate coverage in global and local media outlets.

Chapter 10 Crafting Global News Releases for Mainstream and Social Media

- Examines the 5Ws—who, what, why, where, and when—of how to write and disseminate news releases in global markets.
- Covers the step-by-step process of how to create traditional and social media news releases.
- Addresses content, organization, and formatting, as well as different types of news stories.
- Explains how to select the best images to be used by media in different markets and how to write captions that include necessary facts.

Chapter 11 Composing Global Media Kits and Online Newsrooms

- Provides tips on which media kits formats are best for different situations, as well as creative packaging solutions.
- Covers how to operate a global online newsroom, illustrating best practices in providing global and local contacts, customizing content for various markets, opting for password-protected content, and other considerations in providing comprehensive resources for journalists worldwide.
- Reviews the different types of media kit components to consider and a step-by-step approach to write them, particularly for diverse global markets.
- Illustrates a variety of photography and video footage to illustrate stories, as well as supplemental material for online newsrooms.

Chapter 12 Using Other Media Relations Techniques for Local or Global Campaigns

- Explores how to create story angles to match specific media outlets.
- Explains the value and purpose of conducting events and editorial briefings to meet with the media in person.
- Focuses on how to write materials to encourage the media's participation and how to prepare spokespeople for interviews, particularly outside one's own country.
- Shows how to express opinions and convey thought leadership through letters to the editor, op-eds, and bylined articles.

10 Crafting Global News Releases for Mainstream and Social Media

> "Churnalism" is a news article that is published as journalism, but is essentially a press release without much added.
>
> —Media Standards Trust

10.1 Introduction to News Releases and Industry Issues

The above definition of "churnalism" from the Media Standards Trust reflects the challenges encountered in separating journalism from public relations. The Media Standards Trust is an independent registered charity that aims to be a "think-and-do-tank" by conducting research on such issues as transparency, accountability, and standards in news media. Its website (www.churnalism.com) is dedicated to enabling consumers of mass media to track stories generated from public relations materials by allowing anyone to paste a news release on its website and find copy that overlaps in more than 3 million articles published by national British newspapers, BBC, or Sky News since 2008. The Media Standards Trust (2014) also acknowledges that "not all churnalism is bad" (para. 4), meaning that some news releases share useful information for the public interest.

This website also has been noticed by public relations practitioners around the globe. A public relations industry trade publication expressed concerns about how this website "that exposes journalists recycling press releases is threatening to undermine the PR profession" (Wicks & Kaba, 2011, para. 1). Commentary in the *Columbia Journalism Review*, as well as in blogs and other media outlets, has debated about the reputation of the public relations industry churning out non-news and journalists recycling the content, while others have defended practices in public relations by emphasizing a symbiotic relationship with journalists. Steve Iseman (2011), a communications professor at Ohio Northern University, who also has served on the Public Relations Society of America board of directors, explains the beneficial relationship between journalism and public relations:

> For the most part, PR pros benefit since the information they provide receives the third-party endorsement of established mass-media channels. Journalists, meanwhile, benefit since public relations material helps supplement diminishing journalistic resources in a time of growing content demand. (para. 5)

> And while each has needs that sometimes seem in conflict—one with telling an objective story; the other with telling a persuasive story—both sides have a common goal, which is to provide the public with information they need to make informed decisions. (paras. 5–6)

Experienced public relations professionals understand how to be helpful to journalists and produce relevant news releases that provide useful facts and resources to the media. In fact, most journalists rarely lift news release content verbatim. Well-written and relevant newsworthy releases can provide hard news, such as financial earning announcements or product recall updates; encourage a reporter to include content in a thematic story, such as one on industry trends or roundup stories on a specific topic; offer facts for columns, such as in a calendar listing of upcoming events; or spark an idea for an in-depth feature story.

News releases are also called **press releases** or **media releases**. One of the first news releases is attributed to Ivy Ledbetter Lee, an American journalist who later co-founded one of the first public relations agencies and developed professional standards in conveying accurate, truthful public information. Lee provided written facts to journalists in the form of a news release on behalf of his client, the Pennsylvania Railroad, about a deadly train accident in 1906 (Jarboe, 2006). Since the early 20th century, news releases have been widely used as a common writing technique to share news with journalists worldwide. The practice of news releases continues to be maligned from time to time by journalists and even by a few public relations and communications practitioners. Coca-Cola's head of digital communications and social media stated that he was on a mission to "kill the press release" (Working, 2013, para. 10) after overhauling the company's newsroom and creating its own brand journalism content and eliminating all news releases by 2015. In early 2015, Coca-Cola's online "Press Center" still prominently features releases and includes creative self-produced stories in its newsroom. (Please see Chapter 15 for more on brand journalism and Coca-Cola's newsroom.)

The objectives of this chapter are to demonstrate how news releases can be meaningful to journalists and be written factually and clearly—without churned-out hype—and distributed to appropriate media outlets in multimedia platforms around the globe. News releases are issued by all types of organizations worldwide—governments, nonprofits, educational institutions, trade associations, and privately and publicly held companies—and on behalf of people, whether they are politicians, sports figures, entertainment celebrities, or other public or lesser-known figures. The primary purpose of a news release is to inform journalists representing print, broadcast, and online media outlets about developments. A news release is not a paid advertisement in which one can control how, when, and where the content will be used in a media outlet. Sending news releases to journalists is not a guarantee that any content will be used. Journalists have no obligation to include any of the news release information in a news story. News releases are judged on newsworthiness, timeliness, and their relevance to the media outlet's readers, viewers, or listeners.

The desired end result of a news release is editorial coverage in newspapers, magazines, blogs, e-zines, and radio and television programs. David W. Guth and Charles Marsh (2012), professors at the University of Kansas, explain why media coverage matters:

> . . . one reason media relations is such an important part of public relations is that the news media can provide a **third-party endorsement** or **independent endorsement** of a news story. In public relations, news media are third parties—neither the sender nor the receiver—that can implicitly offer independent verification of a story's newsworthiness. (p. 262)

Many public relations practitioners refer to stories that appear due to their proactive efforts, such as in the form of a news release, as **media placements**. These stories can have a lifespan beyond the air or publication date. Stories in print media can be reprinted, with approval from the publication, and disseminated to a company's sales staff or distributed at trade shows. Excerpts of media commentary also can be incorporated into other forms of print, electronic, or online content to enhance an organization's image and lend credibility. In addition, anyone with Internet access can obtain news releases that are available online.

A few regional and global studies have attempted to capture the usage of releases by journalists:

- A survey of 72 journalists conducted by the London office of Text 100 (2012), a global public relations agency, in 2012 found that 72% of journalists ranked news releases as the "most useful information source" (p. 6).
- A study by another global public relations agency, Oriella PR (2012), spanned 613 journalists in 16 countries. It revealed a decrease in journalists preferring news releases as "your first port of call when researching a story" (p. 6), dropping from 22% in 2011 to 11% in 2012.
- A survey of 1,729 journalists conducted by U.S.-based Bulldog Reporter and Cision (2010), creator of software for communication practitioners, found that 17% of participating journalists rely on news releases or communication professionals for 40% or more of their stories. The major complaint voiced by 59.4% of the journalists was the irrelevancy of the material produced by communication professionals; almost 60% also considered the content advertising focused.
- Research by MediaWise and Cardiff University on British journalism found that 54% of printed stories and 58% of broadcast stories are influenced by public relations activities, including news releases (Lewis, Williams, Franklin, Thomas, & Mosdell, 2008).
- A study by Ipsos Markinor (2011), a South Africa-based research company, investigated not the specific use of news releases, but the relationships between journalists and public relations agencies in the country. On a mean scale of 1 to 10, the media ranked honesty (8.89), followed by providing quality information (8.84), as the most important qualities of public relations companies.

10.2 News Release Strategies

A British contributing editor to *GQ* and other newspapers and consumer magazines was quoted in a public relations trade publication in an article on the relationships between journalists and public relations professionals: "I am not anti-PR. I am anti-poorly targeted PR and, on that score, I am not alone" (Wallace, 2010, para. 3). This journalist had published a list of the names of public relations practitioners who clogged up his email inbox with irrelevant news releases in his blog, which he later removed and apologized for after receiving numerous complaints. This is the type of list that no self-respecting public relations executive would want to be on.

News releases have three objectives. The first objective is to provide relevant content with accurate facts of interest to editors, writers, or producers. The second is to encourage the decision-maker at the media outlet to write or assign the story to someone else. The third is to get the readers, listeners, or viewers of the media outlets to care about the news with a clear end goal, such as to spread awareness or motivate people to do something specific.

Applying the "Si, Lo, Ba, Ti, Un, Fa" (Parkinson & Ekachai, 2006) test can help determine the value of the news content, particularly when communicating with multinational media:

- How **significant** (Si) is the news; how relevant or important will it be to the readers, listeners, or viewers?
- Does it have appeal to the **local** (Lo) market or region? This component is particularly important for editing content to appeal to specific international or multicultural audiences.
- Is the content of the release **balanced** (Ba) with accuracy and without biases? News releases that read like advertisements will be ignored by journalists.
- Is the news **timely** (Ti)? Out-of-date news should not be covered in news releases.
- Does the news convey an **unusual** (Un) event or story? Although not all news releases may have an unusual topic, they still should be relevant and newsworthy.
- Does it involve **famous** (Fa) or **familiar people** that the target audiences will be interested in? These two components may not apply to every news release; yet distinctive stories with well-known people, organizations, or events may generate more interest.

A strong visual metaphor of what a news release should *not* be is "the 'camel' of communications, too often carrying the weight of collective expectations on a journey with no apparent end in sight" (Tritton, 2012, para. 1). Examining the **5Ws**—*who, what, why, where*, and *when*—and *how* components also can help writers figure out what content to include and how best to reach target audiences. Ask these basic questions before writing a release:

- **WHO** is your intended end audience—desired readers, listeners, or viewers of the media outlets you are sending the releases to? What do they care about? What do you know about them or need to find out? Where do they live? What local area, regions, or countries do you need to tap?
- **WHAT** news do you want to convey? What are the core facts and benefits of interest to journalists and the consumers of mass media in that specific market? What does the organization really want to achieve with the news—inspire people to buy a product or use a service, attend an event, vote for a candidate, or volunteer time or donate money to a cause? Who would be the organization's spokespeople, if you want to add quotations from someone? Should you include regional spokespeople? How will you need to localize content for different international or regional markets?
- **WHY** should journalists care to use this information? You only have a few seconds to grab a busy reporter's attention. If you can't answer this question easily, you may want to reconsider writing a news release. Poorly conceived releases are considered spam and will be deleted instantly when received by email. Public relations agencies should avoid distributing a pre-agreed-upon number of news releases on a monthly basis for their clients—and produce releases when actual news value is merited.
- **WHERE** are you sending the release? Which media outlets are you targeting—general interest, special interest, or industry trades? Are they bloggers, freelancers, editors at magazines and newspapers, or producers at television and radio stations? In which countries—or states or regions—are the media located? Releases can be customized to specific types of reporters, such as those who cover financial or lifestyle topics, and to specific geographic areas.

- **WHEN** do you want to share the news? Do you know the best timeframe to connect with specific types of media? When are their deadlines? Knowing the lead time of media outlets is important. Monthly consumer magazines have long lead times, some up to six months or longer in advance. Financial news from publicly held companies must comply with strict distribution times regulated by security exchanges. Some publications also issue editorial calendars on thematic topics and special issues. Are you aware of major holidays in the markets you are trying to reach? Seasoned public relations practitioners plan a calendar of distribution of news to tap both long-lead and short-lead media outlets.
- **HOW** are you planning on sending the release? Are you sending the release by email, posting it on organization's online newsrooms, using a news release distribution service, or sharing content on social networking outlets? Or are you using multiple distribution channels? What visuals do you have to illustrate and support the story?

10.3 Writing Techniques

Does the news release convey hard news or soft news? **Hard news** topics include new products and service announcements, financial earnings, major executive appointments, crisis updates, and other newsworthy events. **Soft feature news** provide tips and how-to advice, survey findings, milestones, case studies, holiday tie-ins, and other created news that still should have value, usually in the lifestyle-related sections, such as food, style, or entertainment. Soft news stories traditionally have more limited distribution to special-interest sections and industry trades, depending on the appeal of the topic. Some public relations practitioners do not make a distinction between the terms "news releases" and "feature releases"; they use the term "release."

10.3.1 News Release Topics

Hard news releases pertain to announcements and updates, many of which can be localized. Each of the following topics includes examples of real-world release headlines that quickly convey the essence of the story and the location as appropriate.

- **Announcements** on new products, services, and developments:

    Headline: New iPad arrives in China on Friday, July 20

    Headline: Hershey unveils world's first public 3-D chocolate candy printing exhibit

    Subhead: Visitors to Hershey's Chocolate World Attraction can experience 3-D chocolate printing

- **Enhancements** of existing products and services:

    Headline: Nestlé continues to develop its operations in Chile with CHF 127 million investment

    Headline: Toyota to expand Lexus RX production in Canada

- **Events**, particularly ones open to the public or widely reported by the media:

    Headline: Biggest icons to switch off for Earth Hour

    (Release announced global Earth Hour events worldwide.)

Headline: China's Yi Siling wins first Gold Medal of London 2012

(News issued from the London 2012 Olympic Games.)

- **Promotions and new hires**, particularly for CEO and executive-level positions; less senior positions or announcements from smaller organizations are more appropriate for industry trade publications and local newspapers:

  Headline: JWT announces executive promotions within the MEA Region

  (Advertising agency release covering news within a specific geographic region.)

- **Awards and other significant honors**, many of which would be of primary interest to specific industry trades and blogs:

  Headline: Four years running: BMW 135i Sport Coupé crowned best sports car
  (Release announced award from Australia.)

- Updates on **bad news** or **crisis situations**, such as product recalls, closures, or interrupted operations:

  Headline: Toyota announces recall of certain RAV4 and Lexus HS 250h vehicles

  Headline: Worldwide pork shortage predicted

  (This release with a provocative headline issued by Britain's National Pig Association sparked worldwide commentary in traditional media and on the Internet. It also generated stories in such outlets as *Slate* [Yglesias, 2012] that disputed the looming bacon shortage.)

- **Financial news** and quarterly financial earnings for publicly held companies, which strictly adhere to regulations by security exchanges:

  Headline: NIKE, Inc. reports fiscal 2015 second quarter results

Another category of news releases is called **soft news** that can cover such topics as follows:

- **Milestones**, such as major anniversaries or sales or social media achievements:

  Headline: Starbucks celebrates 25th anniversary milestone in Canada

  Headline: BMW India records one million fans on Facebook

- **Human-interest** or unusual stories:

  Headline: American cat in Paris to take first-class trip home on Continental Airlines

  (This release explained how an airline reunited a cat that was trapped in a box shipped to France with her owners back in the U.S.)

- **Survey findings**:

  Headline: Microsoft releases national survey findings on how to inspire the next generation of doctors, scientists, software developers and engineers

(The preferred adjective for the survey would be *U.S.,* instead of *national*, for greater clarity since international journalists may read the release.)

- **Tips**, particularly on seasonal themes, whether they are weather-related (gardening, home, and car maintenance), holiday-themed (gift-giving, entertaining, and decorating), or other helpful advice on specific topics, such as on career development, or timing of specific events, such as this example about the Summer Olympic Games:

Headline: Tangoe offers businesses tips to prevent mobile "bill shock" during the Summer Olympic Games

(Release provided tips for businesses to prevent spike in mobile data and avoid excessive costs during the Olympics.)

- **Opportunistic news** based on **trends** or organizations becoming involved with other larger events:

Headline: P&G opens family home to moms & families of more than 10,000 Olympians

Subhead: Celebration welcomes moms of Olympians to London including moms of Sir Chris Hoy, Ryan Lochte, Lin Dan, Nikita Lobinstev, Felipe Franca & Noko Matlou

(This release covered global brand-building awareness during an international event.)

- **Corporate social responsibility** news illustrating how a company is helping others (some of these stories can be both hard and soft news):

Headlines:

Chinese pandas embark on a journey of a lifetime as they board the "FedEx Panda Express" to the United Kingdom

Chinese pandas touch down in Scotland on the "FedEx Panda Express"

Chinese school children send their well-wishes to Beauval ZooParc and its newest residents onboard the "FedEx Panda Express"

("Panda-monium" was part of a series of events that fostered goodwill for FedEx, a multinational company in global transportation and business services, resulting in media relations campaigns that showcased the company's experience in handling precious cargo and its commitment to helping wildlife preservation.)

10.3.2 Content and Considerations

Learning how to write news releases effectively can make the difference in generating news about your organization. John Coventry, a British communications professional, provided a humorous account of how to ensure that journalists discard your news releases in "10 ways to get your press release binned" (2008), which opened with "Keen to have your message ignored by journalists everywhere?" (para. 1). The trade article included ways to irritate journalists from making the text too long and burying the news content to forgetting to proofread and sending too many releases too frequently to all journalists, especially to those who never cover the topic.

So what can public relations writers actually do to bring attention to their news releases? They should consider the following recommendations:

- **Localize content and understand what is relevant to journalists covering specific beats** (subject areas) in specific countries or by regions, provinces, or states. This means investing more time in editing releases to appeal to different outlets, but the effort will be worthwhile. For example, the public relations staff in the headquarters usually prepare a generic news release and then local public relations talent edit— or translate—the release to contain local information, as well as to conform to cultural values and the specific needs of the local media. Local releases should contain as many references as possible relevant in the specific market, whether it's a state, province, country, or region. Quotes should be from local spokespeople, and the boilerplate information should include details about the local market, such as its operations and local contact sources.
- **Be concise and include what is relevant to share about the topic**. Less content may be preferred since reporters are quite busy. Writers, however, should be more concerned about the quality of information versus the quantity of pages. Social media news releases are briefer than traditional releases. Many news release distribution services have fees structured by length of release, so brevity can save the organization money.
- **Consider editing releases for different versions of English**. Executives of global newswire services in a *PR Week* article recommended that American English releases should be changed into the spelling conventions of British English when distributed to current and former British colonies (Lewis, 2007). I would recommend taking this one step further and have the entire document edited by someone who is fluent in that specific version of English. Refer to a stylebook for consistency of the content as well—this is particularly important when press materials are created by multiple authors. English-language stylebooks are covered in depth in Chapter 5.
- **Be mindful of cultural sensitivities**. Be careful to avoid cultural references that may be unclear—or even inappropriate—to different readers. Look out for slang or regional words or expressions that may be confusing to broader audiences. Avoid using humor that may not be universally appreciated. Some releases also may need to be translated, so it is essential to write clear and factual copy—and have the content edited by someone who is fluent in the language and understands current nuances. Refer to Chapter 4 for more insight on intercultural perspectives and Chapter 9 on editing tips.
- **Be aware of potentially hot topics and geopolitics** that may not be politically correct or reflect corporate social responsibility (CSR) in specific markets. In an interview in *PR Week* (a public relations industry trade publication with country-specific editions), the vice president of international distribution for PR Newswire said. "In China, stay away from human rights, disobedience, freedom, and CSR . . . We've had releases refused because of [CSR] information in boilerplates" (Lewis, 2007, para. 3). In the same article, the president of Business Wire Latin America said: "Don't [condescend]. And always be aware of national pride. In Taiwan, if you pitch a company with ties to mainland China, you'll get resistance. Watch geopolitical dynamics" (Lewis, 2007, para. 4).

- **Use short paragraphs**; try not to exceed eight lines. Long paragraphs are too difficult to read and can result in eye fatigue.
- **Be consistent in tone**. Financial releases are very straightforward to convey news to shareholders. Releases distributed from a publicly held company follow strict regulations from stock exchanges and are usually vetted by legal counselors. This particularly applies to news that could affect the buying and selling of the company's stock. Announcements on new products or services need to be factual, yet they can convey the "personality" of the brand. For example, a release issued from a candy manufacturer would have a more playful and whimsical tone than a release issued by a life insurance company. Cause-related releases usually convey an emotional plea to persuade the desired audience to attend an event, volunteer their time, or donate money. In reality, the writing style will be influenced by the organization's decision-makers during the approval process. The positioning and messaging of the specific brand or product also may have glocal variations that should be reflected in country-specific editions of releases.
- **Think search engine optimization** and incorporate key words to make the document easier to find online.
- **Edit, edit, edit . . .** refer to Chapter 9 for more insight on editing and make sure to pay particular attention to the following tips:

  - **Write in the present tense,** so the content does not sound like old news. The future tense can be used, but avoid the past tense (except for quoting from someone, when "said" is the preferred verb).
  - **Use specific timeframes,** such as the exact dates, instead of today, tomorrow, or next week.
  - **Avoid copy with you, your, we, and our**—unless these pronouns are included in a quotation from someone. The third person singular or plural (*he, she, it,* or *they*) is preferable unless the organization has a different policy in pronoun usage.
  - **Purge jargon**, particularly marketing and other industry terms, which the reader may not be familiar with. Be careful to explain abbreviations; spell out the first reference.
  - **Avoid hype**. *Unique, revolutionary, breakthrough, state-of-the-art, innovative,* and *cutting-edge* are just a few examples of words that can be deleted. Use words that describe the attributes, instead of meaningless adjectives that many readers will consider exaggeration. Avoid fluff and clichés that may sound like advertising or sales copy. Puffery should only be used in quotes from the spokesperson— and even then, they can be edited to provide more value.
  - **Delete unnecessary words**. Avoid overusing *there is* and *there are*. Be careful of stating the obvious, such as *Company X is pleased to announce* when *Company X announces* suffices.
  - **Use the active voice** as much as possible.
  - **Proofread carefully** for content, accuracy, grammar, spelling, punctuation, consistency, and formatting. Don't rely on any computerized spell checking and grammar program. The letter *l* left out of the word *public*, for example, will not be flagged as a mistake. Make sure all facts are accurate—particularly dates, prices, telephone numbers, websites, and social media. Journalists will not necessarily complain if a public relations writer overlooks stylebook rules, but they will be unhappy with inaccurate facts.

10.3.3 Organization and Formatting

News releases in all markets traditionally include the following components (please refer to Exhibit 10.1 that highlights the key components with corresponding numbers):

Exhibit 10.1—TRADITIONAL NEWS RELEASE TEMPLATE.

Contact: Name of PR Executive ①
Company or Agency
Tel: XXX-XXX-XXXX
Email: xxxx@xxxx.com

FOR IMMEDIATE RELEASE ②

Headlines convey the essence of the story
Don't exceed 2 Lines, headlines are flush left or centered ③
Subheads can provide supporting facts and are usually italicized ④

CITY WHERE NEWS IS RELEASED, STATE OR COUNTRY, Month Day, Year ⑤ – The opening paragraph is called the lead and should include the essential information—relevant who, what, why, where, when, and how. This content may be the only part used in a story. Avoid hype and superlatives throughout. Paragraphs should not exceed eight lines. ⑥

Supporting paragraphs should be written in the journalistic inverted pyramid style with the information presented in order of importance. Continue to organize information with facts logically. Some releases may require a number of supporting paragraphs to provide the complete story. Subheads can be added to help the reader scan the information. ⑦

Many writers place a quotation from a company spokesperson to express a point of view and provide context to the news being presented. The full name, title, and affiliation of the spokesperson need to be included. If that information is mentioned earlier, only the last name should be indicated. The best verb to use is "said." Follow the stylebook for capitalizations of titles. Some releases may quote from a few different people involved with the news. Try to avoid quoting from more than two people. Quotations must be approved by the spokespeople. ⑧

About the Organization ⑨

The closing paragraph is also called the boilerplate paragraph and includes the essential facts about an organization, such as a brief description, geographic reach, general website, toll-free numbers for consumers, and social media. Publicly held companies may include more details on financials. Some releases may include more than one boilerplate if other organizations are directly involved.

⑩

Add more to the center bottom of continuing page(s), particularly if printed:

- more-

Add a slug line and page number(s) on continuing page(s), traditionally on upper left side:

Abbreviated Name of Release
Page X of X (total number of pages)

Note to Editors: This is optional, but can provide helpful resources to journalists.⑪

1. Public Relations Contacts (required unless posted on an online newsroom containing public relations contacts in another section)

This section provides journalists with the names of the public relations representatives to reach to ask any questions, secure more material or set up an interview; their company or agency affiliations; and telephone numbers, emails, and optional social media. It is important that the contacts are the people who are best equipped to answer calls from journalists. If the contacts are on vacation or out of town, their voice mail and email messages should provide another person to reach for immediate assistance. Releases can include the names and contacts of both the in-house public relations and public relations agency staff. Telephone numbers also should indicate international dialing codes; contact information also can include mobile phones and Skype. Contacts should be localized as much as possible.

Contact information can be located in different places: the upper right or left side of the first page or at the end of the news release. It is recommended to be consistent in whatever style is selected by the organization. Website newsrooms may exclude contact information on the posted news releases. In this case, a section on public relations contacts, preferably by geographic area, is located prominently in the online newsroom. Another option is to include a generic public relations email without specific names, such as publicrelations@companyX. com, but the organization should ensure that someone is regularly monitoring all inquiries.

During a crisis situation, public relations practitioners should set up toll-free media telephone numbers that will need to be monitored frequently and responded to as quickly as possible. Voicemail messages also can be revised as necessary to provide updates and other contacts for immediate assistance. The organization's online newsroom and Twitter (or other microblogs) also can be valuable to provide quick updates to media.

2. Release of Information (required)

This part lets the reader know when the news is available for release. Many writers place the three words—FOR IMMEDIATE RELEASE—in capital letters on the left side of the first page, below the public relations contacts and above the headline, to indicate that the news is available immediately. If facts are embargoed, the information should include the date and time, including the time zone, of the requested release of news. Since most releases are distributed digitally, public relations practitioners rarely indicate date restrictions and, instead, issue them when the news is ready for release to the public. Medical and scientific journals are exceptions; many have signed embargo agreements with specific media outlets (Wenner, 2002).

3. Headline (required)

The headline provides the essence of the news story and should be carefully crafted to encourage journalists to continue reading the release. Avoid exceeding two lines. Headlines do not require full sentences and periods. Most headlines include the name of the organization (or its product, service, cause, or event), and a verb. Localizing headlines also can be beneficial in communicating the relevance to the specific geographic area. Stylebooks contain different writing standards on capitalizing words. The Associated Press, for example, recommends capitalizing only the first word and formal nouns. The placement of the subhead (flush left or centered) and use of boldface text also vary from company to company. Whatever format is selected should remain consistent in all press materials.

4. Subhead (optional)

Although subheads are optional, they can convey supporting information that would otherwise clutter the headline and provide facts to help the reader better understand the topic of the release. Subheads should not exceed two lines and are placed below the headline. This example from the Caribbean-based Captain Morgan brand of rums plays on its pirate heritage by sponsoring an archaeological dig of its namesake's ships. The subhead provides important supporting facts about the archaeological find.

Headline: Underwater archaeologists dig deep for iconic Privateer Captain Henry Morgan's lost fleet in the Caribbean

Subhead: Team recovers sword, chests and wooden barrels from 17th-century shipwreck off the coast of Panama where Morgan lost five ships in 1671

5. Dateline (required)

Datelines indicate where the news is distributed from, such as the location of the organization issuing the news, and when the news is being released. This information is included at the beginning of the first paragraph of the release. Stylebooks indicate how to write datelines. For example, the *Associated Press Stylebook*, which is the most commonly adopted stylebook in the U.S., lists which cities need to include the name of the state or country where the news is disseminated from. It also includes specific guidelines on how to abbreviate names of states and months. Here are a few examples following Associated Press guidelines:

BEIJING, August, 8, 2017—
KYOTO, JAPAN, Sept. 1, 2017—
WHITE PLAINS, N.Y., Dec. 1, 2017—

It is important to avoid using numbers for months when communicating with an international audience to avoid any confusion. In the U.S., dates are written with the month followed by the day, whereas other countries may write the day first followed by the month.

6. Lead Paragraph (required)

The lead paragraph (also spelled **lede** by journalists to avoid confusion with lead or leading, which is the spacing between lines of type in typeset material) refers to the first paragraph. Fran Pelham (2000), a communications professor, identified four types of leads: straight news (5Ws and how), modified straight news (with a main theme), informal lead (arouse interest), and feature lead (human interest).

Most leads traditionally contain the relevant **5Ws**—*who, what, why, where, when*—and sometimes *how*:

- Who is the news about?
- What is happening?
- Why is the news important?
- Where is the news taking place?
- When is it happening?
- How is it being done?

A good lead must tell the story quickly and capture its essence. Reporters are very busy people who are inundated with releases, so clarity is essential. Follow an **inverted pyramid**

journalistic style, with the lead having the core facts of the story and additional information in descending order in supporting paragraphs. A well-written lead paragraph should be able to stand on its own since it may be the only section included in a story.

Let's examine the lead paragraph in the news release issued from DreamWorks Animation (2014):

Headline and Subhead:
How To Train Your Dragon 2 Crosses $600,000,000
Highest Grossing Animated Film of the Year Continues to Breathe Fire Into Global Box Office; Third Chapter of Epic Story Lands on June 9, 2017

Lead Paragraph:
LOS ANGELES, September 2, 2014 /PRNewswire/—DreamWorks Animation's *How to Train Your Dragon 2* continues to breathe fire into the global box office as it officially crossed the $600,000,000 mark on Labor Day. A record-breaking opening in China coupled with phenomenal success in territories around the world have catapulted *Dragon 2* to become the highest grossing animated film of the year and one of the top ten grossing films of the year in any genre.

What are the relevant 5Ws in this release?:

Who?:	DreamWorks Animation
What?:	Box office success of *How to Train Your Dragon 2*
When?:	September 2014
Why?:	Record-breaking opening in China, as well as worldwide popularity
Where?:	Global; company based in California

7. Supporting Paragraphs (as needed)

Content should be shared in descending order of importance of content. Public relations writers can learn a great deal from reading major daily newspapers for insight on how facts are conveyed in a story. They also can read releases distributed by other organizations, particularly a client's competitors.

The supporting paragraphs in a release on the underwater archaeological dig for Captain Morgan's fleet (Diageo, 2012), which was earlier used as an example in the section on headlines and subheads, provided relevant facts on the excavation process.

Release copy:
The search began in September 2010, when the team discovered six iron cannons belonging to Morgan off the coast of Panama, and continued last summer with the discovery of a 17th-century wooden shipwreck, potentially one of the five ships Morgan lost—which included his flagship "Satisfaction"—in 1671 on the shallow Lajas Reef.

This summer, the team returned to Panama to excavate historic artifacts from the shipwreck in hopes of confirming its origin. Throughout the field season, the team recovered a sword, chests, wooden barrels and multiple cargo seals. The artifacts, which are currently housed at Patronato Panama Viejo (Old Panama Trust) in Panama City, will undergo the preservation process before being studied further and verified by London-based experts in English artillery. (paras. 4–5)

In addition, writers can include short subheads throughout longer releases to make the copy easier to follow. Fact sheets also can be sent (or embedded in text with Web links) along with releases to provide important background about an event, a new product or service, or another major component. Releases can include links to the organization's online newsroom to find out more information and download visual imagery.

8. Quotation from Spokesperson (as relevant; recommended to express opinions)
Use relevant quotations from a company spokesperson or spokespeople that express opinions on the news. Writers should be careful to distinguish the differences between facts and opinions; opinions should be used as a quotation written in full sentences, with the name, title, and affiliation of the spokesperson. Read copy carefully for verbs, such as *claim, think, believe, hope, expect,* and *want,* which usually pertain to points of view and not facts. Quotations should not repeat core facts covered elsewhere in the release. This is the only part of the release that should convey points of views and can include puffery; however, better writers can avoid self-serving platitudes and promotional hype—and still explain the value and benefits to the reader. Writers also need to avoid writing negative statements about competitors, governments, and people, particularly comments that could be considered culturally offensive.

Don't feel obligated to provide quotations from all parties involved in a project since too many quotations are distracting to the reader. *Said* is the best verb to use. Avoid the obvious: *Company X is delighted to . . .* or *pleased to . . .* or other empty phrases. Use full sentences when writing quotations. Think sound-bites that would be appealing for a reporter to drop into a story. However, be careful to avoid using brand names and other cultural references that multinational audiences may not recognize. If the organization has a company spokesperson in a specific geographic market, that local person would be more relevant to quote from— and also localize the content and communicate messages appropriate to that market. Although it is not uncommon for quotations to be drafted by public relations professionals, all quotations should be approved by the spokesperson stated in the release.

In a release issued at the Farnborough International Airshow in the south of England, with the headline, "Virgin Galactic reveals privately funded satellite launcher and confirms SpaceShipTwo poised for powered flight," the quotation from Sir Richard Branson expresses his opinions and optimism, as well as benefits of the new product. In this case, using the verb, "revolutionize," can be acceptable since this new air service would be the world's first commercial spaceline. (Branson's full name, title, and affiliation were mentioned earlier in the news release; otherwise, that information would need to be included.)

Quotation:

> "Virgin Galactic's goal is to revolutionize the way we get to space," Branson said. "I'm immensely proud of what we have already achieved as we draw near to regular suborbital flights on SpaceShipTwo. Now, LauncherOne is bringing the price of satellite launch into the realm of affordability for innovators everywhere, from start-ups and schools to established companies and national space agencies. It will be a critical new tool for the global research community, enabling us all to learn about our home planet more quickly and affordably." (Virgin Galactic, 2012, para. 3)

Another example from a news release titled, "Apple announces iPhone 6 and iPhone 6 Plus—the biggest advancements in iPhone history," adds an opinion by the CEO about the impact of Apple's latest smartphones and about the company at large.

Quotation:

"iPhone 6 and iPhone 6 Plus are the biggest advancements in iPhone history," said Tim Cook, Apple's CEO. "The iPhone is the most loved smartphone in the world with the highest customer satisfaction in the industry and we are making it much better in every way. Only Apple can combine the best hardware, software and services at this unprecedented level and we think customers are going to love it." (Apple, 2014, para. 3)

9. Boilerplate Paragraph (recommended)

The closing paragraph, which is called the boilerplate paragraph, traditionally includes core information about the organization, such as a brief description of its products, services, or mission; headquarters, locations, or number of offices or stores; and other resources, such as telephone, website, and social media for public information. Double-check phone numbers, email addresses, and key facts carefully. This content also can be localized to geographic areas by containing facts relevant to that market. Some releases may include more than one boilerplate, if more than one organization is involved with the news.

The boilerplate paragraph from L'Oréal's news release on the launch of its International Awards for Social Responsibility in dermatology starts off with a subhead and includes two paragraphs. The first paragraph gives core information about its number of brands, earnings, global workforce, and distribution of products. The second paragraph covers the company's research and sustainability mission.

Subhead: About L'Oréal

Boilerplate:

L'Oréal has devoted itself to beauty for over 105 years. With its unique portfolio of 28 international, diverse and complementary brands, the Group generated sales amounting to 23 billion euros in 2013 and employs 77,500 people worldwide. As the world's leading beauty company, L'Oréal is present across all distribution networks: mass market, department stores, pharmacies and drugstores, hair salons, travel retail and branded retail.

   Research and innovation, and a dedicated research team of 4,000 people, are at the core of L'Oréal's strategy, working to meet beauty aspirations all over the world and attract one billion new consumers in the years to come. L'Oréal's new sustainability commitment for 2020 "Sharing Beauty With All" sets out ambitious sustainable development objectives across the Group's value chain. (L'Oréal, 2014a, paras. 9–10)

For a news release in the U.S., L'Oréal customized the boilerplate to focus on its U.S. operations.

Subhead: About L'Oréal USA

Boilerplate:

L'Oréal USA is the largest subsidiary of the L'Oréal Group, the worldwide leader in beauty. L'Oréal USA manages a portfolio of 28 iconic global beauty brands, including Clarisonic, Essie Cosmetics, Garnier, Giorgio Armani Beauty, Kérastase, Kiehl's, Lancôme, L'Oréal Paris, Maybelline New York, Redken, Soft-Sheen Carson, Urban Decay and Yves Saint Laurent Beauté. In addition to its corporate headquarters in New York City, L'Oréal USA has Research & Innovation and Manufacturing & Distribution facilities across six other states including Arkansas, Kentucky, New Jersey, Ohio, Texas and Washington with a workforce of more than 10,000 employees. For more information, visit www.LorealUSA.com or follow on Twitter @LOrealUSA. (L'Oréal, 2014b, para. 7)

Publicly held companies may add additional financial information or disclaimers (also called **safe haven legalese**) about **forward-looking statements** and other content. Here is an example of legal content included in a financial release from L'Oréal titled, "First-half 2014 results: A solid first half: Good operating profitability progression growth contrasted by division":

"This news release does not constitute an offer to sell, or a solicitation of an offer to buy L'Oréal shares. If you wish to obtain more comprehensive information about L'Oréal, please refer to the public documents registered in France with the Autorité des Marchés Financiers, also available in English on our Internet site www.loreal-finance.com.

This news release may contain some forward-looking statements. Although the Company considers that these statements are based on reasonable hypotheses at the date of publication of this release, they are by their nature subject to risks and uncertainties which could cause actual results to differ materially from those indicated or projected in these statements."

This is a free translation into English of the First-half 2014 results news release issued in the French language and is provided solely for the convenience of English speaking readers. In case of discrepancy, the French version prevails. (L'Oréal, 2014c, paras. 73–75)

Nonprofits and other types of organizations also use boilerplates in news releases. Here is an example from Partners In Health, a global nonprofit:

Boilerplate:

About Partners In Health: Partners In Health is a global health organization relentlessly committed to improving the health of the poor and marginalized. We build local capacity and work closely with impoverished communities to deliver high-quality health care, address the root causes of illness, train providers, advance research, and advocate for global policy change. For more information please visit www.pih.org. (Partners In Health, 2014, para. 9)

10. Headers and Footers (recommended)

Releases traditionally conclude with an **end mark** of three number signs, which are also called hash characters or pound signs, centered two lines underneath the last paragraph: # # #. If the release is more than one page, many writers add—**more**—to the bottom center of each page that is continuing and include an abbreviated title of the news item (or **slug line**), such as *Company Y Announces Merger with Company Z*, and indicate the page numbers, such as *Page X of X total*, immediately below the slug line on the upper left side. Reporters may have printed out multiple documents and appreciate having each page labeled and numbered. Some public relations writers do not apply recommended headers and footers to news releases posted on online newsrooms.

11. Note to Editors (optional)

Note to editors (also called **note to reporters** or **journalist note**), which is traditionally placed below the end mark, is an option to bring attention to other resources for information or visuals available to journalists. Here is a generic example:

Journalist note: Information about (name of organization) and its products in (name of country) is available to journalists online at (online newsroom in the specific country or region).

Exhibit 10.2 includes other tips on formatting news releases.

Before moving to the next section, try Exercise 10.1 and select a traditional news release, whether you find it on a news release distribution service or on an organization's online newsroom, to analyze the content and determine if you would do anything differently.

10.3.4 Social Media News Releases

As social media innovations continue, new formats and techniques in writing and sharing news release content have been evolving. Best practices of effective writing, however, remain the same. Todd Defren, CEO of SHIFT Communications, a U.S.-based public relations agency, is credited for launching the first **social media release** in 2006. The major differences between social media news releases and traditional releases are enhanced brevity of content with more bulleted copy, serious consideration of key words for search engine optimization, reorganization of core release information (by shortening release copy or segregating it into delineated blocks), and inclusion of multimedia, sharing functions, and interactivity. Social media news releases are abbreviated as **SMNR** or **SMR** for social media releases, and they also may be referred to as **social media press releases**.

Exhibit 10.2—OTHER NEWS RELEASE FORMATTING TIPS.

Writers should consider these pointers when formatting news releases:

- Some organizations add logos and include "News" to their electronic or hardcopy letterhead exclusively for releases.
- Most releases do not exceed two pages, unless you have relevant information to include. One-page releases are perfectly acceptable. The quality of information is the most important factor.
- Most authors use 11- or 12-point type and avoid unusual typefaces, and apply standard margins for traditional releases.
- Copy is traditionally single-spaced for email distribution, online newsrooms, and social and mobile media. Most writers follow block-style paragraphs, with no indentations and one blank line between paragraphs for single-spaced copy. Although the traditional hard copy releases are double spaced, some organizations prefer to single space to save money on printing. If a release is double-spaced, the first line of each paragraph is indented (except for the lead paragraph with the dateline).
- Most copy is flush left and not justified. Whatever style a company chooses should remain consistent in all press materials.
- Words should not be hyphenated to continue on to the next line.
- Some textbooks state that writers should not split sentences or paragraphs between lines. In the professional world, many writers do split them. But don't leave a "widow"—a paragraph with a single line that starts or ends on a page.

Exercise 10.1

Insights: Analysis of News Releases

This exercise will help you better understand news releases. Find a recent news release online about a product, service, personality, or cause that you care about. You can look at the newsroom on the organization's website. Many online media sections are located under "about us" or "company information," or some sites have a separate link called "press room," "news room," "media room," or "for journalists." You also can look at www. prnewswire.com, www.businesswire.com, or another online news release distribution service for recent releases.

Analyze your selected release and answer the following questions:

1. What is the objective of the release? Is it to announce a new development, to increase product sales, to enhance the organization's reputation, to seek donations or volunteers, to change attitudes and behavior, or to increase attendance at an event?
2. What are the key messages communicated in the release?
3. Who is the primary audience? Is the content geared to consumers who may buy a product or service? Or is it aimed at voters, a specific age group or lifestyle, other businesses, etc.?
4. Was the release content localized to a specific geographic area? If not, could the content be edited to appeal to a different market and, if so, how?
5. What does the target audience gain from this product, service, or information? What are the potential benefits and rewards?
6. Does the headline want you to continue reading?
7. Is the most important information placed first in the lead paragraph? Is supporting information organized in descending order?
8. Is there a closing paragraph (boilerplate) with core facts on the organization? Does it have any Web or social media links?
9. Does the release include supporting visuals?
10. If you were a journalist, do you think you would find this release newsworthy and of interest to develop a story or include the news in a column that you write? Explain why or why not. If you think the release needs improvement, what enhancements would you recommend?

Jamie Turner, co-author of *How to Make Money with Social Media*, explained in an interview as part of an article in *Inc.*, a U.S. business magazine:

If you think of a press release as points in time, a social media release is really an evolving continuum . . . The reason for that is that even if you do a social media release that goes out and targets everyone, the nature of social media is that it moves so rapidly between people and the conversation quickly grows organically. You have to engage yourself and evolve the conversation as it's happening, rather than standing by waiting to see what the reaction is. (Dubois, 2010, para. 5)

The template of a social media news release varies in terms of formatting style. Social media releases can include such components as follows:

- **Contact information** of the spokespeople quoted from in the SMNR, in addition to in-house public relations and agency executives (this also could be placed last).
- News release **headline**, which may even be shorter for Twitter retweets, and an optional subhead.
- **Lead paragraph** followed by **brief paragraphs or bulleted highlights**—or just core news facts in bullet points.
- A few **quotes**, usually in bullets, from executives from the organization, and other parties involved with the news announcement, industry analysts, or customers.
- **Boilerplate** (closing paragraph with core information about an organization).
- Embedded **visual galleries** with thumbnail images of photos, logos, infographics, and other visuals, as well as links to videos.
- Additional **links and tagging and sharing options**—such as mobile apps, RSS feeds, social media bookmarks, social networking sites, and links to the online newsroom and the organization's website.
- **Links to the release translated** into other languages.
- **Links to news outlets and blogs** that have covered the story.
- **Comment box**, which can be monitored.
- **Email and print** options.

Look at the social media releases posted on RealWire (www.realwire.com) and Pressitt (pressitt.com), which are two examples of online news release distribution services.

10.4 Imagery and Captions

Images can strengthen a news release and help build on a story. For example, the FedEx Panda Express news releases on shipping animals, which were mentioned earlier, were supported with a variety of photos, as well as video clips posted on the company's multimedia online newsroom. In addition, FedEx arranged photo opportunities for journalists to cover the shipping process (see Figure 10.1). Although many organizations may not have such dynamic imagery to work with, they need to consider images that illustrate components of the story. Images should be available online in the organization's online newsroom or through another online photo sharing library to avoid clogging a journalist's email with large attachments.

Photo captions should be brief and capture the essence of the image, using the present tense. Some writers define **captions** as the headline above a photo and **cutlines** as the descriptive content below images. People should be clearly identified, and group photos should list the names of people from left to right. The text only needs to say "from left." Model releases should be obtained as necessary. Copyright information can be simply stated with the copyright sign © followed by the name of the organization. Photo credits also may need to be attributed to the photographer.

The following types of images can help build a story and be widely used by journalists, as well as consumers:

- **Products**—High-quality photographs that clearly show the product and highlight its most important features should be included in announcements related to the new product or enhancements.

Figure 10.1—A FEDEX PANDA EXPRESS JUST SECONDS AFTER LANDING AT EDINBURGH TURNHOUSE AIRPORT CARRIES TWO GIANT PANDAS TIAN TIAN AND YANG GUANG TO EDINBURGH ZOO IN EDINBURGH, SCOTLAND, ON DEC. 4, 2011. Source: © Michal Kowalski/Shutterstock.com.

Apple's online release about its iPhone 6 and iPhone 6 Plus provided four different images of the smartphones, with simple captions including the product names. In order to download the images, users have to agree to an Image Use Agreement, which in essence indicates that the images must not be altered and will be used exclusively for editorial purposes or by industry analysts, and not for any commercial application.

Honda's online news release worldwide on the debut of its Honda FCV CONCEPT Fuel-Cell vehicle (Honda, 2014) included exterior and interior images of the new vehicle, the external power feeding device, and the new logo. The photo caption includes the same headline, subhead, and date of the news release, along with a few words of the actual image below the photo.

Photo caption of exterior view of vehicle:
Honda Unveils All-New FCV CONCEPT Fuel-Cell Vehicle
—Striving to Realize a CO2-free Society by Combining FCV with an external power feeding device and Smart Hydrogen Station—
Honda FCV CONCEPT

- **Profiles**—Announcements related to people, whether promotions, new hires, awards, or other related news, should include a portrait of the person. Other options can include the person at work or on location. When Walmart announced its new president and CEO of Walmart U.S., the company's news release (Walmart, 2014) included a traditional formal portrait image of the CEO with a suit and tie and another image of him wearing a collared shirt in a less formal setting. The caption is embedded as the name of the file, which is another way of labeling imagery.

Photo caption:
Greg Foran addresses associates during his first town hall meeting as CEO of Walmart U.S.

- **Discoveries and New Developments**—Visual imagery can make a difference in getting the story placed—and grabbing the reader's or viewer's attention. The Hubble Space Telescope, a project of international cooperation between the European Space Agency (ESA) and National Aeronautics and Space Administration (NASA), issued a news release titled, "The riddle of the missing stars: Hubble observations cast further doubt on how globular clusters formed," along with eight images and a few video clips. Here is an example of the text from one of the supporting photo captions (NASA/ESA Hubble Space Telescope, 2014; see Figure 10.2):

Photo Caption and Cutline:
Four globular clusters in Fornax
This NASA/ESA Hubble Space Telescope image shows four globular clusters in the dwarf galaxy Fornax.
New observations of the clusters—large balls of stars that orbit the centres of galaxies—show they are very similar to those found in our galaxy, the Milky Way. The finding is at odds with leading theories on how these clusters form—in these theories, globular clusters should be nestled among large quantities of old stars—and so the mystery of how these objects came to exist deepens.
Left to right: Fornax 1, Fornax 2, Fornax 3 and Fornax 5. Their positions within the galaxy are shown in image G.

Credit:
NASA, ESA, S. Larsen (Radboud University, the Netherlands)

Figure 10.2—FOUR GLOBULAR CLUSTERS IN FORNAX. Source: NASA, ESA, S. Larsen (Radboud University, the Netherlands).

Hubble's newsroom includes strong writing examples of conveying complex news simply to laypeople with limited knowledge of space astronomy.

The National Science Foundation (2014) in the U.S. issued a release titled, "Scientists discover fossil of bizarre groundhog-like mammal on Madagascar: Newly discovered fossil alters thinking on evolution of early mammals," along with renderings of the mammal, and images of the fossil, skull, and scientists at the excavation site in Madagascar. The photo captions include appropriate credits and simple descriptions since the release provides details of the discovery. For example, the image of the model sculpted from a cast of the skull of the mammal, *Vintana sertichi* (see Figure 10.3), contains a simple photo caption: "Artist's reconstruction of the huge groundhog-like animal that once lived on Madagascar," and a credit to the artists at Staab Studios, a company that specializes in creating natural history and prehistoric life models for museums, publishing, and film.

- **Events**—Releases on upcoming events can include imagery of posters, location of event, preparation scenes, or scenes from previous events. Event releases can be followed up with details and success of the actual event, such as the proceeds generated by the fundraiser, as well as imagery of the actual event.

- **Diagrams, Charts, and Infographics**—Quantitative information works more effectively in charts that can illustrate progress and changes over a period of time. Infographics, which are covered in Chapter 11, can creatively provide facts and more context at a glance.

- **Behind-the-scenes** or **Works-in progress Imagery**—More unusual or harder-to-find imagery can show the production of a movie, the preparation of a major public event, the construction of a new building, the creation of a new product, the process of an elaborate meal, or before-and-after transitions over a period of time.

For example, when Corning Museum of Glass (2013), one of the world's leading museums of glass, issued a news release on its major expansion, the release and its online newsroom included a collection of exterior and interior renderings to illustrate

Figure 10.3—ARTIST'S RECONSTRUCTION OF THE HUGE GROUNDHOG-LIKE ANIMAL THAT ONCE LIVED ON MADAGASCAR. Source: Courtesy of Luci Bette-Nash and Gary Staab, Staab Studios.

what the new contemporary glass gallery will look like. See Figure 10.4 of an exterior image that conveys the minimalist white glass building and renovated ventilator building with expanded glass-blowing demonstration space; and refer to Figure 10.5 for an interior image of its new wing, with a sophisticated light-filtering system that uses diffusing skylights to light the works of art.

Figure 10.4—RENDERING OF THE NEW NORTH WING EXPANSION AT THE CORNING MUSEUM OF GLASS, CORNING, N.Y., DESIGNED BY THOMAS PHIFER & PARTNERS. Source: Photo courtesy of Thomas Phifer & Partners.

Figure 10.5—RENDERING OF THE NORTH WING CONTEMPORARY GALLERY, CORNING MUSEUM OF GLASS, CORNING, N.Y. Source: By-Encore.

These are just a few examples of how visuals can bring a story to life and create desirable imagery to build an image library of interest to journalists, as well as to the public. Just as the content can be localized, images should be localized as relevant. Chapter 5 covers visual resources in greater depth, including cultural sensitivities on application of subject matter and colors.

Try Exercise 10.2 and see if you can find a story that was generated from a news releases and any supporting imagery.

10.5 Delivery of News Releases

How do public relations practitioners distribute news releases? Distribution options include paid news release services, Real Simple Syndication (RSS), email blasts, standard mail, Web newsrooms, blogs and microblogs, social networking sites, and mobile apps for smartphones and tablets. Many public relations practitioners use a combination of multimedia distribution methods and also keep track of the individual preferences of journalists, particularly the most influential ones in each market.

News release distribution services can be the fastest method to convey news to the largest number of media outlets worldwide. Many public relations firms and companies pay to have their releases distributed since these services maintain current databases of media contacts, offering multiple media distribution options by industry sector and geographic region, as well as high search engine optimization. A number of news release distribution services around the globe also offer capabilities to prepare and distribute social media news releases with embedded photos and videos, as well as other social networking and bookmarking interactivity.

Here are a few examples of the largest global distribution services that charge fees:

- PR Newswire (www.prnewswire.com) is a global provider of multimedia platforms with clients spanning the globe. It is owned by U.K.-based UBM plc company.

Exercise 10.2

Insights: Media Placements Generated from a News Release

Find a story of interest, particularly on a new product launch, a new CEO, or another major development, that you've seen covered in multiple media outlets. See if you can find a corresponding news release(s) issued by the organization(s) involved. Ask yourself these questions?

1. Was any of the content from the news stories or social media culled directly from the news release?
2. Was the release content localized to that specific market or was it global in scale?
3. Was a quotation from the spokesperson (or spokespeople) in the release included in the aired or published stories?
4. If the release included any images or video links, do you recall seeing those images used in the reporting of the story?
5. Did you find any translated versions of the release?

- Wholly owned subsidiary of Berkshire Hathaway, an American multinational conglomerate in diversified industries, Business Wire (www.businesswire.com) maintains bureaus worldwide and is widely used by publicly held companies.
- Headquartered in Canada and majority-owned by OMERS Private Equity, Marketwire (www.marketwire.com) also has global news release distribution.

Other distribution services offer complimentary services, with some limitations. French-based Kontax (www.kontax.com), for example, states that it has reach in more than 160 countries in over 60 languages. Kontax offers free of charge distribution of multimedia releases in one language, but it charges for translation services.

News releases also can be distributed using the following methods:

- **Emails** can be sent to a customized media list, but the list should be kept up to date with current contacts. Make sure to only send relevant releases to reporters covering those topics. The subject line should include an abbreviated version of the release's headline. Insert the release as text into the email message; avoid sending attachments and PDF files. Reporters will rarely open up unsolicited attachments.
- **Online newsrooms** provide updated and helpful resources to journalists. It is recommended that all releases be posted regularly online. Chapter 11 covers best practices in creating and maintaining online media resources in local and international markets. In the real world, you may have to produce a "vanity release" of no significant news value that your client or company demands—after you have done due diligence trying to persuade your client that the release will be unlikely to receive interest. In this case, the release could be posted in the online newsroom, instead of clogging up reporters' email with content that would be considered spam.
- **Social media news releases** and **links to online traditional releases** also can be incorporated into organizational **blogs**, **microblogs**, such as **Twitter**, and other **social media**. **Real Simple Syndication** (RSS) enables websites to publish content summaries to subscribers who can track updated content and receive feeds of material of interest. Some reporters like to be able to upload news release content on **mobile apps**.
- **Video news releases**, which are created exclusively for television or online videos, and **audio news releases** for radio. However, many public relations practitioners also distribute traditional or social media releases to broadcast media.
- Photocopies of releases in **hardcopy media kits** have not been completely eliminated. Although this is a less common practice, releases may be printed on the company's letterhead or customized news release letterhead and distributed at media-related events or face-to-face meetings with journalists, as well as by mail with product samples. Media kits, whether digital or printed, traditionally include current news releases.
- Some journalists still prefer to receive releases by **fax** and, to a lesser extent, by **regular mail**.

10.6 Learning Objectives and Key Terms

By studying this chapter, readers should be able to:

- Understand what constitutes content for news releases of interest to journalists.
- Apply the "Si, Lo, Ba, Ti, Un, Fa" and 5W techniques to determine news value.

- Identify the differences between hard news and soft news topics.
- Name different methods to disseminate news releases.
- Craft a traditional news releases and know which components can be localized to different markets.
- Edit documents for greater clarity and be aware of cultural sensitivities and geopolitics.
- Convert traditional news release content to a social media news release.
- Select imagery and write captions to accompany news releases.

This chapter contains the following key terms:

News release (p. 236)

Media placements (p. 237)

Soft feature news (p. 239)

Hard news (p. 239)

Contacts (p. 245)

Release timing/embargoes (p. 245)

Headlines (p. 245)

Subheads (p. 246)

Datelines (p. 246)

Leads and ledes (p. 246)

5Ws (p. 246)

Inverted pyramid (p. 246)

Quotations (p. 248)

Boilerplates (p. 249)

Safe haven legalese (p. 250)

Forward-looking statements (p. 250)

Slug lines (p. 250)

End marks (p. 250)

Headers and footers (p. 250)

Notes to editors (p. 250)

Social media news releases (p. 251)

Photo captions (p. 253)

Photo cutlines (p. 253)

News release distribution service (p. 258)

References

Apple. (2014, September 9). Apple announces iPhone 6 & iPhone 6 Plus—the biggest advancements in iPhone history [News release]. Retrieved from https://www.apple.com/pr/library/2014/09/09Apple-Announces-iPhone-6-iPhone-6-Plus-The-Biggest-Advancements-in-iPhone-History.html.

Bulldog Reporter & Cision. (2010). 2010 journalist survey on media relations practices. Retrieved from http://insight.cision.com/content/2010-journalist-audit-bulldog-reporter.

Corning Museum of Glass. (2013, May 30). Corning Museum of Glass unveils final design of its North Wing expansion [News release]. Retrieved from http://www.cmog.org/press-release/corning-museum-glass-unveils-final-design-its-north-wing-expansion.

Coventry, J. (2008, June 4). Third Sector Extra: 10 ways to get your press release binned. *Third Sector*. Retrieved from http://www.thirdsector.co.uk/third-sector-extra-10-ways-press-binned/communications/article/813852.

Diageo. (2012, July 26). Underwater archaeologists dig deep for iconic privateer Captain Henry Morgan's lost fleet in the Caribbean [News release]. Retrieved from http://www.prnewswire.com/news-releases/underwater-archaeologists-dig-deep-for-iconic-privateer-captain-henry-morgans-lost-fleet-in-the-caribbean-163852336.html.

DreamWorks Animation. (September 2, 2014). How to Train Your Dragon 2 crosses $600,000,000 [News release]. Retrieved from http://ir.dreamworksanimation.com/investor-relations/press-releases/press-release-details/2014/How-To-Train-Your-Dragon-2-Crosses-600000000/default.aspx.

Dubois, L. (2010, November 11). How to write a social media press release. *Inc*. Retrieved from http://www.inc.com/guides/2010/11/how-to-write-a-social-media-press-release.html.

Guth, D. W., & Marsh, C. (2012). *Public relations: A values-driven approach* (5th ed.). Boston, MA: Allyn & Bacon.

Honda. (2014, November 17). Honda unveils all-new FCV CONCEPT fuel-cell vehicle [News release]. Retrieved from http://world.honda.com/news/2014/4141117All-New-Fuel-Cell-Vehicle-FCV-CONCEPT/.

Ipsos Markinor. (2011, April 13). Ranking professional communications and PR companies in South Africa: The good, the bad and the lag behind global standards [News release]. Retrieved from http://ipsos-markinor.co.za/news/ranking-professional-communications-and-pr-companies-in-south-africa-the-good-the-bad-and-the-lag-behind-global-standards.

Iseman, S. (2011, March 11). Time for PR to consider impact of "churnalism." *PRSay.* Retrieved from http://prsay.prsa.org/index.php/2011/03/11/impact-of-chunrnalism-pr-journalism/.

Jarboe, G. (2006, October 29). The 100th birthday of the press release. *Search Engine Watch.* Retrieved from http://searchenginewatch.com.

Lewis, J., Williams, A., Franklin, B., Thomas, J., & Mosdell, N. (2008). The quality and independence of British journalism: Tracking the changes over 20 years. Project Report [Online]. MediaWise. *Cardiff University.* Retrieved from http://www.cardiff.ac.uk/jomec/resources/QualityIndependenceofBritishJournalism.pdf.

Lewis, T. (2007, February 12). What's Mandarin for "press release"? As more news releases go global, the rules get more complex. *PR Week* (US), 18.

L'Oréal. (2014a, November 19). L'Oréal announces the launch of its international awards for social responsibility in dermatology [News release]. Retrieved from http://www.loreal.com/press-releases/loreal-announces-the-launch-of-its-international-awards-for-social-responsibility-in-dermatology.aspx?mediaType=cp&returnPage=?parentCategory=&groupBy=&type=cp&startDate=1900-01-01&endDate=2099–12-31&keyword=&cat=&returnTopcode=&sort=.

L'Oréal. (2014b, October 20). L'Oréal USA signs agreement to acquire Carol's Daughter Group. Retrieved from http://www.loreal.com/press-releases/loreal-usa-signs-agreement-to-acquire-carols-daughter.aspx?mediaType=cp&returnPage=?parentCategory=&groupBy=&type=cp&startDate=1900-01-01&endDate=2099-12-31&keyword=&cat=&returnTopcode=&sort=.

L'Oréal. (2014c, July 31). First-half 2014 results [News release]. Retrieved from http://www.loreal-finance.com/eng/news-release/first-half-2014-results-972.htm.

Media Standards Trust. (2014). *Churnalism.com.* Retrieved from http://mediastandardstrust.org/churnalism/.

NASA/ESA Hubble Space Telescope. (2014, November 20). Four globular clusters in Fornax. Retrieved from http://www.spacetelescope.org/images/heic1425a/.

National Science Foundation. (2014, November 5). Scientists discover fossil of bizarre groundhog-like mammal on Madagascar [News release]. Retrieved from http://www.nsf.gov/news/news_summ.jsp?cntn_id=133092.

Oriella PR Network. (2012). The influence game: How news is sourced and managed today. *Oriella PR Network global digital journalism study 2012.* Retrieved from http://www.oriellaprnetwork.com/sites/default/files/research/Oriella%20Digital%20Journalism%20Study%202012%20Final%20US.pdf.

Parkinson, M. G., & Ekachai, D. (2006). *International and intercultural public relations: A campaign case approach.* Boston, MA: Pearson.

Partners In Health. (2014, October 24). Partners In Health names Gary Gottlieb chief executive officer [News release]. Retrieved from http://www.pih.org/press/partners-in-health-names-gary-gottlieb-chief-executive-officer.

Pelham, F. (2000). The triple crown of public relations: Pitch letter, news release, feature article. *Public Relations Quarterly, 45*(1), 38–43.

Text 100. (2012, March). Engaging journalists through social media: How journalists use social media for research and communication in their professional roles. Retrieved from http://www.text100-uk.com/survey/.

Tritton, L. (2012, March 12). How to make your press releases work for you. *bdonline.co.uk*. Retrieved from http://www.bdonline.co.uk/how-to-make-your-press-releases-work-for-you/5033140.article.

Virgin Galactic. (2012, July 10). Virgin Galactic reveals privately funded satellite launcher and confirms SpaceShipTwo poised for powered flight [News release]. Retrieved from http://staging.virgingalactic.com/news/item/xxx/.

Wallace, C. (2010, January 20). Media relations: A perfect match? *PR Week*. Retrieved from http://www.prweek.com/article/978511/media-relations-perfect-match.

Walmart. (2014, July 24). Walmart names Greg Foran president and CEO of Walmart U.S. [News release]. Retrieved from http://news.walmart.com/news-archive/2014/07/24/walmart-names-greg-foran-president-and-ceo-of-walmart-us.

Wenner, K. S. (2002, September). News you can't use: Journalists are questioning the longstanding practice of embargoing news. *American Journalism Review*. Retrieved from http://www.ajr.org/article.asp?id=2597.

Wicks, N., & Kaba, N. (2011, March 4). Industry wary of "churnalism" site. *PR Week*. Retrieved from http://www.prweek.com/article/1057950/industry-wary-churnalism-site.

Working, R. (2013, December 23). Coca-Cola digital chief: "Kill the press release." *Ragan.com*. Retrieved from http://www.ragan.com/Main/Articles/CocaCola_digital_chief_Kill_the_press_release_47600.aspx.

Yglesias, M. (2012, September 26). There will be no bacon shortage: How a British trade association release sent the Internet into a senseless panic. *Slate*. Retrieved from http://www.slate.com/articles/business/moneybox/2012/09/unavoidable_bacon_shortage_u_k_s_national_pig_association_has_everyone_worried_about_the_price_of_pork_.html.

11 Composing Global Media Kits and Online Newsrooms

The two words "information" and "communication" are often used interchangeably, but they signify quite different things. Information is giving out; communication is getting through.

—Sydney J. Harris, journalist and columnist

11.1 Introduction to Newsroom Writing in Public Relations

This quote from Sydney J. Harris (1917–1986), the late American journalist, reflects the distinction between information and communication. Public relations writers must not only be able to provide news and information, but they also must make the connection to communicate and be relevant with journalists. **Media kits** (also called **press kits**) tell the story of an organization and serve as a comprehensive resource for journalists to learn about the multifaceted qualities of an organization. This comprehensive written and visual information can help journalists better understand the scope of an organization, find facts quickly, develop ideas for stories, obtain supporting imagery, and know who to contact for any questions. Practically every organization today has an **online newsroom**—obscure bed-and-breakfasts; small businesses and craftspeople; Internet video cat stars, artists, and entertainers; government offices of all kinds; charities and NGOs; and local, regional, and multinational corporations. Even the British royal family has a "Media Information" section on its website (www.royal. gov.uk) with event engagements, news releases, speeches, images, and comprehensive guidelines on interviewing policies. However, you would not find any less than favorable news. Prince Harry's former escapades in Las Vegas seem to have lived up to the tourist board's tagline: "What happens in Vegas, stays in Vegas." If online newsrooms are not password protected, they can be read by anyone—and organizations may find it beneficial to have consumers access this content, as long as the site includes different contacts for the general public and the journalists seeking more information.

Writing media kit materials can be time-intensive, requiring a communications audit of existing written material and additional research to fill in gaps of information. Public relations writers may be updating and enhancing existing media kit materials by reviewing all online and written materials, reading media coverage over a specific timeframe, and searching other secondary sources from digital libraries and industry trade associations. When starting a new media kit, writers may need to travel on location to conduct interviews and discover firsthand how the organization operates. In some cases, writers may need assistance in translating content for media kits in other languages, as well as for researching information to develop the kit's content. When I was preparing a pre-opening media kit for a conversion of a historic building into a luxury hotel in Budapest, I had to collaborate with someone fluent in Hungarian and English since many of the archival sources were available only in Hungarian.

Media kits should be updated regularly to ensure that the facts and visuals remain current. Public relations executives also may create customized versions of media kits as follows:

- **General corporate story** on the big picture or global reach of the organization, as well as its products, services, evolution, and executives.
- **Brand-specific editions**, particularly for larger companies with diverse products and services.
- **Subject-specific versions** for journalists (consumer information for lifestyle reporters, business and financial content for business reporters), which also can be edited for global needs. Publicly held companies traditionally have financial materials, which may be located in a separate online section on investor relations.
- **Regional- or country-specific versions**, focusing on the operations in that location.
- **Different versions of English** (such as American or British English) and **translated editions** in other languages.

The writing style should reflect the personality of the organization. Content for a chocolatier or a toy company, for example, would be more whimsical than the serious tone required of a financial services company. The tone also changes based on content geared to a specific type of reporter—straightforward financial information for business reporters covering a publicly held company, more conversational tone with how-to decorating tips and visuals for a furniture and home accessories company, or quantitative research for a science reporter investigating an environmental nonprofit.

According to findings from a survey of 120 corporate online newsrooms from six European countries, Singapore, and the U.S., most online newsrooms would benefit with more enhancements, such as greater efficiency, easier navigation, updated resources, and more information and visuals (González-Herrero & Ruiz de Valbuena, 2006). This chapter shows how to create dynamic press content and digital newsrooms that would provide extensive written and visual resources.

11.2 Types of Media Kits

As with news releases, media kits continue to evolve in physical appearance, accessibility, and distribution. Public relations writers can select to use multiple formats based on their budget and type of media relations activities. The required format today is an online newsroom. Tactical media kits, however, may be useful to distribute at media events and to mail to journalists along with product samples.

11.2.1 Printed and Digital Formats

Tactical media kits still apply for such specific circumstances as follows:

- Selective media kit mailings are important when you want journalists to be able to see or experience a product, particularly a new or updated product. Manufacturers of beauty products and cosmetics, food products, and alcoholic and non-alcoholic drinks tend to send samples of their products to journalists. Product samples may be mini-sized, such as the little bottles you find on airplanes or in-room hotel bars or beauty products the size of in-room hotel amenities. Mailings also can be effective to bring attention to a major event. Be careful about sending promotional items to some journalists who may be unable to accept any gift, even an inexpensive logoed coffee mug, bottle stopper, or corkscrew.

- Press events offer you the opportunity to meet face-to-face with journalists. Whether you are hosting a product demonstration at a trade show or a reception with corporate executives, you may want to provide journalists with both printed and digital materials.
- One-on-one press briefings in a journalist's office also would give you the chance to review material in person and leave behind a tactical media kit.

Printed media kits are traditionally packaged in a two-pocket folder, containing written materials and supporting news releases printed on the organization's letterhead. The kit also could include print-outs of reduced sized imagery (also called **thumbnails**), so reporters can quickly see what images are available online, as well as brochures or other relevant materials. The packaging can range from the least expensive option, store-bought four-color paper portfolios with affixed decals of the logo, to more costly four-color customized printed and specially designed fabric with multiple folders. For example, the public relations director of a luxury resort in Bali, Indonesia, hired a local artist to create handmade media kit folders with ikat batik fabric, reflecting the Indonesian textile tradition.

Data storage devices include **USBs** (Universal Serial Bus connectors), which are also called **flash drives**. USBs can be printed with the company's name and logo, as well as custom designed in different shapes, sizes, and colors to reflect the brand. For example, Musikmesse is acclaimed as the largest international festival of musical instruments and the music business held in Germany every year—and its flash drive was the shape of a guitar (see Figure 11.1). Aquatica San Antonio created a flash drive in the shape of a sting ray (see Figure 11.2).

Figure 11.1—MUSIKMESSE USB IN THE SHAPE OF A GUITAR. Source: © USBpromos.com.

© USBpromos.com

Figure 11.2—AQUATICA, A WATERPARK AT SEAWORLD SAN ANTONIO, PROVIDED JOURNALISTS WITH PHOTOS, VIDEOS, AND NEWS RELEASES ON A USB SHAPED LIKE A STINGRAY. Source: Fred Blauth, BizBash Media.

Some companies also have used CDs, with a custom-designed case or a color printed insert for a clear plastic case or another creative approach. Sony, for example, designed a square-shaped cardboard package with two jewel cases containing illustrations of the game characters of its Heavy Rain game for PlayStation 3 (see Figure 11.3). The packaging unfolds like origami, an appropriate design motif for the game's Origami Killer character, with each flap providing content about the game's lead characters.

Figure 11.3—SELF-CONTAINED HEAVY RAIN MEDIA KIT MAILER CONSTRUCTED OF HARD CARDBOARD UNFOLDS INTO A JEWEL-CASE BOX CONTAINING THE SONY PLAYSTATION 3 GAME. Source: Courtesy of wecollectgames.com.

Media kits also can be placed in customized boxes and tote bags with product samples. This technique is popular for food products, wines, spirits, and beauty products. Creativity is essential, particularly when a new product is being launched within a highly competitive marketplace. When the Kraken Black Spiced Rum introduced its Caribbean rum to the U.S., the company hired a Brooklyn-based creative agency to design a limited-edition media kit that would entice journalists to find out more and sample the product. The new product is named after the kraken, a legendary octopus-like sea monster, which is prominently illustrated on the bottle, as well as in its advertising, sales promotional items, and its press materials. This media kit (see Figures 11.4 and 11.5) tells the story of the kraken and invites the journalist who opens the elegantly designed package to experience seven elements of "proof" of the monster's existence. The illustrated box contains a letter from a "noted hoax researcher," along with such evidence as a kraken tooth, a vial of kraken ink—and the final 94% proof of the actual bottle of rum. The designer and art director Charmaine Choi was quoted in *The Future of Ads* (O'Brien, 2013):

> To launch the world's first 94 proof black spiced rum, we developed an integrated campaign based on the sea-beast of myth and legend. We developed an "accurate" history and, quite possibly, real world from which The Kraken Rum, may indeed have come. We created "scientific" movies, a scientific journal and an interactive website to educate the public. (para. 10)

The media kit for introducing Lindt's luxury chocolates (see Figure 11.6) elegantly showcases the new products in a box constructed of a soft brown velvet with gold foil edging, which is wrapped with a brown ribbon printed with the gold Lindt logos. The box unfolds with the four chocolate bars held in place in a row, so you can see the new collection, along

Figure 11.4—KRAKEN BLACK SPICED RUM MEDIA KIT BOX WITH SEVEN FORMS OF "PROOF." Source: Agency, Dead As We Know It; Creative Director Mikal Reich; Copywriters Mikal Reich and Ella Wilson; Art Director and Production Charmaine Choi.

Figure 11.5—KRAKEN BLACK SPICED RUM MEDIA KIT BOX WITH "SCIENTIFIC JOURNAL." Source: Agency, Dead As We Know It; Creative Director Mikal Reich; Copywriters Mikal Reich and Ella Wilson; Art Director and Production Charmaine Choi.

Figure 11.6—LINDT MEDIA KIT PACKAGED WITH CHOCOLATE SAMPLES.
Source: Concept and design by Jo Stedman, SO Creative Studio Limited in London,
www.socreative.co.uk.

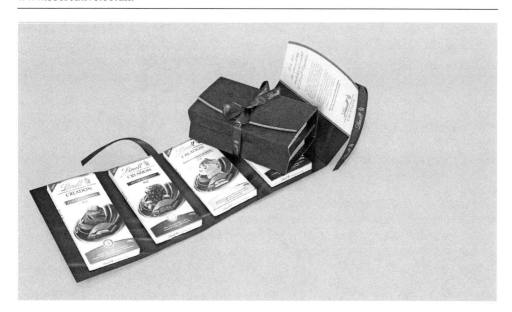

with a written message and a USB containing the media kit. Jo Stedman (2012), founder and
creative director of SO Creative Studio Limited, a London-based design and communications
agency, that created the media kit for the Swiss chocolatier, explained:

> When you launch a food product, try appealing to food lovers' different senses. To launch four new
> flavours for one of Lindt's luxury lines, we produced a luxury press kit in the style of an indulgent
> box of chocolates—in sumptuous cocoa-brown velvet that not only shouted "eat me" but begged to be
> touched. The bespoke concertina piece opened to reveal samples of the four new flavours, supported
> by an informational USB memory stick. Produced to support a launch event at the Dorchester Hotel
> in London, these luxurious press kits were gifted to the attending press. (para. 9)

The media kit to promote Marc Jacobs' Daisy fragrance unveils a surprise when you
open the Daisy-covered box—a logoed cube literally pops into shape (see Figure 11.7). The
"Fiat Experience" media kit showcases an espresso cup and saucer, along with a comprehensive
booklet and USB media kit, to promote its Fiat 500, a car that actually comes equipped with
its own espresso maker (see Figure 11.8).

Media kits for special events also can be packaged creatively. Another engaging example
comes from Universal Orlando to promote its annual Halloween Horror Nights. When you
open the brown shipping box, you find a trunk with an invitation on top, part of which reads
(see Figure 11.9):

Figure 11.7—DAISY MARC JACOBS POP ART EDITION MEDIA KIT. Source: Courtesy of Structural Graphics.

Figure 11.8—FIAT 500 MEDIA KIT. FIAT is a registered trademark of Fiat Group Marketing & Corporate Communication S.p.A., used under license by Chrysler Group LLC. Source: Courtesy of Christian Vitale/Fiat500USA.com.

Figure 11.9—UNIVERSAL ORLANDO'S HALLOWEEN HORROR NIGHTS MEDIA KIT PACKAGED IN A LOCKED TRUNK CONTAINING A FAUX HEAD. Source: Courtesy of Ricky Brigante/InsideTheMagic.net.

Will you survive?
OPEN the box. . .
SEE what awaits. . .
FEEL the fear. . .
Surely, it's not brain surgery.

The trunk wrapped with fake roots has a lock and key and when you open the trunk, the inside lid reads, "What evil has taken root?" Inside you find faux moss on top of a faux bloodied head with a flash drive stuck in its eye socket. This approach is gruesome, but appropriate for the theme park promoting its Halloween events. The previous year's media kit contained bloodstained contents of a faux rotting skull wrapped in a bloody canvas, in which you had to pry the flash drive out of the brain (hence, the reference to "it's not brain surgery" in the newer version's invitation copy).

Nike's 11 "Write the Future" media kits would be considered a collector's item. Each media kit contains six hand-carved crayons by artist Diem Chau of the soccer players in the FIFA World Cup, along with a display stand (see Figures 11.10, 11.11, and 11.12). This was part of an integrative global campaign that attempted to capture the imagination and inspiration of soccer fans through multiple traditional and social media platforms.

Try Exercise 11.1 and prepare creative packaging ideas for a tactical media kit for a fictitious company that aims to introduce its new high-energy drinks to journalists and bloggers.

Figure 11.10—NIKE "WRITE THE FUTURE" WORLD CUP MEDIA KIT. Source: Image provided by Wieden+Kennedy.

Figure 11.11—NIKE "WRITE THE FUTURE" MEDIA KIT ALSO INCLUDED A DISPLAY STAND FOR HAND-CARVED CRAYONS WITH THE LIKENESS OF SIX WORLD CUP SOCCER PLAYERS. Source: Image provided by Wieden+Kennedy.

Figure 11.12—CLOSE-UP IMAGES OF CRAYONS CARVED BY DIEM CHAU IN THE NIKE "WRITE THE FUTURE" WORLD CUP MEDIA KIT. Source: Image provided by Wieden+Kennedy.

Exercise 11.1

Creative Thinking: Tactical Media Kit Ideas

Your client (a fictitious company) is launching a new high-energy beverage, Awesome!, that will contain fewer calories and less caffeine than its competitor's products. The new product line will be sold in five flavors: Crazy Cranberry, Glorious Grape, Lively Lemon, Magic Mango, and Peppy Pomegranate. This new product will be sold in two sizes, 8 fluid ounces (240 milliliters) and 12 fluid ounces (350 milliliters), in recyclable glass bottles. The target markets are college students and busy young professionals on the go, primarily in urban areas. The company is based in San Francisco, California, and has hired artists from five continents to design the labels of its new bottles. Ten percent of all revenues will be donated to a new charity called Awesome! Arts for All, that will provide scholarships to art students and help fund art exhibitions around the world.

Your client wants to introduce this new product to leading food and beverage editors and bloggers, as well as to hosts and producers of TV and radio programs, across the U.S. (The new product will be tested in the U.S. before being available in international markets.) How would you package the products and share information in a tactical media kit to be distributed to bloggers and journalists? You can be as creative as you want.

11.2.2 Online Media Kits and Newsrooms

Online newsrooms can offer engaging experiences for journalists with interactivity and instantly available information and images. Public relations practitioners operate online newsrooms like virtual news bureaus, providing current information that can be easily updated as needed, as well as archival materials. The other benefit is that the content, unless it is password protected, can be read by anyone—potential customers, shareholders, donors, volunteers, and audiences. With the proliferation of smartphones and tablets, public relations practitioners also can convert media kit content to be read and downloaded more easily by journalists and consumers using mobile apps.

Online newsrooms should include the following components:

- An **easy-to-find online newsroom** is a must. For example, the reporter should be able to search and find the newsroom by typing in the name of the organization plus newsroom on Google or on another Web search engine. Websites should clearly identify the newsroom on its opening page, such as "Media," "Press Information," "Press Club," "Newsroom," "Online Newsroom," or "News Center." However, some corporate websites bury the newsroom in the "About Us" section. It can be frustrating for reporters to spend too much time trying to find a newsroom online. Use **tags** to clearly label and identify components of text and visual content for search engine optimization.

- The **landing page** of the newsroom should be well organized and simple to navigate. The site should have a scroll-down menu with a choice of languages, whether global English (usually the English of the country or the organization's headquarters), other English-language versions, and other language versions. This page should serve as a "table of contents" to clearly navigate content. Some newsrooms say "welcome," but I would recommend adding a welcome message.

  Here is an example of an online newsroom's "Welcome" message:

  Welcome to the Virgin Mobile USA Newsroom for use by journalists and analysts. Virgin Mobile USA is one of Sprint's prepaid brands.

  Virgin Mobile USA welcomes contact from members of the press and wireless industry. For answers to specific questions, help researching a mobile industry trend or to set up an interview with a Virgin Mobile USA spokesperson, please email us at: VMUGeneral@sprint.com.

  If you have questions or need more information, please add your name to our opt-in email news list in our "News Alerts" section to keep current on Virgin Mobile USA news.

  Thanks for your interest in Virgin Mobile USA. We're here to be a resource for you. (Virgin Mobile USA, 2014, paras. 1–4)

- **Media and public information or customer service contacts** in the corporate headquarters, as well as in regional or local offices, should be easy to find. Swiss-based Nestlé, for example, contains information in English and links on its global homepage to its corporate communications and media relations team members with photos, titles, time zones, and contact information of each executive. It also includes a scroll-down menu, where you can select the country and business unit of public relations executives around the globe. This section also asks "Not a Journalist?" and includes general information for consumer inquiries and a link to a "Contact Us" form.

- **Interactive features and social media integration** with one-click icon buttons make it easy for journalists to find and share content on social network sites. Make the newsroom simple for the reporter to print out, bookmark, share documents, or communicate by email or on social media, such as Facebook, Google+, or Twitter. Ask journalists if they would like to subscribe to receive news releases and updates by Real Simple Syndication (RSS) feeds. Nestlé, for example, has a simple "Sign Me Up" form on its online newsroom that also allows journalists to customize the type of information they would like to receive and indicate when, such as news when it happens or as a monthly roundup. It also explains how easy it can be to unsubscribe, and the questionnaire includes a privacy statement on the use of the data.

- **News releases** should be easy to search. Many online newsrooms provide the material in reverse chronological order, so you can search by topic and year. Highlighting current news with imagery can make it simple to see the latest developments. News release archives should span at least the past two years. News releases also can be organized by global news, regional or country-specific, or by specific brand or topic.

- **Media kit content** should be easy to find and download. Some online newsrooms allow users to download a complete media kit or specific parts. **Fact sheets** or frequently asked questions provide core information on the organization and its products, services, or resources. **Executive profiles** give biographical details on the founder, CEO, and other key staff. **Backgrounders** can contain more detailed information on specific attributes of an organization. For example, Boeing's online newsroom (http://boeing.mediaroom.com) provides comprehensive information about the company's operations, employment practices, people, awards, history, and corporate social responsibility, as well as product information on each of its commercial and military airlines and out-of-production models.

- **Thumbnail images** make it easy to see what is contained in the visual library. Nissan's Official Media Newsroom in the U.S. includes thumbnails of its car models in alphabetical order by year. When you click on the car icon, you are immediately shown a collection of thumbnails of the entire photo collection of the model in different colors and perspectives, with close-up details of features. Each image should be high quality (preferably offering a choice of imagery for Web and print usages) and be accompanied with a brief caption, required copyright, and credit to the photographer. An image use agreement can be useful to clarify copyright and how the image can and cannot be used. Apple's newsroom (http://www.apple.com/pr/), for example, requires people downloading images to agree to the terms, unless other written permission is signed by the company. The visual library also can include broadcast-quality footage (called B-roll), YouTube and Vine videos, or video or audio podcasts. Nonprofits and governments also can include public service announcements. It is not uncommon for an online newsroom to add an "add to cart" feature for visual imagery that would require ordering high-resolution imagery, which also helps the public relations team monitor image usage and track potential stories.

- Newsrooms also can include **other supporting material**, such as statements, speeches, transcripts of press conferences, white papers, annual reports, digital brochures or magazines, self-produced stories (see Chapter 15 on brand journalism), and information about upcoming events, as well as other relevant content. A tourist board, for example, could add terms and applications for press visits. A publicly held company could add a section on financial information or a link to a separate investor relations section.

Try Exercise 11.2 and investigate an online newsroom about a company, nonprofit, or place that interests you.

11.3 Core Written Media Kit Components

The traditional written content for media kits includes four different types of information:

- **Fact sheets** offer readers easy-to-scan information about an organization, serving as a useful source for journalists and even consumers. Websites may include fact sheets in more than one section, such as in "About Us" and "Newsroom."
- **Executive profiles**, which are also called **profiles** or **biographies**, tell the life story of an executive, celebrity, government official, nonprofit director, or company spokesperson. The content can be presented in different styles, based on the preference of the brand or organization. Many organizations post executive profiles in their online newsrooms, as well as in the "about the company" section.

Exercise 11.2

Insights: Investigating Online Newsrooms

Please find an online newsroom for any company, government entity, or nonprofit of your choice—and then answer the following questions.

1. Was it easy to find the newsroom from the home page of the organization's website? How was the newsroom section labeled? (Some companies may use different names for their newsroom, such as press room, press gallery, media center, media resources, or media information; some media sections are included in the "about the company" section.)
2. Was the newsroom available in other versions of English and other languages? If so, which version did you select?
3. Were the contacts for the public relations staff easy to find? Was a separate contact listed for general public inquiries?
4. How was the newsroom organized?
5. Did you find it easy to navigate and useful in terms of available content for journalists seeking information and trying to develop stories?
6. Did the content include a media kit and an archive of news releases?
7. Was the visual library extensive? Was it easy to scan to find out what images were available? Did the images have captions?
8. What other resources did the newsroom share?
9. How interactive was the site with other social media?
10. Did you feel that the newsroom was missing any content? Would you do anything differently if you were the public relations executive representing this organization?

- **Backgrounders** provide reporters with more in-depth information about specific aspects of an organization, its history and mission, products and services, and other distinctive attributes.
- **Current news releases** also complement media kits, particularly if they are not part of an online newsroom, thereby providing reporters with the latest news and developments. This topic is covered extensively in Chapter 10.

Many organizations add their logos to media kit materials, and some may identify the documents by adding *News Release*, *Facts*, *Profile*, or *Backgrounder*, in a larger font on the top of the first page.

When researching content from other sources, writers should not lift sentences verbatim (except for core facts). For example, if you were writing press material for a university, you could add such details as the number and names of degree programs, number of students, size of campus, contact information, and other facts. Media kit materials traditionally do not use academic citations and references. However, writers should indicate sources for statistics, such as: *A study by the (name of organization) in (year) showed that (number) percent of (specific types of people) prefer (specific quality)*. The entire source could be added: *For more information on the research findings, log on to (name of website)*. If writers find a description from another source that is so specific and perfectly expressed, they can quote from the source, such as: *(name of person or organization) describes the (company, product, service, or person) as ("specific quote")*. Writers should obtain written approval to use quotes from other sources for commercial purposes.

11.3.1 Fact Sheets

Think of a **fact sheet** as part of both a media kit and an online newsroom, so Web links are important to add for supporting detail, such as hours of operations and contact information for multiple resources. Assume the reader knows nothing about the topic, so make sure to provide descriptions for all relevant facts. The most basic fact sheet is a snapshot of the organization. Fact sheets can be organized in many different ways:

- facts at a glance about the overall organization worldwide;
- facts at a glance about the organization's operations in a specific region or country;
- fast facts about a specific product line or service;
- an overview of a particular initiative, such as corporate social responsibility or employee programs;
- fun facts and trivia;
- frequently asked questions; and
- a timeline of its history or major innovations and accomplishments.

A two-column format fact sheet is not required but recommended since it provides easy-to-scan information. This content could be localized to a specific geographic region. Some writers also add extensive imagery to make the fact sheets more colorful. The list below outlines potential components in a corporate fact sheet; the order and subhead titles may change based on the company's priorities and operations. The numbers below follow the fact sheet example in Exhibit 11.1.

Exhibit 11.1—FACT SHEET TEMPLATE (TWO-COLUMN FORMAT).

Contact: Name (PR contact) ①
Affiliation
Email
Telephone

ORGANIZATION X ②

FACT SHEET (or FACTS AT A GLANCE)

Description:	③	This section briefly explains the type of organization (nonprofit, publicly held or private company), its focus in specific industries, scope of products and services, and locations/number of countries served. If the company is publicly held, add ticker symbols for stock exchanges here.
Mission:	④	You may use the word "philosophy" instead. This part explains the goal of the organization. This section can include the organization's entire or shortened mission statement. If the mission/philosophy is lengthy, you also can add the Web link if the media kit is available online.
Categories:	⑤	Breakdown information in logical categories to briefly explain specific product lines or services, corporate social responsibility, etc.
Year Founded:	⑥	Indicate full date or just the calendar year, such as 20XX.
Headquarters:	⑦	Street Address City, State/Province Zip/Postal Codes Country
Offices:	⑧	Include the total number of offices and number of countries.
Management:	⑨	List full names and titles of other key executives, starting with the most senior positions first (CEO, president, or executive director).
Employees:	⑩	Add worldwide numbers; number of employees by specific locations.
Awards:	⑪	List awards and recognitions.
Website:	⑫	Add URL. Indicate sections by specific countries and languages.
Social Media:		List as appropriate
Telephone:		List as appropriate.

⑬

January 20XX ⑭

1. **Public Relations Contact Information** (required for tactical media kit materials)
   This information must be included in tactical media kits. It also should be included in online newsrooms, unless the contact information is clearly indicated elsewhere on the website. Contact information is usually placed at the top or at the end of the document.

2. **Headline** (required for all types of fact sheets)
   The title of a fact sheet usually includes two items: the name of the organization and an indication that it is a fact sheet (or facts at a glance).

3. **Description** (recommended in a general fact sheet about an organization)
   The description would let the reader know the basics—what type of organization it is (public or private company, INGO, nonprofit, government department, etc.) and a brief description of what it does.

4. **Mission** (recommended in a general fact sheet about an organization)
   The mission or philosophy would explain the purpose of the organization.

5. **Products or Services** (recommended in a general fact sheet about a larger organization)
   This section could provide an overview of an organization's products or services, which could be organized by different brand lines, if applicable. A smaller company could provide details on its products or services in section 3.

6. **Year Founded** (recommended in a general fact sheet about an organization)
   This section could include the year or both the month and day the organization was officially launched. The other option is to include some facts about the founder, particularly for long-established organizations.

7. **Headquarters** (recommended in a general fact sheet about a larger organization)
   The location of the headquarters and the complete address can be included here.

8. **Worldwide Scope** (recommended in a general fact sheet about a larger organization)
   This section could include the total number of offices that could be divided by country or region.

9. **Management** (recommended in a general fact sheet about an organization)
   This part could include the name and title of executive management, such as the CEO, president(s), and executive vice president(s) in the corporate headquarters.

10. **Employees** (recommended in a general fact sheet about a larger organization)
    This could include the total number of employees, followed by the number of employees in specific countries or geographic regions.

11. **Awards and Recognitions** (recommended in a general fact sheet about an organization)
    Current awards and other recognitions can be listed. Some writers also may provide context, if the organization has won the award for a number of consecutive years or has received the greatest number of awards in its industry. A separate fact sheet could be created if the organization has received extensive awards.

12. **Information Resources** (required)
    This section could include the organization's website, social media, and toll-free numbers, as well as its headquarters address, if not included earlier. This content also can be easily localized for specific markets.

13. **End Sign** (recommended)

Printed versions traditionally contain three number tags (# # #) centered to indicate the end of document. Some writers also include these symbols in online versions. The same headers and footers as news releases are traditionally added in fact sheets.

14. **Date** (optional)

Some writers include a date, usually placed in the lower left side, so that they know when the document was prepared or updated. (Fact sheets do not require datelines as in a news release.)

Not all copy needs to be completely dry, some fact sheets can be entertaining and share interesting trivia and unusual facts. Here are examples from different organizations:

- Cracker Barrel Old Country Store is a publicly held company in the U.S., with restaurants and retail stores offering packaged foods, nostalgic toys, and other gifts. Its online newsroom contains several different fact sheets on its evolution, philosophy, awards, background on the development of its logo and décor, as well as fun trivia. Here is an excerpt from its section on restaurant fun facts.

  How much did you say? Cracker Barrel fun facts you can share with your friends and readers!
  Restaurant Fun Facts
  On a typical day, Cracker Barrel uses 70,000 pounds of flour to produce our made-from-scratch biscuits and dumplins [sic].
  In a typical year, Cracker Barrel serves:
  13.1 million pounds of chicken tenders
  121 million slices of bacon
  151 million eggs
  11 million orders of Chicken N' Dumplins
  37 million portions of grits
  56 million pancakes. (Cracker Barrel, 2014)

- Con Edison, a utility service in New York City and neighboring areas, includes information on its online newsroom with statistics and fun facts on its electrical, gas, and steam systems. Here is the section on its electrical system fun facts, which uses clever descriptions to explain dimensions:

  The 94,931 miles of underground cable in the Con Edison system could wrap around the Earth 3.8 times.
  Our underground cable could stretch up and down Broadway 7,302 times.
  Our 33,971 miles of overhead cable could make 6 round trips from New York to Los Angeles.
  Our overhead cables could reach from the top to the bottom of the Empire State Building 141,545 times.
  128,902 miles of underground and overhead cables could stretch more than half way to the moon. (n.d., para. 5)

- Intel, an American multinational technology company, attempts to explain the dimensions of nanometers in a fact sheet titled, "Fun facts: Exactly how small (and cool) is 22 nanometers?" (Intel, 2012). Here are two examples, along with footnotes, from the fact sheet:

  More than 6 million 22nm tri-gate transistors could fit in the period at the end of this sentence. (The footnote reads: A period is estimated to be 1/10 square millimeter in area.)

A 22nm transistor can switch on and off well over 100 billion times in one second. It would take you around 2,000 years to flick a light switch on and off that many times. (The footnote reads: Assumes a person can flick a light switch on and off 150 times per minute.)

Try Exercise 11.3 and think about how you would organize a general fact sheet on the higher education institution you are attending or the company you are working at.

11.3.2 Executive Profiles

One of the best ways to start writing an **executive profile** is to obtain the person's resume (also called curriculum vitae) and look at the person's LinkedIn profile. You also can find out if there have been any news release announcements on the person's new job or promotion or previously prepared executive profiles. In many cases, the writer may need to supplement the information by emailing a simple questionnaire or setting up a phone or face-to-face interview. Exhibit 11.2 includes a variety of questions about the person's current and former positions; professional activities, publications, and awards; education; other personal information; and any other relevant information.

Organizations may create bios with their own specific style and templates for staff to follow. For example, some companies do not follow reverse chronological order and may use a more narrative format that tells a story about the person. For new business proposals, public relations agency executives may customize professional and personal information in their profiles that is directly relevant to the prospective client.

Profiles traditionally include a photograph, usually a close-up of the person in business attire or the clothing appropriate in the field (creative staff, for example, may not need to wear formal business attire). Figure 11.13 shows a photograph of a student taken during her last year of college, which she added to her profile on her electronic portfolio. The image projects a professional demeanor yet conveys personality. The other option is to add a second less formal image showing the person at work, such as the chef in the kitchen, the hotel general manager in the lobby, or the musician in the studio or in concert.

A formal executive profile traditionally includes the following content—and please refer to Exhibit 11.3 with corresponding numbers:

1. **Public Relations Contacts** (required, if not available on the online newsroom)
   The public relations contact information should be included. Some writers place the contact details at the end of the document. In online newsrooms, contacts may be a

---

Exercise 11.3

Creative Thinking: Fact Sheet Topics

Let us assume that you are responsible for creating a new general fact sheet about your university or the organization you are working for full time or as an intern. Think about all the important details that you could share in a fact sheet that would be posted on your organization's online newsroom. List the topics you would include in a logical order. Refer to Exhibit 11.1 for ideas.

Exhibit 11.2—SAMPLE OF A BIOGRAPHY QUESTIONNAIRE.

Current Position

What is your job title?

Which office/location are you based in?

What are your major job responsibilities, including geographic areas and number of staff supervised?

Do you have any accomplishments to share, including any factual information with numbers?

Former Positions

If at current organization: What is your job history with the current organization? When did you start with the organization? What other positions/responsibilities have you held? Which offices have you worked at? What accomplishments would you like to highlight?

Outside current organization: What positions have you held at other organizations? Please include titles, responsibilities, locations, total number of years served at each organization, and brief descriptions of organizations. You also can highlight major accomplishments. Please list in reverse chronological order (or if you have extensive work experience, you can provide an overall summary and include more details about the past five years).

Professional Activities, Publications, and Awards

Do you belong to any professional associations? Please list and indicate if you have held any leadership positions.

Have you been published? Please list the book(s) or article titles, names and dates of the publications. Please attach Web links, if available.

Have you been a speaker at conferences or other industry events? Please list the events, locations, and discussion topics.

Have you received any awards or honors? Please list.

Education

Please list university degrees, as well as any certificates, and the names and locations of educational institutions.

Other Personal Information (optional, if the person wants to share these facts)

Where do you live (city, state/province/country)?

What languages do you speak?

What are your hobbies?

Do you want to share any community involvement or volunteer work?

Are you married? How many children do you have?

Miscellaneous (optional)

What other information would be helpful to share about your experience?

Figure 11.13—EXAMPLE OF A PORTRAIT IMAGE FOR A PROFILE, EPORTFOLIO, OR OTHER BIOGRAPHICAL USE. Source: Courtesy of Dominique Brown. Photo by Kristine Tsui.

separate section on the launch page, thereby excluding contact details on press materials.

2. **Headline** (required)
   The headline should include the person's full name, official title, and affiliation.

3. **Current Position** (required)
   Opening paragraph should cover the person's current position and responsibilities. An additional paragraph can be added if the position has extensive responsibilities. Biographies in media kits and online newsrooms are traditionally written in third person (*he*, *she*). After the person's full name is written in the introductory paragraph, all future references should be consistent on a first or last name basis, depending on the preference of the organization.

4. **Professional Experience** (required)
   This section should include the person's prior work history, starting with the most current jobs in reverse chronological order, or organized by type of work experience.

5. **Other Professional Activities and Accomplishments** (recommended)
   This section can include professional memberships, publications, speaking engagements, conference presentations, industry awards, and any other relevant professional experience.

Exhibit 11.3—EXECUTIVE PROFILE EXAMPLE.

Contact: Name (PR contact) ①
Affiliation
Email
Telephone

JUANITA DOE ②

EXECUTIVE VICE PRESIDENT

XYZ COMMUNICATIONS

Juanita Doe joined XYZ Communications, a global public relations agency based in Los Angeles, as executive vice president and director of the Global Consumer Marketing Group in January 20XX. Doe is responsible for managing interdisciplinary and worldwide campaigns for such brands as X, Y and Z, at the company's headquarters and its wholly owned offices in 10 countries. She has been involved in recruiting new talent, building the agency's business and strengthening the agency's presence in the global arena. ③

Throughout her career in public relations, Doe has gained extensive experience in developing global, regional, and local campaigns for leading brands. Prior to joining XYZ Communications, Doe served as senior vice president and deputy director of the Consumer Brands Division of ABC Public Relations in New York from 20XX to 20XX. She also was the director of global public relations for Brand X, a publicly held company, in London for five years. ④

Doe has been a guest speaker at leading international public relations conferences. She has served as vice president of Industry Association X, a leading industry group in global marketing and public relations, where she has set up workshops around the globe on social media engagement and branding strategies. She has received numerous awards for her campaigns, including X, Y and Z. ⑤

She graduated from University X in New York with a bachelor of science in international business and a minor in French, and she received her master's degree in public relations from University Y in London. In addition, she has taken courses in international management and public relations in Singapore. ⑥

Born in Buenos Aires, Argentina, and raised in New York City and Paris, Doe speaks fluent English, Spanish and French. An avid traveler, she has been to more than 30 countries for business or pleasure. With her commitment to community service, she has been a volunteer for X since her college years. She currently resides in Los Angeles with her husband and daughter. ⑦

⑧

January 9, 20XX ⑨

6. **Education** (required)

   This section can cover the person's education, which should include the specific degree and name and location of the educational institution. Certificates and continuing education courses and workshops can be added.

7. **Personal Information** (optional)

   Personal life information can include such facts as place of birth, places lived, current residence, family, travels, hobbies, or volunteer work. This information varies based on the style of the company and the preference of the person. Some companies like to include fun personal facts, such as pets and favorite leisure pursuits. Here is an example:

   Jane has two cats, Felix and Felicia, and a dwarf parrot, Groucho, that can speak 100 words. As an avid fan of Second Life, Jane has built her own island with a Japanese rock garden in this virtual world. Her alter-ego avatar, Okinawa Fox, is a red fox in a kimono, carrying a samurai sword.

   Most organizations, however, do not use humor or personality in bios.

8. **End Notes** (recommended)

   The three number signs (# # #) centered indicate that the document is completed.

9. **Date** (recommended)

   Adding the date when the document was prepared can be helpful since biographies can be updated frequently.

Executive profiles also can be adapted for LinkedIn. In this case, the summary of one's work experience needs to be succinctly edited and written in first person (*I*), while other sections allow one to include such information as professional positions, volunteer experience, education, certifications, honors and awards, languages, patents, publications, memberships, skills, endorsements, and other topics. LinkedIn's features continue to evolve with new sections, and the paid version offers more features while the unpaid version still enables one to provide extensive content.

11.3.3 Backgrounders

Backgrounders provide extensive information and more insight about an organization. Think about the different perspectives you have to share about the organization you are representing. These documents can be customized for different types of journalists (from architecture and business to lifestyle) and specific geographic regions and language editions. Backgrounders are written in prose, using the similar structure of a news release, without the dateline, and more flexibility in the structure of the lead paragraph. Many backgrounders include subheads in the text to make the copy easy to scan. Contacts need to be included and many backgrounders include a boilerplate paragraph (closing paragraph) at the end. The same headers and footers as news releases may apply, depending on the style preference of the organization. Many writers include a date at the end since these documents may be updated.

For example, backgrounders for a resort would highlight the property's major selling features and competitive benefits, such as the following:

- Specific attributes and facilities of the property (on-property options, which could focus specifically on golf courses, tennis courts, water sports, or other recreational sports; dining options and signature dishes and drinks; spa facilities and fitness center; meeting and convention spaces for business or social events; choices of rooms and suites; on-site cultural activities; architecture and interior design; environmentally friendly initiatives and community service; and history for an older property).

- Interests to specific types of people (romantic settings for honeymoons and weddings; what to do with families and supervised children's activities; solo travelers who may want to explore on their own or join groups; retirees who may have more time but may need to be aware of low-impact activities; and business travelers who may be extending their stays or trying to make the most of their spare time between meetings).

- More about the location (destination in general; history and culture, as well as museums, galleries, concerts, theater, and dance performances; the great outdoors and natural attractions; recreation and spectator sports; shopping options; off-property dining options, nearby wineries or farmers' markets; and organized tours).

For the pre-opening media kit of the Four Seasons Hotel Gresham Palace in Budapest, I prepared backgrounders to provide journalists with more context on the building's history and the property's prominent location in the city. Architecture, design, and travel journalists were the primary targets. In addition to a fact sheet on the actual hotel, the pre-opening media kit including the following three documents:

- *Headline/Subhead*: The rebirth of the Greshman Palace: One of the world's finest examples of Art Nouveau architecture restored to its former brilliance
  This backgrounder covered the building's evolution as one of the world's finest Art Nouveau/Secessionist structures (and this claim was not an exaggeration), tracing its history from a life insurance company to a prestigious residence and Communist-era housing, and its restoration as a luxury hotel. The rest of the backgrounder used subheads to explain its evolution with historical facts and details on its architecture and restoration process. As I mentioned earlier, this media kit took extensive time to research—and I collaborated with someone fluent in Hungarian and English, who could translate archival sources only available in Hungarian.

- *Headline*: Historical trivia about Four Seasons Hotel Gresham Palace Budapest
  I also added a two-page hybrid fact sheet/backgrounder that shared fun facts about the people involved with the building during different time periods from high finance to bohemia—financier Sir Thomas Gresham's thoughts on money, an actress who loved not having a kitchen, a World War II spy housed in the building's cabaret, among others—and other points about the Art Nouveau/Secessionist architecture throughout the city, as well as trivia about the nearby landmarks.

- *Headline*: Budapest: One of Europe's most vibrant cities
  Subhead: A city of romance, history, culture, fine food and wine, just outside the doors of the Four Seasons Hotel Gresham Palace Budapest
  This backgrounder emphasized the hotel's prominent location overlooking the Danube. It was structured by what there is to see and do within walking distance and by car or public transportation. In this case, I was able to draw upon my own experiences as a frequent visitor and input from the Hungarian-American translator, as well as from guidebooks.

Creative Thinking: Topics for Backgrounders

Your client is the department of economic development in your city (or choose your state, province, or country) that wants you to create a new media kit to explain how the location is a desirable place to live, work, learn, and visit.

What backgrounders would you need to include that showcase your benefits? Think of the different attributes of your location of appeal to residents, businesses, students, and tourists—such as real estate, arts and cultural offerings, tourist attractions, diversity of businesses and workforce, annual events, sports and recreational activities, educational institutions, and future developments. Prepare a list of headlines and subheads for your thematic backgrounders.

For examples of comprehensive backgrounds, look at Airbus's online newsroom (www. airbus.com/presscentre). Try Exercise 11.4 and brainstorm themes for backgrounder topics to include in a new media kit.

11.4 Audiovisual Libraries for Global and Glocal Media Kits

Media kits also give journalists a variety of photography and video footage to illustrate stories. Documents can further convey company values, such as corporate social responsibility and brand-building messages. Visual and supplemental material can be created for specific international media. As discussed in Chapter 10, imagery should be clearly captioned with copyright information and photo credits. It also should be offered in different resolutions for print and digital usage.

- **People, Products, Places**—Imagery, whether photography or video, should capture people from different backgrounds, ages, and ethnic groups, based on your target audiences, as well as a wide collection of images of products, services, or places that are relevant to illustrating the organization's attributes. Avoid religious icons, unless you are representing a religious organization, and be mindful of body gestures that could be misinterpreted or confusing in other markets.
- **Charts, Graphs, Infographics**—Numbers and timeframes are more easily understood in a chart form. Infographics can effectively explain complex information or even entertaining facts more creatively. The Jelly Belly Candy Company, a privately owned manufacturer of jelly beans and treats, creates colorful yet informative infographics (see Figures 11.14–11.17) about jelly bean facts, fun trivia about the candy worldwide, favorite flavors for adults and children, and public tours of its factory and onsite attractions.
- **What's Being Said**— Supplemental material can consist of digital reprints or links of stories that appeared in blogs, magazines, or newspapers, as well as audio links to radio programs or video links to television segments. Testimonials from satisfied customers can be added. Be mindful of obtaining necessary copyright approvals, some of which may require fees.

Figure 11.14—THE JELLY BELLY JELLY BEAN INFOGRAPHIC. Source: Infographic courtesy of Jelly Belly Candy Company.

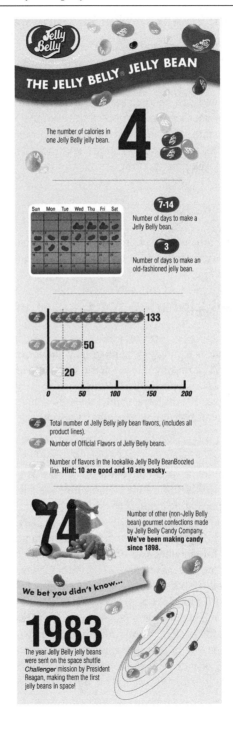

Figure 11.15—SPILLING THE BEANS INFOGRAPHIC. Source: Infographic courtesy of Jelly Belly Candy Company.

Figure 11.16—VISITING JELLY BELLY INFOGRAPHIC. Source: Infographic courtesy of Jelly Belly Candy Company.

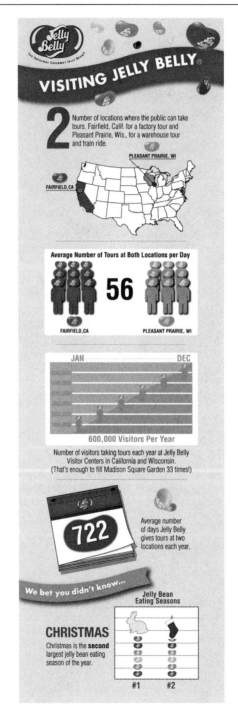

Figure 11.17—LOVE IT OR LEAVE IT? INFOGRAPHIC. Source: Infographic courtesy of Jelly Belly Candy Company.

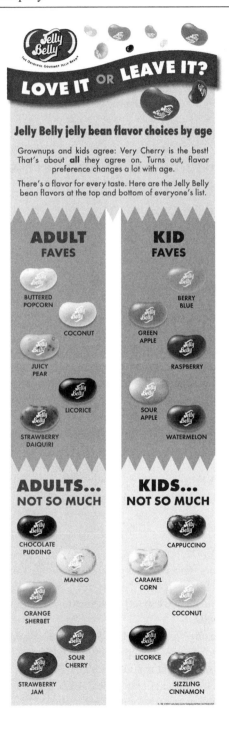

- **Other Organizational Content**—Consider adding other existing material, such as digital brochures and magazines, advertisements, white papers, and copies of speeches.
- **Under Development Content**—Maps, renderings, blueprints, illustrations, or images of models and prototypes can serve as visual imagery when a product, service, or place is in the planning stages.

Selected visual imagery also can be posted on Flickr, Pinterest, Instagram, and other social media platforms. Captions can be adapted to reflect a more conversational tone for the general consumer.

11.5 Learning Objectives and Key Terms

After reading this chapter, you should be able to:

- Understand the purposes of media kits in providing resources to journalists and even to the public.
- Be familiar with the types of material that can be included in a media kit, whether tactical or digital.
- Identify the scope of resources that can be available on an online newsroom, as well as how content can be customized to different markets.
- Prepare a general fact sheet and understand components for a specialized fact sheet.
- Know what type of information should be included in an executive profile and draft a profile for inclusion in a media kit.
- Discuss the purposes of backgrounders and the basics in drafting content.
- Pinpoint other supplemental materials for inclusion in a visual library for global and local media kits.

This chapter contains the following key terms:

Media kits (p. 263)	Press kits (p. 263)
Online newsrooms (p. 274)	Fact sheets (p. 277)
Executive profiles (p. 281)	Backgrounders (p. 285)
Audiovisual library (p. 287)	Infographics (p. 287)

References

Con Edison. (n.d.). Newsroom. Facts & background. Retrieved from http://www.coned.com/newsroom/information_facts.asp.

Cracker Barrel. (2014). Fun facts [Fact sheet]. Retrieved from http://newsroom.crackerbarrel.com/fact+sheets/fun+facts/.

González-Herrero, A., & Ruiz de Valbuena, M. (2006). Trends in online media relations: Web-based corporate press rooms in leading international companies. *Public Relations Review, 32*, 267–275. doi: 10.10161/j.pubrev.2006.05.003.

Intel. (2012). Fun facts: Exactly how small (and cool) is 22 nanometers? [Fact sheet]. Retrieved from http://download.intel.com/newsroom/kits/22nm/pdfs/22nm_Fun_Facts.pdf.

O'Brien, C. (2013). Kraken Rum creates a strong brand for launch. *The Future of Ads*. Retrieved from http://thefutureofads.com/kraken-rum-creates-a-strong-brand-for-launch.

Stedman, J. (2012, July). Insights: A great press kit design can work wonders for your brand. *SO Creative*. Retrieved from http://www.socreative.co.uk/what-makes-a-great-press-kit/.

Virgin Mobile USA. (2014). Newsroom: Welcome. Retrieved from http://newsroom.virgin mobileusa.com/.

12 Using Other Media Relations Techniques for Local or Global Campaigns

This is, without doubt, a challenging time for old media companies as they seek new business models to keep them afloat in the 21st century. While they do, as PR people, we still need to reach the widest and most relevant audience with a carefully crafted message, and traditional media remain very much part of the mix. Combine the mass awareness that they deliver with relevant touch points on digital and social channels and you have the potential to move beyond message delivery to audience engagement and advocacy.

—Helen Nowicka, specialist in strategic digital, social, and mobile engagement

12.1 Introduction to Other Methods of Communicating with Reporters

This quote from Helen Nowicka (2012, p. 33), a digital and social media strategist and former journalist, reflects on evolving technology and emphasizes the reality that traditional media still have significance—and that stories generated from traditional media can be shared, discussed, and debated on blogs, microblogs, and other social media. Beyond news releases and media kits, public relations practitioners utilize other writing techniques to communicate with journalists.

Public relations practitioners must understand how to create **story angles** (also called **news hooks** and **news pegs**) to match print, broadcast, and digital media outlets for broad global media outlets, as well as in specific local and regional markets. In Chapter 10, we reviewed the inverted pyramid approach that is popular in news release writing—with all the most important information first and then in descending order of importance. But should all stories give away all the facts in the first paragraph? Absolutely not; it is similar to telling a joke and starting with the punchline. Consider how stories could lose their suspense, wonderment, and surprise if the ending is told at the beginning. Let us look at a few other approaches to storytelling from a journalistic point of view:

- **The Chronological Narrative**—This storytelling approach follows three sequences: the beginning, the middle, and the end, with the climax.

- **The Hourglass** (see Figure 12.1, or visualize a martini or wine glass, if you prefer)—Writer Roy Peter Clark is attributed as the inventor of the hourglass metaphor, which is a hybrid of the straightforward inverted pyramid news reporting and the more descriptive narrative approach, in 1983 (Scanlan, 2003a). This news writing style requires three steps:

  1. **The top**—Think of the top of the hourglass as the part that contains the essence of the news story, with the relevant 5Ws, thereby providing busy readers with the basics even if they only read the first part of the story.
  2. **The turn**—See the waist part of the hourglass as the transitional phase where the writing style switches to storytelling, usually with quotations from people. For example, in a crime story, the writer would start to share comments from the police and eyewitnesses about the incident. This twist also alerts the reader that a more comprehensive story is ahead, if they want to invest the time to find out more.
  3. **The narrative**—Look at the base of the hourglass and conclude the story by returning to the broad story with a beginning, middle, and end in chronological order, which can be enhanced with quotations and more colorful detail.

The Kabob—Tim Harrower, a journalist and author of *Inside Reporting: A Practical Guide to the Craft of Journalism* (2007), shares a colorful metaphor of a shish-kabob skewer (see Figure 12.2) as one way to craft a story. Think of the cherry tomato on top of that delectable kabob as the compelling beginning in the form of an anecdote about a person or another interesting topic. Then comes the **nut graf** (the essential paragraph)—the morsel that summarizes the story snugly into a nutshell by sharing the pertinent 5Ws. The nut graf is followed by a few chunks of high-grade meat building on the topic. And then the story wraps up with another tomato, seasoned as a quote or an anecdote about the first cherry tomato.

Figure 12.1—HOURGLASS METAPHOR SHOWS A TECHNIQUE IN NEWS REPORTING. Source: © Andrey Burmakin/Shutterstock.com.

Figure 12.2 THE KABOB METAPHOR ILLUSTRATES ANOTHER WAY TO ORGANIZE A STORY. Source: © Africa Studio/Shutterstock.com.

The *Wall Street Journal* is acclaimed to be the creator of the nut graf story. In an article posted on Poynter.org (Scanlan, 2003b), *Wall Street Journal* editor Ken Wells described the importance of the nut graf:

> a paragraph that says what this whole story is about and why you should read it. It's a flag to the reader, high up in the story: You can decide to proceed or not, but if you read no farther, you know what that story's about. (para. 6)

12.2 Global and Glocal Media Relations

Public relations practitioners will not be responsible for writing the complete stories for the journalists, but they need to consider what they can do to spark a journalist's interest in creating a story about the organizations they represent—and what meaningful resources they can provide to assist in making the story come to life. I have developed the following **IDEAS** approach to craft story angles:

- **Interests**—Know what topics are of interest to journalists. What stories would be relevant to their audiences—their readers, viewers, or listeners—who are the consumers of their media outlets?
- **Deadlines**—Know when journalists would be interested in developing the story. Timing is significant whether the story is breaking news or part of the regular news cycle, which could include in-depth features, profiles on people, roundups about trends and how-to stories, or specific items for regular columns.
- **Exclusivity**—Know when a story should be offered as an exclusive. Exclusives can be effective only when the story is of such high-impact that a journalist would want to be the first to report on the topic—whether the reporter is the first person or the only one to interview someone or have access to photography or video footage.

- **Accessibility**—Know what the reporter would need access to. You could arrange interviews with people who are authoritative sources, set up a behind-the-scenes look at something, or invite reporters to attend an event, a product demonstration, or travel somewhere.
- **Sensations**—Know how you can help bring a story alive. Audio sound-bites and visuals in print and video formats can round out a story and engage the senses of the media outlets' readers, viewers, or listeners to care about the topics.

The practice of media relations requires identifying the media of greatest interest to the organizations you are representing. This is not a numbers game, meaning that the quality and relevance of the media outlets are more important than the quantity of media outlets. Understand the media you are trying to reach. Not all media outlets are the same: many have different beats (areas of specialization or topics) and not all relationships between public relations practitioners and media are the same from country to country. In some cases, a personal relationship would need to be established first. For example, the Public Relations Global Network (Carufel, 2014) conducted a survey of different media practices of 165 business journalists from 14 countries in Europe, in which reporters identified the biggest "turnoffs" of public relations practitioners: arrogant behavior (75%), inability to answer critical questions (73%), and speaking in empty platitudes (62%). American public relations practitioners would be surprised to see that 41% of the journalists surveyed always allow the PR representative or CEO to directly review the quotes before publication and 21% allow the entire article to be reviewed in advance. American journalists would consider this an inappropriate request.

Nonetheless, some universal appeals do apply and they can be localized as needed. Here are essentials to follow:

- **Focus on the most relevant media outlets** for the organizations you are representing. Prepare a list of the top 25 and rank them in importance. A story in a high-value outlet can have more impact—the most respected media outlets are like "beacons" to motivate other media in doing the story. You are writing to a specific person at a media outlet, not to the media outlet in general. For newspapers, magazines, e-zines, or even blogs with multiple authors, you need to pitch the specific editor of a section or column or a freelance contributor. It is important to look at the publication and gain familiarity with its content—and the specific writer's interests. Obtain a copy of the outlet or check its website to know its content and style. Many media outlets, whether print, TV, or radio, can be accessed online.
- **Maintain a media database with contacts and notes**. You can develop a targeted media list on your own by researching contact information online, which can be very time-consuming, and not all contacts are publicly available. A more viable option is using a paid service (such as Cision, a global provider of public relations software and services) that provides all contact information, as well as descriptions on the outlets and other intelligence—and enables you to customize lists online. Lists also can include notes on the journalists' editorial interests and preferred methods of contact and best times—and you should personally customize these notes based on your firsthand experiences. Do the journalists prefer to receive material by email, Twitter, or other social media—or even by phone? Are they receptive to interviews or editorial briefings, media events, product demonstrations, or press familiarization trips? Media lists also need to be updated regularly since people move around.

- **Gain familiarity with regular and special sections**. Some media outlets publish annual editorial calendars that indicate regular and special topics. Editorial calendars are actually created for advertisers, not for public relations. It is not uncommon for the topics to change. However, they can serve as a helpful platform. Many lifestyle columns routinely cover the same topics every year, such as the holidays.
- **Keep track of media catching opportunities**. Media catching refers to services that journalists can use to post requests for material needed to produce specific stories—and media catching is beneficial to public relations practitioners who can respond directly to requests for story opportunities. Richard Waters, Natalie Tindall, and Timothy Morton (2010) have researched this trend, stating that "media catching is the turning of the tables of the traditional process" (pp. 242–243). Instead of public relations practitioners proactively pitching story ideas to the media, journalists and bloggers are now requesting specific information and suggestions on people to interview to build their stories from any public relations representatives who are following these online services, such as Help-A-Reporter Out (HARO). Waters et al. concluded that:

  Ultimately, there may even be a shift in the thinking of journalists and public relations practitioners that media relations is becoming more relationship-focused and centered on a continued dialogue rather than a series of one-sided media pitches. (p. 261)

- **Identify the right spokespeople**. The Oriella PR Network Global Digital Journalism Study (2013) found that reporters value conversations, particularly from industry analysts or academics. One of the reasons journalists trust analysts and academics is that they are not paid spokespeople on behalf of an organization, meaning that they traditionally have an unbiased point of view and tend to speak about an industry at large. Organizations also can develop relationships with analysts or academics specializing in particular industries, as well as secure paid spokespeople, whether celebrities or experts on a relevant subject. In many cases, spokespeople for organizations are staff within the company. For example, the CEO, chief financial officer, or head of investor relations would discuss business and financial topics.
- **Offer the most relevant ideas, information, visual resources, and assistance**. While Chapter 10 covers news releases and Chapter 11 examines media kits and online newsrooms, this chapter looks at how to develop media pitches, determine face-to-face approaches to meet with media, and hone other writing techniques. The ideal scenario is to become a valued, reliable resource, who knows not just your clients' businesses, but the industries at large.

12.3 Story Ideas and Pitches

Pitches (also called **media pitches** or **story idea memos**) are personalized communications from public relations practitioners to specific journalists with story ideas. These communiqués are traditionally called "pitches" since publicists are trying to pitch a story idea to a newspaper or magazine editor, blogger, or TV or radio producer or booker. Pitches should provide compelling reasons why a reporter should be interested in covering this particular story. As mentioned earlier, the most effective pitches are targeted and well-informed. Most pitches are sent by email, social media, or by regular mail as a letter, if other product samples or tangible materials are enclosed. Pitches are rarely longer than one page—and the copy also can be edited to one paragraph or to a tweet, if the reporter communicates on Twitter. Seasoned public relations professionals send pitches to carefully selected journalists—and match the story ideas of greatest interest to specific journalists. Think benefits to the journalists in doing the story, not the benefits to your agency or the organizations you are representing. (Just as when you are writing cover letters for an internship or full-time job, you need to address what benefits you offer the employer *not* the career benefits the job directly offers you.) Effective pitch letters are well-researched, so collect all facts, statistics, and other information before you write the story—and know what else you can offer the reporter.

Poorly done pitches are spam and a nuisance. I have seen some public relations agencies count the number of pitches to be disseminated on a monthly basis; this is a practice I would not recommend. I also have experienced a few clients wanting to review all pitch letters in advance—and transform them into brochure copy or advertisements despite pleas from the agency staff—and then wonder why the pitches were unsuccessful. Read the Bad Pitch Blog (http://badpitch.blogspot.com) for cautionary tales.

Let us look at how to prepare and write an email pitch step by step. Please refer to Exhibit 12.1 that corresponds to the numbers below.

1. **The Recipient, a Specific Journalist** (automatic on email)
   A pitch letter is an individual communication from a public relations professional to a journalist. For print, you need to think of what content would build the story in words and supporting imagery—and many print outlets have digital editions. Read the print outlets and understand what the editors like to cover. For TV journalists, you need to think of visual imagery that the camera crew can capture to highlight the story to its viewers and the strengths of the spokespeople to be interviewed on that specific program. You should watch that program to know how to best approach it. You would send the pitch letter to the TV program's producer or booker. For radio, you need to consider the dynamics of sound—and the credibility, relevance, and quality of the spokespeople to be interviewed. Again, it is recommended to listen to the program and look at what the reporter likes to cover.

2. **The Sender, the Public Relations Executive** (automatic on email)
   It is beneficial if the journalist knows you or has worked with you before. As mentioned earlier, public relations executives should invest time in meeting the most significant journalists in the industries and markets they cover. The sender must make sure that the content is relevant with a solid story; if not, do not send the pitch.

3. **The Subject Line** (required)
   The subject line on the email message should be carefully worded to encourage the journalist to read the document. These few words can make a huge difference in getting your email read. The reporter should know if this is an exclusive story. Indicate in the subject line if you are recommending an idea based on the media outlet's editorial calendar or another media catching opportunity.

4. **Date** (automatic on email)
   Before you distribute the pitch letter, you should know the timing. Make sure that news is distributed in a timely fashion, particularly to long-lead time media, such as monthly or quarterly magazines. Conversely, do not send out news too far in advance for newspapers, wires, TV, and radio.

Exhibit 12.1—EMAIL PITCH TEMPLATE.

To: Email of specific journalist, blogger, or producer ①
From: Email from public relations executive ②
Subject: Brief thematic message on content ③
Date: Automatic on email, but be mindful of the best timing ④
CC: Optional; some organizations or agencies may copy or blind copy correspondence
           to the entire team handling media relations ⑤

Dear Mr./Ms./Mrs./Dr. last name of reporter, such as Mr. Doe: ⑥

Single space text and do not indent paragraphs. The first paragraph explains why this story
would be of interest to the specific journalist, as well as to the media outlet's readers, listeners,
or viewers. Consider using a provocative question, sharing interesting facts or statistics, or
offering exclusive access to a person or place. The opening paragraph must be appealing to
attract the reporter's attention. Be mindful that journalists are inundated with material by PR
practitioners—and they have tight deadlines. ⑦

The second paragraph, if needed, should provide supporting details to round out the story
idea. Think sound bites and visuals, based on the type of media you are targeting. Use bullet
points to highlight key facts and points to bring the story alive. You also can use names of
experts who would be available for interviews and able to provide more insight. Images can
be embedded into the message, particularly when the visuals help build on the story. ⑧

The third paragraph, if needed, can offer key supporting details, including additional information
on people to interview to develop the story.

The content of your last paragraph is based on your relationship with the journalist. The final
paragraph traditionally concludes with how you can be of assistance and suggested next
steps, as well as your contact information. You can let the reporter know if you'll be following
up with a phone call. ⑨

Sincerely, ⑩

Your name (first and last) ⑪

Title (optional, avoid using if you are an intern)
Affiliation (name of company or public relations agency)
Public Relations on behalf of Company X (optional; some PR agencies add this detail)

P.S.: You can use a postscript to add an interesting fact. You also can refer the reporter to
your client's or organization's website, particularly the online newsroom, for more information.
Reporters may be reluctant to open up unsolicited email attachments. ⑫

5. **Copies** (optional)

   Some public relations agencies or in-house public relations departments may copy
   (or blind copy) pitch letters with other members of the team who are handling media
   relations.

6. **Salutation/Greeting** (recommended)

   Only use *Dear first name*, such as *Dear John*, if you know the journalist and have an established first-name relationship; some countries prefer a more formal approach. Unless you have a friendly personal relationships with an American journalist, I would recommend avoiding *Hi, John*.

7. **Opening Paragraph** (required)

   For pitch letters, the first sentence must be compelling, such as a provocative question or an interesting fact. Otherwise, the reporter will press the delete button on email. Put yourself in the reporter's place. Why is this story of interest? Will this motivate me to do a story? Has this topic been covered recently? What are you offering the reporter (an exclusive, a complimentary or discount visit, an opportunity to interview executives or a behind-the-scenes peek at something)?

8. **Supporting Paragraphs** (optional, as needed)

   A pitch letter could be condensed into one paragraph. However, you may need to provide additional explanations that would be relevant to the specific outlet. Make the email message visually attractive and easy to scan.

   – Tabulate or use bullets to list a variety of items.
   – Use Web links. Do not include attachments.
   – Break up larger areas of copy with boldface subheadings.
   – Avoid more than eight lines within a paragraph (six lines are preferred).
   – Never reduce type below 11 points or use unusual typefaces.
   – Writers can use "you" and "your" in a pitch letter.

9. **Closing** (required)

   The last paragraph (or last sentence in a one-paragraph pitch) should include a call to action that indicates the next steps:

   – Spokesperson (use full name, title, and affiliation) will be in town next week and available to meet with you at your office.
   – I'll call you shortly to see if you'd like to schedule an interview in person or by phone.
   – I can arrange for you to travel on location for a firsthand experience (if the media outlet can accept subsidized travel).
   – Please look at our online newsroom at (URL) to see video clips of (potential spokesperson) and B-roll footage of (specific topics).

   You should include different options on how you can be reached. You also could indicate that your contact information is below your signature. See item 11 on signature blocks where you can add contacts without cluttering your copy.

10. **Complimentary Close** (required)

    Writers should close with one of the following:

    – Sincerely yours, (more formal and widely accepted)
    – Yours truly,
    – With best regards, (more informal, popular in the U.S.)

11. **Signature/Signature Block** (required)

Include your name below, both first and last names. You should include your title (unless you are an intern), the name of the organization or public relations agency. Some agencies add a line: *Public Relations on behalf of (name of client)* to make it clear who you are representing. This section also can include your address, telephone number, and social media. If you are communicating with a journalist outside of your country, you should add the country code to the telephone number. You can configure your email to set up a signature block with more details on your contact information.

12. **Postscripts** (optional)

Postscripts can be effective in providing additional useful information. You just need to write *PS:* and then the message.

Be prepared to edit your pitch into tweets (for Twitter) and into a brief voicemail message—but avoid reading from the script for a phone message; just have a few key words or sound-bites that you want to share. The reality is that most pitches require follow-up and not all will be successful. Other solutions are creating face-to-face meetings and organizing media events.

12.4 Face-to-Face Media Events

This part explains the value and purpose of conducting meetings and receptions to meet with the media in person. It focuses on how to write materials to encourage the media's participation

Figure 12.3—POPULAR DUTCH DJ ARMIN VAN BUUREN (center) AND ENGLISH MUSICIAN CHRISTIAN BURNS (to his left) SPEAK AT A PRESS CONFERENCE IN MOSCOW. Source: © Editorial Credit: Pavel L Photo and Video / Shutterstock.com.

and how to prepare spokespeople for interviews. International media events can add another level of stress and discomfort for spokespeople, who may have less confidence about their language skills and a lack of knowledge of the local media.

12.4.1 Media Alerts

Media alerts, which are also called **media advisories**, serve as invitations for reporters to cover breaking news, updates on a crisis situation, the launch of a significant new product or service, or an important announcement, such as the appointment of a new CEO or the resignation of a political figure. Media alerts are commonly used for invitations to formal **press conferences** (also called **news conferences**) in which spokespeople make announcements to a group of journalists and, in many cases, also address questions from reporters and provide extra time for individual interviews. Figure 12.3 shows an example of what a press conference can look like. They should be used sparingly and only for newsworthy events.

These documents include only the core essential information on **one page** that is easy to read quickly. Public relations writers provide a quick overview about the event, addressing the important 5Ws, as well as potential audiovisual opportunities for journalists, photographers, or camera crews. They give journalists—whether they are assignment desk editors or reporters from online, print, radio, or television—the essence of the interview opportunities. Media alerts are traditionally sent by email, with the copy embedded in the text, and abbreviated text and links can be shared in other social media and microblogs. These documents also can be posted on the organization's newsroom.

The goal is to interest journalists in attending the event. The details will be provided during the event. Similar events may take place with the same structure in different locations within the same country or be held in a few different countries. In this case, the core media alert can be localized as appropriate.

Writers traditionally follow these steps to prepare a two-column media alert, which align to the numbers in the template in Exhibit 12.2.

1. **Media Alert Heading** (required)
   Use a larger font or boldface type to let the reader know that the document is a media alert. Some authors repeat the words, *media alert*, multiple times on the first line.

2. **Succinct Headline** (required)
   The headline should fit on one line and briefly describe the event. For example, a crisis-related press conference could read: *Update on (crisis incident)*. A launch event for a new product could read: *Launch and demonstration of (name of product)*.

   Body Copy:
   5Ws—Who, What, Why, Where, and When

   The order of the 5Ws—who, what, where, when, and why—can vary based on the importance of each.

3. **What**
   It's not uncommon to see media alerts beginning with *What*, which describes what type of event is being held, whether the event is a press conference on a crisis situation, an announcement of a new political candidate or other major developments, or a new product launch.

Exhibit 12.2—MEDIA ALERT TEMPLATE.

MEDIA ALERT ①

BRIEF HEADLINE THAT GIVES THE ESSENCE OF THE EVENT ②

WHAT: ③   Clearly and succinctly explain what type of event you are inviting journalists to attend (such as a press conference, press preview, or product demonstration) and what the event will focus on (such as to announce a major development, to unveil a new product or service, to update the public on the status of the product recall, etc.). If the event has a name, you would indicate that here.

WHY: ④   Explain more details on the purpose of the event. Add relevant visual opportunities for photographers and camera crews.

Note: In some cases, the "Why" can be covered in the "What."

WHO: ⑤   List the full names, titles, and affiliations of the people who will be speakers or people available for interviews. Start with the names of the most significant speakers first.

WHEN: ⑥   Add day of week, month, day, and year.

Indicate start and end time of event.

Optional: List time in sequence of different activities, such as exact time of conference, time for Q&A, any food or drinks, or other times available for interviews with specific people.

WHERE: ⑦   Indicate name and address of location, as well as the specific floor or room number.

Note: Include brief directions, particularly if held at a lesser-known spot, or cross streets in a city, and relevant parking or nearest public transportation. Also indicate if any form of identification is needed for entry to the location.

CONTACT: First and last name of public relations contact
⑧   Name of company, organization or public relations agency
            Telephone contacts
            Email and other social media

Optional: If this is a large-scale event, consider adding another public relations contact. You only need to place contact information here; no need to use the traditional news release formatting. Most alerts ask for confirmations—and use "RSVP' instead of "Contact," particularly if you are serving food, need to make travel arrangements, or have limited space to accommodate attendees.

⑨

4. **Why**

   The *Why* section explains the purpose of the event, providing more background and context on the event.

5. **Who**

   The *Who* section lists the names, titles, and affiliations of the participants. If well-known people are participating, this section could be the first part of the 5Ws. The list is traditionally organized in order of prominence of the participants. Some media alerts may provide brief biographical information on speakers to provide relevant context on their involvement with the event. For example, a celebrity may be involved with the launch of a new product or nonprofit event, so the copy would indicate that the person is a celebrity spokesperson for the organization. If a moderator conducts the event, his or her name, title, and affiliation may be included and clearly labeled as a moderator.

6. **When**

   The *When* section includes the essential facts on the day of the week, the month, and the day (make sure to spell out the months to avoid any confusion), and the timing of the event. Timing should include the starting and ending time. If the event has specific timeframes for activities, such as tours or meals, they also can be listed separately. Indicate if there will be time after the event for one-on-one interviews with spokespeople. If the event is bilingual or multilingual, it is important to indicate that separate interviews will be held in a specific language.

7. **Where**

   The *Where* section needs to provide the location of the event. Street addresses should include cross streets, as well as the specific floor or room number. Urban locations can include closest public transportation stops. Suburban or rural locations should include driving directions or available public transportation. Details on any required identification and what type should be included, such as two forms of identification, including official photo identification. Any details relevant to satellite or live trucks also can added here, such as required registration, parking with camera equipment, and information on electrical power, particularly for outdoor venues that may have no electricity.

8. **Contact or RSVP** (required)

   The *Contact* section also can be written as *RSVP* when the public relations staff is asking for confirmations, particularly if food and beverages are served, and to make sure that ample seating and arrangements are set up in advance to accommodate participants. In some cases, spacing restrictions may apply and warrant advance confirmation.

   Here are two examples of requesting confirmations; the second example is based on content from a media advisory from the U.S. White House Office of the Press Secretary, which also adds time zones due to international media participation:

   Example 1:

   Registration is required to attend; seating is limited. Please RSVP to (Name) at (Email) or (telephone) by (date). An email confirmation will be forwarded to participating media.

Example 2:

Media Coverage: This event is open to pre-credentialed media. To request credentials, please RSVP online at: (Web link). The deadline to RSVP is (time) (time zone), (day of week), (month) (day).

All names submitted for credentials must be accurate and reflect the identification media presents at check points for entrance. RSVPs do not guarantee access. You will receive a confirmation email if you will receive a credential to cover the event.

Public relations contacts should be included. For large scale events or press conferences on a crisis situation, more than one contact should be added. This part does not require full sentences since the core information just needs to be listed: name, affiliation, office telephone or cell phone, and email. The person's job title and other social media are optional. Some authors place the contact information below the media advisory heading.

Juan Rivera, Agency X
Office telephone: 212–333–444; cell 212–444–5555
Email: jrivera@agencyx.com

9. **Conclusion** (recommended)
    The three number signs (# # #) indicate the conclusion of the document. They are centered and placed two lines below the last part of the media alert.

Another format option for media alerts does not follow the previous example of an easy-to-scan two-column format. This approach may be more useful when the company wants to convey more information. The order may vary based on the preferred style of the organization. Here is a list of the components:

1. **Headline and Subhead** (required)
    In this format, writers may write the headline as follows, starting with the words, media alert followed by a colon, then the headline with core information, and a subhead with supporting facts.

    Media Alert: Press Conference
    Launch of Product X with Demonstration by CEO X

2. **Date of Media Alert** (optional)
    Some writers prefer to include the date when the media alert is distributed. The date is more important to include when the document is posted online and linked to other social media. Email distribution automatically indicates the date of the release of the media alert.

3. **Relevant 5Ws** (required)
    In this format, writers may combine some of the 5Ws. Here is an example based on a media alert posted by NYSE Euronext:

    Who/What:
    On (day of week, month, day), executives of (company, ticker symbol), (brief description of company) will visit the New York Stock Exchange (NYSE) to (purpose of visit).
    To mark the occasion, (full name), (title of company), joined by members of the company's leadership team, will ring The Closing Bell.
    When/Where:

Day of week, Month, Day, Year
NYSE Security Checkpoint/Tent at corner of Exchange Place and Broad Street
3:30 p.m. Media escorted into the building
4:00 p.m. The Closing Bell rings

4. **Photos and Footage** (recommended)
   This separate section gives public relations staff the opportunity to provide more details on available images and footage for journalists. Here is an example based on a media alert by the New York Stock Exchange, which has an established setup in providing the Closing Bell footage:

   Photos/B-roll/Closing Bell Footage:
   Photos available via Associated Press/New York (telephone), Reuters America (telephone), Getty Images (telephone), Bloomberg Photo (telephone) and European Press Agency (telephone). B-roll of the NYSE trading floor and The Closing Bell (starting at 3:56 p.m.) will be available via Encompass 4090 (Full HD), Encompass 4009 (SD) and The Switch. Additional requests should be made through the NYSE Broadcast Center at (telephone).

5. **Social Media** (optional)
   This separate section works when an organization provides frequent updates on press events and resources for media on microblogs and social networking sites.

6. **About the Organization** (optional)
   Some organizations prefer to add a boilerplate paragraph with key facts. This option only works for events focused on one organization or primarily on one. For example, a crisis situation may focus on one entity, yet many other organizations would be involved with the process of the investigation underway. In this case, a boilerplate would not be appropriate.

7. **Public Relations Contacts** (required, the placement may vary)
   Public relations contact information can be added here.

12.4.2 Formal Invitations

Other invitation options include printed invitations, which are more popular for a black-tie gala, an awards ceremony, a fundraising event, or a formal media event. Invitations can be quite formal like a wedding invitation, with a folded invitation, a reply card, and stamped envelope—or more cost-effective and eco-friendly electronic invitations (also called **evites**), which also offer features to easily track responses. Printed invitations can be custom designed, with creative shapes, such as the shape of a fan or any type of silhouette, and contain sound when opened. They also can contain confetti in the envelope, or be creatively packaged. I recall a real estate developer who sent reporters a construction hard hat, with the company's logo, in a box containing an invitation to attend a lunch reception at the construction site. The public relations director of a new spa sent a terry-cloth robe embroidered with the reporter's name, along with an invitation to tour a new luxury spa development. Not all reporters, however, can accept gifts in the form of invitations.

Formal invitations should include the following components, and the order may vary:

1. **Name or Names of Host of Event** (required)
   The host could be the name of the organization or a specific person at the organization.

2. **Clear indication that it is an invitation** (required)

   The wording can vary considerably from less to more formal, such as:

   – Join us in celebrating . . .
   – Please join us in celebrating . . .
   – Name of host . . .
   – . . . invites you and a guest to join our celebration
   – . . . cordially invites you to attend . . .
   – . . . requests the pleasure of your attendance at the . . .
   – . . . would be honored by your presence at the . . .

   Events hosted by government officials, royalty, and nobility require specific wording, so writers should look at the proper protocol guidelines.

3. **Description of Event** (required)

   The invitation needs to indicate what type of event is taking place—press reception, holiday party, dinner reception, lunch reception, new product demonstration, awards dinner, grand opening, premiere of a specific performance, fundraiser for a specific organization or cause, or wine tasting, among others.

4. **Date of Event** (required)

   This part should include the day of the week, month, day, and year (or day, month, year).

5. **Time of Event** (required)

   This should include the beginning time to end time, using the 12-hour or 24-hour clock. If the event has different time periods, the invitation copy should indicate those timeframes.

6. **Other Activities, Refreshments** (as needed)

   It is important to let the invitee know if food and beverages are served, if those facts are not clearly indicated earlier in the description of the event or in the time breakdown of events, such as a lunch or dinner reception. If this is not mentioned earlier, you would add: *Cocktails and hors d'oeuvres will be served.*

7. **Location of Event** (required)

   This part includes the name of the location (such as an office building, hotel, restaurant, or outdoor location), followed by the street address, and city, state, or province. If the location is complex to reach, some invitations may include an insert with details on driving directions and public transportation.

8. **Dress Code** (recommended)

   Indicate the dress code—black tie, business attire, business casual, or informal.

9. **RSVP** (required for most events)

   Letting people know when to respond by is highly recommended. Use a specific name of a person, as well as phone and email contacts. Event planners need to be able to set up properly and have ample food and beverages to accommodate guests. *Please respond by (specific date) at (website and/or social media) or by calling (name) at (number).* Some formal invitations may have a response card in a separate envelope with a stamped envelope. In this case, the deadline for responding would be included here. Avoid saying *regrets only* in business invitations.

10. **Fees** (only for certain events)

    Fundraising events, awards receptions, and industry events may require a fee. Many hosts, however, will cover the costs of the participation of journalists, depending on the media outlet's policies in accepting meals.

11. **Non-transferable** (optional)

    Some invitations indicate if the invitation is not transferable. In other words, the person invited cannot just forward the invitation to another person to attend.

    See Figures 12.4 and 12.5 for an example of an invitation for a U.S. nonprofit that hosts an annual awards reception in New York City.

12.4.3 Media Tours and Editorial Briefings

A variety of events can help an organization meet face to face with influential journalists and bloggers. **Media tour** is the term used for a series of appointments that public relations executives set up for a company spokesperson to meet with journalists. Some media tours can be a few hours, a few days, or for a time period that involves extensive travel within a country or to multiple countries. **Editorial briefing** is the term generally used for a one-on-one meeting with a reporter, usually in the reporter's office.

Helping spokespeople develop a comfort level for conducting media interviews, particularly outside their own country, requires providing helpful written materials and media training. Public relations executives must devote time to preparing the spokespeople for media tours. Interviews will be more successful when spokespeople understand the media outlet's focus and know more about the reporter's background and areas of interest. The level of preparation may be intensified when the spokesperson is traveling to another country. Media tours should be escorted by a public relations representative, which can be a win-win situation

Figure 12.4—FRONT COVER OF INVITATION FOR THE NATIONAL MARITIME HISTORICAL SOCIETY'S ANNUAL DINNER. Source: Courtesy of the National Maritime Historical Society.

Figure 12.5—INSIDE SPREAD OF INVITATION FOR THE NATIONAL MARITIME HISTORICAL SOCIETY'S ANNUAL DINNER. Source: Courtesy of the National Maritime Historical Society.

2014 Award Recipients

Daniel J. Basta, Director of the National Oceanic and Atmospheric Administration (NOAA) Office of National Marine Sanctuaries, will receive the NMHS Distinguished Service Award. Mr. Basta created a Maritime Heritage program to explore, protect and interpret historic sites and artifacts within the National Marine Sanctuaries system; projects include the site of the USS *Monitor*, whaling ships, and the steamer *Portland*. Mr. Basta will be honored for his stewardship of these national treasures and for his continuing work in involving more people and organizations in their management and interpretation.

George W. Carmany III will be receiving the NMHS Distinguished Service Award in recognition of his work furthering the sport of yachting in the 21st Century, and his lifelong work advancing our maritime heritage. Mr. Carmany is a former commodore of the Shinnecock Yacht Club, and a longtime chairman of the America's Cup Committee for the New York Yacht Club. Mr. Carmany has been an active supporter of maritime organizations, including South Street Seaport.

James J. Coleman Jr. will be recognized with the Distinguished Service Award for his leadership in the campaign to build a national Coast Guard museum to honor the commitment, accomplishments, and sacrifices of Coast Guard men and women; this project took a great step forward with a ceremonial groundbreaking this May. Mr. Coleman is chairman of the National Coast Guard Museum Association and is a director of the Coast Guard Foundation and the US Navy League, New Orleans. He is chairman of International Matex Tank Terminals (IMTT) and CEO of International Properties, LLC.

Howard Slotnick will be presented with the David A. O'Neil Sheet Anchor Award. A longtime presence in the maritime heritage community, Mr. Slotnick was one of the co-organizers of the first Operation Sail event, and he was chairman and CEO of OpSail Miami. He is an active leader whose vision has helped in building the strength of the Society. Mr. Slotnick led NMHS in organizing the only Parade of Tall Ships on the Hudson in the last century and served on the team representing us in the War of 1812 Bicentennial Commemoration Advisory Board. He has traveled around the country conducting outreach for the Society, and shepherded the publication of the second and third editions of *The Skipper and the Eagle* and Peter and Norma Stanford's *A Dream of Tall Ships*.

Dinner Chairman is **Clay Maitland**, maritime executive and founding chairman of NAMEPA, and previous recipient of the NMHS Distinguished Service Award. **Richard T. du Moulin**, award-winning yachtsman and previous recipient of the NMHS Distinguished Service Award, will be Master of Ceremonies. The **US Coast Guard Academy Cadet Chorale**, directed by **Dr. Robert Newton**, will provide the evening's entertainment.

The trustees of the
National Maritime Historical Society
cordially invite you to attend the 2014 Annual Awards Dinner on
Thursday, 23 October 2014 to honor:

Daniel J. Basta
George W. Carmany III
James J. Coleman Jr.
Howard Slotnick

Reception at 5:30 PM
Dinner at 7:00 PM
at the New York Yacht Club
37 West 44th Street
New York, New York

NMHS gratefully acknowledges our Corporate Sponsors:
The Artina Group; George W. Carmany III; Coleman, Johnson, Artigues, and Jurisich; the Consortium on International Marine Heritage; the National Marine Sanctuary Foundation and **Howard Slotnick**

Black Tie Optional. Military: Dinner Dress Blue.

$175 of each ticket is the non-tax deductible portion of the cost of the dinner.

Seating is limited; please make your reservation early.
Kindly complete and return the enclosed reservation card in the envelope provided.
Or, you may call in your reservation to 914-737-7878, ext. 0.

for both parties. Out-of-town clients may be unfamiliar with getting around the city and prefer to have public relations experts on hand to help with the interviewing process and provide feedback after each session. Certain situations also may require having an interpreter and translated materials. Public relations executives would have the opportunity to meet reporters face to face, provide guidance during the interview, and follow up with any additional materials.

Written documents traditionally include the following components:

- **A pitch letter** to set up the appointment, which is usually followed up with a phone call or other social media message.

- **A follow-up confirmation with the journalist,** usually by email, that clearly indicates the date and location of the meeting. The message also can include an executive profile of the spokesperson and other supporting background, such as relevant news releases, media kit contents, or links to the online newsroom.
- A confirmation to the spokesperson should include a **media tour itinerary** to help the participant communicate effectively in diverse markets, thereby ensuring that he or she has the necessary background material to be prepared—intelligence on the media outlets, biographies on the reporters, examples of previously published or aired stories, and key messages and talking points for the interview.

A media tour takes time to coordinate and reconfirm all appointments. The itinerary for the spokesperson should be easy to follow and quickly convey the following eight components (which correspond to the numbers in the template in Exhibit 12.3):

1. **Heading**
   This section usually indicates that it is a media tour itinerary and for whom and the date span.
2. **Public Relations Host**
   Many media tours are escorted by public relations executives. Add the name of the person and contact information.
3. **Date**
   Each day should be separated with the day of the week and date.
4. **Specific Times**
   A grid format can work effectively to provide details at a glance. The far left column should list the exact times of each meeting. If a public relations executive is escorting the media tour, you should let the spokesperson know where to meet that person and when every appointment, break, and meal takes place.
5. **Appointments/Journalist, Media Outlet, and Location**
   This next column includes details on the meetings, such as the name and title of the journalist, the media outlet, as well as the address, floor or room number, and the phone number. It also would indicate locations for meals and breaks.
6. **About the Journalist**
   This column can include Web links to the journalist's bio online or LinkedIn. Relevant information on this person's familiarity with the company, product, or service can be helpful to add, if known.
7. **About the Media Outlet**
   This next column provides background information on the media outlet. Minimum facts should include the type of media outlet (magazine, newspaper, wire service, radio, or TV), timing (daily, weekly, monthly, or quarterly, or when the broadcast outlet airs), and circulation and audience figures. It also can include a link to the media outlet's website. Spokespeople may want copies of the most recent print editions, particularly if they are from out of town.
8. **Key Messages**
   This part includes key points that the spokesperson can talk about during the face-to-face meeting. Spokespeople may prefer a separate document with key points by topic, particularly if that person is new to the organization or has less experience with interviews.

Exhibit 12.3—MEDIA TOUR APPOINTMENT TEMPLATE.

Media Tour ①
First and Last Name, Company X
Month Day, 20XX
Name of City

Public Relations Host: ②
Name, Title, Company, Email, Phone

Day of Week, Month Day ③

Time ④	Appointments ⑤	About the Journalist ⑥	About the Media Outlet ⑦	Key Points ⑧
Use 12-hour or 24-hour clock	Meet (name of public relations representative) at (location, such as lobby of hotel) to begin media tour			
Each section should include time	Name of Media Outlet Address Floor/office Telephone Email	Full Name Title Any biographical information relevant to interview; add links to LinkedIn or online biography	Type Frequency Circulation or Viewership Other facts of interest Website	List key messages Add if previous stories have appeared in the media outlet, particularly over the past two years.
Add breaks, meals, next appointments in separate grids				

12.4.4 Statements

Statements are widely used to share timely commentary on a variety of internal or external situations. They can provide an update or perspective about news within the organization, share commentary about a situation outside the organization on breaking news about a crisis or current event, and offer congratulations to someone about a promotion or accomplishment or condolences about an illness or death. They can be issued from a specific person or by the organization in general. Statements also can be edited for senior corporate spokespeople, as well as for local managers, to deliver during press conferences, disseminate to the media on a regional and global basis, and post on websites and other social media. They can be widely quoted from and open to discussion in traditional media and social media.

A blog posting by Lou Hoffman, a public relations CEO, highlighted U.S. President Obama's statement about the death of Harold Ramis, a screenwriter, director, and actor, as an example of a human quote with "storytelling quality" (2014, para. 13), instead of many of the boring canned statements. Here is the full statement released by the White House on February 25, 2014:

> Michelle and I were saddened to hear of the passing of Harold Ramis, one of America's greatest satirists, and like so many other comedic geniuses, a proud product of Chicago's Second City. When we watched his movies—from "Animal House" and "Caddyshack" to "Ghostbusters" and "Groundhog Day"—we didn't just laugh until it hurt. We questioned authority. We identified with the outsider. We rooted for the underdog. And through it all, we never lost our faith in happy endings. Our thoughts and prayers are with Harold's wife, Erica, his children and grandchildren, and all those who loved him, who quote his work with abandon, and who hope that he received total consciousness.

Although the content requires having familiarity with Ramis's movies, the statement brings in Obama's adopted hometown of Chicago and reflects many of the emotions that movie fans share about these films. *Caddyshack* fans may recognize the reference to a memorable line spoken by Bill Murray's character who reminiscences about caddying for the Dalai Lama who bequeaths him "total consciousness" on his deathbed as a "tip." Leading newspapers also ran excerpts of this quote.

The excerpt below is an example of one of the statements titled, "Lack of dedicated resources and funds fuel Ebola crisis," on the Ebola epidemic issued by Kofi Annan (2014). As the former Secretary-General of the United Nations, a Ghanaian, and chairman of the Kofi Annan Foundation, Annan is a well-respected authority on Africa and global issues.

> The Ebola crisis in West Africa is a grave threat to public health and requires a swift and effective response. Unfortunately, measures such as the imposition of travel bans, may hinder rather than help efforts to contain the virus by impeding the flow of expertise and supplies to the affected areas.
>
> A coordinated response from governments, regional and international organisations is essential. Civil society organisations also, have a critical role to play, helping to ensure that communities are well informed and that dangerous misinformation is dispelled.
>
> With the adequate care, contracting the virus is by no means a death sentence. Yet too many people have already died in West Africa in the Ebola outbreak. The economic impact is disastrous for a region that is struggling to deal with severe poverty and the aftermath of many years of armed conflict.
>
> I urge donors and other partners in the international community, together with national governments and civil society organisations across the region, to urgently support the courageous efforts of the first responders who are tackling this crisis. Without adequate and timely support, the crisis is likely to worsen and create further misery and anguish in West Africa and beyond.

The most scrutinized statements, however, are during a crisis situation or incident that can impact an organization's reputation and affect many people—such as product recalls, computer malfunctions, severe weather, layoffs and closures, health outbreaks, accidents, and criminal activities, among others. The most severe situations are loss of life.

I am drawing primarily from my experience in the airline industry, which is an industry that is traditionally well prepared and trained in crisis preparedness and crisis communications since serious accidents can result in loss of life for passengers and crews from many countries.

Accidents also involve many other emergency services and investigation organizations. I am also reflecting back on other situations involving health, crime, and labor disputes, as well as acts of gods, a term that refers to non-manmade situations, such as severe weather conditions. I have represented tourist offices around the globe in locations that faced droughts, floods, earthquakes, and hurricanes.

Statements should express the facts known at that time, the process underway in investigating and resolving the situation, the resources available to the media and any affected parties, and reflect compassion and concern about the situation. Let us look at these four parts in more depth:

1. **The Facts**—Statements must only provide the facts known in real time—and avoid any speculation about what may have happened. If you were representing an airline and one of its planes has crashed and you know no details, you can only provide confirmed facts: the number of the flight and the aircraft manufacturer, the takeoff time from the airport and its intended flight path, the number of passengers and crew on the flight and their nationalities; and you may be able to add the age of the aircraft and last maintenance check, and the captain's flight experience.

   Example (excerpt from a statement by Joseph Lhota, who was then the Metropolitan Transportation Authority's chairman and chief executive officer, about Hurricane Sandy's impact on the New York City subway in 2012):

   The New York City subway system is 108 years old, but it has never faced a disaster as devastating as what we experienced last night. Hurricane Sandy wreaked havoc on our entire transportation system, in every borough and county of the region. It has brought down trees, ripped out power and inundated tunnels, rail yards and bus depots.

   As of last night, seven subway tunnels under the East River flooded. Metro-North Railroad lost power from 59th Street to Croton-Harmon on the Hudson Line and to New Haven on the New Haven Line. The Long Island Rail Road evacuated its West Side Yards and suffered flooding in one East River tunnel. The Hugh L. Carey Tunnel is flooded from end to end and the Queens Midtown Tunnel also took on water and was closed. Six bus garages were disabled by high water. We are assessing the extent of the damage and beginning the process of recovery. Our employees have shown remarkable dedication over the past few days, and I thank them on behalf of every New Yorker. In 108 years, our employees have never faced a challenge like the one that confronts us now. All of us at the MTA are committed to restoring the system as quickly as we can to help bring New York back to normal. (as cited in Johnston, 2012, paras. 3–4)

2. **The Process Underway**—A crisis incident does not operate in isolation since many organizations may be involved in investigating the situation, providing emergency resources, and trying to resolve the immediate problem. An organization can discuss how it is cooperating with authorities and thank them for their support—and defer to those experts. If a hotel experienced an incident of salmonella, the local health authority would be involved immediately to investigate the situation. In the case of a plane crash, airline executives would be involved in cooperating with aviation authorities, safety and transportation boards, search and rescue missions by the military and other parties, police and fire departments, and investigation authorities on crimes and terrorism, among others. Crisis training in aviation emphasizes the investigation process, which means that spokespeople cannot speculate or offer

opinions about what others are doing or provide any information that may hinder the process underway. Queries about the accident investigation team and the police, for example, should be directed to those parties.

Example (excerpt from one of the statements issued on the day of the crash of AirAsia Indonesia Flight QZ8501):

At this time, search and rescue operations are being conducted under the guidance of The Indonesia Civil Aviation Authority (CAA). AirAsia Indonesia is cooperating fully and assisting the investigation in every possible way. (AirAsia Indonesia, 2014, para. 6)

3. **The Resources**—Organizations need to provide immediate informational resources for different audiences. Airlines, for example, during an emergency situation would have different toll-free numbers (also called call centers) set up worldwide for media inquiries and for loved-ones of passengers and crew. Emergency centers are set up for families and friends of passengers. Frequent press conferences are set up to provide updates to the media and the public. A darkroom on the airline's website would be activated with content exclusively on the situation, as well as emergency resource contacts. Other social media may also offer resources.

Example (excerpt from a statement regarding a pet food recall):

We encourage consumers who have purchased affected product to discard the food or return it to the retailer for a full refund or exchange. We have not received any reports of injury or illness associated with the affected product. The lot codes indicated below should not be sold or consumed.

At Mars Petcare, we take our responsibility to pets and their owners seriously. We sincerely apologize for this situation and encourage you to reach out to us at 1–800–305–5206 from 8:00 a.m.—7:00 p.m. CST if you have questions. (Pedigree, 2014, paras. 4–5)

4. **The Compassion**—Spokespeople must express sympathy for all parties concerned, and apologize, as appropriate. Serious crisis situations are emotionally charged— and the people affected by the situation and the general public want to hear concern, empathy, and reassurance. An airline crash, for example, is a serious tragedy for the family, relatives, friends, and colleagues of the victims, as well as for all of the employees of the airline.

Example (excerpts from one of the statements released on the day of the plane crash issued by AirAsia Indonesia Flight QZ8501):

Sunu Widyatmoko, CEO of AirAsia Indonesia, said, "We are deeply shocked and saddened by this incident. We are cooperating with the relevant authorities to the fullest extent to determine the cause of this incident. In the meantime, our main priority is keeping the families of our passengers and colleagues informed on the latest developments." (AirAsia Indonesia, 2014, para. 2)

We will release further information as soon as it becomes available and our thoughts and prayers are with those on board QZ8501. (AirAsia Indonesia, 2014, para. 9)

A statement should contain the following five core components, as illustrated in the template in Exhibit 12.4 (with corresponding numbers in circles):

1. **Headline**

   Indicate that the document is a statement. If it is to be delivered at a press conference, write *Press Conference Statement.*

2. **Source/Spokesperson or Organization**

   At a press conference, a statement is traditionally issued by a specific person, followed by the person's title and affiliation. Statements posted online or distributed to the media may use a person's name or the company in general.

3. **Date, Time, and Time Zone**

   Statements include the full date, followed by the exact time of release and the time zone, particularly since the statement may be read by people in different time zones. Many situations are updated frequently, so the time is a significant detail.

4. **Body Copy**

   This part needs to include the four parts discussed earlier. The opening part usually focuses on the situation, providing the facts. The second part can focus on the investigation underway and efforts to return to normalcy. The third part can express sympathy and appropriate apologies (this part also can be placed earlier). The next-to-last part usually includes resources for the public.

5. **Conclusion**

   During an actual press conference, the last part can be a conclusion, whether to introduce the next speaker, open the floor to questions and answers, or indicate that the conference has concluded and that updates will be provided as new developments are confirmed. If the next press conference is confirmed, the last speaker also could share the details.

Exhibit 12.4—STATEMENT TEMPLATE.

Press Conference Statement by: ①

Name of Person ②

Title, Affiliation

Date (Month, Day, Year), **Time** (Hour, Minute, using 12-hour or 24-hour clock), **Time Zone** (of where your press conference is being held since crises can impact multiple time zones, and the information would be updated regularly in the real world) ③

Most press conference statements are double spaced since they are easier to read aloud from than single-spaced documents. Provide the facts—without speculation, humanize the situation (apologies, if necessary, as well as acknowledgment of concern and sympathy, as relevant to the situation), explain the process underway and your specific role (such as investigations and activities to resolve the situation), and give toll-free numbers and social media for affected parties to find out more information (as well as customer service contact information or how to contribute to an emergency relief fund, if relevant). ④

Not every press conference participant needs to repeat contact information. Each speaker needs to provide facts that are relevant to the involvement of the specific organization. You can add more detail about the organization's involvement with the process and investigation

continued

—and its overall mission, as relevant. These facts can help provide context to how this organization is helping with the situation.

Each speaker must express sympathy. Press conferences traditionally conclude with a question-and-answer session. More serious press conferences are broadcast live and can be repeated, along with footage of the actual tragedy. Some statements also are posted on websites and social media, distributed to the media or used as stand-by comments, if reporters contact the organization requesting an update.

Conclude by introducing the next speaker, including the person's name, title, and affiliation, and add what that person will address. The last person speaking should start a question-and-answer session for the journalists. ⑤

Exhibit 12.5 is an example of a statement about a fictitious plane crash that would be distributed to the media and posted on the company's website and other social media.

Exhibit 12.5—EXAMPLE OF A STATEMENT.

This is an example of a statement by a fictitious person and company that could be posted on the company's website and online newsroom, as well as distributed to media.

Scenario: You can confirm that no one died in the plane crash, but the accident resulted in a few minor injuries. You have set up a support center and toll-free numbers.

Statement issued by Terry Greene, CEO World Airways

January 1, 20XX

New York, 10:30 a.m. EST

World Airways flight WA358 flying from London to Toronto had an accident while landing at Toronto Pearson Airport in Canada.

The aircraft, an Airbus A340, carried 297 passengers and 12 crew members. Everyone on board the jet was able to get off the plane. Twenty-two passengers suffering minor injuries are treated at area hospitals in Toronto.

This is very sad situation, but we are thankful that there were no deaths or serious injuries. We credit the emergency evacuation procedures and training followed by our cabin crew.

World Airways is doing everything possible to give assistance to passengers who were on board flight WA358.

World Airways has established a passenger information center, and a toll-free number is available for family and friends of those who may have been on board WA358.

The toll-free numbers are as follows:

For those calling in the U.S. and Canada: 800–888–1212

For those calling from outside North America: 01–1-800–888–1212

# # #

Exercise 12.1

Insights: Press Conferences

Press conferences are effective formats to convey breaking news to a large group of journalists from diverse print and electronic media outlets. They traditionally conclude with a question-and-answer session. Press conferences are most widely used to provide updates on significant news stories that will impact organizations (such as mergers or resignations of key executives or officials) and are particularly useful during crisis incidents (severe weather, product recalls, crime or major accidents) to provide updates. Politicians also hold press conferences (also called briefings) regularly to discuss major developments and offer their perspective on major news.

Think of a recent news incident that you have followed or one that you have heard about — and find a press conference video clip to watch. (Good sources include online editions of TV news programs and YouTube.)

1. Which press conference did you select? Please add the URL.
2. What was the major topic of the press conference?
3. What other issues were addressed?
4. Who was involved in sharing the news?
5. Was the delivery credible?
6. What other factors influenced your opinion of the press conference?
7. Do you have any other observations to share? Would you have done anything differently?

Most statements are edited to conform to other communications platforms, particularly microblogs and social networking sites. Twitter, in particular, has become a useful resource for posting updates and resources for additional information.

Find a press conference online on a topic that interests you and answer the questions in Exercise 12.1.

12.4.5 Press Familiarization Trips

Providing journalists with samples of products is a common tactic in public relations. Some experiences are more challenging to distribute to the media as "samples." How can one best convey the travel experiences of a country, the vineyards of a wine-producing region, a behind-the-scenes look at how a product is made, or the music and cultural performances at an annual festival? Media kit materials, brochures, video footage, and photography can breathe life and insight into services and products. Yet promotional materials and events are not substitutes for covering stories on location that would result in in-depth stories. **Press trips** (also known as **press familiarization visits**, **press fams** or **junkets**) serve as a public relations tactic to provide journalists with firsthand experiences.

This technique is particularly popular with travel-related organizations. Public relations practitioners coordinate pre-arranged itineraries for journalists on a group or individual basis to showcase airlines, travel destinations, hotels or resorts, cruise lines, restaurants, theme parks, recreational activities and sports, scenic beauty and natural attributes, and cultural and historical attractions. Many press trips are hosted by the travel-related organization exclusively or in cooperation with a variety of travel-related services on a complimentary or discount basis. For example, a public relations representative for a tourist board would arrange transportation, accommodations, food and beverages, sightseeing and recreation, and other activities and services in that specific destination. Public relations representatives for hotels or resorts would provide accommodations and amenities on property. To defray the cost of hosting the trip, they would seek the support of airlines and other travel partners and attractions to round out the experience.

In addition to the travel, hospitality, and aviation industries, these trips are hosted by many different types of organizations:

- A car manufacturer launching a new product line would invite journalists to see how the vehicles are made and tested for safety.
- An international nonprofit could show how it has improved a community and arrange for journalists to tour the resources and meet the people responsible and local residents.
- A major event, such as a film festival, could invite journalists to review creative work or cover the event.
- A regional group of vineyards could arrange a tour of the vineyards, where the journalists could see the winemaking facilities, meet the winemakers, and partake in wine tastings, as well as sample local restaurants that feature the wines.

Public relations practitioners need to check the media policies on subsidized travel arrangements. Some media outlets are unable to accept stories resulting from complimentary or discount travel offered by a company or its public relations firms. The New York Times Company, for example, addresses travel specifically: "No writer or editor for the Travel section, whether on assignment or not, may accept free or discounted services of any sort from any element of the travel industry" (New York Times Company, 2004, p. 13).

"Do free press trips allow for greater access, or biased coverage?" was the first sentence of an article on a BBC blog (Haq, 2013). "Truth in travel" has remained *Condé Nast Traveler*'s motto since the U.S. travel magazine's inception in 1987, which also influenced the press trip policies of other travel-related publications that used to allow subsidies. However, the magazine's new editor-in-chief Pilar Guzman in 2014 had to face economic realities and re-examine its no-freebies policy. In a *Travel Weekly* article, she explained the editorial changes:

> We will never abandon "Truth in Travel," Guzman said. "The only thing we are softening is that we will accept [discounted] press rates. Not junkets; we will pay our way. But I was finding that we weren't covering a lot of properties that we should have because they were prohibitively expensive, or [writers were] staying only one night or just visiting the lobby. That's the truth." (Weissmann, 2014, para. 8)

Australian-based Lonely Planet states its travel guides are impartial with no advertising and no subsidized travel on its website: "Lonely Planet authors are not allowed to accept free accommodation or meals in exchange for favourable write-ups, so their recommendations are honest and objective" (2014, para. 3).

Before you write materials for a press trip with international journalists, you need to consider the following components:

- What languages do the media participants speak? If you are hosting a large international group with journalists from different countries, you can split up the group into different sections or host them separately.
- What are the dress codes? Explain dress codes clearly. What constitutes business casual or formal attire may mean different things. Indicate what to bring for weather conditions.
- What are the passport or visa requirements? Some countries also issue press visas and that process may be quite complex and time-consuming. Also, don't assume that a journalist residing in a particular place carries a passport from that country.
- What are the hosts offering on a complimentary basis? Being clear on what is covered can avoid surprises and potential disappointments. Usually air travel, all meals, transportation, and activities outlined in the itinerary, such as admission fees and ground transfers, are covered. Spell out what is not covered, such as dry cleaning and laundry; telephone, Internet access, and hotel business center fees; hotel mini-bar, meals and drinks on one's own; any independent travel during free time; passport and visa fees; travel to and from local airports; and any other personal expenses.

Most press trip invitations are handled like a pitch email. In this case, the content would focus on the dates, highlights of the itinerary, and key points on why the invitee should consider attending. The call to action is the press trip with a clear respond-by date. Be prepared to make follow-up calls to journalists.

The most time-intensive written document is the itinerary, in which writers need to spell out when and where every scheduled activity takes place. The following components should be included (please note that the order may vary). Please refer to Exhibit 12.6, which is an example of the first few days of a fictitious press trip to South Africa. The numbers in the exhibit follow these key itinerary components:

1. **Heading and Date Range** (required)
   Indicate the name or theme of the trip, the location(s), and the entire date range.
2. **Public Relations Escort/Local Contacts** (recommended)
   Many trips are coordinated by a public relations representative who will be traveling with the group. If this is the case, add that person's cell phone. The trip may have a local contact whose name and contact information could be added.
3. **Day of Week, Date** (required)
   Each day should be clearly indicated.
4. **Timing of Each Activity** (required)
   Each activity that has a specific time should be indicated on the left side. Use the clock time that most of the participants are familiar with or what is commonly used in the country they are visiting.
5. **Activity Details** (required)
   On the right side, list the major activities for each time slot.
6. **Transportation Details** (required)
   The first day must include the travel arrangements to the location. In many cases, press trips may have people traveling from different airports or driving from different

Exhibit 12.6—PRESS TRIP ITINERARY EXAMPLE.

International Press Group to South Africa

11–20 November, 20XX ①

Host Contacts: ②

Name, Title, Affiliation, Cell

Name, Tile, Affiliation, Cell

Sunday, 11 November ③

④   ⑤

Arrive at Johannesburg International Airport on South African Airways flight (see your attached flight itinerary for international arrivals/departures). ⑥

Meet representative from X Tours (cell phone) at Baggage Claim who will be holding a sign "International Press Group" for transfer to your hotel to check in. ⑦

Rest and enjoy free time (see media kit or ask hotel concierge for ideas). ⑧

19:30   Meet in hotel lobby ⑦ for transfer to Restaurant X and dine with Name, Title, Affiliation. ⑨

Dress code: business casual (no jeans, shorts, or T-shirts). ⑩

Overnight at Hotel X, address, telephone. ⑪

Monday, 12 November

Breakfast on your own by room service or in hotel restaurant.

10:00   Meet X Tours representative in hotel lobby for a full-day tour of Soweto and Funda Centre where you will meet with Name, Title, Affiliation. ⑫

Dress: Casual (bring comfortable walking shoes) for full-day tour.

13:00   Lunch at X Restaurant; continue tour of Soweto and meet Name, Title, Affiliation.

16:30   Transfer to X Cultural Village for walking tour, followed by an evening cultural performance and dinner with Name, Title, Affiliation.

Overnight at Hotel X.

Tuesday, 13 November

Breakfast on your own by room service or in hotel restaurant; check out of hotel.

08:45   Meet X Tours (cell phone) for transfer to Johannesburg International Airport for your SA XXX flight to Skukuza with group in Terminal X.

Note that only 15 kgs (33 lbs) of luggage per person is permitted; all other luggage to be stored at the airport in Terminal X; take malaria precaution (if not taken earlier).

11:40   Arrive at Skukuza Airport where you will be met by your rangers for transfer to the X Safari Lodge.

continued

Exhibit 12.6—Continued

12:30   Lunch at X Safari Lodge with Name, Title, Affiliation.

13:30   Free time: Relax or take escorted nature walk with ranger or enjoy spa treatments.

17:00   Meet in lobby for evening game drive followed by a braai (barbecue) at X Safari Camp. *Dress: Casual, bring binoculars and a jacket.*

Overnight at X Safari Lodge, address, telephone.

Wednesday, 14 November

05:30   Join group in dining room for light breakfast followed by early morning game drive followed by al fresco brunch.

Dress: Casual, bring binoculars and wear layers.

11:30   Return and check out of lodge.

12:00   Meet in lobby for transfer to Skukuza Airport for your flight to Johannesburg SA XXX, collect luggage in storage, and check in for your South African Airways flight to Cape Town SA XXX.

17:00   Arrive in Cape Town with group and meet X Tours for transfer to your hotel.

20:00   Dinner at Wine Estates X with Name, Title, Affiliation.

Dress: Business formal (suit and tie required for men).

Overnight at Hotel X, address, telephone.

---

locations. The email or letter to the individual journalist would include those facts. If there is one group all arriving together at the same time, you can list the flight or other form of transportation. Also add any details on local travel arrangements. The last item in an itinerary is the departure travel arrangements.

7. **Meeting Places** (required)

Add the meeting place for all activities and be as specific as possible, such as where at the hotel or at the airport. Indicate relevant information about people they will be meeting.

8. **Free Time** (required)

Let the participants know when they have free time. Itineraries should allow free time so journalists can deal with their pending work and their offices, as well as have time to spend time interviewing people or exploring on their own. Free time should be allocated on the first day when journalists are arriving from long-haul flights.

9. **Meals** (required)

Make sure to indicate when meals take place. Also add names of anyone who will be joining the group. In some cases, meals may be on their own. For example, some itineraries will offer flexible arrangements for breakfast either by room service or in the hotel restaurant during a specific timeframe. Clearly indicate if any meals are not complimentary.

10. **Dress Codes** (recommended)

    Let people know what the dress codes are for dining and events. It is also helpful to indicate clothing for touring, such as comfortable walking shoes, and for specific activities.

11. **Overnight Arrangements** (required)

    Let the group members know where they will be staying each day. Make sure to include the full contact information of the hotel, resort, or place with addresses and telephone numbers. Some writers include all hotel contacts in a separate sheet, if there is extensive travel.

12. **Tours and Events** (as needed)

    Indicate when each activity will take place, as well as names of specific people the group will be meeting and recommended attire.

12.5 Techniques for Voicing Opinions in Media Outlets

Three important methods to express opinions are letters to the editor, op-eds, and bylined articles. Op-ed columns and letters to the editor allow you to share your opinion and frame a debate with the consumers of the media outlets. This commentary also can spread on other social media. It is not uncommon for public relations executives to scout opportunities, develop story ideas, and draft comments for other people, whether they are company executives, clients, or influential industry experts. Credentials count—and when you look at the authors, you will see many names of authoritative sources from politicians, academics, scientists, corporate executives, directors of nonprofits, or lesser-known people who have fascinating and relevant firsthand experiences to share.

12.5.1 Letters to the Editor

Letters to the editor (also referred to as **LTEs**) can be valuable in adding another perspective, or strongly disagreeing or agreeing with previously published stories. (If the goal is to correct a simple fact that ran in a story about your organization, the public relations executive should contact the editor responsible for another section called "Corrections.") Look at the submission guidelines for letters to the editor issued by the specific media outlet, most of which are posted on the outlet's website. The word count and process can vary.

This editorial section encourages submission from non-editorial staff. Researcher and editor Rasmus Kleis Nielsen (2010) determined that the majority of Danish newspaper editors selected letters to the editor on the value of six considerations, which could apply to newspapers in any location:

- **Value of the news**, such as "novelty and originality" (p. 26) related to current news.
- **Textual quality**, meaning "letters that strike a balance between the personal and the professional" (p. 27) and a brief and concise style.
- **Speed** in terms of submissions received quickly while the subject is directly related to today's news.
- **Individualized representation** in terms of points of view, instead of collective opinions from a group, such as the government or another authority.

- **Fairness** in which the editors select letters that reflect different viewpoints on the same topic.
- **Disagreement,** such as debates and criticism, on how a newspaper is reporting on a topic.

Kleis Nielsen also identified three genres of letters to the editor, which also apply to letters to the editor anywhere: **storytelling**, primarily based on personal experience; **criticism** on a previously published story; and **appeal letters** on general topics and public figures, as well as a suggested course of action.

In fact, editors may select a balance of letters, whether negative, neutral, or positive. These letters must be submitted quickly since the content traditionally addresses current articles or timely events. Consider responding within the same day to newspapers, within two days to weeklies, and so forth. Many letters to the editor are under 150 or 200 words, so within that limited word count, writers must consider the following:

- Follow the submission guidelines. Stick to the word count; you can write less but not more.
- Refer back to the story you are commenting on without repeating the content, but the copy needs to be easily understood by the reader who may not recall the story you are referring to.
- State your point of view right away. You need to stick to a consistent tone—are you providing a rebuttal, adding another perspective, or strongly agreeing with the original letter? As with all openings, the first sentence must be compelling to encourage readers to continue reading.
- Support your point of view with a few key points or observations. Do not rant.
- Close with a well thought-out statement.

12.5.2 Op-Eds

Opposite-the-Editorial pages, which are referred to as **op-eds** (or **guest editorials** or **guest commentary**), can be a powerful way to express points of views that can be widely read in some of the most respected English-language outlets, appealing to diverse global audiences. Although op-eds are treated like "exclusives," the topic can be adapted, edited, and localized for media in different geographic markets. Op-eds allow people who are not on staff to express their points of view in short essays. Most op-eds are authored by people who have expertise with the topic. Contributors also may include staff editors and regular columnists of the specific media outlet.

Significant current events are the most common topics addressed in the op-ed pages. Politicians comment frequently on issues, as do industry experts and academic researchers. Firsthand experiences with a slice of reality can be compelling. Trends in any areas—whether business, dining, education, fitness, fashion, science, or you-name-it—can make interesting fodder for op-eds. Other considerations include timing, such as holidays, seasons, anniversaries, and major milestones.

Let us look at a few real-world examples:

- "A plea for caution from Russia: What Putin has to say to Americans about Syria" was the title of a *New York Times* op-ed by Vladimir V. Putin (2013). The Russian president discussed his opinions on a diplomatic solution, rather than military intervention, in Syria following the Syrian government's use of chemical weapons. This controversial op-ed became a story in itself—in media and blogs around the globe. Ketchum, the public relations agency of the Russian government, also received praise and criticism for helping to place this prominent op-ed.

- "What did Edward Snowden get wrong? Everything" was the title of an op-ed in the *Los Angeles Times* by Andrew Liepman (2013). The author's name is not as instantly recognizable as the leader of a country. However, Liepman has strong credentials as a senior analyst at Rand Corp. and a former CIA officer and former deputy director of the National Counterterrorism Center, which make him an appropriate source to comment on Snowden, the American computer systems administrator who leaked classified documents from the National Security Agency.

- Firsthand experiences from an unknown person can work effectively, as long as other people can relate to the topic. Willetta Dukes (2013), a Burger King employee in the U.S., wrote an op-ed in the *Guardian* titled: "Why I'm on strike today: I can't support myself on $7.85 at Burger King." She shares her life story as a single mother struggling to support her two sons on her low income and the reasons why fast food workers are striking.

- Here is an example on timing. Ruth Chang (2015), a professor of philosophy at Rutgers University, wrote an op-ed titled "Resolving to create a new you" in the *New York Times*, three days after the new year when many have pledged resolutions. Chang's byline also includes an interesting detail: her TED (Technology, Entertainment, Design) talk, "How to make hard choices," which she draws upon in the op-ed, has been viewed more than 2.8 million times.

   THE annual ritual of the New Year's resolution—I'll lose 10 pounds, get my finances in order, be more patient with my family, feel more grateful—misses the point. We try to steel our wills to do what we already know we should be doing. Kick-in-the-pants reminders, however stern, are missed opportunities for genuine self-renewal. (Not to mention that the shelf life of any motivational juice we generate in January tends to expire in February.) (para. 1)

To develop a viable op-ed, I would recommend the following steps in targeting specific outlets, keeping abreast of news, determining topics, and following submission guidelines:

- **Step 1:** Read the outlets of interest frequently, including their news stories and op-ed columns. Develop a targeted list of media outlets and find out the submission guidelines. Rely on local public relations talent who can identify media outlets that may restrict freedom of expression or have unwritten rules on political correctness. Also read the "masters," such as the staff columnists at the *New York Times*—Maureen Dowd, David Brooks, Bob Herbert, and Thomas L. Friedman, among others.

- **Step 2:** Stay current with news in your field and follow topics that would be relevant to your organization or clients in your home country and in other markets. Make sure your op-ed topic is timely and relevant, and presents strong arguments. Avoid promotional news that sounds like a news release. Even though you are expressing an opinion, you will need to justify it with researched facts and credibility. The Earth Institute (2010) explains in its guide on writing op-eds "Passion and strong opinion are prerequisites; but they are not enough" (p. 2).

- **Step 3:** Follow the outlet's guidelines. Draft the copy. Write a colorful headline that makes the editor want to read more. Don't be surprised, however, if the headline of a published article is different. Provide a compelling introductory paragraph. Supporting paragraphs should provide evidence to justify your point of view. Avoid using too many quotes from other sources. Use vivid examples; avoid too many statistics. Instead of including academic citations and references, writers should indicate the source where the facts are from. The last paragraph should provide a conclusion, as well as a relevant call to action or things to consider.

Unless you are writing an op-ed on your own, you will then need to make sure you follow the approval process with your client or company, making it clear that the op-ed draft is time-sensitive material.

- **Step 4:** Most op-eds are submitted by email—and are considered exclusives so you can only submit to one outlet at a time. You can, however, edit content extensively for a different geographic market from a local author. A brief cover note should explain why the author is qualified to write this op-ed, unless the person is a public figure or well-known authority. Do not expect a response for rejections—and most op-ed editors will not take phone calls or respond to follow-up emails.

Try Exercise 12.2 and evaluate an op-ed that interests you.

Exercise 12.2

Insights: Op-eds

An op-ed is a column or guest essay published in the opinion section of a newspaper (Opposite-the-Editorial page). Find an op-ed in any media outlet—most major daily newspapers or even your student paper may publish opinion pieces. Answer the following questions:

1. Which publication did you find the op-ed in?
2. Did the headline persuade you to read more?
3. How is the author qualified to discuss the topic? What are his or her credentials?
4. What do you think is the objective of the op-ed?
5. What are the key messages communicated in the op-ed?
6. Did you find it well written? What qualities did you like?
7. How was it relevant or timely?

An excellent online resource is the OpEd Project (www.theopedproject.org), which is a nonprofit committed to encouraging women in diverse fields to submit op-eds. The nonprofit states that: "Our world conversation is currently an echo chamber that reproduces the same narrow range of (85% male) voices over and over" (OpEd Project, n.d., para. 4). Even though the organization's goal is to gain a higher share of female voices in opinion pieces, its website contains useful information and how-to advice for any type of op-ed writer.

12.5.3 Bylined Articles

Bylined articles are published stories in newspapers, magazines, or blogs, in which the author receives credit. These can be an important writing tactic in public relations campaigns. Unlike op-eds, which are opposite the editorial pages, bylined articles are on the editorial pages. Not all publications will accept bylined articles since they prefer articles prepared by staff editors or regular contributors. Industry trade publications are among the most viable outlets to place bylined articles by experts and respected sources. Other possibilities include local, regional, or national publications on general news or business, as well as guest blogs. Bylined articles cannot serve as advertisements, so writers must avoid promotional copy and overt references to their companies. These articles usually provide insight into the industry, helpful advice, and case studies.

The following steps can help writers determine topics and media outlets, edit the copy, and promote the published article:

- **Selection of Media Targets**—Look at outlets read by your audiences and identify the most important trade publications in the specific industry. If you are helping someone else prepare the bylined article, you'll need to convey to the author the benefits of preparing targeted media outlets ranked in order of priority.
- **Determination of Topic**—Read the content in recent issues to find out what topics have been recently covered and the editorial style and tone.
- **Find out the Guidelines**—See if an editorial calendar and editorial submission guidelines on stylebooks, citations, and word count are posted online; if not, contact the publication to find out. Some editorial calendars may be under "media kits" or "advertising."
- **Draft the Article**—Some articles are ghostwritten with input and final approval from the identified bylined author. You probably will be writing the story for someone else, such as your client or a corporate executive. The public relations writer will most likely have to interview the person to find out any unique angles or points of view. Be prepared to discuss a few story topics in advance. A client who has authored a new book, for example, could edit material for a bylined story. Determine the story themes and prepare an outline for the author's review.
- **Send a Query Letter and Follow Up**—Find out if the story would be of interest for consideration to publish. You will need to share the theme, key points, and why the author is qualified. Be prepared to follow up by phone or email, and make any suggested changes on the topic. If rejected, you can move on to the next media outlet on your list.
- **Edit and Submit the Article**—Work in collaboration with the author to finish the article. This process may be time-consuming. Submit the article for editorial review and be prepared that the editor may ask for additional content or changes. Submitting an article is also no guarantee for publication.
- **Promote the Bylined Article After it is Published**—The publication owns the copyright, so you would need approval to make reprints, which will most likely require a fee. The story may be useful to the company's sales force for sales calls and trade shows, as well as to its employees and customers. You also would need approval to post the entire article on the company's website. You can include the article link, if available. You also can spread the word through blogs, microblogs, and other social media.

12.6 Learning Objectives and Key Terms

After reading Chapter 12, you should be able to:

- Develop story angles for journalists.
- Describe different approaches in news reporting.
- Compose pitch letters to propose story ideas to journalists.
- Write media alerts to invite media outlets to events.
- Draft invitation copy for formal printed or electronic invitations.
- Craft a statement that could be delivered at a news event, posted online, or shared with the media and the public.
- Prepare an itinerary for a press familiarization trip.
- Understand the differences between letters to the editor and op-eds.
- Determine topics for bylined articles and understand the process in preparing and submitting these stories.

This chapter covers the following key terms:

Story angles (p. 294)	News pegs (p. 294)
Chronological narrative (p. 294)	Hourglass metaphor in news (p. 295)
Kabob metaphor in news (p. 295)	Nut graf (p. 295)
Pitches (p. 298)	Media alerts/advisories (p. 303)
Formal invitations (p. 307)	Media tours (p. 309)
Editorial briefings (p. 309)	News/press conferences (p. 303)
Statements (p. 312)	Press familiarization trips (p. 318)
Letters to the editor (p. 323)	Op-eds (p. 324)
Bylined articles (p. 327)	

References

AirAsia Indonesia. (2014, December 28). *AirAsia Indonesia Flight QZ8501. Issued at 11:40PM (GMT+8) on 28th December 2014* [Statement]. Retrieved from http://qz8501.airasia.com/28-dec-2014/index.html.

Annan, K. (2014, September). Lack of dedicated resources and funds fuel Ebola crisis —Statement by Kofi Annan on the Ebola crisis [Statement/news release]. *Kofi Annan Foundation*. Retrieved from http://kofiannanfoundation.org/newsroom/press/2014/09/lack-dedicated-resources-and-funds-fuel-ebola-crisis-statement-kofi-annan.

Carufel, R. (2014, May 30). Global PR: Do you think your CEO is prepared to be interviewed by European journalists? Execs should expect different media practices, reports new study by PRGN. *Bulldog Reporter's Daily Dog*. Retrieved from http://www.bulldogreporter.com/daily dog/article/pr-biz-update/global-pr-do-you-think-your-ceo-is-prepared-to-be-interviewed-by-euro.

Chang, R. (2015, January 4). Resolving to create a new you [Op-ed]. *New York Times*. Retrieved from http://www.nytimes.com/2015/01/04/opinion/sunday/resolving-to-create-a-new-you.html.

Dukes, W. (2013, August 29). Why I'm on strike today: I can't support myself on $7.85 at Burger King [Op-ed]. *Guardian*. Retrieved from http://www.theguardian.com/commentis free/2013/aug/29/fast-food-worker-protest-minimum-wage.

Earth Institute. (2010, February). *Writing and submitting an opinion piece: A guide.* Columbia University. Retrieved from https://www.google.com/webhp?sourceid=chrome-instant&ion=1&espv=2&ie=UTF8#q=earth%20institute%20%2B%20passion%20and%20strong%20opinion%20are%20prerequisites.pdf.

Haq, H. (2013, May 1). The bottom line of travel writing. *BBC The Passport Blog.* Retrieved from http://www.bbc.com/travel/blog/20130501-the-risk-of-accepting-free-travel.

Harrower, T. (2007). *Inside reporting: A practical guide to the craft of journalism.* New York, NY: McGraw-Hill.

Hoffman, L. (2014, February 25). The next time you're crafting executive quotes, consider this. *Ishmael's Corner* [blog]. Retrieved from http://www.ishmaelscorner.com/2014/02/.

Johnston, G. (2012, October 30). MTA Chairman: Hurricane Sandy a devastating disaster for mass transit. *Gothamist.* Retrieved from http://gothamist.com/2012/10/30/mta_chairman_sandy_a_devastating_di.php.

Kleis Nielsen, R. (2010). Participation through letters to the editor: Circulation, considerations, and genres in the letters institution. *Journalism, 11*(1), 21–35. doi: 10.1177/1464884909350641.

Liepman, A. (2013, August 10). What did Edward Snowden get wrong? Everything [Op-ed]. *Los Angeles Times.* Retrieved from http://articles.latimes.com/2013/aug/10/opinion/la-oe-0811-liepman-snowden-and-classified-informat-20130811.

Lonely Planet. (2014). *About Lonely Planet: Our books.* Retrieved from http://www.lonelyplanet.com/about/our-books/.

New York Times Company. (2004). *Ethical journalism: A handbook of values and practices for the news and editorial departments.* Retrieved from http://www.nytco.com/wp-content/uploads/NYT_Ethical_Journalism_0904–1.p.

Nowicka, H. (2012). Integrating traditional and social media. In Stephen Waddington (Ed.), *Share this: The social media handbook for PR professionals.* Chartered Institute of Public Relations (CIPR). Chichester, West Sussex: John Wiley & Sons.

OpEd Project. (n.d.). About. Retrieved from http://www.theopedproject.org.

Oriella PR Network. (2013). The new normal for news: Have global media changed forever? *Oriella PR Network Global Digital Journalism Study 2013.* Retrieved from http://www.oriellaprnetwork.com/sites/default/files/research/Brands2Life_ODJS_v4.pdf.

Pedigree. (2014, August 13). *Recall notice* [Statement]. Retrieved from http://www.pedigree.com/update/.

Putin, V. V. (2013, September 11). A plea for caution from Russia: What Putin has to say to Americans about Syria [Op-ed]. *New York Times.* Retrieved from http://www.nytimes.com/2013/09/12/opinion/putin-plea-for-caution-from-russia-on-syria.html?pagewanted=all&_r=0.

Scanlan, C. (2003a, June 18). The hourglass: Serving the news, serving the reader. *Poynter.org.* Retrieved from http://www.poynter.org/news/media-innovation/12624/the-hourglass-serving-the-news-serving-the-reader/.

Scanlan, C. (2003b, May 19). The nut graf, part 1. *Poynter.org.* Retrieved from http://www.poynter.org/news/media-innovation/11371/the-nut-graf-part-i/.

Waters, R. D., Tindall, N. T. J., & Morton, T. S. (2010). Media catching and the journalist-public relations practitioner relationship: How social media are changing the practice of media relations. *Journal of Public Relations Research, 22*(3), 241–264. doi: 10.1080/10627261003799202.

Weissmann, A. (2014, February 17). Redefining truth in travel. *Travel Weekly.* Retrieved from http://www.travelweekly.com/Arnie-Weissmann/Redefining-truth-in-travel/.

Part Five

CONNECTING ONLINE AND USING EXTERNAL COMMUNICATION TOOLS GLOBALLY

This section includes three chapters that investigate writing for the Web and social media, crafting speeches and scripts, and developing controlled-content written tools.

Chapter 13 Writing for the Internet and Social Media Worldwide

- Discusses effective writing styles in connecting with people on social media, including how to write hashtags.
- Provides examples of corporate blogs and shows how to write in a more informal, less corporate language to communicate with readers.
- Highlights how to use microblogs effectively to reach various audiences and engage participation.
- Covers the power of storytelling in social media, with compelling imagery and well-written captions.
- Addresses the issues of transparency and conflict of interest in posting content on Wikipedia.

Chapter 14 Shaping Speeches and Scripts

- Covers the preparation process, structural and presentation considerations, and the benefits of learning from the masters past and present in delivering speeches.
- Examines speechwriting for audiences with diverse levels of fluency in English.
- Discusses how to evaluate the receptivity of the audience, goals of the organization, timing and setup, considerations for supporting visuals, speaking skills and delivery style of the speaker, and other components to craft a speech that would resonate with the listeners.

- Looks at how speeches in English and in translated versions can have a lifespan on the Web and be distributed to the media and other stakeholders.
- Shows how to make introductions, based on the needs of specific international organizations and audiences.
- Reviews how to write for the ear and eye, with a look at broadcast-quality video, video news releases, public service announcements, and video-sharing social media applications.

Chapter 15 Controlling Content with Brand Journalism and Corporate-Produced Materials

- Explores controlled content and brand journalism opportunities for public relations writers.
- Examines printed and online magazines and newsletters produced by international organizations.
- Shows how online newsrooms also can function like media outlets with staff reporting on current events and covering human interest stories that can be posted with supporting visual imagery.
- Describes the value of printed brochures (also called leaflets or pamphlets) and posters and why they make sense when reaching people who may not have Internet access or for wired audiences who may benefit by receiving tactical information that they may not seek online.
- Explains how white papers can be useful tools to share opinions and position an organization as a thought leader to diverse international markets.
- Discusses advertorials and native advertising that look like editorial but are paid-for placements.

13 Writing for the Internet and Social Media Worldwide

Ultimately, however, good writing rests on craft and always will. I don't know what still newer electronic marvels are waiting just around the corner to make writing twice as easy and twice as fast in the next 25 years. But I do know they won't make writing twice as good. That still will require plain old hard work—clear thinking—and the plain old tools of the English language.

—William Zinsser, author of *On Writing Well*

13.1 Introduction to Web Writing for Public Relations

The quotation above is from William Zinsser, the late American writer and teacher, in *On Writing Well: The Classic Guide to Writing Nonfiction* (2001, p. xii), a helpful book on writing nonfiction. Zinsser confronts the reality that clear and compelling writing transcends any medium. More than 40% of the world has Internet access as of July 1, 2014 (Internet Live Stats, 2015), a percentage that will most likely continue to surge. The penetration of the Internet globally presents public relations practitioners with benefits and challenges.

James E. Grunig, the public relations scholar renowned for encouraging **two-way symmetrical dialogue** between organizations and audiences, stated: "If the social media are used to their full potential, I believe they will inexorably make public relations more global, strategic, two-way and interactive, symmetrical or dialogical, and socially responsible" (2009, p. 1). I agree that social media offer a dialogue for organizations and their constituents, whether they are journalists, customers, employees, and other audiences anywhere. Organizations are able to share visual and verbal content in multiple platforms, while having a conversation with stakeholders, learning about their sentiments, and identifying their preferences and potential issues of concern. Social media outlets are like virtual customer service counters open to the public. While we can control the words and imagery we post, we cannot control the commentary and reactions. We have to monitor the exchange, while truly listening and learning from the interchange. And we need to pay attention to changing trends in usage of existing social media platforms while exploring new innovations. The most popular platforms today may become passé quickly.

In addition, social media engagements complement traditional media relations activities since more and more journalists are seeking content from blogs, microblogs, and social networking sites. Brunswick Research (2011), a global financial and corporate communications firm, conducted a worldwide media poll on business journalists, with the majority of respondents from Europe and North America, on the impact of social media in reporting stories. It discovered that two-thirds of journalists claimed to cover stories that originated from social media, with blogs being the primary source to investigate an issue or form the foundation of a published story, followed by microblogs, social networking sites, and message boards. The top four social media information sources were Twitter, blogs, Facebook, and LinkedIn. Regional differences indicated that North American journalists were more receptive to using and believing social media sources than journalists from other areas.

13.1.1 Strategic Considerations

Regardless of the social media platform, public relations writers need to consider the following factors:

- **Strategic Goals and Time Investment**
  Before engaging in any social media platform, you must be able to pinpoint what you hope to accomplish with social media and identify your audiences and the specific social media platforms they spend time on—not just for personal use, but to communicate with brands, companies, nonprofits, or public figures. You also need to identify how much time and resources you have to devote to the platforms by posting content, responding to comments, and monitoring content. For global public relations campaigns, the social media platforms may be quite diverse and in different languages. Frankly, organizations may be better off not engaging a specific platform, if they are unable to invest the time in doing it well.
- **Guidelines and Policies**
  With multiple authors in the same organization—in-house staff, paid spokespeople, and outside consultants, such as public relations, advertising, or digital agencies—being involved with social media engagement, organizations should develop clearly written social media guidelines for use on a local, regional, or global basis. Written standards can apply to all Web and social media platforms, covering such topics as consistency, decorum, and approval processes. Ethical and legal issues should cover copyrights, trademarks, libel and defamation, rights of privacy, and proprietary information. Each social media outlet also posts its own guidelines on terms of service, which also address rules on promotions.
- **Names for Websites, Blogs, and Hashtags**
  Be careful to select domain and hashtag names carefully, so that the words in English cannot be misinterpreted. You should also explore if the words could have other meanings in different languages, particularly in markets where you are promoting products or services. Naming URLs is a challenge since many of your choices may be taken and spaces between words are not allowed. Andy Geldman (2010) coined the word **slurls** for poorly worded domain names and created a website (www. slurls.com) and wrote *Slurls: They Called Their Website What?! The World's Worst Internet URLs from effoff.com to penisland.net*. By examining parts of URLs, you may discover how words can be read different ways, with completely different meanings: Is it *pen island* or *penis land*? *Therapist* or *the rapist*? *Gored foxes* or *go red foxes*? *IT scrap* or *its crap*? *Who represents* or *whore presents*? *Childrens laughter* or *children slaughter*?

A **hashtag** is simply the symbol # (also called a pound or number sign, but not in social media) before a word, words, or phrases that can be capitalized or not and include numbers, but a hashtag cannot contain spaces or other punctuation marks. Longer names can be abbreviated to avoid taking up too much space. Hashtags are beneficial in categorizing topics, organizing conversations, and following trends. While hashtags started on Twitter, they are now popular for posts on other social media sites, such as Vine, Facebook, Instagram, and Google+.

Writing hashtags can take time—and be prepared to participate in brainstorming sessions with many people making contributions. See Figure 13.1 for a look at how cartoonist Tom Fishburne captures how difficult it can be to create brief hashtags that can satisfy all parties involved. Business hashtags can be named many ways:

- After a person (#lionelmessi)
- An organization, which also can use a well-known acronym (#UN)
- A product or service (#iPad)
- A promotion or contest (#MTVHottest, #GlobalSelfie)
- A theme (#CookieHQ for Hershey's chocolates)
- An event (#olympic; or a more specific hashtag with country and year, such as #Rio2016; or by a team, such as hashtag, team, country, #TeamUSA or #TeamCanada; or even a theme for Canada, #WeAreWinter).

Online resources can help you find out which hashtags are trending in real time: www.twitter.com/trending topics or @TrendingTopics, www.hashtags.org, and www.trendsmap.com, among others.

Figure 13.1—CARTOON ILLUSTRATES THE CHALLENGES IN CREATING HASHTAGS. Source: © Tom Fishburne.

Exhibit 13.1—WRITING TIPS ON BLOGS, MICROBLOGS, AND SOCIAL MEDIA.

- Write strong headlines to motivate the reader to continue.
- Avoid long paragraphs—consider six lines or less ample.
- Use the pronouns *you* and *your* frequently, as well as *we* and *our* when talking about your organization.
- Use imperative verbs—find out more. . .click on. . .share your thoughts.
- Apply contractions regularly.
- Feel free to ask questions.
- Avoid ranting and being defensive.
- Use positive language.
- Localize content as much as you can to connect with that audience.
- Use bullets that make information easy to scan.
- Edit copy for different platforms. Blog content can be more in-depth, followed by shorter copy on Facebook, and under 140 characters on Twitter.

- **Dynamic and Interactive Written and Visual Content**
  Social media give you the opportunity to tell stories about the multi-dimensions of a personality, a brand, and any type of organization. Unlike journalistic and formal business writing, social media writing demands a conversational tone, greater immediacy, and relatable verbal and visual content that people find of value to look at, share with others, comment on, or bookmark. Social media content must avoid sounding like "approved by the corporate marketing department" copy. Exhibit 13.1 includes other writing tips for social media.

  While content should reflect the company's image positively, it needs to convey a human voice that connects with people. The storytellers can be people beyond the corporate staff—personalities, experts, and everyday people with interesting experiences to share. Public relations writers need to figure out what their audiences will care about—and match the content to their interests.

  Ideal content is catchy, and so appealing that it spreads rapidly throughout multimedia online platforms—in other words, goes **viral**. Jonah Berger (2013), a marketing professor at the Wharton School of the University of Pennsylvania, developed a six-step STEPPS principle that explains how content can become contagious, which is based on his book *Contagious: Why Things Catch On*:

  1. Social currency (what people feel gives this status and positive associations).
  2. Triggers (what makes people recall and talk about your brand).
  3. Emotion (what emotions your products or services generate).
  4. Public (what people notice and observe about your brand publicly).
  5. Practical value (what practical value your brand offers).
  6. Stories (what narratives people like to share about your brand).

  His website (http://jonahberger.com/) features online resources that are helpful to public relations practitioners.
- **Newsjacking**
  David Meerman Scott, author of *The New Rules of Marketing & PR* (2013), coined the term **newsjacking**, which means taking advantage of a prominent news story by

finding connections to your organization. Scott explains this concept: "If you have a legitimate tie to a breaking news story and you react in real-time—by providing additional content in a blog post, tweet, video, or media alert—journalists may find you while they are researching material for their story" (p. 349). He shares an example of how Oreo cookies created its own story about the power outage during the Super Bowl XLVII in 2013. It became the #BlackoutBowl on Twitter and social media. Oreo tweeted: @Oreo "Power out? No problem," along with a photo of an Oreo cookie on a table in a dark room with the caption "You can still dunk in the dark" (p. 347). This newsjacking story resulted in more than 14,000 retweets, received more than 20,000 likes on Facebook, and generated mainstream media exposure. The president of Oreo's digital agency explained the importance of flexibility and speedy responses in a BuzzFeed post: "You need a brave brand to approve content that quickly. When all of the stakeholders come together so quickly, you've got magic" (Sanders, 2013, para. 7).

Not all newsjacking is an automatic success, however. The worst examples attempt to capitalize on crisis situations or react without significant knowledge about why the story is trending. Here are two cautionary tales. Kenneth Cole, the fashion retailer, tweeted this message at the onset of the Egyptian protests in 2011 (Sweet, 2011):

Millions are in uproar in #Cairo. Rumor is they heard our new spring collection is now available at http://bit.ly/KCairo-KC.

The company tweeted an apology within an hour:

Re Egypt tweet: we weren't intending to make light of a serious situation. We understand the sensitivity of this historic moment-KC.

Another example also illustrates the perils of not knowing what is behind a trending story. Even if you are based in a country outside of the situation, you still can find news coverage about what is happening around the world. Celeb Boutique, an online clothing store based in the U.K., issued the following tweet on July 20, 2012:

#Aurora is trending, clearly about our Kim K inspired #Aurora dress.

Why was this tweet problematic? The Colorado town was trending that day because a gunman opened fire at a movie theater in Aurora, killing 12 people and wounding 70. The retailer's public relations team deleted the tweet and apologized, claiming that it was not U.S. based and unaware of the situation (Miltenberg, 2012).

- **Brevity**

Social media text needs to be brief and digestible yet vivid and compelling. Wanting more time to write less is a centuries-old lament. Garson O'Toole (2012) maintains a website aptly named the Quote Investigator (http://quoteinvestigator.com), and he researched the origins of the "If I had more time, I would have written a shorter letter" quote. He tracked the first reference to the quote with essentially the same meaning to Blaise Pascal, the French mathematician and philosopher, in the mid-1600s, and validated sources attributed to such luminaries as John Locke, Benjamin Franklin, Martin Luther, Henry David Thoreau, and Woodrow Wilson, among others.

Brevity in social media writing does not mean texting and turning a popular verse from Hamlet into 2b?Ntb?=? The exception would be if you were discussing or promoting the work of John Sutherland, professor emeritus of University College London, who has been transforming English literature classics into text messages as educational tools (Wainwright, 2005). Can you decipher this text translation from Scott Fitzgerald's *Great Gatsby*: MembaDatAlDaPplnDaWrldHvntHdDaVantgs UvAd?[1]

You can shorten website addresses by using a service like bitly (https://bitly.com). Shorter links can significantly reduce character counts in microblogs.

- **Frequency**
  Social media require a frequent dialogue to post content, respond to comments, and monitor sentiment to uncover positive points and areas of concern. The 24/7 instant accessibility presents challenges too. Speed does not mean that one should communicate instantly with stream of consciousness instead of careful thinking. Insightful and thoughtful commentary will have greater impact. A level of respect and decorum needs to be maintained at all times, particularly when addressing negative commentary. During a crisis situation, social media enable organizations to share updates in real time, respond to questions or complaints, and detect public sentiment, as well as misinformation or rumors.

  Many public relations agencies have been struggling to accomplish more with fewer resources and shrinking staff with more demanding clients, thereby blurring the lines between work and the employee's own life outside the office. No one should work nonstop; a separation should be maintained between one's professional and business life. Staff should be able to take a real break with vacations that do not require keeping in touch with the office. Collaborative tools, such as Hootsuite (www.hootsuite.com), can help people organize social media engagement and set up content in advance to be live at a specific time. Editorial calendars on social media content also can establish a steady stream of content for specific times. Setting up realistic time guidelines on responding to social media can help as well. Some agencies arrange for people on an alternate basis to be on call during specific weekends based on their schedules, particularly to contact during a crisis situation.

13.2 Blogs and the Blogosphere

Blogs (originating from **Web logs**) debuted in the 1990s, enabling anyone with Internet access to share their experiences like a personal diary, express their opinions, and report on stories the same way a journalist would cover topics from recipes to serious global issues. They are essentially websites that let bloggers post text, photos, and videos; add links to other websites; and have a dialogue with commentators.

Whether written by CEOs, employees, or third parties, blogs share points of view and also can spark a dialogue with constituents worldwide. Bloggers not only bypass the traditional "gatekeepers" of the editorial review process, they are competing with old-guard newsrooms. Bloggers also have turned into amateur journalists by being able to report on the scene of an incident, sharing their perspectives and fact-checking, and reporting a current event in real time. In the U.S., bloggers were instrumental in leading to the resignation of two mainstream news leaders. Dan Rather, a veteran news reporter and former anchor of a major U.S. network news program, was blamed for sloppy reporting and a liberal bias by bloggers during the 2004 U.S. presidential election. In a *Washington Post* article titled, "After blogs got hits, CBS got a black eye," Howard Kurtz (2004) wrote: "It was like throwing a match on kerosene-soaked wood. The ensuing blaze ripped through the media establishment as previously obscure bloggers managed to put the network of Murrow and Cronkite firmly on the defensive" (para. 4). Typography experts on the blogosphere quickly disputed the CBS television report, claiming that President George W. Bush failed to fulfill his National Guard obligation in the 1970s, based on inauthentic memos. The following year, Eason Jordan resigned as CNN's chief news executive after the blogosphere attacked his controversial comments about American journalists being killed by U.S. soldiers in Iraq (Kurtz, 2005).

For public relations professionals, blogs also can be a powerful way to engage with influential audiences and develop a dialogue as "electronic word-of-mouth." Stories and opinions can be shared without pitching traditional media outlets. People with unique perspectives and knowledge can gain attention as "thought leaders," attracting followers online. Blogs are inexpensive to maintain and provide customer research that can uncover trends and issues in real time. In addition, many mainstream media outlets now have blogs that enable more personalized reporting and in-depth coverage—and other opportunities for publicity too.

Setting up a blog is a relatively simple process. The challenge is time: keeping content fresh and posting frequently. The process entails the following steps:

- **Strategy**
  Figure out who you want to reach and define your goals. Do you want to develop a dialogue with current consumers, potential volunteers and donors of a nonprofit, trade association members, educators and administrators, or employees? Are you trying to educate, inform, entertain, or set up a forum to share ideas?
- **Theme and Content**
  Determine the theme of your blog and the type of content that would appeal to your readers. Look at content that you have a wealth of knowledge to draw from, as well as topics and news that you will be able to invest the time in following and researching. Blogs should express the author's personality and share opinions, insights, trends, and issues.
- **Solo or Multi-Authored**
  Decide if the blog will be solo- or multi-authored. Bloggers need to speak with a human voice, not sound like bureaucrats or company executives with blatant promotional messages.
  They need to be able to write about topics beyond the organization and share expertise about the industry at large or issues affecting their customers, employers, and community.
- **Guidelines**
  Set guidelines for blogging; this is essential if you have more than one author. IBM, an early adaptor of blogging and other social media, has made its social computing guidelines public. (See http://www.ibm.com/blogs/zz/en/guidelines.html.)
- **Name and Registration**
  Give your blog a name. You can register a unique domain name (the Internet address), which is a popular choice for most organizations. It is worth investing the time to come up with the best name—or names since many blog names have been taken— to express the personality of the blog and a name that would be easy for people to remember. The other choice is to use a hosted blog service, which would include the host service's name in the URL.

- **Blog Provider**
  Select a hosted blog provider or a stand-alone blog provider in which you have the domain name. Some hosted blogging platforms are free or the monthly fees are nominal. For example, **WordPress** (2015) hosts blogs in more than 120 languages, with 71% in English, and claims that 409 million people read more than 19 billion blog pages monthly. The basic service is free, yet it offers limited space and no video storage, and shows advertisements. You also would have to create a blog name ending with WordPress.com. Premium upgrades allow custom domains and provide video storage, advanced customization, and other features. **Tumblr** may be another platform to consider when the content is rich with dynamic imagery. Social marketer and blogger Jason Keath (2011) explained: "Photos, videos, quotes and questions are the currency in the Tumblr ecosystem" (para. 5). Fashion designers, art museums, publishing houses, and broadcast media are examples of industries that are prevalent on Tumblr.
- **Interactivity and Sharability**
  Use RSS feeds and incorporate other social media, such as Twitter, Facebook, and Pinterest, and make it easy to share content.
- **Schedule and Frequency**
  Start blogging and work out a frequent schedule, at least weekly. Look at other blogs and sources for inspiration. Line up guest bloggers with bylines.
- **Promotion**
  Publicize your blog and link with other social media on an ongoing basis. You can add your blog URL to your business card and email signature. Word of mouth is also powerful.
- **Monitoring Responses**
  Monitor commentary and respond quickly. Moderation settings allow you to approve comments before they are public on your blog. Track usage and make any adjustments to draw readers and spark dialogue. Consider developing your blog in other languages.

13.2.1 Best Practices in Blogging

Blogging for businesses or nonprofits anywhere should achieve the following qualities:

- **Transparency: Identify the Authors**
  The bloggers should be identified, as should the organization behind the blog, if that is the case. The multinational discount retail chain Walmart was criticized for hiding the identity of the bloggers, who were positioned as a couple in their new recreation vehicle who claimed to be writing about their positive experiences while parking at Walmart stores and engaging with the chain's cheerful staff in their blog titled "Walmarting Across America." Their rosy stories were prepared by a photographer and journalist paid on behalf of the retailer. Fake blogs are called **flogs**.
- **Authenticity: Avoid Promotional Hype**
  The voice should seem real and sincere, not just another way to repeat news release content and promote a company's products and services. The blog also should be written by a person who is identified as its author; public relations staff, however, can help provide story ideas and editing assistance. Create an authentic voice that reflects your perspective, while maintaining a personal and professional tone. The preferred voice is first person (*I*).

A good example is a blog by J. W. "Bill" Marriott, Jr., chairman of Marriott International, which is listed in a number of best blog rankings and articles for its authenticity. Apparently, Mr. Marriott, who was born in 1932, writes his own personal stories and industry perspectives in "Marriott on the Move."

In the public relations field, a popular CEO blog is authored by Richard Edelman, president and CEO of Edelman, an international public relations agency. You can read his blog on http://www.edelman.com/conversations/6-a-m/.

- **Timeliness: Keep Readers Updated**
  Blogs give you the opportunity to provide your readers with frequent and relevant updates and address current events as they are happening. The American Red Cross blog (see Figure 13.2) provides frequent updates on events in real time from different volunteers, and it seeks the engagement of socially wired Digital Disaster Volunteers. The blog also incorporates imagery, videos, and interactivity with other social media, including Twitter, Facebook, and Google+. The American Red Cross clearly states the goals of its official blog as follows:

  1. To inspire you to talk to each other and your networks about issues we care about.
  2. To offer you immediate actions you can take (online or offline) to help people prevent, prepare for, and respond to emergencies.
  3. To give you valuable information about preventing, preparing for, and responding to emergencies.
  4. To have a little fun and find areas of collaboration with you. (n.d., para. 2)

- **Relevance: Connecting the Organization**
  Although a hard-sell approach would be ineffective in a corporate blog, the content still should have relevance to the organization's mission. GE Global Research's blog, "Edison's Desk" (see Figure 13.3) explains its purpose on its landing page: "Curious about researchers' minds? Here, you'll find reflections on new discoveries, with random variation to keep things interesting." The content engages technology enthusiasts worldwide on topics related to multiple industries, thereby positioning General Electric's leadership as an innovator of diverse products and services.

- **Connectivity: Compelling Reasons to Comment**
  Blogs should give readers encouragement to post their own comments and give feedback to others, even when facing negativity. Devereux and Peirson-Smith (2009) recommend that successful bloggers should "stifle the instinct to please everyone. Blandness is a blogging death sentence" (p. 185). Their principle also overlaps with authenticity in being able to accept the fact that people may disagree with you. This approach has some merit, although some corporations may be less receptive to it. The appealing feature of "My Starbucks Idea" is that it serves as a forum for Starbucks' customers to openly share their ideas or comments about new products, store experiences, and community involvement suggestions in the U.S. and worldwide. Mark Schaefer (2011), a marketing consultant, educator, and blogger, said in his blog about Starbucks as one of the top 10 corporate blogs: "They are leading the way in social media marketing but the unexpected aspect of their blog is that it only tangentially has anything to do with coffee. Instead, Starbucks employs its blog as a global brainstorming platform" (para. 11). Although the design is simple and understated, the blog is easy to navigate. Visitors can view the most popular, most recent, and most commented on ideas. The "Ideas in Action" section includes posts

Figure 13.2—AMERICAN RED CROSS BLOG SCREENSHOT. Source: © American Red Cross.

Figure 13.3—EDISON'S DESK BLOG SCREENSHOT. Source: © GE Global Research.

Exercise 13.1

Insights: Blogs

Identify a blog—one that is created on behalf of a business, nonprofit, or government—that interests you. Look at the reasons why this blog appeals to you and answer the following questions:

1. Which blog did you select?
2. What is the theme of the blog?
3. Who is the author or is it multi-authored? What credentials do the authors have?
4. What type of content is covered in the blog—observations on a specific industry, current events, reviews on something, firsthand experiences, etc.?
5. Who is the blogger trying to reach? Which audiences and where?
6. What do you think of the writing style?
7. How frequent are the posts?
8. Do the posts encourage you to comment or share content with others?
9. Do you think this blog is sustainable?
10. What other observations do you have to share?

---

from Starbucks' staff who explain the status of the customers' suggestions, whether their ideas are being launched, coming up soon, or under review.

- **Localized: Different Content for Specific Geographic Markets**
  Lenovo, the Chinese multinational technology company, provides a choice of blogs by such topics as design and education, and by different geographic areas, including the U.S., U.K., and Australia/New Zealand. The content is presented as a digital magazine, with interviews, current news, and business tips from identified Lenovo staff and guest bloggers. The blog (http://blog.lenovo.com/) enables viewers to search topics easily and interact with other social media.

Take a moment and reflect on blogs you like to follow, and try Exercise 13.1 by selecting a blog hosted by a business or nonprofit and think about the reasons why this blog resonates with you.

13.3 Microblogs and the Twitterverse

Twitter, Chinese Weibo, and other **microblogs** offer quick ways to communicate. The largest microblog in English, **Twitter**, which was founded in 2006, allows a maximum of 140 characters. From a historical perspective, writing abbreviated copy is not new. You may not remember telexes or telegrams. Western Union sent its last message in 2006, yet iTelegram still exists (Tynan, 2010). The difference is the delivery system—and now anyone can read microblogs online if they are public.

In the public relations field, many online newsrooms integrate Twitter to communicate with journalists and use other Twitter accounts to connect with consumers or other audiences.

According to Twitter (2015), the microblog has more than 300 million monthly active users, sending 500 million tweets daily, with 77% of its accounts outside the U.S. Twitter also supports more than 30 languages. eMarketer (2014) estimates that Twitter's greatest growth area will be the Asia-Pacific region, leading with a projected 40.1% share of total users worldwide in 2018, with Twitter populations in India and Indonesia rising the most.

Fortune Magazine publishes its annual list of the 500 wealthiest American corporations and also studies their social media use. A 2014 study (Barnes & Lescault, 2014) revealed that 83% of the Fortune 500s have a Twitter account, with a tweet over the past 30 days, which is a 6% increase from the previous year. A number of other studies have attempted to capture the most effective techniques in communicating on Twitter:

- According to a report on Twitter by Salesforce Marketing Cloud (2012), the following best practices apply: weekends are most popular, but pay attention to patterns by industry; tweet between 7 a.m. and 8 p.m.; tweet no more than four times daily; add links for more retweets; include hashtags, but only one or two; add images; indicate to retweet; and write tweets under 100 characters.
- Dan Zarrella is a specialist and author on social media who has studied **clickthrough rates** (**CTRs**), which he calculated "as the number of clicks on a tweeted link divided by the number of followers the account had when it tweeted that link" (n.d., para. 2). Here are highlights of Zarrella's findings on tweets receiving higher CTRs: tweets between 120 and 130 characters; links located approximately one-quarter of the way through the tweet; weekends, particularly during the afternoon; more adverbs and verbs versus nouns and adjectives; and tweets with such words or symbols as via, @, RT, please, and check.

Twitter posts its "Top 100 Most Followers" (http://twittercounter.com/pages/100), where you can find out who has the greatest number of followers worldwide. It is not surprising that celebrities dominate the list followed by other social media sites and news companies. American singer and actress Katy Perry held the no. 1 position with more than 70 million followers in June 2015. American actress and TV personality Ellen DeGeneres broke the retweet records in 2014 when she hosted the 86th Academy Awards, widely known as the Oscars. Her selfie packed with A-list talent—Angelina Jolie, Jennifer Lawrence, Brad Pitt, Julia Roberts, Kevin Spacey, and Meryl Streep—generated 871,000 retweets in less than an hour, eclipsing the 777,000 retweets held by former record holder President Barack Obama, hugging his wife on election night. Actor Bradley Cooper snapped the Oscars' ceremony image, and DeGeneres wrote the caption: "If only Bradley's arm was longer. Best photo ever. #oscars" (Fisher, 2014, para. 2).

Twitter is not just a hub for voices of celebrities. Global public relations agency Burson-Marsteller conducted an annual global survey called *Twiplomacy*, investigating how world leaders and diplomats use Twitter. The executive summary states: "For many diplomats Twitter has become a powerful channel for digital diplomacy and 21st century statecraft and not all Twitter exchanges are diplomatic, real world differences are spilling over reflected on Twitter and sometimes end up in hashtag wars" (Lüfkens, 2014, p. 2). The numbers on the diplomatic Twitterverse are impressive: 83% of the 193 United Nations member countries are on Twitter, 68% of heads of state or governments have personal accounts, and more than 50% of the world's foreign ministers and their institutions are active on Twitter. World leaders collectively have sent more than 1.9 million tweets, averaging four daily tweets (as of June 25, 2014). While they communicate in 53 languages, English ranks as the lingua franca in total number of accounts and followers, yet the Spanish-language accounts are the most active with the greatest number of tweets, and French ranks third.

13.3.1 Taste and Judgment

Some of the most challenging content to share locally, regionally and, particularly, globally is wit. Humor on Twitter may not be easy to convey since it is so subjective and may not travel beyond an area's borders. I would like to share a few examples that show relevant humor and two that demonstrate poor taste and judgment.

Starting with a positive example, the Central Intelligence Agency in the U.S., which is better known as the CIA, debuted on Twitter with the handle @CIA in 2014 with a surprisingly witty tweet: "We can neither confirm nor deny that this is our first tweet."

This quintessential evasive non-answer is also called the "Glomar Response," named after the Glomar (contraction of global and marine) Explorer, a salvage vessel on a convert mission to find a sunken Soviet submarine with nuclear missiles in the 1970s. The CIA responded to media inquiries about the operation with the statement: "We can neither confirm nor deny the existence of the information requested but, hypothetically, if such data were to exist, the subject matter would be classified, and could not be disclosed" (as cited in Shin, 2014, para. 4). The Cold War is long gone, yet governments still use this ambiguous expression when responding to public or media inquiries about secretive undertakings.

The CIA Director John Brennan provided a rationale for engaging Twitter: "We have important insights to share, and we want to make sure that unclassified information about the Agency is more accessible to the American public that we serve, consistent with our national security mission" (Central Intelligence Agency, 2014, para. 2).

Two cautionary examples are from a corporation and an individual. As part of its social media campaign in South Africa, Durex set up a #DurexJokes hashtag to post and collect jokes. The theme was logical for a company that is one of the leading manufacturers of condoms. An executive in its Durex South Africa office tweeted: "Why did God give men penises? So that they'd have at least one way to shut women up." The company soon afterwards commented after receiving negative feedback: "Apologies go out to @FeministsSA, but also thanks. You reminded us that rape and violence against women is still a major concern in SA" (Copeland, 2011, para. 4). Durex also subsequently issued slightly better apologies, tweeting: "We're really sorry for causing offence today, not intentional. We believe in the rights of woman and safe sex. Thanks for putting us right." And later: "As a brand respected by millions, we wld like 2 take this opportunity 2 apologize 4 the jokes posted on our timeline yesterday" (Kelley, 2011, para. 9).

Public relations professionals also need to be mindful about their own tweets. A public relations executive from a well-known media company quickly became an ex-employee when she sent a racist tweet about AIDS in Africa that went viral around the world: "Going to Africa. Hope I don't get AIDS. Just kidding. I'm white!" Nsenga Burton (2013), a communications professor and digital expert, explained the magnitude of the comment's impact in which the executive "managed to do something that is really hard to do—insult a race of people, a nation and an entire continent simultaneously" (para. 1).

13.4 Social Networking and Photo and Video Sharing Sites

Organizations also can connect with people on a variety of **social networking** and **visual imagery sharing sites**. This section looks at some of the most popular English-language sites. Many organizations may have a presence on a few different sites, with each having different capabilities and audiences. Innovations abound and evolve, so it is important for public relations practitioners to keep abreast of enhancements and new developments, including additional language capabilities, as well as changes in user terms on such items as promotions and contests.

Every social networking site contains useful tips overall and specifically on business applications—with many explaining how to get started and providing case studies from different industries on how to communicate more effectively—to better understand what you can do to maximize your presence and engage with people. Exhibit 13.2 includes tips on visual and written content directly from social networking sites, industry studies, and other sources on communicating on specific platforms.

According to **Facebook** (2015) as of March 2015, this social networking site has approximately 1.44 billion monthly active users and 1.25 billion monthly mobile users, including an average of 936 million daily active users and 798 million mobile daily active users, of which 82.2% are based outside of North America. Facebook has capabilities in 70 languages (Statistics Brain Research Institute, 2015). In 2011, Google introduced its own social networking site, **Google+** (also called Google Plus), which has more than 300 million users as of March 2015, ranking as the ninth leading social network worldwide by number of active users, after Facebook, QQ, WhatsApp, QZone, Facebook Messenger, WeChat, LinkedIn, and Skype (Statista.com, 2015). The seventh largest social networking site is **LinkedIn**, which was officially launched in 2003 (Statista.com, 2015). LinkedIn states that it has more than 364 million registered members worldwide, including more than 100 million in the U.S. alone, in over 200 countries and territories, of which more than 67% reside outside the U.S. (LinkedIn, 2015; LinkedIn Corporate Communications Team, 2014). In addition, LinkedIn is available in 24 languages and has more than four million company pages—and can legitimately claim to be the Internet's largest professional network worldwide (LinkedIn, 2015).

Telling brand stories with visual imagery of all kinds has become easier with visual sharing sites. Cartoonist Jerry King shares a humorous approach on how not all images should be posted (see Figure 13.4). However, public relations executives need to invest time and care in selecting the best images to tell their stories on the most appropriate sites. Established in 2010 and acquired by Facebook in 2012, **Instagram** (2015) claims that it has more than 300 million Instagrammers, with 70% outside of the U.S., sharing more than 70 million photos and videos (3-to-15 seconds in length) from their mobile devices daily. With more than 70 million users, **Pinterest** has 40 million monthly active users of which 80% are female (Digital Insights, 2014), with content in English and 25 other languages. Launched in 2010, Pinterest enables users to upload, share, and manage images (pins) on pinboards. **Flickr**, which was established in 2004 and acquired by Yahoo in 2005, has 92 million users in 63 countries (Smith, 2015) and allows people and organizations to make photos available online.

Founded in 2005 and acquired by Google in 2006, **YouTube** claims to draw more than 1 billion users, with 300 hours of videos uploaded every minute. The impact of YouTube

Exhibit 13.2—TIPS ON VISUAL SHARING SOCIAL MEDIA SITES.

- A study by Curalate (2013a), an Internet marketing services company, examined more than a half-million images on **Pinterest** and 30 different visual characteristics to understand what type of content users pin, repin, and like. Highlights of the findings showed the following:

  - colorful images, particularly red, orange, and brown, are preferred over blue—and multicolored imagery has a likelihood to be repinned 3.25 more times than an image with one dominant color;
  - images of medium lightness are repinned 20 more times than an image primarily in black and eight times higher than predominately white images;
  - images with limited backgrounds, under 30%, are repinned the most; the more background the less likely to be repinned;
  - vertical (portrait) images are more popular than horizontal (landscape) images;
  - brand images without faces generate 23% more repins—and under one-fifth of images on Pinterest contain faces.

- According to Jess Loren and Edward Swiderski (2012), who co-authored a book on business uses of **Pinterest**, captions should be one or two sentences, while writing with a professional, positive, and respectful tone to connect with viewers. "Communicate your point without being too dry or predictable, but also avoid being over-the-top" (p. 192).
- **Pinterest** posts an online guide for businesses and recommends best visual images, such as vertical pins, and supporting text, emphasizing descriptions that provide timeless context and information to suggest what to do with the pin.
- Curalate (2013b) also examined visual imagery on **Instagram** and discovered that the following characteristics generated more likes: imagery with high lightness, more background space, a single dominant color, blue as the dominant color versus red, low-saturated colors, diverse textures, as well as duck-faced selfies.
- **Flickr**'s online advice on best practices for businesses reiterates that photo and video imagery should be "to share photos, not to sell things" (2015, para. 6)—this advice pertains to any business application on visual-sharing sites:

  Upload fresh, authentic material rather than product shots or staged, over-produced content that would be more at home in your product catalog or latest advertising campaign.

  Photos that show off your organization's culture and personality will help you build loyalty for your brand and tell your story. For example, sharing behind-the-scenes photos of your products being made or of customers engaging with your organization will show what you stand for and more importantly that you're interesting and human. It's not rocket science; the more unique, interesting content you share, the more interest you'll receive in return. (paras. 3 and 4)

Sources

Curalate. (2013a, June 6). New Curalate research reveals how different image characteristics drive social engagement: Study of a half a million photos points to psychology behind images and the actions they trigger [News release]. *BusinessWire*. Retrieved from http://www.businesswire.com/news/home/20130606005065/en/Curalate-Research-Reveals-Image-Characteristics-Drive-Social#.VK664ivF-So.

Curalate. (2013b). [Study] 6 image qualities which may drive more likes on Instagram. Retrieved from http://curalate.tumblr.com/post/68079619904/study-6-image-qualities-which-may-drive-more.

Flickr. (2015). Best practices for organizations using Flickr. Retrieved from https://www.flickr.com/bestpractices/

Loren, J., & Swiderski, E. (2012). *Pinterest for business: How to pin your company to the top of the hottest social media network*. Indianapolis, IN: Que Publishing.

Figure 13.4—CARTOONIST DEPICTS HOW CLICHÉD CONTENT ON INSTAGRAM CAN BE. Source: © Jerry King.

"Charlie, not every meal is an Instagram opportunity."

cannot be disputed—its global impact is enormous, with its content localized in 75 countries and in 61 languages. In addition, "60% of a creator's views comes from outside their home country" (YouTube, 2015).

YouTube can work effectively in public relations programs in multiple ways. Instead of hosting a formal press conference, spokespeople also can share their opinions directly on YouTube. When Domino's Pizza, a publicly held company with operations in more than 75 countries, faced a crisis situation after bored employees adulterated food in the kitchen of one of its restaurants in North Carolina and posted their pranks on YouTube, the chain decided to post its side of story by "fighting viral with viral." The president of Domino's USA issued a video statement that provided the public with an update on the isolated incident and emphasized the company's mission and passion for quality.

Video content also can include interviews with people on any topic of interest to an organization's stakeholders, as well as behind-the-scenes imagery, how-to examples, and comprehensive information. Footage can be posted on the company's website and newsroom and shared with others on social media and traditional media outlets.

The Twitter equivalent of video sharing is **Vine**, which was established in 2012 and acquired by Twitter the same year. Vine enables smartphone users to record and share brief, looping video clips lasting up to six seconds. With more than 40 million users (Twitter, 2015), Vine offers storytelling platforms for quick visual imagery, such as brief soundbites from someone; before-and-after imagery; and progressive scenes, usually within three scenes, such as stop-gap action. Timeliness also can be an important factor in Vine content. Honda created an amusing VACula, the "nemesis" of its HondaVAC, thereby bringing attention to its built-in vacuum cleaner during Halloween (see Figure 13.5 and 13.6). The American Red Cross also used Vine to raise awareness of its blood drives during Halloween (see Figure 13.7).

Figure 13.5—HONDA CELEBRATES HALLOWEEN ON VINE WITH VACULA; SCREENSHOT NO. 1. Source: Courtesy of American Honda Motor Company, Inc.

Figure 13.6—HONDA CELEBRATES HALLOWEEN ON VINE WITH VACULA; SCREENSHOT NO. 2. Source: Courtesy of American Honda Motor Company, Inc.

Figure 13.7—THE AMERICAN RED CROSS ALSO CELEBRATES HALLOWEEN ON VINE. Source: © American Red Cross.

Quit, a U.K.-based nonprofit dedicated to educating children about the dangers of smoking cigarettes, created a Vine channel (https://vine.co/QUIT) with 6-second videos that illustrate the health problems as part of its World No Tobacco Day May 31 campaign. Each video caption reads "Every 6 seconds, someone dies from smoking," along with a series of hashtags: #WorldNoTobaccoDay #smoking #fail #relatable #every6seconds. One video, for example, shows a young woman smoking with the caption, "Before this video starts again, another smoker will die," and the next frame reads, "Don't be one of them," and then adds the word "Quit." The videos were created pro bono by M&C Saatchi, Sydney. The channel has generated 100,000 likes and more than 68,000 revines (as of March 2015).

Complete Exercise 13.2 and identify a company, personality, or cause that you follow on a social networking site—and look at what draws you to this specific site.

13.5 Wikipedia

Wikipedia (see Figure 13.8) debuted on January 15, 2001 as a free, open-source Web-based multilingual encyclopedia, written collaboratively by a community of volunteers who can remain anonymous or use a pseudonym or real name. The name is a portmanteau of *wiki*, the Hawaiian word for *quick*, and *encyclopedia*. Wikipedia is available in more than 285 languages, with English the most extensive content of all Wikipedia languages, with more than 4.8 million English-language articles (Wikipedia, 2015a). The scope of Wikipedia is impressive: it draws 470 million unique visitors every month, ranking as the seventh most popular website in the world—after the top six in order, Google, Facebook, YouTube, Yahoo, Baidu, and Amazon (Alexa, 2015). Have you noticed how many times Wikipedia is the first or one of the top 10

Exercise 13.2

Insights: Organizational Social Networking Sites

Identify a social networking site by a business, celebrity, or nonprofit that you enjoy and visit regularly. Please answer the following questions.

- What is the name of the site?
- How did you discover this site? (word of mouth, ad, article, blog, etc.)
- How often do you visit it?
- How much time do you spend on it during an average visit?
- What are the appeals of this site? What makes you re-visit it?
- Have you added comments or shared content with others?
- What target market(s) is this site aiming to reach?
- Have you ever read, seen, or heard stories about this site in print or broadcast media, blogs, or microblogs? Can you recall which media outlets?
- How do you think this site will evolve over the next few years?

results for practically any Google search of a noun, phrase, or a well-known person or organization? From a public relations standpoint, Wikipedia can play an important role in sharing information about people, products, services, and organizations to a wide global audience in English, as well as translated content to reach other local markets.

The founder of Wikipedia, Jimmy Wales (Wikipedia Foundation, 2012), explains: "Wikipedia is something special. It is like a library or a public park. It is like a temple for

Figure 13.8—WIKIPEDIA WEBSITE. Source: © Ingvar Bjork/Shutterstock.com.

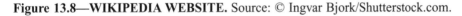

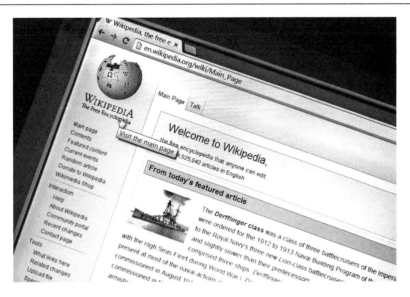

the mind. It is a place we can all go to think, to learn, to share our knowledge with others" (para. 4). Wikipedia is a nonprofit called the Wikimedia Foundation, which accepts donations, and does not allow advertising.

This website also does not accept content that sounds like hype or advertisements. Guidelines require that contributors cite from reputable sources—not just voice their opinions or unsubstantiated facts. Wikipedia has its own in-depth style manual, editing guidelines, and policies on etiquette and acceptable content. Its guidelines state: "Wikipedia has many policies and guidelines about encyclopedic content. These standards require verifiability, neutrality, respect for living people, and more" (Wikipedia, 2015b, para. 21). In essence, Wikipedia's policies and guidelines recommend clarity, conciseness, maintenance of scope, as well as avoidance of redundancy, overlinking, and contradictions.

Editorial administrators use software programs to help monitor content and handle disputes and abuses, following an editorial review board with specific focuses, such as the Neutrality Project and Cleanup Taskforce. New articles posted by anyone can be rejected, primarily for unverified facts and lack of citations.

Wikipedia also has conflict of interest policies about paid advocates, including public relations representatives. Some public relations agencies have pledged publicly to follow Wikipedia's rules. Terms of use require that paid contributors disclose their roles by applying at least one of the following statements (Wikipedia, 2015c):

- a statement on your user page,
- a statement on the talk page accompanying any paid contributions, or
- a statement in the edit summary accompanying any paid contributions. (para. 3)

How to Post Content on Wikipedia

Let us look at steps qualified writers can take to post content on Wikipedia:

- Search Wikipedia and see if there is any existing content about the topic.
- Look at Wikipedia content of existing relevant topics, paying attention to how information is worded and cited. Also refer to Wikipedia's style, editorial, and conflict of interest guidelines.
- Determine if you have opportunities to edit content on existing Wikipedia articles.
- Follow Wikipedia's procedures to register to create a new article, if necessary.
- Research references from credible sources—magazines, newspapers, TV and radio programs, journals, and books (not vanity publications). Wikipedia does not consider blogs, personal websites, social networking sites, and message boards reliable sources.
- Double-check accuracy of information and references, as well as Wikipedia policies, paying particular attention to notability guidelines used by its editors to determine if the topic deserves its own article.
- Post the article first on your own user space as a subpage.
- Review any commentary posted by Wikipedia editors. If your article is rejected, it will be deleted. You can ask for feedback and try to re-submit.
- Consider translating approved copy. Some editing may be required to provide more local context and references in other languages.
- Monitor pages on a regular basis to suggest any additions or editorial corrections for accuracy to new comments, as needed.

You probably have heard from your professors to not cite directly from Wikipedia in an academic report. Accuracy is an issue. Columnist and author Thomas Friedman (2007) also cautions that Wikipedia "is not all sweetness and light, and it does not always control itself" (p. 123):

> I like Wikipedia. I have used it in writing this book. But I use it with the knowledge that the community is not always right, the network doesn't always self-correct—certainly not as fast as its errors can get spread. It is not an accident that IBM today has a senior staffer who polices Wikipedia's references to IBM and makes sure that everything that gets in there is correct. More young people will learn about IBM from Wikipedia in coming years than from IBM itself. (p. 124)

13.6 Learning Objectives and Key Terms

After reading Chapter 13, you should be able to:

- Discuss the importance of using multiple online platforms in public relations writing to connect with audiences.
- Appreciate the evolving innovations in technological platforms and the need to stay current with new developments.
- List the considerations in using online platforms effectively from goals to guidelines for multiple authors.
- Characterize the differences in writing social media content from journalistic writing styles.
- Select names for websites and hashtags.
- Explain how to create dynamic written and visual content on multiple online platforms.
- Describe the term newsjacking and articulate some of the benefits and potential issues.
- Address best practices in developing content for blogs for business.
- Determine ways to communicate to the public and media on microblogs.
- Use social networking to share news and content and tell stories.
- Understand the value and range of supporting visual imagery options.
- Follow guidelines on posting content on Wikipedia.

This chapter covers the following key terms:

Two-way symmetrical dialogue (p. 333)	Hashtags (p. 335)
Viral (p. 336)	Newsjacking (p. 336)
Blogs (p. 338)	Flogs (p. 340)
Microblogs (p. 343)	Twitter (p. 343)
Click-through rates (p. 344)	Image and video sharing sites (p. 346)
Social networking sites (p. 346)	Wikipedia (p. 350)

Note

1   Answer to *Great Gatsby* quote in text abbreviations: "Whenever you feel like criticizing anyone, just remember that all the people in this world haven't had the advantages that you've had."

References

Alexa. (2015). The top 500 sites on the web. Retrieved from http://www.alexa.com/topsites.

American Red Cross Blog. (n.d.). About. Retrieved from http://redcrosschat.org/about/#sthash. AUVaSklT.dpbs.

Barnes, N. G., & Lescault, A. M. (2014). The 2014 Fortune 500 and social media: LinkedIn dominates as use of newer tools explodes. *University of Massachusetts Dartmouth.* Retrieved from http://www.umassd.edu/cmr/socialmediaresearch/2014fortune500and socialmedia/.

Berger, J. (2013). *Contagious: Why things catch on.* New York, NY: Simon & Schuster.

Brunswick Research. (2011). *Use of social media among business journalists.* Retrieved from http://www.brunswickgroup.com/publications/surveys/social-media-survey/.

Burton, N. (2013, December 27). Justine Sacco: AIDS is no laughing matter. *Huffington Post.* Retrieved from http://www.huffingtonpost.com/nsenga-burton/justine-sacco-aids-is-no-_b_4499428.html.

Central Intelligence Agency. (2014, June 6). CIA launches new social media accounts [Press release & statement]. Retrieved from https://www.cia.gov/news-information/press-releases-statements/2014-press-releases-statements/cia-launches-new-social-media-accounts.html.

Copeland, D. (2011, November 28). Durex ribs on Twitter in South Africa—but not for her pleasure. *The Daily Dot.* Retrieved from http://www.dailydot.com/news/durex-condom-twitter-controversy/.

Devereux, M. M., & Peirson-Smith, A. (2009). *Public relations in Asia Pacific: Communicating effectively across cultures.* Singapore: John Wiley & Sons.

Digital Insights. (2014). Social Media 2014 Statistics—an interactive Infographic you've been waiting for! Retrieved from http://blog.digitalinsights.in/social-media-users-2014-stats-numbers/05205287.html.

eMarketer. (2014, May 27). *Emerging markets drive Twitter user growth worldwide: More than 40% of Twitter users worldwide will be in Asia-Pacific by 2018.* Retrieved from http://www.emarketer.com/Article/Emerging-Markets-Drive-Twitter-User-Growth-World wide/1010874.

Facebook. (2015). Company information. Retrieved from http://newsroom.fb.com/company-info/.

Fisher, L. (2014, March 2). Ellen's Oscar selfie most retweeted tweet ever. *ABC News* [Blog]. Retrieved from http://abcnews.go.com/blogs/entertainment/2014/03/ellens-oscar-selfie-most-retweeted-tweet-ever/.

Friedman, T. L. (2007). *The world is flat: A brief history of the twenty-first century* (3rd ed.). New York, NY: Picador.

Geldman, A. (2010). *Slurls: They called their website what?! The world's worst Internet URLs from effoff.com to penisland.net.* London: Angel Internet Press.

Grunig, J. E. (2009). Paradigms of global public relations in an age of digitalisation. *PRism, 6*(2). Retrieved from http://www.prismjournal.org/fileadmin/Praxis/Files/globalPR/GRUNIG. pdf.

Internet Live Stats (2015). Internet usage & social media statistics. Retrieved from http://www.internetlivestats.com/.

Instagram. (2015). Stats. Retrieved from http://instagram.com/press/.

Keath, J. (2011, April 1). 60 brands using Tumblr. *Socialfresh.com*. Retrieved from http://social fresh.com/60-brands-using-tumblr/.

Kelley, L. (2011, November 28). Durex Condoms' unfunny Twitter "joke": God created penises to shut women up? *AlterNet*. Retrieved from http://www.alternet.org/newsand views/article/740447/durex_condoms'_unfunny_twitter_%22joke%22%3A_god_created_ penises_to_shut_women_up.

Kurtz, H. (2004, September 20). After blogs got hits, CBS got a black eye. *Washington Post*, p. C01.

Kurtz, H. (2005, February 12). CNN's Jordan resigns over Iraq remarks: News chief apologized for comment on troops. *Washington Post*, p. A01.

LinkedIn. (2015). About LinkedIn. Retrieved from https://press.linkedin.com/about-linkedin.

LinkedIn Corporate Communciations Team. (2014, April 18). LinkedIn reaches 300 million members worldwide [Online newsroom]. Retrieved from https://press.linkedin.com/site-resources/news-releases/2014/linkedin-reaches-300-million-members-worldwide.

Lüfkens, M. (2014, July). Twiplomacy: Heads of state and government and foreign ministers on Twitter. *Burson-Marsteller*. Retrieved from http://twiplomacy.com/blog/twiplomacy-study-2014/.

Miltenberg, B. (2012, August 2). PR News hotlist: Top 10 PR blunders of 2012, part 1. *PR News*. Retrieved from http://www.prnewsonline.com/water-cooler/2012/08/02/pr-news-hotlist-top-10-pr-blunders-of-2012-part-1/.

O'Toole, G. (2012, April 28). If I had more time, I would have written a shorter letter: Blaise Pascal? John Locke? Benjamin Franklin? Henry David Thoreau? Cicero? Woodrow Wilson? *Quote Investigator*. Retrieved from http://quoteinvestigator.com/2012/04/28/ shorter-letter/.

Salesforce Marketing Cloud. (2012). Strategies for effective tweeting: A statistical review. Retrieved from https://www.salesforcemarketingcloud.com/wp-content/uploads/2013/03/ Strategies-for-effective-tweeting.pdf.

Sanders, R. (2013, February 3). How Oreo got that Twitter ad up so fast. *BuzzFeed*. Retrieved from http://www.buzzfeed.com/rachelysanders/how-oreo-got-that-twitter-ad-up-so-fast#. lnJo56917.

Schaefer, M. (2011, January 5). The 10 best company blogs in the world. *(Grow) blog*. Retrieved from http://www.businessesgrow.com/2011/01/05/the-10-best-corporate-blogs-in-the-world/#disqus_thread.

Scott, D. M. (2013). *The new rules of marketing & PR: How to use social media, online video, mobile applications, blogs, news releases & viral marketing to reach buyers directly* (4th ed.). Hoboken, NJ: John Wiley & Sons.

Shin, H. B. (2014, June 6). The CIA's secret history of the phrase "can neither confirm nor deny." *ABC News*. Retrieved from http://abcnews.go.com/US/cias-secret-history-phrase-confirm-deny/story?id=24033629.

Smith, C. (2015, May 23). By the numbers, 14 interesting flickr stats. *DMR-Digital Marketing Ramblings*. Retrieved from http://expandedramblings.com/index.php/flickr-stats/.

Statista.com. (2015). Leading social networks worldwide as of March 2015, ranked by number of active users (in millions). Retrieved from http://www.statista.com/statistics/272014/ global-social-networks-ranked-by-number-of-users/.

Statistics Brain Research Institute. (2015). Facebook statistics. *Statisticsbrain.com*. Retrieved from http://www.statisticbrain.com/facebook-statistics/.

Sweet, K. (2011, February 14). Kenneth Cole Egypt tweets ignite firestorm. *CNN.com*. Retrieved from http://money.cnn.com/2011/02/03/news/companies/KennethCole_twitter/.

Twitter. (2015). About. Retrieved from https://about.twitter.com/company.

Tynan, D. (2010, July 4). 10 technologies that should be extinct (but aren't). *PCWorld*. Retrieved from http://www.pcworld.com/article/200325/10_technologies_that_should_be_extinct.html.

Wainwright, M. (2005, November 17). If you don't want to know how Bleak House ends, look away now. *Guardian*. Retrieved from http://www.theguardian.com/technology/2005/nov/17/news.mobilephones.

Wikipedia. (2015a, January 11). About. Retrieved from https://en.wikipedia.org/wiki/Wikipedia:About.

Wikipedia. (2015b, January 15). Wikipedia: Policies and guidelines. Retrieved from http://en.wikipedia.org/wiki/Wikipedia:Policies_and_guidelines.

Wikipedia. (2015c, September 6). Wikipedia: paid-contribution disclosure. Retrieved from https://en.wikipedia.org/wiki/Wikipedia:paid-contribution_disclosure.

Wikipedia Foundation. (2012). From Wikipedia founder Jimmy Wales. Retrieved from http://wikimediafoundation.org/wiki/WMFJA085/en/US.

WordPress. (2015). A live look at activity across WordPress.com. Retrieved from https://wordpress.com/activity/.

YouTube. (2015). Statistics. Retrieved from https://www.youtube.com/yt/press/en-GB/statistics.html.

Zarrella, D. (n.d.). How to get more clicks on Twitter [Infographic]. *Danzarrella.com*. Retrieved from http://danzarrella.com/infographic-how-to-get-more-clicks-on-twitter.html.

Zinsser, W. K. (2001). *On writing well: The classic guide to writing nonfiction*. New York, NY: HarperCollins.

14 Shaping Speeches and Scripts

Tell me a fact and I'll learn. Tell me a truth
and I'll believe. But tell me a story and it
will live in my heart forever.

—Native American Proverb

14.1 Introduction to Writing for the Ear

Storytelling skills are particularly significant when writing for the ear, whether you are preparing a speech or copy for an audio or video clip. Copy in print or in a digital format allows one to go back over and re-read sections. When writing for the ear, you do not have that luxury, so you have to get it right the first time. A number of techniques can help writers convey information for the ear, whether they are writing speeches or scripts for podcasts, video news releases, or public service announcements.

Let us start with **speaking rates**. According to Toastmasters International (2011), the desirable speaking rate is between 120 and 160 words per minute. Auctioneers and actors, particularly those who recite the disclaimers on pharmaceutical television advertisements, probably talk the fastest. The speed can vary by geographic area and proficiency in the language. Long-time residents in New York City, in general, are notorious for speaking quickly. I have heard non-native English speakers talk too slowly or too rapidly, if they are nervous.

Engaging the audience is essential. The reality is that many speakers addressing international audiences are usually traveling to another country and crossing multiple time zones—and people in the audience may be jet-lagged too. You do not want to see your audience nodding off or even snoring loudly.

Consider the following tips when writing for the ear, which I have organized in alphabetical order by topic:

- **Acronyms**—Avoid acronyms that the audience may not understand. In this case, use the full name of the organization.
  Centers for Disease Control instead of the *CDC*.
- **Active vs. Passive Voice**—Using the active voice is easier to hear.
  We know that . . . instead of *It has come to our attention that . . .*

- **Contractions**—Use common contractions, such as *don't* or *can't*. However, avoid using too many contractions with an international audience. *I'll*, for example, may be misheard.
- **Conversational Tone**—Avoid using bureaucratic-sounding language. George Orwell's translation of Ecclesiastes 9:11 from the Bible into bureaucratic English is a classic example.

  Try reading the following paragraph aloud to someone, and see how well they understand the content:

  > Objective considerations of contemporary phenomena compel the conclusion that success or failure in competitive activities exhibits no tendency to be commensurate with innate capacity, but that a considerable element of the unpredictable must invariably be taken into account. (Orwell, 1946, para. 17)

  A speech sounding like this would lose the audience instantly. Always read your speeches aloud, preferably to someone else, before you test them on a live audience.

  Try reading this excerpt aloud titled "How schools kill creativity" delivered by Sir Ken Robinson (2006), an author and educator, at a TED conference.

  > I heard a great story recently—I love telling it—of a little girl who was in a drawing lesson. She was six and she was at the back, drawing, and the teacher said this little girl hardly ever paid attention, and in this drawing lesson, she did. The teacher was fascinated. She went over to her and she said, "What are you drawing?" And the girl said, "I'm drawing a picture of God." And the teacher said, "But nobody knows what God looks like." And the girl said, "They will in a minute." (2006, 3:30–4:06)

  You must have noticed a huge difference between the two examples. The second excerpt uses the first person and simple language—and encourages you to pay attention to the story about the child. Sir Ken's speech has drawn more than 33 million views on TED Talks (https://www.ted.com/talks), which is a website worth spending time on to listen to how experts from around the world share their knowledge in under 18 minutes. Speeches can be sorted by topics, languages, duration, most recent or viewed, and other qualities.
- **Localize**—Localize content for your audience. Marvin Sissey (2012), CEO, *Business Insider Africa*, shares good advice about localizing content:

  > Choose your analogies and metaphors carefully. Sports are a fertile ground for analogies. Try to know which sport applies where and how to use them. Cricket is big in India. Rugby is adored in South Africa. Football is loved in Nigeria. Learn whatever tickles their fancy. Use it accordingly. (paras. 25–26)

- **Nouns vs. Pronouns**—Use nouns more often than third-person pronouns. The listener may not know who the pronouns—particularly *it*, *he*, *she*, or *they*—are referring to. However, speakers should use first person (*I* or *we*) and second person (*you* or *your*) frequently.
- **Numbers**—Rounded-up numbers are easier to understand.
  Nearly one million. . . instead of *nine hundred and fifty-six thousand. . .*
  Also when writing speeches, it is easier to read numbers that are written out—and also spell out currency figures.
  Three million dollars is easier to read aloud than *$3 million.*

- **Positive Words**—Be careful of using negative words. *I would not be unsatisfied*. If someone is not listening carefully, it could be misinterpreted as *I am unsatisfied*.
  I am content instead of *I would not be discontent*.
- **Pronounciation Cues**—Adding phonetics to words you are concerned about mispronouncing can be helpful. These cues are particularly important for names of people, places, or organizations—or any words the speaker may struggle with. This technique can be particularly useful for people who may be less comfortable speaking in English. These cues should be deleted in a written version that may be shared with others.
- **Prompts**—Other cues can indicate body language, speaking emphasis, and usage of props. These notes also should be deleted in any shared versions of the speech.
- **Simpler Words**—Avoid complex multisyllabic words—without sounding like a children's book. The exception would be for words commonly used in a specific industry, such as a speech for a medical convention or for an academic audience.
- **Titles**—Put titles before names when talking about a person since the listener will not see the punctuation.
  Vice President of Marketing Jane Doe versus *Jane Doe, vice president of marketing.*

14.2 Speeches for Glocal and Global Audiences

According to most studies, people's number one fear is public speaking. Number two is death. Death is number two. Does that sound right? This means to the average person, if you go to a funeral, you're better off in the casket than doing the eulogy. (Jerry Seinfeld, an American comedian, actor, writer and TV producer)

You can easily search the Internet and find many articles on the fear of public speaking—I just did a Google search on this topic that yielded more than 27 million results in 45 seconds. Although many public relations executives may be more proficient in public speaking than people in other professions, their clients may have anxiety about speaking. Public relations practitioners not only need to write their own speeches, they also craft speeches for personalities, corporate executives, nonprofit directors, or government officials who may not be comfortable up at the podium. And nervousness can be magnified when speakers present outside their native tongue—and even native speakers may experience more jitters when they address multicultural audiences, inside or outside of their own country.

Speechwriting is an important skill in public relations and one that requires application of multicultural insight to deliver effectively. This particularly applies when writing for speakers, whether English is their first, second, or sixth language, who may be addressing diverse audiences locally or abroad. Many occasions warrant speeches: press conferences and receptions, employee events, panel discussions, conference presentations, celebratory occasions, eulogies, commencements and convocations, farewells and resignations, and award acceptances, among others. The experience can be quite exhilarating when the audience applauds enthusiastically (see Figure 14.1).

14.2.1 The Preparation Process

Whether you are writing a speech for yourself or someone else, the best place to start preparing a speech is to collect information and to answer the following questions about the occasion

Figure 14.1—RECEIVING ENTHUSIASTIC APPLAUSE AFTER YOU SPEAK CAN BE REWARDING. Source: © Volt Collection/Shutterstock.com.

and purpose of the speech, the style and skill level of the speaker, the audience, the setup and equipment, and the format and timing of the event:

1. **The Purpose**

   – What is the occasion?
   – What is the goal of the speaker's presentation? Is it to entertain, generate enthusiasm, share insight, provide advice, or persuade people to do something?
   – What are the key messages the speaker wants to convey?
   – Will the speaker make some remarks in another language or languages? Will the same presentation be used at another time in another language?
   – Will the speaker require an interpreter?
   – Does the speaker intend to post the speech online, share it on social media, or publicize it to the media? Will it be edited for YouTube and Vine for quick soundbites?
   – Will the speech be translated afterwards?

2. **The Speaker**
   If you are writing the speech for yourself, you will have to conduct an honest assessment about your experience, strengths, and weaknesses. If you are preparing the speech for someone else, you will need to find out more about the speaker.

- What is the speaker's experience in presenting speeches—and for which occasions and what types of audiences?
- How comfortable is the speaker presenting overall?
- Has the speaker ever had presentations recorded? If you are writing for someone else, you should ask to see or hear these recordings. You also can ask for transcripts of the speeches.
- Has the speaker presented in English before? What is the speaker's native language? What languages does the speaker know—and what levels of fluency?
- What is the speaker's delivery style?
- How familiar or comfortable is the speaker with the topics to be addressed?
- What is the speaker's relationship with the audience? Has the speaker addressed this group before? How well does the speaker know the audience or some of the audience members?
- Will the speaker be able to rehearse? This step is highly advisable.
- Will the speaker be able to see the venue and setup before the presentation? Again, this preview can increase the speaker's comfort level.
- Will the speaker be traveling to give this speech? How many time zones? It is advisable that a speaker traveling by air should arrive the day before, if not earlier. Weather conditions and other air travel delays can make a trip on the same day risky. If that is the case, the speaker should arrange for a substitute speaker as a backup.

Figure 14.2—KNOWING THE SETUP OF WHERE YOU WILL BE SPEAKING IS ESSENTIAL. Source: © Elena11/Shutterstock.com.

3. The Audience

–   What is the motivation of the audience to participate? Is their participation voluntary or mandatory? Did they pay to participate?
–   How receptive or interested in the topics are the audience members?
–   What is their educational level? Professions? Other demographics?
–   Is English their first language? If not, what is their proficiency in English? What languages do they speak?
–   Will the entire audience be present in person? If not, how will other participants be involved? Some events are hybrid formats, with some people participating by videoconferencing or teleconferencing or other virtual formats.
–   Will the audience receive any materials in advance or during the presentation?

4. The Physical Setup and Equipment

–   What type of venue is being used?
–   Where will the speaker present from? Will the setup have a podium? Microphone? Teleprompter?
–   What is the room layout? Will the audience be seated or standing? Will the audience be eating during the speech?
–   Will a supporting presentation, such as PowerPoint, need to be set up? What other props could be used? Figure 14.2 shows a setup in which the speaker could potentially be overshadowed by the large screen.
–   Will video monitors be set up for people to view the speech (a format used in a larger room)?
–   What other activities (or distractions) are there?
–   What other audiovisual or interactive capabilities are available? Will there be a TweetDeck or other interactive social media engagement during the presentation? If so, make sure that someone is dedicated to monitoring the social media and keeping the conversation on track.
–   Will the event be videotaped or streamed live?
–   Will microphones be available in the room for audience members to ask questions?

5. The Event Format and Timing

–   When will the speech take place?
–   How much time will the speaker have?
–   Who will introduce the speaker? Will there be a master of ceremonies to make
–   introductions?
–   Who else will be speaking and in what order? What are their topics?
–   Is there a question-and-answer session afterwards—or will the audience be able to ask questions throughout the presentation?

14.2.2 Structural and Presentation Considerations

One of the simplest structures is the **1-3-1 approach** (Kerrigan, 2014): one key point that should be introduced during the opening of your speech; three supporting themes, each with a clear rationale that can be explained with interesting facts and brief stories; and one conclusion where you can reiterate your key point and provide a relevant wrap-up, whether you are trying to encourage people to vote for your candidate, donate money or volunteer for a nonprofit, or think about things differently in the future. You should be able to answer these questions:

- What are your key points?
- What supporting themes do you have to back up your key points?
- What facts can you find and from what sources?
- Will you need to interview others to develop more supporting details?
- What stories can you draw upon, whether from firsthand experience or culled from someone else's?
- What message do you want to conclude with?
- What do you want the audience to do or consider? Is there a plea for action?

For an actual real-world presentation, you could add **visual displays** to illustrate key points or include imagery. You also can use other simple **props**. Consider using relevant props, which can be visual or even audio. I once had introduced an award winner at an industry trade event and provided background on the sponsor of the award who had passed away a few decades earlier. I found out interesting trivia about him by interviewing one of his closest friends. He shared with me a fun fact that the sponsor frequently whistled a tune called the "Colonel Bogey March" made famous by the film *The Bridge on the River Kwai*. I had mentioned this detail during the speech and, to my surprise, a few people in the audience starting whistling the tune and almost everyone in the room joined in.

When Bill Gates, co-founder of Microsoft and a leading philanthropist, spoke about the importance of malaria prevention at the Technology, Entertainment and Design conference, TED2009, he opened up a jar of mosquitos on stage to dramatize his point that not only the poor should be at risk from the disease. This conference attracts an affluent and elite crowd of influentials in multiple industries. Although Gates quickly assured the audience that the mosquitos were not carrying malaria, the stunt backfired with negative commentary in mainstream and social media. The curator and host of the conference, Chris Anderson, reportedly quipped that the title of the video clip of Gates's speech on the conference's website should read "Gates releases more bugs into the world" (Musil, 2009, para. 4). The actual video clip on www.TED.com was titled "Bill Gates: Mosquitos, malaria and education."

14.2.3 Benefits of Learning from the Masters

Watch video clips, listen to audio clips, or read transcripts of speeches that you admire, whether they are past or present. Examine the purpose of the speech and the audience—and how the speaker resonated with the audience. Let us take a look at excerpts of a few English-language speeches.

Speaker: Reverend Martin Luther King, Jr.
Speech Theme: "I have a dream" speech
Occasion: U.S. civil rights movement march
Date/Location: August 28, 1963 at the Lincoln Memorial, Washington, D.C., USA (see Figure 14.3 of the Lincoln Memorial plaque that commemorates the location where the "I Have a Dream" speech was delivered)
Audience: Estimated 250,000 participants in the march; speech broadcast live on network television and radio, reaching millions

Word count: The entire speech is approximately 1,652 words; this excerpt is 144 words.

I have a dream that one day this nation will rise up, live out the true meaning of its creed: "We hold these truths to be self-evident that all men are created equal."

I have a dream that one day on the red hills of Georgia, the sons of former slaves and the sons of former slave-owners will be able to sit down together at the table of brotherhood. I have a dream that one day even the state of Mississippi, a state sweltering with the heat of injustice, sweltering with the heat of oppression, will be transformed into an oasis of freedom and justice.

I have a dream that my four little children will one day live in a nation where they will not be judged by the color of their skin but by the content of their character. I have a dream . . . (King, 1963, pp. 4–5)

Figure 14.3—SPOT WHERE "I HAVE A DREAM" SPEECH WAS DELIVERED BY AMERICAN CIVIL RIGHTS ACTIVIST MARTIN LUTHER KING, JR. ON AUGUST 28, 1963, FROM THE STEPS OF THE LINCOLN MEMORIAL IN WASHINGTON, D.C. Source: © njene/Shutterstock.com.

What do you notice about this speech? The words were powerful, carefully chosen, and he used a rhetorical technique, **anaphora**, by repeating words effectively.

Speaker: J. K. Rowling, English author (shown at another event in Figure 14.4)
Speech Theme: The Fringe Benefits of Failure, and the Importance of Imagination
Occasion: Honorary degree acceptance speech/commencement speech, Harvard University, Cambridge, Massachusetts
Audience: Harvard University administration, faculty, staff, students, and parents and friends of students
Date: June 5, 2008
Word Count: 2,824 words; the following excerpt contains 231 words:

So why do I talk about the benefits of failure? Simply because failure meant a stripping away of the inessential. I stopped pretending to myself that I was anything other than what I was, and began to direct all my energy into finishing the only work that mattered to me. Had I really succeeded at anything else, I might never have found the determination to succeed in the one arena I believed I truly belonged. I was set free, because my greatest fear had been realised, and

Figure 14.4—AUTHOR J. K. ROWLING AT THE PRESS CONFERENCE FOR AN EVENING WITH HARRY, CARRIE AND GARP AUTHOR BOOK READINGS TO BENEFIT DOCTORS WITHOUT BORDERS, RADIO CITY MUSIC HALL, NEW YORK, IN 2006. Editorial Source: © Everett Collection/Shutterstock.com.

I was still alive, and I still had a daughter whom I adored, and I had an old typewriter and a big idea. And so rock bottom became the solid foundation on which I rebuilt my life.

You might never fail on the scale I did, but some failure in life is inevitable. It is impossible to live without failing at something, unless you live so cautiously that you might as well not have lived at all—in which case, you fail by default.

Failure gave me an inner security that I had never attained by passing examinations. Failure taught me things about myself that I could have learned no other way. I discovered that I had a strong will, and more discipline than I had suspected; I also found out that I had friends whose value was truly above the price of rubies. ("Fringe benefits of failure, and the importance of imagination," 2008, paras. 19–21)

Rowling's speech was structured around two themes, as noted in its title, in which she shared two lessons in life based on her experiences: failure, with an unusual twist on its positive sides; and imagination, which surprisingly did not focus on her bestselling books, but reflected instead on her experience as a researcher at Amnesty International.

Speaker: Steve Jobs, co-founder of Apple

Speech Theme: "You've got to find what you love"

Figure 14.5—CLOSE-UP OF AN APPLE iMAC COMPUTER DISPLAYING THE WWW.APPLE.COM FRONT PAGE TRIBUTE TO FORMER CHIEF EXECUTIVE STEVE JOBS, WHO DIED ON OCTOBER 5, 2011. Source: © antb/Shutterstock.com.

Occasion: Commencement speech at Stanford University
Audience: Stanford University students, faculty and administration, as well as parents and friends of new graduates, many from multicultural and international backgrounds
Date/Location: June 12, 2005/Stanford University, Stanford, California
Word Count: 2,246 words; excerpt contains 168 words

No one wants to die. Even people who want to go to heaven don't want to die to get there. And yet death is the destination we all share. No one has ever escaped it. And that is as it should be, because Death is very likely the single best invention of Life. It is Life's change agent. It clears out the old to make way for the new. Right now the new is you, but someday not too long from now, you will gradually become the old and be cleared away. Sorry to be so dramatic, but it is quite true.

Your time is limited, so don't waste it living someone else's life. Don't be trapped by dogma—which is living with the results of other people's thinking. Don't let the noise of others' opinions drown out your own inner voice. And most important, have the courage to follow your heart and intuition. They somehow already know what you truly want to become. Everything else is secondary. ("'You've got to find what you love,' Jobs says," 2005, paras. 22–23)

This speech used personal stories and learning experiences in three phases: connecting the dots, telling the story of his birth, adoption, and college experience; second story on love and loss about starting up Apple and later getting fired from the company he co-founded; and the third phase was about death, in which he shared his experiences coping with cancer and mortality, as noted in the excerpt. Steve Jobs died in 2011 (see Apple's tribute in Figure 14.5).

Many political figures have delivered moving speeches that you can find online or on a library database. Read or listen to any available video clips of the speeches from Winston Churchill, Charles DeGaulle, Mahatma Gandhi, John Fitzgerald Kennedy, Golda Meir, Nelson Mandela, and Jawaharlal Nehru. Also consider reading speeches delivered by Demosthenes, Isocrates, and other Ancient Greek orators.

14.3 The Art of Making Short Introductions

Many public relations practitioners introduce speakers or write speeches for other people making introductions at events for employees, consumers, business partners, and other stakeholders. Introductions set the stage before the main speaker begins. Your goal is to get the audience excited about hearing from the speaker, not to reiterate his or her résumé. Look at the Nobel award ceremony presentation speeches for the Nobel prizes in physics, chemistry, medicine, literature, peace, and economic sciences. When you log on www.nobelprize.org, you can chose from a list of Nobel prizes and laureates past and present by category of award, organizations, women awardees, age, and country of birth. Some also include video clips that you can watch. These examples show core principles in how to share background information on people. As you will see, their résumés are not repeated; instead, their accomplishments are highlighted with enough background for anyone to understand their contributions in these categories. After the presentation speeches at the ceremony in Oslo, the Nobel Laureates receive their diplomas and medals from His Majesty the King of Sweden.

Organize the speech in three parts:

- **The opening** captures the audience's attention and makes a connection on the importance of the speaker and the topic. You can use a personal story or anecdote, share a relevant quotation or statistic, oppose a popular opinion, tell a humorous yet tasteful story, ask a thought-provoking question, or arouse curiosity. The style will depend on the audience's relationship with the speaker. Do they know the speaker personally or is the audience aware of his or her accomplishments?

- **The body** highlights the speaker's credentials and relevance to the audience. You want the audience to like and respect the speaker. Instead of reciting a résumé, you can bring the speaker's experiences alive and share outstanding achievements and interesting and significant information. You can share your experiences with the speaker as well. If you have no prior experience with the speaker, you may want to interview someone who knows the speaker well. You also can talk to the person you will be introducing by phone or in person (or by email) to find out more interesting details. Your goal is to get the members of the audience excited about the benefits the speaker offers them.

- The **conclusion** provides a summary, makes the speaker feel welcomed, and the audience feel enthusiastic. It also leads to applause (see Figure 14.6) as the speaker walks up to the stage, podium, or front of the room. You also can give the upcoming speaker's presentation a title. You can establish whether or not the speaker will be able to take questions during the presentation or hold a question-or-answer session at the end of his or her speech.

Beyond the actual words of the speech, the delivery comes into play. **Paralanguage** (also called **paralinguistics**) refers to the nonverbal parts of a speech. Nuances of voice apply to

Figure 14.6—CONNECTING WITH YOUR AUDIENCE IS ESSENTIAL. Source: © Rawpixel/Shutterstock.com.

the volume, pace, pitch, and emotional range, as well as any gasps and silent breaks, in the delivery of speech. Body language covers the use of space by the speaker, as well as facial and hand gestures, posture, and eye contact with the audience. And when presenting to an international audience, speakers should be mindful that that "pitch, stress, volume, and speed with which language is spoken, lends itself readily to misinterpretation cross-culturally" (Bennett, 1998, p. 11).

Having a speech, preferably a rehearsal, videotaped can be an effective training tool, particularly for a new or less seasoned speaker. By watching the footage, preferably with another person, you may be able to identify any nervous gestures and areas for improvement.

14.4 Video Applications in Public Relations

Public relations practitioners can produce original video content to support their campaigns. Footage can support media relations activities, particularly for television and online newsroom resources, as well as business-to-consumer and business-to-business relations on multiple platforms.

Video can simply show what something looks like, but it also can capture many experiences of a brand, a product, a service, a place, or a person, such as the following:

- **Behind-the-scenes** imagery can show how something is made or created—an artist in her studio at work, a wine maker crafting the latest vintages, or a manufacturer showing how the factory operates.
- **How-to videos** on any topic can share tips or provide step-by-step instructions—how to tie a scarf, how to set a table for a formal party, how to paint a wall, how to do a simple car repair, how to use a digital single lens reflex camera, or how to do almost anything.
- **Highlights of events** can capture the most exciting scenes and incorporate soundbites from participants at trade shows, product demonstrations, fundraisers, awards ceremonies, or any kind of public or private event.
- **New product or service launches** can be supported with video that shows different dimensions, such as product choices and demonstrations, as well as explain how the product was developed and incorporate interviews with the creators and other spokespeople.
- **Commentary** provides a personal touch with soundbites from company spokespeople, celebrities, experts, customers, or others who can share meaningful content. They can address facts and provide resources, offer congratulations and support to someone or something, comment on current events, provide testimonials, give advice on specific topics, answer frequently asked questions, or tell inspirational stories.

Before creating the video ideas and scripts, you need to be able to answer the following questions:

- **Goals**—How would the video support your public relations campaign objectives? How will it help to enhance your brand and share your story to the public and journalists?
- **Audiences**—Who are your target audiences? Are they internal or external? Are they the general public, a specific group, the media, or all of them? Where do they live? Will you need to translate the content for other markets by adding subtitles or will

you produce different language-editions for specific geographical areas? How much of the footage will you have to edit or reshoot for local editions?

- **Accessibility**—Where do you think your target audiences would find and view the footage—the organization's website, social media, vodcasts, traditional media, or blog and microblog links?

- **Messages and Imagery**—What messages do you want to convey? What imagery do you want to capture? Do you have any existing footage, whether new or archived, that could be used? Where will you find new footage?

- **Storytellers**—Who would tell the story on camera or narrate the script? You may need to hire a seasoned actor to be the narrator and read from your script. Writers should provide questions to address and suggested soundbites for on-air interviews by spokespeople. Interview segments seem more convincing when the person is not reading from a script or a teleprompter.

- **Usages**—How will you repurpose the footage? You can edit footage for longer or shorter segments, as well as edit video created for media usage for consumer viewing on your website, social networking sites, YouTube, or even a six-second Vine episode.

- **Budget**—How much money do you have to spend? High-quality video footage is costly. If your company or agency does not have in-house talent, you most likely will have to hire videographers to film, produce, and edit the content. Other expenses could include music, on-location shooting permits, stock footage, and on-air talent, such as actors.

14.4.1 B-Roll Footage and Video News Releases

Video plays an important role in media relations, providing additional imagery to build stories on television programs, as well as on blogs and online content by other traditional media outlets. **B-roll** is the term used for broadcast-quality footage that can be dropped into a television news segment. This footage should look "raw," meaning not staged or produced like a sales promotional video with attractive models and perfectly orchestrated scenes. This imagery works effectively as a backdrop for on-air interviews with spokespeople. For example, a TV news segment of an interview with an automaker executive could show footage of the new car being tested or assembled. This footage also can be posted on an online newsroom and on YouTube.

    Video news releases (commonly referred to as VNRs) are the video equivalent of a news release, but be careful not to have the copy sound like a commercial. In the real world, VNRs are very costly and seriously need to be evaluated for effectiveness. Not all television outlets will use VNRs, so the footage may only be used by smaller news programs in potentially less relevant target markets. The issue of transparency has been widely addressed by the public relations industry and government agencies. The Public Relations Society of America addresses transparency in video news releases in its ethical standards advisories. The trade group also provides background on the practice of VNR production for over 40 years, including the widespread dissemination of VNRs during the George W. Bush administration (two terms from 2001 to 2009). The Center for Media and Democracy, a public relations watchdog group, brought attention to the practice of what it considers fake news in its *PR Watch* publication in 2005 and the following year issued its first report, "Fake TV news: Widespread and undisclosed," that documented how 77 television stations in the U.S. have used undisclosed video news releases, as well as footage from satellite media tours, over a 10-month period in their reporting. The report concluded:

In sum, television newscasts—the most popular news source in the United States—frequently air VNRs without disclosure to viewers, without conducting their own reporting, and even without fact checking the claims made in the VNRs. VNRs are overwhelmingly produced for corporations, as part of larger public relations campaigns to sell products, burnish their image, or promote policies or actions beneficial to the corporation. (Farsetta & Price, 2006, para. 18)

These initiatives have led to more scrutiny by the Federal Communications Commission, a U.S. government agency that is responsible for regulating "interstate and international communications by radio, television, wire, satellite and cable in all 50 states, the District of Columbia and U.S. territories" (Federal Communications Commission, n.d., para. 1). The Public Relations Society of America delivered testimony in 2005 to the Federal Communications Commission, of which the following excerpt is from its Ethical Standards Advisory ES-13, as well as concluding comments about the importance of transparency:

"In a free society, almost any subject matter could be deemed controversial or political in nature by some individual or special interest organization." Public relations professionals are urged to make full disclosure of sources in all VNRs and accompanying material, and to include contact information. (2009, para. 2)

In 2011, for example, the Federal Communications Commission levied a USD4,000 fine against a TV station in Minneapolis for airing a video news release from a car manufacturer on the popularity of convertibles without sponsorship identification. The TV station maintained that using a VNR is the same as using content issued from a news release and that it had paid its parent network for the footage. The Federal Communications Commission rejected the station's arguments, claiming that the news story content by General Motors was more than "disproportionate to the subject matter of the news report" (Silverman, 2011, para. 2) and that the network received unsolicited corporate footage for free.

A post on the Broadcast Law Blog explained how the FCC actions warrant that TV stations will need to pay attention to usage of commercial footage:

If a station's use of such video contains anything more than "transient or fleeting" images of commercial products, sponsorship identification may well be required. In this case, the station could have complied merely by providing a visual credit stating "Video provided by General Motors." (Silverman, 2011, para. 5)

Public relations practitioners should investigate any government requirements and restrictions in the countries where they plan to release video news releases, as well as their usage by television news stations in those markets.

14.4.2 Writing Audiovisual Scripts

Writing for video requires seeing content from two perspectives: **visual imagery** of what the viewer will see and **audio** of what the viewer will hear. The best way to prepare the script is to use two columns, for visuals and audio, and think through each frame of what will be captured on film. See Exhibit 14.1, which has corresponding numbers to show how to prepare a video news release script. This basic format can be adapted for any type of footage.

Exhibit 14.1—VIDEO NEWS RELEASE TEMPLATE.

Title of VNR ①	Total Running Time: ②
Name of Organization ③	Producer: ④
Date ⑤	Email ⑥
	Telephone

Suggested Anchor introduction: ⑦

Brief copy provides a synopsis of the story and wording to introduce the story on air.

VISUALS ⑧	AUDIO ⑨
Slate #1 Column describes visual imagery for each scene. Indicate camera angles as desired: • CU (close up) • DIS (dissolve) • ECU (extreme close up; the E can be used to indicate other extreme shots) • EXT (exterior) • INT (interior) • LS (long shot) • WS (wide shot) • MS (medium shot)	Type of Sound#1: Column describes the sound or includes quotations from on-air spokespeople or narrator. More detail on the sound can be added as follows: • SOT (sound on tape, particularly referring to what is spoken on camera; commonly used when someone is interviewed or seen on camera; some writers use soundbites of quotes from spokespeople seen on camera) • SFX (sound effects) • VO (voice over from narrator, who is usually not visually shown; some writers use SOT/VO) • NATSOUND (means natural sound)
Slate #2 Each grid should describe a new visual backdrop.	SOT #2: Explain audio for each new visual scene.

Suggested anchor close: A few sentences can provide an interesting fact or tell viewers where to find out more information—toll-free telephone, website, or social media. ⑩

Additional Soundbites: Additional footage or soundbites that the television station could use. ⑪

1. **Title** (required)
   This section simply includes the title of the video news release, which traditionally includes the name of the company/government agency and a brief description of the topic.

2. **Running Time** (required)

This section should include the total running time in minutes and seconds. Some producers create edited video segments in different lengths to easily drop into news stories.

3. **Sponsor** (required)

This part lists the name of the organization sponsoring the VNR. In some cases, two different organizations may be involved, so the lead organization could be listed here or both names could be added.

4. **Producer** (required)

The name of the producer would be the public relations agency or in-house public relations contact who would be the primary person to contact for additional information or to answer any questions.

5. **Date** (required)

The date when the video is distributed.

6. **Contact Information** (required)

This part would include the telephone and email of the producer, as well as other social media.

7. **Suggested Anchor Opening** (optional)

Writers may opt to include copy for a suggested opening for the on-air story.

8. **Visuals** (required)

VNRs traditionally have two columns; the left side usually describes visual imagery. Text should indicate what is shown for every numbered slate (every scene of different imagery), such as:

- Images of spokespeople with full name, title, and affiliation, as well as the setting, if needed.
- Footage of specific scenes, activities or montages.
- Types of charts, diagrams, maps, or illustrations.
- Logos of organizations.
- Words on screen (also called chyron to indicate text-based graphics).

Use standard acronyms in the broadcasting industry to help the reader better understand the imagery, without taking up too much space in the script.

- CU (close up)
- DIS (dissolve)
- ECU (extreme close up; the E for "extreme" can be used to indicate other extreme shots)
- EXT (exterior)
- INT (interior)
- LS (long shot)
- WS (wide shot)
- MS (medium shot).

9. **Audio** (required)

This column is traditionally on the right side and includes text or a description of what the viewer can hear, such as:

- VO: Text from the voice over from the narrator, who is usually not shown on camera.
- Soundbite: Quotations from spokespeople seen on camera.
- SFX: Briefly describe the sound effects that one can hear.
- NATSOUND: Natural sound that can be heard on camera.

10. **Anchor Close** (optional)

This section can provide the broadcaster with suggestions on closing the segment. This could include additional facts of interest or more information about the organization and its website or toll-free number.

11. **Additional Soundbites** (optional)

This part could include extra soundbites from on-camera interviews or additional footage of scenes that were not included in the actual VNR, but still have merit for potential viewing. You also can add the length of footage. The television news station also may add this footage to the VNR content, or use this footage, instead of the packaged VNR, to build its own story.

For soundbites, writers should include the name of the person, title, and affiliation, as well as the quotation. For visual imagery, add a brief description of the footage.

14.4.3 Public Service Announcements

Public service announcements (also called **public service advertisements** or **public information films**) are created by governments, charities, and nongovernmental organizations that bring attention to important and timely issues affecting residents of a community, state, province, region, or country. The Federal Communications Commission in the U.S. defines a PSA as:

> A PSA is any announcement (including network) for which no charge is made and which promotes programs, activities, or services of federal, state, or local governments (e.g., recruiting, sale of bonds, etc.), or the programs, activities, or services of nonprofit organizations (e.g., United Way, Red Cross blood donations, etc.) and any other announcements regarded as serving community interests, excluding time signals, routine weather announcements, and promotional announcements.
> (Dessart, 2013, p. 1849)

PSAs must be non-commercial, non-denominational, and non-political; in other words, they are not advertisements that directly promote a product, service, or a political candidate. PSAs convey educational messages, bring attention to serious issues, and communicate resources to the public. PSAs can be in print form in newspapers and magazines or in audio-visual formats for television or radio programs. Most producers of PSAs produce multiple formats for media outlets to select from based on their space or air availability. Print PSAs would be in different sizes, black and white, or color. Radio can be distributed as suggested copy for an anchor to read from or a pre-taped actuality, with a voice over narrator and sound effects in different time slots. Producers of PSAs for television usually produce 10-, 30-, and 60-second versions. Longer versions also can be produced for movie theaters and the organization's website and social media.

Unlike print, radio, or television commercials where one buys the space or air time to determine when and where the ads will air, PSAs are placed in unsold advertising space. Although PSAs are free to place, they are costly to produce. The actual creators of PSAs may be advertising professionals, instead of public relations executives who still may have input on the process. The practice of PSAs goes back to World War II with the War Advertising Council in the U.S. and the Central Office of Information in the U.K. The War Advertising Council was renamed the Ad Council and remains the leading producer of PSAs in the U.S. Its website (http://adcouncil.org/) serves as an excellent resource with a comprehensive library of current and classic PSAs. The Central Office of Information was dissolved in 2011, with the Cabinet Office procuring creative work from outside advertising agencies on behalf of the U.K. government. The National Archives' website (http://www.nationalarchives.gov.uk/films/) contains public information films produced by the Central Office of Information from 1945 to 2006.

Government communication regulations vary, so public relations practitioners should investigate the rules in specific countries. In addition, company websites and YouTube are ideal locations to post public service announcements. PSAs also can be shared on blogs, social media, or on online versions of traditional media.

The goals are to figure out your key messages and the final call to action. Effective PSAs tell stories that inspire people to think about something or even change their behavior, using the following techniques:

- **Fear factor** with cautionary tales and dramatizations of what could happen if you text and drive, drive too fast, take drugs, smoke cigarettes, or partake in other dangerous behavior.
- **Humor** that makes you laugh even when addressing a serious topic.
- **Inspirational stories** that show how people overcome challenges or make a difference in their communities and touched others.
- **Celebrity appeals** from well-known public figures or authoritative sources who share insight or make a plea for viewers to care and do something.

Try Exercise 14.1 and select a PSA that you found engaging—you may be surprised to discover how much talent around the world goes into creating fascinating PSAs. My personal

Exercise 14.1

Insights: Public Service Announcements

Search for a public service announcement made for television or another video platform (such as YouTube) that you found appealing. Answer the following questions:

1. Which PSA did you select? Please add the link.
2. Where did you find the PSA?
3. Which organization issued the PSA?
4. What was the mission/cause of the PSA?
5. Who were the target audiences and in which geographic area(s)?
6. How were the words delivered—by narrator or cast (actors or real people), or written on the screen?
7. What did you think about the background sound or music?
8. Did the PSA make you want to listen and care about the topic? Please explain.
9. Do you have any other observations to share?

Figure 14.7—"DUMB WAYS TO DIE" SCREENSHOT OF PUBLIC SERVICE ANNOUNCEMENT CREATED BY METRO TRAINS MELBOURNE, AUSTRALIA, TO PROMOTE RAIL SAFETY. Source: © Metro Trains Melbourne, Dumb Ways to Die™ All Rights Reserved.

favorite is "Dumb ways to die," a PSA created by McCann Melbourne, an advertising agency, for Metro Trains Melbourne (see Figure 14.7). This humorous and memorable PSA promotes train safety subtly *without* being morbid or preachy. Geared to a younger audience, the PSA shows animated cartoon blobs that die in whacky ways, such as swimming with piranhas, gulping superglue, and playing with a wasp nest, and later doing dangerous things at the train station. The catchy song, "So Many Dumb Ways to Die," accompanies the animation and uses repetition effectively. It is not surprising that this PSA has won a variety of awards, including the Cannes Lions Grand Prix. As of June 2015, this PSA, which is 3 minutes and 2 seconds in length, has drawn more than 104 million views on YouTube.

14.5 Learning Objectives and Key Terms

After reading Chapter 14, you should be able to:

- Understand the key differences in writing for the ear versus the eye.
- Describe the preparation process in setting up and writing a speech.
- Write a brief introduction speech in any business setting.
- Discuss how videos can help share stories with the public on company websites, blogs, microblogs, and social networking sites.
- Characterize how videos can support media relations activities in placing stories on television, as well as in blogs and online editions of print media.
- Explain the differences between B-roll and video news releases.
- Address transparency issues in the use of video news releases on television.

- Develop a script for a video news release or a public service announcement using the two-column approach for describing visuals and audio.

This chapter covers the following key terms:

Speaking rates (p. 357)
Anaphora (p. 365)
B-roll (p. 370)
Audiovisual scripts (p. 371)

1-3-1 approach in speeches (p. 362)
Paralanguage (p. 368)
Video news releases/VNRs (p. 370)
Public services announcements/PSAs (p. 374)

References

Bennett, M. J. (1998). Intercultural communication: A current perspective. In Milton J. Bennett (Ed.), *Basic concepts of intercultural communication: Selected readings* (pp. 1–34). Yarmouth, ME: Intercultural Press.

Dessart, G. (2013). Public-service announcement. In H. Newcomb (Ed.), *Encyclopedia of Television/Museum of Broadcast Television*, 2nd ed. (pp. 1849–1850). Abingdon, Oxon: Routledge.Yarmouth, ME: Intercultural Press.

Farsetta, D., & Price, D. (2006, November 3). Still not the news: Stations overwhelmingly fail to disclose VNRs. *PRWatch*. Retrieved from http://www.prwatch.org/fakenews2/execsummary.

Federal Communications Commission. (n.d.). What we do [Website]. Retrieved from http://www.fcc.gov/what-we-do.

Fringe benefits of failure, and the importance of imagination. (2008, June 5). *Harvard Magazine.* Retrieved from http://harvardmagazine.com/2008/06/the-fringe-benefits-failure-the-importance-imagination.

Kerrigan, B. (2014, September). Structure your speech for success. *Toastmaster*, p. 15. Retrieved from http://www.toastmasters.org/~/media/6CD7345EC44945FE966AD225F2A6AF5F.ashx.

King, Jr., M. L. (1963). "I have a dream . . ." Speech by the Rev. Martin Luther King at the "March on Washington." *National Archives and Records Administration*. Retrieved from http://www.archives.gov/press/exhibits/dream-speech.pdf.

Musil, S. (2009, February 4). Gates spreads malaria message with mosquitoes. *CNET*. Retrieved from http://www.cnet.com/news/gates-spreads-malaria-message-with-mosquitoes/.

Orwell, G. (1946, April). Politics and the English language. *Horizon*. Retrieved from http://www.orwell.ru/library/essays/politics/english/e_polit/.

Public Relations Society of America. (2009, October). *Ethical standards advisory ES-13: Use of video news releases as a public relations tool*. Retrieved from http://www.prsa.org/about prsa/ethics/ethicalstandardsadvisories/#.VKsEFSvF-So.

Robinson, K. (2006, February). How schools kill creativity [Transcript]. *TED Talks*. Retrieved from https://www.ted.com/talks/ken_robinson_says_schools_kill_creativity/Transcript?language=en.

Silverman, D. (2011, July 8). FCC confirms $4000 fine for televising video news release without sponsorship ID. *Broadcast Law Blog*. Retrieved from http://www.broadcastlawblog.com/2011/07/articles/fcc-confirms-4000-fine-for-televising-video-news-release-without-sponsorship-id/.

Sissey, M. (2012, September 20). Perfect speech for a global audience. *Business Daily Africa*. Retrieved from http://www.businessdailyafrica.com/Opinion-and-Analysis/Perfect-speech-for-a-global-audience/-/539548/1513106/-/item/1/-/9h7852z/-/index.html.

Toastmasters International. (2011). Your speaking voice: Tips for adding strength and authority to your voice. Retrieved from http://www.toastmasters.org/~/media/B7D5C3F93FC3439 589BCBF5DBF521132.ashx.

"You've got to find what you love," Jobs says. (2005, June 14). This is a prepared text of the commencement address delivered by Steve Jobs, CEO of Apple Computer and of Pixar Animation Studios, on June 12, 2005. *Stanford Report*. Retrieved from http://news.stan ford.edu/news/2005/june15/jobs-061505.html.

15 Controlling Content with Brand Journalism and Corporate-Produced Materials

Brand journalism is storytelling meant to draw readers to a company's field of expertise, without laying on the hard sell.

—Ira Basen, CBC Radio producer and journalist

15.1 Introduction to Brand Journalism

This quote above from Ira Basen, a Canadian journalist and radio producer, comes from his story, "Is that an ad or a news story—and does it matter which?" (2012) from *The Globe and Mail*, Canada's national daily newspaper. Basen discusses how Cisco Systems hired leading journalists to write content for its website and the evolution of **brand journalism**, particularly online channels bypassing traditional journalism. The blurring of journalism and advertising started in the late 19th century with self-produced magazines, the first one of which, *The Furrow*, was published by John Deere. It continues to flourish with new platforms on the Web and social media. This area opens up opportunities for not just advertisers, but also for public relations practitioners worldwide. Brand journalism falls into the category of **controlled media**, meaning that you determine the words, the visuals, and the distribution. These tactics also require greater expenditures.

Let us look at a few trends in how consumers are valuing information:

- Although more than three-quarters of Canadians considered traditional media a reliable source, almost a quarter of Canadian 18- to 34-year-olds trusted company websites and social media as credible news sources, versus 10% of adults over the age of 55 (Canadian Council of Public Relations Firms, 2012).
- The Gallup poll (Mendes, 2013) reported that less than half of Americans expressed a great deal or a fair amount of trust and confidence in the accuracy of mass media reporting: 44% in 2013, which was the same as 2011, yet an increase from 40% in 2012. Since 1997 when Gallup began tracking Americans' impressions of media annually, 45% to 65% of respondents have indicated not very much or no trust at all

in media reporting. Republican and independent voters expressed the highest dissatisfaction, claiming a liberal bias in the media.

- The Edelman Trust Barometer (2015) surveyed people ages 25 to 64 in 27 countries and revealed that 60% of countries distrust the media, while online search engines have surpassed traditional media as a trusted source for information and general news. In fact, 64% of the general public and 72% of millennials considered search engines the most trusted source.

Communicators need to complement traditional media and social media outreach by connecting with audiences through other forms. Although so much content in public relations trades and books focuses on the Internet, public relations practitioners cannot ignore the fact that not everyone is online. While approximately 40% of the world's population has Internet access (Internet Live Stats, 2014), around 60% of the public worldwide does not have access to digital technology, meaning that a substantial number of audiences need to be reached by non-electronic means, such as printed material.

This chapter looks at other print and digital communiqués that can be produced directly by organizations: magazines and newsletters, self-produced online news stories, white papers, brochures and posters, and advertorials and native advertising.

15.2 Organizational Magazines and Newsletters

Organizational-produced magazines, whether print or digital, go beyond inflight magazines and in-room hotel magazines to many types of industries and nonprofits. Many self-produced publications started out small and expanded with more content and wider distributions with editions in other languages. In fact, the cost of producing these magazines can be offset with advertising revenues. Let us look at the evolution of corporate- or nonprofit-produced magazines from the beginning with examples from different industries.

Considered the first brand magazine, *The Furrow* debuted in 1895 as a resource for farmers by John Deere, which is now a publicly held corporation and a global supplier of agricultural, construction, and forestry equipment. The company's Publications Manager David Jones explained the magazine's ongoing success in an article in *The Content Strategist*: "Telling stories that folks enjoy reading—and that they can use in their own operations—has been the recipe since the beginning" (Gardiner, 2013, para. 2). The magazine has evolved with the times, from just print to both print and digital editions (www.deere.com/furrow), from English to 12 languages, and from longer to shorter stories with more visuals. What has not changed is the editorial focus on the farmers, not on the company itself and its products. Jones added, "We've always been able to convince the management that the content shouldn't be about John Deere equipment. We've stuck to that over time" (Gardiner, 2013, para. 9). See Figure 15.1 for an example of an early issue and Figure 15.2 for a more recent edition of *The Furrow*.

Five years after *The Furrow* debuted, the Michelin brothers, renowned as tire manufacturers, printed 35,000 copies of the *Michelin Guide* to help motorists find places to stay and refuel their cars in France, as well as to provide tips on tire maintenance and repair. The *Michelin Guide* exists today—and no longer for free—covering 23 countries and sold in approximately 90 countries (Michelin, 2009).

An excellent example of a cross-cultural magazine produced by a corporation is *AramcoWorld*, which started out as an interoffice newsletter for employees of the Arabian

Figure 15.1—FRONT PAGE OF *THE FURROW* **FROM 1897.** Source: Used with permission of Deere & Company's The Furrow Magazine.

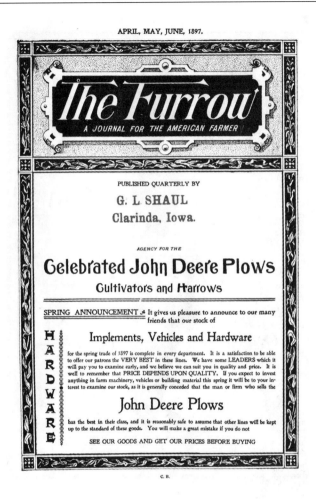

American Oil Company (Aramco) in 1949. As more Americans relocated to work in Saudi Arabia, the publication expanded into a bimonthly educational magazine to help people unfamiliar with the culture gain a better understanding of life past and present in Saudi Arabia. *AramcoWorld* now reaches audiences beyond the oil company's staff with more than 160,000 subscribers in more than 125 countries. The content also expanded to cover all Islamic countries. A digital edition (www.saudiaramcoworld.com) also was launched in 2004. The magazine explains it goal: "to increase cross-cultural understanding by broadening knowledge of the histories, cultures and geography of the Arab and Muslim worlds and their global interconnections, past and present" (*AramcoWorld*, 2015, para. 1).

BMW rebranded its original customer magazine, *BMW Magazine*, that debuted in 1989, with a new lifestyle format and layout with the motto, *DRIVEN*, focusing on "international stories about people whose visionary ideas change our lives" (BMW, 2012, para. 1) in 2012.

Figure 15.2—COVER PAGE OF *THE FURROW*, SEPTEMBER/OCTOBER 2014 ISSUE.
Source: Used with permission of Deere & Company's The Furrow Magazine. Copyright 2014, all worldwide rights reserved.

According to a news release issued by BMW, the twice yearly print edition has a circulation of 3.8 million, along with an online edition, in 25 languages, reaching customers in more than 150 countries.

Procter & Gamble relied on its custom quarterly magazine about its beauty products to reach mommy bloggers in the U.S. The company expanded its Canadian quarterly magazine *Rouge*, which debuted in 2005, to the U.S. in 2009. An *AdAge* reporter explained the appeal to bloggers: "It's available at the internet's favorite price (free) and comes loaded with coupons, which happen to drive much of the routine chatter regarding package-goods brands in social media" (Neff, 2009, para. 3).

One of the largest international agency holding groups, Interpublic Group, launched *Stronger*, a magazine in both print and digital versions on the company's corporate citizenship in 2014 (see Figure 15.3). Originally, Interpublic produced a printed report on sustainability and later sought after a new platform. In an interview in the *New York Times* (Elliott, 2014), Interpublic's vice president for communications and strategy explained how the original report "didn't have a soul" (para. 10), and the print magazine can "allow agencies' voices, people's voices, to come through, and make it feel more grass-roots" (para. 13).

The Australia and New Zealand Banking Group Limited, commonly called ANZ, added an online publication, *BlueNotes*, with the tagline, "connecting news and insights," to its online newsroom in 2014 (see Figure 15.4). With an award-winning journalist and former editor of the *Australian Financial Review* serving as managing editor, the publication covers content beyond its own company and its website statement claims to seek "a more frequent and candid conversation with you about our business and the contribution we make to our clients and to the economies and communities in which we work across Australia, New Zealand and the Asia Pacific region" (ANZ, n.d., para. 4). ANZ's group head of strategic content and digital

Figure 15.3—COVER OF *STRONGER*, AN INTERPUBLIC PUBLICATION ON CORPORATE CITIZENSHIP, FROM 2014. Source: © Cover by Robert Landau/Corbis.

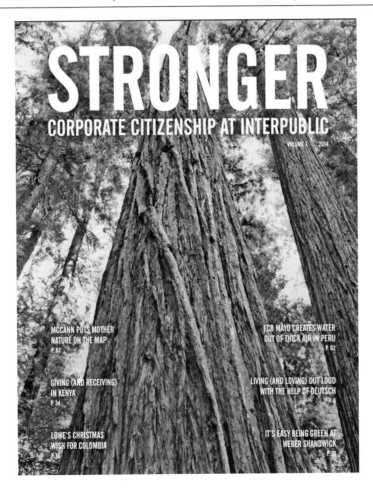

Figure 15.4—SCREENSHOT OF *BLUENOTES*, AN ONLINE PUBLICATION POSTED ON ANZ'S NEWSROOM. Source: With permission of BlueNotes, the ANZ newsroom.

media stated in an article in *The Australian* how the publication operates like an actual media newsroom, "We will also be breaking our own stories . . . our aim is to work hand-in-hand with (traditional media) journalists" (Sinclair, 2014, para. 8).

Even children can receive free custom-produced magazines. The *LEGO® Club Magazine* features its constructed toys with comics, games, and puzzles. Print editions can be mailed to a child's home, with email approval by a parent or guardian, in the U.S., Canada, Denmark (where the company is based), and other European countries. An online interactive edition is also available, with a link for residents of Australia and New Zealand (LEGO, n.d.).

Many nonprofits also offer magazines as membership incentives and fundraising generators with advertising revenues. One of the leading global nonprofits and masters of storytelling, the National Geographic Society reaches 30.9 million through its audited multimedia—print and digital editions, websites, social media, apps, and newsletters—plus 33 local-language editions, read by more than 60 million people each month worldwide. The National Geographic Channel also reaches approximately 440 million people in 171 countries (National Geographic, 2012). Its original journal, *National Geographic*, began in 1888 in English.

Public relations practitioners may want to propose company-produced magazines for their clients or organizations as a viable tactic. If the organization has an existing publication, public relations executives can make the following contributions:

- Promote the publication on the organization's website and social media.
- Use excerpts of stories and images, following copyright guidelines, in other corporate digital media and social media.
- Write your own stories or find a freelance writer to contribute stories. Most editors of corporate publications prepare editorial calendars. Public relations staff also could

make suggestions to enhance editorial calendar themes and content, particularly to build more content about specific countries.

- Pitch story ideas about the publication to non-competing media and set up interviews with the editors of the publications as experts in writing company-produced magazines. I had included a few quotes earlier from editors at newspapers and industry trades who covered stories on corporate publications.
- Share copies with audiences at events.

Another less complicated publication to produce is a **newsletter**, which can be exclusively digital or print or both. And newsletters are not yet dead or on life support, particularly ones distributed by email. As reported in an article titled, "For email newsletters, a death greatly exaggerated," in the *New York Times*: "Email newsletters, an old-school artifact of the web that was supposed to die along with dial-up connections, are not only still around, but very much on the march" (Carr, 2014, para. 2). The article addresses how publishers, such as the *New York Times* itself, *Bloomberg*, and *Fast Company*, continue to connect with their email newsletter subscribers, whether unpaid or paid, who are experiencing Internet information overload, and appreciate receiving news summaries and relevant insight on current events.

Newsletters can be produced internally as a way to share news about the organization and its employees worldwide, thereby providing a more personal touch and goodwill between the company and its staff. External newsletters can be helpful to communicate with business-to-business or business-to-consumer customers; members of a club or society; volunteers or contributors to a nonprofit or NGO; or residents of a condominium, retirement community, or other real estate development.

Newsletters should contain the following elements:

- **Masthead** with the publication's name that has its own logo or incorporates the organization's logo.
- **Consistent format** with regular columns and editorial guidelines that encourage submissions.
- **Opportunity for readers to provide feedback**, whether online or through letters to the editor as a regular column.
- **Regular distribution**, such as twice a year, quarterly, or monthly, depending on the volume of news and resources.
- **Different English-language editions and translated versions with more local content**, particularly for a multinational organization.

15.3 Branded Online Newsroom Content

Public relations writers can enhance content on **online newsrooms** with **self-produced stories** presented as editorial, as well as supporting content in video reports. The *Financial Times* published a story titled, "Nissan's PR mimics the newsroom" (Reed, 2011), that covered how Nissan hired in-house journalists and camera crews to develop self-produced materials when its CEO visited its plant in Iwaki, Japan, that was damaged by the earthquake. A few hours after the event, the in-house journalists of the car manufacturer ran "Nissan Recovery Stories: Iwaki Factory" videos on its online newsroom and streamed videos on YouTube. Nissan is not the only multinational company expanding its corporate communications staff to produce its own journalistic content online, thereby reducing the reliance on traditional media outlets to produce stories. A reporter for *Ragan's PR Daily* provides a clear rationale: "As newsrooms shrink and the public relations industry continues to grow its influence, the two are becoming increasingly indistinguishable" (Allen, 2011, para. 1).

Cisco, the global information technology company, transformed its newsroom into *The Network*, which includes its own self-produced feature stories and video clips, and other traditional newsroom content, such as news releases, and social media (see Figure 15.5). Cisco engaged its 180,000 Facebook followers to vote on the new name of its former newsroom, News@Cisco. Cisco's corporate communications director discussed the mission of its newsroom in a Cisco blog:

> We will create, share and curate content on these topics as a part of our overall Cisco voice. We have commissioned world-class reporters who have worked at Fortune, Forbes, BusinessWeek, Wall Street Journal, AP and more to create content on our core technology news topics. The purpose of these stories isn't to showcase Cisco, but to create compelling content in the topical areas that we care about. We are supporting the generation of this content in the hopes that our audience shares it and becomes more educated on the topics that are important to Cisco and to our customers. (Earnhardt, 2011, para. 4)

Figure 15.5—SCREENSHOT OF *THE NETWORK,* CISCO'S TECHNOLOGY NEWS SITE. Source: With permission of Cisco—The Network.

Coca-Cola also revamped its corporate website (www.coca-colacompany.com) as an online magazine called *Coca-Cola Journey*, which was the original name of its former employee publication, with the slogan "refreshing the world one story at a time." The effort pulls in resources from four dedicated staff members, its corporate marketing and public relations staff, and 40 freelance writers and photographers. Coca-Cola's director for digital communications and social media explained in a *New York Times* interview: "We have this belief in great, real content and creating content that can be spread through any medium as part of our 'liquid and linked' strategy" (Elliott, 2012, para. 9). The company claims to attract more than 1.2 million unique visitors per month to its website. Its current website has global English content and other country-specific versions. *Coca-Cola Journey* also has a link to its Press Center, which contains company-produced stories, along with traditional newsroom resources.

15.4 White Papers

White papers (also called **positioning papers**) originally started as official government reports, based on the term white book. One of the most widely referenced early white papers was written by Winston Churchill, which is also called the British White Paper of 1922, on the future of Palestine. Not only politicians issue white papers; business executives also find white papers to be useful tools to share opinions and position an organization as a thought leader to diverse local and international markets, particularly for business-to-business communication. These documents also can be adapted for specific regions or countries in different versions of English or translated into other languages.

Eccolo Media, a San Francisco-based communications company specializing in technology, conducted an online survey on business-to-business collateral affecting purchases by U.S.-based buyers of technology products. Its fifth annual survey found that "white papers continue unchallenged as the collateral most frequently ranked as the number one most influential content type" (2012, p. 8).

Writing a white paper requires significant time that in-house public relations staff may not be able to invest in. It is not uncommon for these writing projects to be assigned to freelance writers or industry experts. However, the public relations executive will need to communicate clearly the goals of the organization or client, draft an outline of the paper, provide information, contacts of people to interview to include quotes, and oversee all details of the project, including timetables, review of deliverables, feedback from all parties, and the editing process.

Before writing a white paper, you should have answers to the following questions:

- **What is the objective of the white paper**—to increase customer loyalty, to attract new customers, or to gain recognition as a thought leader in a particular area by sharing insights? In some cases, you may have more than one objective.
- **Who are your intended readers**—current or prospective customers, bloggers and journalists, or other stakeholders? Where are they located? Which customers would most likely use your products or services?
- **What do you want to convey**—what are your key themes and topics? A white paper cannot use language as in an advertisement or a news release. You cannot just promote the organization or its products or services; you need to convey value to the reader, who is probably a professional interested in career enhancement, time-saving measures, solutions to problems, current trends, and other ways to be more

effective. Are you sharing original research undertaken by your company, synthesizing new trends of interest to your customers, explaining how to do something more effectively, or offering new solutions to your customers' needs? What existing material do you have to draw from? Do you have relationships with authoritative sources to interview? Answering these questions would help determine if you have primary research to draw from and how much secondary research would need to be investigated.

- **Why are you qualified to write the paper**—or do you need to find someone else within your company or an outside expert? What topics do you have experience with? It would be worthwhile to see if any other white papers exist on the subjects, particularly by your competitors.

- **When is the best time to release the white paper**? How timely are the issues you are addressing? When would your readers be more receptive to reading your white paper? Is there a major industry conference being held?

How to Write a White Paper

The structure in writing a white paper varies considerably. Many white papers read like a blend of an article in a business or industry trade publication and an academic research paper. Here is an overview of a format to follow.

- **Title Page** (required)
  The cover page includes the title of the paper, the logo of the sponsoring organization(s), and the authors. I highly recommend that names of a specific author or authors be used, instead of the name of the company. Dates should be added to white papers.

- **Acknowledgements** (optional)
  This part gives the author or authors the opportunity to acknowledge the contributions of people who helped during the research, writing, and approval process.

- **Table of Contents** (recommended for longer papers)
  This section would include the titles and subtitles of each section and their corresponding page numbers. Longer reports benefit from a table of contents to make it easier for readers to find specific sections of interest.

- **Introduction** (recommended)
  This part also could be called an Executive Summary that gives the reader an overview of the content and also can share benefits in reading and sharing the content with others.

- **Body Copy** (required)
  This section should be logically structured and include subheads throughout. White papers also should include sidebars, charts, diagrams, and other relevant imagery. For example, the International Olive Council (2012) released a white paper titled, "The emerging health attributes of the Mediterranean diet and olive oil," that shared scientific evidence on the benefits of olive oil consumption while providing an overview on different fats and their impact on health. After the introduction and before the conclusion, the paper is structured into four parts with the following subheads:

  - *Making Sense of Fats—The Good, the Bad and the Ugly*
    This part describes the sources of healthy and unhealthy fats and their impact on our health, while segueing to the good fats in olive oil.

- *Olive Oil and Inflammation*
  This section looks at causes of acute and chronic inflammation and the preventative dietary measures, including highlights of research on the consumption of olive oil and its effect on the immune system.
- *Olive Oil and Brain Function*
  This part highlights scientific research that shows how diet also impacts cognitive functions, while weaving in the positive contribution of olive oil.
- *Quality of Life*
  This section discusses how a new study concluded that the Mediterranean diet improves one's physical and emotional well-being.

- **Conclusion** (required)
  This part provides a recap of the key points, as well as key messages or a call to action. For example, the conclusion of the white paper issued by the International Olive Council reads as follows:

  Scientific research is continuously providing more evidence to support the benefits of dietary and lifestyle choices on health, including the Mediterranean diet and olive oil. Emerging research is finding the diet to have positive effects on inflammation, cognitive health, neurological disease, depression and overall quality of life. As a dietary pattern, the MD confers several health benefits augmented by including olive oil. The mechanisms are not fully understood, but are attributed in part to oleic acid and phenolic compounds in olive oil. Diet cannot completely prevent aging, but it can promote healthy aging. Furthermore, choosing a healthy diet, physical activity and maintaining a healthy weight are factors that people can control to help fight chronic disease and may help mitigate factors that are more difficult to control such as environmental factors and genetic predisposition. (p. 10)

- **References** (required)
  White papers must be well researched just like academic reports and follow a specific stylebook for citations within the text and references at the end of the paper. Some of the most popular stylebooks for research are the *Chicago Manual of Style*, the *Publication Manual of the American Psychological Association*, and the *MLA Handbook*.
- **About the Organization** (recommended)
  This is the only place where information about the company should be included. Some writers place this part after the acknowledgements. This section should be quite brief. Websites and other social media should be included.

  How to disseminate and promote the final white paper is just as important as writing the paper on a relevant topic. The following steps can make the difference in getting people to read your work:

  - Post the white paper on the organization's website and newsroom section. An option is to require registration for people to download the entire white paper, which is a technique that can help generate sales leads. Keep the registration process simple; a longer, more complex process may discourage people.
  - Send printouts of the white paper with a brief cover note by regular mail or write email pitches to bloggers and other traditional media to generate stories or to add quotes from the paper in thematic round-up articles.
  - Distribute by mail or email to clients, customers, sales representatives, and other stakeholders.

– Forward links with a cover note by email to all employees, post on the Intranet or other internal communiqués, and consider sending hardcopies to key staff along with a cover memo.
– Send follow-up thank you emails and links of the white paper (or letters and hardcopies) to the people who made a contribution to the process of preparing the white paper.
– Bring copies of the white paper to speaking engagements and editorial briefings with journalists.
– Add the white paper (title and link) to the authors' LinkedIn.

See Exhibit 15.1 for examples of companies that issue white papers on topics related to the public relations industry. Try Exercise 15.1 and analyze a white paper on any topic that interests you.

Exhibit 15.1—RESOURCES CONTAINING WHITE PAPERS ON PUBLIC RELATIONS. This list includes examples of public relations services that post white papers on industry topics.

Company	White Papers	Website
BurrellesLuce claims to be the U.S. leader in media monitoring content from local and national print, online, broadcast, and social media sources.	White papers organized by topic: media monitoring, media measurement, media outreach, and social media. Required registration for free content.	http://www.burrellesluce.com/resources/white-papers
Businesswire, a Berkshire Hathaway company, claims to be the global leader in news release distribution and regulatory disclosure.	Organized by public relations/marketing and investor relations.	http://www.businesswire.com/portal/site/home/white-papers/
Cision offers global public relations software and services.	Library of resources includes white papers, along with tip sheets and case studies.	http://www.cision.com/us/resources/
PR Newswire positions itself as the premier global provider of multimedia platforms, including news distribution.	Online "Knowledge Center" includes white papers, along with articles, cases studies, and events.	http://www.prnewswire.com/knowledge-center/
Vocus offers cloud-based public relations and marketing software with offices in North America, Europe, and Asia.	Organized in reverse chronological order.	http://www.vocus.com/resources/the-guides/

Exercise 15.1

Insights: Evaluation of White Papers

Select a white paper on any topic that you can find online and answer the following questions.

1. What organization wrote or commissioned the white paper?
2. Why do you think the organization issued the white paper? Is it trying to generate more sales, position itself as a thought-leader, or serve what other purpose?
3. Who are the target audiences and from which geographic areas?
4. Is there a specific name of an author or authors? What are their credentials?
5. What is the title of the white paper?
6. What is the white paper's theme? How does it relate to the sponsoring organization?
7. How is it organized? Did you find it well structured?
8. What do you think of the quality of the writing?
9. What other observations do you have to share?

15.5 Brochures and Posters

Brochures (also called **leaflets**, **circulars**, **handouts**, **handbills**, or **pamphlets**) and **posters** fall into the category of **marketing communications materials** (also called **sales promotional literature**). Printed brochures still exist and make sense when reaching people who may not have Internet access and for wired audiences who may benefit by receiving tactical information that they may not seek online. Brochures can be useful in communicating events, products, and services, and in encouraging people to volunteer or donate money for nonprofits. They also have value during face-to-face business events, such as at trade shows and conferences, as well as at public events or venues that display information on what to see and do in the area, such as hotels, bed-and-breakfasts, or tourist information centers.

When Volkswagen launched its Jetta TDI Clean Diesel,[1] the German automaker hired a Canadian brand consulting and design agency, Cause+Affect, to promote the new environmentally friendly product in Canada with "a holistic VW branded green experience" (Cause+Affect, 2010, para. 2). As part of the "Green Guts" campaign, the agency designed custom-designed brochures shaped like leaves that conveyed an organic theme and were integrated seamlessly within the VW exhibition spaces, where consumers could pick the brochures from white stalks on the display case, where they looked like sprouting plants. The leaf brochure unfolded to explain clean diesel and the new car, while the other side provided tips on buying a green car. Refer to Figures 15.6, 15.7, 15.8, and 15.9 for images of the brochures and the exhibition spaces where the brochures were displayed.

Posters work effectively to promote time-sensitive content within a specific community—upcoming special events, festivals, movies, concerts, theater performances, art gallery openings, guest lectures, fundraisers, or other activities in which the call to action is to attend something. If you are a student, you probably see posters plastered throughout campus in public spaces

Figure 15.6—VOLKSWAGEN "GREEN GUTS" BROCHURE; FRONT AND BACK COVERS. Source: Courtesy of Cause+Affect.

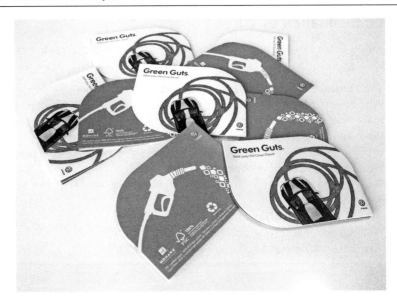

Figure 15.7—VOLKSWAGEN "GREEN GUTS" BROCHURE SHOWN OPENED FRONT AND BACK PANELS. Source: Courtesy of Cause+Affect.

Figure 15.8—VOLKSWAGEN "GREEN GUTS" BROCHURE ON DISPLAY AT CONSUMER SHOW EXHIBITIONS IN TORONTO AND VANCOUVER. Source: Courtesy of Cause+Affect.

Figure 15.9—CLOSE-UP IMAGE OF VOLKSWAGEN "GREEN GUTS" BROCHURE ON DISPLAY AT CONSUMER SHOW EXHIBITIONS IN TORONTO AND VANCOUVER. Source: Courtesy of Cause+Affect.

from dormitories and cafeterias to classrooms and office hallways. Posters also can convey public services to a community, such as health, housing, or educational resources.

WWF's Earth Hour started as a symbolic lights-off event in Sydney in 2007 to build awareness on climate change. The event has grown into a global movement driving tangible environmental outcomes and uniting people, businesses, organizations, and iconic landmarks to act for our planet in more than 162 countries and territories worldwide. Visual imagery, including posters, plays an important role in bringing attention to the cause Earth Hour represents and in mobilizing the public to celebrate the annual events and be a part of the broader movement. Given its open source nature, any individual and organization around the world can download the Earth Hour Starter Kit from its website (www.earthhour.org) that includes posters, logos, Web banners, videos, and social media strategies to help promote the world's largest grassroots environmental movement's mission of "Uniting People to Protect the Planet" and inspiring them to use their power to "Change Climate Change." See Figure 15.10 for an example of an Earth Hour poster.

Creating these visual materials requires synergy between the written copy and the visual imagery. Public relations writers usually work in collaboration with graphic designers, as well as with photographers and illustrators, if new visual materials need to be created. Affordable photography, illustrations, and vector graphics (high-resolution computer graphics that are infinitely scalable) can be purchased from stock photo houses.

Free options do exist yet they may have restrictions on use and choices. The cheapest choices, yet limited in customization, are the free online templates for creating brochures and posters. Free online clipart has serious limitations—and many of the images scream "clipart," making your final product look low budget. Historical archives or material in the public domain may be available for free, but you do need to check any disclaimers about commercial use, copyright, and credits to the organization, the artist, or photographer. Trying to gain approval for using imagery for free from other outside sources takes a great deal of time—and be prepared for many rejections or requests to pay for usage. In this case, signed consent forms are essential that outline the terms of usage.

Before concentrating on the writing and design, writers need to start with considering the usage.

- What are you trying to accomplish? Promote an upcoming event, provide additional resources about a product or service, or entice people to do something.
- What messages and information do you want to convey?
- Who are you trying to reach?
- Will the material be focused on one area or will you need to customize the content for a specific geographic area?

Figure 15.10—EARTH HOUR POSTERS. Source: Courtesy of Earth Hour.

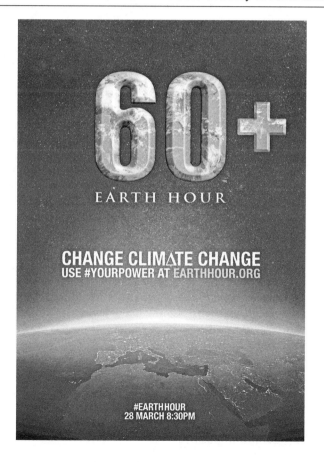

- Where do you plan on distributing the material? Sales promotional literature cannot be displayed everywhere; some public spaces have restrictions and require advance approvals or even a fee. When do you need to distribute the material? You will need to factor in the writing and design mockups, final approval process, and the printing time.

After you have answers for how the material will be used, you can then focus on determining the budget, which is a huge variable. How much time do you have to spend to create the materials? Rush printing jobs can be extremely costly, so the best approach is to give yourself ample advance time. Obtaining high-quality and high-resolution visual imagery is extremely important. You will need to look at the existing photography, illustrations, cartoons, or other imagery—and then determine how much more you need to create. Most printers will not accept digital photographs less than 300 dpi (dots or pixels per inch). Will you need to hire outside experts to help with the design and the copy? Will the copy need to be translated and the imagery customized for specific geographic areas? What will the printing costs be? Prices vary considerably based on the quality of paper, type of printing process, and types of folds and binding. How many copies do you need to print? How much will you need to pay for shipping materials? Don't underestimate this cost. Paper products in bulk are quite heavy and costly to mail.

Now that you know what you need to accomplish and how much you have to spend, the next step is to draft the copy and figure out the layout and imagery. Let us start with the jargon of printing production and, unfortunately, not all printers are consistent with their definitions of terms:

- **Paper Stock**—Although stock is the general term for the printed surface, it also refers to the texture of the paper, which can range from a visible pattern that can be felt to one that is invisible and smooth. The weight of the paper is measured in pounds or grams per square meter in the metric system. **Caliper points** (also called points or calipers) describe the thickness of a sheet of paper measured by micrometers. The finish of the paper is called the **coating**. Coated papers can be on one or both sides and range from a shiny gloss surface to a non-shiny matte surface.
- **Paper Sizes**—Not all paper sizes are universal worldwide, so I would recommend checking with your printer on exact sizes and costs. The International Organization for Standardization (ISO) has attempted to standardize paper sizes worldwide, with a series called A and B (ISO 216 sizes) and C (ISO 269 sizes). However, North America uses its own paper standards with such terms as letter, legal, ledger, and tabloid. Many of these terms primarily cover stationery letterhead and envelopes.
- **Colors**—The most expensive printing is the four-color process, which really means full color, followed by three- or two-color, and then one-color as the least expensive option. And then inks have a layer of complexity. **Pantone**® is the industry standard worldwide for color selection, ensuring universal accuracy of color. Metallic ink is more expensive to use.
- **Folds**—The choices of printing folds require serious consideration, particularly for writers and designers, since these details determine the number of surfaces for copy and imagery, and the end-user experience in viewing the content. Standard folds range from the simple four-panel half-fold brochure and six-panel gate or trifold to multi-panel Z-folds, which are also called accordion folds that can expand like the instrument (see Figures 15.11 to 15.15) to costly customized pieces. Ask your printer for samples of different brochures.

Figure 15.11—HALF-FOLD BROCHURE. Source: © totallyPic.com/Shutterstock.com.

Figure 15.12—SIX-PANEL GATE FOLD BROCHURE. Source: © Soulart/Shutterstock.com.

Figure 15.13—TRI-FOLD BROCHURE. Source: © Soulart/Shutterstock.com.

Figure 15.14—Z-FOLD BROCHURE. Source: © Gepardu/Shutterstock.com.

Figure 15.15—MULTI-PANEL ACCORDION-FOLD BROCHURE. Source: © John T Takai/Shutterstock.com.

- **Binding**—**Saddle stitching** is the term used to describe pages stapled in the middle, such as some magazines, which can work only for increments of eight pages. **Perfect binding** is a printing process in which an adhesive binding holds pages together at the spine, such as most paperbacks. Binding terms also have nuances, whether the stock is coated and uncoated, as well as other more costly options.
- **Digital Printing or Offset Printing**—Although digital printing is cheaper, the quality of the color ink may be inconsistent. Offset printing ensures consistent Pantone coloration.

For inspiration, you may want to look at some of the graphic design competitions, many of which have categories in brochures and posters. See Exhibit 15.2 for a list of examples of design organizations worldwide, many of which display award-winning creative work online.

- **The Cover**—Think of this part as the first impression. You want to compel someone to pick up the brochure and look at it. For fliers and rack cards, which can be printed on one side or both front and back sides, the front display side needs the greatest attention. Consider where the material will be displayed and how. How much of the front surface will be viewed when the documents are placed in displays? In this case, the top quarter of the first page needs the greatest emphasis. For posters, the cover is everything.
- **The Brochure Folds**—Figure out how each fold will be opened—and then determine how each fold will share the information with the reader. The best way to do this is to fold up the paper the way the final product will appear and label each panel: cover, inside flap #1, outer flap #2, and so forth, and then the back panel.
- **Draft Copy**—Clearly label each page for copy and then indicate where to insert the specific image. The artist can then tweak the final document—or the writer may complete the entire project on a desktop publishing software program.
- **Translation Considerations**—Translating material into other languages may require reconfiguring the copy and design layout. Many Western languages, including Russian, read horizontally from left to right. Arabic and Hebrew read horizontally from right to left, which would affect the layout considerably. If you were to show a before-and-after image, for example, you would need to switch the order. Chinese, Japanese, and Korean alphabets can be read horizontally or vertically from top to bottom. However, the Western horizontal writing in Korea has become more mainstream

Exhibit 15.2—RESOURCES ON GRAPHIC DESIGN ASSOCIATIONS AND AWARDS WORLDWIDE.

Organization	Website
American Design Awards	http://www.americandesignawards.com
AIGA American Institute of Graphic Arts	http://www.aiga.org
Australian Graphic Design Association	http://www.agda.com.au
Art Directors Club	http://www.adcglobal.org
Association of Professional Design Firms	http://www.apdf.org
Association Typographique Internationale	http://www.atypi.org
Color Marketing Group	http://www.colormarketing.org
Design Council	http://www.designcouncil.org.uk
Design Management Institute	http://www.dmi.org
Designers without Borders	http://www.designerswithoutborders.org
Graphic Artists Guild	http://www.graphicartistsguild.org
Graphic Designers of Canada	http://www.gdc.net
Grolier Club	http://www.grolierclub.org
IAPHC/Toronto Craftsmen Club	http://www.iaphc.ca
International Color Consortium	http://www.color.org
International Council of Design	http://www.ico-d.org
Letter Exchange	http://www.letterexchange.org
National Association of Photoshop Professionals	http://members.photoshopuser.com
One Club, The	http://www.oneclub.org
Organization of Black Designers	http://obd.org
Printing Industries of America	http://www.gain.net
RGD Registered Graphic Designers	http://www.rgd.ca
Society for Experiential Graphic Design	https://segd.org
Society for News Design	http://www.snd.org
Society of Illustrators	https://societyillustrators.org
Society of Illustrators, Artists and Designers	http://www.siad.org
Society of Publication Designers	http://www.spd.org
Type Directors Club	https://www.tdc.org

(Kim-Renaud, 2009). Switching the layout from horizontal to vertical readers would require significant restructuring.

• The other consideration for translations from English to another language is including ample room to allow more text. Some languages may require more words or longer words to express the same content adapted from the original English copy. For example, Portuguese requires approximately 15% more space, Czech 15 to 20%, and Polish 20%, while Dutch, French, and Spanish require 20 to 25% more room than English (Singh, 2012).

15.6 Advertorials and Native Advertising

A *Washington Post* journalist called **advertorials** "the chameleons of the media business," whereby sophisticated ones "can lull readers into believing that they're consuming articles with the same neutrality, authority and credibility as an adjacent news or feature story" (Farhi, 2013, p. C1). Well-written and designed advertorials can be as well done as editorial pieces. Although these ads may be written to resemble editorial copy, they are identified as advertorials and are paid-for placements (although some advertorials may be labeled inconspicuously).

Organizations may have their advertising agency or in-house advertising department, not their public relations agency or in-house staff, write and place advertorials. Some media outlets may offer services in writing and designing the advertorial for client approval, as part of the placement cost. This more expensive option may be a solution for organizations that want to dictate the text, imagery, and placement completely. Since they are paying for the placement, they would have complete control, within the regulations of the media outlet. Advertorials are placed by diverse organizations from controversial religious groups, such as the Church of Scientology, and consumer products to governments, such as countries touting their benefits for economic development.

Advertorials go beyond print into digital media. The widely used term for digital advertorials is now **native advertising**, which is sponsored content that blends in naturally with the online platform's physical layout and editorial, unlike disruptive banner ads and pop-ups. The business magazine *Forbes*, for example, changed its original AdVoice in 2012 to BrandVoice, a digital publishing platform of content produced by marketers. Some of the paid-for stories have topped its most popular module over editorial content. A *Forbes* editor describes the benefits of native advertising to the magazine and in general:

> The mission of journalism is to inform, and that requires observation, selection and interpretation, with all the biases that entails. The business of journalism is to provide marketing partners with new ways to reach consumers. BrandVoice aims to achieve both. It helps makes a wide array of credible information easily accessible and fosters connections between journalists, consumers and marketers. (DVorkin, 2012, para. 10)

BuzzFeed, a social news and entertainment website, found that one of its sponsored content stories went viral, attracting more than 2,000 Facebook likes and approximately 330,000 views from people sharing the post on other social media (Hagey, 2012). The posting was titled, "11 things no one wants to see you Instagram," a sponsored story from Virgin Mobile.

Find an advertorial in a magazine or newspaper or online native advertising example—and complete Exercise 15.2.

Exercise 15.2

Insights: Assessment of Advertorials or Native Advertising

Find an advertorial from a magazine or newspaper or a native advertising example online. Please answer the following questions:

1. Which advertorial or native advertising example did you select? Please add the URL, if available online.
2. Where did you find the advertorial or native advertising?
3. Was it clearly labeled as an ad? How was the identification worded?
4. Who sponsored the advertorial? Or were a few organizations involved?
5. What target audience or specific geographic area(s) is the advertorial trying to reach?
6. What is the theme of the advertorial?
7. How is the copy promoting the brand, product, service, or organization? What messages are conveyed?
8. What type of visual imagery supports the advertorial?
9. Do you think it was well written?
10. What other observations would you like to share?

15.7 Learning Objectives and Key Terms

After reading Chapter 15, you should be able to:

- Understand the applications of controlled content—and the distinctions between controlled and uncontrolled tactics—in public relations writing.
- Be familiar with the term brand journalism and its implications in public relations.
- Discuss the evolution of company-produced magazines, both print and digital, and how they could be used in communicating with specific audiences.
- Appreciate how stories could be packaged in company-produced magazines and newsletters.
- Identify online branded content and explain how this content could work effectively on online newsrooms.
- Develop, structure, and promote white papers.
- Describe the considerations and process in preparing brochures, fliers, and posters.
- Explain how advertorials and native advertising work in different media platforms.

Chapter 15 covers the following key terms:

Controlled media (p. 379)	Brand journalism (p. 379)
Organizational publications (p. 380)	Newsletters (p. 385)
Online branded newsrooms (p. 385)	White papers (p. 387)
Marketing communications (p. 391)	Paper stock (p. 396)
Caliper points (p. 396)	Pantone colors (p. 396)
Folds (p. 396)	Binding (p. 398)
Digital and offset printing (p. 398)	Advertorials (p. 400)
Native advertising (p. 400)	

Note

1   The Volkswagen "Green Guts" visual imagery was selected prior to the September 2015 announcement of irregularities concerning software used in diesel engines.

References

Allen, K. (2011, June 13). Journalist turned PR pro: "Traditional PR is . . . potentially unwatchable and unreadable." *Ragans's PR Daily*. Retrieved from http://www.prdaily. com/Main/Articles/Journalist_turned_PR_pro_Traditional_PR_is_potenti_8565.aspx.

ANZ. (n.d.). About BlueNotes. Retrieved from https://bluenotes.anz.com/about-bluenotes/.

AramcoWorld. (2015). Introduction: The magazine of Arab and Islamic cultures and connections. Retrieved from https://www.saudiaramcoworld.com/about.us/.

Basen, I. (2012, August 3). Is that an ad or a news story—and does it matter which? *The Globe and Mail*. Retrieved from http://www.theglobeandmail.com/arts/books-and-media/ is-that-an-ad-or-a-news-story-and-does-it-matter-which/article4461877/?page=all.

BMW. (2012, September). The new BMW Magazine—DRIVEN: New lifestyle concept for BMW customer magazine [News release]. Retrieved from https://www.press.bmwgroup. com/global.

Canadian Council of Public Relations Firms. (2012, January 24). For shoppers: Media opinions are #1 influence [News release]. Retrieved from http://ccprf.ca/2012/01/24/for-shoppers- media-opinions-are-1-influence-2/.

Carr, D. (2014, June 29). For email newsletters, a death greatly exaggerated. *New York Times*. Retrieved from http://www.nytimes.com/2014/06/30/business/media/for-email-a-death- greatly-exaggerated.html?_r=0.

Cause+Affect. (2010). Volkswagen. Retrieved from http://cargocollective.com/causeandaffect/ Volkswagen-Green-Guts.

DVorkin, L. (2012, October 3). Inside Forbes: The birth of brand journalism and why it's good for business. *Forbes*. Retrieved from http://www.forbes.com/sites/lewisdvorkin/2012/ 10/03/inside-forbes-the-birth-of-brand-journalism-and-why-its-good-for-the-new- business/.

Earnhardt, J. (2011, June 18). Introducing: "The Network: Cisco's technology news site." *Cisco blog: The Platform*. Retrieved from http://blogs.cisco.com/news/introducing-the-network- cisco%E2%80%99s-technology-news-site/.

Eccolo Media. (2012). *Eccolo Media B2B technology collateral survey report*. Retrieved from www.eccolomedia.com.

Edelman. (2015). *Edelman trust barometer 2015: Annual global study*. Retrieved from http://www.edelman.com/2015-edelman-trust-barometer.

Elliott, S. (2012, November 11). Coke revamps web site to tell its story. *New York Times*. Retrieved from http://www.nytimes.com/2012/11/12/business/media/coke-revamps-web- site-to-tell-its-story.html.

Elliott, S. (2014, April 21). Interpublic Group joins ranks of publishers with report in magazine form. *New York Times*. Retrieved from http://www.nytimes.com/2014/04/21/business/ media/interpublic-group-joins-ranks-of-publishers-with-report-in-magazine-form.html?_ r=0.

Farhi, P. (2013, January 16). Sneaking past the gates of journalism. *Washington Post*, p. C.1. Retrieved from http://www.washingtonpost.com/lifestyle/style/atlantic-fiasco-renews-ethics-concerns-about-advertorials/2013/01/15/24287dfc-5f5f-11e2-9940-6fc488f3fecd_story.html.

Gardiner, K. (2013, October 3). The story behind "The Furrow." *Contently*. Retrieved from http://contently.com/strategist/2013/10/03/the-story-behind-the-furrow-2/.

Hagey, K. (2012, October 7). The advertorial's best friend: BuzzFeed site relies on sponsored content shared by visitors on social media. *The Wall Street Journal*. Retrieved from http://www.wsj.com/articles/SB10000872396390443493304578034732867593920.

International Olive Council. (2012). The emerging health attributes of the Mediterranean diet and olive oil [White paper]. Retrieved from http://www.addsomelife.org/wp-content/uploads/IOC_WhitePaper22.pdf.

Internet Live Stats. (2014). Internet users. Retrieved from http://www.internetlivestats.com/internet-users/.

Kim-Renaud, Y. (2009). *Korean: An essential grammar*. New York, NY: Routledge.

LEGO. (n.d.). LEGO Club: Interactive magazine. Retrieved from http://club.lego.com/en-us/interactive-magazine.

Mendes, E. (2013, September 19). In U.S., trust in media recovers slightly from all-time low: More Americans say media are too liberal than too conservative. *Gallup*. Retrieved from http://www.gallup.com/poll/164459/trust-media-recovers-slightly-time-low.aspx.

Michelin. (2009, February 3). The MICHELIN Guide: 100 editions and over a century of history. Retrieved from http://www.viamichelin.co.uk/tpl/mag6/art200903/htm/tour-saga-michelin.htm.

National Geographic. (2012, September 24). National Geographic shows 30.9 million worldwide audience via consolidated media report: ABC releases audited data from print editions, social media, apps and more [News release]. Retrieved from http://press.nationalgeographic.com/2012/09/24/national-geographic-shows-30-9-million-worldwide-audience-via-consolidated-media-report/.

Neff, J. (2009, October 7). P&G to launch custom beauty magazine Rouge in U.S.: Package goods giant plans to build database by relying on mommy bloggers to spread the word. *AdAge*. Retrieved from http://adage.com/article/media/media-p-g-launch-custom-beauty-magazine-rouge-u-s/139515/.

Reed, J. (2011, June 10). Nissan's PR mimics the newsroom. *The Financial Times*. Retrieved from http://www.theglobeandmail.com/report-on-business/international-business/nissans-pr-mimics-the-newsroom/article615946/.

Sinclair, L. (2014, April 14). ANZ to launch Blue Notes as brand journalism strikes a chord. *The Australian*. Retrieved from http://www.theaustralian.com.au/media/anz-to-launch-blue-notes-as-brand-journalism-strikes-a-chord/story-e6frg996-1226883579270.

Singh, N. (2012). *Localization strategies for global e-business*. Cambridge: Cambridge University Press.

Part Six

WRITING INTERNATIONAL PLANS, REPORTS, AND BUSINESS CORRESPONDENCE

The last part of the book covers how to write and present public relations plans; how to craft business correspondence, particularly new business letters and responses to complaints; how to prepare meeting agendas and record minutes; and how to handle activity and monitoring reports in public relations.

Chapter 16 Creating and Presenting Public Relations Plans for Local or Global Markets

- Explains how to write and present recommendations for an international public relations plan, which would apply to both public relations agencies (pitching new clients or renewing contracts) and to in-house public relations staff at multinational organizations (providing plans to decision-makers, who could be the CEO, executive management, marketing executives, or board of directors).
- Reviews tips on writing for potential clients or in-house staff members, who may not be native English speakers and may lack familiarity with public relations terms.
- Covers how to write a public relations plan from start to finish—executive summary, situation analysis, target audiences, objectives, strategies, tactics, timetable, measurement and evaluation, budget, staffing, and agency credentials.
- Provides tips on how to adapt a proposal to PowerPoint (or other visual presentation formats) with brief bullet points and imagery to serve as a visual guide and emphasize key points.
- Covers suggestions on presenting to diverse audiences, who may benefit by hearing more definitions of terms and receiving presentation hand-outs.

Chapter 17 Preparing Global Business Correspondence and Internal Reports

- Shows how to write clear correspondence for specific purposes, including how to respond to a complaint in writing and how to write compelling sales letters from a public relations agency to a prospective client.
- Reviews tips on writing business correspondence and emails for multinational audiences.
- Shows how to prepare easy-to-follow meeting agendas for different audiences.
- Demonstrates how to capture the essence of a meeting, including an overview of key discussion points, decisions made, and immediate next steps and responsibilities.
- Covers the reporting process to document accomplishments, work in progress, and other activities undertaken by local and international staff.
- Discusses the benefits of evaluating work that could be adapted for other markets, identify problem areas, and communicate results for case studies and award opportunities.

16 Creating and Presenting Public Relations Plans for Local or Global Markets

> You can have brilliant ideas, but if you can't get them across, your ideas won't get you anywhere.
>
> —Lee Iacocca, retired business executive and former CEO of Chrysler

16.1 Introduction to Public Relations Proposals

This quote from Lee Iacocca, former president of Ford Motor Company and CEO of Chrysler, applies to practically any industry, but it is particularly relevant in writing and presenting creative ideas to decision-makers—whether you are on the public relations agency side or in-house public relations staff. The proposal-planning process can be exhilarating, testing one's knowledge and strategic abilities. A well-written proposal explains how a public relations campaign would solve the organization's problems, overcome challenges, find new opportunities, and meet marketing objectives. It "walks" the client through the entire process with clear ideas that demonstrate why, how, where, and when the campaign would be undertaken and how much it would cost.

New business development is the lifeblood of the public relations agency world. Bringing in new accounts can result in increased revenues, client base expansion, and staff retention and new hires. In reality, most PR proposals are competitive, and clients receive numerous proposals to select from. Many larger new business prospects issue a **Request for Proposal** (RFP) that outlines the organization's interests in receiving bids from public relations agencies. The process may require multiple steps: a first step may request agency credentials to determine whether the agency's capabilities match the client's needs; then a short list of agencies are invited to prepare public relations recommendations; and the last step is the invitation to meet and present creative ideas to the prospective client. Some prospective clients may require a simpler process: an initial proposal with both agency credentials and creative concepts; and then the finalists present their proposal to the decision-makers.

Not all new business prospects follow the formal RFP process. In some cases, agencies may be approached directly by prospective clients, usually by referral, or the agency executives proactively seek prospective clients. In many of these cases, the agency still would be required to submit a public relations proposal.

New business development can present challenges too. Agencies need to make informed decisions on the amount of staff time and out-of-pocket expenses that should be devoted to a specific new business opportunity. The process requires finding out the answers to many questions.

- Do you know who is currently representing the client?
- Is this a real search for a new agency or pro forma, in which the incumbent will most likely keep the business?
- What other agencies are competing for the business, if known?
- What do you think is the likelihood of getting the account?
- How much is the potential business worth?
- Do you have the in-house expertise or wholly owned or affiliate arrangements with other agencies in geographic areas the potential client is interested in reaching?
- Is this new business opportunity a potential conflict with any of your existing clients? Many contracts include non-compete clauses.

The time invested in developing new business proposals is non-billable from an agency's perspective, meaning that staff involved with the project will be interrupted from their billable work with existing clients. Winning the new business, however, is a time-intensive proposition—and the process can be quite stimulating, requiring creative, strategic planning, and problem-solving skills.

16.2 The New Business Planning Process

I have dealt with new business from both the client and agency side. I have written RFPs, selected agencies to bid on the business, read stacks of proposals, and sat through new business presentations by agencies in different countries. In the agency world, I have deciphered RFPs, written new business proposals with feedback from offices around the world, and presented with diverse teams. As a professor, I also bring in real-world organizations as "clients" for students to create and present public relations proposals to as a final project.

Culled from this firsthand experience, I believe the following four steps can help expedite the process and make it more productive and less stressful:

1. **Maintain a Current Database of Agency Information and Create Templates**
    Having an instantly available database, whether on the Intranet or in another digital format, of up-to-date information about the public relations agency is essential. Time and energy can be misspent when the proposal writer is grappling with trying to find and update basic information about the public relations agency—instead of working on the creative strategy for a new business proposal. It is worth the effort to create templates for all staff worldwide to prepare the following content:

    - Agencies should maintain a list of current clients by office, as well as a list of former clients by industry and pro bono clients.
    - Staff biographies with photographs of all staff members should be consistent in tone, structure, and visual layout.
    - Case studies also should be consistent in content and layout. They should emphasize the situation, strategies, deliverables, and results, as well as include supporting visual imagery. Ideally, case studies should be easy to access by name of client, type of industry, geographic markets (global, region, country, or city), and type of campaign (such as social media, event planning, investor relations, consumer marketing, etc.).

– A list of awards and other accolades achieved by the agency should remain current at all offices worldwide.

– Speeches, white papers, published articles, and blogs also should be tracked and readily available as useful new business tools. They may address issues of particular interest to the prospective client.

– A fact sheet should cover at a glance the agency operations and credentials overall, including total number of offices, locations, areas of expertise, industries, awards, websites, and other relevant information. In addition, separate fact sheets on local agency operations by country should be compiled.

– A database of older new business proposals can be useful to generate ideas. However, a proposal writer should not attempt to just search the name of the older prospect and replace it with the new one. The new plan must match the client's specific needs. Generic plans, just like generic pitch letters, do not work as effectively.

– Agencies should invest time in creating a well-designed template with the agency's logo—and a place for the prospective client's logo—for the written proposal and visual presentation.

2. **Develop a Relationship with the Prospective Client—and Ask Questions**
   RFPs traditionally include a contact person who would be more than willing to answer relevant and intelligent questions posed by public relations agencies—not questions to which the answers are stated in the RFP or could be easily uncovered by reading the prospective client's website. Agency executives must avoid making assumptions about the client's business. Writers must put themselves in the prospective client's place and try to write the plan with all the necessary information for the decision-makers to evaluate your public relations recommendations—and inspire the client to approve the plan. The prospective client representatives are the decision-makers about the selection of creative agencies; they can be CEOs, entrepreneurs, managing directors, general managers, marketing or sales executives, or in-house public relations staff.

3. **Involve Relevant Contributors**
   Determine the staff members who can make a meaningful contribution to the planning, preferably executives who would be representing the client, and the presentation team. Many clients want to meet the people who will be on the account, as well as one of the agency partners. High power-distance clients will want to meet the most senior person or people; whereas low power-distance clients will care more about being introduced to the staff they will interact with on a daily basis. The more money at stake, the more agency staff will want to be involved—and this can present time and management challenges. Some agencies have a dedicated new business development team who may be able to offer creative solutions and packaging. The challenge is that they may have limited knowledge about the client's business.

4. **Be Organized**
   Work out a simple timetable to prepare the proposal and determine responsibilities and deadlines for each person's contribution from every office. Although brainstorming sessions can be beneficial, some agencies spend too much time in meetings to discuss ideas and cut back on the time actually writing and preparing the proposal. Since new business development can take time away from existing clients, agency

executives may have limited time during the day to focus on the plan. They may need to spend extra time on evenings and weekends to complete the proposal. All-nighters can be counterproductive; the quality of work usually suffers. With advance planning, executives should be able to minimize the stress and develop a stronger proposal. The planning process should include the feedback of the agency principal, director of the practice group, or other senior executives responsible for reviewing the draft and providing input within a realistic timeframe—but not the night before the plan is due. Last-minute changes with extensive rewrites and additional content can result in confusion and potentially costly mistakes. The reality, however, is that some new business opportunities can arise with limited advance time for planning. When the new business process is well organized, the process can be rewarding with creative energy and collaboration.

16.3 Writing Public Relations Proposals for Local or Global Campaigns

Tom Sant (2012), author of a book on writing proposals, illustrates his principle on trust with a quasi-equation on how important it is for new business to include credibility on qualifications *and* rapport on how your expertise matches your prospective client's specific needs, thereby "minimizing the customer's perception of risk in doing business with us" (p. 39).

$$\frac{\text{Credibility} \times \text{Rapport}}{\text{Trust}} = \text{Risk}$$

Make sure to apply a non-judgmental tone—and use positive language even when addressing negative points. For example, you may feel that the client's current online newsroom is weak or the social media engagement is off target. You could recommend *enhancements* to existing Web content. Diplomacy is vital—you don't know if the client had written the copy or made decisions about the existing website, press materials, brochures, or other projects.

Public relations writers usually team up with a designer who can create a template while the document is being written. The other consideration is how the proposal is packaged. How will it be bound? Will it be placed in a binder? I recall an agency that liked to customize the look of every proposal. A proposal for a private jet company was packaged in a sleek aluminum binder. A proposal for a leather apparel company was packaged in a high-quality leather binder. Be wary of cute gimmicky packaging for some clients. When I was on the client side for a luxury travel company, I received a small overnight bag packed with samples of the agency's other products, which were mostly inexpensive beauty products and over-the-counter pharmaceutical brands that emphasized the agency's primary client base—and not its experience with premium brands.

16.3.1 Step-by-Step Guidelines on Proposal Writing

Writing a public relations proposal traditionally includes the following 15 components. The order may change, particularly if the agency is responding to an RFP that requests a particular structure. In this case, the first part may need to focus on the agency's credentials and capabilities.

1. **Cover** (required)

   The cover of the public relations proposal may be the first impression, particularly if the public relations agency team members have not met with the prospective client. Many agencies invest time in creating a color design with their logo and the prospective client's logo, as well as other relevant graphics. Compelling visual imagery can make your proposal stand out among the stacks of proposals from other agencies—and motivate the prospective client to read the contents. (See Figure 16.1 of an example of a well-designed public relations proposal cover created by a graduate student for a real-world presentation with an organic food company.) The design template also should be consistent throughout, incorporating colorful headers and footers.

   The content should include the following copy:

   – **Title of the proposal** and a **subhead** can help convey the major goal or umbrella theme of the campaign. The title also can include the word global, if it covers multiple countries, or list the specific countries or regions. For example:

   > Public Relations Proposal for X (name of prospective client):
   > Differentiating Your Brands in a Competitive Marketplace
   > in North and South America

   – **Date of submission**—and make sure to spell out the month.
   – **Name of agency**, unless the logo is used, and clearly states the name.

Figure 16.1—COVER OF PUBLIC RELATIONS PROPOSAL FOR EMMY'S ORGANICS. Sources: Courtesy of Enrique Nunez, designer of proposal, and Emmy's Organics.

2. **Contact Information** (recommended)

Instead of cluttering the cover with contact information, writers can add a separate contact information page, with the names of the public relations agency executives to contact, along with their addresses, telephone numbers, emails, and optional social media. This section also could include a photograph of the proposed account team in the lead office, as well as other offices. I have seen some agencies create back covers with contact information; the challenge is that the prospective client may not see that section and believe that the contact information is missing.

3. **Table of Contents** (required for longer documents)

Tables of contents include the headings for each section. Some writers may want to incorporate more creative wording of each section, based on the industry. Try Exercise 16.1 to write your own headings for a table of contents.

Exercise 16.1

Creative Thinking: Preparing Colorful Table of Content Headings

Table of contents can be written factually or they can be written creatively. For example, if you were preparing a public relations proposal for the launch of a new restaurant chain as a prospective client, you could write more interesting headings with a food-related theme. Here are a few examples: *Our Menu: Introducing Recipes to Success* for the Executive Summary; *Three-Course Menu*, with three separate sections, such as *Appetizers: Pre-Opening Tactics*, *Entrees: Opening Tactics*, and *Desserts: Post-Opening Tactics* for the section on Tactics; *Cooking Time: Getting it Right* for the Timetable; *Measuring Cups: Featuring Precision* for Measurement and Evaluation, and *Our Kitchen Crew: Offering the Finest Talent* for the Agency Staff; and *Freshest Ingredients: Supplying the Goods* for Agency Credentials.

Your client is an auto manufacturer that is launching a new luxury sports car—and you are preparing a global public relations plan to introduce the new product. Customize the following headings (and you can add subheads) in the Table of Contents to be more expressive and reflective of the product or industry:

1. Executive Summary
2. Situation Analysis
3. Target Audiences
4. Objectives
5. Strategies
6. Tactics
7. Timetable
8. Measurement and Evaluation
9. Budget
10. Agency Team and Management
11. Agency Credentials
12. Appendix.

Double-check the page numbers—before the document is printed or sent electronically—in the final version since many edits can be made during the preparation process. Include only the starting page number of each section and align numbers so that they are easy to read. Make sure that the headings for each section exactly match the wording in the Table of Contents.

4. **Executive Summary** (recommended)

   Otherwise known as the introduction or overview, the Executive Summary describes briefly how the plan addresses the client's needs, overcomes challenges, or seeks new opportunities. This section can demonstrate how the plan can make a difference from a local, regional, country-specific, or global basis. It also gives the public relations agency the opportunity to thank the prospective client or other people who were helpful during the planning process. This section can reiterate why your public relations agency is the best fit—be careful to match specific needs of the client, not generic attributes of the agency. This section should be written last. It is worth spending time on it since it is widely read by decision-makers. Another option is to substitute the Executive Summary with a cover letter on the agency's letterhead signed by the principal or senior executive.

5. **Situation Analysis** (required)

   A well-developed plan explains the current situation the organization faces, including its strengths, benefits, and current and future opportunities, particularly if the prospective client is approaching new markets. Avoid making assumptions or repeating obvious facts about the client's business—look at what the agency can add and why those markets could be of value. This section helps to explain your rationale for making specific decisions.

   This process requires undertaking research to further develop the plan and make informed decisions in multiple markets. Here are a few options:

   – Research **media coverage** of articles in blogs, magazines, and newspapers, as well as TV and radio programs, over the past two years in the specific countries. Google News and online library databases can be useful. You also can examine media coverage on the organization's leading competitors. Try to incorporate those findings into the plan, particularly if you can develop other story ideas and identify new media targets.

   – Look at the client's **engagement on social media**, as well as its competitors' social media, to get an indication of volume, interactivity, and sentiment. Explain similarities and differences between the prospective client and its competitors.

   – Research any **industry trends** in secondary sources that may impact the client's business or operations, particularly in the specific geographic markets.

   – Add a **competitors' analysis** by examining the issues of greatest importance to the prospective client, such as price, location, product offerings, or other points of difference or similarity. Many prospective clients will identify their competitors in their RFPs.

   – Consider conducting **primary research** to help substantiate your recommendations. Online surveys, such as SurveyMonkey or Qualtrics, can be helpful. Use charts to make quantitative information easier to understand and help illustrate specific points.

   – Add the full survey and raw data in the Appendix.

– Consider conducting **soft-soundings**—which are informal conversations, following the same questions by telephone or by email, with journalists, industry experts, or opinion leaders.

– Include a **SWOT analysis**—internal **S**trengths and **W**eaknesses, and external **O**pportunities and **T**hreats—by using a grid format that summarizes the findings and is easy to read. Include regional versions of the SWOT analysis, if the situation is dramatically different in other markets.

– Consider recommending **future research** using a market research company that the client may want to undertake in specific markets as part of the plan.

– Include **closing commentary** on your findings and why they are relevant to your recommendations.

A more complex situation analysis can start off with a **global overview** followed by a **country-specific or region-specific analysis** of major competitors, the marketplace situation, the company's selling features in that market, as well as specific challenges and opportunities. Writers may need to add more information and justification about a specific geographic area, if the prospective client is entering a new market.

Writers explaining considerations about a new geographic market for a client may want to look at the **CAGE dimensions** developed by Pankaj Ghemawat (2007), author of *Redefining Global Strategy*. The CAGE framework examines four areas of dimensions of countries:

– **C**ultural distance, such as language, ethnicities, religious differences, preferences, and tastes.

– **A**dministrative/political distance, such as policies and laws that present barriers to selling products and enforce quality standards, and protectionism of tariffs.

– **G**eographic distance affecting trade and transportation of goods and services.

– **E**conomic distance, such as income levels, competition, labor, capital, and foreign investment.

6. **Target Audiences** (required)
Audiences are the "who" portion that the plan is designed to reach. For regional or international plans, audiences can be organized by geographic area and can include both primary and secondary target audiences. Be as specific as possible to illustrate the characteristics—demographics and psychographics—of your target audiences. Here are hypothetical examples of target audiences for a hotel company.

The public relations campaign will reach the following target audiences:

– Upscale travelers between 39 and 49 years old, with an average annual household income of more than USD175,000, who are married or partnered with young children, and likely to hold a post-graduate degree.

– Emphasis on the male traveler with 60% of the current customer base comprised of men, mostly employed in financial services, professional services, IT, and telecommunications.

– Also outreach to introduce more women to the brand, including both female business travelers and family vacationers, seeking a resort stay or a weekend break in a luxury urban hotel.

–   Americans who are frequent fliers on United, American, and Southwest; likely to drive Ford, Toyota, and Chevrolet; who enjoy spending time with the family, learning new things, investing in stocks, dining out, going to beaches and lakes, and visiting museums.

You also can add narrative examples of hypothetical people who illustrate the characteristics of your target audience. You can tell their story in a colorful way to indicate how they would connect with the brand, product, service, place, or cause.

Most plans include traditional media outlets by geographic area, whether they are local, regional, and national newspapers, magazines, radio, television, e-zines, radio and TV programs, as well as blogs. Provide a few examples of media outlets within each category, which can be organized by type of media (newspapers, magazines, etc.), by topic (business, lifestyle, etc.), or by geographic area (by city, country, or region). This part can be included in the section in Target Audiences or add a separate section called Target Media. It is recommended to include only the most relevant and influential traditional media. Some writers also list target social media outlets in this section—and then elaborate in the section on Tactics.

7. **Objectives** (required)

What will the public relations plan achieve after the program is completed? Focus on a few clearly expressed objectives the public relations campaign plan can accomplish, including how they may differ in various markets. Emma Daugherty (2003), a communications professor at California State University, Long Beach, recommends a strategic planning matrix that explains the problem based on facts, outlines an achievable goal, quantifies a marketing objective, explains a communication objective, which may be informational or quantifiable, followed by strategy and tactics. Let us look at a hypothetical example:

–   **Problem**: (Name of country) is experiencing a decline in tourist arrivals after a major hurricane. (In some cases, the situation may not be a problem but a new opportunity.)
–   **Goal:** To increase the number of tourist arrivals.
–   **Marketing objective:** To attract (a specific percentage) of tourists from (specific countries or regions) within two years.
–   **Communication objective:** To educate repeat and new travelers about the country's restored hotels, resorts, and tourist attractions, as well as new and upcoming tourism developments.

The other approach is to provide the overall global objectives and then divide objectives by specific countries or markets. Here are a few generic examples of both quantifiable and communication objectives:

Quantifiable objectives:

–   Increase revenues of product by X percent.
–   Raise the volume of traffic on the company's website and interactivity on social media outlets.
–   Increase the number of volunteers by X percent.
–   Raise more money than in the previous year to support the nonprofit's new program within the community.

Communication objectives:

- Craft a personality for the brand by creating compelling social media content that consumers will want to save, share, and comment.
- Change the perceptions of the organization's image.
- Decrease negative news coverage and social media sentiment on (specific topics).
- Educate target audiences of the benefits of the company's or product's (specific attributes).
- Differentiate the company from its competitors and identify its unique selling propositions to customers in (specific markets).

Be conservative if you use estimates on percentage increases. It is preferred to try to achieve—and preferably to exceed—results. Higher estimates may not be readily achievable. Make sure you have an understanding of what the numbers mean. For example, if you estimate that your plan would result in increasing volunteers by a specific percent, you should find out how many current volunteers are helping the nonprofit.

8. **Strategies** (required)

Strategies explain how the objectives will be realized. They also can be organized by global strategies, applying to all markets, and then by specific geographic markets. Here are a few generic strategies:

- To undertake an extensive media relations campaign to generate stories in print, broadcast, and online media read, seen, or heard by the company's target audiences.
- To use all relevant social media outlets to create engagement with the company's target audiences.
- To create high-profile events to launch the company's new products.
- To develop new communication tools to share key messages about the company's products and services.
- To distinguish the company's services from its competitors on its website and through all social media.
- To elicit positive reviews from industry analysts.
- To position the company's management as opinion leaders and share their opinions and visions at consumer and industry events, as well as through social media outlets and industry trades.

9. **Tactics** (required)

The "nuts and bolts" are tactics, which are the specific activities undertaken based on your objectives and strategies, such as news releases, events, or social media. This section reviews the scope of tactics to consider, as well as different approaches in creatively and logically explaining these ideas. It also reviews approaches to express core global and glocal strategies. This does not mean that you have to provide a step-by-step process on how you will implement the tactic; you need to explain the value of each tactic and how it will achieve results.

Tactics can be organized different ways:

- **By objective** (tactics to achieve each stated objective).
- **By type of tactic** (social media, traditional media, events, etc.).

- **By type of audience** (tactics to reach the media, residents in the community, or online community, and other target audiences addressed in the plan).
- **By geographic area** (tactics to reach North America, South America, Europe, Africa and the Middle East, and Asia-Pacific; or by specific countries).

The types of tactics covered vary based on the scope of the program. Here are suggested elements to add in this section:

- Create an umbrella theme to package the "big idea," which can be very effective.
- Consider adding key messages that would be communicated through different tactics, as well as in different geographic areas.
- Provide recommendations on social media (Facebook, Twitter, YouTube, etc.)—look at the client's existing social media and include enhancements—and investigate other social media that the client may want to tap and why.
- Include ideas to generate traditional media coverage in newspapers, magazines, TV and radio outlets—tactics can include ideas for story angles, news releases, media kit materials, interviews with company spokespeople, press invitations to events, or press visits, among others.
- Investigate existing events that the client is involved with and include enhancements—or provide ideas for newly created events that would build awareness of the client's products or services.
- Explore promotions—contests, cooperative incentives with complementary but noncompetitive organizations—or fundraisers or community relations.
- Look at the client's existing communication materials—website, brochures, fliers, posters, newsletters, and sales promotional merchandise—and make recommendations for enhancements or creation of new ones.
- Indicate what the potential results could be when discussing tactics.
- Include a few creative examples to illustrate your ideas. If you are showing how a social networking site could be enhanced, try to show a before-and-after example. Creative examples can be included in each appropriate section in Tactics—or placed in the Appendix. Be consistent in organizing information with whatever approach you decide to take. If creative examples are included in the Appendix, you need to let the reader know that each creative example is in the Appendix. And consider saving a few creative examples for the in-person presentation to share with the prospective client. See Exhibit 16.1 for a list of different types of tactics that a public relations proposal may include.

10. **Timetable** (recommended)

The timetable highlights when each activity will be undertaken throughout the timeframe of the plan. Charts and grids can show projected timing of activities succinctly and clearly, particularly with diverse global markets. Another approach is a start-up calendar, with action, responsibilities for multiple offices, and targeted dates. Some include an account checklist for the first 30, 60, or 90 days. Fit the timetable into one page (minimum) or a maximum of two pages.

- Explain when each activity would be undertaken—and make sure that you include each recommended tactic in the proposal.

Exhibit 16.1—SCOPE OF PUBLIC RELATIONS TACTICS. This list in alphabetical order includes examples of the variety of different tactics that could be covered in a public relations proposal, many of which may include an integrated marketing communications approach with advertising and digital branding. This list does not include all tactical options in the industry.

- Advertisements
- Advertorials and native advertising
- Blogs
- B-roll
- Brochures
- Bylined articles
- Contests
- Editorial briefings
- Employee communications
- Events (for the public, media, or industry groups)
- Fundraisers
- Interviews
- Letters to the editor
- Magazines (self-produced)
- Market research
- Media kits
- Media relations
- Media training
- Message development
- Microblogs (such as Twitter)
- News releases
- Newsletters

- Online newsrooms
- Op-eds
- Podcasts
- Posters
- Press conferences
- Press visits
- Promotions (cooperative, online, radio, retail, etc.)
- Public service announcements
- Sales promotional materials
- Social media news releases
- Social networking (such as Facebook)
- Speaking engagements
- Speechwriting
- Statements
- Story ideas
- Video news releases
- Visual imagery sharing (such as YouTube and Pinterest)
- Website enhancements
- Web stories (brand journalism)
- White papers.

- Ensure that activities are spread throughout the year—in the real world, a plan would have activities every month—and some activities may be ongoing.
- Show how you would accomplish this work on a quarterly basis (every three months) for **one year**, unless the plan is for a campaign that has to be executed within a shorter or longer timeframe.
- Write copy that is extremely brief and easy to scan.
- Use nouns or active verbs and be consistent in use of language, such as write press materials, escort press trip, revamp website, conduct special event, follow up with media, update social media, etc.

11. **Measurement and Evaluation** (required)

How will the success of the campaign be determined? Will the campaign be evaluated differently in specific markets? What is the return on investment? This part examines how the campaign will be evaluated to determine its success, covering outcomes, not just outputs, and how to measure the return on investment. This area has been widely discussed and disputed in the public relations industry. In an effort to create a universal framework with consistent professional industry standards, five public relations groups collaborated and established the **Barcelona Declaration of Measurement Principles** at a conference hosted by the International Association for the Measurement and Evaluation of Communication (also called AMEC) and the Institute for Public Relations (IPR), which was held in Barcelona, in 2010. They determined seven principles (AMEC & IPR, 2010) that are outlined in Exhibit 16.2.

The industry has been debating the usage of **advertising value equivalencies** (AVEs) as a measurement tool. AVEs mean that the publicity generated in traditional media is measured in terms of how much advertising would have cost for the same exposure. These numbers have many pitfalls: How can you compare advertising expenditures with the relative value of stories generated on the editorial side, which are higher in credibility? How does the number really measure the results in achieving the company's business objectives? In addition, the practice of traditional media relations is not the only part of the public relations process.

Another perspective is the **IOIO (Input-Output-Impact-Outcome)** model of measurement (Devereux & Peirson-Smith, 2009, p. 206) that determines results by evaluating the following:

- **Input**—the measurement of the quantity of an activity, such as a specific number of news releases distributed, number of events coordinated, number of social media posts, etc.
- **Output**—the immediate results of the activities, such as the total circulation of readers or number of viewers or listeners of media outlets, number of participants at events, website and social media traffic, or number of toll-free telephone calls.
- **Impact**—the effect of the output, such as positive messages and sentiment.
- **Outcome**—how the program impacted the company's business objective or goals of a nonprofit. Did the company's revenues increase? Did the campaign increase the number of volunteers, donors, or corporate sponsors? Did the musicians perform in sold-out concert halls?

Exhibit 16.2—BARCELONA DECLARATION OF MEASUREMENT PRINCIPLES.
Source: AMEC & IPR. (2012). *Barcelona declaration of measurement principles*. Retrieved from http://amecorg.com/2012/06/barcelona-declaration-of-measurement-principles/.

Five public relations industry groups—Global Alliance for Public Relations and Communication Management, International Communications Consultancy Organisation, Institute for Public Relations, Public Relations Society of America, and AMEC (International Association for the Measurement & Evaluation of Communication) U.S. & Agency Leaders Chapter—presented and finalized these seven principles on July 19, 2010.

1. Importance of Goal Setting and Measurement
2. Measuring the Effect on Outcomes is Preferred to Measuring Outputs
3. The Effect on Business Results Can and Should Be Measured Where Possible
4. Media Measurement Requires Quantity and Quality
5. AVEs are Not the Value of Public Relations
6. Social Media Can and Should Be Measured
7. Transparency and Replicability are Paramount to Sound Measurement.

12. **Budget** (required)

Budgets in public relations proposals include both **agency staff fees** and **estimated expenditures**. As one of the most scrutinized parts of a public relations plan, this section needs to explain how staff fees are billed, whether on a monthly retainer or hourly basis, and to provide estimates on out-of-pocket expenses for the proposed tactics in the proposal.

Agencies traditionally bill like lawyers, with an hourly rate per position, which can vary from country to country due to local operational costs, benefits, and salaries. Expenses for events, printing, and other activities also can be quite different in specific locations. The staff and out-of-pocket estimates are traditionally prepared by a senior executive who has experience in managing and budgeting teamwork in multiple offices in different countries. That person also would request estimates from staff in specific offices to determine potential expenses.

The traditional approach is to provide estimates in the local currency of the agency where the work would be undertaken, along with conversion rates in the currency of the location of the client's headquarters. It is essential to provide the source of the conversion and clarify that the rate applies to the exchange at a specific time since rates can fluctuate. The preferred way to designate the type of currency being used is the three-letter International Organization for Standardization 4217 currency codes to avoid any confusion. For example, an Australian public relations agency preparing estimates for an American client would need to indicate the costs in American dollars (USD) or Australian dollars (AUD). Make sure to include a grand total.

You also can include a pie chart to indicate the percentage breakdown on how you would spend the money, such as 25% on events, etc.—and be careful to use clearly distinguishable colors to make the information easy to read.

13. **Agency Team and Management Structure** (required)

This section is an important selling feature for public relations agencies in demonstrating the depth of knowledge of the prospective account team and how the team will be structured, as well as accountability and reporting. A management account chart can visually show the reporting structure with multiple offices and levels of expertise required to execute the program.

Avoid such hackneyed phrases as "experienced team of professionals," "dedicated team with personalized service," and "exceptional talents." Explain your experience, how you would work with the client, and highlight the team members' talents.

Biographies should be organized in order of rank, then in alphabetical order by last name. The content can follow the executive profiles in Chapter 11 or the style of the specific agency. Most biographies include the professional's full name, title, location of office, scope of responsibilities, career with agency, prior work history, awards and publications, professional memberships, and education. Some agencies may include more personal background and add a personal touch relevant to the client, such as the staff member's experience with the brand, product, service, cause, or place. Biography lengths can vary based on titles, with the more senior staff having longer bios than the junior staff.

Consider adding a photograph of each staff member in his or her biography— or a photo of the entire team in each office involved with the campaign. Be mindful

Figure 16.2—CREATIVE EXAMPLE OF A BIO IN THE FORM OF A MOTORCOACH TICKET. Source: © Ella Sciocchetti.

Wanderlust Public Relations

ELLA SCIOCCHETTI
Class of 2017
Major: Integrated Marketing Communications
Minor: Honors

Reservation # 45ACJ
PAID

ELLA SCIOCCHETTI

Departure
ALBANY, NY

Arrival
ITHACA, NY

Favorite Travel Destination: Berlin, Germany
Favorite Part about Ithaca: the waterfalls and gorges

Reservation at the Tenwood Lodge in Ithaca, NY
Room of choice: Bunkhouse Mini-Master

of the culture of the country of the client. For example, women should avoid wearing short-sleeved or sleeveless clothes or miniskirts for clients from Islamic countries. More formal cultures would be less appreciative of staff wearing casual attire. Biographical images that show personality or action need to be carefully considered and relevant to the potential client.

Another creative approach is to package the information differently. For example, a team of students in my class prepared their bios as nutritional labels for a yogurt manufacturer. For a country inn, the students converted their bios into bus tickets since that it is one of the most popular ways for visitors to travel from major cities nearby to this destination (see Figure 16.2).

14. **Agency Credentials**

If the RFP required a first step of agency credentials that were previously submitted, this part can be extremely brief and emphasize key points. Otherwise, public relations agencies can feature credentials in new business plans, showcasing their scope of services and resources in multiple markets, areas of specialization, awards and accomplishments, current client list, and case studies to prospective clients. If time is permitted, writers may want to edit the generic information and make the content as relevant as possible to the client. If you know which agencies you are competing with, you can provide points of differences. For example, you may know that the prospective client is currently represented by a small, independent agency and your agency is a large conglomerate. You may want to emphasize high-quality service and the scope of services offered throughout the agency.

15. **Appendix** (optional)

If creative mockups were not included in Tactics, you can include that material here and let the reader know that creative samples are in the Appendix. Adding a glossary of terms in the Appendix can be useful to international clients, who may be less familiar with terms in the public relations industry. If you have conducted informal research, you may want to include the complete survey findings here as well.

16.4 Presenting Public Relations Plans

Let us assume that your prospective client liked your proposal and your agency made it to the short list. Now you and your team have to figure out how to best present your creative ideas and highlight your agency's capabilities and achievements. Effective presentations can make the difference in winning a new account or renewing an existing account on the agency side, thereby maintaining the viability of an agency's profitability and expansion plans. On the corporate side, in-house staff may need approvals and support from many decision-makers—the CEO, marketing and public relations executives, regional sales directors, among others—for new public relations plans, budgets, and staffing.

As with preparing public relations proposals, the public relations writer needs to find out key facts before starting to put the presentation together.

- **Know who will be listening to the presentation**—Feel free to ask the prospective client who will be attending the presentation. You can try to find biographical information on the organization's website and LinkedIn. Knowing how many people are attending can help you work out the physical setup and any food and beverages needed.

- **See if the list of competitors is public**—Prospective clients may share the short list of agencies with all presenters. In some cases, you can ask the prospective client, but be aware that the question may not be answered. However, it is not uncommon for large-scale competitive agency reviews to be covered in public relations industry trades.

- **Find out where you will be presenting**—The ideal scenario for many agencies is hosting the prospective client in the agency's office. This is not unusual since many clients want to see the agency's office and meet with the entire team. The second most common situation is traveling to the prospective client's office. Not all prospective clients will cover transportation, hotels, and meals for the presenting team. This means that the agency has to consider carefully how much it is willing to spend for travel and how many people should travel and from which offices. In this case, the agency team members must arrive the day before the presentation. Traveling on the same day can be risky; inclement weather and unexpected travel delays may result in missing the presentation time. The third option is for the client to host the agency meetings at a hotel or meeting space either in a major city or in the client's home city. The team also needs to find out what the presentation setup is like and when the room is available.

- **Determine your presentation team**—Know who will be presenting and determine what section each person will be presenting. Everyone attending the presentation should make a contribution and speak—avoid "mute" participants. Preferably the person who researched or prepared specific sections should be the one to discuss those parts. Longer sections can have more than one presenter at a time. Determine the "clicker"—will it be one person responsible or will each presenter advance his or her slides? Remote clickers are worth using. All presenters should review the slide copy in advance, thereby allowing them to make any edits before rehearsals. Be prepared to have one person responsible for editing the final presentation during the rehearsals when the presentation team members may make additional changes. Make sure you have the right number of people to present—and the right range of titles. I recall how a single presenter—the principal of an independent agency—with no visual materials won a lucrative new business presentation over an "army" of mid-level executives at a large agency that was part of an international conglomerate, with splashy visuals and props. Why? The single presenter was the founder and the highest-ranking person at the agency—and she developed a rapport with the prospective client during a lively interchange and convinced the client that her agency had the best resources, talent, and ideas to make the campaign a success.

- **Identify the primary editor and designer**—Many agencies have in-house talent who can focus on the visual design while the writer devotes time to the text. Also consider any handouts for the prospective client. You may want to distribute storyboards of the presentation and images of the presenting team, with their names and titles.
- **Figure out the setup**—Having the presentation held in one's own office has benefits, enabling the public relations team to stage the setting. What type of food and beverages will be served? One agency, for example, arranged for a well-respected restaurant to serve lunch in its conference room. Do you want to display your work? Some conference rooms may already be decorated with excellent work and awards. I recall how an agency pitching an airline papered the conference room walls with First Class airline tickets as a backdrop to illustrate that its public relations strategy would sell high-yield seats. The agency did win the business.

  Make sure you have the right number of chairs and the seating arrangements in advance. Table tents with everyone's name and title can work effectively. If not, a handout of the presentation team with their photographs can be distributed to the prospective client representatives. Some cultures like to receive gifts and, in this case, the agency may want to give logoed gifts or locally made food or products from the area. But do double-check the cultural customs for gift-giving courtesies. If the prospective client representatives are from out of town, you may want to offer to drive, arrange a car service, hail a taxi, or escort the guests to the nearest public transportation. To conclude, do not underestimate the power of staging and hosting prospective clients.

16.4.1 How to Avoid "Death by PowerPoint" Presentations

"Death by PowerPoint" has been joked about by cartoonists illustrating long-suffering meeting participants collapsing to the floor. Do whatever you can to avoid this infliction in whatever form of presentation software you choose. PowerPoint is still quite popular with its customized features, while Prezi presentation software can be effective yet some people say it makes them dizzy. The benefits of visual presentations, however, are still numerous. They can serve as prompts for the speakers and help your audience remember key points and show visual examples. The disadvantages still exist; PowerPoint (or any other presentation software) can distract the audience, if it is poorly executed. Let us look at techniques for visuals:

- **Easy-to-scan text** serves as guideposts for the speaker and audience. If the visual presentation contains too much text, the audience may spend too much time reading instead of listening to the presenters. Keep it short since the presenters will provide more details. Use phrases instead of complete sentences—be consistent and start with verbs or nouns—don't mix and match them. Avoid complete sentences, unless you are quoting from someone. Avoid exclamation marks; instead use your voice to emphasize key points. Proof and edit copy. No one can rely on computerized spell check programs.

- **Aesthetically pleasing design** should be relevant to that audience. Use color combinations that are easy to read on the projected screen, not just on your smaller laptop screen. Soft yellow text on a white background will not be easy to read. Other eye-straining combinations can be purple text on a black background. Double-check any potential cultural interpretations of colors. Be consistent visually with fonts, colors, and template design. Make sure the right images are used. I recall a lost new business prospect when an agency used the company's old logo that was updated six months earlier. Charts and graphs package research and numbers more effectively than just text. Photos or videos can illustrate creative concepts and break up the visual monotony—but be careful of cartoons and humor that may not be understood by your audience.
- **A backup of the presentation** can help you be prepared for the worst-case scenario—a power failure can derail a stunning visual presentation. Bring along a few presentation print-outs.

Although a stunning visual presentation is important, the prospective clients will focus more on the proposed agency talent, who will need to develop a rapport and convince the decision-makers that they have the experience, knowledge, and enthusiasm to manage the account. The intangible quality of chemistry is essential.

- **Make eye contact** with the audience. The presenters must avoid relying too heavily on the screen and note cards. Avoid reading verbatim—you are not paying attention to the audience when you are reading from the screen or cards. The only time reading should be permitted is when you are sharing a quoted source or referring to numbers.
- **Rehearse** and make sure each presenter knows what each team member is doing. Present with enthusiasm and confidence. Be animated—but be mindful of cultural considerations—and show interest with energy. Pick up on cues from your audience. Stand tall and straight.
- **Dress appropriately**. Most new business presentations require formal business clothes, not business casual attire. I recall members of a management team of a company in a South American country who were distracted by the business casual attire of the American agency presenters. They felt the agency expressed a lack of consideration and awareness of business etiquette in their country. The agency did not win the account.
- **Time your presentation.** Allocate time for a question-and-answer session. Running out of time is less desirable than ending early, which would give you more time for the question-and-answer session. If the prospective client has few or no questions, you can ask questions to spark a conversation.

The public relations proposal presentation will not be won just on the supporting visual presentation alone. Exhibit 16.3 includes considerations on the content and flow for the visual presentation, including text and imagery, and tips for the presenters of each section.

Exhibit 16.3—CONSIDERATIONS FOR PUBLIC RELATIONS PROPOSAL PRESENTATIONS.

Section	Text and Visual Considerations for Presentations	Considerations for Presenters
Introduction	The first slide should include the name of the public relations proposal, preferably with a subhead on the umbrella theme or goal of the campaign.	The most senior person traditionally kicks off this section, welcomes the clients, and expresses thanks for the opportunity. When presenting to representatives from a high power-distance culture, the person with the highest rank should be the lead presenter, whereas people from a low power-distance culture would prefer to hear more from the person who will be the day-to-day account supervisor.
		If someone on the agency team speaks the native language of the client representatives, that person could provide the introductions in that language—and then the next presenter would continue in English.
		If the prospective client representatives are given any handouts, that presenter should discuss what they are for.
Agenda	The agenda slide should list the topics the presentation will cover.	The person handling the introduction also can provide a quick overview of what the presentation will cover in the allotted time. This part is also an opportunity to set up guidelines, such as how questions can be addressed during the presentation or to please hold questions until the end of the presentation in which a question-and-session will be held for a specific timeframe. Allowing the decision-making team members to ask questions can make the presentation more interactive, yet this approach can derail the flow and may result in running out of time to discuss all components.
Team Introductions	This slide should include the names and titles of the team and their photos (or the management chart).	The lead speaker also can introduce the proposed account team members and their roles. The preferred method is to have each team member presenting make a few comments how his or her experience is
	You also can drop in video clips, particularly of key staff from other	

continued

Exhibit 16.3—Continued

	offices, if some teams are not available to travel. (You also could try video conferencing, but this approach may have technical issues.)	relevant to the client and their role with the account.
		A personal touch can make a difference— yet be cautious with humor. For example, presenters could talk about their experience with the brand or their favorite product option.
About the Agency	This section should be quite brief and highlight what would interest the prospective client.	A senior person should lead this part and try to match the agency's expertise with the client's specific needs.
	More time should be spent on what the agency can do for the client— some agencies invest too much content here and lose the audience.	
Situation Analysis	This section can highlight what you have learned from primary or secondary research. Charts can work effectively in conveying numbers. SWOT analysis works effectively in a grid format.	Another presenter can address the core findings of the situation analysis and how it impacted the campaign planning elements. Be careful to avoid making assumptions about the client's business.
Target Audiences	For target audiences, images of potential audiences can work effectively—or list the key audiences with a few points.	The presenter could talk about why these target audiences are important. If the plan is addressing new geographic markets, a local executive from that market could cover that specific section. The presenter also could use a narrative approach by telling a hypothetical story about specific people, who would be fictitious, but descriptive of the target audience.
	For target media, the slide can show logos of different media outlets that the agency will approach. This can read more effectively than just listing names of examples of media.	
Objectives	This slide can contain a list of the objectives that can be numbered.	The same person who handled the audiences could continue this part.
	Use active verbs.	
Strategies	This slide can include a bulleted list, which also could be numbered in order of importance.	The same person who discussed audiences and objectives could handle this part.
Tactics	This section is considered the "heart" of the campaign since it outlines what activities will take place. Since the written proposal contains details,	This part should be presented by team members who will be hands-on with the account. The section on tactics is usually the longest, so a tag-team approach with

continued

Exhibit 16.3—Continued

	the text on the tactics should be logically organized—by geographic region, by audience, by type of tactic, or by strategy.	two or more presenters can work effectively.
	Elaborate on the best ideas. Before-and-after examples work effectively. Include any creative examples in this part. Add as many images as you can. If you are recommending an event, show an image of the venue or location.	Based on the timeframe, the agency presenters may not be able to discuss every recommendation, but they should explain why specific tactics are worthwhile and their potential results.
Timetable	This part should be presented simply with text in active verbs or nouns in a grid format for a specific timeframe. Make sure the timetable can be read clearly when viewed on the screen.	The focus should be on the key initiatives, not every single detail. If something is ongoing, let the audience know that.
Evaluation	Quick bulleted text can emphasize how the plan will be measured and evaluated.	A senior person should discuss this part and emphasize how the campaign's success will be evaluated.
Budget	List numbers separately for staff and expenses, including a total for each. Make the currency clear.	A senior person should handle this part.
	Use a pie chart that can be viewed clearly on the projected screen to show how the budget will be allocated for out-of-pocket expenses. This section can be quite complex, particularly if the prospective client did not share a specific budget with the agency.	
Conclusion	The last slide can simply say "thank you" with logos of the agency and the prospective client.	The most senior person (or the first presenter) usually returns to say a few closing remarks and begins a question-and-answer session.
	Some agencies also like to add messages about the future relationship, such as "we want to be your public relations partner."	

The reality is that no public relations agency will win every new business opportunity. Use each experience as an opportunity to be reflective and learn from it. Even if you are rejected, you can contact the former prospective client and ask to meet in person, set up a phone call, or ask questions by email. Some people may not respond, but others may really appreciate the interest and provide valuable feedback.

16.5 Learning Objectives and Key Terms

After reading Chapter 16, you should be able to:

- Be best prepared for new business development by creating internal templates and guidelines for public relations agency resources.
- Pinpoint the traditional components in a public relations plan.
- Understand editorial considerations for each section.
- Know how to prepare for a public relations proposal presentation.
- Organize visual and written content for a public relations proposal presentation.
- Identify considerations in selecting the presentation team who would be responsible for each section during the presentation.

Chapter 16 contains the following key terms:

Request for proposal (p. 407)	Situation analysis (p. 413)
Soft soundings (p. 414)	SWOT analysis (p. 414)
Target audiences (p. 414)	CAGE dimensions (p. 414)
Marketing objectives (p. 415)	Communication objectives (p. 415)
Quantifiable objectives (p. 415)	Strategies (p. 416)
Tactics (p. 416)	Timetable (p. 417)
Measurement and evaluation (p. 418)	Barcelona Declaration of Measurement
IOIO model (p. 419)	principles (p. 419)
Staff time/budget (p. 420)	

References

AMEC & IPR. (2010, July 19). *Barcelona Declaration of Measurement Principles*. Retrieved from http://amecorg.com/wp-content/uploads/2012/06/Barcelona_Principles.pdf.

Daugherty, E. (2003). Strategic planning in public relations: A matrix that ensures tactical soundness. *Public Relations Quarterly, 48*(1), 21–26.

Devereux, M. M., & Peirson-Smith, A. (2009). *Public relations in Asia Pacific: Communicating effectively across cultures*. Singapore: John Wiley & Sons.

Ghemawat, P. (2007). *Redefining global strategy: Crossing borders in a world where differences still matter*. Boston, MA: Harvard Business School Publishing Corporation.

Sant, T. (2012). *Persuasive business proposals: Writing to win more customers, clients, and contracts* (3rd ed.). New York, NY: AMACOM.

17 Preparing Global Business Correspondence and Internal Reports

> Meetings are often scheduled "just because," and dysfunctional meeting behavior is on the rise. At one company, about 1 in 5 meeting participants sent an average of three or more emails for every 30 minutes of meeting time. At a sample 10,000-employee business, $60 million—20 percent of the total cost of meetings—was squandered in unproductive activity.
>
> —Bain & Co., a global management consulting firm

17.1 Introduction to Business Communication in Public Relations

Bain & Co., a global business consulting firm, investigated time usage of 17 large corporations and found that 15% of staff time collectively is spent in meetings, with senior executives devoting more than two days per week to meetings with colleagues. The survey also revealed that executives receive an average of 30,000 external communications per year, meaning that more than one day each week is required to manage the volume (Bain & Co., 2014).

Other surveys also reveal the perils of time wasted in attending meetings and sorting through emails, many of them unnecessary.

- Thirty percent of 2,000 managers surveyed by *Industry Week* declared meetings a waste of time, while 20 to 50% of executives in an EM Meeting Network survey also made the same claim (Williams, 2012).
- A survey by Atos Origin, a global information technology company, found that employees waste 40% of their time reading internal emails of no value (Atkin, 2012).
- A reporter for *Management Today* (Burn-Callander, 2013) summed up the reality of meeting mania in the U.K.: "That's four hours of pointless meetings every week. Or a weekly *Gone with the Wind* screening" (para. 3). The 1939 historical romance film lasts 3 hours and 58 minutes. She summed up the time wasted throughout the average office worker's career as "a full year and ten days spent twiddling their thumbs" (para. 4).

Have you ever found yourself sitting in meetings that you thought were poorly planned or lasted too long? Think about all the email messages you receive from internal and external sources. Have you found that you have been copied in on messages that have no direct relevance to you? Have you received unsolicited spam? Unnecessary meetings and emails are major culprits in the workforce. I suspect that many executives in the corporate world have already or will encounter the "corporate sadist," who enjoys stifling and strangling valuable staff time with meaningless meetings and emails, as well as brain-numbing reports. Try Exercise 17.1 and reflect on meetings that you have attended.

Exercise 17.1

Insights: Your Experiences with Meetings

Reflect upon experiences you have had either organizing or attending meetings of any kind, whether for a job or internship, for a student organization or class project with team members, or for volunteer work. Please answer the following questions:

1. What do you consider the characteristics of a successful meeting?
2. What about the opposite—what characterizes an unproductive meeting? What would you have done to improve these meetings?
3. Have you had the opportunity to coordinate and conduct a meeting? If so, what did you learn from those experiences?
4. Have you ever prepared written agendas or meeting minutes? Did you receive any feedback from the participants?

Scott Adams' Dilbert cartoons (www.dilbert.com) bring humor to the downside of office culture (see Figure 17.1). Adams drew from his work experiences at a bank and a telecommunications company before he was able to leave his day job and become a full-time cartoonist. It is not surprising that his cartoons have appeared in more than 2,000 newspapers in 65 countries—and became the first syndicated cartoon strip on the Web in 1995.

Learning how to communicate effectively, particularly with internal communications, can make you a more effective manager who knows how to write clearly, how to coordinate productive meetings, and how to prepare collaborative reports that share meaningful information. These skills will save time and money for all parties. Your colleagues at all levels will thank you. Michael Mankins, leader of Bain's Organization Practice in the Americas,

Figure 17.1—DILBERT CARTOON CAPTURES HOW MEETING TIME CAN BE MISUSED. DILBERT © 2001 Scott Adams. Used by permission of UNIVERSAL UCLICK. All rights reserved.

said, "Innovative companies are fostering cultures where time is treated as a scarce resource and invested as prudently as capital" (Bain & Co., 2014, para. 9).

This chapter covers how to prepare business correspondence from formal business letters to email messages, as well as how to write new business letters and responses to complaints; how to craft meeting agendas and minutes; and how to prepare public relations activity reports and media monitoring updates.

17.2 Business Correspondence

Business writing style varies from the corporate culture within a company, as well as the cultural differences based on the office's location. This section looks at how to prepare three types of basic business correspondence: formal letters, memos, and emails.

17.2.1 Preparing Formal Business Letters

Although routine correspondence is most often sent by email, circumstances may require more formal letters that are printed out and mailed to the recipients or sent as an attachment by email. In the public relations business, executives may use formal letters for the following purposes, among others:

- Confirmations of job offers, including the job title, responsibilities, salary and benefits, work hours, paid vacation days, and other details.
- Confirmations of project work with freelancers or outside specialists.
- Sales letters to prospective clients by public relations agencies seeking new business.
- Cover letters prepared by organizations with Request for Proposals seeking public relations services.
- Cover letters from public relations agencies responding to Request for Proposals to bid on new business.
- Confirmations of renewals or new public relations contracts with clients, accompanying legal contracts.
- Pitch letters to journalists with product samples and printed media kits or other forms of tactical materials.
- Important correspondence to clients with supporting materials, such as plans or comprehensive reports, sent by mail or courier.
- Recommendation letters that require a signature on company letterhead.
- Job resignations or terminations, resignations from clients for public relations representation, or public relations agencies resigning accounts.

How to Format a Formal Business Letter (for mail or as a PDF attachment)

Since many people today are accustomed to texting and writing emails, this section explains the parts of a formal letter. Please refer to Exhibit 17.1 that shows how a block-style letter is formatted; the number codes listed in the step-by-step guidelines match the circled numbers in the exhibit.

1. **Sender's Address** (required, unless on letterhead or digital macro)
   Letterhead traditionally includes the organization's logo, name, address, telephone number, email, and website (and other social media). Some companies also create personalized letterheads for senior executives, with their name, title, and direct

contacts. If you are sending personal correspondence and do not have letterhead, you can download templates free from Microsoft Word and other online sources. The other option is to write your address at the top of the letter, leaving at least two lines between the last line of the address and the date.

Exhibit 17.1—TRADITIONAL BUSINESS LETTER FORMAT IN BLOCK STYLE.

Sender's Address (if letterhead is not used)
Full Name of Sender (some writers exclude name and title in sender's address)
Title
Name of Organization
Street Address
City, State/Province Postal/Zip Code ①

Date (Month Day, Year in the U.S.; Day Month Year outside of the U.S.) ②

Mr. or Ms. or Dr. (or other title) First and Last Name (of recipient) ③
Title of Person
Affiliation
Street Address
City, State or Province, Postal or Zip Code
COUNTRY

Re: Topic (optional "with regard to"; also can list subject title) ④

Dear Mr./Ms./Miss/Mrs./Dr. Last Name (use first name only if you are on a first-name basis with the recipient; otherwise, use the last name): ⑤

Single space the body copy of your letter and add one blank line between each paragraph in a block-style format. Avoid writing paragraphs over eight lines. Left justify your letter. The first paragraph should provide an introduction to why you are writing—or it should be edited to different cultural norms. ⑥

Each supporting paragraph should focus on one theme. You also can use bullets to emphasize key points.

The last paragraph should reiterate key points and close with any next steps; it also can include the sender's telephone number and other contact information.

Sincerely yours, ⑦

Handwritten Signature ⑧

Typed Signature (full name of the person sending the letter)
Title (if not printed on letterhead)

P.S.: (optional postscript) ⑨

XX/xx (optional, signature initials/typist initials, if typed by another person) ⑩

Enclosures (if you are enclosing material with the letter) ⑪

CC: (if other people are receiving the letter, list their names, titles and affiliations) ⑫

2. **Date** (required)

Letters must include the date when the document is sent. Make sure to spell out the month to avoid confusion; *1/7/16* could mean *January 7* or *July 1*. American correspondence writes the date in order of month day year, such as *January 7, 2016*, whereas other countries usually indicate the date as day month year, *7 January 2016*, with no punctuation. Also be mindful of time considerations when the letter is sent. Avoid sending correspondence that would arrive on major holidays when offices are closed or peak vacation seasons when recipients may be away from their office.

3. **Inside Address** (required)

This part refers to the address of the person who will be receiving the letter.

Dr. John Brown	Courtesy title and full name of recipient
Managing Director	Title of recipient
John Brown Global Ltd.	Name of organization
East Tower, Suite 200	Street address and any room number
24 Kings Road	
Markham, Ontario L3R 9Z7	Town/city, state/province, and postal/zip code
CANADA	Country, usually written in capitalized letters, if mailed outside the sender's country

Please note that some countries may write their addresses differently, particularly the placement of the postal codes.

Although this part may seem simple, writers must make sure to follow protocol when writing the name and title of the recipient. Some places, such as Hungary and many countries in Asia, use the last name first, so double-check that you have the right order and don't make assumptions. Are you certain about the gender of the recipient? You may not be familiar with the name or it could be a unisexual name, and some women and men may have first names that are more traditional for the opposite gender. For men, the choice is simple: *Mr.* For women, however, there are three options: *Ms.*, *Miss*, or *Mrs.* In the U.S., *Ms.* is used frequently, whether or not the person is married. Be mindful that some cultures prefer to use *Mrs.*, if the person is married, or *Miss*, with no punctuation, if the person is single. Oxford English also does not use punctuation for courtesy titles (*Mr, Mrs,* or *Dr*).

Be mindful of official forms of address in which you may need to use another title to reflect someone's academic degree, profession, or social status. Would you know how to address a letter to a queen, a military general, an ambassador, or a president or premier of a country? Make sure to follow the proper traditional protocol, even when it is optional. For example, the official website of the British monarchy clearly indicates that all correspondence to a member of the royal family must be by letter—not by email or telephone. It advises that letter writing does not need to adhere to strict protocol, but that writers may prefer to observe traditional forms.

4. **Reference Line** (optional)

The **reference line** (also called **attention line** or **subject line**) can be helpful if you want the recipient to quickly know the purpose of the letter. In American correspondence, the abbreviation *Re:* is used followed by a colon, such as *Re: Public Relations Recommendations for Company X.* Outside of the U.S., the subject alone could be listed, such as *Public Relations Recommendations for Company X.* If you are referring back to correspondence that was coded, either with numbers, letters, or a combination, from your company (*Our reference AB123*) or the sender's company (*Your reference CD234*), you can add this information in the reference line. Some authors may place the reference one blank line below the date or below the salutation.

5. **Salutation** (required)

The **salutation** (also called **greeting**) traditionally begins with *Dear* followed by the person's courtesy title and last name (surname), such as *Dear Mr. Jones* (do not write *Dear Mr. John Jones* since the first name is not necessary in this section). Make sure that you are using the correct courtesy title. Only use the first name, such as *Dear John*, if you have established a first-name relationship with the recipient. People in more formal cultures may be offended by the use of first names. If you do not know the name of the person, you can write *Dear Sir* for a man and *Dear Madam* for a woman. Most letters in public relations, however, will be addressed to a specific person.

American English business correspondence traditionally uses a colon after the person's name in business correspondence (*Dear Mr. Jones:*), and British English correspondence applies a comma (*Dear Mr Jones,*) or no punctuation, which is also referred to as open punctuation (*Dear Mr Jones*).

Traditional protocol also has rules on how to write salutations for officials, royalty, and nobility.

6. **Body Paragraphs** (required)

Body refers to the text of the letter. Letters in Western cultures tend to be polite yet direct, with the opening paragraph clearly explaining the purpose of the letter, supporting paragraphs in order of importance, with the closing indicating a call to action.

The direct style may be considered too blunt or even inconsiderate in other cultures, where a quasi-inductive style that delays the purpose of the letter may be preferred. For example, a study on Thai and non-Thai cross-cultural business letters of request revealed that Thai letters state their intent in the middle or second to last part, and they contain more expressions of gratitude and politeness throughout. Thai letters also "seem to be oriented towards emotional appeal, collectivism and relationship building" (Chakorn, 2006, p. 144). Japanese business letters tend to start with a comment about the season and include compliments about the recipient's health, and his or her company's prosperity, and thankfulness for the business relationship (Barešová, 2008; Johnston, 1980).

7. **Complimentary Close** (required)

The most commonly used **complimentary close** (also called **closing** or **sign off**), which is the closing before your signature, is *Yours sincerely* in business letters. Other options include *Sincerely, Yours faithfully,* or *Respectfully*. Americans tend to use more informal closings, such as *Cordially* and *With best regards*. The first words of the complimentary close are capitalized. In American correspondence, a comma is used after the complimentary close (*Sincerely,*); in British English, the comma is optional. Traditional protocol also has guidelines for complimentary closes in letters addressed to government, diplomatic, military, and religious leaders, as well as to royalty and nobility.

8. **Signature Block** (required)

Signatures are customarily handwritten three blank lines below the complimentary close, and above the signer's typed name; this section is referred to as the **signature block** (or **signature line**). The next line includes the person's title, unless personalized stationery indicates the sender's title. In some cultures, the person's name may be followed with academic degrees and other designations. In British society, the traditional order is military and civil orders and decorations, degrees and diplomas, memberships, and letters indicating professions (Scott, 1998). Look at how the recipient identifies himself or herself.

Writer Mary A. De Vries (1994) recommends that women include their preferred title in parentheses before the typed signature line in international business correspondence. Adding the title—*(Mrs.) Jane Doe* or *(Ms.) Jane Doe* or *(Miss) Jane Doe*—would help the recipient know how to address the person properly.

In British correspondence, the initials *p.p.* (meaning *per pro*) may be typed before the sender's typed name to indicate that the letter was signed by someone else on behalf of the sender. Refer to identification initials in section 11 for the style used in the U.S.

Who the letter is from can make the difference in it being read by the recipient in high power-distance cultures when the status of the sender is extremely important.

9. **Postscript** (optional)

Postscripts are quite common in American correspondence, using the abbreviation *P.S.:* followed by a colon. Postscripts can add an interesting detail or emphasize a key point. People tend to read these. Fundraising letters use postscripts effectively:

P.S.: Let me urge you to send your most generous gift today—$25, $50, $100 or whatever you can contribute. Any amount you give will help us!

10. **Identification Initials** (optional)

Identification initials (also called **reference initials**) are applied in American correspondence to indicate if the letter was typed by someone else, such as an administrative assistant. The first two initials of the sender's name are capitalized followed by a colon and lower-case initials of the typist, such as *JD:ef*. This identification line is traditionally placed one blank line below the signature block, if there is not a postscript. Refer to item 8 for British correspondence usage of identification initials.

11. **Enclosure Notations** (optional)

Enclosure notations let the recipient know that other documents are accompanying the letter. If your letter includes enclosures, you should write *Enclosure* or *Enc.* If you have more than one enclosure, you should indicate the number of enclosures in parentheses, such as *Enclosures (3)*, or list the contents, such as:

Enclosures: Public Relations Recommendations for Company X
       Agency XYZ's Capabilities and Global Offices
       Agency XYZ's Standard Contract

12. **Copy Notations** (optional)

If the letter is being distributed to another person or people, the abbreviation followed by a colon *CC:* (meaning *courtesy copy* or *carbon copy*) is used followed by the name or names of the other recipients. The term **carbon copy** is still widely used, even though the practice is archaic (placing carbon paper between the top and bottom sheets of paper and rolled into a typewriter, or written over with a pen or pencil, to make duplicate copies). In dialogue, many English speakers say "CC" as a verb. For correspondence outside of English-language countries, write *Copy* or *Copies*. When writing to more formal cultures, be mindful to list the names in order of hierarchy by title, with the most senior titles followed by less senior positions in descending order. If copies are distributed to multiple organizations, writers should include the name of the organization after each person's name. The other option is to list the titles and offices, without specific names, starting with the most senior titles.

Blind copies refer to documents that do not identify the distribution of recipients receiving copies. If this is the case, type *BCC:* (which used to mean *blind carbon copy* or *blind copy circulation*) and list the name or names only in the letters that are blind copies.

If your letter exceeds two or more pages, you can include page numbers on the upper-left side of each page, such as *Page 2 of 2* or *Page X of X* (total pages of document).

Letter writers also should consider the following components:

- **Formatting**—A block-style letter is illustrated in Exhibit 17.1, when indentations are not used. Other options are semi-block, in which the date, complimentary close, and signature block are indented to the center of the page; or modified-block, in which the first line of each paragraph also is indented five spaces. Formal stationery would include printed letterhead with the organization's logo and general contact information, along with matching envelopes with pre-printed addresses and logo, as well as mailing labels for larger envelopes and packages. Some stationery also is personalized with the executive's name and title, and direct contact information. Letters sent as a PDF email attachment should include a digital version of the organization's letterhead and logo. You may be required to scan letters with signatures for electronic distribution.

- **Style Guides**—Companies may have style guides that cover the font size and preferred format for formal correspondence. In the U.S., for example, 12-point or 11-point type is commonly used. Avoid type sizes under 11 points, which may be too small to read. Margins should be one inch on all sides; avoid extending margins to keep copy on one page.

- **Proper Protocol**—If you are communicating with government officials, members of the diplomatic corps, religious leaders, military officers, certain professions (such as medical doctors), royalty and nobility, you will need to follow proper protocol in forms of address. This etiquette should be followed when making face-to-face introductions and in all forms of written correspondence, such as in invitations and letters, which most likely would be sent to the recipients' administrative assistants or private secretaries (secretaries may seem to be "extinct" or have become "endangered species" in some fields, but not in all). In letters, proper forms of address apply to the courtesy title in the address, the salutation, and complimentary close, as well as the accompanying envelope. You will need to check the rules for specific countries since the wording may vary from country to country. Exhibit 17.2 includes a list of sources for books and online resources for formal protocol.

Exhibit 17.2—RESOURCES FOR FORMAL TITLES OF ADDRESS.

Resource	Brief Description	Website
Debrett's	British etiquette and forms of address; also publishes books on manners and etiquette.	www.debretts.com
Emily Post Institute	American etiquette and forms of address; also publishes books on manners and etiquette.	www.emilypost.com
A Protocol Guide to Forms of Address	PDF from protocol handbook for Queensland Government Offices in Australia; also covers the U.S. and countries in Asia.	www.premiers.qld.gov. au/publications/ categories/policies-and-codes/assets/att1-forms-of-address.pdf
Protocol Red Book	Diplomatic protocol and etiquette; U.S. focus, not country specific; limited content on website.	protocolredbook.com
The Protocol School of Washington's Honor & Respect: The Official Guide to Names, Titles, and Forms of Address	U.S. and international forms of address; also publishes a book.	www.formsof address.info

17.2.2 Crafting Business Memos

Although email is more frequently used for interoffice correspondence, memos (also called memoranda) are still used for interoffice communication, particularly when printed copies of reports or other documents need to be distributed or when a major announcement or important policy needs to be emphasized. With the increasing volume of email, recipients may not read all messages and could overlook an important message.

The traditional format for memos includes the following components:

1. **Clear Identification of Memo** (required)
   MEMO or MEMORANDUM in capitalized letters is in larger font and usually centered or placed flush left.
2. **Recipient or Recipients** (required)
   The *TO*: line is placed flush left followed by name or names of recipients. For memos distributed to numerous people, their first and last names are listed in alphabetical order by last name or by rank, which is an important detail in a hierararchial culture, with the more senior titles listed first. Some writers may just list their titles in rank and office locations, if sent to multiple departments or offices. Courtesy titles are usually not used.

| | TO: | Terry Black, John Brown, Ann Green, Lee White |

or

	TO:	Corporate Marketing Senior Vice President
		Corporate Marketing Vice President
		Corporate Public Relations Vice President
		Corporate Public Relations Director
		Public Relations Managers, North America, Caribbean and Central America, South America, Europe, Middle East and Africa, Asia and Pacific

3. **Sender** (required)

The sender line traditionally includes the first and last name. The title is optional, but it would be essential if the recipients do not know the sender.

| | FROM: | Juan Rivera |

or

| | FROM: | Juan Rivera, Executive Vice President/Corporate Marketing |

4. **Date** (required)

The date line should spell out the month to avoid any confusion.

| | DATE: | January 2, 20XX (or 2 January 20XX) |

5. **Subject** (required)

The subject line should be concise with a few words that describe the topic of the memo.

| | SUBJECT: | 20XX Marketing Plan for Company X |

6. **Body Copy** (required)

Memo copy can be quite brief and to the point. It also should reflect an appropriate tone for the audience. Add one blank line between paragraphs.

We are pleased to share the marketing plan for our new product launch. We would like to thank our marketing, advertising, and public relations staff in the corporate headquarters and throughout the field for their contributions. 20XX should be an exciting year as we announce our new product line in the coming months. If you have any questions, please send me an email at (email) or call me at (telephone number).

7. **Complimentary Close** (optional)

Not all memos close with a complimentary close, such as *Sincerely* or *With best regards*. Refer to item 7 in formal business letter guidelines (p. 434 above).

8. **Signature** (optional)

If a complimentary close is included, a signature would be required. Some authors prefer to sign their memos or add a typed full name and title below the signature. See item 8 on signature blocks in the formal guidelines on business correspondence.

9. **Notations** (optional)

See the formal business letter guidelines, items 10 through 12, for identification notations, if the sender did not type the letter; if enclosures are noted; and if blind copies are distributed.

17.2.3 Writing Business Emails

Even when communicating by email (and texting) in business, writers should maintain a professional demeanor and be clear and concise. Email dialogue with public relations agencies and their clients may cover such topics as approvals for plans, projects, written materials, and budgets; requests for facts, visuals, or interviews; confirmations for interviews and appointments; updates on work completed or in progress; and responses to requests from clients.

Business netiquette remains necessary even in a digitally distracted world when we need to be aware of content read on multiple platforms. Be respectful of people's time. The reader is most likely contending with hundreds of messages, so avoid rambling and clearly express your thoughts.

1. **Recipient(s)** (automatic on email)
   The distribution line (*TO:*) only should include people who need to review the message or respond to it. If you are emailing many people, you need to be sensitive to hierarchy in high power-distance cultures by listing names in order of title. Low power-distance recipients can be listed in alphabetical order to make it easier for the recipients to see who else is receiving the message.

2. **Date** (automatic on email)
   Email automatically sets the date, but be mindful of the recipient's schedule and of time zones. For example, if you have a deadline for *today*, it could be *yesterday* or *tomorrow* depending on the time zone of the location of the recipient of your message.

3. **Copies (CC:) or (BCC:)** (optional)
   Only copy people who should be aware of the message, but do not have to respond or act upon the content. Blind copies (*BCC.:*) should be used when the distribution list is confidential or unnecessary to share. Some public relations agencies set up a generic account email, such as clientX@agencyX.com, to track all relevant activities about a specific account. This process can help with the preparation of activity reports, which will be covered later in this chapter.

4. **Subject** (required)
   Be specific with a few words in the subject line of an email, so the recipient instantly knows the topic of the message. Never leave a subject line blank.

5. **Attachments** (optional)
   The attachment icon is automatically included when attachments are posted. Be sure to identify attachments. Avoid naming an attachment just "Resume"; write Jane_Doe_Resume. Double-check that you are including the correct attachment. Large files should be zipped or distributed by an external drop box since they may exceed the recipient's email size limits or take too long to load. Journalists, as well as some business executives, may avoid opening up attachments. You can use links in your messages to available online content.

6. **Salutation** (recommended)
   Write *Dear X*, unless the person you communicate with uses a more informal tone, such as *Hi X* or *Hello X*, which is a less formal style popular in the U.S. Avoid using first names unless you have an established first-name basis with the recipient. This is particularly important for correspondence outside of the U.S., Australia, New Zealand, and parts of Europe.

7. **Message** (required)

Body content should be brief and professional. Avoid paragraphs over eight lines. The tone can vary based on your relationship with the recipient and the preferred communication style of the company and country. Be as succinct and clear as possible. Remember that many people are inundated with emails. Write in proper English—not just in all lowercase or uppercase letters. Capitalized words can be interpreted as yelling at someone. Avoid emoticons and multiple exclamation marks.

Remember any email you send can be shared easily with others, so use professional language, double-check the facts for accuracy, and proofread the content. Confidential information should be sent by interoffice or regular mail or by courier. Consider making a phone call to share negative news or criticism. Avoid writing messages when you are angry or upset. Hold off sending content until you are confident that the message is clear and appropriate.

If by chance you have sent a message with a mistake, you can resend it and indicate in the subject line—*Updated message on (specific topic)*, and let the reader know that he or she should disregard the previous message and read the current version.

8. **Complimentary Close** (recommended)

Close with *Sincerely yours* or another formal complimentary close (*Yours truly,*), particularly for external email outside your organization. Use the less formal—*All the best, Thanks, With warm regards*—for internal communications or with organizations that prefer an informal style. Keep closings with *Love* or *XOXO* (not all audiences would recognize that the Xs and Os stand for hugs and kisses) exclusively for friends and family members.

9. **Signature** (recommended)

Even when composing emails, writers should add their names. More formal correspondence warrants using both first and last names. The other option is to use an email signature block setting; see number 10.

10. **Email Signature Block Setting** (recommended)

Emails can be customized at the end of your message automatically for outgoing messages. You can include your name, title, affiliation, address, telephone, and optional social media or professional memberships. Students also can use this function with their full name, class year, major and minor, and preferred contact information, as well as a list of membership and leadership roles in clubs and associations. This step is highly recommended since recipients may be less familiar with you or they may want to contact you by mail or phone.

11. **Email Disclaimers** (optional)

Companies may have a policy that requires a disclaimer on confidentiality and liability for computer viruses.

12. **Out-of-Office Automatic Replies** (recommended as needed)

If you are out of the office on business, vacation, illness, or for other personal reasons, you should update your out-of-office automatic responses to let senders know that you are away and when you will be returning. It is recommended to provide an alternate contact for immediate assistance. Make sure to identify the intermediate contact with the full name, title, and both email and phone contacts.

I will be on vacation from June 1 to 14. If you need immediate assistance while I'm away, please contact John Doe, administrative assistant in Corporate Communications, at jdoe@company.com or by phone at 111–222–3333.

17.3 New Business Letters and Responses to Complaints

This section covers how to write two particularly challenging letters: 1) sales letters to prospective clients, which can help bring in new business to a public relations agency; and 2) responses to complaints, particularly those that require a formal written response.

17.3.1 Preparing Sales Letters in Public Relations

New business letters are sales letters from public relations agencies to prospective clients. A public relations agency may send an unsolicited sales letter to a prospective client, requesting an opportunity to meet and present ideas. These letters are traditionally sent by regular mail, and may be accompanied by a brochure or an example of the agency's work. Sales letters sent by email could be quarantined as spam or easily ignored by the recipient.

Be careful of gimmicks in new business letter writing. For example, a public relations agency used "missed opportunities" as ploys to attract the attention of marketing executives by sending a sales letter along with round-up articles in influential media that excluded mention of the prospective client's company or its products or services. The letter touted that this public relations agency would not miss such important story opportunities for its clients. What are the challenges of such a strategy? The in-house public relations staff may be offended by this approach, considering it a criticism of their work, or this tactic could be regarded as naïve since that agency would not be aware of the reasons why the company was excluded from a specific article. The reality is that no company will be covered in every possible story. The other two important issues are that media relations is only one part of most public relations campaigns, and no agency can guarantee placement in any specific blog, newspaper, magazine, or TV or radio program, unless paying for an advertisement or advertorial.

Sales letters also serve as **cover letters** in response to Requests for Proposals (RFPs), which are documents prepared by all type of organizations that outline the type of services needed by creative agencies. Some RFPs can be quite detailed, providing insight on the organization's business goals, competition, and future plans, as well as budgetary parameters and requested public relations credentials. As reviewed in Chapter 16 on public relations proposals, more extensive RFPs can have three phases:

- Request for agency credentials, so the potential client can prepare a short list based on the agency's capabilities, industry experience, and current client list.
- A part two when short-list agencies are invited to submit a public relations proposal, outlining creative ideas to implement for a specific timeframe.
- The last part is when the finalists are traditionally asked to present their creative in person to a team of decision-makers. Some companies also may ask the public relations agencies to address a potential what-if scenario to solicit recommendations on handling a potential crisis or tapping a new market.

If English is not your prospective client's first language, you can use more formal and simpler English, while avoiding slang and colloquialisms. However, be careful to avoid choppy and overly simplistic sentences that would be found in a textbook on English for beginners. If your agency has staff members fluent in the language of the prospective client, you may want to have the cover letter translated.

The following guidelines can help make a sales letter more resonant and stand out among the competition.

- **Salutation**

  Make sure to double-check that the prospective client's name is spelled properly and the correct title is used. These simple details create a first impression—and mistakes over basic information will not be viewed favorably. (When I was on the client side, I recall receiving correspondence from prospective agencies with my first name misspelled.)

- **Opening**

  The first paragraph of your business letter should provide an introduction to why you are writing. This is a "sales" letter, so you need to emphasize why your agency is excited about this new business opportunity and what you can offer the prospective client.

- **Supporting Paragraphs**

  - *What your agency can accomplish*

    You also can highlight a few ideas about how you can help the prospective client reach its goals, particularly if you are sending a cover note to a completed RFP response. This gives you an opportunity to explain what you can do to solve the prospective client's challenges and be a meaningful partner.

  - *Why your agency is truly qualified*

    How can you make your company stand out? Provide more information and specific facts about why your agency is qualified. Think specific benefits to the client—you need to match the client's needs to your capabilities and services. You also can use bullets or supporting paragraphs to emphasize the following points of relevance; however, be careful that the letter does not read like a generic fill-in-the-blank new business letter to any prospective client. Here are some facts you can include that should be tailored to the specific needs of the client:

    - Key benefits and features about your company (but focus on what is relevant to the client; avoid generic "laundry lists").
    - Overall geographic reach and pinpoint where you have offices of geographic interest to the client.
    - Areas of specialization that would be of interest to your prospective client.
    - Current and former clients, particularly names that would appeal to your potential client and not be considered current competitors. Status-seekers want to make sure that they are in good company with other high-profile organizations.
    - Highlights of success stories, particularly if relevant to the client.
    - Awards to show that you have earned the respect of your peers.
    - Other distinctive selling propositions that would make the prospective client interested in meeting with you.

- **Closing Paragraph**

  The last paragraph of your letter should reiterate the reason you are writing and thank the reader for reviewing your Request for Proposal or other enclosed material. If your letter is accompanying an RFP response, your goal is to make it to the next round in the competitive agency review and be invited to present your ideas in person to the prospective client. If this is an unsolicited sales letter, you would need to offer options to meet in person, set up a phone call, or indicate other next steps to showcase your agency and how your staff and services can make a difference.

- **Complimentary Close and Signature**
  High-power distance clients respond better to letters sent from a high-ranking executive. In some cases, the letters would be ghostwritten by a less senior person for approval by the senior person.

17.3.2 Responding to Complaints in Writing

Responses to complaints are the most challenging letters to write—and the author must determine if a written response is the best decision, when a telephone call or face-to-face discussion could be a preferred option. For example, a public relations agency may receive a complaint in writing by a client about service issues. Public relations professionals also may be called upon to prepare letters to address serious customer service issues that would be widely distributed to customers. Remember these documents can be shared easily with anyone and disseminated through social media.

This four-step response process applies to a written response in which the sender wants to satisfy the customer and attempt to regain the person's loyalty to your business, product, or service. You could be an agency partner wanting to restore a client's confidence and improve the working relationship or an executive desiring to keep your customers using your service after an operational glitch. Please refer to Exhibit 17.3 for an example of an email template response to a complaint.

1. **First Paragraph: Gratitude and Apology**
   Thank the customer or client for writing to you and expressing his or her opinion, even if you do not agree with it. The opening paragraph also gives you an opportunity to apologize for the situation or inconvenience.

2. **Second Paragraph: Empathy**
   Explain how you understand the situation. Stress relevant high standards in customer service or client satisfaction. You can add former accomplishments achieved over the years. Avoid reiterating negative comments; you do not need to grovel too much.

3. **Third Paragraph: Solution**
   This paragraph should offer a solution or incentive and then explain what immediate next steps will be taken to resolve the situation. Indicate what you are offering, such as a free month of client service or other financial incentive, replacement of the product, or a coupon or discount for future purchases. Also, you can use bullet points to outline immediate next steps to work out a solution that relates directly to the customer's specific concerns. You do not need to refer again to the existing problems or issues, just focus on solutions moving forward.

4. **Last Paragraph: Conclusion**
   If this letter is to one person or to a few people, you can indicate that you will call to discuss this further and answer any other questions or concerns the customer or

client may have. If feasible, you may want to meet in person, even for lunch or dinner, to discuss the situation and solution further. If the person is out of town, you could arrange for a local company representative to meet with the customer. If this letter is sent to a larger group of people, you can provide customer service representatives contacts. Regardless of the volume of recipients, writers should close positively and reiterate care and concern.

Exhibit 17.3—RESPONSE TO A COMPLAINT TEMPLATE (BY EMAIL).

To: Name of person who sent the complaint
From: Your name or the person you are writing on behalf of
Date: Timeliness is important in addressing complaints
CC: Copy all relevant parties
Subject: Be diplomatic and concise in the subject line

Dear X:

Thank the person or persons for sharing their opinions with you. Explain what complaint you are responding to and apologize in the first paragraph. Don't argue or be defensive. ①

The second paragraph should explain how you understand the situation. Stress your high-standards in customer service or client satisfaction, if relevant. You can add former accomplishments achieved for the client or customers over the years. Avoid reiterating negative comments. Never criticize your colleagues, even if they made mistakes. ②

Offer a solution or incentive and indicate next steps to resolve the situation. If you are investigating the problem at this time and have insufficient information, you should explain the process underway. Let the recipient know if you will be offering a financial incentive, such as a reimbursement or a discount on a future purchase or service. You also can use bullet points to outline immediate next steps to work out a solution that relates directly to the client's or customer's specific concerns. You don't need to repeat problems or issues, just focus on solutions moving forward. ③

If you are writing to one person, you should conclude that you will call to discuss this further and answer any other questions or concerns the client or customer may have. It is preferred to try to meet in person, even for lunch or dinner, particularly if the situation is with a significant client or customer. If this is a generic customer service response, you will need to explain who to contact to receive financial rewards or to discuss further. In both cases, close on a friendly note—reiterate care and concern.④

Sincerely,

Name

Title

Affiliation

Address

Telephone

Email

17.4 Written Materials for Meetings

Public relations executives need to write meeting agendas for both internal and external meetings. A clearly written, well-organized meeting agenda can make a meeting run more smoothly by helping presenters be prepared for the meeting and by providing information at a glance so all attendees will know where the meeting will be held, the purpose of the meeting, what will be covered, and for how long. These steps can make the difference in having an engaging meeting with greater interactivity and enthusiasm from all meeting participants (see Figure 17.2).

Before preparing your agenda, you should be able to answer the following questions:

- **Goal of Meeting**—What is the purpose of the meeting? Is it to receive approval from clients or decision-makers on your public relations planning and budget? Is it to brainstorm ideas? If you can't answer these questions, you should reconsider hosting a meeting.
- **Topics to Cover**—What items do you need to cover and who will be responsible for each item. Make sure to share the agenda in advance for approval with decision-makers.
- **Participants**—Who do you need to invite? Relevant participants include the presenters, the appropriate decision-makers, and people directly involved with the projects covered in the agenda. Will you have to invite people from multiple offices and organizations?

Figure 17.2—LEARNING HOW TO WRITE CLEAR AGENDAS AND MINUTES CAN MAKE MEETINGS MORE PRODUCTIVE FOR ALL PARTICIPANTS. Source: © Konstantin Chagin/Shutterstock.com.

Are all people joining the meeting in person or participating by teleconference or videoconference? Make sure you have the correct spellings and titles of participants. Avoid inviting people who will not be actively involved; they can read the minutes.

- **Preparation**—What information do you need to share or obtain in advance? People responsible for presenting material or facilitating specific discussion topics should receive ample time to prepare. Non-presenters also prefer to receive material that requires time to review in advance.

- **Timing**—When should the meeting be held and at what time? Does it need to be face-to-face or will a conference call or Skype be sufficient? Be mindful of holidays celebrated in your country and the countries of other participants. Try to avoid hosting a meeting the day after a long holiday or during peak vacation seasons when participants may have other plans. If participants are traveling from out of town, try to host the meeting the day after arrivals. For shorter-haul travel, look at hosting the meeting later in the afternoon and be prepared for travel delays. Be judicious with everyone's time; shorter meetings are preferred. The major exceptions in public relations are annual planning sessions or new business strategy sessions.

- **Location and Setup**—Where should the meeting be held? Once you know how many participants will be invited, you can select the best location in your office or secure another meeting location, such as a nearby hotel or conference site. Look at the seating arrangements in advance, particularly for hierarchical groups. Know how much you can spend or bill back to the client. What audiovisual equipment do you need? Are you serving any food or drinks? If you are serving meals and beverages, consider any special dietary restrictions of the participants. Also, some companies prefer working lunches to continue discussions while others like to take a break and make the meal more social.

17.4.1 Preparing Meeting Agendas

Meeting agendas should be easy to scan and understand. Public relations agencies and in-house public relations departments should create a template to follow for all meetings. Some clients may prefer a specific format. Exhibit 17.4 illustrates a more formal meeting agenda with specific timeframes, and Exhibit 17.5 shows a meeting agenda without specific time blocks.

Meeting agendas traditionally include the following content; the numbers match the items shown in the exhibits:

Part A: Heading

1. **Title** (required)
   A concise title should indicate the purpose of the meeting, followed by the name of the organization or organizations participating in the meeting.
2. **Location** (required)
   Add where the meeting is held, including the name of the office or other meeting location, the street address, and room or suite number.
3. **Timing** (required)
   This section includes the day of the week, month (spelled out), day, and year, followed by the starting time to ending time (use the 12-hour or 24-hour clock based on what is most frequently used by the majority of the attendees).

Exhibit 17.4—EXAMPLE OF MEETING AGENDA WITH SPECIFIC TIMES.

Agenda for 20XX Public Relations Planning Session
Client X and Public Relations Agency Y ①
Agency Y, 200 Main Street, Second Floor, Anywhere City ②
Monday, December 1, 20XX
9 a.m. to 2 p.m. ③

④   ⑤

9:00 a.m.:	**Welcome Remarks and Introductions by CEO Alexander Doe** ⑥
9:15 a.m.:	**Overview of 20XX Public Relations for Client X** ⑦

Opportunities and Challenges by Vice President Terry Jones (30 minutes)

- Social Media and Media Relations Achieved in 20XX by Account Supervisor Sam Brown (30 minutes)
- Events and Promotions Undertaken in 20XX by Account Executive Donna White (15 minutes)

10:30 a.m.:	**Break** ⑧
10:45 a.m.:	**Client X Update on 20XX Marketing Plan by Executive Vice President Marketing Barbara Smith**

- Goals and Objectives (10 minutes)
- New Target Markets (20 minutes)
- Overview of Competition (10 minutes)
- New Announcements and Developments (20 minutes)

11:45 a.m.:	**Client X Update on Internal Public Relations by Vice President Public Relations Chris Young**
12:15 p.m.:	**Break**
12:30 p.m.:	**Working Lunch and Brainstorming Session on Next Year's Planning Led by Vice President Terry Jones**
1:45 p.m.:	**Closing Remarks by Executive Vice President Marketing Barbara Smith** (15 minutes) ⑨

Participants: ⑩

Client X: Barbara Smith, Executive Vice President Marketing; Chris Young, Vice President Public Relations; Robert Johnson, Public Relations Manager

Agency Y: Alexander Doe, CEO; Terry Jones, Vice President; Sam Brown, Account Supervisor; Donna White, Account Executive; Lee James, Assistant Account Executive

Notes: Continental breakfast will be available from 8:30 a.m. to after the first break; lunch of assorted sandwiches and salads with beverages will be served in meeting room ⑪

Attachments: 20XX Marketing Plan ⑫

Exhibit 17.5—EXAMPLE OF MEETING AGENDA WITHOUT SPECIFIC TIMEFRAMES.

Agenda for 20XX Public Relations Planning Session ①
Client X and Public Relations Agency
Agency Y, 200 Main Street, Second Floor, Anywhere City ②
Monday, December 1, 20XX ③
9 a.m. to 2 p.m.

④   ⑤

I.   **Welcome Remarks and Introductions** by CEO Alexander Doe ⑥

II.   **Overview of 20XX Public Relations for Client X** ⑦
            Opportunities and Challenges by Vice President Terry Jones

          A.   Social Media and Media Relations Achieved in 20XX by Account Supervisor Sam Brown

          B.   Events and Promotions Undertaken in 20XX by Account Executive Donna White

          Break ⑧

III.   **Client X Update on 20XX Marketing Plan and Developments** by Executive Vice President Marketing Barbara Smith

          A.   Goals and Objectives

          B.   New Target Markets

          C.   Overview of Competition

          D.   New Announcements and Developments

IV.   **Client X Update on Internal Public Relations** by Vice President Public Relations Chris Young

          Break

V.   **Working Lunch and Brainstorming Session** led by Vice President Terry Jones

VI.   **Closing Remarks** by Executive Vice President Marketing Barbara Smith ⑨

Participants: ⑩

Client X: Executive Vice President Marketing Barbara Smith, Vice President Public Relations Chris Young, Public Relations Manager Robert Johnson

Agency Y: CEO Alexander Doe, Vice President Terry Jones, Account Supervisor Sam Brown, Account Executive Donna White, Assistant Account Executive Lee James

Notes: Continental breakfast will be available at 8:30 a.m.; lunch of assorted sandwiches and salads with beverages will be served in meeting room. ⑪

Attachment: 20XX Marketing Plan ⑫

Part B: Agenda Items (required)

This section succinctly lists the topics to be covered during the meeting. Writers usually follow two typical formats. One is a more flexible timeframe that lists agenda items in order of importance; traditionally using Roman numerals as a structure (refer to Exhibit 17.5 as an example of a meeting agenda without specific time allotments per agenda item). This format would be more effective for groups that prefer flexibility and would most likely ignore scheduled time slots. The role of the facilitator and timekeeper still would be important to attempt to cover all slotted agenda items. The other format includes specific time allotments (see Exhibit 17.4 as an example of a meeting agenda with clear timeframes), with a two-column format. This structure works best for highly organized groups that prefer to follow a structured order with clear timeframes. In either case, no agenda item should exceed 90 minutes; many meeting agendas items can be covered in shorter timeframes.

4. **Recommended Flow** (required)
   Place **time allotments** on the left side. If most meeting attendees are North American, use the 12-hour clock (a.m. and p.m.); if not, use the 24-hour clock. The meeting agenda without specific timeframes should use Roman numerals to indicate preferred order of discussion topics.

5. **Topics** (required)
   Agenda topics are listed on the right side. Use simple descriptions that are easy to understand. Be consistent in use of capitalization.

6. **Opening** (recommended)
   Welcome remarks and introductions are recommended to start a meeting. This kick-off portion is usually handled by the most senior person or the person most involved with the agenda items would serve as the meeting facilitator. This person should set ground rules, such as guidelines on use of smartphones or laptops. If participants are requested to turn off their phones, the meeting facilitator should let them know when breaks will be held. If attendees have not met the participants, they all should be introduced (also consider using tent cards with each person's name, title, and affiliation, if multiple companies are involved). The goal of the meeting should be addressed. Any self-service or served food and beverages also should be mentioned.

7. **Other topics** (required as relevant)
   Other discussion topics should follow a logical flow. If a natural flow is less obvious, Barbara Streibel (2003), a management consultant, recommends agenda items to follow any or all of these sequences: "difficulty: hard vs. easy; time: long vs. short; energy: intensive vs. light; and emotions: hot vs. cool" (p. 25). These items can be listed by brief categories, such as Public Relations Plan for 20XX or Review of 20XX Public Relations Results, and include the names of people responsible for discussing these topics; their titles and affiliations should be included for more formal meetings and particularly in settings when not everyone knows one another. If announcements are covered, writers may consider placing this section near the end since new information can change the focus of a meeting.

8. **Breaks** (required for meetings over 2 hours)
   Breaks should take place every 1.5 hours or 2 hours at the maximum for longer meetings.

9. **Conclusion** (recommended)

The last section is the **conclusion** or **closing remarks**, in which the meeting facilitator can reiterate key items discussed, determine action items and responsibilities, and set up a time for the next meeting.

Part C: Participants, Optional Notes, and Attachments

10. **Names of Participants** (recommended)

List **meeting participants** by titles in order of rank for a large-scale meeting, such as vice presidents or group directors. For smaller meetings, list the full name, followed by title, and office, starting with the most senior titles. Names of participants also may be organized by specific company, if multiple organizations are involved. Some companies also include the names and roles of the meeting facilitator, timekeeper, and notetaker.

11. **Notes** (recommended as needed)

Notes can indicate if any **food and beverages** are served and from what time.

12. **Attachments** (recommended as needed)

Attachments can include electronic copies of material for review before the meeting or supporting documents to review during the meeting.

17.4.2 Recording Meeting Minutes

Meeting minutes (also called **conference reports**) should capture the essentials—key discussion points, major decisions, change of plans, immediate next steps and responsibilities, and the date for the next meeting, if confirmed. Not all companies today have experienced secretaries or administrative assistants to serve as the notetakers. I have seen many public relations agencies delegate the writing of minutes to an intern or to another least senior participant. Without proper training and a structured template to follow, that person may not be able to produce a high-quality product, which could result in even more time invested by other staff members revising the minutes. The best solution is to provide the assigned writer with a template, an example of previous minutes for the same client (if feasible), and to set up a clear approval process before the final minutes are shared with all parties. The writer preparing the minutes also should receive notes taken from other attendees, particularly from colleagues from the same public relations agency. For more senior-level meetings, without administrative support, a senior-level executive with the most relevant experience would be responsible for the notetaking and preparation of the minutes. Recording tools, software, or smartpens can help with the process; some writers prefer to use their laptops or tablets to record key points as they are addressed.

I highly recommend that the writing of the minutes take place as soon as possible, preferably the same day since details may fade with time. Minutes do not need to be a transcription of every spoken word; they should capture the essentials of a meeting. Many companies use simple grids that provide scannable information that can be understood quickly. Other organizations may prefer a more detailed approach that outlines who presented which section and who shared commentary, along with full sentences. Exhibit 17.6 is an example of more detailed minutes, yet easy to scan, while Exhibit 17.7 illustrates a briefer format that captures the essence and focuses on the immediate next steps (both examples use fictitious company names, situations, and people). The numbers in the exhibits correspond to the following components:

Exhibit 17.6—MEETING MINUTES TEMPLATE WITH MORE DETAILS.

Meeting Minutes on Topic ①
October 1, 20XX, 8 a.m. to noon ②
Held at Agency Y, Street, City ③

Participants: ④

Company X Paris:	Full names in alphabetical order or by title
Company X NY:	Full names in alphabetical order or by title
Agency Y:	Full names in alphabetical order or by title
Distribution:	The above, all Company X public relations directors worldwide ⑤

This report covers key points and actionable items discussed during the crisis communications planning meeting. The goal was to finalize the 20XX crisis communications plan and determine the roles of in-house and agency public relations staff in different markets. ⑥

Topic	Action/Major Discussion Items ⑦
This column includes a brief description of the topic covered **Crisis Communications Seminar**	This column includes more details on the topic followed by discussion points and next steps listed in bullets. • (Name) presented the draft of the Crisis Communications Seminar presentation, which will be held in Paris on (Date). She discussed crisis communications guidelines, including the role of the Press Office; invariable aspects, franchises and code-share partners, and roles and responsibilities of local communications officers. **Discussion Points:** • Agency Y and local communications officers will contact the Press Office, not the Crisis Center, during a crisis. (The previous plan presented will be modified accordingly). **Next Steps/Responsibilities/Deadlines:** ⑧ ⑨ ⑩ • (Names) will update crisis plan and share with all parties by (date). • (Names) will participate in crisis communications seminar in Paris on (date).
Next Topic Description	Same format as above

Exhibit 17.7—EXAMPLE OF AT-A-GLANCE MEETING MINUTES.

Conference Report ①
Account Update Meeting
Client Y and Agency X
Monday, June 30, 20XX ②
Held at Agency X, Location of Office ③

Attendees: ④
Client Y: CEO Pedro Filipe, Marketing Director Dina Greene
Agency X: Senior Vice President Renee Dubois, Account Supervisor Juan Roya

Distribution: ⑤
The Above; Account Executives Donato Bell and Renata Gomez

Major Goals: To create a new social media campaign to connect Client Y with target audiences in South America; to generate media coverage in targeted traditional media and blogs in the U.S. and specific markets in South America; to position the CEO as a thought leader in the industry through bylined articles and white papers; to build momentum with industry analysts. ⑥

Decisions: Filipe approved the third-quarter public relations plan. ⑦

Next Steps

Action ⑧	Responsibility ⑨	Due Date ⑩
Translate English-language content into Spanish for client review	JR, DB	August 10
Review translated material and provide any comments for editorial changes to Agency X	DG	August 20
Prepare media lists for new markets	RG	August 5
Research editorial calendars in trade publications for potential bylined articles	DB	August 20
Draft suggested topics and message points for bylined articles in specific trade publications	RD, DB	August 30
Review bylined recommendations and provide comments to Agency X	DG	September 5
Develop themes and outlines for white papers	RD, DB	September 5
Review white paper ideas and provide feedback to Agency X	DG	September 10
Compile target list of industry analysts	RG	September 10

Next Meeting: September 15, 20XX; details to follow. ⑪

1. **Title of the Report** (required)
   Indicate that the report is minutes recorded for a specific meeting; some companies use the term "conference report."
2. **Date and Time** (required)
   Indicate when the meeting was held; some writers include the exact times.
3. **Location of the Meeting** (required)
   Add where the meeting took place, such as the name of the office or meeting space, as well as the city, if the meeting included participants from other locations.
4. **Attendees** (required)
   List all attendees (who also can be referred to as participants). If the meeting included many attendees from different offices who may not know one another, list their names, titles, and companies. Most public relations agency minutes record meetings between the agency staff and the client. Err on the more formal side by listing the most senior person first and the rest in descending order by title. Start with the client first.
5. **Distribution** (as needed)
   Write "The Above" to indicate distribution to all meeting participants. If the minutes need to be shared with others who were not in attendance, list their names, as well as titles and affiliations for multi-office meetings.
6. **Brief Description** (recommended)
   You can include a brief description of the purpose of the meeting. Some writers prefer to include major goals of the meetings.
7. **Discussion Points** (required as needed)
   Some companies prefer to indicate what was accomplished, preferably following the order of the meeting agenda, as well as key action items, discussion points, and any major approvals, or results of votes. Exhibit 17.7 sums up the decisions in one line since the previous section on major goals provided an adequate summary of the meeting. This section should not include shared opinions or debates. The moment you write the verbs—*believe*, *feel*, *consider*, or *think*—delete the comments since they do not reflect decisions.
8. **Next Steps** (required)
   Use active voice and write phrases, unless the company prefers a more detailed approach with full sentences, to indicate next steps.
9. **Responsibilities** (required)
   This part should indicate who will be responsible for the specific next steps, which may include more than one person. Minutes may include the person's initials for smaller meetings. If all the attendees do not know one another, use the person's last name in descending order by rank or in alphabetical order.
10. **Deadlines** (recommended)
    Due dates can help keep people on track. Although it is not uncommon to read minutes with "as soon as possible," this approach is not as effective as indicating a specific date.
11. **Next Meeting Date** (optional, if confirmed)
    Add the date and location of the next meeting, if confirmed. This part also can include any agenda items that were not covered or will need to be discussed further.

Although less commonly used in the corporate world, the other structure is the more formal ***Robert's Rules of Order***, which is widely used in academic departmental and committee meetings and board of director meetings for nonprofits, among other voluntary associations. Robert's Rules Online (http://www.rulesonline.com) gives an overview of rules named after Brigadier General Henry M. Robert of the U.S. Army. When Robert served as chair for his local church, he was so frustrated by his first 14-hour nonproductive meeting that he vowed to work out an organized structure of rules to run and record meetings based on the U.S. House of Representatives. His first book was published in 1876 for the lay person and continues to be published today with revisions.

17.5 Public Relations Reporting

The most commonly used written reporting structures in the public relations industry are **activity reports** and **media monitoring updates**.

17.5.1 Preparing Activity Reports

Both public relations agencies and in-house public relations departments write **activity reports** to provide an update on their accomplishments, scope of activities undertaken, and work in progress during specific timeframes. Public relations agencies typically submit monthly activity reports to their clients along with their monthly invoice; although some clients may prefer more frequent yet briefer weekly **status reports** or more comprehensive **quarterly reports**. Global agencies conducting work in multiple markets usually combine activity reports into one consolidated document that incorporates feedback from each office.

In-house public relations departments may prepare reports on a monthly or quarterly basis. These reports can include activities undertaken by both the internal staff in the headquarters and field offices, as well as from external public relations agencies.

The format varies considerably in terms of structure and level of detail required. Government accounts, for example, may be quite bureaucratic and require specific guidelines and forms that must be adhered to. Preparing activity reports can be considered one of the most mundane and routine tasks in the public relations business. Both agency and in-house staff members may complain that this process takes valuable time away from more meaningful projects. However, these reports are not optional. Consider these reports an opportunity to accomplish the following goals:

- To **showcase the accomplishments of the public relations team**, particularly to the decision-makers, whether they are your agency's clients or in-house marketing executives. The content should be clear and meaningful to those people who approve public relations plans and expenditures. The most important part will be how the work undertaken is evaluated and measured. Are the readers of the report low context or high context? Clients or in-house marketing staff can pay strict attention to previously submitted annual or project plans, so the public relations team should refer back to those documents and address any change in plans. Try to match the scope of information that would best suit the readers' interests. In addition, readers of a multinational report may not be familiar with or understand the value of traditional or social media in specific markets. The report needs to contain enough content to explain the relevance of the agency's work on behalf of the client.

- To **acknowledge high-quality work and share best practices** with the public relations team members in all markets. Projects that were effective in one location could be adapted to the needs of other city, country, or region. Conversely, the reports can help executives identify areas of improvement. In this case, the account team supervisor may want to communicate directly with those staff members on an individual basis.
- To **explore other ways that you can share news about the team's work**. For example, the company's sales force may benefit from receiving highlights of "what's being said" by media outlets or key points on social media engagement and sentiment. Major feature stories in blogs, magazines, or newspapers can be reprinted or shared online, with copyright permission and some will require fees. Some of the content could be added to your online newsroom or shared on social media. Consider submitting exceptional work for industry awards on a global, regional, or local basis as another way to gain peer-review recognition—and award-winning campaigns also generate favorable attention. The report content can be used for developing case studies, particularly for public relations agencies, that can be posted on their websites and serve as valuable new business tools.

The reporting process can be a great deal less time-consuming and stressful by establishing easy-to-follow guidelines for all participants:

- Design a **template** for the final report, including a well-designed cover page, which could include a montage of media placements and events undertaken during the time period. The cover also could be quite simple and include the reporting period, date of submission, and logos of all parties.
- Develop a **format structure**, using easy-to-fill-in grids, and style guidelines for all participating staff internally and externally to follow, so that all the information is written and presented consistently. Be clear on how completed work should be evaluated and measured. Multinational reports may require more context and detail. Keep in mind that writers from some countries may provide what is viewed by others as too much information or an insufficient amount. Make sure that the guidelines include written examples and suggestions on the amount of copy for each section. This step can save a great deal of time during the editing process. The consolidated report should have a consistent, unified appearance in content and layout, even if 50 or more people from multiple internal and external offices around the world have made contributions.
- Establish **guidelines** on what type of supporting material is required and in what digital format. Do you want to include examples of completed written documents, such as news releases; copies of stories that appeared in blogs, newspapers, magazines, or transcripts from television and radio programs; highlights of microblogs and social media; and visual imagery of events, such as the invitation, guest list, and images of scenes from the event? Should major stories be translated into English or into other languages?
- Organize a **system** so that each person involved fills in his or her activities and provides supporting documentation. Google Docs, for example, can be a useful tool for collaborative work in progress.

- Determine clear **submission deadlines**. Keep in mind that the primary office responsible for coordinating one master report should receive feedback from other offices in advance to complete the final document.
- Set up a structured **editorial review process** that involves only a few people to approve the final report.
- Ensure that you have an **updated distribution list**, so that the right people receive the report, which usually includes executive management and the marketing staff at the headquarters and other field offices. Determine how you will distribute the report—email, Intranet, or hardcopies. Consider setting up a way to solicit feedback, even if the executive summary concludes with a primary contact to reach for comments. Make sure that the report is also distributed electronically to all participating public relations staff, so that they see what every office is undertaking.

How to Structure an Activity Report

Although some organizations may have specific requirements for structuring activity reports, the documents traditionally include the following components:

- **Title** (required)
  The first page should include a brief title of the report, indicating which geographic regions or countries, reporting time period, and name of organizations involved:

Public Relations Activity Report for Asia and Europe
for Company X
January 20XX
Submitted by Public Relations Agency Y

  Longer reports would require a separate cover page, which can be straightforward with the logo of the company and agency, or it can be creatively designed and visually show highlights of work achieved.
- **Table of Contents** (optional; recommended for longer reports)
  A table of contents, including numbers of the starting pages of each section, is preferred for longer reports, so the reader can easily find specific sections.
- **Executive Summary** (recommended; required for longer reports)
  This introductory section gives the reader an overview on key achievements and immediate next steps. This section may be the only part read by a busy executive. This section is worth spending the most time on. It can start with a brief overview on major accomplishments and include subheads on work undertaken and achieved in specific markets. This part also can explain any reasons why the activities changed due to new opportunities, challenges, crisis situations, or mandates from the client. The concluding paragraph also could address upcoming work.
- **Results** (required)
  Quantify information as much as possible. All results should be consistent in formatting, writing style, and how activities are measured and evaluated. This section on accomplishments can be divided many ways:

  - By type of **traditional media** (magazines, newspapers, TV, and radio), which should include at the minimum the name of the outlet, title of story, date of story, and audience (circulation and viewership). Other suggested content should explain what type of story—cover, feature, round-up, or mention. Stories also can be tracked by type of messaging. International reports could include more detail on the significance of the media outlet to provide context to the reader who may not be familiar with the media outlets in that particular country.

- By type of **social media** (Facebook, Twitter, Instagram, etc.).
- By type of **activity** (news releases, media tours, events, promotions, etc.) and include examples of news releases and written materials, screen grabs, and other relevant visuals (or place in the Appendix).
- By specific **markets, regions, or specific countries**.

- **Work in Progress** (required)
  This section also should be logically organized, such as by pending placements, upcoming social media activities, and events or other activities.
- **Administrative** (recommended)
  This section can cover meetings and other administrative tasks that took time to undertake.
- **Immediate Next Steps** (optional)
  Some clients prefer to add a section on next steps to outline work to be undertaken within a specific timeframe.
- **Appendix** (optional, if not included in earlier sections)
  This section can include copies of news clippings, screenshots of blogs and social media, examples of written materials, and other tactical work undertaken. Some reports may include examples of work in the results section.

17.5.2 Documenting Media Monitoring Updates

Media monitoring updates (also called **tracking reports**) provide frequent updates on traditional media coverage and social media content, whether it is positive, negative, or neutral. This intelligence helps the public relations staff, whether in-house or agency, track coverage of media relations activities and find out what stories have appeared in various media. Monitoring also should include social media engagement and sentiment. Media monitoring is traditionally conducted daily by outside monitoring services or during the workdays by in-house or public relations agency staff, which are usually interns or junior staff who come in a few hours earlier to complete this work.

Media monitoring services can be quite worthwhile on a regular basis—and essential during a crisis situation. Services can save the public relations staff time and enable them to undertake other proactive activities, and they also can provide simple to sophisticated reports that can track both traditional and social media by volume and sentiment by specific terms (such as names of the organization, products, services, or competitors), track trends that can identify issues, analyze delivery of messages, and develop customized metrics relevant to the needs of the organization. The public relations team would need to provide clear direction on what to monitor and how to evaluate and share the findings. **Boolean logic** can be helpful in determining the right terms to track, thereby saving time and money. Let us assume you are trying to find stories about bats—the mammals that fly; not bats used in sports such as baseball and cricket, or a stick—without attempting to modify the search, you would receive many irrelevant stories. Using AND, OR, and NOT can help customize your searches. Google's online support explains techniques to narrow searches with punctuation and symbols. You also can determine whether or not you want to receive all mentions in any type of story, particularly multiple copies of the same wire service story.

At the most simplistic level, traditional media monitoring reports can be developed by using **Google News**, particularly by personalizing content to view and receive alerts on specific topics. This free solution will not cover all media outlets, however. Online library databases, such as **LexisNexis**, can be used for a fee and cover more media worldwide. The most basic paid media monitoring services also can track stories, using specific search terms, which can be emailed regularly to the public relations staff.

Google Analytics features a free Google Analytics Individual Qualification course and exam to learn how to use the service, which has a free level and a more extensive paid premium level. Here you can obtain data to track Web traffic and discover where visitors are coming from, what are the most popular content and search terms, among other intelligence. In addition, paid measurement and analysis communication services can set up customized metrics of both social media and traditional media worldwide and in multiple languages.

No matter whether the traditional and social media monitoring is done in-house or by an outside service, the following considerations need to be made since this intelligence can monitor results, gauge sentiment, identify new opportunities, and flag problem areas:

- **When/Timeliness**—determine the frequency when information is shared. Be mindful of time differences with international teams. During a serious incident or crisis situation, the frequency should increase.
- **Who/Distribution List**—make sure that you have an updated list of all people who receive the reports—particularly public relations in-house and agency staff worldwide and other important decision-makers.
- **What/Content and Topics**—ensure that you are tracking the right terms related to the organization, its competitors, and relevant industry trends that would impact the business.
- **Where/Accessibility and Archival Intelligence**—keep all reports on file in a location that others can find and include older reports that may need to be referred to or incorporated into other activity reports.
- **Why/Impact of Findings**—Analyze the information and decide how to use the knowledge to make changes to any public relations activities.
- **How/Formatting Facts**—work out an easy-to-share report that can be scanned easily by readers and provide context on findings. People receiving the information are busy, so make sure that the content is useful and presented in a quick-to-grasp format. Content may need to be translated as well. For example, the staff may be unable to translate an entire article or blog post, but they could provide a brief paragraph giving the essence.

17.6 Learning Objectives and Key Terms

After reading this chapter, you should be able to:

- Write a formal business letter.
- Craft memos and email messages for business usage.
- Draft a new business letter to a prospective public relations client.
- Prepare a response to a complaint in writing.
- Be aware of cultural nuances in business correspondence.

- Structure a formal and less structured media agenda.
- Understand what content to capture and how to prepare meeting minutes.
- Name components for inclusion into a public relations activity report.
- Appreciate the importance of monitoring traditional and social media.

This chapter covers the following key terms:

Salutation/greeting (p. 434)	Complimentary close (p. 434)
Signature block (p. 435)	Postscripts (p. 435)
Identification notations (p. 435)	Copy notations (p. 435)
Enclosure notations (p. 435)	Proper protocol (p. 436)
New business letters (p. 441)	Meeting agenda (p. 446)
Conference reports (p. 450)	Meeting minutes (p. 450)
Robert's Rules of Order (p. 454)	Activity reports (p. 454)
Boolean logic (p. 457)	Tracking reports (p. 457)
Media monitoring updates (p. 457)	Google Analytics (p. 458)

References

Atkin, N. (2012, December 17). 40% of staff time is wasted on reading internal emails: As Generation Y begins to dominate the workplace, Halton Housing Trust says it's time to break our addiction to email. *Guardian*. Retrieved from http://www.theguardian.com/housing-network/2012/dec/17/ban-staff-email-halton-housing-trust.

Bain & Co. (2014, May 6). Busy CEOs spend nearly one day each week managing communications, two days in meetings [News release]. Retrieved from http://www.bain.com/about/press/press-releases/Busy-ceos-spend-nearly-one-day-each-week-managing-communications.aspx.

Barešová, I. (2008). *Politeness strategies in cross-cultural perspective: Study of American and Japanese employment rejection letters* (1st ed.). Olomouc, Czech Republic: Palack_ University.

Burn-Callander, R. (2013, March 18). UK workers waste a year of their lives in useless meetings. *Management Today*. Retrieved from http://www.managementtoday.co.uk/bulletin/mtdailybulletin/article/1175002/uk-workers-waste-year-lives-useless-meetings/.

Chakorn, O. (2006). Persuasive and politeness strategies in cross-cultural letters of request in the Thai business context. *Journal of Asian Pacific Communication, 16*(1), 103–146. doi: 10.1075/japc.16.1.06cha.

De Vries, M. A. (1994*). Internationally yours: Writing and communicating successfully in today's global marketplace*. Boston, MA: Houghton Mifflin Company.

Johnston, J. (1980). Business communication in Japan. *The Journal of Business Communication, 17*(3), 65–70. doi: 10.1177/002194368001700307.

Scott, J. C. (1998). Dear???: Understanding British forms of address. *Business Communication Quarterly, 61*(3), pp. 50–61. doi: 10.1177/108056999806100305.

Streibel, B. J. (2003). *The manager's guide to effective meetings*. New York, NY: McGraw-Hill.

Williams, R. B. (2012, April 15). Why meetings kill productivity: Cancel 50 percent of your meetings and you'll get more work done. *Psychology Today*. Retrieved from http://www.psychologytoday.com/blog/wired-success/201204/why-meetings-kill-productivity.

Appendix *A*

Examples of English-Language Public Relations Industry Trade Outlets

Outlet	Description/Website	Country of Origin
B&T and B&T Magazine	Website with streaming content, blog, and a searchable database of more than 50,000 articles. Covers marketing, advertising, media, and PR. www.bandt.com.au/home	Australia
	Subscription magazine on the marketing, advertising, and media industry, including PR, in Australia. www.bandt.com.au/home	
Behind the Spin	Online magazine for PR students and young practitioners, supported by the Public Relations Consultants Association. www.behindthespin.com	U.K.
Brand Republic	Online content on advertising, marketing, media, and PR in the U.K. Subscription-based online and magazine packages. www.brandrepublic.com	U.K.
Bulldog Reporter	News and content for public relations and corporate communication professionals. Subscriber-based Inside Health Media and Media Pro Pitching Alert. Also offers webinars, PR databases, and other services. www.bulldogreporter.com	U.S.
Campaign	Weekly subscription-based print magazine and online edition covers the communications industries with an emphasis on advertising in the U.K. www.campaignlive.co.uk	U.K.
Campaign Asia-Pacific	Asia and the Pacific edition in English of the U.K.'s Campaign for advertising and media industries. www.campaignasia.com	Hong Kong and Singapore
Campaign India	India edition in English of the U.K.'s Campaign. www.campaignindia.in	India

Outlet	Description/Website	Country of Origin
Campaign ME	Middle East edition in English of the U.K.'s Campaign. http://campaignme.com	U.A.E.
Communicate Magazine	Subscription-based monthly digital magazine. www.communicatemagazine.co.uk	U.K.
Communication Director	Quarterly magazine for corporate communications and public relations in Europe. Published in English; partner with the European Association of Communication Directors. Subscription-based. www.communication-director.eu	Germany and Belgium
Communication World	Bimonthly publication for members of the International Association of Business Communicators. IABC also has a blog (http://cafe.x.iabc.com). cw.iabc.com	U.S.
Holmes Report	Online news on global PR industry, annual report card on PR agencies worldwide, SABRE awards, blogs, and other special reports. www.holmesreport.com	U.S.
Marketing Magazine	Online content on advertising, marketing, media, and PR in Canada. Subscription-based magazine. www.marketingmag.ca	Canada
O'Dwyer's PR Website, Blog, Monthly Magazine, and Newsletter	Website has blog, PR firm rankings, and PR job listings. www.odwyerpr.com O'Dwyer's Monthly Magazine; subscription. www.odwyerpr.com Also publishes annual directory of more than 1,400 PR firms in the U.S. and abroad. Some content is posted free. www.odwyerpr.com/pr_firm_rankings/independents.htm Jack O'Dwyer's Newsletter; subscription, weekly eight-page newsletter on PR industry distributed by email. www.odwyerpr.com	U.S.
PR News	Online content on PR news, awards, jobs, and other content. Subscription-based magazine and subscriber-only online section. www.prnewsonline.com	U.S.
PRWeek (U.K.)	Online news, blogs, rankings, job listings, and other PR-related content, focusing on the U.K. Subscription-based publication. Also covers Asia (www.prweek.com) and German-language content (http://prreport.de/). www.prweek.com/uk	U.K.
PRWeek (U.S.)	Online news, blogs, rankings, job listings, and other PR-related content, focusing on the U.S.; subscription for monthly magazine and more news access. www.prweek.com/us	U.S.

Outlet	Description/Website	Country of Origin
The Public Relations Strategist	Magazine geared to executive-level PR management. Published by Public Relations Society of America. Included in membership; subscriptions for non-members. www.prsa.org/Intelligence/TheStrategist	U.S.
Public Relations Tactics	Monthly newspaper published by Public Relations Society of America. Included in membership; subscriptions for non-members. www.prsa.org/Intelligence/Tactics	U.S.
Ragan Report	Ragan.com and Ragan's PR Daily Ragan's Health Care Communication News, among others. Paid subscriptions and memberships; some free online content. www.ragan.com	U.S.

Appendix *B*

Public Relations Industry Groups Worldwide

Geographic Area	PR Industry Group	Website (or email or Facebook)
International	Global Alliance for PR and Communication Management	http://www.globalalliancepr.org
	International Association of Business Communicators	http://www.iabc.com
	International Communications Consultancy Organisation	http://www.iccopr.com
	International Public Relations Association	http://www.ipra.org
Africa and the Middle East	African Public Relations Association	http://afapr.org
	Middle East Public Relations Association	http://www.mepra.org
Bahrain	Bahrain Public Relations Association	http://prbahrain.org
Ghana	Institute of Public Relations Ghana	http://www.iprghana.com
Israel	Israel Public Relations Association	http://www.ispra.org.il
Kenya	Public Relations Society of Kenya	http://www.prsk.co.ke
Nigeria	Nigerian Institute of Public Relations	http://www.nipr-ng.org
	PR for Africa	http://prforafrica.org
South Africa	Public Relations Institute of Southern Africa	http://www.prisa.co.za
Syria	Syrian Public Relations Association	http://www.spra-sy.com
Uganda	Public Relations Association of Uganda	http://www.prauganda.com
Zambia	Zambian PR Association	https://sites.google.com/a/zambiapra.org/zapra
Asia	Asian Institute for Development Communication	http://www.aidcom.unisel.edu.my

Geographic Area	PR Industry Group	Website (or email or Facebook)
China	China International Public Relations Association	www.cipra.org.cn
	Shanghai Public Relations Association	http://www.chspra.com
Hong Kong	Hong Kong Public Relations Professionals' Association	http://www.prpa.com.hk
India	Public Relations Consultants Association of India	http://www.prcai.org
	Public Relations Society of India	http://www.prsi.co.in
	PRromise Foundation	http://promisefoundation.com/index.php
Indonesia	Public Relations Association of Indonesia	http://www.perhumas.or.id
	Public Relations Society of Indonesia	http://www.prsociety.or.id
Japan	Public Relations Society of Japan	http://www.prsj.or.jp/en
Malaysia	Public Relations Consultants' Association of Malaysia	http://www.prcamalaysia.org
	Institute of Public Relations Malaysia	http://www.iprm.org.my
Pakistan	Council of Public Relations Pakistan	https://www.facebook.com/CPR.Pakistan
Philippines	Public Relations Society of the Philippines	https://www.facebook.com/PRSPnews
Singapore	Institute of Public Relations of Singapore	http://www.iprs.org.sg
South Korea	Korea Public Relations Association	http://www.koreapr.org
Thailand	Thailand Public Relations Association	http://www.prthailand.com
Caribbean, Central and South America	Inter-American Confederation of Public Relations (Confederação Interamericana de Relações Públicas)	confiarpsecretariageneral@gmail.com
Argentina	Professional Council of Public Relations of Argentina (Consejo Profesional de Relaciones Públicas de la República Argentina)	http://www.rrpp.org.ar

Geographic Area	PR Industry Group	Website (or email or Facebook)
Brazil	Associação Brasileira de Comunicação Empresarial	http://www.aberje.com.br
	Regional Council of Public Relations Practitioners	http://www.conferp.org.br
Chile	Instituto Chileno de Relaciones Públicas	http://www.rrppchile.com
Colombia	Centro Colombiano de Relaciones Públicas y Comunicación Organizacional	http://www.cecorp.com.co
Cuba	National Committee of Public Relations from the Cuban Association of Social Communicators	http://www.accs.co.cu
Mexico	PRORP: Asociación Mexicana de Profesionales de Relaciones Públicas	http://www.prorp.org.mx
Puerto Rico	Asociación de Relacionistas Profesionales de Puerto Rico	http://www.relacionistas.com
Uruguay	RR.PP. Asociación de Relaciones Públicas Uruguay	rrppuruguay@rrppuruguay.com
Europe (including Russia and Turkey)	European Public Relations Education and Research Association	http://www.euprera.org
	European Association for Internal Communication	http://www.feiea.com
	European Association of Communication Directors	http://www.eacd-online.eu
Austria	Public Relations Association of Austria	http://www.prva.at
Belarus	Institute of Public Relations Belarus	http://www.ipr.by
Belgium	Belgium Association of Public Relations Consultancies (BGPRA) Association Belge des Conseils en Relations Publiques	http://www.bprca.be
Bulgaria	Bulgarian Public Relations Association	http://www.bapra.bg
Croatia	Croatian Public Relations Association	http://www.huoj.hr
Czech Republic	Association of Public Relations Agencies	http://www.apra.cz/en

Geographic Area	PR Industry Group	Website (or email or Facebook)
Denmark	Danish Association of Communication Professionals	http://www.kommunikations forening.dk/
	Danish Association of PR Consultancies	http://www.publicrelations branchen.dk/
Estonia	Estonian Public Relations Association	http://www.epra.ee
Finland	Finnish Association of PR Consultancies	http://www.procom.fi
France	Syndicat National Des Attachés De Presse et Des Conseillers en Relations Publics	http://www.synap.org
	Conseil en Relations Publics	http://www.syntec-rp.com
Germany	German Public Relations Consultancies Association	http://www.gpra.de/?L=1
	Deutsche Public Relations Gesellschaft e.V.	http://www.dprg.de
Greece	Hellenic Association of Advertising-Communications Agencies	http://www.edee.gr
Hungary	Hungarian Public Relations Association	http://www.mprsz.hu
Iceland	Public Relations Association of Iceland	http://athygli.is
Ireland	Public Relations Consultants Association of Ireland	http://www.prca.ie
	Public Relations Institute of Ireland	http://www.prii.ie
Italy	Federazione Relazioni Pubbliche Italiana	http://www.ferpi.it
Latvia	Latvian Public Relations Association	http://www.lasap.lv
Lithuania	Lithuanian Public Relations Professionals' Union	http://www.lrvs.lt
Luxembourg	National Association of Public Relations of Luxembourg	http://www.cenarp.lu
Netherlands	Logeion, Association for Communication	http://www.logeion.nl
	Netherlands Association of Public Relations Consultants	http://www.vpra.nl/en
Norway	Norwegian Communication Association	http://www.kommunikasjon.no

Geographic Area	PR Industry Group	Website (or email or Facebook)
Poland	Polish Association of Public Relations	http://www.polskipr.pl
	Polish Public Relations Consultancies Association	http://www.zfpr.pl
Portugal	Associação Portuguesa de Comunicação de Empresa	http://www.apce.pt
Russia	Russian Public Relations Association	http://www.raso.ru
Serbia	Serbian Society for Public Relations	http://pr.org.rs
Slovenia	Public Relations Society of Slovenia	http://www.piar.si
Spain	Asociación de Directivos de Comunicación, Dircom	http://www.dircom.org
Sweden	Swedish Public Relations Association	http://www.sveriges kommunikatorer.se
	Public Relations Consultancies in Sweden	http://www.precis.se/
Switzerland	Swiss Public Relations Association	http://www.prsuisse.ch
	Swiss Public Relations Institute	http://www.spri.ch
	Harbour Club (Chief Communication Officers of Swiss organizations)	http://www.harbourclub.ch
Turkey	Turkish Public Relations Association	http://www.tuhid.org/tr
Ukraine	Ukrainian Association of Public Relations	http://www.uapr.com.ua/en
United Kingdom	Chartered Institute of Public Relations	http://www.cipr.co.uk
	Public Relations Consultants Association	http://www.prca.org.uk
North America		
Canada	Canadian Public Relations Society	http://www.cprs.ca
United States	Public Relations Society of America	http://www.prsa.org
	Public Relations Student Society of America	http://www.prssa.org
	Arthur W. Page Society	http://www.awpagesociety.com

Geographic Area	PR Industry Group	Website (or email or Facebook)
	Entertainment Publicists Professional Society	http://www.eppsonline.org/home
	Institute for Public Relations	http://www.instituteforpr.org
	National Association of Government Communicators	http://www.nagconline.org
	National Black Public Relations Society	http://www.nbprs.org
	PR Council	http://prfirms.org
	Public Affairs Council	http://pac.org
Oceania		
Australia	Public Relations Institute of Australia	http://www.pria.com.au
New Zealand	Public Relations Institute of New Zealand	http://www.prinz.org.nz

Appendix *C*

Examples of English-Language Television Broadcasters

TV Network Website	Headquarters	International Reach (facts from websites)
Agence France-Presse www.afp.com/en	France	2,260 staff members cover the world 24 hours a day in six languages, including English. 200 bureaus cover 150 countries across the world.
Al Jazeera English www.aljazeera.com	Qatar	24-hour English-language news and current affairs TV channel and website. Sister channel of Al Jazeera America. Worldwide reach.
Associated Press Television News www.aptn.com	U.S. (AP); U.K. (APTV)	AP content published in newspapers, websites, and TV and radio outlets worldwide. Network of staff in more than 280 locations. Global customers.
Australian Broadcasting Corporation tv.australiaplus.com	Australia	Provides radio and television services within Australia and overseas. Promotes Australia's musical, dramatic and other performing arts. Australia Plus TV beams to countries in the Asia-Pacific region.
BBC www.bbc.com	England	10 national TV channels plus regional programming,10 national radio stations, 40 local radio stations, and an extensive website.
		BBC World Service broadcasts to the world on radio, on TV and online, providing news and information in English and in 27 languages.
		BBC World News is the BBC's commercially funded international news and information television channel, broadcasting in English 24 hours a day in more than 200

TV Network Website	Headquarters	International Reach (facts from websites)
		countries and territories worldwide, around 300 million households and 1.8 million hotel rooms.
Bloomberg TV www.bloomberg.com/tv/shows	U.S.	Global television network available in more than 360 million homes worldwide across more than 70 countries.
CBC News Network www.cbc.ca	Canada	Service is available worldwide, with the exception of documentary programming, which is only available to viewers inside Canada.
CCTV english.cntv.cn	China	English-language 24-hour news channel of China Central Television (CCTV), the nation's largest national broadcasting network. Free-to-air satellite signals can be received by more than 85 million viewers, in over 100 countries and regions.
CNBC www.cnbc.com	U.S.	15 live hours a day of business programming in North America with business news and real-time financial market coverage to more than 370 million homes worldwide, including more than 100 million households in the U.S. and Canada. CNBC World provides 24-hour digital television network offering live, global financial market information and programming. Daily business updates to 400 million households across China.
CNC World www.cncworld.tv	China	24-hour English-language channel operated by China Xinhua News Network Corporation. Cable and wireless digital TV networks in more than 60 countries and regions, including parts of Asia-Pacific, Africa, North America, Central America, Europe, the Middle East, and Oceania.
ChannelNews Asia www.channelnewsasia.com	Singapore	English-language channel reports on global developments with Asian perspectives. Based in Singapore with correspondents in major Asian cities and key Western ones, including New York, Washington DC, London, and Brussels.
CNN www.cnn.com	US	Staffed 24 hours, seven days a week in CNN's world headquarters in Atlanta,

TV Network Website	Headquarters	International Reach (facts from websites)
		Georgia, and in 36 bureaus and 4,000 employees worldwide. CNN's combined branded networks and services available to more than 2 billion people in more than 200 countries and territories.
DD News www.ddinews.gov.in	India	Currently producing news content in Hindi, English, Urdu, and Sanskrit languages. Over 17 hours of LIVE transmission include telecast of more than 30 news bulletins in these languages.
Deutsche Welle www.dw.de	Germany	Germany's international broadcaster with 3,000 staff employees and hundreds of freelancers from 60 countries working in its headquarters in Bonn and Berlin. Television channels around the world; a comprehensive website with content in 30 languages and radio broadcasts that reach out to listeners in Africa and parts of Asia. Launched a new 24-hour global English-language news and information TV channel in June 2015.
France 24 www.france24.com/en	France	Three separate TV channels broadcast in French, English, and Arabic. Broadcasts 24 hours a day, seven days a week to 250 million TV households in 177 countries around the world.
NDTV www.ndtv.com	India	NDTV 24x7 is the only English News Channel from India which is beamed in the U.K., U.S., Canada, South Africa, Middle East, Australia, New Zealand, Mauritius, and most of the SAARC Countries to reach out to the Indian Diaspora.
NHK World www3.nhk.or.jp/nhk world	Japan	NHK operates international television, radio, and Internet services. NHK World TV provides latest information from Japan, Asia, and the rest of the world, as well as a wide variety of programming, 24 hours a day; available to more than 273 million households in more than 140 countries/regions through local satellite services and cable service providers.

TV Network Website	Headquarters	International Reach (facts from websites)
Reuters TV www.reuters.tv	U.S.	Reuters World News Service covers major international news event, with its on-the-ground television crews working with over 200 Reuters bureaus globally.
Russia Today rt.com	Russia	Three global news channels broadcasting in English, Spanish, and Arabic. RT has 22 bureaus in 19 countries and territories, with a presence in Washington, New York, London, Berlin, Gaza, Cairo, Baghdad, and other key cities. Global reach of over 650 million people in 100+ countries, or more than 25% of all cable subscribers worldwide, and is now available in more than 2.7 million hotel rooms.
Sky News news.sky.com	U.K.	UK's first dedicated 24-hour news channel reporting news live across all its platforms— TV, mobile, online, radio, and iPad. Sky News reaches over 107 million homes across 118 countries around the world.
Times Now www.timesnow.tv	India	24-hour English News channel operates out of Mumbai, with presence in 15 other cities. Channel can be viewed live outside of India on www.watchindia.tv with a broadband connection.

Appendix *D*

Answers to Selected Exercises

Chapter 1

Answers to Exercise 1.1: Origins of English Words

1. Agile, t. Latin; 2. Algebra, c. Arabic; 3. Amok, u. Malay; 4. Bigot, j. French; 5. Boss, h. Dutch; 6. Berserk, w. Old Norse; 7. Boomerang, d. Australian Aboriginal; 8. Catamaran, cc. Tamil; 9. Catastrophe, m. Greek; 10. Coach, p. Hungarian; 11. Face-Off, e. Canadian English; 12. Fest, l. German; 13. Galore, k. Gaelic; 14. Ghetto, r. Italian; 15. Gung-ho, v. Mandarin; 16. Hurricane, y. Spanish; 17. Juggernaut, o. Hindi; 18. Kayak, q. Inuit; 19. Ketchup, f. Cantonese; 20. Khaki, dd. Urdu; 21. Klutz, ee. Yiddish; 22. Lanai, n. Hawaiian; 23. Ombudsman, aa. Swedish; 24. Robot, g. Czech; 25. Safari, z. Swahili; 26. Sauna, i. Finnish; 27. Terrapin, b. Algonquin; 28. Trek; a. Afrikaans; 29. Troika, x. Russian; 30. Tycoon, s. Japanese; 31. Yogurt, bb. Turkish.

Chapter 3

Answers to Exercise 3.2: Self-Evaluation: Ethical and Legal Issues in Public Relations

1. The practice of arranging press visits on a complimentary or discount basis is not unethical. You would need to know the ethical policies of the media outlets, some of which do not allow their editors, producers, or freelance writers to accept subsidized travel arrangements.
2. You would need to check your contract with the existing client. Contracts should indicate other competing organizations that the public relations agency would be unable to represent. Your loyalty should be with the existing client.
3. Images should not be altered that would change the decision-making process in buying or leasing real estate, in this case, which would be misleading to the public. This situation is not only unethical but could have legal implications as well.
4. You could only include activities that have not been undertaken as "immediate next steps" for future work in an activity report.
5. Your client contract most likely would indicate that confidential information cannot be shared at any time, even after you no longer represent the client. Confidential content would not have an expiration date.

6. You would need to check your employment contract, which most likely would include a non-compete clause within a specific timeframe in which you would be unable to solicit existing accounts for another agency.

7. Buying expensive gifts for journalists would be considered unethical. In fact, some media outlets have a code of ethics that would not allow any staff member to accept gifts.

8. You can include puffery as an opinion in a quotation from a company spokesperson in a news release. However, most writers would avoid making unsubstantiated claims.

9. Sharing information that affects the trading of securities before it is disclosed to the public would be considered insider trading, a very serious offense. Securities and exchange commissions have strict rules to prohibit insider trading.

10. You would need to check who holds the copyright of the artwork and then contact that person or organization for permission in writing that would stipulate the usage, timing, distribution, and any fees.

11. You would need to check the estate of the deceased public figure to request permission and determine licensing fees with specific terms stipulated in a contract.

12. Posting false reviews online falls into the category of astroturfing, which is named after AstroTurf, the synthetic grass. The name evolved from contrived grassroots initiatives, particularly ones created by the self-interests of organizations that pay people for pretending to be supportive of the cause, company, or politician. Astroturfing could not only damage the organization's reputation, the practice could result in penalties by many countries that have enacted new laws to prohibit this practice.

13. You would need to gain approval from the media outlet in order to post the entire story or make reprints of the article. This process would most likely require a fee and a contract outlining the terms.

14. You should try to find another positive quote from another source. The Federal Trade Commission in the U.S., for example, has jurisdiction to determine that the public is not being misled by false publicity and advertisements, which would apply to incomplete review quotes that alter the original meaning.

Chapter 4

Exercise 4.1: Circles Test on Perception of Time: Past, Present, and Future.

Please refer to the section on long-term or short-term orientation in Chapter 4 or read the original research by Cottle:

Cottle, T. J. (1967). The circles test: An investigation of perceptions of temporal relatedness and dominance. *Journal of Projective Techniques and Personality Assessment, 31*(5), 58–71. doi:10.1080/0091651X.1967.10120417

Suggested Answers to Exercise 4.2: Self-Evaluation: Writing with Diplomacy and Tact

The responses below are suggestions since there could be different responses. The goal, however, is to be more diplomatic and considerate while avoiding negative language.

1. I'm available at (dates/times). Please let me know if any of these times are convenient for you. (Focus on when you are available, not when you are unavailable. Remember to ask if suggested times work in your client's schedule.)
2. I'm sorry but I was just about to leave for an appointment. Would it be possible for me to call you back at (time) or may we schedule another time that works for you? (Apologize and work out another time; or take the time to talk at that moment.)
3. Thank you for sharing your ideas. We would like to suggest another approach that we believe would work effectively. (Provide positive feedback and work out other solutions, preferably collectively.)
4. We would need to research the costs involved in undertaking (specific activity) since that project falls outside of our current work. We will provide you with cost estimates by (time). (Explain the reasons why you would need more funding or suggest a substitute for a current project. If you're a junior-level staff member, you also could explain that you would need to check with your account supervisor—or have the account supervisor contact the client to discuss the budget.)
5. We would like to suggest (specific date) as a feasible deadline to complete the project and achieve high-quality results. (Explain the benefits of requesting more time or change the priorities of current projects.)
6. We would like to recommend a few enhancements to your (specific social media platform). (Avoid criticizing the existing social media. Use positive language to show how the social media could be improved.)
7. (Name of journalist) is working on a tight deadline and would appreciate receiving an answer by (a specific time). (Explain the benefits of a story in that specific media outlet. Make suggestions on how to expedite an answer.)
8. I will need to check on (specific topic), and I will provide you with the answer by (specific time). (Instead of admitting that you do not know the answer, you should take the initiative to find out the answer.)

Chapter 5

Answers to Exercise 5.1: Self-Evaluation: Cross-Cultural Interpretations of Hand Gestures

1. Offensive ("your wife is unfaithful"); 2. Salute to the Longhorns football team; 3. Offensive; 4. Approval; 5. Offensive ("get lost"); 6. Money; 7. Victory; 8. Offensive; 9. Offensive ("you're stingy"); 10. Offensive ("you're an idiot")

Sources:

Cotton, G. (2013, June 13). Gestures to avoid in cross-cultural business: In other words, "keep your fingers to yourself!" *Huffington Post*. Retrieved from http://www.huffingtonpost.com

Lefevre, R. (2011). *Rude hand gestures of the world: A guide to offending without words*. San Francisco, CA: Chronicle Books.

Chapter 7

Answers to Exercise 7.1: Self-Evaluation: American (Webster's) and British (Oxford) English Spelling

American English to British English: 1. Practice (noun and verb), practice (noun), practise (verb); 2. Organization, organization or organisation; 3. Counseling, counselling; 4. Cozy, cosy; 5. Honor, honour; 6. Mustache, moustache; 7. Acknowledgment, acknowledgement; 8. Skeptic, sceptic; 9. Airplane, aeroplane; 10. Artifact, artefact.

British English to American English: 11. Pyjamas, pajamas; 12. Tyre, tire; 13. Haulier, hauler; 14. Paralyse, paralyze; 15. Marvellous, marvelous; 16. Paediatrics, pediatrics; 17. Savour, savor; 18. Skilful, skillful; 19. Plough, plow; 20. Fibre, fiber.

Chapter 8

Answers to Exercise 8.1: Self-Evaluation: Pronouns

1. I (subjective case pronoun); 2. he (subjective case pronoun); 3. I (subjective case pronoun); 4. me (objective case pronoun); 5. me (objective case pronoun); 6. me (objective case pronoun); 7. my (possessive case); 8. its (possessive case); 9. examines (each is singular); 10. is (everyone is singular); 11. is (everybody is singular); 12. was (singular when meaning not one person); 13. was (both nouns are singular); 14. are (both nouns are plural); 15. who (subjective case); 16. whom (objective case).

Answers to Exercise 8.2: Self-Evaluation: Punctuation

1. Let's eat, grandpa. 2. It was a moose with huge antlers. Using binoculars, we have all seen it in the woods at the nature reserve. 3. The chef finds inspiration in cooking, her family, and her dogs. 4. A woman: without her, man is nothing. 5. A woman, without her man, is nothing. 6. Colin said, "I'm trying to understand the differences in punctuation between American and British English." 7. Colin said, 'I'm trying to understand the differences in punctuation between American and British English'. 8. She will re-sign as soon as she can. 9. The agency executive said, "The client was challenging."

Chapter 9

Answers to Exercise 9.1: Self-Evaluation: Geographic Knowledge of Religions of the World

1. Indonesia; 2. India; 3. Latin America and the Caribbean; 4. Tel Aviv; 5. New York City; 6. Thailand; 7. India and Nepal; 8. India; 9. Japan; 10. China.

Answers to Exercise 9.2: Self-Evaluation: Cross-Cultural Meanings of English Words

1. Apartment, H. Flat; 2. Baby carriage, R. Pram; 3. Closet, Z. Wardrobe; 4. Cookie, C. Biscuit; 5. Diaper, O. Nappy; 6. Drug store/pharmacist, F. Chemist; 7. Dumpster, V. Skip; 8. Eggplant, A. Aubergine; 9. Elevator, M. Lift; 10. Eraser. T. Rubber; 11. Exhausted, L. Knackered; 12. Fall, B. Autumn; 13. Flashlight, W. Torch; 14. Garbage, U. Rubbish; 15. Gas, P. Petrol; 16. Hood, D. Bonnet; 17. Line, S. Queue; 18. Pacifier, G. Dummy; 19. Period, I. Full stop; 20. Sneakers, X. Trainers; 21. Steal, Q. Pinch; 22. Subway, Y. Underground; 23. Sweater, K. Jumper; 24. Truck, N. Lorry; 25. Trunk, E. Boot; 26. Vacation, J, Holiday.

Index

achievement versus ascription orientations 90, 99, 101
acronyms 15, 176, 194, 219, 357, 373
active vs. passive voice 192, 243, 357, 453
activity reports 431, 439, 454–7
Ad Council 375
Adams, Scott 430
adjectives 184, 186–7, 189, 192–3, 199, 201–2, 204, 216, 243, 344
adverbs 184, 186, 193, 201, 344
advertising: brand journalism 379–80, 384, 400; campaigns 123–4, 132, 152, 267; communication conglomerates 32–3; glocalization 38; industry 31, 142; media ethics 73, 75–6; public relations-related 237, 243, 347, 375–6, 418–19; storytelling 132; style guidelines 163, 175
advertising value equivalencies (AVEs) 419
advertorials 75, 380, 400–1
affective versus neutral cultures 89, 96, 100
African Public Relations Association 37, 464
AirAsia Indonesia 315
Airbus 15–16, 287, 317
American English: education 19, 164; evolution 9–10; style 172; *see also* English language
American Red Cross 341–2, 349, 350
ampersands 195, 204
anaphora 365
animals: storytelling 133, 138–41; symbolism 106, 124–6
Annan, Kofi 313
apostrophes 195, 204
Appadurai, Arjun 29–30, 48
Apple, Inc. 56, 248–9, 254, 275, 366–7
appositives 185
Arabic language 12, 17, 44, 123, 398
AramcoWorld 380–1
Asia Pacific Communication Universe model, 98
Associated Press Stylebook and Briefing on Media Law 173-4, 180, 197, 199, 201, 204, 217-18, 245-6
Association of Religion Data Archives 216
astroturfing 71, 475
audiences: blogs 339; bylined articles 327; multicultural/international 29, 42, 87–8, 176, 187, 189, 202, 208–9, 211, 213, 219; internal/external 64, 175; media kits 287; media relations 59, 296, 315; microblogs 343; news releases 238, 242–3, 246, 248; op-eds 324; public relations plans 414–17;

public relations presentations 423–4, 426–7; social media 333, 336, 346; speeches 358–63, 367–9; storytelling 133, 135; video 369–70; Wikipedia 351
audiovisual scripts 371–4
authenticity 38, 340–1
Australian Bat Clinic & Wildlife Trauma Centre 143–4

backgrounders 275, 277, 285–7
Barcelona Declaration of Measurement Principles 419
BBC News Styleguide 163, 174
Berne Convention 68
biographies *see* executive profiles
blogs: ethics 71; evolution 338–9; public relations applications 113, 135, 143, 145, 151–2, 236, 240, 253, 258–9, 287, 294, 297, 299, 309, 325, 327, 333, 341–3, 370, 375, 382, 386–7, 389, 409, 413, 415, 418, 452, 455, 457–8; setup process 334, 339–40; statistics 3, 60, 334, 340; style 175; writing guidelines 210, 336-7
BlueNotes, ANZ 383–4
BMW Magazine 381
body language 96, 106–7, 110, 113–14, 359, 369
Boolean logic 457
brackets, punctuation 202, 204
brand journalism 379–80
Breast Cancer Awareness Month 153
British English: education 15, 163–4, 167; evolution 9, 164–6, 168–9; *see also* English language
British Petroleum 224
broadcast media 42, 58–9, 61, 259, 340
brochures: copy, design, production 394–400; media kits 265; newsrooms 275, 292; purposes 391
B-roll footage 275, 301, 307, 370
budgets 32, 219, 420, 422, 427, 439
Burberry 148
Bush, George W. 109–10, 339, 370
Business Wire 242, 259
bylined articles 135, 323, 327

CAGE dimensions 414
Canadian Public Relations Society 36, 468
capitonyms 220
Captain Morgan Rum, 246–7
captions *see* photo captions

careers, global 42–7
Carter, Kevin 105-6
Cawdrey, Robert 164
Center for Media and Democracy 370
Central Intelligence Agency 345
charity: water 137
Charter on Media Transparency 73, 76
Chartered Institute of Public Relations 36, 468
Chase's Calendar of Events, 153
cheong 62
Chicago Manual of Style 173–4, 389
Chile's English Open Doors 18
Chinese language 3, 12, 16–17, 21, 41, 44, 118, 120,
    193, 224–5, 398
chronological narrative 294
churnalism 235
Cisco 379, 386
Cision 237, 297, 390
citizen activism 57
citizen journalists 57
civil society organization 31
clichés 208, 210–11, 243
clickthrough rates 344
client contracts 72
CNN 61, 139, 224, 339
Coca-Cola 40–1, 149, 158, 224–5, 236, 387
colloquialisms 210, 212, 441
colons, punctuation 195, 197–8, 204
colors *see* cultural interpretations
commas 185, 194–5, 198–9, 203–5
commercial regulations 70–1
Commission on Public Relations Education 43
communication conglomerates 32–3
computer spell check 219, 227, 243, 424
Con Edison 280
Condé Nast Traveler 319
conference reports *see* meeting minutes
conjunctions 183, 186, 193–4
consumer empowerment 57
Continental Airlines 141, 240
controlled media 379
contronyms 220
convergence 53, 57
copyright 62, 65, 68–9, 72–3, 167, 253, 275, 287, 327,
    334, 384, 395, 455
Corning Museum of Glass 256–7
corporate culture 87, 89, 431
Cracker Barrel Old Country Store 280
Crayola 115–16
crisis: communications 32; incidents/situations 57, 92,
    121, 224; media alerts 303, 306–7; monitoring
    457–8; newsjacking 337; news releases 239, 240,
    245; public relations plans, 456; social media 338,
    348; statements 312–15
culture, definitions 83–7

cultural interpretations: colors 41, 106, 114–18, 145,
    424; cultural icons 123–4; hand gestures 107–9,
    126–7; numbers 118–20; *see also* animals; flowers;
    religious symbols; national/political symbols
Cupertino effect 227
Curalate 347
customized style guides 175–6

Daimler AG 15
dashes, punctuation 195, 199–200, 204
databases 34, 65, 258, 408–9, 413, 458
defamation 62, 65, 69–70, 334
Dela 152–3
Delta Air Lines 13
Dentsu 32–3
dictionaries, English-language: evolution 164, 166–9,
    171; Jamaican English 168, 170; Macquarie 168,
    170, 172, 177; Merriam-Webster 54, 59, 170–2,
    167–8, 211, 220; Oxford 12, 54, 59, 164, 168, 170,
    178, 200, 209, 211–12; worldwide 170
Disneyland Paris 40–1
dogberryism 222
Dove Campaign for Real Beauty 142
dpi (dots or pixels per inch) 396
DreamWorks Animation 247
Durex 345

Early Modern English 5, 8–9
Early Old English 5–6
Earth Hour 239, 394–5
economics: English-language 3, 8, 14; globalization
    29–30, 38–9, 83, 414
Edelman, Richard 341
Edelman Trust Barometer 380
editing: clarity 214–16; confused words 219–23;
    correct terms 216–18; expressions 210–13;
    importance 208–9; numbers and abbreviations 219;
    sports references 211, 258; tone and relevance
    209–10; transcultural gaps 213–14; translation
    issues 223–5
editorial briefings 297, 309, 390
editorial calendars 239, 298, 327, 338, 384
eggcorns 222
Elements of Style 208
email, writing 439–40, 443–4
employment agreements 71–2
English language: differences between American and
    British/Oxford English 94, 163–5, 167, 180, 182,
    185, 187, 193, 199, 202–4, 221–2, 227, 242, 264,
    433–4; evolution 5–10, 12; other English variations
    18–19, 163–9
English-language education: Business English as a
    Lingua Franca (BELF) 17; English as a Business
    Language (EBL) 17; English as a Foreign Language
    (EFL) 15; English as a Global Language (EGL) 15;

English for International Business (EIB) 17; English as an International Language (EIL) 15; English as a Lingua Franca (ELF) 15; English as a Mother Tongue (EMT) 17; English as a Second Language (ESL) 15

Esperanto 21

ethics: corporate 87; journalism 73–6; public relations 37, 64–7, 75–7; strategic 64

ethnocentric theory 85

euphemisms 210–11

exclamation marks 183, 200, 424, 440

executive profiles 275–6, 281–5

Facebook: evolution 56–7, 346; hashtags 335; public relations applications 138, 148–9, 275, 337, 340–1, 386, 400, 417–18, 457; rankings/statistics 334, 346, 350; writing 334–8

fact sheets 248, 275–81

fair use 68

Fairy Liquid 142

feature news 239, 240–1

Federal Communications Commission 371, 374

FedEx 138, 241, 253–4

Fiat 123, 269–70

flack 131

Flickr 56, 292, 346–7

flowers, symbolism 124–6

Forbes 386, 400

foreign-language education 15, 20–1

formal letters 431–2, 433–6

Fortune 500 89, 344

forward-looking statements 71, 209, 250

France Telecom 118

French language 5, 9–10, 12–13, 21, 164, 193, 250, 345, 400

FreshIntelligence 41

Freytag, Gustav 132

Freytag's dramatic storytelling sequences 133

Friedman, Thomas L. 39, 53, 325, 352

Furrow, The 379–82

gatekeepers, media 53

Gates, Bill 363

General Electric 341–2

generic principles 41

geographic indications 68–9

geopolitics 242

Ghonim, Wael 57

GLAAD Media Reference Guide 218

Global Alliance for Public Relations and Communication Management 37–8, 50, 64–5, 419

global communications: evolution 52–6; trends 56–8; media 58–62

global cosmopolitans 47–8

global cultural flows 29–30

Global Language Monitor 10

global media ethics, 73, 75

global village 52–3

globalization 19, 27, 29–31, 38–9, 53, 156, 208

globish 3, 22–4

glocalization: defined 38; public relations 41–2; think locally, act globally 38–9; think globally, act locally 39–41

Glomar response 345

Google 13, 42, 54–6, 187, 193, 274, 346, 350, 457

Google Analytics 458

Google Docs 455

Google News 413

Google+ 56, 275, 335, 341, 346

government regulations 62, 65, 70–1, 73

grammar: archaic 194; common errors 182–6; importance 178–80; organic 205; parts of speech 186–94; prescriptive 205; sentences 181–3

graphic design associations worldwide 398–9

Grunig, James 41, 333

guanxi 62

guest commentaries *see* op-eds

Gutenberg Press 52

Hall, Edward T. 88–9, 91, 95, 113

Hampden-Turner, Charles 88–91, 96, 98–9, 102

haptics 107

hard news 236, 239–40

hashtags 334–5, 344, 350

headlines, news releases 239, 241, 245, 336

Hebrew language 164, 193, 398

Hewlett–Packard 137

high- and low-context cultures 89, 95–6, 100, 454

Hofstede, Geert 88–90, 96, 98–9, 102

homographs 220

homonyms 220, 222

homophones 220

Honda 254, 349

hourglass metaphor 295

Hubble Space Telescope 255

humor 86, 209–11, 242, 345, 424

hyphens 195, 199–202, 204

IBM 21, 89, 155–7, 339, 353

idioms 210–11

IKEA 112–13

imagery: auditory 145; gustatory 145; kinesthetic 145; olfactory 145; organic 145; tactile 145; visual 145; *see also* visuals/visual imagery

indefinite articles 194

independent service contracts 72

Index on Censorship 73

individualism and communitarianism dichotomies 89, 98

individualism versus collectivism dimension 89, 98, 101

indulgence versus restraint dimension 89, 101-2

infographics 106, 253, 256, 287

Instagram 56, 292, 335, 346–7, 400

Institute for Public Relations 419, 469

Intel 280

intellectual property 62, 65, 68–9

Inter-American Confederation of Public Relations 37, 465

intercultural communication: air traffic control and cockpit 13; cultural dimensions and considerations 100–1; cultural generalizations 84; diplomacy and expressiveness 95–6; language policies in multinationals 15; multiculturals 47; rules and traditions 99, 102; scholars 89–90; sense of power and control 96–9; time orientation 88, 90–4

intergovernmental organizations 31

interjections 186, 194

internal versus external control dichotomies 90, 99, 101

International Agency for Research on Cancer 153

International Association of Business Communicators 37, 462, 464

International Association for the Measurement and Evaluation of Communication 419

International Civil Aviation Organization 13

International Communications Consultancy Organisation 29, 37, 419

International Consumer Protection and Enforcement Network 71

International Longevity Center 230

International Monetary Fund 12

international nongovernmental organizations (INGO) 27, 31

International Olive Council 388–9

International Organization for Standardization (ISO): currency 219, 420; paper sizes 396

international public relations: culture 83–5, 123; definition 28; ethics 64–7; trade groups 35–7, 73, 76, 464–9; services 32, 34

International Public Relations Association 36, 64, 66–7, 73, 76, 464

International Trademark Association 69

Internet: business 31, 39; English 3, 12, 182; ethics 66; global 3, 10, 21, 27, 53, 57; issues 53, 57–8; law 71; news releases 237, 240, 250; rankings/statistics 54–5, 333, 346, 380; storytelling 133, 138–9

Interpublic Group 32–3, 382

introduction speeches 367–9

invasion of privacy 57, 65, 69–70, 112

invitations, formal 307–9

IOIO model 419

Japanese language 11, 17, 38, 118, 120, 139, 191, 398

jargon 208, 210, 212–13, 243

Jelly Belly Candy Company 287, 288–91

Jobs, Steve 134, 366–7, 367

John Deere 379–80

journalism: brand 379, 400; definition 59; global ethics 73, 75–6; global trade groups 73–4; political 62; public relations 235–7; style manuals 173–4, 218; surveys 60–1, 237, 298, 379; writing techniques 294–5

kabob metaphor 295–6

Kachru, Braj 18–19

Kenneth Cole 337

kinesics 107

King, Jr., Martin Luther 363–4

kisha kurabu 62

Kontax 259

Korean Air 13–14

Korean language 398

Kraken Black Spiced Rum 267, 267–8

languages: living languages 15, 18; most widely spoken 15, 17

Late Modern English 5, 9–10

Later Old English 5–6, 8

Latin language 5–6, 8–10, 21, 92, 164, 187, 203–4, 219, 227

leads, news releases 246–7, 253, 368, 389

Lee, Ivy Ledbetter 236

legal considerations 62, 64, 68–73

LEGO® Club Magazine, 384

Lenovo 15, 343

letters *see* email; formal letters; memos

letters to the editor 323–4, 385

Lindt 267, 269

lingo 210, 212–13

lingua franca: defined 3; English 3, 12, 15, 17, 20–1, 345; Latin 6, 21; French, 21

LinkedIn 56, 281, 285, 311, 334, 346, 390, 422

literacy rates 178

Lonely Planet 319

long-term versus short-term orientation 88-9, 100

L'Oréal 48, 249–50

Madrid System of International Registration of Marks 69

magazines: bylined articles 327; ethics 73; media relations 53, 59, 131, 287, 292, 297, 298–9; native advertising 400; news releases 236–9; online newsrooms 287; organizational–produced 379–87; PSAs 374; trends 60

malapropisms 221–2

Mandela, Nelson 23, 367

Marc Jacobs' Daisy 269

Marketwire 259

Marriott 341

Mars Petcare 315
material announcement 71
material culture 85
McDonald's 40, 69, 123, 211
McLuhan, Marshall 52–3
measurement and evaluation 32, 418–19, 427, 458
measurements and dimensions 219
media alerts 303–7
media catching 298–9
media kits: online newsrooms 274–6; purposes 263–4; tactical and digital 264–73; visuals 287–92; written components 276–87
media monitoring 390, 454, 457–8
media placements 237, 455
media relations: cultural differences 42, 62; defined 59; importance 235–6; public relations plans 416–19; public relations tactics/techniques 241, 264, 274, 296–8, 300, 333, 369–70, 441, 457
media tours 309, 311–12, 370
meeting agendas 445–50
meeting minutes 450–4
Melbourne Mandate 37–8
memos 437–8
Metro Trains Melbourne 376
Metropolitan Transportation Authority, New York 314
Michelin Guide 380
microblogs: evolution 343; public relations applications 245, 258–9, 294, 303, 307, 318, 327, 370, 418, 455; style guides 175; surveys/trends 60, 333–4; writing considerations 336–8
Microsoft Office 169
Middle English 5, 8
misplaced modifiers 185–6
MLA Handbook 173, 389
mobile apps 253, 258–9, 274
model of three concentric language circles 18–19
Modern English 5, 9
mondegreens 222
monochromatic versus polychromatic cultures 89, 91–2, 100
multiculturals 47–8
multinational corporations 3, 14–15, 30–1, 87, 224, 263, 385
Murray, James A. H. 164, 168–9
Musikmesse 265

National Aeronautics and Space Administration 226, 255
National Archives (U.K.) 375
National Association of Black Journalists 218
National Council of Teachers of English 218
National Geographic 384
National Maritime Historical Society 309–10
National Olympic Committees 5
national/political symbols 121–3

National Science Foundation (U.S.) 256
native advertising 380, 400–1
negative language 214–16
neologisms 210, 213
Nerrière, Jean-Paul 21-2
Nestlé 16, 31, 274–5
new business letters 431, 441–3
New Oxford Style Manual 173–4
news conferences *see* press conferences
news release distribution services 239, 242, 251–3, 258–9, 390
news releases 139, 141, 175, 209; delivery 258–60; issues and trends, 235–7; media kits 263–5, 275, 277; media tours 311; strategies 237–9; structure 241–51, 294; topics 239–41
newsjacking 336–7
newsletters 380, 384–5, 417
newspapers: activity reports 455–6; imagery 105; media relations 151, 236–8, 240, 247, 287, 297–9, 311, 323–4, 327, 385; public relations plans 413, 415, 417; PSAs 374; style guides 173; surveys/trends 60–1
newsrooms *see* online newsrooms
Nike 41, 69, 123, 224, 271–3
Nissan 275, 385
Nobel prizes 367
Nokia 15, 41
nominalizations 186
nongovernmental organizations 27, 30–1, 87, 374
North Atlantic Treaty Organization 13
nouns 184–9, 192–7, 202, 215–16, 218, 220, 245, 344, 358, 418, 424, 427
numbers *see* cultural interpretations
nut graf 295–6
Nutella 148–50

Obama, Barack 224, 313, 344
objective culture 85
oculesics 107
Olay Eyes of Arabia 113
Old Spice 137–9
Omnicom 32–3
online newsrooms: branded content 383, 385–7; components 274–6; guidelines 175; media relations 301, 311; news releases 239, 245, 248, 250–1, 253, 275, 277; public relations plans 455; purpose 259, 263; social media 275, 343; surveys 264; visual imagery 106, 253, 256, 275, 287, 369–70; written documents 277–87
op-eds 323–6
Oped Project 326
Oreo 337
Organisation for Economic Co-operation and Development 13
Organization of the Petroleum Exporting Countries 13

organizational publications 380–5
Orwell, George 358
Oxford Corpus 12
oxytocin 132

Pantone 396, 398
paper, printing: binding 398; coating 396; colors 396;
    folds 396–8; sizes 396
paralanguage 368–9
parallelism 186
past-present-future orientation 90–1
Pepsi Max 148
periods, punctuation 195, 197, 202–4
photo captions 253–8
photo cutlines 253
phrasal verbs 215
phrases 182, 184–6, 193, 210, 212–13, 222, 248, 335,
    420, 424, 453
Pinterest 56, 292, 340, 346–7
Pitches 145, 298–9, 300–2, 389
Plato 52
Pollock, Jackson 180–1
polycentric model 85
polysemic words 209–10, 219–20
positioning papers see white papers
posters 256, 380, 391, 394–6, 398, 417
power distance dimension 89, 96–7, 100
PowerPoint 362, 423–4
PR Newswire 258, 390
Pre-English Period 5–6
prepositions 186, 193
press 59–62
press conferences: newsrooms 275; media alerts 303–6;
    purpose 303; speeches 359; statements 312, 315–18;
    YouTube 348
press familiarization trips 297, 318–20, 321–3
press releases see news releases
print media 12, 59, 237
printing process 396
Procter & Gamble 112, 142, 382
professional culture 87
pronouns 98, 178, 186–90, 243, 358
proofreading 209, 225–9
proper protocol 308, 433–4, 436–7
proxemics 89, 113
public affairs 31
public domain 68, 395
public relations agencies: conglomerates 32–3;
    credentials 407, 409–10, 421; English proficiency
    15; ethics 64; global expansion 27, 31–2; global and
    glocal operations 41–2; independent agencies 32;
    international services 32; law 62, 71; meetings 446,
    450; new business 407–10, 431, 441; rankings 35;
    reporting 454–5; surveys 29, 237
public relations associations worldwide 36–7, 64, 73

public relations definitions 27-28; see also international
    public relations
Public Relations Institute of Australia 36, 469
public relations proposals: planning/process 407–10;
    presentations 422–8; structure 410–22
Public Relations Society of America (PRSA) 27–8, 36,
    156, 370–1, 419, 463, 468
public relations trade publications worldwide 34–5,
    461–3
public service announcements (PSAs) 132, 209, 275,
    332, 357, 374–6
public speaking 359–62
Publication Manual of the American Psychological
    Association 173
Publicis Groupe 32–3
publicity 53, 339, 419
Pulitzer Prizes 105–6
Puma 122–3
punctuation 176, 178–80, 184, 194–205, 226, 228, 359,
    433–4
Putin, Vladimir 324–5

question marks 182–3, 189, 191, 203–4
quotation marks 195, 198, 203–4

radio: audio news release 259; ethics 73; evolution 9,
    60; issues 52; media relations 59, 132, 236, 238,
    287, 297–9, 303, 311; PSAs 374; style guides 163
Rakuten 15–16
Real Simple Syndication (RSS) 258–9, 275
Red Bull 141–2
regionalisms 210, 212
religious symbols 121–2
Request for Proposals (RFPs) 407–10, 421, 441–3
research: library databases 413, 458; primary research
    388, 413; secondary research 135, 388; soft
    soundings 414; see also Google Analytics; media
    monitoring
right of publicity 70
response to complaint letters 443–4
Rouge, Procter & Gamble magazine 382
Rowling, J. K. 365–6

safe haven legalese 250
Samsung 16, 71, 87
search engine optimization 243, 251, 258, 274
security and exchange regulations 71
self-reference criterion 83–4
semantics 213
semicolons 203–5
sentences: editing 208; errors 182–5; structure 180,
    182; types 183
sequential versus synchronic cultures 90–1, 100
service marks 69
Shakespeare, William 5, 9, 12, 24, 130, 166, 222

Singapore Speak Good English Movement 17
situation analysis 412–14, 426
slang 10, 168, 171, 178, 208–10, 212–13, 223, 242, 441
slurls 334
social media: brand journalism 379–80, 382, 384, 386–7; business correspondence 431, 440, 443; editing 209–10, 214, 224, 226; ethics and law 68, 70–1; evolution 10, 56; grammar 178, 187, 191, 194; media kits 271, 279; media relations 297–8, 302–4, 306–8, 310, 312, 315–17, 323, 327; native advertising 400; news releases 236, 240, 242–5, 249, 251–3, 258–9; newsrooms 275, 292; nonverbal 106, 109, 113; proofreading 226–7, 229; public relations industry 32, 42, 54, 56–7; public relations plans 410, 412–13, 415–19; punctuation 195; storytelling 129, 132, 135, 137, 139, 142–3, 145, 148, 151, 156; style 163, 171–3, 175; trends/surveys 56, 60–1, 344, 379; white papers 389–90; writing 333–45, 347
social media news releases 242, 251–3, 258–9
soft news 239–41
Sony 99, 155, 266
soundbites 348, 360, 369–70, 372–4
Spanish language 9, 12–13, 17–18, 44, 69, 118, 193, 345, 400
speaking rates 357
specific versus diffuse cultures 90, 95–6, 100
speechwriting: 1-3-1 approach 362–3; examples 363–7; introductions 367–9; preparation 359–62; structure 362–3
spokespeople: law 70–1; media events 303, 305, 309, 311–12; media relations 59, 191–2, 276, 298–9, 301, 417; news releases 238, 242–4, 248, 253; social media 334, 348; statements 312–15; video 369–70, 372–4
Starbucks 341, 343
statements, media 275, 312–18
status reports see activity reports
stereotypes 84
story angles 294, 296–7
storytelling: benefits and brand messages 141–3; brand journalism 384; evolution 6, 129–30; journalism 294–7; letters to the editor 324; participatory 148–53; people and animals 133–41; public relations 129–32; sensory experiences 143–8; timeliness 153–7; Vine 348; writing for the ear 357
strategic ethics 64
strategies 38, 41–2, 237, 394, 408, 412, 416, 426
story idea memos see pitches
style guides 69, 173–6, 218, 436
subculture 85
subjective culture 85
SWOT analysis 414, 426

symbolism 111, 114, 124–5; see also cultural interpretations

tactics 416–18, 426–7
technological innovations 3, 9–10, 36, 53, 56–7, 209
television: B-roll 370; commercials 112, 123, 137–8; evolution 9, 53; global broadcasters 470–3; issues 52; media alerts 303; newsrooms 287; PSAs 374; surveys and trends 60–1; VNRs 259, 369–75
Thai language 191, 434
third culture 48
third-party endorsement 235–6
thumbnails, images 253, 265, 275
time: business hours 94; clock time 92–3; Coordinated Universal Time 93; dates 92, 118, 246, 433; seasons 94, 133, 324, 446; time zones 93–4, 245, 274, 275, 305–6, 316, 357
timetables 417–18, 427
Toastmasters International 357
TOMS Shoes 149, 151
tone: conversational 57, 191, 292, 336, 358; visual 145; written 95, 175, 208–10, 243, 264, 324, 340, 408, 410, 438–40
Tourism Australia 151–2
Tourism Queensland 151–2
Tourism New Zealand 154–5
tracking reports see media monitoring
trade shows 237, 327, 369, 391
trademarks 65, 68–9, 175–6, 197, 200, 334
translation 12, 42, 223–5, 398, 400
transparency 57, 64, 73, 75–6, 235, 340, 370–1, 376, 419
Trompenaars, Fons 88–91, 96, 98–9, 102
Truss, Lynne 180, 198
Tumblr, 56, 340
Twiplomacy 344
Twitter: evolution 56, 171, 343–4, 348, 417; public relations applications 138, 245, 253, 259, 275, 297, 299, 302, 318, 334–5, 340–1, 417–18, 457; statistics/trends 60, 334, 344–5; writing considerations 334–8, 345
Two-way symmetrical dialogue 333

uncertainty avoidance 89, 99, 101–2
United Nations 4–5, 12, 31, 35, 64–6, 151, 344
United States Department of Education 20
Universal Orlando 269, 271
universalism and particularism dichotomies 89, 101–2
URLs 301, 334, 339–40; see also websites

verbs 132, 180, 184, 186–8, 190–2, 215, 248, 336, 344, 418, 424, 426–7, 453
video news releases (VNRs) 259, 357, 370–4
Vine 56, 275, 335, 348–50, 360, 370

viral 132, 336, 345, 348, 400
Virgin Galactic 248
Virgin Mobile 274, 400
visuals/visual imagery: activity reports 455–7; audiovisual scripts 371–4; brand journalism 380; brochures and posters 394, 396; cultural considerations 42, 110–14, 117–18, 120–1, 258, 287; customized style guides 175–6; events 148; laws 64, 69–70; media alerts 303; news releases 239, 248, 250, 253, 255; newsrooms 263–5, 274–5, 292; pitches 298–9; public relations overall 105–6; public relations plans 408–9, 411, 420, 423–7; social media 56, 333, 336, 346–8; speeches 363
Volkswagen 391–4

Walker Art Center 138–9, 140
Walmart 30, 255, 340
Weber Shandwick 10X10 87
websites: dark rooms 315; law 68–9; naming 334; public relations applications 32, 34, 106, 245, 253, 259, 274, 276, 297, 311–12, 317, 327, 334, 348, 370, 375, 389, 409–10, 418–19, 455
Webster, Noah 5, 9, 164, 166–8
White, E. B. 208

white papers 135, 173, 209, 275, 380, 387–90, 409
Wikipedia 56, 350–3
Willis Group 137
WordPress 340
World Association of Newspapers and News Publishers 60–1
World Bank 12–13, 31
World Economic Forum 68
World Englishes 18
World Intellectual Property Organization 65, 68–9
World No Tobacco Day 350
World Trade Organization 13
WPP 32–3
writing for the ear 357–9
writing terms: age 218; gender 217–18; nations 217; race 29, 218–19; religions 216; sexual orientation 29, 217–18

Yahoo 346, 350
YouTube: media usage 60; public relations applications 138, 148, 275, 348, 360, 370, 375–6, 385, 417–18; rankings/statistics 346, 348, 350

Zamenhof, Ludwig L. 21